Multisensory Teaching
of Basic Language Skills

Multisensory Teaching of Basic Language Skills

edited by

Judith R. Birsh, Ed.D.

Teachers College
Columbia University
New York

·P A U L·H·
BROOKES
PUBLISHING Cº

Baltimore • London • Toronto • Sydney

Paul H. Brookes Publishing Co.
Post Office Box 10624
Baltimore, Maryland 21285-0624

www.brookespublishing.com

Typeset by Brushwood Graphics, Inc., Baltimore, Maryland.
Manufactured in the United States of America by
The Maple Press Co., York, Pennsylvania.

The individuals and situations described in this book are based on the authors' and volume editor's actual experiences. In all instances, names have been changed; in some instances, identifying details have been altered to protect confidentiality.

Several glossary definitions are adapted from Hensyl, W.R. (Ed.). (1990). *Stedman's Medical Dictionary* (25th ed.). Baltimore: Lippincott Williams & Wilkins. Copyright © Williams & Wilkins; adapted by permission.

Table 5.2 copyright © 1991 by Houghton Mifflin Company. Adapted and reproduced by permission from *The American Heritage Dictionary, Second College Edition.*

Second printing, April, 2000.

Library of Congress Cataloging-in-Publication Data

Multisensory teaching of basic language skills / edited by Judith R. Birsh.
    p.   cm.
  Includes bibliographical references and index.
  ISBN 1-55766-349-1
  1. Dyslexic children—Education—United States. 2. Dyslexics—Education—United States.
  3. Language arts—United States.
I. Birsh, Judith R.
LC4708.85.M85 2000   99-21233
371.91′44—dc21   CIP

British Library Cataloguing in Publication data are available from the British Library.

Contents

About the Editor

Judith R. Birsh, Ed.D., Adjunct Assistant Professor of Education, Department of Curriculum and Teaching, Teachers College, Columbia University, Box 31, 525 West 120th Street, New York, NY 10027-6625, founded and has directed the Multisensory Teaching of Basic Language Skills Series in the Program in Learning Disabilities of the Department of Curriculum and Teaching since 1985. Her primary interests are the teaching of reading and the preparation of teachers to work with individuals with dyslexia. She is a consultant to public and private schools as well as a certified academic language therapist.

Dr. Birsh was educational consultant on two Vineyard Video Productions videotape series for teachers and parents, *Teaching the Learning Disabled: Study Skills and Learning Strategies* (1991) and *Learning Disabilities/Learning Abilities* (1997; available from Paul H. Brookes Publishing Co.). She is former president of the New York Branch of the International Dyslexia Association and was the 1995 recipient of their award for achievement in the field of dyslexia education.

About the Contributors

Kay A. Allen, M.Ed., Associate Director, Neuhaus Education Center, 4433 Bissonnet Street, Bellaire, TX 77401-3233, has taught Orton-Gillingham–based teacher courses since 1982 and has worked for the past 20 years with adult students on improving their written language skills. She is an Academic Language Therapy Association Qualified Instructor, a certified academic language therapist, Secretary of the International Multisensory Structured Language Education Council, and co-author of *Multisensory Reading and Spelling* (Apple Core Press, 1993).

Holly Baker Hill, M.A.T., Doctoral Candidate, Department of International and Transcultural Studies, Teachers College, Columbia University, Box 211, 525 West 120th Street, New York, NY 10027-6625, is completing a dissertation on required reading classes for elementary education majors in three large university education departments in the United States, Australia, and New Zealand. Mrs. Baker Hill has taught in special education classes at all levels in the United States and internationally. She has been a research assistant for the District of Columbia National Institute of Child Health and Human Development Early Intervention Project and has taught reading and special education teacher training courses at the university level.

Marilyn C. Beckwith, B.A., Associate Director (Retired), Neuhaus Education Center, 4433 Bissonnet Street, Bellaire, TX 77401-3233, has had a 35-year interest in the relationship of spoken language to written language, which resulted in her using multisensory structured techniques to teach basic language skills to both dyslexic and nondyslexic individuals. This interest also resulted in her following related research made possible by advancing technology, which confirms the principles taught to teachers at the Neuhaus Education Center.

Susan H. Blumenthal, Ed.D., Licensed Clinical Psychologist, Private Practice; Founder, The Learning Difficulties Program, Institute for Contemporary Psychotherapy, 280 Ninth Avenue, 3F, New York, NY 10001, specializes in psychoeducational evaluations and cognitive remediation for adults and adolescents with learning difficulties and academic work output problems. She started an innovative program at the Institute for Contemporary Psychotherapy to train psychotherapists to work with adult patients with learning disabilities. In addition, she has trained teachers at Teachers College, Columbia University; Hunter College; and Manhattanville College.

Suzanne Carreker, B.A., Director of Teacher Development, Neuhaus Education Center, 4433 Bissonnet Street, Bellaire, TX 77401-3233, was a classroom teacher and consultant at the Briarwood School in Houston, Texas, for 13 years and has worked privately with students who have learning disabilities for more than 20 years. She has authored several systematic, multisensory curricula on teaching basic language skills. Her current interest is family literacy.

Mary L. Farrell, Ph.D., Professor, School of Education, Fairleigh Dickinson University, Bancroft Hall, Room 310, 1000 River Road, Teaneck, NJ 07666-1914, is director of Fairleigh Dickinson's Learning Disabilities Program, which offers the Dyslexia Specialist Certificate Program, which trains teachers in the Orton-Gillingham approach to teaching reading, spelling, and handwriting. Dr. Farrell also directs the Regional Center for College Students with Learning Disabilities, a comprehensive support program.

Dorothy Flanagan, M.S., Co-Director and Co-Founder, Stratford Friends School, 5 Llandillo Road, Havertown, PA 19083-5319, has supported the founding of several schools for children with learning differences. She has given numerous workshops for teachers and parents. Her interests include thematic/interdisciplinary studies; math; multisensory learning; multicultural education; Friends School education; and nurturing the spiritual lives of children as well as their academic, physical, social, and emotional lives.

Anne M. Glass, M.Ed., Educational Therapist, 382 Central Park West, Apartment 16G, New York, NY 10025, earned her master's in education in reading and learning disabilities from Teachers College, Columbia University. Her research and clinical interests include assessment of and remediation for children with learning difficulties.

Marcia K. Henry, Ph.D., Professor Emeritus and Former Director, Center for Educational Research, San Jose State University, 1 Washington Square, San Jose, CA 95192-0078, received her doctorate from Stanford University and was a Fulbright Lecturer/Research Scholar at the University of Trondheim, Norway, in 1991. Dr. Henry served as president of the International Dyslexia Association for 4 years.

Judith C. Hochman, Ed.D., Head of School, Windward School, Windward Avenue, White Plains, NY 10605-5398, holds a doctor of education in curriculum and instruction from Teachers College, Columbia University. She has been a teacher, administrator, and consultant in both mainstream and special education settings and has a particular interest in the teaching of expository writing. She regularly offers teacher training courses in written language and is the author of *Basic Writing Skills* (GSL Publications, 1995), which is used extensively by educators throughout the country in all grades. Dr. Hochman has been the Head of Windward School, an independent school for students with learning disabilities, since 1988. In 1998, she received the New York Branch Award of the International Dyslexia Association for her years of leadership in advancing the needs of people with dyslexia.

Joan R. Knight, M.A., M.S., President, Knight Education, Inc.; Director, Starting Over of New York, Inc., 317 West 89th Street, #9E, New York, NY 10024-2137, is the author of two textbooks, *Starting Over: A Combined Teaching Manual and Student Text for Reading, Writing, Spelling, and Handwriting* (Educators Publishing Service, 1986), and *Adults with Dyslexia* (The International Dyslexia Association, 1997). She has been supervisor of staff development in the New York City Adult Basic Education program, and as a consultant to schools, unions, and government agencies, she now designs literacy programs for children and adults and trains teachers. Her Starting Over teacher education course is accredited by the International Multisensory Structured Language Education Council.

Betty S. Levinson, Ph.D., Licensed Clinical Psychologist, Private Practice; Founder and Former Co-Director, TRI-Services Center for Children and Adults with Learning Disabilities, 19 Hawthorn Court, Rockville, MD 20850-2028, has wide clinical and teaching experience in the psychology of children and adults and in psychotherapy. Dr. Levinson has been a consultant on child abuse to local and state governments. Among other honors, she has been appointed to the Section Committee on Psychology of the American Association for the Advancement of Science, is on the Board of Directors of the International Dyslexia Association, and chairs the Committee of Children and Adolescents of the Board of Social Responsibility for the Maryland Psychological Association.

Shary Maskel, Ed.D., Director, The Hill Center, 3130 Pickett Road, Durham, NC 27705-6008, has worked in the field of learning disabilities for almost 30 years. She has experience as a classroom teacher, reading teacher, parent educator, school psychologist, and university professor and has served as Director of The Hill Center since 1985.

Louisa C. Moats, Ed.D., Project Director, District of Columbia National Institute of Child Health and Human Development Early Intervention Project, 4545 Connecticut Avenue, NW, Apartment 1020, Washington, DC 20008-6042, is director of the Washington, D.C., site of a large-scale, longitudinal study of early reading instruction supervised by Dr. Barbara R. Foorman. Dr. Moats has worked as a teacher, neuropsychology technician, and specialist in learning disorders. She was a licensed psychologist in private practice for 15 years in Vermont and a graduate instructor at Harvard University and at St. Michael's College. Specializing in reading development, reading disorders, spelling, and written language, she has written and lectured widely throughout the United States and abroad. Her publications include journal articles, book chapters, a classroom basal spelling program, and *Spelling: Development, Disability, and Instruction* (York Press, 1995).

Claire Nissenbaum, M.A., Director, Atlantic Seaboard Dyslexia Education Center, Rockville, MD 20850-2028, is Vice President of the International Multisensory Structured Language Education Council, which accredits professional training programs in dyslexia. She is a member of Academic Language Therapy Association, is a Fellow of the Academy of Orton-Gillingham Practitioners and Educators, and serves on the Information and Referral Committee of the International Dyslexia Association. She has been a dyslexia specialist for more than 30 years and co-founded the TRI-Services Center for Children and Adults with Learning Disabilities in Rockville, Maryland, which received national recognition for its programs. She has received the John Dewey Award for Outstanding Service to Public Education from the American Federation of Teachers.

Cecily Selling, M.S., Teacher, Stratford Friends School, 5 Llandillo Road, Havertown, PA 19083-5319, has been an elementary school teacher in several private schools in the Philadelphia area. She uses multisensory, interdisciplinary education in her classroom and shares these techniques with other teachers at local educational workshops.

Margaret Jo Shepherd, Ed.D., Founder, Program in Learning Disabilities, and Professor Emeritus, Department of Curriculum and Teaching, Teachers College, Columbia University, Box 31, 525 West 120th Street, New York, NY 10027-6625, is a teacher educator with more than 30 years of experience. Her professional interest is the education of teachers of students with learning disabilities. Dr. Shepherd and a long-time colleague, the late Dr. Jeannette Fleischner, created the Program in Learning Disabilities and the Special Education Child Study Center at Teachers College in 1967. In 1996, they began requiring enrollees in the Program in Learning Disabilities to take a course on multisensory instruction. Dr. Shepherd currently is involved in a variety of in-service professional development activities for experienced teachers.

Margaret Taylor Smith, M.Ed., Executive Director, EDMAR Educational Associates, Inc., 201 Elm Street, Forney, TX 75126-8649, has served as a classroom teacher and a dyslexia remediation teacher during 16 years of experience in public education. She trained teachers at the Dean Learning Center Teacher Training Department in Dallas, Texas. She co-founded EDMAR Educational Associates, Inc., in 1982, and has since acted as a consultant to numerous public and private schools in the United States.

Lydia H. Soifer, Ph.D., Language and Speech Pathologist, The Soifer Center for Learning & Child Development, 333 Old Tarrytown Road, White Plains, NY 10603; Assistant Clinical Professor of Pediatrics, Albert Einstein College of Medicine of Yeshiva University, Jack and Pearl Resnick Campus, 1300 Morris Park Avenue, Bronx, NY 10461-1926, is also a faculty member of the Early Intervention Training Institute of the Rose F. Kennedy Center for Research in Mental Retardation and Human Development. The focus of Dr. Soifer's work with children, parents, and professionals has been the developmental needs of children regarding learning, behavior, and communication and the nature of language functioning in academic performance and success.

Lynn Stempel-Mathey, M.A., Registered Professional Educational Diagnostician (Retired), Texas Scottish Rite Hospital for Children, Child Development Division, 2222 Welborn Street, Room 425, Dallas, TX 75219-3924, is a certified academic language therapist and is now in private practice as an educational diagnostician. She co-authored the *Children's Handwriting Evaluation System* (CHES, 1985) and has served as adjunct professor in the Learning Therapist Program at Southern Methodist University. She is currently a board member of the Academic Language Therapy Association.

Margaret B. Stern, M.Ed., Consultant in Mathematics Education to the National Council of Teachers of Mathematics and the International Dyslexia Association, 116 Pinehurst Avenue, Apartment J 44, New York, NY 10033-1755, is co-author of the Structural Arithmetic program (HarperCollins, 1971), which earned two grants from the Carnegie Foundation. She has received awards for achievement in education from the New York State Branch of the International Dyslexia Association and the Bank Street College of Education. At present, she is a math education consultant to schools in the New York City area.

Joanna K. Uhry, Ed.D., Assistant Professor of Education, Graduate School of Education, Fordham University, 113 West 60th Street, New York, NY 10023-7404, teaches literacy education to graduate students. Her research interests include dyslexia as well as the underlying cognitive processes used by young children who are learning to read and how these processes are supported by instruction.

Beverly J. Wolf, M.Ed., Dean of Faculty, Slingerland Institute for Literacy; Director Emeritus, Hamlin Robinson School for Dyslexics, 14702 Southeast 105th Street, Renton, WA 98059, has worked with children and adults with language disabilities for more than 30 years. As a teacher, program administrator, school head, and dean of faculty of the Slingerland Institute for Literacy, she has provided instruction both for students and their teachers. She is a member of the adjunct faculty of Seattle Pacific University and has served on both local and national boards of the International Dyslexia Association. She is also author of independent activity and language materials for classroom use.

Introduction

it is Thursday at 4:am and I can't sleep and I can't come this weekend. Michelle is having a terrible time at school this year—honors math teacher doesn't want her in the class Michelle can't go fast enough—english teacher thinks her students are cheater and treat them that way what a mess history teacher is a cow boy and relates all history to sports and lectures the whole period michelle is a visual learning

we had a meeting with them at the opening of school and it fell on deaf ears

I only wish I could find orton teacher in the content areas these teachers DON'T have a clue how to break down the learning

so what do we do well right now kevin and I take turns doing her homework with her she knows it at home and then at school she draws a blank—they say she didn't study I want to kill them

Do you see why you need to be at Columbia and you have to be a beaken so teachers know teaching is more that opening a book and presenting Long winded . . . I need to look into another school I will visit today or back to home schooling.

I received from an academic language therapist, who is dyslexic, this despairing e-mail about her daughter, who also has dyslexia. I use it with her permission because it highlights poignantly the relentless frustration that the parents of a dyslexic child experience, even if they themselves are knowledgeable about their dyslexic child's needs, as they try to ensure that their child receives an appropriate education. This e-mail makes clear two questions: Why is valuable information about how this child learns best not taken seriously by her teachers? Can parents learn ways to communicate with teachers that will yield better results? Moreover, the e-mail emphasizes the common finding of the lack of teacher knowledge and preparation to meet the range of abilities in the classroom. Unfortunately, it is often assumed that one kind of instruction will fit all. If Michelle's teachers had considered using some multisensory techniques such as the ones outlined in this book, she as well as others no doubt would have benefited. From teaching practice and research results, we now know that the best way to teach children with a broad range of skills and weaknesses in language and reading abilities is to provide effective instruction "that is explicit, systematic and sequential" and, "is active and engaging, emphasizes discovery and understanding, and is aided by frequent opportunities to practice" (Brady & Moats, 1997, pp. 9–10). Teacher modeling, using step-by-step prompts, direct questioning, and individualization are other ways teachers can make instruction effective.

Also evident in this e-mail is the persistence of the learning disability at each level of language complexity in school. Here we see the need for an informed developmental perspective that is sustained and carefully monitored throughout the child's school-the child's schooling. The demand for higher level problem-solving skills increases in adolescence even though the student may still have difficulties with reading and spelling. The e-mail message, which was written by a parent who is dyslexic, contains errors typical of dyslexia. Thus, the message conveys the hereditary component of dyslexia as well as the strengths and weaknesses of the writer's daughter. The e-mail I received reinforces the importance of promoting knowledge and understanding among all of the people in the child's life so that the individual who has dyslexia or is struggling to grasp the essential skills to function in life can thrive rather than fail unnecessarily.

THE NEED FOR THIS TEXTBOOK

Reading itself does not develop naturally and calls on many areas of language processing and adept instruction for a successful outcome. So, teachers who work with students at risk of failing to learn to read or with those already falling behind need a wide range of experience and a strong knowledge base from which to make judgments about what to teach, how to teach it, when to teach it, and to whom. When a child struggles with written language, none of the myriad layers of language processing can be taken for granted. Each individual is different and brings to the task unique cognitive and linguistic strengths and weaknesses. Therefore, teachers who work at prevention, intervention, or remediation require a foundation as broad and complex as reading itself.

This text on multisensory structured language education (MSLE) provides that foundation and offers components of instruction and effective teaching strategies that teachers can put into practice for students with dyslexia and others struggling to learn to read, write, and spell. It is a guide to helping students become literate by providing teachers and teacher educators models of recommended practices essential for preparation in the complicated task of literacy instruction.

The idea for the book evolved from a gathering of forces beginning in 1990. The Committee on Teacher Education Initiatives of the International Dyslexia Association (IDA; formerly called the Orton Dyslexia Society), 60 teacher trainers representing MSLE programs in the preparation of teachers and academic therapists, met yearly to create an accrediting body for organizations that prepare specialists in the education of individuals with dyslexia. Their aim was to set high professional standards for teachers, clinicians, and teacher education programs in the field of dyslexia in college and university programs, hospitals, and other institutions that have MSLE preparation as their function. By 1995 the group was incorporated as the International Multisensory Structured Language Education Council (IMSLEC) and is presently accrediting programs to assure individuals who need effective intervention and their families that programs are indeed providing well-prepared specialists who have been held to exemplary standards of teaching.

FILLING THE NEEDS OF TEACHER PREPARATION

During these collaborative forums of expert teacher trainers and therapists, it became clear that there was a great need for a comprehensive textbook for teacher preparation that would present research in reading and learning disabilities and would also grow out of the group members' long years of professional experience in the classroom and in one-to-one and small-group practice.

Until now, no one text has brought together research and clinical experience of the second half of the 20th century to teach written language skills to children and adults with dyslexia, the most prevalent learning disability. The information had appeared in fragmented form in journal articles and in teacher-authored workbooks and manuals tied to particular systems or methods. This, however, is the first general text on multisensory teaching. Each chapter begins with a conceptual framework based on research in a specific area, followed by content knowledge and explicit how-to information based on working model programs. This presentation of the essence of multisensory instruction is suitable for use as a core text in university education courses, as a handbook for teacher practitioners, as a source of parent information, and as a guide to the field of dyslexia studies. It will be a highly useful resource for schools of education, professional development personnel, and teacher training organizations because it offers in-depth treatment of all aspects of written language instruction; references, illustrations, and examples of hands-on procedures; a glossary of key terms; and an extensive appendix of materials and sources. Terms defined in the glossary are set in boldface on first occurrence in the text. Throughout the book, phonic symbols (e.g., /b/, /ǎ/, /th/) are used, except when phonetic symbols (International Phonetic Alphabet; e.g., /æ/, /θ/) appear in a figure reprinted from another source. This was done because teachers and remedial specialists are more familiar with phonic symbols and use them with their students.

Major topics include a historical and empirical perspective on multisensory instruction; the relationship between spoken and written language development; phonological awareness and training; knowledge of the alphabetic/phonemic system; insight into the history of English and its impact on learning to read, write, and spell; lexical knowledge; spelling rules and patterns; reading fluency; comprehension strategies; handwriting instruction; understanding of grammar; writing processes; math instruction; and study skills. Additional topics of interest are use of an interdisciplinary approach for in-depth study of a subject that includes multisensory teaching and learning; assessment gained through history, clinical observation, and testing; the complexities of transition from intensive assistance to general class inclusion; ways to help adults cope with long-standing issues of learning difficulties; and how professionals can aid parents in helping their child. The text explains specific multisensory methods and how to apply this knowledge during instruction with a variety of tested materials. Each step along the way to literacy and academic achievement is carefully outlined and illustrated with the sequence of necessary steps laid out within the framework of multisensory teaching.

DEFINITION OF DYSLEXIA

The definition of dyslexia used in this book is the one agreed on in 1994 by the Research Committee of the Orton Dyslexia Society and adopted by the National Institute of Child Health and Human Development (NICHD):

> Dyslexia is one of several distinct learning disabilities. It is a specific language-based disorder of constitutional origin characterized by difficulties in single word decoding, usually reflecting insufficient phonological processing abilities. These difficul-

ties in single word decoding are often unexpected in relation to age and other cognitive and academic abilities; they are not the result of generalized developmental disability or sensory impairment. Dyslexia is manifested by variable difficulty with different forms of language, often including, in addition to problems reading, a conspicuous problem with acquiring proficiency in writing and spelling. (as cited in Lyon, 1995b, p. 9)

MAIN CHARACTERISTICS OF DYSLEXIA

It is important to recognize the main characteristics of dyslexia, which affects 80% of those identified with learning disabilities (Lerner, 1989). It is typical that an individual with dyslexia will have some but not all of the problems described because of individual differences and access to early remediation.

The present working definition, based on empirical support, emphasizes that dyslexia runs in families, is inherited with genetic origins, and is associated with abnormalities in the language areas of the brain. It is manifested by weaknesses in phonological awareness, which prevent easy and early access to letter–sound correspondences and decoding strategies for automatic word recognition. This leads to overreliance on context and guessing instead of use of the alphabetic principle to decode words. Slow and inaccurate reading means that poor readers do not get to the meaning of the text, avoid reading, and fail to develop from text exposure the necessary vocabulary for comprehension and enjoyment of reading. Associated phonological weaknesses, short verbal memory span, and difficulty with word retrieval have also been identified in poor readers. These deficits can affect listening and reading comprehension. Students with dyslexia may spell poorly and have difficulty with the motor aspects of writing. Poor pencil grip and messy handwriting persist. Expression of ideas clearly in both written and oral form is slow to develop.

Other manifestations of dyslexia in early childhood are difficulty learning to talk along with lack of correct pronunciation of words. Following directions, retrieving names of things such as letters of the alphabet, sequencing, and/or forming letters or numbers can be areas of poor functioning. Characteristics that may accompany dyslexia include time management problems, lack of social awareness, and poor spatial sense. Attention disorders and organization difficulties are also associated with language-based reading disability.

Perhaps what puzzles teachers and parents the most is that students who fail to learn how letters represent speech sounds and how sounds are represented by the letters in words is that in other aspects of development these children often are good thinkers and are talented. They may excel in the arts, sports, computer technology, mechanics, or science, for example. Although boys are identified as having dyslexia four times more often than girls are, there are as many females as males with dyslexia. It affects people of all levels of intelligence. Dyslexia is a lifelong issue of constitutional origin that cannot be cured. With the right early intervention and prevention programs, students with dyslexia and other poor readers can increase reading skills to at least average levels. Such programs must combine instruction in phoneme awareness, phonics, spelling, reading fluency, and reading comprehension strategies taught by teachers who have in-depth research-based and experiential knowledge about reading development and difficulties.

Older individuals with dyslexia can also improve with intervention that focuses on remediation of reading and writing skills and other areas of weakness. Effective programs involve direct teaching using an MSLE approach. Modifications and accommodations, while not a substitute for remediation, along with the use of technology to support learning, can pave the way for many poor readers to gain information, expand their world knowledge, and be successful at school or work.

Approximately 17%–20% of school-age children are affected to some degree by deficits in phonological awareness (Lyon, 1999). Phonological awareness plays a vital role in learning to read because it helps children connect spoken language to written language. In kindergarten it predicts growth in word reading ability (Torgesen, Wagner, & Rashotte, 1994). When children do not have good word identification skills, they fall behind in reading and without appropriate intervention have only a one in eight chance of ever catching up to grade level (Juel, 1994). Without the ability to think about and manipulate the individual sounds in words, beginning and remedial readers risk falling behind or never catching up to their peers. Reading disability has far-reaching consequences, which is why we must be prepared to intervene early and intensively until the reader is on target for success. It is important for in-service and preservice teachers to be prepared to work directly with children with reading, writing, and spelling disabilities who also may have other co-occurring difficulties, such as difficulties with arithmetic calculation and mathematical reasoning. Without question, both general and special education teachers need the tools to identify students with language-based learning disabilities, to intervene with explicit instructional procedures, and to continue to sustain their students with intensive support for as long as they need it. Lyon stressed that

> Even children with relatively subtle linguistic and reading deficits require expertise of a teacher who is well trained and informed about the relationships between language development and reading development. Unfortunately, such teachers are in short supply, primarily because of a lack of professional certification programs providing this training. (1996, p. 67)

RESEARCH IN READING AND LEARNING DISABILITIES

Research since the 1980s and the experience of many professionals in the field of learning disabilities tell us that early and appropriate intervention can make a difference. Deficits in phonological awareness can be detected as early as kindergarten and first grade, and appropriate training programs can be provided that prepare children to be successful in reading and spelling. Contrary to that outcome is the bleak prospect of the findings from NICHD-supported research that 74% of the children with disabilities in reading who are not identified until third grade continue to have reading disabilities in the ninth grade although they may be in special education classes (Lyon, 1995b). Unfortunately, most children with learning disabilities are not identified until the third grade (Lyon, 1996). Colleges of education have a grave responsibility to improve the expertise of all teachers so that they really know how to address learning difficulties in accordance with research and years of clinical experience described in this book.

Table 1 summarizes research on beginning reading instruction. Teachers can use it as a reference to check their understanding of accepted principles of teaching reading from kindergarten through third grade. It can also serve as a point of reference for the typical progression of reading development. Table 2 is a compilation of the major findings from research programs in reading development, reading disorder, and reading instruction supported by the NICHD (Lyon, 1996; Shaywitz, 1998). This information needs to be disseminated and used as the foun-

Table 1.   What research is telling us about beginning reading instruction

Long before children begin to read, they need language and literacy experiences at home and in preschool to develop a wide range of knowledge that will support them later in acquiring linguistics skills necessary for reading. These include language play, such as saying nursery rhymes; writing messages; listening to and examining books; developing oral vocabulary and verbal reasoning; and learning the purposes of reading. Exposure to oral reading and language play fosters development of phonemic awareness.

It is essential that children learn the alphabet and be able to say the letter names in sequence, to recognize letter shapes, and to write the letters. These skills are powerful predictors of reading success.

Reading development depends on acquiring phonemic awareness and other phonological processes. *Phonemic awareness* is the ability to understand the sound structure in spoken words. To learn to read, however, children must be able to pay attention to the sequence of sounds or phonemes in words and to manipulate them. This is difficult because coarticulation means that separate sounds in words cannot be heard easily. Children learn to do this by engaging in intensive oral play activities, such as rhyming, alliteration, syllable counting, hearing and blending sounds, and analyzing initial and final sounds of words of sufficient duration, before beginning to learn to read. This training facilitates and predicts later reading and spelling achievement.

Along with the letter names, children need well-designed and focused phonics instruction to learn the sounds that the letters most commonly and consistently represent.

Fast and efficient decoding and spelling rest on the *alphabetic principle:* how the written spellings of words systematically represent the phonemes in the spoken words. The beginning reader must begin to connect the 26 letters of the alphabet with the approximately 44 phonemes of the English language.

Having command of the most frequent sight words (e.g., *of, from, the, once, only, are, to, and*) is important so that children can read more than just controlled texts when they are ready.

Children need to practice new sounds and letters using materials that directly reinforce the new information and that review what they already know for maximum gains in fluency and automaticity.

Fluency and comprehension depend on the ability to recognize words almost instantly and effortlessly. Slow decoders are poor at comprehension due to reduction in attentional and memory resources needed. Systematic word-recognition instruction on common, consistent letter–sound relationships supports successful word recognition skills.

Opportunities to apply phonetically regular spelling patterns and rules that match the reading patterns being learned give children a double immersion in the information. When children are familiar with the spelling regularities of English, their reading and writing are strengthened.

Instructional procedures should ensure that students in a literature-rich environment understand what has been read. Comprehension depends on activation of relevant background knowledge and is related strongly to oral language comprehension and vocabulary growth. Therefore, a balanced approach that includes strategies such as predicting, making inferences, clarifying misunderstandings, and summarizing while reading aids comprehension.

(continued)

Table 1.   *(continued)*

Readers with learning disabilities need highly systematic, structured, explicit, and intensive multi-sensory one-to-one or small-group instruction that matches their developmental level in phonological awareness, word recognition, and comprehension processes.

Whole-language instruction used in isolation has been found to be counterproductive with children with learning disabilities or children at risk of not learning to read and been found to produce fewer gains in word recognition and decoding skills than does instruction based on phonics.

Well-trained, accomplished teachers who can analyze instruction and achievement, who can set goals, and who can continue to learn about effective practice are the mainstay of children's success in learning to read.

Based on Adams (1990), Center for the Improvement of Early Reading Achievement (1998), and Lyon (1999).

dation for curriculum planning in teacher preparation as well as for prevention, intervention, and remediation of dyslexic learners.

THE NEED FOR WELL-PREPARED TEACHERS

There is abundant evidence that teachers generally are not taught what they need to know about learning to read and spell (Brady & Moats, 1997; Moats, 1994; Moats & Lyon, 1996) and that many teachers come to the classroom woefully unprepared in reading instruction to teach this extremely complex skill to their students. Teachers require a broad base of conceptual knowledge that informs them about what, when, and whom to teach, and, most important, how to teach in ways that motivate and help children learn. In 1979, Bateman called inadequate teacher preparation "the single greatest obstacle to successful reading instruction for learning disabled children." Long before reading, spelling, and writing become accurate and fluent, many steps need to be taken. The concern of this textbook is the steps of effective instruction, especially for children and adults with the most prevalent type of learning disability, dyslexia.

GAPS IN TEACHER PREPARATION

What has been lacking in teacher training is strong preparation in the structure of the English language and the linguistic insights to understand the phonological, morphological, syntactic, and semantic systems, all of which underlie written language instruction. One specific deficiency pointed out by Brady and Moats (1997) and Moats (1994) is that teachers rarely are informed of how to identify and categorize speech sounds. Such knowledge is essential for teaching phonemic awareness and letter–sound correspondences to children, particularly those at risk for reading difficulties (Cox, 1992). Moats (1994) noted that teachers are not taught the basics of phonemic awareness or the nature of sound–symbol correspondences nor are they familiar with how spelling represents spoken language. Familiarity with the history of the English language and its polyglot nature is helpful in explaining the organization of spelling patterns. Knowing the origins of words can provide a framework for teaching decoding skills throughout the grades (Henry, 1993). Other areas lacking in teacher preparation are handwriting instruction, organization and study skills, expository writing, and comprehension strategies. Adult educators are seldom given any insight into the primary difficulties of their adult students who struggle with undiagnosed learn-

Table 2.   Major findings from research programs in reading development, disorder, and instruction supported by the National Institute of Child Health and Human Development (NICHD)

Converging evidence from longitudinal and population-based data indicate that at least 17%–20% of children have significant reading disability. Among these children, there is a dispro-portionate representation of children from low-income families, from racial minorities, or who are nonnative speakers of English. However, large numbers of children from all socioeconomic groups, races, and ethnic groups have significant difficulties with reading.

Learning to read is not a natural process. Most children require systematic and explicit instruction (see Table 1).

Children most at risk for reading failure have limited exposure to English; little understanding of phonemic awareness, letter knowledge, print awareness, and the purposes of reading; and lack oral language and vocabulary skills. Children raised in poverty, children with speech and hearing impairments, and children whose parents or caregivers have weak reading skills are also at risk for reading failure.

As many females as males manifest dyslexia; however, schools identify three to four times more dyslexic boys than girls.

Children with reading disability differ from one another *and* from other readers along a continuous distribution and do not aggregate together to form a distinct "hump" separate from the normal distribution.

Definitions that measure the discrepancy between IQ scores and achievement do not adequately identify learning disabilities, particularly in the area of beginning reading skills. Plus, differences on measures of decoding and word recognition skills have not been found between children with reading disabilities with high IQ scores and children with lower scores.

All individuals with reading disabilities show similar profiles when examined for accurate and rapid reading of single words. A common characteristic is slow, labored reading of words.

Providing oral language and literacy experiences from birth onward, including reading to children, playing with language through rhyming and games, and encouraging writing activities, are impor-tant to vocabulary development and enhance verbal reasoning, semantic, and syntactic abilities.

Early identification and intervention is essential to successfully treat children who are at risk for reading failure. There are accurate and reliable identification procedures that are linked to preven-tion programs.

Converging evidence from prevention and intervention studies shows that for children at risk for reading failure, highly direct and systematic instruction to develop phonemic awareness and phonics skills, reading fluency and automaticity, and reading comprehension strategies within a literature-rich environment are required to obtain maximum gains.

A reading disability reflects a persistent deficit rather than a developmental lag. Longitudinal stud-ies show that of those children who have a reading disability in the third grade, approximately 74% continue to read significantly below grade level in ninth grade. Without informed teaching they are unlikely to catch up.

As children get older, the intensity and duration of reading intervention must increase exponen-tially to achieve the same improvement that is possible with younger children.

Dyslexia is familial with a risk factor from 23% to 65% for a child who has a parent with dyslexia. There is strong evidence for a genetic basis for reading disabilities with deficits in phonological awareness reflecting the greatest degree of heritability.

Neurobiologic investigations show that there are differences in the temporoparietal and occipital brain regions among people with dyslexia and poor readers without dyslexia.

The ability to decode single words accurately and fluently is dependent on the ability to segment words and syllables into phonemes. Failure to develop adequate phonemic awareness is the core deficit contributing to reading disability. Speed and accuracy of single-word reading is predicted by facility in phonemic awareness, which poor readers have difficulty developing.

(continued)

Table 2. (*continued*)

The best predictor of reading ability from kindergarten and first-grade performance is phoneme segmentation ability. The development of phonemic awareness is necessary but not the sole component of learning to read. From the beginning, reading instruction must include attention to phonics principles for accurate and rapid decoding and active use of comprehension strategies.

The ability to read and comprehend is dependent on rapid and automatic recognition and decoding of single words. Slow and inaccurate decoding are the best predictors of deficits in reading comprehension.

Additional factors impeding reading comprehension include the following: vocabulary deficits, lack of background knowledge for understanding text information, deficient understanding of semantic and syntactic structures, insufficient knowledge of writing conventions for different purposes, lack of verbal reasoning ability, and inability to remember and/or retrieve verbal information.

Dyslexic readers may also have difficulties with the processes underlying the rapid, precise retrieval of visually presented linguistic information; measures of letter, digit, and color naming are predictors of later reading ability (see Wolf, 1997, for more on the non–NICHD-funded research in this area).

Approximately 15% of students with reading disability also have a disorder of attention. Approximately 35% of students with disorders of attention also have a reading disability. Reading disabilities and disorders of attention, however, are distinct. Disorders of attention exacerbate the severity of reading disability.

Longitudinal data indicate that systematic phonics instruction results in more favorable outcomes for individuals with reading disabilities than does an approach emphasizing context (whole-language approach).

Instruction by expert teachers with proper training and skills can prevent reading failure by emphasizing early development of phonemic awareness and, with intensive, direct instruction over a sufficient duration, can remediate deficient decoding and word recognition skills. The children with the most severe impairments, however, respond more slowly.

There still is serious underpreparation among teachers regarding language instruction. Teachers need to have multiple layers of expertise on how children acquire reading, the relationship between oral language development and reading development, the characteristics of reading disabilities, and the basic tenets of reading instruction methodologies. There needs to be serious reform in colleges of education.

Based on Lyon (1996, 1999); Shaywitz (1996); and Snow, Burns, and Griffin (1998).

ing disabilities in literacy programs. High-functioning dyslexics often need expert assistance as they continue to cope with their lifelong condition in their professional and personal lives.

A MANDATE FOR WELL-PREPARED TEACHERS

The National Commission on Teaching and America's Future (NCTAF) stated, "What teachers know and can do is one of the most important influences on what students learn" (as cited in Darling-Hammond, 1998, p. 6). This teacher resource is directed to this aim. The NCTAF examined studies and found that student achievement was determined most often by teacher expertise. Along with the positive influence of small class and school size, which allow teachers to know students well, teachers who know a lot about what and how they teach are a critical element of successful learning (Darling-Hammond, 1998). Knowledge of subject matter, student learning and development, and teaching methods are part and parcel of successful teacher preparation. The more time teachers spend on understanding the art and science of teaching, learning their chosen discipline, and training in teaching methods, the better they are at presenting subject matter clearly and making the "teachable moment" successful. This book is designed to help implement this model of teacher preparation.

MULTISENSORY STRUCTURED LANGUAGE EDUCATION

The proposals to improve practice, which are supported by the authors of this volume, agree with the content to be learned and principles of instruction adopted by IMSLEC for training specialists who work with individuals with dyslexia. Table 3 outlines what teachers need to understand about the linguistic units of speech and print. The areas of expertise listed in Table 3 are both the background information for teaching and the basis of the curriculum in MSLE for students with dyslexia. The principles of multisensory instruction outlined in Table 4 work in tandem with the content of instruction listed in Table 3.

Originally devised by Anna Gillingham, a school psychologist, and her colleague, Bessie Stillman, a remedial teacher, the basic multisensory, step-by-step approach to language learning was based on Dr. Samuel T. Orton's educational recommendations for remediating dyslexia and on his neurological theories. He advocated breaking language down into its smallest units and, at the same time, using all sensory pathways to learning (hands, eyes, ears, and voice) in order for the student to benefit from language training. Gillingham published her program of a phonics approach with specific multisensory procedures that integrated the teaching of reading, spelling, and handwriting in 1936. Gillingham's organization

Table 3.   Multisensory structured language programs: Content of instruction (what is taught)

Phonology and Phonological Awareness: Phonology is the study of sounds and how they work within their environment. A phoneme is the smallest unit of sound in a given language that can be recognized as being distinct from other sounds. Phonological awareness is the understanding of the internal linguistic structure of words. An important aspect of phonological awareness is the ability to segment words into their component phonemes [phonemic awareness].

Sound–Symbol Association: This is the knowledge of the various sounds in the English language and their correspondence to the letter and combinations of letters that represent those sounds. Sound–symbol association must be taught (and mastered) in two directions: visual to auditory and auditory to visual. Additionally, students must master the blending of sounds and letters into words as well as the segmenting of whole words into the individual sounds.

Syllable Instruction: A syllable is a unit of oral or written language with one vowel sound. Instruction must include the teaching of the six basic types of syllables in the English language: closed, open, vowel-consonant-*e,* *r*-controlled, and vowel pair [or vowel team]. Syllable division rules must be directly taught in relation to the word structure.

Morphology: Morphology is the study of how morphemes are combined to form words. A morpheme is the smallest unit of meaning in the language. The curriculum must include the study of base words, roots, and affixes.

Syntax: Syntax is the set of principles that dictate the sequence and function of words in a sentence in order to convey meaning. This includes grammar, sentence variation, and the mechanics of language.

Semantics: Semantics is that aspect of language concerned with meaning. The curriculum (from the beginning) must include instruction in the comprehension of written language.

From McIntyre, C.W., & Pickering, J.S. (1995). *Clinical studies of multisensory structured language education for students with dyslexia and related disorders* (p. xii). Poughkeepsie, NY: Hamco Corp; reprinted by permission.

Table 4. Multisensory structured language programs: Principles of instruction (how they are taught)

Simultaneous, Multisensory (VAKT): Teaching is done using all learning pathways in the brain (visual, auditory, and kinesthetic-tactile) simultaneously in order to enhance memory and learning.

Systematic and Cumulative: Multisensory language instruction requires that the organization of material follows the logical order of the language. The sequence must begin with the easiest and most basic elements and progress methodically to more difficult material. Each step must also be based on those [elements] already learned. Concepts taught must be systematically reviewed to strengthen memory.

Direct Instruction: The inferential learning of any concept cannot be taken for granted. Multisensory language instruction requires the direct teaching of all concepts with [continual] student–teacher interaction.

Diagnostic Teaching: The teacher must be adept at prescriptive or individualized teaching. The teaching plan is based on careful and [continual] assessment of the individual's needs. The content presented must be mastered to the degree of automaticity.

Synthetic and Analytic Instruction: Multisensory structured language programs include both synthetic and analytic instruction. Synthetic instruction presents the parts of the language and then teaches how the parts work together to form a whole. Analytic instruction presents the whole and teaches how this can be broken down into its component parts.

From McIntyre, C.W., & Pickering, J.S. (1995). *Clinical studies of multisensory structured language education for students with dyslexia and related disorders* (p. xii). Poughkeepsie, NY: Hamco Corp; reprinted by permission.

of the language for teaching in subsequent editions became the basis for teacher training and influenced the creation of many MSLE programs that developed specifically to remediate dyslexia and to prevent students from failing (Colony, 1995; Richardson, 1995). Thus, the Orton-Gillingham approach was established as a different way to learn language than had been used in the general classroom. Teacher training programs and curricula that reflect this orientation are listed in Appendix B, page 505.

CHAPTER SUMMARIES

Chapter 1—Multisensory Instruction

Chapter 1 introduces the definition, history, and efficacy of multisensory teaching. Over time, practitioners have learned that parsing language into small pieces with the aid of multisensory experiences and direct, systematic, sequential, and cumulative teaching allows struggling students to learn basic language skills. Following a careful analysis of the research literature, the chapter contains suggestions as to what research is needed to support the use of MSLE approaches. The use of such instruction to educate novice or poor readers in language concepts and associations integrating the senses—visual, auditory, kinesthetic, and tactile—is a focus of the chapter.

Chapter 2—Development of Oral Language and Its Relationship to Literacy

Language is perceived and used by humans on many levels and for many purposes, including reading. This chapter tackles language and its relationship to literacy and learning from both a developmental and a pedagogical point of view and describes the stark differences and the similarities of oral and written language. Chapter 2 focuses on making teachers aware of the role that language plays as a child learns to decode words and comprehend the meaning of written text. It details the components of language—form (phonology, morphology, and syntax), content (semantics), and use (pragmatics). For each of these components, the patterns of typical and disordered development and their parallel relationships to reading and writing are explained. The chapter also discusses the possible effects of middle-ear infections on overall language and academic development and offers suggestions for working with children with recurrent middle-ear infections.

Chapter 3—Phonological Awareness and Reading: Research, Activities, and Instructional Materials

When children can pay attention to the structure of oral language, they have acquired phonological awareness. This skill often is a stumbling block for children with dyslexia, and unless they receive explicit phonological awareness instruction before and while they are learning to read, their attempts may be extremely frustrating. This chapter describes the attributes and development of phonological processing, reviews research on the benefits and effectiveness of phonological awareness instruction, and explains the link between phonological awareness and reading. In addition, Chapter 3 suggests a number of screening tests that use phonological tasks as benchmarks. Then, several programs are presented that may be useful with all children but are critical to the reading success of children at risk for reading failure.

Chapter 4—Alphabet Knowledge: Letter Recognition, Naming, and Sequencing

Chapter 4 assembles a significant amount of evidence that letter recognition and naming are essential components in learning to read and gain access to information in our culture. Students with dyslexia especially need to have facility with the dictionary to check their work. The first section of this chapter advocates teaching accurate and fast letter recognition and letter naming when reading instruction begins. The second section of the chapter presents a variety of multisensory lessons, activities, and games to help students with dyslexia to develop reliable and rapid letter–sound associations. Many activities are derived from the experience of clinical practitioners and involve guided discovery teaching in which the teacher leads the learner to make discoveries through careful questioning based on the learner's knowledge. The final section of the chapter describes activities to teach alphabetizing skills. After acquiring alphabet skills, it is not unusual for students with dyslexia to excel at them and gain a sense of confidence when dealing with word sources.

Chapter 5—A Short History of the English Language

Gillingham and Stillman (1956, 1997), whose work is the foundation of MSLE, deemed it essential that both the teacher and the remedial student be aware of the history of the English language. Keeping with that tradition, this chapter explains that instruction in phonics alone is not sufficient. Once students have learned the basics of the letter–sound correspondences, syllable types, and syllable division patterns, they will need to gain facility with words with Latin and Greek origins. Addressing the history of English in MSLE also provides a framework for teaching a decoding and spelling curriculum based on word origin and word structure. Students will be able to analyze numerous kinds of multisyllabic words more easily. Teachers who understand the origins of words can enhance their presentation of reading instruction, improve their assessment skills, communicate clearly about the features of the language, and convey useful strategies to their students. Chapter 5 outlines events in the development of English and then describes the letter–sound correspondences, syllable patterns, and morpheme patterns unique to English words of Anglo-Saxon, Latin, and Greek origin. This chapter also presents sample lesson plans centered around words from these origin languages.

Chapter 6—Teaching Reading: Accurate Decoding and Fluency

The heart of MSLE is reading instruction. Accurate and fluent reading should be the outcome of a well-structured research- and language-based reading program. Chapter 6 presents a blueprint for such a program and discusses both the developmental stages of learning to read and a precise, step-by-step curriculum appropriate for a range of students. Chapter 6 first delineates the key elements of a multisensory, structured presentation of decoding instruction, phonemic awareness, and letter recognition. Next, this chapter explains how to introduce the concepts of vowel and consonant sounds and blending sounds. Decoding instruction can easily be incorporated into a literature-based reading curriculum, and an example of a daily lesson plan is provided. The chapter also describes syllable types in English and how to introduce them to students. Morphology units (prefixes and suffixes) and syllable division are given the same careful analysis. In addition, the chapter presents a specific procedure of teaching irregular words and gives suggestions for the development of fluency in both oral and silent reading.

Chapter 7—Teaching Comprehension from a Multisensory Perspective

Comprehension is the primary goal in purposeful reading. To comprehend is to assemble many complex linguistic and cognitive processes, such as using background knowledge; making predictions; summarizing, analyzing, and evaluating ideas; and drawing conclusions. Chapter 7 opens with a historical overview of comprehension instruction; an overview of various approaches to teaching comprehension; and a discussion of intra-learner factors that can affect its development. The chapter addresses when to begin comprehension instruction and what materials to use. The chapter also contains an explicit model showing a teacher talking through the thinking process of getting meaning from the text, followed by detailed analysis and description of how to introduce, review, and practice comprehension in a multisensory framework. The chapter progresses from the introduction of the noun and words in other grammatical classes, to the teaching of sentence elements, to the introduction of links between comprehension and written composition and then presents outstanding examples of how to teach the elements of both narrative and expository texts.

Chapter 8—Teaching Spelling

Learning to spell is not simply a by-product of learning to read; it plays an important role in learning to read and enhances reading proficiency by reinforcing letter patterns. Spelling, however, is a far more difficult skill to learn than reading. Chapter 8 explains how spelling requires explicit instruction supported by the teacher's knowledge of how spelling develops, the structure of spoken and written language and how the orthography is represented in our alphabetic language. Therefore, this chapter describes spelling development and explores the problems of poor spellers, such as difficulties with phonological processing and with memory for letter patterns. Next, the chapter outlines the knowledge necessary for teaching spelling, such as an understanding of the sounds of the English language and how they are produced and a handle on the patterns and rules that govern how words are spelled. The chapter suggests an order of presentation in spelling instruction and many examples of discovery teaching procedures.

Chapter 9—Teaching Handwriting

In most books on reading and learning disabilities, handwriting instruction is given scant attention; in contrast, this chapter gives the rationale for placing handwriting in a prominent position as a vital component of MSLE. Handwriting instruction reinforces reading and spelling and provides practice in a skill with which students with dyslexia often struggle. In addition, fluent handwriting aids note-taking, test-taking, and other daily activities. Learning the shapes of each letter through analysis of strokes and structured practice promotes the integration of the visual, motor, and phonological characteristics of letters and often leads to improvement in spelling. Multisensory instruction in both print and cursive handwriting is presented in this chapter with rationales for teaching each. Chapter 9 also outlines the stages of handwriting development. Proper paper, pencil, and body position are explained; pointers on working with left-handed students are given as well. The last section offers detailed lessons in print and cursive handwriting along with helpful charts that contain models of upper- and lowercase letter shapes with teacher verbalizations to promote consistency during lessons.

Chapter 10—Composition: Expressive Language and Writing

One of the difficulties that individuals with dyslexia have is a "conspicuous problem with acquiring proficiency in writing" (The Orton Dyslexia Society Research Committee, 1994, as cited in Lyon, 1995b, p. 9). Primary grade teachers need to teach written language skills as they begin teaching reading, spelling, and handwriting. Chapter 10 provides a program in composition instruction with clear guidelines and goals and addresses what to teach. This chapter describes sentence activities that use scrambled sentences, different sentence types, sentence kernels, and frequently used conjunctions and transition phrases. Then, the chapter provides paragraph activities that involve topic sentences and supporting details. Next, activities geared toward writing various kinds of longer expository compositions are given. Three useful outline forms are described with preliminary activities and directions to accomplish these sequenced steps in writing. The chapter suggests techniques for revising and editing and lists many questions that teachers can use to help students focus on ways to improve and correct their work.

Chapter 11—Multisensory Mathematics Instruction

The difficulties that children with learning disabilities have with language concepts and associations, with memory, and with sustained attention also affect their grasp of mathematical concepts. This chapter explains a teaching approach that helps children discover mathematical concepts and relationships through student and teacher manipulation of multisensory materials such as blocks, numbered tiles, and trays of various sizes. The chapter first describes children's exploration of the materials and the many things they can do with numbers. They develop a language of mathematics as they naturally express their thoughts about their discoveries. The next step is to record the ideas with math symbols. Then, students learn number patterns, which they later relate to addition and subtraction facts, and they learn all of the combinations that make up 10. They also learn how to record math facts as equations. The chapter explains numerous games and activities so that students can gain confidence in such concepts as place value, zero, and the meaning and structure of two-digit numerals. Next, students learn the concept of regrouping for addition and subtraction. The chapter then suggests a sequence for teaching the multiplication tables. Division, including division with a remainder and word problems, is addressed in the final section of the chapter.

Chapter 12—Applying Multisensory Techniques to Interdisciplinary Studies

This chapter illustrates how the in-depth study of a topic can help students capture the connections among subject areas in school and avoid fragmented learning. Rather than rely on abstract textbook descriptions of a topic, dyslexic students can engage in real-life presentations of materials. In addition, students are more likely to remember the information and feel in control of learning. Children with weak reading and writing skills can participate using well-developed skills in other areas such as art, music, drama, or crafts. Chapter 12 explains ways to choose what to study in a thematic unit based on the style of education in the school, the expectations of the community, and, most of all, the needs of the students and teachers. Through examples from actual classes of students with learning disabilities, the chapter also demonstrates how a unit of interdisciplinary studies can be taught at many different levels. The chapter also addresses how to wrap up a thematic unit so that students can share their knowledge with others and how to evaluate students using multisensory methods instead of traditional testing only. The chapter ends with a discussion of ways teachers can gain support for multisensory, interdisciplinary teaching.

Chapter 13—Organization and Study Skills

This chapter focuses on the techniques for training students in organization, time management, and specific learning strategies and study skills, which can be adapted immediately and applied to content subjects. The chapter details the typical difficulties of dyslexic adolescents and the effect of these difficulties on learning and academic success. Next, tips on working with preadolescent and adolescent dyslexic students are described, followed by a description of the materials to be used and the specific way in which to arrange them. Then, the chapter describes learning strategies and study skills techniques. The first phase of study skills training consists of "Quick Tricks" to help improve the student's relationship with his or her teachers. The second phase of study skills training comprises "Advanced Quick Tricks" to clear up high-frequency spelling and mechanics errors and to give the student strategies for completing work and dealing with long texts in emergencies. The third phase of study skills training attends to critical thinking and developing higher order language skills, such as proofreading, using memory aids, writing summaries, and creating outlines.

Chapter 14—Assessment of Progress

The first section of Chapter 14 discusses a diagnosis of dyslexia as a disorder that is separate from other reading and spelling problems. Case studies illustrate the academic achievements and lifelong language difficulties of three college students with dyslexia. The second section of the chapter describes the sources of information, including different kinds of tests, school records, and a detailed family history, that are used to make a diagnosis of dyslexia. The third section of the chapter describes information needed to assess a student's progress, such as skill at reading single words, knowledge of letter–sound associations, and spelling proficiency. This section also names checklists and inventories that teachers may use to obtain this information. This chapter provides a useful overview of diagnostic evaluation of dyslexia and its usefulness to individuals, parents, and educators.

Chapter 15—Transition to the General Classroom and Content Areas

Chapter 15 discusses how educators can prepare a student with learning disabilities to make the transition from receiving remedial language training in a separate classroom to attending the general classroom on a full-time basis. The chapter begins with a review of the laws mandating accommodations during and after transition and a description of different combinations of MSLE in remedial pullout programs and general classrooms, followed by a case study of how one school handles remedial language training and transition. Next, the chapter offers specific tips on adapting multisensory strategies in general classrooms and meeting the needs of students with learning disabilities. In addition, the chapter discusses when a student is ready for transition, what planning must take place, and how to help students become self-advocates.

Chapter 16—Reading and Writing Instruction in Adult Basic Education

It is now known that dyslexic children who do not receive remediation have as adults the same inadequate phonological awareness abilities and poor decoding skills that they had when they were younger. This chapter explains some of the difficulties encountered by adults with dyslexia, such as inability to focus while listening or reading. Chapter 16 describes two examples of the Starting Over (Knight, 1986) program, developed to diagnose and provide remediation using MSLE methods for adult readers with phonological awareness deficits and decoding weaknesses. The Starting Over diagnostic session asks the prospective student to complete tasks such as segmenting and counting sounds in words, naming the letters for sounds heard, and spelling words and numbers. Subsequent Starting Over classes include phonological awareness exercises, blending letters and word parts, spelling, defining words and finding techniques for remembering them, and writing sentences. This chapter contains a sample lesson plan followed by case studies of adults who have succeeded in Starting Over classes.

Chapter 17—Working with the High-Functioning Dyslexic

Many high-functioning adults with dyslexia seek to move on in their academic work or careers yet suffer from chronic feelings of inadequacy, stress, and low self-esteem in relation to their ability to learn, read, or write. Among them, difficulty in the early grades and uneven functioning throughout school are common experiences. Chapter 17 outlines how remedial specialists can work with these individuals on a one-to-one basis, starting with an assessment that includes tests and a writing sample from the individual that recounts school memories. This written passage provides a rich source of diagnostic information and a way to get to know the client. This chapter presents excerpts from four adults' writing samples that illustrate the painful experiences and feelings arising from early schooling that have had an impact on these four adults to this day. The chapter explains the areas in which high-functioning dyslexic adults often need help and names goals of remediation: helping the individual perceive him- or herself as a person who can learn, teaching the individual awareness of his or her thinking process, and reducing learning-related anxiety. The chapter gives pointers on how to achieve these goals and concludes with two case studies.

Chapter 18—Parenting the Child with Dyslexia

Chapter 18 emphasizes the importance of guidance and counseling for parents and caregivers of dyslexic children to help them deal with the many social, emotional, and behavioral issues that arise at home and at school because of the nature and implications of dyslexia. The chapter offers information on matters such as enhancing communication; working with parents who may also have dyslexia; helping families with organization, time management, and prioritization; and helping parents who feel overwhelmed. Also included in the chapter are a suggested training regimen for professionals, including the knowledge and experience needed to work effectively with parents and families, and a recommended library of key books and resources.

REFERENCES

Adams, M.J. (1990). *Beginning to read: Thinking and learning about print*. Cambridge: The MIT Press.

Bateman, B. (1979). Teaching reading to learning disabled and other hard-to-teach children. In L.B. Resnick & P.A. Weaver (Eds.), *Theory and practice of early reading* (Vol. 1., pp. 227–259). Mahwah, NJ: Lawrence Erlbaum Associates.

Brady, S., & Moats, L.C. (1997). *Informed instruction for reading success: Foundations for teacher preparation*. Baltimore: The International Dyslexia Association.

Center for the Improvement of Early Reading Achievement. (1998). *Improving the reading achievement of America's children: 10 research-based principles* [On-line]. Available: http://www.ciera.org/resources/principles/principles.html

Colony, B. (1995). The history of Orton-based multisensory structured language methods. In C.W. McIntyre & J.S. Pickering (Eds.), *Clinical studies of multisensory structured language education for students with dyslexia and related disorders*. Poughkeepsie, NY: Hamco Corp.

Cox, A.R. (1992). *Foundations for literacy: Structures and techniques for multisensory teaching of basic written English language skills*. Cambridge, MA: Educators Publishing Service.

Darling-Hammond, L. (1998). Teachers and teaching: Testing policy hypotheses from a national commission report. *Educational Researcher, 27*(1), 5–15.

Gillingham, A., & Stillman, B.W. (1956). *Remedial training for children with specific disability in reading, spelling, and penmanship*. Cambridge, MA: Educators Publishing Service.

Gillingham, A., & Stillman, B.W. (1997). *The Gillingham manual: Remedial training for children with specific disability in reading, spelling, and penmanship* (8th ed.). Cambridge, MA: Educators Publishing Service.

Henry, M.K. (1993). Morphological structure: Latin and Greek roots and affixes as upper grade code strategies. *Reading and Writing: An Interdisciplinary Journal, 5*, 227–241.

Juel, C. (1994). *Learning to read and write in one elementary school*. New York: Springer-Verlag.

Knight, J.R. (1986). *Starting Over: A combined teaching manual and student textbook for reading, writing, spelling, and handwriting*. Cambridge, MA: Educators Publishing Service.

Lerner, J.W. (1989). Educational interventions in learning disabilities. *Journal of the American Academy of Child and Adolescent Psychiatry, 28*, 326–331.

Lyon, G.R. (1995a). Research initiatives in learning disabilities: Contributions from scientists supported by the National Institute of Child Health and Human Development. *Journal of Child Neurology, 10*, 120–126.

Lyon, G.R. (1995b). Toward a definition of dyslexia. *Annals of Dyslexia, 45*, 3–27.

Lyon, G.R. (1996). Learning disabilities. *The Future of Children: Special Education for Students with Disabilities, 6*(1), 54–76.

Lyon, G.R. (1999). The NICHD research program in reading development, reading disorders, and reading instruction: A summary of research findings. In *Keys to successful learning: A national summit on research in learning disabilities*. New York: National Center for Learning Disabilities.

McIntyre, C.W., & Pickering, J.S. (1995). *Clinical studies of multisensory structured language education for students with dyslexia and related disorders*. Poughkeepsie, NY: Hamco Corp.

Moats, L.C. (1994). Knowledge about the structure of language: The missing foundation in teacher education. *Annals of Dyslexia, 44*, 81–102.

Moats, L.C., & Lyon, G.R. (1996). Wanted: Teachers with knowledge of language. *Topics in Language Disorders, 16*(2), 73–86.

Richardson, S.O. (1995). Specific developmental dyslexia: Retrospective and prospective views. The history of learning disabilities. In C.W. McIntyre & J.S. Pickering (Eds.), *Clinical studies of multisensory structured language education for students with dyslexia and related disorders*. Poughkeepsie, NY: Hamco Corp.

Shaywitz, S.E. (1998). Dyslexia. *The New England Journal of Medicine, 338*(5), 307–312.

Snow, C., Burns, S., & Griffin, V. (1998). *Preventing reading difficulties in young children*. Washington, DC: National Academy of Sciences Press.

Torgesen, J.K., Wagner, R., & Rashotte, C. (1994). Longitudinal studies of phonological processing and reading. *Journal of Learning Disabilities, 27*(5), 276–286.

Wolf, M. (1997). A provisional, integrative account of phonological and naming-speed deficits in dyslexia: Implications for diagnosis and intervention. In B. Blachman (Ed.), *Foundations for reading acquisition and dyslexia* (pp. 67–92). Mahwah, NJ: Lawrence Erlbaum Associates.

Acknowledgments

I wish to dedicate this book to the teachers and future teachers who are actively searching for knowledge about what students with dyslexia need to master, to succeed in school and beyond. My experience tells me that teachers also want to learn different kinds of effective methods that will help them deliver appropriate instruction to all students. I extend my deep gratitude to the many extraordinary teachers and researchers who inspired me to reach for the best to help individuals with learning difficulties: Marilyn J. Adams, Alice Ansara, Connie S. Burkhalter, Jeanne S. Chall, Sally Childs, Aylett R. Cox, Jeannette Fleischner, Alice Garside, Jeannette J. Jansky, Diana H. King, Shirley Kohn, Alice Koontz, Isabelle Y. Liberman, G. Reid Lyon, Louisa C. Moats, Cecile Pollack, Margaret B. Rawson, Hyla Rubin, Roger Saunders, Margaret Jo Shepherd, Arlene Sonday, and Joanna P. Williams. I have been privileged to know and work with Mary Hercus-Rowe, Ethel L. Kasten, and Irene Michaud in the Multisensory Teaching of Basic Language Skills Series at Teachers College, Columbia University; and Lenox Reed, executive director of the Neuhaus Education Center. The rigorous standards they all have applied to their own work have been transmitted to their willing students and set an example for us to emulate. Acceptance of the status quo is anathema. They believe in paying close attention to clinical experience and ongoing research so that what they teach gives substance to their efforts to train teachers appropriately for the challenging task of working with students with language-based learning difficulties.

I want to thank the contributors to this book who willingly shared their expertise so that future teachers could be adequately prepared and teachers in the field could benefit from continuing professional development. They worked hard to encapsulate their ideas and firsthand knowledge into individual chapters so that a broad representation of necessary information could be included.

My graduate students in the Program in Learning Disabilities at Teachers College, Columbia University, deserve special thanks for their assistance in reviewing draft chapters. They made sure that the materials made sense to the intended audience. Anne M. Glass created the glossary and assisted in the fine details of checking references and permissions to reprint. I was able to have her assistance through the generosity of the San Marcos Civic Foundation of Austin, Texas, who provided the funding. Holly Baker Hill coded student responses to the draft chapters and organized the information in Appendix B. To both graduate students and to the foundation, I extend my deep gratitude.

I have been favored with many generations of family members who worked proudly as teachers. Teaching came naturally as a profession to me. Because dyslexia runs in my family, however, I was inspired to pursue the mysteries and the revelations of how to help people with language-based learning difficulties. I have had firsthand encounters with the joys and frustrations of learning how to meld the exciting, creative inside world with the often confusing outside world. As my daughter once said, "When you know what something is, it really looks like it!" Opening the doors to literacy for those who have inordinate difficulties with the written word is a deeply rewarding experience. Helping to enhance the many gifts and talents that people with dyslexia bring to the world is equally rewarding.

The staff at Paul H. Brookes Publishing Company have given me and all of the contributors sustaining support and encouragement during the time it took to bring all of the parts of the book together. Their expertise helped make the process both stimulating and challenging. I want to thank Elaine Niefeld, who had the original vision for the book. I gained a friend while Lisa Benson carried out her patient, generous, and skillful editing. Lisa Yurwit's support during the editing phase has been much appreciated. And, finally, my admiration goes to Mika Sam, a truly talented copy editor. She has seen that the book speaks with a vigorous and consistent voice.

With love and gratitude to my children, Andrew, Philip, and Joanne,
and to their children, Alexander, Abigail, Mark, and Neena,
who have all taught me so much

Multisensory Teaching
of Basic Language Skills

1

Multisensory Instruction

Louisa C. Moats and Mary L. Farrell

Multisensory teaching is commonly endorsed and practiced by teachers of students with a wide range of learning difficulties. Although multisensory teaching practices have been embraced by clinicians and teachers since the earliest teaching guides were written (e.g., Fernald, 1943; Gillingham & Stillman, 1960; Montessori, 1912; Strauss & Lehtinen, 1947), they have seldom been well defined or adequately validated by sophisticated research methods. This chapter defines what *multisensory education* means, discusses how it has been implemented in the past, evaluates what direct and indirect evidence there is for its efficacy, and describes what other research might be needed to validate the beliefs and practices of experienced clinicians.

DEFINITION AND HISTORY

The term *multisensory* has been used to refer to any learning activity that includes the use of two or more sensory modalities simultaneously to take in or express information. In education parlance, the term sometimes is used loosely to mean *multimedia*, as in playing videocassettes or audiocassettes, or to refer to generic hands-on activities in the classroom that engage the **tactile** (touch) or **kinesthetic** (movement) senses. The use of the term *multisensory* and the concern of this volume are more specific to the instruction of novice or poor readers in language concepts and associations that frequently involves a "hand-kinesthetic" component as language structure is learned. For example, alphabet letters are learned by feeling and naming three-dimensional forms; paragraph structure is modeled with Tinker Toys; or speech sounds are segmented by feeling and seeing the position of the mouth, lips, and tongue (see Figure 1.1).

Teacher:	Today we're going to learn a new sound. Listen and say these words while you watch your mouth in the mirror. Mop, mess, milk, mat, mud. What sound is your mouth making when you get ready to say those words?
Student:	Mop, mud, milk. [Says /m/]
Teacher:	What part of your mouth moved when you started those words?
Student:	My lips!
Teacher:	Were your lips closed or open when you started those words?
Student:	Closed.
Teacher:	Is the sound blocked or unblocked?
Student:	Blocked.
Teacher:	Right. Where does the air come out?
Student:	I don't know.
Teacher:	Hold your nose, and try to say /m/. Where does the air need to come out?
Student:	[Holding nose, says /m/] Through my nose.
Teacher:	Hold your throat. Is your throat buzzing? Are your vocal chords buzzing?
Student:	[Holding throat, says /m/] Yes.
Teacher:	What letter makes that sound, /m/?
Student:	M.
Teacher:	Vowels are open, and consonants are blocked. Is M a vowel or a consonant?
Student:	A consonant.
Teacher:	[Shows the M card; helps student discover a key word; asks student to trace the letter on a rough board, chalkboard, or salt tray while saying the name of the letter, the key word, and the sound it makes]

Figure 1.1.   Illustration of a multisensory sound–symbol activity.

Multisensory instruction is one dimension of the practices and approaches useful with students who have problems with learning that are described in this book. Although some traditional methods (Fernald, 1943) have not emphasized the structure of spoken and written language, most programs following Orton-Gillingham principles for teaching language-related academic skills (see Clark & Uhry, 1995) have emphasized that the core content for instruction is the structure and use of sounds, **syllables,** words, sentences, and written discourse. Orton-based methods place equal emphasis on the necessity for instruction to teach language structure explicitly; to be systematic, cumulative, direct, and sequential; and to employ multisensory strategies. It is the combination of these principles, according to clinical consensus (see McIntyre & Pickering, 1995), that will facilitate students' ability to learn and recall information.

The idea that learning experienced through all senses is helpful in reinforcing memory has a very long history in pedagogy. Educational psychologists of the late 19th century promoted the theory that all senses, including the kinesthetic sense, are involved in learning. The second volume of James's (1890) *The Principles of Psychology* discussed Binet's theory that all perceptions, in particular those of sight and touch, involve movements of the eyes and limbs and that because such movement is essential in seeing an object, it must be equally essential in forming a visual image of the object. This theory was illustrated through descriptions of typical individuals who used tracing to bolster visual memory. Consistent with this theory were observations that the loss of acquired reading ability as a result of impaired visual memory in adults with brain injury could be bypassed through the use of a kinesthetic **modality** (tracing letters).

> Individuals thus mutilated succeed in reading by an ingenious roundabout way which they often discover themselves: It is enough that they should trace the letters with their finger to understand their sense. The motor image gives the key to the problem. If the patient can read, so to speak, with his fingers, it is because in tracing the letters he gives himself a certain number of muscular impressions which are those of writing. In one word, the patient reads by writing. (James, 1890, p. 62)

The late 19th-century medical literature also contained discussions about individuals who had lost their ability to read because of cerebral dysfunction (Berlin, 1887; Dejerine, 1892; Morgan, 1896). Hinshelwood (1917) was the first physician to advocate a specific instructional approach for written language disorders in children identified as "word blind." On the supposition that reading failure was due to underdevelopment or injury of the brain, he recommended instruction using an alphabetic method in a manner that would appeal to as many cerebral centers as possible.

S.T. Orton, a neurologist, was the first person to report in the American medical literature on **word blindness** (1925, 1928). He proposed that there was a physiological failure of the brain to develop a clearly dominant language hemisphere to subsume reading, writing, and spelling (1937). The lack of dominance, he hypothesized, led to an unusual persistence of symbolic reversals in dyslexic individuals. Like Hinshelwood (1917), he advocated the use of all sensory pathways to reinforce weak memory patterns. Orton (1928) called for education methods based on simultaneous association of visual, auditory, and kinesthetic fields, for example, by having the person sound the visually presented word and establish consistent **directionality** by following the letters with the fingers during sound synthesis of syllables and words. He stressed the unity of the language system and its sensorimotor connections and stated that listening, speaking, reading, and writing were interrelated functions of language that must be taught in tandem.

Both the medical and psychological literature of the early 19th century influenced educational practice. Hunt (1964) reported that in the early 20th century, motor response was considered extremely important in learning. Fernald (1943) described how the kinesthetic aspect of multisensory learning, primarily used for reinforcing word recognition through writing, was incorporated into the approaches of many leading practitioners of the time, including Dearborn (1929); Gates (1927); Hegge, Sears, and Kirk (1932); and Monroe (1932). The methods that have come to be most strongly associated with multisensory instruction today, however, are those developed by educators such as Montessori (1912), Fernald and Keller (1921), and Strauss and Lehtinen (1947), who were challenged by children with **dyslexia, learning disabilities,** and **attention disorders.**

The methods for the teaching of reading developed by Montessori, Fernald and Keller, and Strauss and Lehtinen are summarized in Table 1.1. A review of their methods reveals the multisensory nature of their instruction and, in particular, the strong role that the kinesthetic component plays in the learning process. Their rationales for tactile and kinesthetic teaching methods reflected their belief in the tenacity of muscular memory (Montessori, 1912) and the belief that children with nonspecific, developmental neurological impairments would profit from compensatory or bypass techniques used effectively with children with brain injury (Fernald, 1943; Strauss & Lehtinen, 1947). Fernald also asserted the need for tactile experience in word learning and reported the learning rate to be much more rapid when finger tracing was used than when a stylus or pencil was used. She quoted the work of Husband (1928) and Miles (1928) on maze learning to support her assertion.

The authors who are listed in Table 1.1 all reported very positive results in the educational growth of individual students and attributed their success to the use of kinesthetic methods. In each method, however, there was also an emphasis on language components and systematic, sequential, organized teaching. Fernald's (1943) technique differed from the others in that whole words or whole syllables were taught, not individual phoneme–grapheme relationships (apparently she had a hearing impairment and was unable to perform phoneme **segmentation** tasks herself). In contrast, Montessori (1912) and Strauss and Lehtinen (1947) did emphasize direct teaching of **phonics.**

Given the multiple factors that may have accounted for these practitioners' successes with individuals, including the intensity of their small-group and individual interventions, their case study reports and anecdotal claims cannot be taken as proof of the efficacy of multisensory instruction. Even Strauss and Lehtinen (1947) acknowledged that the effect attributed to multisensory teaching could be a primary consequence of augmented attention rather than of kinesthetic learning per se.

In her doctoral research, Bryant (1979) continued to explore these questions. The introduction to her dissertation provided a history of the use of multisensory instruction up to 1979, a summary of the research examining the theoretical assumptions underlying multisensory approaches, and a review of empirical studies on the use of multisensory instruction in reading with individuals with reading disabilities.

Bryant (1979) reported that until the 1970s, teachers of special education students firmly believed in the value of kinesthetic reinforcement, and she cited a number of well-known names in the fields of reading and learning disabilities who stressed the importance of multisensory approaches (Ayres, 1972; Cruickshank, Betzen, Ratzeburg, & Tannhauser, 1961; Dearborn, 1940; Frostig, 1965; Gates, 1935; Hegge, Kirk, & Kirk, 1940; Johnson, 1966; Kephart, 1960; Money, 1966; Monroe, 1932; Strauss & Lehtinen, 1947; Wepman, 1964). Bryant also found that teacher textbooks on the treatment of learning disabilities typically recommended the use of multisensory techniques in word-recognition instruction and for other domains of symbolic and conceptual learning.

Table 1.1. Overview of early 20th-century multisensory programs

Montessori (1912)	Fernald & Keller (1921)	Strauss & Lehtinen (1947)
Population: Children, 3–7 years old, from the tenements of Rome	*Population:* Nonreaders, that is, children of typical intelligence who failed to read after individual instruction by other recognized methods in Fernald's clinic	*Population:* Children with brain injury, that is, with organic impairment resulting in neuromotor disturbances in perception, thinking, and/or emotional behavior
Cause of disability: Economic and cultural deprivation	*Cause of disability:* "Certain variations" (Fernald, 1943, p. 164) in the integrated brain functioning of the same region in which lesions are found in acquired alexia	*Cause of disability:* Disturbances caused by accidental damage to the brain before, during, or after birth
Method:	*Method:*	*Method:*
1. Daily practice with pencil is given in nonwriting activities to develop muscles for holding and using pencil.	1. Word that child requests is written in large script. Child repeatedly traces word with index and middle fingers, saying it over to himself until he can write it from memory. Word is erased and child writes it, saying the syllables to himself as he writes. If word is incorrect, the process is repeated until the word can be written without the script copy. After a few words are learned, child is asked to read the word in print as well as script and then in print only. If incorrect, word is retaught as in the first presentation.	1. Readiness exercises "emphasize perception and integration of wholes; visual discrimination of forms, letters, and words; organization of space; [and] constructing a figure against a background" (p. 176) as well as "ear training" (p. 177).
2. Child is prepared to write through daily use of light sandpaper. Vowels are taught, and then consonants are begun.		2. Child learns to discriminate and reproduce sounds and to blend orally. Next, child learns to associate visual symbols and writing with sounds. Child learns to articulate sound(s) while writing single letters and then pairs. Child attends to auditory components and visual words, makes words on cards or paper with a stamping set, copies them with crayons emphasizing significant features with color, writes them on the blackboard, and builds them with letter cards.
• Teacher presents two vowel cards and says sounds. Child traces letter repeatedly, eventually with eyes closed.		
• Teacher asks child to give her cards corresponding to two sounds she pronounces. If child does not recognize letters by looking, then he traces them.	2. Child starts writing stories initially on subjects of interest to him and then, as his skill increases, on projects in the various school subjects. Child asks for any word he does not know how to write, and it is taught to him as described before he uses it. After the story is finished, child files new words under the proper letters in his word file.	3. Before child reads a story, he will have learned approximately 10 words in the story as single words, simple sentences, or phrases. They are later presented in varying contexts or exercises to check comprehension. Child is not expected to conform to
• Teacher asks child to give sounds for letters she presents.		
• When child knows some vowels and consonants, teacher dictates familiar words that child "spells" by selecting cardboard letters from a set containing only letters he knows.		
3. After about 1 month (for 5-year-olds), child spontaneously begins to write; that is, he uses a pencil for composing words.		

(continued)

Table 1.1. (continued)

4. When child knows all of the sounds, he reads slips of paper with names of objects that are well known or present.

Length of training: Average time for learning to read and write, starting from moment at which child writes, is about 2 weeks. Child begins reading phrases that permit teacher and child to communicate; they play games in which child solely reads directions and then implements them.

Curriculum control: Although Montessori reported no control for difficulty of words, there is strict control of phonograms written and read through prep stages. Child then reads only familiar words only after learning all of the sounds.

Phonics: Within the writing program, presentation is of phonograms is sequential and cumulative.

Kinesthetic component: "There develops, contemporaneously, three sensations when the teacher shows the letter to the child and has him trace it: the visual sensation, the tactile sensation, and the muscular sensation. In this way the image of the graphic sign is fixed in a much shorter space of time than when it was, according to ordinary methods, acquired only through the visual image. It will be found that the muscular memory is in the young child the most tenacious and, at the same time, the most ready. Indeed, he sometimes recognizes the letters by touching them, when he cannot do so by looking at them. These images are, besides all this, contemporaneously associated with the alphabetical sound." (p. 277)

Length of training: Average tracing period is about 2 months, with range of 1–8 months. After period of tracing, child develops ability to learn any new word by simply looking at word in script, looking at copy, and saying each part of word as he writes it.

Curriculum control: Because child usually is able to recognize words after he has written them, this provides a reading vocabulary that usually makes it unnecessary to simplify the content of the first reading.

Phonics: Sound of each letter is never given separately, yet child is instructed to segment the word into syllables as he writes.

Kinesthetic component: "Individuals who have failed to learn to read by visual and auditory methods show a spurt of learning as soon as the kinesthetic method is used. . . . The end product is a skill equal to that of individuals who learn by ordinary methods" (Fernald, 1943, p. 168). Fernald and Keller reported that the learning rate is much more rapid when using tracing with finger contact than when using a stylus or a pencil.

absolute standards of accuracy while reading words.
4. Child composes short story to be dictated to teacher. These are then written, lettered, or typed with primer typewriter to be read again.

Length of training: Not specified

Curriculum control: "The child's study of phonics is systematically enlarged. He prepares study materials for himself in the form of lists, cards, sliding devices, booklets, etc. using the phonograms which he encounters in his reading lesson. The work is extrinsic, i.e., the phonic study is supplemental to the reading lesson but closely correlated with it." (p. 180)

Phonics: No phonics training given

Kinesthetic component: "The reading instruction emphasizes accurate perception of words and very early attempts to make the relationship between visual and auditory perception a functioning one. In as many ways as possible, his attention should be drawn to the components of a word, both visual and auditory. He should build words from copy, making them on cards or paper with a stamping set; he should copy them with crayons, emphasizing significant features with color, write them on the blackboard, and build them with letter cards." (p. 179)

6

Bryant (1979) noted that popularity of both generic and reading-specific multisensory practices was attributable primarily to reports of success rather than to empirical evidence supporting either the theory or the practice of multisensory teaching. At the time, the prominent rationales offered to account for the power of multisensory instruction were 1) the notion of delayed cerebral lateralization for speech and language, 2) the idea that visual-perceptual skills were deficient in children with learning disabilities, and 3) the theory of deficient **cross-modal integration.** However, Bryant's review and subsequent reviews of the research literature in learning disabilities (e.g., Lyon & Moats, 1988; Moats & Lyon, 1993; Torgesen, 1991) failed to muster evidence in support of any of these explanations of learning or reading disorders. In addition, the existing studies of multisensory teaching methods were either conflicting or inconclusive. Bryant herself compared visual-auditory-kinesthetic word-study techniques with visual-auditory word-study techniques and concluded that young readers responded equally well to both. Other principles of good instruction, including enhancing student attention, providing feedback and modeling, avoiding overloading the student, giving sufficient practice, and providing effective reinforcement, accounted for student success.

Almost a decade after Bryant's (1979) review and intervention study, Clark (1988) also concluded that despite the widespread inclusion of multisensory techniques in remedial programs for dyslexic students and strong belief among practitioners using these techniques that they work, there was little empirical evidence to support the techniques' theoretical premises. Although many of the programs incorporating these strategies have been effective according to clinical reports, the specific contribution of multisensory methods to the overall success of those programs has not been adequately documented through rigorous manipulation of instructional conditions and subsequent measurement of outcomes.

A compilation of clinical studies on the effectiveness of multisensory, structured language teaching with students with dyslexia and learning disabilities has been published by McIntyre and Pickering (1995). All of the studies subscribed to the following principles of instruction: 1) simultaneous employment of visual-auditory-kinesthetic-tactile (VAKT) **linkages;** 2) systematic and cumulative organization of content; 3) direct, teacher-led instruction; 4) diagnostic teaching to mastery; and 5) **synthetic** and **analytic** presentation. These studies reflected the positive results typically reported by clinicians working with a wide range of students in varying environments. The lack of controlled comparisons with other approaches, however, weakens the claim that multisensory, structured language teaching is superior to other intensive, structured approaches. Furthermore, it is not possible to pinpoint which of the five major principles of instruction reflected in these studies accounts for the reported gains in reading or which programs of those described might be the most efficacious for certain types of children in specific environments.

STATE OF METHODS RESEARCH IN TEACHING READING

Traditionally, methods for teaching reading in an **alphabetic language,** beginning with the methods used by teachers in ancient Greece, have included direct teaching of the links between sounds and symbols (Matthews, 1966). The extensive literature on teaching reading, which includes hundreds of studies, has undergone several comprehensive reviews since the late 1960s, including Adams (1990); Anderson, Hiebert, Scott, and Wilkinson (1985); and Chall (1967, 1983), all of which concluded that direct, systematic teaching in phonics for beginning and remedial readers, along with much practice in text reading and instruction in various comprehension skills, is a necessary component of effective instruction. The studies reviewed reflect a variety of research methodologies, including small, well-controlled laboratory experiments and large-scale, multiple-classroom research. None of the major, comprehensive evaluations of research in reading instructional methods has concluded that phonics is unnecessary or unimportant in elementary instruction. Children with direct instruction in speech–print correspondences learn to read words, spell, and define vocabulary better than children who do not receive such instruction, especially if they are defined as "at risk" for failure (Adams, 1990; Snow, Burns, & Griffin, 1998). The evidence supporting the systematic teaching of sound–symbol correspondences and orthographic structure within a balanced instructional program is very strong (Snow et al., 1998).

Research has contributed an explanation of why such instruction is necessary and effective for learning to read alphabetic **orthography** and of which skills are necessary before children can respond to phonics teaching. Hundreds of studies have revealed the nature of skilled reading and the reading acquisition process (see, e.g., Adams, Treiman, & Pressley, 1998; Gough, Ehri, & Treiman, 1992; Perfetti, 1985; Share & Stanovich, 1995; and Vellutino et al., 1996, for reviews). Beginning readers must be aware or must learn that words are made up of individual speech sounds (**phonemes**). They must be able to represent in their minds the **linguistic** structure of words they are learning to read, primarily at the phoneme level but at other levels of language structure as well. Although it appears that good readers guess at words or that they read whole words as units, good readers in fact process virtually every letter of the words they read and are able, on demand, to translate print to speech rapidly and efficiently. It is the fluency of this translation process that permits a good reader to attend to the meaning of what is read. Therefore, it is logical that effective instruction with poor readers would seek to increase their awareness of phonemes and other linguistic units and that the speech-to-print translation process would become a focus of teaching until the children read fluently enough to focus on comprehension.

Indeed, a wide range of studies have shown that poor readers are marked by weaknesses in phoneme awareness, slow and inefficient decoding skills, inaccurate spelling, and related language-processing difficulties (see Lyon, 1995a, 1995b, for a synthesis of the research supporting these definitional aspects of dyslexia). Their problems are linguistic in nature and are related both to inaccurate and to inefficient linguistic coding at very basic levels of word and subword processes. When readers cannot **decode** print accurately, comprehension is impaired; too much mental energy is being used to recode the message, and too little is available for making meaning. Effective instruction addresses these issues as directly and systematically as possible (Vellutino et al., 1996).

National Institute of Child Health and Human Development Intervention Studies

In 1985 the federal government, through the National Institute of Child Health and Human Development (NICHD), assumed the challenge of understanding learning disabilities, with a focus on language and reading problems. Following the recommendation of a task force that defined the research agenda in learning disorders, which were regarded as a major public health problem (Alexander, 1996), longitudinal and epidemiological studies were funded to address basic questions still unanswered at that time: How many children have learning disorders? What are their characteristics? How should we define and differentiate various disorders? What will ameliorate them? These questions had not been addressed previously on the scale and with the scientific methodology that would be necessary to answer them (Lyon & Moats, 1997; Moats & Lyon, 1993). Five university-based projects were funded in 1987. These projects and three intervention studies that are still underway as of 1999 (see Lyon, Alexander, & Yaffe, 1997, for descriptions of these projects) have offered the following findings: **reading disability** (in particular, dyslexia) is the most prevalent learning disorder; it occurs equally often in girls and boys; reading disabilities and attention-deficit/hyperactivity disorder are highly heritable; most children do not recover spontaneously from early academic problems; and language processing, especially at the **phonological** level, is a primary causal factor in how well students learn to read and spell.

A new focus now characterizes the NICHD research program in learning disabilities: controlled comparisons of classroom and remedial intervention techniques for students with well-defined characteristics. The major intervention studies were directed by Foorman, Fletcher, and Francis at the University of Houston (Foorman, Francis, Beeler, Winikates, & Fletcher, 1997); Torgesen, Wagner, and colleagues at Florida State University (Torgesen, Wagner, Rashotte, Alexander, & Conway, 1997); Scanlon and Vellutino at the State University of New York at Albany (Scanlon & Vellutino, 1997; Vellutino et al., 1996); Berninger and colleagues at the University of Washington; and Morris, Wolf, and Lovett at Georgia State University, Tufts University, and the University of Toronto, respectively. Preliminary findings in Florida, New York, and Texas confirm that in kindergarten and first and second grades, systematic, direct teaching of phoneme awareness and phonics produces reading gains more quickly in children who are at risk for academic failure than do approaches that are indirect, implicit, unsystematic, whole-word oriented, or focused exclusively on comprehension. Many but not all children who are significantly below average in reading in third to fifth grade can be brought up to grade level if they are given intensive, linguistically informed teaching for up to 2 hours per day (Torgesen et al., 1997). Several methods seem to be equally effective, but all that are effective include direct teaching of language structure with an emphasis on decoding fluently and accurately. Ample practice with skill application in meaningful contexts is a component of effective teaching. Multisensory instruction, however, has not been a controlled variable in this research, although one of the approaches that is bringing positive results in students is the Lindamood Sequencing Program for Reading, Spelling, and Speech (LiPS; Lindamood & Lindamood, 1998), formerly called Auditory Discrimination in Depth, which emphasizes explicit, multisensory teaching of **phonology.**

As these projects continue, they will address questions about the relationship between the characteristics of individuals and their response to instruction; the relationship among reading, spelling, and writing practice in interventions for reading disability; the relationship of teacher knowledge to children's progress;

the timing, intensity, and duration of instruction necessary for improvement to occur in children with varying characteristics; and the relationship between learning and changes in brain function visible in **neuroimaging** studies. Given the state of intervention research, it is not surprising that formal, controlled studies that meet rigorous methodological standards have not yet addressed some of the subtle questions of teaching, such as why or whether multisensory presentation is superior to unisensory teaching or for whom it might be necessary.

Absence of evidence does not mean that the approaches lack efficacy; however, before the validation of experimental science is achieved, teachers must continue to practice with the tools deemed most efficacious by experienced clinicians. In the case of multisensory teaching, the collective experience of thousands of practitioners affirms the power of these techniques. In addition, what is already known about cognition, memory, and **neuropsychology** provides at least theoretical support for multisensory teaching.

Theoretical Support

Several lines of argument can be used to explain why multisensory teaching strategies appear to work. Well-known facts about the nature of attention, memory, verbal learning, and brain organization and function can explain the power of these techniques. All other things being equal, why would multisensory presentation and practice result in more rapid, effective, and enjoyable learning in students who have learning disabilities? If instruction is already systematic, direct, sequential, and focused on the structure of language, why might multisensory involvement add something vital to the learning process? One source of explanation is the design of memory itself.

The Nature of Memory   According to Wagner's (1996) overview of research on memory processes, **short-term** and **long-term memory** are not separate functions that reside in different circuits or locations in the brain. Rather, short-term memory, or working memory, is most likely the temporary activation of selected and established long-term memory stores. During the conscious learning of any new information, a large number of organized patterns of neural networks are activated temporarily. This activation of selected circuitry lasts as long as attention is focused on a specific bit of information; otherwise, the activation pattern decays quickly as attentional shift occurs. Control processes such as selective attention, attentional shift, and employment of strategies for remembering such as **verbal rehearsal** or use of imagery are features of working memory as well.

Within working memory, which is important in reading, are specialized storage mechanisms including a **phonological loop** that can store small bits of speech information as they are being processed and a **visuospatial loop** that can store print or graphic information. The functional separation of these parts of working memory have long been evident in various experiments, including those that show that it is easier to integrate multiple sources of information during learning when the material is physically integrated, auditorily and visually, than when information is presented to each modality separately (Mousavi, Low, & Sweller, 1995).

Bits of speech information held in the phonological loop are interpreted in a different workspace that subsumes comprehension or the construction of meaning. Previous knowledge of the domain of information being processed determines comprehension more than any limitation of working memory capacity. Therefore, the processes of initial word identification and subsequent interpretation of those words are served by different functions within working memory, and comprehension is very much a product of prior knowledge. Storage and retrieval of knowledge from long-term memory improve with practice and vary with subject-matter familiarity. Long-term memory content is created differently according to the different types and purposes of memories, including experiential, semantic, procedural, and automatic response memories.

The phonological loop is the special part of working memory that has been implicated in dyslexia or reading/spelling disabilities. It is responsible for such feats as remembering a novel list of unrelated digits or words or a novel phonological string such as a **nonsense word** or an unfamiliar word from a foreign language. According to Torgesen's (1996) review, the phonological loop includes a phonological memory store to hold speech information for a brief period while speech is being interpreted and an articulatory control process that activates speech-motor programs. This articulatory control process is central, not peripheral, in its location and function: It is functionally dissociated from the parts of the brain that control speech musculature and the peripheral hearing mechanism. One can have a severe disorder of speech production and/or a hearing loss but have intact central articulatory control processes.

Items such as names of letters, individual speech sounds (phonemes), and words are represented in the phonological memory store as a set of distinctive features. For example, the /m/, /n/, and /ng/ phonemes all are **nasal stop** consonants that differ only in place of articulation. Research has shown that when features are shared among phonemes, those units of sound are likely to be confused with one another. When a child says "aminal" for "animal," or when the child spells "con" for "comb," the exact features of the nasal consonants in those words are not being processed accurately in the phonological memory store. To improve pronunciation, word recognition, or spelling, the child needs to establish memories for words with nasal consonants in which the features of sounds are fully specified and differentiated from one another. To reduce the possible confusion of speech sounds with shared features, a speech-motor program that provides an internal "image" of the gestures involved in saying the phonemes can be deliberately engaged. There is evidence that children with phonological disabilities improve in **phoneme awareness,** reading, and spelling when they actively study and feel the precise articulatory gestures involved in word production (Torgesen et al., 1997).

In brief, memories for phonological units are deficient in children with reading disabilities, in that the units are not fully specified as sets of distinctive features. Memories are likely to be strengthened by a conscious awareness of articulation mechanisms and attention to the distinguishing features of similar, confusable units. In this way, listening, speaking, reading, and writing, along with other related tactile and kinesthetic activities, could produce multiple representations of linguistic units in working memory that would improve the explicitness, completeness, and durability of what is stored in long-term memory.

Lessons from Neuropsychology   Studies of humans who have sustained brain injury and studies of animals with acquired lesions indicate that there are at least two forms of long-term memory processes that involve different neural systems (Bachevalier, Malkova, & Beauregard, 1996). One subsumes incremental learning of habits and skills, such as are involved in classic conditioning of one association to another, perceptual learning of feature discrimination, and even complex problem solving that is habituated (performed automatically). The other type of long-term memory involves recall of episodes and situations including memory of having engaged in a learning activity and memory of sets of procedures that are consciously employed to solve problems or to execute tasks. Only the latter type of long-term memory is affected in amnesia (acquired memory loss). Patients with amnesia have been able to learn habits and skills (conditioned, associative learning) even though they have no recall of having engaged in the learning experience (declarative, explicit recall). Both of these long-term memory systems depend on the integrity of many areas of the brain and the connecting circuits between them.

The discovery of these two types of long-term storage processes suggests that the practice of teaching motor habits and associations through conscious or explicit verbalization and analysis, such as the formation of letters, could be effective for students with deficits in symbolic association ability. Students would learn to employ one type of memory process to compensate for a weakness in the other.

Functional Neuroimaging   There is substantial evidence that students with specific language-based reading disabilities demonstrate neural abnormalities in the language areas of the left cerebral hemisphere (Rumsey, 1996). **Functional neuroimaging,** in which images are constructed of the brain activity of subjects performing specific tasks while awake, can provide concrete evidence of how the brain is organized for reading (Shaywitz et al., 1996). Multiple sites and multiple connections among those sites are activated during typical reading. The brain does not store information in localized compartments but rather establishes highly specialized and widely distributed networks that can be interrupted when damage occurs to specific areas. Messages from print are processed first in the visual (occipital) cortex, then in the **left angular gyrus,** which is linked to the left hemisphere's speech-processing centers. The left angular gyrus is the primary location for translating visual-orthographic information into phonological representations (linking symbol to sound). The nearby language association areas connect meaning to those phonological codes. Other connections also link the visual association cortex to speech-processing areas. (Figure 1.2 shows the areas of the brain that are involved in reading.) The neural connections for reading are so specialized that the type of word one is reading—for example, a noun or an adjective, will affect the exact sites that are activated for processing. Processing proceeds simultaneously and interactively, even though specific modules or neural connections are highly specialized for processing jobs (Rumsey, 1996). During reading, when compared with children without reading disabilities, children with poor phonological processing show reduced cerebral blood flow in the left temporal cortex (where incoming language is coded and interpreted) and reduced activation of language areas normally involved in reading. Underactivation of left hemisphere language areas and abnormal activation patterns continue to characterize dyslexic adults, even when they have learned to read reasonably well.

From this functional neurological model, a working hypothesis would be that dyslexic individuals learn to read by establishing alternative circuits for word recognition. Alternative pathways could be established when multiple representations of language (phonological, orthographic, motoric, **semantic,** syntactic) are stimulated during multisensory instruction.

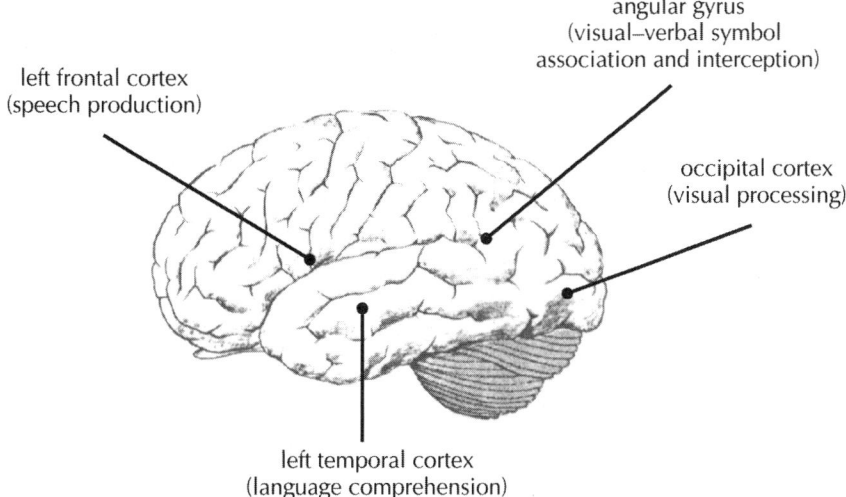

angular gyrus
(visual–verbal symbol
association and interception)

left frontal cortex
(speech production)

occipital cortex
(visual processing)

left temporal cortex
(language comprehension)

Figure 1.2. Left cerebral hemisphere, areas subsuming reading. (From an illustration by Bunji Tagawa in Llinas, R.R. [1975]. *Scientific American, 232[1],*59; adapted by permission from the Estate of Bunji Tagawa.)

Principles of Cognition   Even before so much was known about the nature of linguistic deficits in reading disabilities, there was substantial evidence that successful instructional practices with students who had learning disabilities included deliberate provision of reinforcement and conscious employment of responsive, strategic learning (Lyon & Moats, 1988; Swanson, 1989; Wong, 1991). As cognitive psychologists have repeatedly demonstrated, learning is an active, constructive process in which new information is linked with established **schemata** (Wittrock, 1992). The brain transforms new information in accordance with stored information that it has activated during the learning process. Active learning is that which causes the learner to mentally search for connections between new and already-known information. That is, instruction that includes teaching of **metacognition**—the deliberate rearrangement, regrouping, or modal transfer of information, and the conscious choice of and evaluation of the strategies used to accomplish a task—is more effective than rote or passive memorization approaches in almost every domain of learning. For example, students who create their own mnemonic strategies tend to learn from those more readily than students who are provided with a mnemonic strategy. Students who "think aloud" while working remember more and make fewer errors. Students who respond motorically, who must do something as they learn, attend better to the details and meaning of a stimulus and are likely to remember more.

Adams and her colleagues (1998) completed an extensive review of the research literature on reading comprehension instruction. They concluded that the active (vocal) modeling and rehearsal of basic comprehension functions such as summarizing, questioning, and predicting during an interaction among a teacher and group of students was much more effective in improving comprehension than was structured seatwork or independent silent reading. The high rate of active response on the part of students, the combination of reading and verbalization of ideas, and the emphasis on deliberate employment of learning strategies characterized instructional conditions that resulted in retention and generalization of comprehension ability.

SUMMARY

Multisensory teaching links listening, speaking, reading, and writing. The simultaneous and alternative deployment of visual, auditory, kinesthetic, and tactile sensory modalities has traditionally been a staple of remedial and preventive intervention for students with learning disabilities and/or dyslexia. Multisensory methods support the connection of oral language with visual language symbols and can involve the use of touch and movement to facilitate conceptual learning in all academic areas. The appeal of multisensory instruction endures even though it has been poorly defined and is not well validated in existing intervention studies.

As noted previously, multisensory techniques have been cited and recommended by experts in learning disorders before and throughout the 20th century. Although respected instructional programs incorporate similar instructional principles, research has contributed more to the definition and explication of the nature of dyslexia and learning disorders than it has contributed to remedial intervention. Science has substantially redefined the nature of dyslexia and learning disabilities. In other words, practitioners' beliefs about what works have remained quite stable even though conceptualizations of dyslexia and learning disabilities have changed substantially.

Prior to the conceptualization of dyslexia as a language-based disorder of phonological origin (Lyon, 1995a; Vellutino & Scanlon, 1991), many proponents of structured, multisensory, explicit language teaching endorsed the view that reading disability was primarily a visually based disorder. For many years, practitioners invoked various theories of modality preference, modality bypass, interhemispheric dominance, intersensory integration, and other ideas alluding to neurological organization to justify and explain the power of multisensory, structured teaching of language organization and other content. Most of those theories have been decidedly disproved or radically revised to accommodate the findings of cognitive, neuropsychological, neurological, and psycholinguistic research.

It is ironic that research-based conceptions of reading and language-based learning disabilities may provide a better theoretical rationale to explain why multisensory instruction works than are provided by the theories of the methods' originators. It is known that poor and novice readers at risk for reading and spelling difficulties are usually lacking in phonological skill and often have related problems with short-term memory of verbal information and rapid retrieval of verbal information. In addition, at least one third of children with language-based learning disabilities also have coexisting attention disorders. Such learners benefit when the structure of spoken and written language, beginning with phonemes, is represented for them explicitly, sequentially, directly, and systematically, in the context of balanced and comprehensive reading instruction. Multisensory experiences with linguistic units such as single phonemes, letters, **morphemes,** words, and sentences may in fact activate more circuitry during language learning than unisensory experiences.

Conceptions of memory organization, neural activation patterns in language processing, and the importance of metacognition are consistent with the efficacy of multisensory techniques. New neural networks, which in the human brain are highly specialized for certain processing functions, are established through repeated activation. When attention to linguistic detail is enhanced through multisensory involvement, a more complete and explicit registration of linguistic information (phonological and other) is likely to occur in the learner's working memory. Those transient associative memories are more likely to be stored in connection with existing information in the language processor if other movement or sensory events occur with them. Most likely, it is not simply the multimodal nature of such practice that explains its power but the mediating effect of various sensory and motor experiences on attention and recall.

Knowledgeable clinicians have been hoping for a scientific explanation for accepted instructional practices for many years. Eventually, cognitive psychology, educational psychology, and the neurosciences may provide more definitive support. Eventually, research may also provide more definitive answers to the question of what to do, for what types of children, when, how much, for how long, and in what environments. Until science delivers, there is no choice but to rely on common sense, good judgment, and the collective wisdom of many experienced teachers.

REFERENCES

Adams, M.J. (1990). *Beginning to read: Thinking and learning about print.* Cambridge: The MIT Press.

Adams, M.J., Treiman, R., & Pressley, M. (1998). Reading, writing, and literacy. In I. Sigel & A. Renninger (Eds.), *Handbook of child psychology: Volume 4. Child psychology in practice* (5th ed., pp. 275–355). New York: John Wiley & Sons.

Alexander, D. (1996). Learning disabilities as a public health concern. In S. Cramer & W. Ellis (Eds.), *Learning disabilities: Lifelong issues* (pp. 249–253). Baltimore: Paul H. Brookes Publishing Co.

Anderson, R.C., Hiebert, E.H., Scott, J.A., & Wilkinson, I.A.G. (1985). *Becoming a nation of readers: The report of the commission on reading.* Washington, DC: U.S. Department of Education, The National Institute of Education.

Ayres, J. (1972). Improving academic scores through sensory integration. *Journal of Learning Disabilities, 5*(6), 338–343.

Bachevalier, J., Malkova, L., & Beauregard, M. (1996). Multiple memory systems: A neuropsychological and developmental perspective. In G.R. Lyon & N.A. Krasnegor (Eds.), *Attention, memory, and executive function* (pp. 185–198). Baltimore: Paul H. Brookes Publishing Co.

Berlin, R. (1887). *Eine besondere art der wortblindheit: Dyslexia* [A special kind of word blindness: Dyslexia]. Wiesbaden, Germany: J.F. Bergmann.

Bryant, S. (1979). *Relative effectiveness of visual-auditory vs. visual-auditorykinesthetic-tactile procedures for teaching sight words and letter sounds to young disabled readers.* Unpublished doctoral dissertation, Teachers College, Columbia University, New York.

Chall, J.S. (1967). *Learning to read: The great debate.* New York: McGraw-Hill.

Chall, J.S. (1983). *Stages of reading development.* New York: McGraw-Hill.

Clark, D.B. (1988). *Dyslexia: Theory and practice of remedial instruction.* Timonium, MD: York Press.

Clark, D.B., & Uhry, J. (1995). *Dyslexia: Theory and practice of remedial instruction* (2nd ed.). Timonium, MD: York Press.

Cruickshank, W.M., Betzen, F.A., Ratzeburg, F.H., & Tannhauser, M.T. (1961). *A teaching method for brain-injured and hyperactive children: A demonstration–pilot study.* Syracuse, NY: Syracuse University Press.

Dearborn, W.F. (1929). Unpublished paper presented at the Ninth International Congress of Psychology, Yale University, New Haven, CT.

Dearborn, W.F. (1940). On the possible relations of visual fatigue to reading disabilities. *School and Society, 52,* 532–536.

Dejerine, J. (1892, February 27). Contribution a l'étude anatomo-pathologigue et clinique des différentes variétés de cécité verbale [Contribution to the anatomopathological and clinical studies of different types of word blindness]. *Mémoriale Société Biologigue*, 61.

Fernald, G.M. (1943). *Remedial techniques in basic school subjects*. New York: McGraw-Hill.

Fernald, G.M., & Keller, H. (1921). The effect of kinesthetic factors in development of word recognition in the case of non-readers. *Journal of Educational Research, 4,* 355–377.

Foorman, B.R., Francis, D.J., Beeler, T., Winikates, D., & Fletcher, J.M. (1997). Early interventions for children with reading problems: Study designs and preliminary findings. *Learning Disabilities: A Multidisciplinary Journal, 8*(1), 63–71.

Frostig, M. (1965). Corrective reading in the classroom. *The Reading Teacher, 18,* 573–580.

Gates, A.I. (1927). Studies of phonetic training in beginning reading. *Journal of Educational Psychology, 18,* 217–226.

Gates, A. (1935). *The improvement of reading: A program of diagnostic and remedial methods*. New York: Macmillan.

Gillingham, A., & Stillman, B. (1960). *Remedial training for children with specific disability in reading, spelling, and penmanship*. Cambridge, MA: Educators Publishing Service.

Gough, P.B., Ehri, L.C., & Treiman, R. (Eds.). (1992). *Reading acquisition*. Mahwah, NJ: Lawrence Erlbaum Associates.

Hegge, T.G., Kirk, S.A., & Kirk, W.D. (1940). *Remedial reading drills*. Ann Arbor, MI: George Wahr.

Hegge, T.G., Sears, R., & Kirk, S.A. (1932). Reading cases in an institution for mentally retarded problem children. In *Proceedings and addresses of the fifty-sixth annual session of the American Association for the Study of the Feebleminded, 15,* 149–212.

Hinshelwood, J. (1917). *Congenital word blindness*. London: H.K. Lewis.

Hunt, J.M. (1964). Introduction: Revisiting Montessori. In M. Montessori, *The Montessori method*. New York: Schocken Books.

Husband, R.W. (1928). Human learning on a four-section elevated finger maze. *Journal of General Psychology, 1,* 15–28.

James, W. (1890). *The principles of psychology* (Vol. 2). New York: Henry Holt & Co., Inc.

Johnson, M. (1966). Tracing and kinesthetic techniques. In J. Money (Ed.), *The disabled reader: Education of the dyslexic child* (pp. 147–160). Baltimore: The Johns Hopkins University Press.

Kephart, N.C. (1960). *The slow learner in the classroom*. Columbus, OH: Charles E. Merrill.

Lindamood, P., & Lindamood, P. (1998). *Lindamood sequencing program for reading, spelling, and speech: Teacher's manual for the classroom and clinic*. Austin, TX: PRO-ED.

Lyon, G.R. (1995a). Research initiatives in learning disabilities: Contributions from scientists supported by the National Institutes of Child Health and Human Development. *Journal of Child Neurology, 10,* 120–126.

Lyon, G.R. (1995b). Toward a definition of dyslexia. *Annals of Dyslexia, 45,* 3–27.

Lyon, G.R., Alexander, D., & Yaffe, S. (1997). Progress and promise in learning disabilities research. *Learning Disabilities: A Multidisciplinary Perspective, 8,* 1–6.

Lyon, G.R., & Moats, L.C. (1988). Critical issues in the instruction of the learning disabled. *Journal of Consulting and Clinical Psychology, 56,* 830–835.

Lyon, G.R., & Moats, L.C. (1997). Critical conceptual and methodological considerations in reading intervention research. *Journal of Learning Disabilities, 30,* 578–588.

Matthews, M.M. (1966). *Teaching to read: Historically considered*. Chicago: University of Chicago Press.

McIntyre, C.W., & Pickering, J.S. (1995). *Clinical studies of multisensory structured language education*. Poughkeepsie, NY: Hamco Corp.

Miles, W. (1928). The high finger relief maze for human learning. *Journal of General Psychology, 1,* 3–14.

Moats, L., & Lyon, G.R. (1993). Learning disabilities in the United States: Advocacy, science, and the future of the field. *Journal of Learning Disabilities, 26,* 282–294.

Money, J. (Ed.). (1966). *The disabled reader: Education of the dyslexic child*. Baltimore: The Johns Hopkins University Press.

Monroe, M. (1932). *Children who cannot read*. Chicago: University of Chicago Press.

Montessori, M. (1912). *The Montessori method*. New York: Frederick Stokes.

Morgan, W.P. (1896, November 7). Word blindness. *British Medical Journal, 2*, 1378.

Mousavi, S.Y., Low, R., & Sweller, J. (1995) Reducing cognitive load by mixing auditory and visual presentation modes. *Journal of Educational Psychology, 87*, 319–334.

Orton, S.T. (1925). "Word-blindness" in school children. *Archives of Neurology and Psychiatry, 14*, 581–615.

Orton, S.T. (1928). Specific reading disability—strephosymbolia. *JAMA, 90*, 1095–1099.

Orton, S.T. (1937). *Reading, writing, and speech problems in children.* New York: W.W. Norton.

Perfetti, C.A. (1985). *Reading ability.* New York: Oxford University Press.

Rumsey, J.M. (1996). Neuroimaging in developmental dyslexia: A review and conceptualization. In G.R. Lyon & J.M. Rumsey (Eds.), *Neuroimaging: A window to the neurological foundations of learning and behavior in children* (pp. 57–77). Baltimore: Paul H. Brookes Publishing Co.

Scanlon, D., & Vellutino, F. (1997). A comparison of the instructional backgrounds and cognitive profiles of poor, average, and good readers who were initially identified as at-risk for reading failure. *Scientific Studies of Reading, 1*, 191–215.

Share, D., & Stanovich, K.E. (1995). Cognitive processes in early reading development: Accommodating individual differences into a mode of acquisition. *Issues in Education: Contributions from Educational Psychology, 1*, 1–57.

Shaywitz, S.E., Shaywitz, B.A., Pugh, K.R., Skudlarski, P., Fulbright, R.K., Constable, R.T., Bronen, R.A., Fletcher, J.M., Liberman, A.M., Shankweiler, D.P., Katz, L., Lacadie, C., Marchione, K.E., & Gore, J.C. (1996). The neurobiology of developmental dyslexia as viewed through the lens of functional magnetic resonance imaging technology. In G.R. Lyon & J.M. Rumsey (Eds.), *Neuroimaging: A window to the neurological foundations of learning and behavior in children* (pp. 79–94). Baltimore: Paul H. Brookes Publishing Co.

Snow, C.E., Burns, M.S., & Griffin, P. (1998). *Preventing reading difficulties in children.* Washington, DC: National Academy Press.

Strauss, A., & Lehtinen, L.E. (1947). *Psychopathology and education of the brain-injured child.* New York: Grune & Stratton.

Swanson, H.L. (1989). Strategy instruction: Overview of principles and procedures for effective use. *Learning Disability Quarterly, 12*, 3–14.

Torgesen, J. (1991). Learning disabilities: Historical and conceptual issues. In B. Wong (Ed.), *Learning about learning disabilities* (pp. 3–37). San Diego: Academic Press.

Torgesen, J., Wagner, R., Rashotte, C.A., Alexander, A.W., & Conway, T. (1997). Preventive and remedial interventions for children with severe reading disabilities. *Learning Disabilities: A Multidisciplinary Journal, 8*, 51–61.

Torgesen, J.K. (1996). A model of memory from an information processing perspective: The special case of phonological memory. In G.R. Lyon & N.A. Krasnegor (Eds.), *Attention, memory, and executive function* (pp. 157–184). Baltimore: Paul H. Brookes Publishing Co.

Vellutino, F., & Scanlon, D. (1991). The preeminence of phonologically based skills in learning to read. In S. Brady & D. Shankweiler (Eds.), *Phonological processes in literacy: A tribute to Isabelle Liberman* (pp. 237–252). Mahwah, NJ: Lawrence Erlbaum Associates.

Vellutino, F.R., Scanlon, D.M., Sipay, E.R., Small, S.G., Pratt, A., Chen, R., & Denckla, M.B. (1996). Cognitive profiles of difficult to remediate and readily remediated poor readers: Early intervention as a vehicle to distinguish between cognitive and experiential deficits as basic causes of specific reading disability. *Journal of Educational Psychology, 88*, 601–638.

Wagner, R. (1996). From simple structure to complex function: Major trends in the development of theories, models, and measurements of memory. In G.R. Lyon & N.A. Krasnegor (Eds.), *Attention, memory, and executive function* (pp. 139–156). Baltimore: Paul H. Brookes Publishing Co.

Wepman, J.M. (1964). The perceptual basis for learning. In H. Robinson (Ed.). *Meeting individual differences in reading.* Chicago: University of Chicago Press.

Wittrock, M.C. (1992). Generative learning processes of the brain. *Educational Psychologist, 27*, 531–541.

Wong, B.Y.L. (1991). Assessment of metacognitive research in learning disabilities: Theory, research, and practice. In H.L. Swanson (Ed.), *Handbook on the assessment of learning disabilities: Theory, research, and practice* (pp. 265–283). Austin, TX: PRO-ED.

2

Development of Oral Language and Its Relationship to Literacy

Lydia H. Soifer

Imagine the elegant intricacies of Beethoven's "Ode to Joy" or Mozart's Serenade in G Major (*Eine Kleine Nachtmusik*) played captivatingly by an artist. It is as beguiling to the experienced listener as to the naive ear. Now imagine pages of musical notation, an array of dots and lines splayed across a page, interrupted by assorted squiggles and swirls. If you can read music, then you may sense the beauty in your mind's ear, much the way Beethoven did. Can't read music? Then what remains is a morass of dots, lines, squiggles, and swirls. The same is true with language, an amazing latticework of interrelated complexities in which the oral (spoken) and aural (heard) in combination with memory, sensory, and motor function; environment; and culture form the basis from which literacy evolves. The challenge of teaching about language is that the language itself is the vehicle for learning. Thus, in large part the very thing that you are attempting to learn about consciously in this chapter is exactly what you are experiencing spontaneously as you comprehend or generate language. Learning about language is a **metalinguistic** task in which language is analyzed and considered as an entity and behavior. When a person speaks or listens, reads or writes, and effectively communicates or understands a particular purpose or intention, the language system has performed efficiently.

Mattingly suggested that there was something "devious" (1972, p. 133) about the relationship between the processes of speaking and listening and the process of reading. Listening and reading both are linguistic processes but are not really as parallel or analogous as many people assume. The differences are in the form of information being presented (complex auditory signals versus more static visual symbols), in the linguistic content (additional information available from the intonational and speech patterns that can be perceived in listening versus the many possible pieces of phonological information contained in one symbol), and in the relationship of the form to the content (enormous variation in what can be produced by voice versus alphabets with limited information carried by any single symbol). Listening and speaking are automatic and natural ways of perceiving and using language, acquired as part of a developmental process. In contrast, the written form of a language must generally be taught, and not all individuals are able to learn it with ease. In addition, not all spoken languages have a written form.

There is agreement that reading is a language-based skill (Catts & Kamhi, 1986; Liberman, 1983; Perfetti & Lesgold, 1977; Snyder, 1980; Vellutino, 1979) and that the relationship between oral language and reading is reciprocal (Kamhi & Catts, 1989; Stanovich, 1986; Wallach & Miller, 1988), with each influencing the other at different points in development (Menyuk & Chesnick, 1997; Snyder & Downey, 1991, 1997). Oral and written language, although intimately and intricately related, are not the same. Teachers need to be aware of the similarities and differences (Moats, 1994; Moats & Lyon, 1996) so that they can facilitate language learning and academic success (Bashir & Scavuzzo, 1992). This chapter helps to foster in teachers an awareness of the inextricable role of language in learning to decode and comprehend. The processes of language learning (on which reading is based) begin long before children receive reading instruction. This chapter provides an insight into each component of the language system, including patterns of normal and disordered development and their analogous relationships to the higher-level language skills of reading and writing. In this chapter, oral and written language are viewed as a continuum, and the varying influences of oral language knowledge and use on the development of early decoding processes and subsequent comprehension processes are considered. Furthermore, to enhance teachers' ability to be informed observers and, as a result, more effective in planning instruction, this chapter offers a discussion of the oral–written language connection; the different levels of language processing; and the effects of chronic, intermittent, conductive hearing loss secondary to **otitis media** (middle-ear infections).

LANGUAGE: A DYNAMIC, RULE-GOVERNED PROCESS

Learning to talk appears easy but in fact is enormously complex. The marvel is that most children learn to talk so well and so quickly (Hart & Risley, 1999). The enormity of the task is confounded by the fact that most children are not taught to use language but rather discover the rules that govern language in the context of social interaction as they strive to understand and to convey meaning.

What is language? Bloom and Lahey offered a superb definition of language: "Language is a code whereby ideas about the world are represented through a conventional system of arbitrary signals for communication" (1978, p. 4). The key concepts to be considered are *communication, ideas, code, system,* and *conventional.* The purpose of language is *communication.* We use language for a variety of purposes in vastly different ways according to our needs, the needs of the listener, and the circumstances surrounding us. Language enables us to express an array of *ideas.* We have ideas about objects, events, and relationships. Our ability to express those ideas through language is different from the objects, events, or relationships themselves. Think about the page you are reading and the words you have available to represent your ideas about the page, what is on it, what you are doing with it, and your relationship to it. Each is different than the page itself, the writing on it, the act of reading, and how you are relating to the page by viewing it or touching it. In this way, language is a *code*, a means of representing one thing with another in a predictable and organized system. There are many different codes, from maps, to Morse code, to words spelled in a book. Sounds may be combined into words, words into sentences, and sentences into conversation. The rule-governed predictability of the *system* enables us to understand it and learn how to use it.

Consider the following:

> 'Twas brillig, and the slithy toves
> Did gyre and gimble in the wabe:
> All mimsy were the borogoves,
> And the mome raths outgrabe. (Carroll, 1865/1960, p. 134)

If asked, one could identify the parts of speech, noun (*toves, raths*), verb (*gyre, gimble*), adjective (*outgrabe*), or adverb (*brillig*); the subject, predicate, and object; have a reasonable idea of how to pronounce these novel words; and answer comprehension questions ("Were the borogoves mimsy?"). All of these tasks are possible because Carroll used the predictable, rule-governed nature of the sounds and grammar of English to create *The Jabberwocky*.

The code of language is also *conventional*. It consists of a socially based, tacitly agreed-on set of symbols and rules that govern their permissible combinations. The conventions of language allow users to share their ideas. Linguistic competence is a person's implicit knowledge about the rules of the language. Possessed of linguistic competence, a child or an adult has the knowledge to be a competent language user. In general, unless called on to do so specifically, a language user need not state the rules of language explicitly. The ability to generate an infinite number of sentences and understand varying forms of language across a plenitude of environments is demonstration of the rule knowledge.

THE COMPONENTS OF LANGUAGE

Bloom and Lahey (1978) conceptualized three major, interactive components of language: form, content, and use (see Figure 2.1). Each component is governed by a complex set of rules that together compose language.

Language Form

Language form consists of the observable features of language. It includes the rules for the combination of sounds (**phonology**), the structure of words (**morphology**), and the order of words in sentences (**syntax**). These features and their development and the relationship of disorders in these elements of language form are described in the sections that follow.

Phonology   Phonology is the sound system of a language. It comprises **suprasegmental** aspects (intonation, **stress,** loudness, pitch level, **juncture,** and speaking rate) and **segmental aspects** (phonemes: **vowels** and **consonants**).

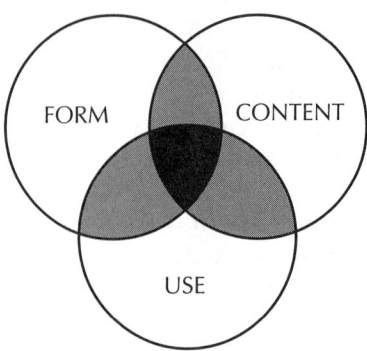

Figure 2.1. Venn diagram illustrating language form/content/use. (From Bloom, L., & Lahey, M. (1978). *Language development and language disorders* [p. 22]. Copyright © 1978 by Allyn & Bacon. Adapted by permission.)

The *suprasegmental*, or paralinguistic, aspects of phonology provide the melody of speech. They are related to speech because they are produced by the vocal tract but are concerned with larger units of production: syllables, words, phrases, and sentences. They are significant in our ability to communicate emotions and attitudes. These suprasegmental features help us to recognize different sentence types, declarative (*Joshua eats pizza.*), interrogative (*Does Russell like ice cream?*), or imperative (*Sit down now!*). Awareness of phrase structure helps us to understand where a comma might be placed in a sentence. These suprasegmental aspects also permit us to say the same sentence and communicate markedly different meanings. Varied aspects of **prosody** (the suprasegmental features of language) are used in talking to different people of different ages and status. Consider the number of ways to say, "Don't be silly," to a baby, to a spouse, or to an employer. At a conversational level, the suprasegmental characteristics of language also may be used to convey sarcasm, to tease, and to mock.

The suprasegmental aspects of phonology are influential in reading. When reading aloud, fluent readers read with full intonation communicating an understanding of the intent of the author. Early readers or those who struggle to decode may read each word individually, then, having derived meaning, will reread with appropriate inflection. Inefficient readers may pause with a downward intonation at the end of a printed line of words rather than at the end of the sentence. Thus, the suprasegmental features of language play an essential role in comprehension.

Vowels and consonants compose the *segmental* features of language. Each language has a set of vowels and consonants, or phonemes, that may be combined to form words. A phoneme is the smallest linguistic unit of sound that can change meaning in a word. Consider the word family of *fat, bat,* and *sat,* which contains five different phonemes: /b/, /f/, /s/, /ă/, and /t/. A change in any of them would change the meanings of the words.

Standard English orthography has only 26 letters with which to represent the approximately 44 phonemes of English. More striking still, there are only 5 vowel letters available to represent the 15 vowel sounds. Knowledge of phonemes and their role in language and reading is essential for teachers. Long before children are able to recognize, write, and read the letters that represent the sounds of English, they must begin to master the elaborate task of making those speech sounds correctly so that they are able to clearly produce the sounds of the language. Children learn each of those 44 sounds and the possible variations on them by exposure to them, by hearing others speak, and by storing information about the qualities that make up each sound. It is an unconscious and intricate task.

Speech production is the complex coordination of respiration (breathing), phonation (the vibration of the vocal folds), resonation (the quality of voice affected by the shape and density of the neck and cavities of the head), and articulation (the rapid, alternating movements of the jaw, tongue, lips, teeth, and soft palate). When we speak, the flow of speech is generally uninterrupted. Speech is produced in breath groups ("Whenneryagoin'?") rather than in individual words ("When   are   you   going?"). Yet early readers decode word by word and, at times, sound by sound. Liberman noted that "if speech were like spelling, learning to read would be trivially easy" (as cited in Brady & Shankweiler, 1991, p. xv). Awareness that the flow of coarticulated, overlapping phonemes can be segmented into sounds, syllables, and words is a precursor to "cracking the code" of language in print (see Chapter 3 in this book for an extended discussion of phonological processes). Although speech and reading are clearly related, they are not equal. Oral language, of which speech is the observable form, is learned naturally. Reading is not (Liberman & Liberman, 1990). A bounty of literature, however, emphasizes the role of **phonological awareness** (the ability to attend to and recognize the sound structure of language) in the acquisition of early reading (Adams, 1990; Blachman, 1989, 1991; Blachman, Ball, Black, & Tangel, 2000; Stanovich, 1987; Wagner & Torgesen, 1987).

The speech-sound segments, vowels and consonants, may vary in their productions (**allophones**) and are guided by a set of rules for their production and placement in words. From the earliest moments of life, babies are acquiring information about the sounds of their language (Eimas, Siqueland, Jusczyk, & Vigorito, 1971). Through continuous exposure, babies acquire the set of acoustic features that define the sounds of their language. Over time the speakers of a given language come to recognize the possible variations in phoneme production while remaining able to recognize the specific phoneme. For example, the phoneme /p/ is a voiceless stop plosive (i.e., there is no vocal fold vibration, it is not produced in a long stream as /s/ is, and it produces a puff of air). Yet the production of /p/ varies by the amount of **aspiration** (puff of air) produced according to where it appears in a word. Pronounce *pot* and *spot* aloud to feel the different amount of aspiration. Nonetheless, speakers of English recognize these variations as the phoneme /p/. Moreover, any of the plosive sounds /p/, /b/, /t/, /d/, /k/, and /g/ must be produced with an accompanying vowel sound, the **schwa** (/ə/), typically produced as "uh." This is particularly relevant for teachers; as Liberman noted, "The word is 'bag,' not 'buh–a–guh'" (as cited in Brady & Shankweiler, 1991, p. xv) The distortion can be so great for some children that they are unable to recombine the sounds into the word *bag* that is readily recognizable to most. Combining /b/ and /ă/ in a smooth, connected production eliminates the /ə/. In addition, by not producing the /g/ with an overemphasis, the /ə/ is once again reduced, thus allowing the word being analyzed and synthesized to sound more like its real-world production. This enables the young reader to use language knowledge of the word to recognize it as a phonological/phonemic phenomenon.

Other **phonetic** distinctions may be made by limitations of the vocal tract. These distinctions may become important for spelling, particularly for children with vulnerabilities in phonological awareness. Plurals, possessives, and the third-person singular marking of the verb all are accomplished by the addition of *-s* (or *-es* for certain plurals) when being spelled. The sounds produced, however, may be /z/ or /s/. This is determined by the nature of the preceding phoneme. **Coarticulation** with a **voiced consonant** (one produced with the vocal folds closed) or a vowel will create /z/ or /ĭz/. Say *hugs, kisses,* and *hits* aloud to hear and feel the distinctions. A similar pattern emerges for the creation of the regular past tense, typically created in print as *-ed.* In speech, however, it may be produced as /d/, /t/, or /ĭd/, as in *hugged, kissed,* or *lifted.*

Vowels and consonants, which combine to form syllable structures, are separated into distinct classes by the nature of their production. A vowel is typically "formed as sound energy from the vibrating folds escapes through a relatively open vocal tract of a particular shape" (Bernthal & Bankson, 1988, p. 12). The tongue, jaw, and lips serve to create the shape of the vocal tract. Because the jaw and tongue work together, vowels are classified by identifying the position of the tongue during articulation (front or back, high or low) and the lips (rounded or unrounded). Vowels may also be tense or lax. **Tense vowels** (e.g., /ē/ in "bee") are longer in duration; **lax vowels** (e.g., /ĭ/ in "bin") are shorter in duration. Figure 2.2 demonstrates the position in the mouth of each vowel's production. Table 2.1 shows the spellings of different vowels. Moats's (1997) view of sound production in its relationship to spelling gives an accompanying image of the appearance of vowels (see Figure 2.3).

Consonants, unlike vowels, are created by either a complete or a partial constriction of the air stream along the vocal tract. The closure is affected by the position of the lips and the placement of the tongue in relation to the teeth and position in the mouth. Consonants are classified as *stops* (*t, k*), *nasals* (*n, m*), *fricatives* (*f, z*), *affricates* (*ch, j*), *glides* (*w, y*), or *liquids* (*l, r*).

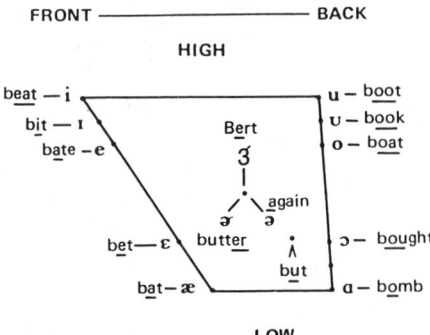

Figure 2.2. Vowel chart. (From Bernthal, J.F., & Bankson, N.W. [1998]. *Articulation and phonological disorders* [4th ed., p. 16]. Needham Heights, MA: Allyn & Bacon; reprinted by permission.)

Table 2.1. American English vowels

Phonetic symbol	Phonic symbol	Spellings
/i/	ē	beet
/ɪ/	ĭ	bit
/e/	ā	bait
/ɛ/	ĕ	bet
/æ/	ă	bat
/ɑj/	ī	bite
/ɑ/	ŏ	bottle
/ʌ/	ŭ	butt
/ɔ/	aw, ô	bought
/o/	ō	boat
/ʊ/	o͝o	put
/u/	o͞o	boot
/ə/	ə	between
/ɔj/	oi, oy	boy
/æw/	ou, ow	bow

From material prepared by Louisa Cook Moats for the Comprehensive Leadership Program, California State Board of Education, 1997.

Table 2.2 provides a clear view of where consonants are produced in the vocal tract. In addition, consonants may be described as voiced (caused by vibrations of the vocals folds when closed) or **voiceless** (open vocal folds). Several sets of phonemes, called **voiced–voiceless cognates,** are produced in the same place in the mouth, in the same manner, but vary only in the voicing characteristic. They are /p/ and /b/, /f/ and /v/, /t/ and /d/, /s/ and /z/, /k/ and /g/, /th/ (*th*ink) and /t̶h̶/ (*th*is), /sh/ and /zh/ (trea*s*ure), /ch/ and /j/. (The distinction between a voiceless and voiced phoneme can be felt as well as heard by placing the fingers gently against the throat. Start to say /s/, and without altering the position of the tongue and jaw, then say /z/.) In addition, the environment in which a consonant or vowel exists, that is, the other phonemes near it, may vary its production. The relationship of vowel, consonant, and syllable production and discrimination and phonological awareness leading to more effective reading and spelling is significant.

In addition to rules for the production and perception of phonemes, there are rules that apply to how phonemes may be combined into meaningful words. These rules allow some sounds to appear in certain positions in a word but not in others. For example, in English, /ng/ may appear in the middle or at the end of a word but never at the beginning. Furthermore, certain combinations of sounds are restricted so that /ts/ may occur at the end of a word but not at the beginning. This set of **phonological rules** has implications for early reading and spelling as children learn to segment the flow of speech and recognize and represent it in print.

Phonological Development   Traditionally speech-sound development was thought to occur through unit-by-unit learning of each phoneme in a developmental sequence. In fact, phonological development is integrally related to the language system as a whole. Phonological development progresses with physical

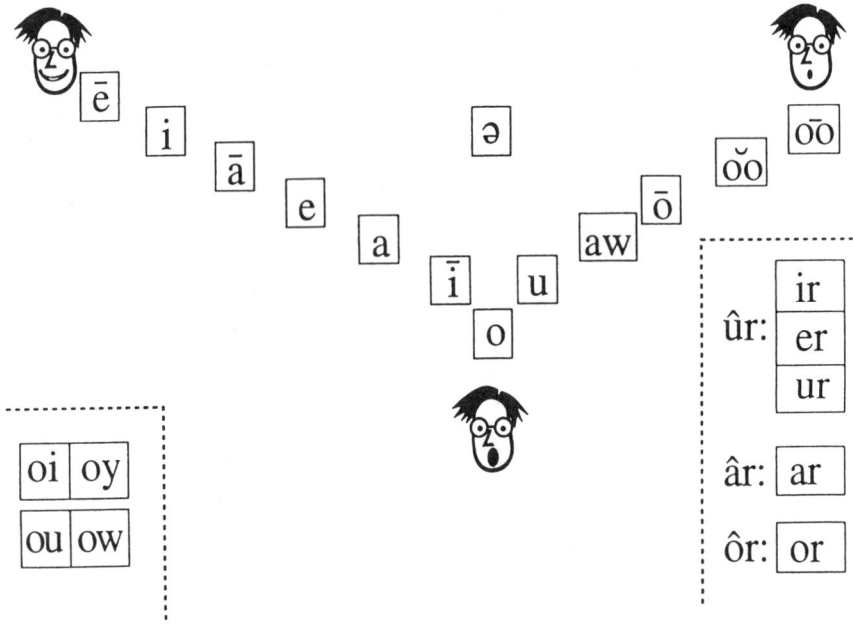

Figure 2.3. Vowel spellings by mouth position. (From material prepared by Louisa Cook Moats for the Comprehensive Leadership Program, California State Board of Education, 1997.)

maturation, the mastery of sound features and phonological processes that reflect the linking of sounds to words and meaning, and the growth of semantic syntactic rule knowledge and ability. Children employ phonological or natural processes to master adult-level speech productions.

Typically, children produce their first recognizable words by 12–18 months of age. The ability of toddlers to make themselves fully understood (without available **context clues**) is often limited by inadequate production of sounds. However, 3-year-olds are generally intelligible and by age 4 have "suppressed" or eliminated the remaining phonological processes that hinder their intelligibility (Hodson, 1994; see Table 2.3 for a summary, with examples of common phonological processes).

Typically developing children are able to produce speech sounds adequately by age 4 and require additional time (until age 7) for complete mastery, including the elimination of lisps and the production of **multisyllabic** words (see Table 2.4).

Relationship of Phonological Disorders to Literacy When preparing to teach early reading skills, teachers should be aware of two areas of consideration: intelligibility of speech production and its relationship to phonological awareness. Children who have problems with speech-sound production at the time they are being introduced to reading instruction or who have a history of such difficulties have been shown to be less adept at tasks of phonological awareness than their typically developing peers (Webster & Plante, 1992). Webster and Plante explained that "productive phonological impairment may hinder performance in phonological awareness because it precludes efficient phonological coding in working memory" (p. 176). In the same vein, Fowler (1991) suggested that articulation ability may be an important prerequisite for acquiring an awareness of phoneme structures.

Table 2.2.   American English consonants (phonic symbols)

Class of consonant	Lips	Lips/ teeth	Tongue between teeth	Tongue behind teeth	Roof of mouth	Back of mouth	Throat
Stop	/p/			/t/		/k/	
	/b/			/d/		/g/	
Nasal	/m/			/n/		/ng/	
Fricative		/f/	/th/	/s/	/sh/		
		/v/	/th/	/z/	/zh/		
Affricate					/ch/		
					/j/		
Glide					/y/	/wh/	/h/
						/w/	
Liquid				/l/			
				/r/			

From material prepared by Louisa Cook Moats for the Comprehensive Leadership Program, California State Board of Education, 1997.

Consider the dilemma of a child who does not have a stable speech production system. Certain speech production problems may be caused by neurological oral-motor dysfunction, including weaknesses of the musculature necessary for making the coordinated movements to produce speech (**dysarthria**). Other speech problems may be caused by sensorimotor disruptions in which the signals to the muscles necessary for speech production are not consistently or efficiently received (**dyspraxia**). When children encounter a new word, they must be able to store it in phonological short-term (working) memory as part of the process of creating a phonological representation for it. Children who have speech articulation difficulties, however, are at a disadvantage: What they are able to say may not match what they have heard. In the phonological awareness tasks of rhyme, segmentation, and **blending** and in spelling tasks, being able to rehearse a word with proper production plays a contributing role in the successful completion of those tasks. Thus, for some children, speech disorders are a hidden contributor to the apparent phonological processing and spelling difficulties (Stackhouse & Wells, 1997).

Children with reading disabilities have been found to make more speech production errors than their typical peers (Catts, 1986; Snowling, 1981). This difficulty has been found to exist in college-age dyslexic students (Catts, 1989). The college-age dyslexic students had greater difficulty in repeating complex phrases rapidly and made significantly more errors than their typical peers. It is hypothesized that children and adults with reading difficulties have more difficulty in encoding phonological information and in planning (for articulation) of complex sequences of sounds (Catts, 1989).

Phonological processing difficulties may manifest differently across the developmental continuum. They may stem from a variety of causes and vary in severity (Spear-Swerling & Sternberg, 1994). In the preschool years the development of oral language may be related to slower vocabulary growth (Catts, Hu, Larrivee, & Swank, 1994), and children may be less sensitive to rhythm, alliteration and nonsense words (Fey, Catts, & Larrivee, 1995). During the elementary

Table 2.3.   Common phonological processes

Process	Example	
Syllable structure processes—simplication of words to either consonant-vowel (CV) syllables or CVCV structures	1. reduplication 2. final consonant deletion 3. cluster reduction 4. deletion of unstressed syllables	/dæ dæ/ for *daddy* /kʌ/ for *cup* /tɑr/ for *star* /efɪnt/ for *elephant*
Substitution processes—one sound is substituted for another depending upon the position in a word	1. fronting 2. stopping 3. gliding	/tʌp/ for *cup*; /dʌn/ for *gun* /dʊt/ for *juice* /wæ bɪt/ for *rabbit*
Assimilation processes—two phonemes in a word become alike	1. consonant harmony 2. prevocalic voicing	/gɔ gi/ for *doggy* /dʌb/ for *tub*

From Edwards, M.L., & Shriberg, L.D. (1983). *Phonology: Applications in communicative disorders* (p. 91). San Diego: College-Hill Press; reprinted by permission.

school years, children with phonological processing difficulties may be weaker in using segmentation strategies to analyze phonemic structure and slower in word recognition secondary to reduced awareness of the relationship between phonemes and the alphabet (Catts, 1989; Ehri, 1989). If a child persists in having significant speech production difficulties, spelling ability may be affected (Clark-Klein & Hodson, 1995). Reduced rate of vocabulary acquisition and difficulty acquiring words with **multiple meanings** and figurative language as well as word-retrieval difficulties may become obvious (Catts, Hu, Larrivee, & Swank, 1994; Milosky, 1994; Snyder & Godley, 1992). Comprehension problems may begin to emerge both orally and in print (Catts, 1996; Snyder & Downey, 1991).

In the 1990s, a great deal of attention was generated by the concept of *temporal auditory processing deficits* and their role in language and reading disabilities as well as their remediation by a specialized computer program commercially mar-

Table 2.4.   Phonemic acquisition—age at which 75% of children tested correctly articulated consonant sounds

Age	Sounds
2.0	m, n, h, p, ŋ, (ri*ng*)
2.4	f, j, k, d
2.8	w, b, t
3.0	g, s
3.4	r, l
3.8	ʃ (*shy*), tʃ (*chin*)
4.0	ð (fa*ther*), ʒ (mea*s*ure)
4.0+	dʒ (*jar*), θ (*thin*), v, z

From Prather, E., Hedrick, D., & Kern, C. (1975). Articulation development in children aged two to four years. *Journal of Speech and Hearing Research, 40;* reprinted by permission.

keted as Fast ForWord (Scientific Learning Corporation) (Merzenich et al., 1996; Tallal et al., 1996). A temporal auditory processing deficit is said to occur when a child has difficulty rapidly processing the acoustic (sound energy) changes that occur between sounds in connected speech. An increasing amount of anecdotal evidence indicates positive changes in the language abilities of those children who participate in the highly intensive and restrictive computer training program that requires involvement with the computer program for 1 hour and 40 minutes daily for 6 weeks. As of 1999, however, no other studies have been published with data providing evidence of what the program actually remediates, for which specific population of children it works, and of exactly why it is effective other than because of the great amount of time that must be invested. Fast ForWord has been written about in many magazines and newspapers and offers hope to those with language and reading disabilities and to children who have autism and related disorders. It has been sharply criticized, however, in scientific journals that are subject to peer review (judgment by others in a particular scientific discipline), most particularly by researchers in the field of speech science (Mody, Studdert-Kennedy, & Brady, 1997; Studdert-Kennedy, 1998; Studdert-Kennedy et al., 1994–1995; Studdert-Kennedy & Mody, 1995). The most serious criticism by Studdert-Kennedy is of enormous concern: that the concept of *temporal auditory processing deficits* on which Fast ForWord is predicated is a false one. The design of the studies on which Fast ForWord has been based as well as the interpretation of the results has been severely questioned. Further research and documentation are necessary before a full evaluation of this controversial conceptualization and approach can be made.

Phonological awareness abilities (see Chapter 3) have been identified as critical to the development of early reading. The evidence is so strong that commercial materials have begun to appear with increasing regularity to aid educators in identifying weaknesses in phonological awareness abilities (Robertson & Salter, 1997) and in developing these skills (Adams, Foorman, Lundberg, & Beeler, 1998; Catts & Vartiainen, 1997). The main point of the research is not only that phonological skills underlie early reading but also that they can be taught. Catts (1997) developed a checklist to aid in the early identification of language-based reading difficulties. The value of the checklist is twofold. The first benefit is in its structure, which identifies six significant areas of observation for the teacher: speech-sound awareness, word retrieval, verbal memory, speech production and perception, comprehension, and expressive language. The second benefit is that when such a checklist is used in collaboration with a speech-language pathologist, it can be of enormous value in targeting students who may be vulnerable to reading difficulty and in pinpointing their particular areas of need (see Figure 2.4).

Phonology is too often simplified to its superficial relationship to speech or phonics instruction. In reality it has far-reaching significance for the rate of language acquisition (Paul & Jennings, 1992), vocabulary size (Stoel-Gammon, 1991), **working memory** (Adams & Gathercole, 1995), word retrieval (Katz, 1986; McGregor, 1994), and phonological awareness skills (segmentation, sound deletion, blending, and counting) that are believed to underlie early literacy (Catts, 1993). Expressive phonological disorders have negative effects on early literacy (Bird & Bishop, 1992; Bird, Bishop, & Freeman, 1995) and spelling (Moats, 1995). The relationship between speech and print is anchored by an understanding of phonology and phonological processes. For children, making this connection is a

---

Early Identification of Language-Based Reading Disabilities: A Checklist

Child's name:_____   Birthday: _____
Date completed: _____   Age: _____

This checklist is designed to identify children who are at risk for language-based reading disabilities. It is intended for use with children at the end of kindergarten or beginning of first grade. Each of the descriptors listed below should be carefully considered and those that characterize the child's behavior/history should be checked. A child receiving a large number of checks should be referred for a more in-depth evaluation.

Speech Sound Awareness
- ☐ Doesn't understand and enjoy rhymes
- ☐ Doesn't easily recognize that words begin with the same sound
- ☐ Has difficulty counting the syllables in spoken words
- ☐ Has problem clapping hands or tapping feet in rhythm with songs and/or rhymes
- ☐ Demonstrates problems learning sound–letter correspondences

Word Retrieval
- ☐ Has difficulty retrieving a specific word (e.g., calls a sheep a "goat" or says, "you know, a woolly animal")
- ☐ Shows poor memory for classmates' names
- ☐ Speech is hesitant, filled with pauses or vocalizations (e.g., "um," "you know")
- ☐ Frequently uses words lacking specificity (e.g., "stuff," "thing," "what you call it")
- ☐ Has a problem remembering/retrieving verbal sequences (e.g., days of the week, alphabet)

Verbal Memory
- ☐ Has difficulty remembering instructions or directions
- ☐ Shows problems learning names of people or places
- ☐ Has difficulty remembering the words to songs or poems
- ☐ Has problems learning a second language

Speech Production/Perception
- ☐ Has problems saying common words with difficult sound patterns (e.g., animal, cinnamon, specific)
- ☐ Mishears and subsequently mispronounces words or names
- ☐ Confuses a similar sounding word with another word (e.g., saying, "The Entire State Building is in New York")
- ☐ Combines sound patterns of similar words (e.g., saying "escavator" for escalator)
- ☐ Shows frequent slips of the tongue (e.g., saying "brue blush" for blue brush)
- ☐ Has difficulty with tongue twisters (e.g., she sells seashells)

Comprehension
- ☐ Only responds to part of a multiple element request or instruction
- ☐ Requests multiple repetitions of instructions/directions with little improvement in comprehension
- ☐ Relies too much on context to understand what is said

(continued)

Figure 2.4. Checklist for early identification of language-based reading disabilities. (From Catts, H.W. [1997]. Appendix A: Early identification of language-based reading disabilities. A checklist. *Language, Speech, and Hearing Services in Schools, 28,* 88–89; reprinted by permission. Some descriptors have been taken from *Language for learning: A checklist for language difficulties,* Melbourne, Australia: OZ Child.)

Figure 2.4. (*continued*)

- ☐ Has difficulty understanding questions
- ☐ Fails to understand age-appropriate stories
- ☐ Has difficulty making inferences, predicting outcomes, drawing conclusions
- ☐ Lacks understanding of spatial terms such as left-right, front-back

Expressive Language

- ☐ Talks in short sentences
- ☐ Makes errors in grammar (e.g., "he goed to the store" or "me want that")
- ☐ Lacks variety in vocabulary (e.g., uses "good" to mean happy, kind, polite)
- ☐ Has difficulty giving directions or explanations (e.g., may show multiple revisions or dead ends)
- ☐ Relates stories or events in a disorganized or incomplete manner
- ☐ May have much to say, but provides little specific detail
- ☐ Has difficulty with the rules of conversation, such as turn taking, staying on topic, indicating when he/she does not understand

Other Important Factors

- ☐ Has a prior history of problems in language comprehension and/or production
- ☐ Has a family history of spoken or written language problems
- ☐ Has limited exposure to literacy in the home
- ☐ Lacks interest in books and shared reading activities
- ☐ Does not engage readily in pretend play

Comments

_____

_____

_____

---

vital step in the development of literacy. For teachers, understanding this connection brings power of knowledge to teaching.

Morphology Language form, one of three major components of language (Bloom & Lahey, 1978), also includes a set of rules for the formation of words. *Morphology* is the study of word formation, or how *morphemes* (the smallest units of meaning in language) combine to form words. Morphemes (unlike phonemes) are endowed with meaning. Words are made up of one or more morphemes. A morpheme that can stand alone, such as *smile, book,* or *cute,* is called an *unbound morpheme.* Another group of morphemes, called **bound morphemes,** must be attached to other words (unbound morphemes). Bound morphemes are typically the **affixes** of a language, such as *un-* and *-ing* for the word *unsmiling,* -s in the plural *books,* and *-est* in the superlative *cutest.* Unbound morphemes have **lexical** (word) meaning of their own. They are the content words of the language: nouns, main verbs, adjectives, and adverbs. Other morphemes, called *function words* or *grammatical morphemes,* such as prepositions, articles, conjunctions, and auxiliary verbs, serve grammatical functions in a sentence by creating the connection between lexical morphemes. Bound morphemes may be either inflectional or derivational. *Inflectional morphemes* modify tense (*-ed* in *played*), possession (*-'s* in *Vicki's*) or number (*-s* in *dollars*). The acquisition of inflectional morphemes is a hallmark of early language development and reflects a child's increasing analysis of the structure and meaning of words. *Derivational morphemes* change one part of speech to another; for example, the verb *argue* plus *-ment* becomes the noun *argument*, and the adverb *happy* plus *-ness* becomes the noun *happiness*. The changes in spelling that result are another indication of the underlying complexity of the relationship between speech and print. Morphemic structure allows the language user to extend and modify meaning. Young language learners, making their way through the dense forest of sounds, words, and meanings, learn to "mark" the differences in tense, number, or possession by attending to the ends of words. Older children learn to recognize the relationships among words (e.g., *nation, national, nationality, nationalism, nationalistic*). Indeed, **prefixes** and **suffixes,** which are most commonly derived from Greek and Latin, permit a learner to extend lexical knowledge (White, Power, & White, 1989; see Chapter 5).

A further intrigue exists in the morphophonemic relationship: change in pronunciation caused by change in the **morphological** structure in a word, such as the changes that occur when the following words are said aloud: "sign," "signature"; "medicine," "medical." Although phonemically such pronunciation changes may seem irregular, from a morphological view many of these changes are predictable.

Morphological Development   In the earliest stages of language development, morphological development is measured by the acquisition of the first 14 morphemes that emerge in children's language (Brown, 1973). As morphemes may either be words (unbound) or affixes (bound), the first 14 morphemes range from the present progressive marker *-ing*, to the use of the irregular third-person singular verb form *has*, to the contracted copula (*to be*) such as *-'m* in *I'm going*. These acquisitions generally occur between the ages of 2 or 2½ years and 4 years. Brown identified this initial phase of acquisition as occurring across five stages of development that span the period of approximately 1½–5½ years of age. During early language development, children acquire pronouns, articles, and adjective and noun suffixes. At a certain point in early development, morphological and syntactic development merge as indicated by the development of the negative forms no and not that become part of the evolution of negative sentence structures.

Later morphological development involves the acquisition of comparatives (*-er*) and superlatives (*-est*), irregular forms (*children*), and advanced prefixes and suffixes (*un-, dis-, -ness, -ment*) including those that mark noun (*-er* in *baker*) and adverb derivation (*-ly* in *slowly*). Spelling and pronunciation are affected by the structure of more advanced morphological development (e.g., *child/children, happy/happiness*). Wiig and Semel provided a sequence of acquisition of morphological or word formation rules:

> 1) Regular noun plurals, 2) noun–verb agreement for singular and plural forms of irregular nouns and verbs in the present tense, 3) regular noun possessives in the singular and plural form, 4) irregular noun plurals, 5) irregular noun possessives, 6) regular past tense verbs, 7) irregular past tense verbs, 8) adjectival inflections for the comparative and superlative forms, 9) noun and adverb derivation, 10) prefixing. (1980, p. 50)

Carlisle (1988), in her studies of fourth, sixth, and eighth graders, demonstrated that children know more about derivational morphology than they use in their spelling. Her recommendation was for direct instruction of words that undergo both phonological and orthographic changes (e.g., *deep/depth*) as opposed to those that undergo only phonological change (e.g., *equal/equality*).

Morphology plays an interesting role in language development and growth. From its earliest role in the emergence of grammar as a child passes beyond the single-word stage to the adolescent's urgent need to master Greek and Latin **roots** and affixes in preparation for the Scholastic Aptitude Test, morphological knowledge and mastery contribute to vocabulary growth, spelling, comprehension, and the richness of a child's written language.

Relationship of Morphological Disorders to Literacy   Children with language learning disabilities often present with impairments in reading as their primary academic problem. The rate of morphological acquisition is slower for these children than for their typically developing peers. Although morphological acquisition has not been widely studied, several investigations have pointed to the relationship between morphological awareness and literacy. Mahoney and Mann (1992) found positive correlations between second graders' ability to appreciate phonologically and morphologically based puns and their reading ability. Ruben, Patterson, and Kantor (1991) reported a relationship between morphological knowledge and spelling ability in typically developing second graders, children with learning disabilities, and adults with literacy problems. Ruben and colleagues demonstrated that the morphemic errors made in writing reflected impairments in both the implicit and explicit levels of morphological knowledge. What was most striking, however, was their evidence that these impairments do not resolve simply by maturation and increased exposure to written language. Furthermore, underlying phonological weakness may contribute to the difficulty poor readers have with certain morphological relationships. Fowler and Liberman (1995) found that poor readers have greater difficulty in producing morphological forms that involve a phonological change (e.g., *courage/courageous*) than they do when there is no phonological change (e.g., *danger/dangerous*).

Morphology is relevant to both reading and spelling for several reasons. Among those reasons concerning English morphology, Elbro and Arnbak (1996, p. 212) identified the following:

- The role morphology plays in orthography;
- The value of morphemes as indicators of meaning;
- The economical nature of storing words in written lexicon as morphemes rather than as wholes (because of the relative unpredictability of sound to letter accuracy);
- Morpheme analysis and recognition as a reading strategy may provide a more direct route to the lexicon of the spoken word; certain reading and spelling errors are morphologically based, e.g., "proceedure"/"proceed."

Morphological awareness has been shown to be a strong indicator of reading comprehension (Carlisle, 1995), and morphological awareness training has been shown to have a positive effect on comprehension (Elbro & Arnbak, 1996). Morphological awareness, however, is not seen as fully independent from phonological awareness (Fowler & Liberman, 1995). Although researchers endeavor to determine the specific nature and interrelatedness of the systems of language that influence reading, teachers must remain conscious of the constant reciprocity among language components.

Syntax   Syntax is a third aspect of language form. *Syntax* is the system of rules that directs the comprehension and production of sentences. Syntax (sometimes referred to as *grammar*) specifies the order of words and the organization of words within a variety of sentence types. Syntactic rules allow the user to combine words into meaningful sentences and to alter the form of a sentence; for ex-

ample, *The boy is walking* may be transposed into *Is the boy walking?* Despite a fi-
nite set of sentence types, an infinite number of sentences can be generated. In addition, syntactic knowledge allows a language user to decide whether sentences
are grammatical.

Syntactic Development   Typically developing children acquire the rudiments
of syntax early in the language acquisition process. As they progress beyond the
basic form of noun phrase and verb phrase, children master the variety of sentence types common in preschool language: negative, interrogative, and imperative forms. Subsequently they begin to develop the earliest complex sentence
structures of coordination demonstrated by the use of *and* ("Joshua went to
grandma's house *and* had a good time"); complementation, indicated by the use
of a clause structure that modifies the verb ("Tell me *what he is eating*"); and rela-
tivization, in which a clause restricts or modifies the meaning of another portion
of the sentence ("The boy *who ate the cake* has a tummyache"). Use of early complex sentence structures generally emerges at approximately 3 years of age and is
mastered by age 5 or 6. Complex sentence development continues through the
school years. Embedding of clauses, either parallel ("She gave him a toy *that he
did not like*") or nonparallel ("He called the man *who walked away*"); the use of
gerunds (verbs with *-ing* that function as nouns; e.g., "Cooking is fun"); and passive structures ("The cookie *was* eaten by the boy") continue to emerge across the
school years with mastery of some forms as late as 11 years old. Other, more mature grammatical structures also evolve with the mastery of new forms such as
more sophisticated conjunctions ("although," "nonetheless"), mass nouns and
their quantifiers ("*How much* water do you want?" versus "*How many* water do
you want?"), and the use of reflexive pronouns ("himself," "herself"). The mature
language user can use sentence complexity to convey numerous relationships
among actions, ideas, and locations.

Sentence complexity continues to grow through the high school years, with
increased maturation reflecting the development and influence of written language skills. Sentence length continues to increase slowly but steadily through
the adolescent years at approximately one word per year as formally measured
(Scott, 1988). Changes in the sophistication of noun and verb phrases and the development of nominal, adverbial, and **relative clauses** contribute to the growth in
complexity of syntax. Chaney (1992) suggested the value of good syntactic
knowledge in reading comprehension and reported that readers with better
awareness of grammatical structure have better paragraph comprehension, possibly because they are able to use strong grammatical knowledge to monitor comprehension.

The ability to deconstruct sentences for comprehension or to construct them
either orally or in writing to convey meaning is dependent on knowledge of syntactic rules. In addition, to some extent syntactic interpretation relies on the ability to maintain sentences in working memory (Adams & Gathercole, 1995) and to
exploit phonological memory (Montgomery, 1996).

Whereas phonological knowledge and skills are relevant to early decoding,
morphological and syntactic knowledge are significant to **fluency** and comprehension in later reading development. Beyond the initial stages of reading, most
typically in second grade (Chall, 1983), increased fluency and comprehension become the focus of reading instruction. Knowledge of syntax enables readers to

make predictions from among a set of possibilities about what type of word or words must be coming next. This can be easily demonstrated using the **cloze technique** (fill-in-the-blank technique) common to research designs in the study of syntax: *Sam gave Ida the* ____. Knowledge of syntactic structure helps an individual to predict the likelihood of either an adjective or a noun or both. This predictive ability aids in **automaticity.**

Relationship of Syntactic Disorders to Literacy   For children who have difficulty with expressive or receptive syntax, the impact on reading may not become obvious until later in elementary school when the emphasis shifts from decoding to comprehension. Moreover, comprehension difficulties may not emerge until the density of text increases beyond the reader's syntactic knowledge limits. As with all aspects of language, there is a continuum that reflects both a developmental sequence and degree of complexity (from single words to complex sentences). A parallel continuum involves the degree of severity and pervasiveness (one particular aspect or all aspects) of the language difficulty.

Studies of early syntactic delay were predictive of subsequent reading disability (Scarborough, 1990), as were studies of children identified more globally as having language impairments in which disordered syntax was a characteristic (Aram & Hall, 1990). Other research has shown that children with reading difficulties have sentence comprehension problems as well. In particular, children and adolescents have difficulty interpreting later occurring complex structures such as those that contain **embedded** or relative clauses (Byrne, 1981; Morice & Slaghuis, 1985; Stein, Cairns, & Zurif, 1984). Reliance on semantic (meaning) strategies and limitations in working memory that would enable the child to retain the sentence for a sufficient period of time to analyze are possible contributing factors to difficulty in sentence comprehension.

Lahey and Bloom (1994) offered that sentence comprehension is far more complex than issues of working memory limitations would imply. As always, they considered a more encompassing view of sentence comprehension that includes working memory capacity, the ability to automatically retrieve the language knowledge needed to construct in mind what the sentence (and its parts) is representing, the nature of the material being processed (in or out of a context familiar to the child), and the availability and strength of any context cues. Sentence comprehension is not a simple process for anyone, but for a youngster with learning and language difficulties, it is an even greater task. What remains unclear is the nature of the relationship between syntactic comprehension problems and reading disability, although there is sufficient evidence to suggest that they coexist.

Comprehension of spoken syntax is supported by the discourse (conversational) structure of the interaction as well as by the paralinguistic and situational cues. Far fewer cues are available to the reader, and, as such, failure to accurately analyze sentence structure can result in deficient comprehension.

The elements of language form (phonology, morphology, and syntax) have clear relationships to one another as one aspect of the foundation on which literacy is built. Early reading ability is strongly connected to phonological knowledge, as is the later development of spelling. Morphological knowledge adds to the skills required for spelling and comprehension. Later reading development, fluency, and comprehension have their roots in morphology and syntax while continuing to rely on efficient phonological processing.

Language Content

Language content, often referred to as *semantics,* is the meaning component of language. Language content reflects our world knowledge, what we know about objects, events, and relationships. The study of semantics is concerned with the meanings of words and the relationship between and among words as they are used to represent knowledge of the world. As explained by Lahey (1988), language content involves both the endless number of particular topics that can be discussed and the general categories of objects, actions, and relationships. Thus, all children of different cultures or experiences will talk about content in terms of the objects, events, and relationships of their world, but the topics within each of these categories will be different. Children raised in Mexico City or in Brooklyn will talk about food (object), eating (action), and possession (relationship) but are likely to ask for different foods.

Language content involves not only individual word meanings, as in the analysis of a child's "vocabulary," but also the understanding of the meaning features that compose a word; how a word may (or may not) be used in a phrase, a sentence, or discourse; and the literal and figurative meanings of words. Words are composed of clusters of meaning features that allow us to define words and to differentiate among them. Most often our knowledge of these features is unconscious. Try, for example, to define the word *walk.* Although all of us know what it means, and most are able to demonstrate it, defining *walk* is quite difficult. Furthermore, when asked, "What does *draft* mean?" one could potentially supply six different responses ranging from *conscription* (being drafted into the military) to *an alcoholic beverage* (an ice-cold draft beer). Thus, determining whether a person knows a word extends beyond checking his or her ability to point to a picture of it or even to use it in a sentence. Moreover, knowledge of the world and the words used to represent that knowledge grows continuously across the life span. Over time, a person may come to associate varied meanings with each word because of increased exposure to assorted usage or varied personal experience. With exposure to print, a person may read about places, events, or people not directly experienced but may acquire new knowledge as well as the **lexicon** (vocabulary) that represents the experience.

In addition, there are rules that govern how words may be used in combination. Consider, for example, *The bachelor's wife is beautiful.* Although superficially the sentence is grammatically acceptable, the relationship between *bachelor* and *wife* raises a serious question as to the meaning of the sentence. Furthermore, the varying roles that words may play in a sentence can result in ambiguity that requires the language user to consider not only word meaning but also context. Consider the sentence *Visiting relatives can be a nuisance.* The meaning varies depending on the grammatical role ascribed to *visiting* as either a gerund or an adjective. These rules for the use of words in combination begin to develop quite early in a child's language acquisition process and form part of the basis for later semantic knowledge.

Word meaning may be literal or figurative. Part of the richness of language is in the imagery that it can create to express the more emotional and ethereal aspects of the human experience. Whether one has *had a ball* (had a good time at a party or possessed a baseball at some time) or *opened a can of worms* (went fishing or unintentionally caused a problem), the semantic knowledge and use are reflected in the way in which meaning is colored.

Meaning in language is conveyed through the use of words and their combinations. Language content is the knowledge of the vast array of objects, events, and relationships and the way they are represented.

Semantic Development   People talk or write to communicate meaning just as we listen or read to determine meaning. The process of learning to assign meaning begins in infancy during the preverbal stages of development. Meaning can be represented in a word, in a sentence, or across sentences, as well as in nonlinguistic ways.

Each of us has a lexicon, a mental dictionary within our semantic memory. Individual word meanings as well as how words may be used are found in the lexicon. In early development children may ascribe a "word" to represent a variety of objects or events or relationships. Thus, in the single-word stage of language development, *cup* pronounced as "kuh" may mean a request for a drink or a request that a fallen cup be returned to the tray of the highchair. In early stages of language acquisition, word meaning may be overextended so that, for example, any four-legged furry animal is called "cat." Obviously, children and adults do not use words in the same way. Although a child may use a word such as *cat* taken from adult lexicon, the meaning may be different as reflected in the overextensions of meaning that children make. Fortunately, word meanings are consistently refined over time so that speakers of the same language share common definitions for words.

In the early single-word stages of language development, children have already begun to code meaning for the words they use. They will use a word to indicate a variety of semantic categories such as existence (indicated by looking at, naming, touching, or referring to an object that exists in their world), nonexistence or disappearance (an object expected to be seen does not appear, "byebye"), or recurrence (the reappearance of an object or the recurrence of an event, "more").

As children progress to the two-word stage of language development, new semantic relations emerge, both individually and in combination. Between 18 and 36 months of age, children steadily acquire an increasing number of meaning relations that they can represent, such as agent–action ("Russell kiss") or attribute–entity ("big book").

With continued development children begin to acquire vocabulary at a very rapid rate. From the toddler years through first grade, children acquire new words at a pace of approximately 9 words per day. The vocabulary of a 6-year-old may be as large as 14,000 words (Carey, 1978). It is a massive task and remarkable feat to acquire sufficient information from interacting with the world (with little direct instruction) to develop a lexicon of nouns, verbs, adjective, adverbs, and prepositions, as well as the words to represent a huge array of concepts such as time, space, and causality.

The learning of a word is a long-term developmental process. It includes determining that a set of sounds are a word; learning the word's meaning components, privileges, and restrictions on its use; and learning its syntactic properties (parts of speech, how it may be used in a sentence) and the conceptual foundations on which that word is based. Not only must children develop word meanings, but they also must learn contextual meaning. In the preschool years words and sentence meaning expand. Later, children must learn to discern meaning from context (both linguistic and nonlinguistic) as well as to use later developing, more sophisticated cohesive devices to connect sentences into discourse.

Cohesive devices (Halliday & Hasan, 1976) include the use of pronouns or definite articles that refer to someone or something previously mentioned. This process is called **anaphora** (e.g., "Marsha was hungry. *She* went out to get lunch"). Another cohesive device, **ellipsis,** is the deletion of information available in a portion of the discourse immediately preceding (e.g., "Can you ice skate? I can"). Still another cohesive device, called **lexical cohesion,** involves the use of synonyms that refer to previously identified referents (e.g., "The *puppy* excitedly chased his tail. Our new *pet* was very entertaining").

In addition to relational meanings and contextual meaning, children must master the nonlinguistic aspects of meaning. **Deictic terms** are words that shift in meaning depending on how the nonlinguistic context changes. The meanings of words such as *I, you, here,* and *tomorrow* depend on who is speaking, where the participants are, and when the words are spoken.

Children acquire meaning of words and sentences and meaning across sentences in discourse. They must master a vast amount of information about the semantic and syntactic roles of words and about contextual and nonlinguistic aspects of meaning. It is amazing that much of this is accomplished in the preschool years. Later semantic development is concerned with continued refinement of previous content knowledge as well as with ongoing growth in vocabulary and in the mastery of **nonliteral language** such as **metaphors,** idioms, proverbs, and humor. As children become literate, the opportunities for growth in semantic knowledge grow considerably. After children learn to read, reading becomes a vehicle for learning.

Relationship of Semantic Disorders to Literacy   There is more to reading than decoding (determining the pronunciation of words by noting the positions of vowels and consonants). The proof of a skilled, fluent reader may be the ability to read a professional manual filled with unfamiliar technical jargon. Being able to decode the words may very well be insufficient to provide the intended meaning or comprehension of the text. Once the reader has gained access to the word through decoding, the meaning of the words and sentences must be analyzed and synthesized for comprehension to occur. Comprehension in reading then is dependent on semantic, syntactic, and world knowledge. Consider *diadochokinesis,* a word unfamiliar to most. A strong decoder can syllabicate and decode the word syllable by syllable, a likely approach given the length of the word, but may not be able to guess the meaning (rapid alternating movements such as those associated with speech articulation).

Gough and Tunmer (1986) made reference to two sets of skills in reading: decoding and linguistic comprehension. Reading is not a unitary action, nor is the use of oral language. Rather, both activities reflect a complex integration of skills. When looking at different groups identified as having reading disorders, dyslexia, language disorders, or "specific language impairment," it is important to consider the criteria that are selected to define the group and which skills are under investigation before generalizing the implications of research findings.

During a consideration of semantic deficits in vocabulary and word knowledge, word retrieval, and the relationship to syntax and sentence comprehension, it is necessary to be concerned with the dynamic relationship of form, content, and use. Specifically, weak phonological coding may be related to the establishment of poorer networks of word meanings as well as poorer access to those words. Thus, facility or difficulty in one aspect of language as it relates to reading does not preclude the same ease or difficulty in the other aspects of reading. Some good decoders have poor comprehension, just as in the early stages of reading mastery, poorer decoders may have adequate comprehension. Swank (1997) demonstrated that in addition to phonological coding, meaning and grammar are important to the decoding abilities of kindergarten and first-grade readers. Similarly, Nation and Snowling (as cited in Snowling & Nation, 1997) wrote that syntactic and semantic information derived from sentences allowed children to alter their inaccurate pronunciation of decoded target words so that the words made sense in the context of the sentence. In older children with reading difficulties, semantic deficits may be the result of what Vellutino, Scanlon, and Spearing referred to as having "accrued" (1995, p. 76) as a consequence of prolonged decoding difficulty in which poor readers are denied access to semantic information about word meaning and use. Early in their school careers children learn to read and for the remainder of their academic years, read to learn (Chall, 1983). Nippold suggested a "symbiotic" (1988, p. 29) relationship between literacy and learning during the later school years.

By fourth grade, reading becomes the primary means of acquiring new vocabulary. When children have inherent language deficits, semantic functions may be restricted, thus influencing learning to read as well as later reading to learn. Semantic deficits may manifest at different times in the reading process, dependent in part on the kind of reading instruction a child receives. Emphasis on **phonetics** in a highly structured sound–symbol system in which word identification is emphasized may allow comprehension difficulties based on semantic deficits to go unnoticed for longer periods of time. When text-based approaches to early reading are stressed, semantic deficits are more likely to be exposed earlier in the process of learning to read.

Semantic competence involves a high degree of organization among the concepts that are being accumulated in the semantic system. Semantic networks must be formed to provide the structure for the concepts that a child is learning. Children who are weaker at concept formation are likely to have less robust vocabulary and weaker semantic networks. Lack of exposure to concepts or difficulties in concept formation or in the organization of the concepts may result in less effective reading comprehension. So, children with ongoing oral language difficulties remain at higher risk for reading comprehension difficulties if their oral language deficits result in depressed semantic knowledge.

Children with reading deficits have been shown to have difficulties in vocabulary, word categorization, and word retrieval. Many children with reading impairments have more difficulty than same-age peers in providing accurate definitions for words. Hoskins (1983) reported that children with reading impairments were more likely to offer descriptions and examples of words they were asked to define rather than to provide more formal, specific definitions. This is a frequently observed clinical behavior. It reflects one level of general comprehension of word meaning and use (e.g., "I know how to use it but I can't really tell you what it means"). For teachers who are concerned about the reading comprehension abilities of their students, defining versus describing is a skill to watch for.

Categorization, or word association, abilities, another semantic skill reflecting a knowledge base, is also frequently deficient in children with reading difficulties. Children with reading and other learning disabilities often demonstrate restricted word meanings as well as weakly developed associations among words and classes of words. Limitations in reading comprehension may result from restricted word meanings that reduce the reader's ability to interpret sentences; reduced vocabulary knowledge so that less-familiar, multisyllabic words are more difficult to decode; and poorly developed semantic networks between word meanings and categories.

Other than word meaning itself, it is necessary to consider several other important aspects of semantics. Understanding a word also requires knowledge of **synonyms, antonyms,** and **multiple meanings** for a word. At higher levels of abstraction, semantic knowledge includes the appreciation and use of humor, slang, idioms, **similes,** and **metaphors** (Roth & Spekman, 1989). World knowledge also plays a considerable role in how semantics functions in reading comprehension. Lack of world knowledge means that a decoding error is more likely to remain uncorrected when reading on an unfamiliar topic. Lack of an adequate knowledge base to judge the content that is being read may result in comprehension errors as well.

Another frequently observed semantic deficit that affects literacy is word retrieval problems. Word retrieval problems may be described as a person's difficulty in gaining access to a specific, intended word from his or her vocabulary. So, despite knowledge of the word, there is a disruption in recovering or retrieving the phonetic structure (sound pattern) of the word to express it in spontaneous production. Common behaviors of people with word retrieval difficulties are delay in retrieving the word; substitution of other, similar words; circumlocutions (descriptions of aspects of the word, as when a person says, "You know, the place where you swim," but means *pool*); the use of gestures or demonstration to represent the word; and the substitution of nonspecific words (e.g., "thing," "stuff," "the place") for the specific word. Children with reading disabilities have been shown to have a slower rate of naming, more frequent naming errors, and longer delays before responding (Denckla & Rudel, 1976; German, 1982; Wiig, Semel, & Nystrom, 1982).

Children with word-retrieval difficulties may read less fluently, with many hesitations and rephrasings. A youngster may look at a word and offer a definition but be unable to say the specific word. Given the frequent substitution of similar or related words, comprehension may not be seriously affected; however, the dilemma may be in demonstrating comprehension when specific words are not readily accessible.

Finally, as children become more adequate decoders, they, similar to mature readers, read for meaning across sentences and through extended text rather than from individual words. At this juncture semantic knowledge must become integrated with syntactic knowledge and the more pragmatic, or discourse-related, aspects of language that include a knowledge of narrative structure and the ability to determine the writer's intent.

Language Use

Language use is frequently referred to as *pragmatics.* Pragmatics involves a set of rules that dictate communicative behavior in three main areas: reasons for which we communicate, called *communicative functions* or *intentions;* different codes or styles of communication necessary in a particular context; and conversation or discourse. Each person speaks for a variety of purposes with an assortment of intentions. These intentions refer to the speaker's goals in talking. For example, one may speak to greet, to inquire, to answer, to request a behavior or information, to negotiate, or to teach, among many other possibilities.

Success in communicating intentions depends on several factors. A speaker must choose the appropriate code or style from among the variety of ways in which something can be said. To make that decision, a speaker must consider the context and the listener's needs. The words and sentences that are chosen to formulate the thought depend on the ages, knowledge bases, and relative status of speaker and listener. Imagine using the greeting, "Hi sweetie!" uniformly when greeting your 3-year-old, your pharmacist, and your boss. Similarly, the words chosen depend on what is occurring or what is present at the time the words are spoken. Two people standing on a train platform at 7 A.M. on a weekday would find it appropriate to hear, "Here it comes." The same utterance while standing in line at the supermarket might be met with a quizzical, "What?"

Finally, pragmatics involves rules of conversation or discourse. To communicate effectively, a speaker must be able to start a conversation, enter a conversation in process, and appropriately remain in a conversation. Moreover, competent communicators must be able to take turns within a conversation, recognize the need for clarification and provide it, change the subject appropriately, listen and respond meaningfully, and tell a coherent and cohesive story (narrative). The minutiae of competent conversation and narrative is an extensive area of study because of its significance in the social and academic lives of children (Applebee, 1978; Brinton & Fujiki, 1989; Dore, 1978; Halliday, 1975; Prutting & Kirschner, 1987; Rees, 1978).

Mastering the social uses of language is an ongoing process for young language learners. In school, classroom discourse patterns and a literate level of talking and understanding represent a level of language use that is critical for academic success. The difference between everyday discourse and the language of the classroom and **expository writing** is dramatic. Although a youngster may have adequate linguistic ability for everyday conversational interactions, the same youngster may not have achieved a level of language use that is necessary to comprehend the language of instruction, which requires an understanding of more sophisticated vocabulary, words with multiple meanings, figurative usages, more varied and complex sentence structures, the distinction between what the sentence is saying and what it is intended to have the listener do, and the higher (less direct in interpretation) levels of understanding. Such a vulnerability can be easily overlooked and is seriously deleterious to a child's learning ability.

Pragmatic Development   The earliest observations of communicative development can be made during the period between birth and approximately 10 months of age. This stage of preverbal communication is the first of three periods identified by Bates, Camaioni, and Volterra (1975). In this earliest period the child is not aware of the communicative impact of his or her behavior. Although a child might point or reach toward an object of interest, he or she does not do this to elicit an adult's attention or action. In the next stage of communicative development, the one-word stage, between 10 and 15 months old, a child more definitely intends to communicate with the adults around him or her. Although these attempted communications may not involve speech, they are clearly recognized by both the baby and the adult as having intent. These attempts may be gestural and/or gestural and vocal (as differentiated from verbal attempts alone). Once a baby begins to use words to communicate, he or she is at the multiword stage, the third stage of this early period of communicative development. The baby's set of intentions previously was conveyed by gesture and vocalization. Now, more conventional word forms begin to serve similar purposes. As the use of words accomplishes goals for an infant or a toddler, the child begins to monitor and learn from the listener's reactions. The baby begins to see the effects of his or her utterances; as such, social interaction provides the context for learning about communication.

Roth and Spekman (1984) identified three sets of categories of intentional behavior for children in preverbal, one-word, and multiword stages of development. During the preverbal period children have many preverbal intentions, including attention-seeking (to self and to objects, events, or other people), requesting (objects, actions, information), greetings, transferring (giving someone a toy that they were holding), protesting or rejecting, responding/acknowledging, and informing. The most fascinating bit of knowledge is that children can and do communicate these intentions before they are talking! As children acquire words, naming and commenting are added to the list of intentions, and the others already available during the preverbal stage become refined. For example, with words a child can request objects that are present (saying "Cookie" while pointing to the package) or absent (saying "Truck" while pulling Mom into another room where the truck can be found). By the time children are producing multiword utterances, their intentions are more varied and refined. Now, when requesting information a child may be asking permission ("May I have more?"), requesting confirmation ("That's Daddy's?"), or requesting a repetition ("What is that?"). Moreover, statements or comments may now express rules or facts or opinions. At the multiword stage children have a better ability to regulate or control conversational interactions, and they have more facility for teasing, warning, claiming, or being humorous with words in a more adultlike manner.

As these multiword toddlers become preschoolers, they begin to learn more complex ways of using language for social purposes. Their conversational skills grow as do their discourse skills, such as telling stories, describing with greater clarity, and recounting personal experiences. As children's language skills grow, language can be used for an increasing number of school-related skills, such as instructing or reasoning. As they progress toward the school years, children begin to use their pragmatic skills for an ever-growing number of purposes at a higher, more refined level. Now language used to plan and organize must help to construct narratives of greater density and longer sequences of events. An increasing number of communicative intentions, more sophisticated conversational skills, and improved narrative (storytelling skills) all mark the development of language use in preschoolers.

Conversational skills develop further during the school years. In the preschool years conversation between children and adults is often supported by the adult. If a preschooler has not effectively communicated his or her intent, and a clarification is requested, most typically the youngster will repeat what he has just said. By the early elementary school years, however, a youngster will not only repeat but also will elaborate in an attempt to be more clear for the listener.

By the middle elementary school years, a child can not only elaborate but also explain, provide additional background information, and monitor the listener's comprehension in an ongoing way (Brinton, Fujiki, Loeb, & Winkler, 1986). Conversation among school-age children also involves the mastery of slang. In addition children speak to each other in sentence structures that are more complex, elaborate, and varied than they do when speaking to adults. This is consistent with parents' observations of the difference in the way children talk at home versus how they communicate among friends (Owens, 1996). Certainly, among teenagers the use of language for social purposes becomes more crucial. Also important is the ability to effectively shift from one conversational style (social) to another (academic) in order to meet the higher expectations of teachers for a fully literate style of language use (Larson & McKinley, 1995).

The school-age years bring with them another level of maturation and an increased demand on children's pragmatic abilities. During the school years several important changes take place in pragmatic development and use. The number of communicative functions must expand. Children have to use their language skills but must do so with increased levels of appropriateness and often more indirectly. The demands on narrative production increase steadily. Preschoolers' simple storytelling of one or two facts or events grows to become the requirements of show-and-tell as well as book reports and essays. Children who have heard stories read and told throughout their lives come to these school-based narrative tasks better equipped than peers with fewer literacy experiences (Linder, 1999). There is a structure and pattern to the ways stories are constructed (Stein & Glenn, 1979). When children have been exposed to this pattern frequently because they have been read to on a regular basis, they come to school with a tacit knowledge of the structure of stories that becomes more available to them as it is required in the school environment.

The language of the classroom is greatly different from the everyday language that is used for social interaction. In school there is a greater degree of formality. The choice of words is often more abstract and unfamiliar; sentence structures are more complex; the interactions are planned and controlled; the topics, which are also controlled, are often related to texts; the rate of speech is faster; and, above all, the language of the classroom is decontextualized (Nelson, 1986). When language is decontextualized there are few contextual clues that children can use to understand the language of the classroom. As communicators people are supported by context in the form of such cues as facial expressions, gestures, intonational patterns, and the presence of the object being discussed. Unlike conversation, instructional discourse provides less meaning and support from context. Understanding is more fully dependent on the words. The purposes of language in the classroom are more instructive, regulatory, and acknowledging and are far less individualized and supportive than in conversation. There is a communicative imbalance that is particular to the classroom. Teachers control topics and turns. They ask questions to which they already know the answers (and judge the responses) and create an environment with the language of authority. Britton has written that in a conversation the partners both are participants who have a generally equal role in the course and direction of the conversation. He described another style of conversation in which one partner is dominant and the other is more of a "spectator" (1979, p. 192). Spectators, he noted, "use language to digest experience" (p. 192). Indeed, when considering classroom discourse, students most frequently play the role of spectators.

The differences between social discourse and instructional discourse can be highlighted by comparing a request for information and its aftermath in a social context and in a classroom environment. A special form of instructional dialogue exists within classrooms (Cazden, 1988; Nelson, 1985), referred to as the *initiation-response-evaluation interaction pattern* that consists of teacher initiation, student response, and teacher evaluation. Thus, in a classroom one might hear the following:

Teacher: [Initiating] What is the capital of California?
Student: [Responding] Sacramento.
Teacher: [Evaluating] That's right. Very good.

In a social environment a similar exchange would end somewhat differently:

Speaker 1:   What is the capital of California?
Speaker 2:   Sacramento.
Speaker 1:   Thanks.

In the classroom the question is a test, although it is phrased as a request for information. In an everyday interaction the request for information is a genuine request. (See Table 2.5 for a discussion of the differences between oral language and literate [classroom] language.)

Relationship of Pragmatic Disorders to Literacy   The emphasis on the relationship between language and reading has grown ever stronger (Catts, 1996; Catts & Kamhi, 1986; Greene, 1996). For certain children whose oral language skills are age appropriate when they enter school, early literacy acquisition and accommodation to school discourse may not be negatively affected. Yet as the demands of the curriculum escalate, these same children may not have developed enough linguistically to meet expectations. Skills that were adequate in early grades when the emphasis was on decoding and when instruction was more experiential in nature are now insufficient as reading to learn (Chall, 1983) becomes the expected mode. Moreover, as the curriculum expands, topics become less familiar; new vocabulary and more complex sentences, paragraphs, and texts must be analyzed and interpreted; more reading and writing are expected; and the cognitive demands become more abstract.

Reading comprehension is an enormously complex integration of high-level linguistic ability and problem-solving skills. Approaching reading with the intent to understand and gain information and with the expectation that the text will make sense are the behaviors of good readers. They recognize that the goal of reading is to comprehend, and to that end they monitor their own comprehension. Poor readers, by contrast, will often perceive the purpose of reading as sounding out and saying the words aloud. The expectation or intent to understand what has been decoded is sharply reduced or is not a concern of poorer readers (Bos & Filip, 1982; Brown, 1982; Myers & Paris, 1978; Owens, Peterson, Bransford, Morris, & Stein, 1980).

An essential higher-order linguistic ability in text comprehension is the aspect of language use called *discourse*, which includes both conversational and

Table 2.5. Oral/literate language differences

Oral language	Literate language
Function	
Talking to regulate social interaction—requesting, commanding, protesting, seeking interaction	Talking to reflect on the past and future—predicting, projecting into thoughts and feelings of others, reasoning, imagining
Questions generally asked by speakers to gain information they do not have	Pseudoquestions asked to get the listener to perform for the speaker who knows the answers
Used to share understanding of the concrete and practical	Used to learn and teach
Symmetrical communication—everyone has an equal right to participate in the conversation; participants collaborate on the discourse	Asymmetrical communication—one person has the floor and is responsible for organizing the entire discourse
Topic	
Talk is about the here and now—the concrete	Talk is about the there and then—the past and future; the abstract
Topic associative organization; chaining of ideas or anecdotes	Topic-centered organization; explicit, linear description of single event
Meaning is in the context (shared information or the environment)	Meaning is in the text
Structure	
Use of pronouns, slang, and jargon; expressions known only to the in-group	Use of explicit, specific vocabulary
Familiar words	Unfamiliar words
Repetitive syntax and ideas	Minimal or no repetition of syntax and ideas
Cohesion based on intonation	Cohesion based on formal linguistic markers (because, therefore, and so forth)

From Westby, C. (1995). Culture and literacy: Frameworks for understanding. *Topics in Language Disorders,* *16*(1), 59; reprinted by permission; © 1995 Aspen.

narrative ability. Numerous higher-order language and cognitive skills are necessary for text comprehension including the following (as identified by Roth & Spekman, 1989): understanding the relationship between words and word parts, grasping sentence cohesion (i.e., the relationship between two sentences or parts of a sentence as signaled by cohesive devices), identifying words based on context or familiarity, determining vocabulary meaning based on context (including multiple meaning words and figurative language), understanding at different levels from literal to inferential (identifying main ideas, summarizing, predicting, and determining character traits and emotions), determining the communicative intent of the author, identifying and retaining relevant information, and using knowledge of narrative structure.

Knowledge of narrative structure and determining the author's intent can play crucial roles in comprehension when other syntactic (sentence structure) and semantic (meaning aspects) are otherwise intact. Recognizing narrative structure and the intention of the writer is part of the active construction of comprehension that extends beyond the interpretations of the grammatical and meaning components of a piece of writing.

The ability to appreciate and use narrative structure in comprehension (and oral/written production) has been studied in children with reading problems.

The use of story grammars that describe the internal structure (both the components of the story and the rules for the order and relationship among the story components) of a story has been the most common way of analyzing narratives (Mandler & Johnson, 1977; Stein & Glenn, 1979).

Stein and Glenn's (1979) story grammar consists of a setting category and a system for ordering episodes within the story. They are easily recognizable to those with the tacit knowledge of narrative structure and familiarity with literature. They are as follows: *setting statements* (*Marsha looked out across the expanse of land that she knew could now be hers*), *initiating events* (*The matching numbers were so unexpected*), *internal responses* (*Marsha remained numbed by the news*), *plans* for obtaining a goal (*Marsha started a telephone list. There was little time to waste*), *attempts* at achieving the goal (*Call after call, Marsha reported the news*), *direct consequences* of the attempts to reach the goal (*Everyone had been reached. They would arrive within 2 days*), and *reactions* that describe the emotional response (*With a grin on her face, she dropped into her favorite chair, exhausted and exhilarated!*).

Children with language and reading disabilities have less appreciation for narrative structure as defined by story grammar. Poorer understanding of temporal and causal relationships, limited detail, mistaken information, shorter retellings, and difficulty with inferential questions were also observed in children with language disorders (Gerber, 1993; Roth, 1986). Westby (1989) reported that children with language disorders tell shorter stories with fewer complete episodes, use a more restricted vocabulary, and have less well-organized stories than their peers who use language more typically.

In addition to knowledge and use of narrative structure, another, very pragmatically based aspect of comprehension is an understanding of the intent of the writer (or speaker, in oral discourse). This involves appreciating information that is not presented explicitly. This grasp of suggested or implied information, called *presupposition*, is necessary for the message being communicated to be understood (Bates, 1976; Rees, 1978). In order to be a successful communicator, it is necessary to have sufficient language flexibility to adjust what is being said according to the needs of the listener. That may mean altering word choice, sentence structure, gestures, and paralinguisitc features such as intonation patterns based on a variety of characteristics including age, relative status (of speaker and listener), intellectual level, and awareness of the listener's prior knowledge of the topic. Sociolinguist Dell Hymes (1972) offered a definition of pragmatics as "knowing what to say to whom, how and under what circumstances." A listener must monitor his or her comprehension and request clarification if necessary.

The parallels of pragmatics of oral language or discourse to reading are strong. Written language can be used for a variety of purposes with different intentions. In writing, one can request, create, solicit, inform, educate, entertain, describe, and persuade, among a lengthy list of other purposes. For the reader the mandate is to discern the communicative intent of the author in nonfiction and of the author and characters in fiction. When children have vulnerabilities in determining a speaker's intent in oral discourse, they are clearly at risk for failing to make these determinations from print. So much emphasis is placed on the decoding process in the early school years that the functional and communicative intents of writing are often neglected (Creaghead, 1986). Children who are weaker in understanding implied meaning in conversation (e.g., the sarcasm in "Nice haircut" said with a sneer) may struggle later on when they are expected to interpret humor, sarcasm, figurative language (idioms), metaphors, and other less explicitly stated intended meanings. Moreover, in reading, the physical and environmental cues on which speakers and listeners depend, such as an arched eyebrow, a falsetto voice, or the gape of onlookers, are absent or may be reflected in more abstract ways (should the author choose to do so) as italics or punctuation (! ; ? "). In conversation the speaker may recognize a furrowed brow as confusion and attempt to clarify before asked to do so. No such author-given support is available to the reader. As an educator, the author of this chapter has lost track of the number of times she has needed to help students recognize the need to actively construct their comprehension because Edgar Allan Poe, O. Henry, or Guy de Maupassant is "unavailable" to explain himself! Conversely, the children can be motivated to consider the needs of their reader (typically a teacher) when writing an assignment via a reminder that the teacher is unlikely to call them at home and ask, "Just what did you mean in the second paragraph on page 3?" It is crucial for teachers to recognize and remember that when children have vulnerabilities in discourse, they are at risk for comprehension difficulties with conversation and narrative despite having decoding skill. Active participation in the process of comprehending what is read involves a complex amalgam of skills among which language use or pragmatics is a subtle and often unrecognized vulnerability. When a youngster has adequate social language skills, the more hidden pragmatic weakness that can negatively affect comprehension may be overlooked easily. Direct instruction in narrative structure via story grammars and in identifying and interpreting the communicative intentions of the author can markedly improve a student's level of reading comprehension.

Metalinguistic Development   At the most developed level of language use, beyond the basic pragmatic skills required for conversation and narrative is another tier of language competence called *metalinguistic abilities* (Miller, 1990). Metalinguistic abilities permit a child to view language as an entity, something to talk about and think about. Metalinguistic skills enable a child to use language to talk about language. In preschoolers, language is viewed primarily as a means of communication, not as an object of consideration. During the school-age years, however, children become increasingly able to reflect on language and make conscious decisions about their own language and how it works. This is different from having tacit, underlying knowledge that allows the generation of sentences with specific words that are appropriate to a situation. Metalinguistic skills are essential to successful school learning because they influence a number of school-based tasks and are particularly important to the development of early decoding ability. Bunce (1993) identified the diverse nature of the metalinguistic skills required for literacy acquisition, comprehension, and successful school learning. At a phonological level a child must be able to segment a word into its sounds and determine whether two words have the same sound. Another metalinguistic task is to determine whether two sentences have equal meaning or to identify a sentence by its syntactic form (e.g., declarative, interrogative). Recognizing multiple meanings, summarizing, and analyzing information are metalinguistic tasks as well.

Wallach and Miller (1988) established a sequence in the development of metalinguistic skills that evolves from 1½ to 10 years of age and older. In the earliest stages children learn to recognize some printed symbols, such as McDonald's signs or the first letter of their name. By the beginning of the later stages of metalinguistic awareness, between 5 and 8 years of age, children's metalinguistic knowledge becomes an essential part of learning to read. Among these skills are those associated with phonological awareness, such as rhyming, segmentation, and phoneme deletion. It is widely agreed that phonological awareness makes a major contribution to early decoding ability. Well-developed metalinguistic skills are as crucial to early reading ability as they ultimately are to classroom success in understanding the discourse patterns of the classroom and the ongoing need to analyze the language being used to teach the language that must be learned.

When children have weaker skills in language comprehension and use, they are at risk for academic difficulty at many levels. For some children the shift from contextualized, social, familiar, adult-supported language to the decontextualized, pedagogic, novel, adult-directed, evaluative, metalinguistic language of the classroom is overwhelming. Such language difficulties can be virtually invisible in a child whose speech is clear and whose demeanor is undemanding. A common misperception is that these children lack motivation or interest; rather, their skills are not on the same level as the language and communication demands of the classroom. Language is a part of every aspect of the school day, and what appears to be inattention or lack of motivation may in fact be a lack of comprehension of the level of language presented and the rules of classroom discourse.

OTITIS MEDIA AND SPEECH, LANGUAGE, AND LITERACY

While you quietly read this chapter, it is easy to take normal hearing and sound **discrimination** (the ability to determine the difference between two sounds so that *whisper* is not processed as *whisker*) abilities for granted. Classrooms are rarely as quiet as libraries or studies, and so for a youngster with a conductive hearing loss secondary to ear infections or allergies, the background noise and acoustic lapses of a classroom, such as open doors, many windows, and uncarpeted floors (which allow for scraping and echoing) can be an obstacle to learning.

Otitis media is inflammation of the middle ear. This inflammation can be accompanied by fluid in the middle ear. If the fluid is not infected, the inflammation is called *otitis media with effusion (OME)*. When an infection exists in the middle ear, it is called *acute otitis media.* Many children shift back and forth between OME and acute otitis media. Fluid in the middle ear may persist for weeks or months after the onset of acute otitis media. When fluid persists for more than 3 months, the OME is said to be chronic. Although some children display signs and symptoms of the discomfort associated with fluid and/or infection in the middle ear, others are asymptomatic. Infected or not, symptomatic or not, when there is fluid in the middle ear, a child will generally have a mild to moderate conductive hearing loss as fluid blocks the normal transmission of sound through the middle ear. Put your fingers in your ears, or try listening to music in the bathtub with your ears below the surface of the water. The experience will provide a sense of how arduous listening and learning are to a child who is experiencing a conductive hearing loss. The conductive hearing loss associated with OME can fluctuate. This poses an additional dilemma for the young student. The teacher's voice may not be heard at a consistent level. Depending on the level of fluid, a child may have better or worse hearing on a given day. He or she cannot predict what he or she will be able to hear. Furthermore, because this type of hearing loss is often "invisible," teachers may be unaware of a child's need for additional support and accommodation. Children may appear uninterested or inattentive when they cannot adequately hear what is being said.

There is controversy regarding the effects of early otitis media on later language and academic development. A large body of research has provided evidence that children with persistent OME during their early years perform more poorly on tests of speech production (Roberts, Burchinal, Koch, Footo, & Henderson, 1988), speech processing (Gravel & Wallace, 1992), expressive language (Friel-Patti & Finitzo, 1990), and academic achievement (Silva, Chalmers, & Stewart, 1986). Children who have a history of otitis media are more frequently described by teachers as having behavioral and attentional problems (Roberts et al., 1989; Silva, Kirkland, Simpson, Stewart, & Williams, 1982).

Although many studies support the relationship between OME and subsequent difficulties in speech, language, and learning, other studies fail to show a significant link between OME and difficulties in the same cluster of skills and abilities, such as speech production and reception, receptive and expressive language, and academic achievement (Bishop & Edmundson, 1986; Lous, Fiellau-Nikolajsen, & Jeppeson, 1988; Roberts, Bailey & Nychka, 1991; Wallace, Gravel, McCarton, & Ruben, 1988).

The conflicting findings are in part a function of the ways in which the studies were conducted, either retrospectively or prospectively. It is important to consider the differences. Retrospective data collection relies on recall of events that may have occurred years before during episodes of OME as well as on review of medical records. The opportunity for error is great. Prospective data collection involves following the course of the child's experience from the time of the earliest incidence of OME through the development of language and academic experience. More prospective studies are needed to identify further the nature of the relationship between early OME and later learning. One study, Friel-Patti and Finitzo (1990), provided support for the logical assumption that the relationship between OME and language is bridged by hearing. Thus the relationship between OME and language is indirect but assumes the more direct relationship between OME and hearing and between hearing and language. Crucial to this point is the importance of repeated measures of OME, hearing, and language ability taken both concurrently and prospectively, given the unquestioned relationship between hearing and language and oral language and reading.

Although treatment of OME is a medical responsibility, teachers can play an important role in facilitating learning for children who have OME. Ear infections and hearing loss, particularly the mild to moderate losses associated with OME, can be unobserved in a classroom environment. The inattentiveness of a child with a mild to moderate hearing loss can easily seem behavioral or emotional. Table 2.6 provides suggestions for teachers working with children with OME to help make the learning experience more positive and robust.

The Oral–Written Language Connection

Literacy is much like a great pyramid. It is built on a broad foundation that is linguistic, sociological, cognitive, and pedagogic. Literacy evolves from well-developed oral language abilities; exposure to written language that gives rise to

Table 2.6.   Suggestions for teachers and daycare providers working with children with OME

1. Be aware of the signs of an ear infection (e.g., ear pain, pulling on ear, discharge from outer ear, hearing loss, congestion related to cold, decreased attentiveness), and let parents know when you observe that the child may have an ear infection.

2. Be aware that children experiencing OME may have a related fluctuating mild hearing loss and thus may exhibit difficulties hearing others talking or paying attention.

3. Recognize that children with a history of chronic OME may exhibit language and learning problems related to earlier OME, although they may not presently have frequent ear infections.

4. Provide an optimal language-learning environment by being responsive to the child.

5. When talking, face the child and talk at his or her eye level.

6. Speak clearly, repeating important words but using a natural intonation.

7. Gain the child's attention before telling information to ensure that the child has the opportunity to hear what you are saying.

8. Optimize the listening situation for the child who has attention difficulties by providing reminders to pay attention.

9. Provide visual supports for verbal-learning situations; for example, for the school-age child give written instructions along with oral instructions.

10. To provide a more quiet listening environment, reduce background noise and room echo, for example, by using carpeting and draperies and closing the door.

11. Give the child preferential seating to provide the clearest auditory signal. Allow the child to sit close to the teacher but in a position where the child can see other students (e.g., at the side of the room).

12. Be sure that the child is close to the person speaking (not more than 5 feet away).

13. Provide opportunities for small group and one-on-one interactions.

14. Refer the child to a speech-language pathologist and other appropriate specialists (e.g., psychologist, special educator) when a child experiencing OME or with a history of OME is having difficulty learning classroom material.

From Roberts, J., & Schuele, M. (1990). Otitis media and later academic performance: The linkage and implications for intervention. *Topics in Language Disorders, 11*(1), 58; reprinted by permission, © 1995 Aspen.

a child's notions of how print works and what it can do, called *emergent literacy* (Sulzby & Teale, 1991; Van Kleeck, 1990); a level of cognitive maturation that allows for metalinguistic awareness that permits a youngster to view language as an entity, something to be considered and analyzed; and a reasonable quality of instruction that can provide varying degrees of facilitation and support.

Language is the vehicle that drives curriculum. Although one may study aspects of the language in discrete ways (e.g., phonics, grammar, vocabulary), even then the very language being studied is the one that is employed to learn. In no instance does this resonate with greater truth than in the acquisition of literacy skills—reading and writing. "Learning to read and write is part of, not separate from, learning to speak and comprehend language" (Wallach & Butler, 1994, p. 11). Despite whole-language arguments to the contrary, however, "learning to read is not the same as learning to speak" (Wallach, 1990, p. 64).

Indeed, Van Kleeck (1990) allowed that the foundations of literacy are created at birth and are interrelated with the evolution and fullness of a child's oral language because reading is a language-based skill dependent on a set of well-developed oral language abilities. Language learning and literacy learning are actually reciprocal. That is to say the relationship between the two is dynamic and changes over time with each influencing the other at different developmental stages (Kamhi & Catts, 1989; Sawyer, 1991). Nonetheless, there are very considerable differences between language learning and literacy learning (Scott, 1994) because reading is not just speech written down (Liberman, Shankweiler, Camp, Blachman, & Werfelman, 1980).

Understanding oral language requires a well-integrated knowledge of the form, content, and use of the language. Recognizing word patterns, word structure, and sentence forms; knowing the meaning of words, how words relate to one another, and how they are influenced by their position in the sentence; and interpreting the intent of the speaker with the context and in relationship to your own knowledge base enable a listener to understand. Understanding written text requires the same linguistic knowledge that is necessary for understanding spoken language. The analogy of hearing spoken language to decoding print serves quite well; "I heard what you said, but I don't know what you mean" is similar to the phenomenon of asking a youngster to tell about what he or she has just read and being met with a look of noncomprehension that implies, "I know that I read [decoded] it, but I don't know what it means!" As described throughout this chapter, deficits in oral language, syntax, morphology, semantics (word meaning and relationships), pragmatics, and narrative structure will have a negative impact on reading comprehension.

In addition to oral language skills, emergent literacy is a foundation for literacy development (see Van Kleeck, 1990, for an extended discussion of emergent literacy). Emergent literacy is an outgrowth of **"literacy socialization"** (Snow & Dickinson, 1991). When children are exposed to print by being read to, whether from books, signs or instructions, or birthday cards, they begin to develop a sense that the marks on the page, box, or card are related to the words being said (Linder, 1999). They also begin to develop an awareness of how books are manipulated, literally which way is up and in which direction the text flows and the pages turn. Children who have been exposed to print in early caregiver–child interactions also benefit from the positive emotional connection between reading and nurturing experiences. Provided with literacy socialization experiences and as a result the emergent literacy skills that precede learning to decode, children who have been read to as preschoolers unquestionably find the process of learning to read an easier experience (Dickinson & McCabe, 1991; Wolf & Dickinson, 1993).

Metalinguistic ability, as discussed previously, permits a child to focus on language from a distance; to view language as an object of consideration; and to reflect on its discrete, particular aspects and characteristics. It is metalinguistically that children recognize word boundaries; make sound–letter correspondences; consider which printed sequences of letters represent which words and meanings; and analyze, blend, and reconstruct words. Little, if anything, in the oral language experience prepares children to view words as discrete units (e.g., sit) to isolate the parts of each unit (e.g., s-i-t) in order to reformulate and orally produce (e.g., "sit"). Certainly, phonological awareness activities are dependent on metalinguistic skills. Beyond the task of decoding, conscious use of linguistic knowledge strongly influences reading comprehension. Oral language development, however, does not require these metalinguistic abilities. The speech stream is continuous with boundaries that are not discrete, and the context is immediate and supported environmentally by the situation in which the talking is occurring. In oral language development, reflection on linguistic knowledge is not part of the process until a fair degree of cognitive maturity and linguistic sophistication has been attained.

Literacy is built on good oral language abilities, literacy awareness, metalinguistic ability, and for the most part, good teaching. Moats and Lyon (1996) strongly urged changes in teacher education related to reading instruction to place a greater emphasis on knowledge of language structure. They cited very disturbing findings in a survey of 103 teachers in which fewer than one third were proficient in basic knowledge of language structure, such as identification of an inflected ending (-ed in *instructed*) or the number of phonemes in words such as *ox, precious,* or *thank.* Teaching children to read requires teaching them language at a higher and conscious level. Successful teaching, particularly of those children who bring linguistic, experiential, cognitive, or environmental vulnerabilities to the task, requires a powerful, integrated knowledge of the language that is being taught.

ORAL–WRITTEN LANGUAGE DIFFERENCES

There is no doubt that reading is a language-based skill, yet there are numerous and obvious differences between oral and written language. These differences have been considered from a variety of different vantage points, either as parallels or continua (Horowitz & Samuels, 1987; Kamhi & Catts, 1989; Rubin, 1987; Scott, 1994; Wallach, 1990; Westby, 1985). In the course of human development, literacy is recent. Learning to read and write does not come naturally to everyone, and these skills are not a requirement in every society. Writing, as anyone who has ever struggled with a blank page or experienced "writer's block" well knows, requires a much greater effort than does producing oral language. Rubin highlighted his difficulty when he wrote that "no one is a native speaker of writing" (1987, p. 3). Human beings are socialized to communicate, and they have a biological predisposition to oral language that enables societal groups to have and pass on oral language systems. Reading and writing are deliberately, rather than spontaneously and more naturally, acquired. The differences are in the aspects of production, influences of context, grammar and vocabulary, and the degree of explicitness.

Oral language is transient and ephemeral. It exists only at the moment when it is spoken. It can be repeated or clarified, but that occurs on the request of the listener. Written language is permanent and more enduring than oral language, except when the latter is audiotaped or videotaped. Print allows the reader multiple opportunities for exposure and decision-making authority regarding the rate and depth of analysis with which the text is read. In oral language, the rate of presentation is at the discretion of the speaker. In oral language, temporal sequencing is most crucial, but in print, spatial sequencing is important. Print can be revisited more readily. A word, sentence, or paragraph can be reread or rewritten. It is rather a different experience to have someone attempt to repeat, exactly, the sentence just uttered.

Most oral language occurs face to face. Reciprocity exists between the speaker and listener. Interpersonal context and situational support exist in the form of vocal, facial, and physical gestures. When people are engaged in conversation or discussion, less needs to be explicitly stated and sentence structures can be more fragmentary. Vocabulary and syntax can be more familiar and less sophisticated. To appreciate the lack of explicitness, as well as the fragmentary, familiar, and contextually and physically supported nature of oral language, request a transcript of a television talk show that you have watched. While watching and listening to the discussion, you probably had little difficulty understanding the ebb and flow, intent, and effect of the exchanges among the participants. Reading the transcript of the same exchange will provide an immediate insight into the significant differences in the explicitness of a written text and the literate, grammatically dense nature of written language versus oral language that has been written down. In oral language, cohesion between sentences and ideas can be established grammatically or paralinguistically through physical signals such as the shrug of a shoulder or a pregnant pause. In a written text the cohesive devices and transitional markers that bind ideas or shift focus must be conveyed concretely and explicitly through a careful choice of words. The conventions of punctuating written language that are communicated orally through intonational gestures must be taught specifically; however, written text does provide other cues to organization and meaning through the structure of paragraphs and the use of boldface, italics, and underlining.

Although written language contains the intent to communicate with another or others or to interpret another person's message, the experience is generally more solitary and involves only the reader and the book, the blank page, or the computer screen. The interaction between writer and reader is limited and is *decontextualized*—separated by time and distance. In print it is necessary for the communicator to be more explicit and succinct.

Written language relies on the lexicon to create the melody and meaning provided by the intonation, stress, pause, and juncture patterns of spoken language as well as the vocal characteristics of the speaker. An anxious tone, a sinister laugh, or a lascivious lilt can be heard, recognized, and interpreted without being explicitly stated by the speaker as such. What is said and meant can be potently influenced by how it is said, and thus the message and intent of the speaker and the response of the listener may vary. The most literate of writers attain a level of mastery that enables them to arrange, adapt, maneuver, integrate, and entwine words and sentences in ways that communicate so effectively that it seems as though they are talking. With that level of written language mastery, it is possible to write the same thing in so many different ways, ranging from the most informal to the most deliberately formal tone.

Following a consideration of the oral–written continuum, it is important to look at writing itself. Writing is the most sophisticated, complex, and formal aspect of language. Even the most well-read and literate individuals may not have equivalent skill in expressing thoughts on paper. Writing is a dynamic interaction among cognitive and linguistic factors and motor skills and emotional considerations. The most sophisticated language act, writing, involves the simultaneous convergence of cognitive factors (abstracting, generating, and ordering ideas), linguistic factors (arriving at semantic and syntactic production appropriate to the nature of what is being written, such as a thank-you note versus an expository paragraph), narrative considerations (structuring information for varied purposes), **graphomotor** skills (recalling, planning, and executing complex motor acts), visual ability (recalling sequences of letters with phonetic rules for spelling), and temporal factors (writing legibly and appropriately under specific time constraints) while controlling for the emotional factors involved in risk, exposure, and evaluation of the final product. It is readily apparent why many children (and adults) might prefer to speak rather than to write! The teaching of writing can be an art form (see Chapter 10 for a discussion of teaching the writing process).

CLOSING THOUGHTS

Consider once more the marvelous melodies and harmonies of *Eine Kleine Nachtmusik*. There are but eight notes in the musical scale, yet the combinations and permutations are endless. In a similar vein, a language system has a set of components that are conceptualized as form, content, and use. Within each of these components are an uncountable number of combinations and variations that function alongside rules and regularities, permitting the language user, young or old, to communicate. No child is like every other child. Genetics, personality, experience, emotion, developmental patterns, intellect, neurology, perception, memory, and **linguistics** intertwine so that in every case, the whole is greater than the sum of its parts. Still, there are certain regularities in language development that teachers must know so as to enrich the understanding of how language influences a child's ability to learn. Simultaneously, the variability from one child to another must be kept in mind so that teachers focus on the child and not only on the task. At times, the child's knowledge and ability as well as the task itself influence performance and learning.

Throughout this chapter, four strands of research have been woven into a braid: language and speech-language pathology, learning disabilities, reading, and education. In-depth knowledge of oral language development and language related to learning and reading comes from the discipline of speech-language pathology. An understanding of the many aspects of learning and flexibility in skill and strategy development emerges from the study of learning disabilities. Reading research and instruction provide an intense consideration of all aspects of the enormous task of "breaking the code" and then encoding to complete the reading process. Educational theory and practice offer a wide array of techniques for encouraging and facilitating learning. For teachers an awareness and integration of this information offers the opportunity for greater power in teaching.

Language is omnipresent in education. It is an immutable aspect of literacy, a treasured gift that many but not all of us share. By understanding and appreciating the role that language plays in learning and literacy and by thinking about the needs of one child at a time, teachers have a greater opportunity to share the gift.

REFERENCES

Adams, A., & Gathercole, S. (1995). Phonological working memory and speech production in preschool children. *Journal of Speech and Hearing Research, 38,* 403–414.

Adams, M. (1990). *Beginning to read: Thinking and learning about print.* Cambridge: The MIT Press.

Adams, M.J., Foorman, B.R., Lundberg, I., & Beeler, T. (1998). *Phonemic awareness in young children: A classroom curriculum.* Baltimore: Paul H. Brookes Publishing Co.

Applebee, A. (1978). *The children's concept of story.* Chicago: University of Chicago Press.

Aram, D., & Hall, N. (1989). Longitudinal follow-up of children with preschool communication disorders. *School Psychology Review, 18,* 487–501.

Bashir, A., & Scavuzzo, A. (1992). Children with language disorders: Natural history and academic success. *Journal of Learning Disabilities, 25*(1), 53–65.

Bates, E. (1976). Pragmatics and sociolinguistics in child language. In D. Morehead & A. Morehead (Eds.), *Normal and deficient child language* (pp. 411–463). Baltimore: University Park Press.

Bates, E., Camaioni, L., & Volterra, V. (1975). The acquisition of performatives prior to speech. *Merrill-Palmer Quarterly, 21,* 205–226.

Bernthal, J.E., & Bankson, N.W., (1998). *Articulation and phonological disorders* (4th ed.). Needham Heights, MA: Allyn & Bacon.

Bird, J., & Bishop, D. (1992). Perception and awareness of phonemes in phonologically impaired children. *European Journal of Disorders of Communication, 27,* 289–311.

Bird, J., Bishop, D., & Freeman, N. (1995). Phonological awareness and literacy development in children with expressive phonological impairments. *Journal of Speech and Hearing Research, 38,* 446–462.

Bishop, D., & Edmundson, A. (1986). Is otitis media a major cause of specific developmental disorders? *British Journal of Disorders of Communication, 21,* 321–338.

Blachman, B. (1989). Phonological awareness and word recognition: Assessment and intervention. In A.G. Kamhi & H.W. Catts (Eds.), *Reading disabilities: A developmental language perspective* (pp. 138–158). Boston: Little, Brown.

Blachman, B. (1991). Early intervention for children's reading problems: Clinical applications of the research in phonological awareness. *Topics in Language Disorders, 12*(1), 51–65.

Blachman, B.A., Ball, E.W., Black, R., & Tangel, D.M. (2000). *Road to the code: A phonological awareness program for young children.* Baltimore: Paul H. Brookes Publishing Co.

Bloom, L., & Lahey, M. (1978). *Language development and language disorders.* New York: John Wiley & Sons.

Bos, C., & Filip, D. (1982). Comprehension monitoring skills in learning disabled and average readers. *Topics in Learning and Learning Disabilities, 2,* 79–85.

Brady, S., & Shankweiler, D. (Eds.). (1991). *Phonological processes in literacy: A tribute to Isabelle Y. Liberman.* Mahwah, NJ: Lawrence Erlbaum Associates.

Brinton, B., & Fujiki, M. (1989). *Conversational management with language impaired children: Pragmatic assessment and intervention.* Rockville, MD: Aspen Publishers.

Brinton, B., Fujiki, M., Loeb, D., & Winkler, E. (1986). Development of conversational repair strategies in response to requests for clarification. *Journal of Speech and Hearing Research, 39,* 75–82.

Britton, J. (1979). Learning to use language in two modes. In N. Smith & M. Franklin (Eds.), *Symbolic functioning in childhood* (pp. 185–198). Mahwah, NJ: Lawrence Erlbaum Associates.

Brown, A. (1982). Learning how to learn from reading. In J. Langer & M. Smith-Burke (Eds.), *Reader meets author: Bridging the gap.* Newark, DE: International Reading Association.

Brown, R. (1973). *A first language: The early stages.* Cambridge, MA: Harvard University Press.

Bunce, B.H. (1993). Language of the classroom. In A. Gerber (Ed.), *Language related learning disabilities* (pp. 135–159). Baltimore: Paul H. Brookes Publishing Co.

Byrne, B. (1981). Deficient syntactic control in poor readers: Is a weak phonetic memory code responsible? *Applied Psycholinguistics, 3,* 201–212.

Carey, A. (1978). The child as word learner. In M. Halle, J. Bresnan, & G. Miller (Eds.), *Linguistic theory and psychological reality* (pp. 264–293). Cambridge: The MIT Press.

Carlisle, J. (1988). Knowledge of derivational morphology in spelling ability in fourth, sixth and eighth graders. *Applied Psycholinguistics, 9*(3), 247–266.

Carlisle, J. (1995). Morphological awareness and early reading achievement. In L.B. Feldman (Ed.), *Morphological aspects of language processing.* Mahwah, NJ: Lawrence Erlbaum Associates.

Carroll, L. (1960). *Alice's adventures in wonderland and through the looking glass. A*

Signet Classic. New York: The New American Library, Inc. (Original work published 1865)

Catts, H. (1986). Speech production/ phonological deficits in reading disordered children. *Journal of Learning Disabilities, 19*, 504–508.

Catts, H. (1993). The relationship between speech and language impairments and reading disabilities. *Journal of Speech and Hearing Research, 36*(5), 948–958.

Catts, H. (1996). Defining dyslexia as a developmental language disorder: An expanded view. *Topics in Language Disorders, 16*(2), 14–25.

Catts, H. (1997). The early identification of language-based reading disabilities. *Language, Speech, and Hearing Services in Schools, 28*, 86–89.

Catts, H.W. (1989). Phonological processing deficits and reading disabilities. In A.G. Kamhi & H.W. Catts (Eds.), *Reading disabilities: A developmental language perspective* (pp. 101–132). Boston: Little, Brown.

Catts, H.W., Hu, C.-F., Larrivee, L., & Swank, L. (1994). Early identification of children with speech-language impairments. In R.V. Watkins & M.L. Rice (Eds.), *Communication and language intervention series: Vol. 4. Specific language impairment in children* (pp. 143–160). Baltimore: Paul H. Brookes Publishing Co.

Catts, H.W., & Kamhi, A. (1986). The linguistic basis of reading disorders: Implications for the speech-language pathologist. *Language, Speech and Hearing Services in Schools, 17*, 329–341.

Catts, H.W., & Vartiainen, T. (1997). *Sounds abound.* East Moline, IL: LinguiSystems.

Cazden, C. (1988). *Classroom discourse: The language of teaching and learning.* Portsmouth, NH: Heinemann.

Chall, J. (1983). *Stages of reading development.* New York: McGraw-Hill.

Chaney, C. (1992). Language development, metalinguistic skills, and print awareness in 3 year old children. *Applied Psycholinguistics, 13*, 485–514.

Clark-Klein, S., & Hodson, B. (1995). A phonologically based analysis of misspellings by third graders with disordered-phonology histories. *Journal of Speech and Hearing Research, 38*, 839–849.

Creaghead, N. (1986). Comprehension of meaning in written language. *Topics in Language Disorders, 6*(4), 73–82.

Denckla, M., & Rudel, R. (1976). Rapid "automatized" naming (RAN): Dyslexia differentiated from other learning disabilities. *Neuropsychologia, 14*, 471–479.

Dickinson, D., & McCabe, A. (1991). The acquisition and development of language: A social interactionist account of language and literacy development. In J. Kavanagh (Ed.), *The language continuum: From infancy to literacy.* Timonium, MD: York Press.

Dore, J. (1978). Requestive systems in nursery school conversations: Analysis of talk in its social context. In R. Campbell & P. Smith (Eds.), *Recent advances in the psychology of language: Language development and mother–child interaction* (pp. 271–292). New York: Plenum .

Edwards, M.L., & Shriberg, L.D. (1983). *Phonology: Applications in communicative disorders.* San Diego: College-Hill Press.

Ehri, L. (1989). Movement into word reading and spelling: How spelling contributes to reading. In J. Mason (Ed.), *Reading and writing connections* (pp. 65–81). Needham Heights, MA: Allyn & Bacon.

Eimas, P., Siqueland, E., Jusczyk, P., & Vigorito, J. (1971). Speech perception in infants. *Science, 171*, 303–306.

Elbro, C., & Arnbak, A. (1996). The role of morpheme recognition and morphological awareness in dyslexia. *Annals of Dyslexia, 46*, 209–240.

Fey, M.E., Catts, H.W., & Larrivee, L.S. (1995). Preparing preschoolers for the academic and social challenges of school. In M.E. Fey, J. Windsor, & S.F. Warren (Eds.), *Communication and language intervention series: Vol. 5. Language intervention: Preschool through elementary years* (pp. 3–37). Baltimore: Paul H. Brookes Publishing Co.

Fowler, A. (1991). How early phonological development might set the stage for phoneme awareness. In S. Brady & D. Shankweiler (Eds.), *Phonological processes in literacy: A tribute to Isabelle Y. Liberman* (pp. 97–117). Mahwah, NJ: Lawrence Erlbaum Associates.

Fowler, A., & Liberman, I. (1995). Morphological awareness as related to early reading and spelling ability. In L. Feldman (Ed.), *Morphological aspects of language processing* (pp. 157–188). Mahwah, NJ: Lawrence Erlbaum Associates.

Friel-Patti, D., & Finitzo, T. (1990). Language learning in a prospective study of otitis media with effusion in the first two years of age. *Journal of Speech and Hearing Research, 33*, 188–194.

Gerber, A. (1993). *Language-related learning disabilities: Their nature and treatment.* Baltimore: Paul H. Brookes Publishing Co.

German, D. (1982). Word-finding substitution in children with learning disabilities. *Language, Speech, and Hearing Services in Schools, 13*, 223–230.

Gough, P., & Tunmer, W. (1986). Decoding reading and reading disability. *Remedial and Special Education, 7*, 6–10.

Gravel, J., & Wallace, I. (1992). Listening and language at four years of age: Effects of early otitis media. *Journal of Speech and Hearing Research, 35*, 588–595.

Greene, J. (1996). Psycholinguistic assessment: The clinical base for identification of dyslexia. *Topics in Language Disorders, 16*(2), 45–72.

Halliday, M.A.K. (1975). *Learning how to mean: Explorations in the development of language.* London: Edward Arnold.

Halliday, M.A.K., & Hasan, R. (1976). *Cohesion in English.* London: Longman Group, Ltd.

Hart, B., & Risley, T.R. (1999). *The social world of children learning to talk.* Baltimore: Paul H. Brookes Publishing Co.

Hodson, B. (1994). Helping individuals become intelligible, literate and articulate: The role of phonology. *Topics in Language Disorders, 14*(2), 1–16.

Horowitz, R., & Samuels, J. (1987). Comprehending oral and written language: Critical contrasts for literacy and schooling. In R. Horowitz & J. Samuels (Eds.), *Comprehending oral and written language* (pp. 1–52). San Diego: Academic Press.

Hoskins, B. (1983). Semantics. In C. Wren (Ed.), *Language learning disabilities* (pp. 85–111). Rockville, MD: Aspen Publishers.

Hymes, D. (1972). On communicative competence. In J.B. Pride & J. Holmes (Eds.), *Sociolinguistics* (pp. 269–293). London: Penguin Books, Ltd.

Kamhi, A.G., & Catts, H.W. (1989). Language and reading: Convergences, divergences and development. In A.G. Kamhi & H.W. Catts (Eds.), *Reading disabilities: A developmental language perspective* (pp. 1–34). Boston: Little, Brown.

Katz, R. (1986). Phonological deficiencies in children with reading disability: Evidence from an object-naming task. *Cognition, 22*, 225–257.

Lahey, M. (1988). *Language disorders and language development.* New York: John Wiley & Sons.

Lahey, M., & Bloom, L. (1994). Variability and language learning disabilities. In G. Wallach & K. Butler (Eds.), *Language learning disabilities in school-age children and adolescents: Some principles and applications* (pp. 354–372). Needham Heights, MA: Allyn & Bacon.

Larson, V., & McKinley, N. (1995). *Language disorders in older students, preadolescents and adolescents.* Eau Claire, WI: Thinking Publications.

Liberman, I. (1983). A language-oriented view of reading and its disabilities. In H. Myklebust (Ed.), *Progress in learning disabilities* (Vol. 5, pp. 81–102). New York: Grune & Stratton.

Liberman, I., & Liberman, A. (1990). Whole language vs. code emphasis: Underlying assumptions and their implications for reading instruction. *Annals of Dyslexia, 40*, 51–76.

Liberman, I., Shankweiler, D., Camp, L., Blachman, G., & Werfelman, M. (1990). Steps toward literacy. In P. Levinson & C. Sloan (Eds.), *Auditory processing and language: Clinical and research perspectives* (pp. 189–215). New York: Grune & Stratton.

Linder, T.W. (1999). *Read, play, and learn!: Storybook activities for young children. Teacher's guide.* Baltimore: Paul H. Brookes Publishing Co.

Lous, J., Fiellau-Nikolajsen, M., & Jeppeson, A. (1988). Secretory otitis media and verbal intelligence: A six year prospective case control study. In D. Lim, C. Bluestone, J. Klein, & J. Nelson (Eds.), *Recent advances in otitis media with effusion* (pp. 185–203). Philadelphia: Decker.

Mahoney, D., & Mann, V. (1992). Using children's humor to clarify the relationship between linguistic awareness and early reading ability. *Cognition, 45*, 163–186.

Mandler, J., & Johnson, N. (1977). Remembrance of things parsed: Story structure and recall. *Cognitive Psychology, 9*, 111–151.

Mattingly, I. (1972). Reading, the linguistic process and linguistic awareness. In

J. Kavanagh & I. Mattingly (Eds.), *Language by ear and by eye: The relationship between speech and reading* (pp. 133–144). Cambridge: The MIT Press.

McGregor, K. (1994). Use of phonological information in word finding treatment of children. *Journal of Speech and Hearing Research, 37*, 1381–1393.

Menyuk, P., & Chesnick, M. (1997). Metalinguistic skills, oral language knowledge and reading. *Topics in Language Disorders, 17*(3), 75–87.

Merzenich, M., Jenkins, W., Johnston, P., Schreiner, C., Miller, S., & Tallal, P. (1996). Temporal processing deficits of language-learning impaired children ameliorated by training. *Science, 271*, 77–80.

Miller, L. (1990). The roles of language and learning in the development of literacy. *Topics in Language Disorders, 10*, 1–24.

Milosky, L. (1994). Nonliteral language abilities: Seeing the forest for the trees. In G. Wallach & K. Butler (Eds.), *Language learning disabilities in school-aged children and adolescents: Some principles and applications* (pp. 275–303). Needham Heights, MA: Allyn & Bacon.

Moats, L.C. (1994). Honing the concepts of listening and speaking: A prerequisite to the valid measurement of language behavior in children. In G.R. Lyon (Ed.), *Frames of reference for the assessment of learning disabilities: New views on measurement issues* (pp. 229–241). Baltimore: Paul H. Brookes Publishing Co.

Moats, L.C. (1995). *Spelling: Development, disability, and instruction.* Timonium, MD: York Press.

Moats, L.C., & Lyon, G.R. (1996). Wanted: Teachers with a knowledge of language. *Topics in Language Disorders, 16*(2), 73–86.

Mody, M., Studdert-Kennedy, M., & Brady, A. (1997). Speech perception deficits in poor readers: Auditory processing or phonological coding? *Journal of Experimental Child Psychology, 64*, 199–231.

Montgomery, J. (1996). Sentence comprehension and working memory in children with specific language impairment. *Topics in Language Disorders, 17*(1), 19–32.

Morice, R., & Slaghuis, W. (1985). Language performance and reading ability at 8 years of age. *Applied Psycholinguistics, 6*, 141–160.

Myers, M., & Paris, S. (1978). Children's metacognitive knowledge about reading. *Journal of Educational Psychology, 70*, 680–690.

Nelson, N.W. (1985). Teacher talk and child listening: Fostering a better match. In C. Simon (Ed.), *Communication skills and classroom success: Assessment of language-learning disabled students* (pp. 65–102). San Diego: College-Hill Press.

Nelson, N.W. (1986). Individualized processing in classroom settings. *Topics in Language Disorders, 6*(2), 13–27.

Nippold, M. (1988). The literate lexicon. In M. Nippold (Ed.), *Later language development: Ages nine through nineteen* (pp. 29–47). San Diego: College-Hill Press.

Owens, R. (1996). *Language development: An introduction* (3rd ed.). Columbus, OH: Merrill/MacMillan.

Owings, R., Peterson, G., Bransford, J., Morris, C., & Stein, B. (1980). Spontaneous monitoring and regulation of learning: A comparison of successful and less successful fifth graders. *Journal of Educational Psychology, 72*, 250–256.

Paul, R., & Jennings, P. (1992). Phonological behavior in toddlers with slow expressive language development. *Journal of Speech and Hearing Research, 35*, 99–107.

Perfetti, C., & Lesgold, A. (1977). Discourse comprehension and sources of individual differences. In M. Just & P. Carpenter (Eds.), *Cognitive processes in comprehension* (pp. 141–184). Mahwah, NJ: Lawrence Erlbaum Associates.

Prather, E., Hedrick, D., & Kern, C. (1975). Articulation development in children aged two to four years. *Journal of Speech and Hearing Research, 40*, 179–191.

Prutting, C., & Kirschner, D. (1987). A clinical appraisal of the pragmatic aspects of language. *Journal of Speech and Hearing Disorders, 52*, 105–119.

Rees, N. (1978). Pragmatics of language: Applications to normal and disordered language development. In R. Schiefelbusch (Ed.), *Bases of language intervention* (pp. 191–268). Baltimore: University Park Press.

Roberts, J., Bailey, D., & Nychka, H. (1991). Teachers' use of strategies to facilitate the communication of preschool children with disabilities. *Journal of Early Intervention, 15*, 369–376.

Roberts, J., Burchinal, M., Collier, A., Ramey, C., Koch, M., & Henderson, F.

(1989). Otitis media in early childhood and cognitive academic and classroom performance of the school-aged child. *Pediatrics, 83,* 477–485.

Roberts, J., Burchinal, M., Koch, M., Footo, M., & Henderson, F. (1988). Otitis media in early childhood and its relationship to later phonological development. *Journal of Speech and Hearing Disorders, 53,* 416–424.

Roberts, J., & Schuele, M. (1990). Otitis media and later academic performance: The linkage and implications for intervention. *Topics in Language Disorders, 11*(1), 53–62.

Robertson, C., & Salter, W. (1997). *The phonological awareness test.* East Moline, IL: LinguiSystems.

Roth, F. (1986). Oral narratives of learning disabled students. *Topics in Language Disorders, 7*(1), 21–30.

Roth, F., & Spekman, N. (1984). Assessing the pragmatic abilities of children: Part I. Organizational framework and assessment parameters. *Journal of Speech and Hearing Disorders, 49,* 2–11.

Roth, F., & Spekman, N. (1989). Higher order language processes and reading disabilities. In A.G. Kamhi & H.W. Catts (Eds.), *Reading disabilities: A developmental language perspective* (pp. 159–198). Boston: Little, Brown.

Ruben, H., Patterson, P., & Kantor, M. (1991). Morphological development and writing ability in children and adults. *Language, Speech, and Hearing Services in Schools, 22,* 228–235.

Rubin, D. (1987). Divergence and convergence between oral and written communication. *Topics in Language Disorders, 7*(4), 1–18.

Sawyer, D. (1991). Whole language in context: Insights into the great debate. *Topics in Language Disorders, 11*(3), 1–13.

Scarborough, H. (1990). Very early language deficits in dyslexic children. *Child Development, 61,* 1728–1743.

Scott, C. (1988). Spoken and written syntax. In M. Nippold (Ed.), *Later language development: Ages nine through nineteen* (pp. 49–96). San Diego: College-Hill Press.

Scott, C. (1994). A discourse continuum for school-aged students: Impact of modality and genre. In G. Wallach & K. Butler (Eds.), *Language learning disabilities in school aged children and adolescents: Some principles and applications* (pp. 219–252). Needham Heights, MA: Allyn & Bacon.

Silva, P., Chalmers, D., & Stewart, I. (1986). Some audiological, psychological, educational and behavioral characteristics of children with bilateral otitis media with effusion: A longitudinal study. *Journal of Learning Disabilities, 19*(3), 165–169.

Silva, P., Kirkland, C., Simpson, A., Stewart, I., & Williams, S. (1982). Some developmental and behavioral problems associated with bilateral otitis media with effusion. *Journal of Learning Disabilities, 15*(7), 417–421.

Snow, C., & Dickinson, D. (1991). Skills that aren't basic in a new conception of literacy. In A. Purves & E. Jennings (Eds.), *Literate systems and individual lives: Perspectives on literacy and schooling.* Albany: SUNY Press.

Snowling, M. (1981). Phonemic deficits in developmental dyslexia. *Psychological Research, 43,* 219–234.

Snowling, M., & Nation, K. (1997). Language phonology and learning to read. In M. Snowling & C. Hulme (Eds.), *Dyslexia: Biology, cognition and remediation* (pp. 153–166). San Diego: Singular Publishing Group.

Snyder, L. (1980). Have we prepared the language disordered child for school? *Topics in Language Disorders, 1*(1), 29–45.

Snyder, L., & Downey, D. (1991). The language of reading relationship in normal and reading disabled children. *Journal of Speech and Hearing Research, 34,* 129–140.

Snyder, L., & Downey, D. (1997). Developmental differences in the relationship between oral language deficits and reading. *Topics in Language Disorders, 17*(3), 27–40.

Snyder L., & Godley, D. (1992). Assessment of word finding in children and adolescents. *Topics in Language Disorders, 12*(1), 15–32.

Spear-Swerling, L., & Sternberg, R. (1994). The road not taken: An integrative theoretical model of reading disability. *Journal of Learning Disabilities, 27,* 91–103.

Stackhouse, J., & Wells, B. (1997). How do speech and language problems affect literacy development? In M. Snowling & C. Hulme (Eds.), *Dyslexia: Biology, cognition and intervention* (pp. 182–211). San Diego: Singular Publishing Group.

Stanovich, K. (1986). Matthew effects in reading: Some consequences of individual differences in the acquisition of literacy. *Reading Research Quarterly, 21,* 360–407.

Stanovich, K. (Ed.). (1987). Introduction: Children's reading and the development of phonological awareness [Special issue]. *Merrill-Palmer Quarterly, 33*(3).

Stein, C., Cairns, H., & Zurif, E. (1984). Sentence comprehension limitation related to syntactic deficits in reading disabled children. *Applied Psychology, 5,* 305–322.

Stein, N., & Glenn, C. (1979). An analysis of story comprehension in elementary school children. In R. Freedle (Ed.), *New directions in discourse processing* (pp. 53–120). Greenwich, CT: Ablex Publishing Corp.

Stoel-Gammon, C. (1991). Normal and disordered phonology in two year olds. *Topics in Language Disorders, 11*(4), 21–32.

Studdert-Kennedy, M. (1998, Winter). Letter to the editor. *Asha,* 7.

Studdert-Kennedy, M., Liberman, A., Brady, S., Fowler, A., Mody, M., & Shankweiler, D. (1994–1995). Lengthened formant transitions are irrelevant to the improvement of speech and language impairments. *Haskins Laboratory Status Report on Speech Research,* SR-119/120, 35–38.

Studdert-Kennedy, M., & Mody, M. (1995). Auditory temporal perception deficits in the reading impaired: A critical review of the evidence. *Psychonomic Bulletin and Review, 2*(4), 508–514.

Sulzby, E., & Teale, W. (1991). Emergent literacy. In R. Barr, M. Kamil, P. Mosenthal, & P. Pearson (Eds.), *Handbook of reading research* (Vol. 2, pp. 727–757). Reading, MA: Addison-Wesley-Longman.

Swank, L. (1997). Linguistic influences in the emergence of written word decoding in first grade. *American Journal of Speech-Language Pathology, 6*(4), 62–66.

Tallal, P., Miller, S., Bedi, G., Byma, G., Wang, X., Nagarajan, S., Schreiner, C., Jenkins, W., & Merzenich, M. (1996). Language comprehension in language-learning impaired children improves with acoustically modified speech. *Science, 271,* 81–84.

Van Kleeck, A. (1990). Emergent literacy: Learning about print before learning to read. *Topics in Language Disorders, 10*(2), 25–45.

Vellutino, F. (1979). *Dyslexia: Theory and research.* Cambridge: The MIT Press.

Vellutino, F., Scanlon, D., & Spearing, D. (1995). Semantic and phonological coding in poor and normal readers. *Journal of Experimental Child Psychology, 59,* 76–123.

Wagner, R., & Torgesen, J. (1987). The nature of phonological processing and its causal roles in the equation of reading skills. *Psychological Bulletin, 101,* 192–212.

Wallace, I., Gravel, J., McCarton, C., & Ruben, R. (1988). Otitis media and language development at 1 year of age. *Journal of Speech and Hearing Disorders, 53,* 245–251.

Wallach, G. (1990). Magic buries Celtics: Looking for broader interpretations of language learning in literacy. *Topics in Language Disorders, 10*(2), 63–80.

Wallach, G., & Butler, K. (1994). Creating communication, literacy and academic success. In G. Wallach & K. Butler (Eds.), *Language learning disabilities in school-age children and adolescents: Some principals and applications* (pp. 2–26). Needham Heights, MA: Allyn & Bacon.

Wallach, G., & Miller, L. (1988). *Language intervention and academic success.* Boston: Little, Brown.

Webster, P., & Plante, A. (1992). Effects of phonological impairment on word, syllable and phoneme segmentation and reading. *Language, Speech, and Hearing Services in Schools, 23,* 176–182.

Westby, C. (1985). Learning to talk—talking to learn: Oral literate language differences. In C. Simon (Ed.), *Communication skills and classroom success: Therapy methodologies for language learning disabled students* (pp. 181–213). San Diego: College-Hill Press.

Westby, C. (1989). Assessing and remediating text comprehension problems. In A.G. Kamhi & H.W. Catts (Eds.), *Reading disabilities: A developmental language perspective* (pp. 199–260). Boston: Little, Brown.

Westby, C. (1995). Culture and literacy: Frameworks for understanding. *Topics in Language Disorders, 16*(1), 59.

White, T., Power, M., & White, S. (1989). Morphological analysis: Implications for teaching and understanding of vocabulary growth. *Reading Research Quarterly, 24,* 283–304.

Wiig, E., & Semel, E. (1980). *Language assessment and intervention for the learning disabled.* Columbus, OH: Charles E. Merrill.

Wiig, E., Semel, E., & Nystrom, L. (1982). Comparison of rapid naming abilities in language learning disabled and academically achieving eight year olds. *Language, Speech, and Hearing Services in Schools, 12,* 11–23.

Wolf, M., & Dickinson, D. (1993). From oral to written language: Transitions in the school years. In J. Gleason (Ed.), *The development of language.* Columbus, OH: Charles E. Merrill.

3

Phonological Awareness and Reading

Research, Activities, and Instructional Materials

Joanna K. Uhry

Phonological awareness is a crucial factor in predicting how easily young children will acquire reading. Furthermore, phonological awareness can be taught. When children receive instruction in phonological awareness at about the same time that they learn to read, they tend to read more skillfully than children without this instruction. Children with dyslexia tend to have very poor phonological awareness and other forms of phonological processing skills. Direct instruction in phonological processing strategies is particularly beneficial to them. This chapter describes a model for the link between phonological awareness and reading, reviews research suggesting the benefits of phonological awareness instruction, and then describes several programs that may be useful to all children but are critical to reading success for children at risk for reading difficulties.

PHONOLOGICAL AWARENESS AND READING THEORY

Stanovich defined *phonological awareness* as "conscious access to the phonemic level of the speech stream and some ability to cognitively manipulate representations at this level" (1986, p. 362). This is different from what is meant by the term *phonics*, which is a paired association between letters and letter sounds. Phonological awareness need not even involve written letters. Simply put, phonological awareness involves attention to the sound structure of oral language. This can involve being able to focus on the sounds of words in sentences; to focus on syllables in multisyllabic words; or, at the most sophisticated level, which is called *phonemic awareness*, to pay selective attention to phonemes rather than to the meaning of a word. Actually, phonemes and word meanings are two language elements that are linked because the phoneme is the smallest unit of sound that can change the meaning of a word. Note that the initial phonemes make the spoken words "hug" and "bug" distinguishable. Toddlers can tell the difference between "Give me a hug" and "Give me a bug." They can hear this fine distinction in sounds and can correctly interpret the meaning of either sentence. Stanovich's definition of phonological awareness, however, uses the words "conscious access to the speech stream." This definition goes beyond equating phonological awareness with auditory discrimination. Children with well-developed phonemic awareness can do more than interpret meaning based on phoneme distinctions. They can segment, identify, locate, and sequence the phonemes that make this key difference. They know that *hug* starts with the sound /h/ and *bug* starts with /b/. They know that /h/ and /b/ come at the beginnings of the words and that the medial and final sounds of both words are the same. These are crucial understandings for anyone engaged in learning how spoken words map onto print. In other words, children need to know more about oral language (i.e., gain phonological awareness) in order to learn to read and write than they need to know in order to learn to talk and listen (Liberman & Liberman, 1990).

Phonics

Phonological awareness is only one of the skills necessary for beginning reading. English is an alphabetic language, meaning that **graphemes** (letters) represent phonemes. In addition, English is a complex language drawn from a number of other languages, with 26 letters that, either alone or in combination, represent roughly 44 phonemes (Moats, 1995). Because there is more than one way to spell some of these 44 phonemes and more than one way to pronounce some of these letters, there are 98 different phoneme–grapheme associations that children need to learn in order to learn to read and spell in English. Knowledge of *phonics* refers to knowledge of these pairs. Some children acquire this knowledge almost by intuition, simply by noticing print while listening to stories read aloud or by noticing ways in which words are alike and different while learning to read. Some children, however, do not acquire this knowledge on their own and need carefully sequenced direct instruction.

The Alphabetic Principle

In order to utilize phonological awareness and phonics knowledge, children need additional understanding; they need to know how phonemes map onto letters in words. The term *alphabetic principle* refers to an understanding of the relationship between letters ordered left to right in a written word and phonemes ordered in a specific temporal sequence in spoken language. Knowledge of how to isolate and manipulate phonemes is critical to understanding the relationship between speech and print. That is, beginning readers need 1) phonological awareness or conscious access to the speech stream, 2) phonics knowledge, and 3) knowledge of how the speech stream relates to print.

Development of Phonemic Awareness

Phonemic awareness is a precursor to reading and begins to develop during the preschool years. Adams (1990) described phonemic awareness as progressing hierarchically through five levels of difficulty.

An Ear for Rhymes   The first level in the development of phonemic aware-ness involves a sensitivity to rhyme. British researchers Maclean, Bryant, and Bradley (1987) followed preschoolers from age 3, when they found differences in the children's ability to memorize nursery rhymes, up through school age, when previous ability with rhymes was found to be correlated with reading ability. Children who can hear rhymes can intuitively recognize that part of the word, the onset (initial phoneme), is exchanged for another phoneme in rhyming words. Although 3-year-olds cannot consciously segment the initial phoneme, they are acquiring what Adams called "an ear for the sounds of words" (1990, p. 80).

Matching Words by Rhyme and Alliteration   The second level of phonemic awareness involves matching two spoken words either by alliteration (i.e., simi-lar onsets) or by rhyme. This can be assessed through use of a research task de-signed by Bradley and Bryant (1983) that is called an *oddity* or *odd-one-out task*. For example, with alliteration as the focus, a child would be asked to listen to the words *ball, bat, tub,* and bird and identify the odd one out (tub).

Segmenting Onsets   Adams (1990) described the third level of phonemic awareness tasks as syllable splitting. At this point, phonemes are not merely intu-ited but are consciously segmented off from spoken words. The most common first attempts at segmenting involve the initial phoneme. Researchers have evi-dence that words break apart most easily at the onset–rime division, the point at which the initial phoneme can be separated from the middle vowel and ending consonant, or the rime (Treiman, 1985). That is, it is easier to segment *map* into /m/-/ăp/ than into /mă/-/p/. Kindergarten children exhibit this level of phonemic awareness when they segment initial phonemes and represent them with letters in invented spellings. For example, kindergarten children have spelled *picking as p* and *dress* as j, the closest letter-name sounds to the initial phonemes in these two words (Morris & Perney, 1984).

Segmenting is difficult because of a phenomenon known as *coarticulation.* Vowel sounds can exist on their own as short words or syllables (e.g., *oh, a, I*), but consonant sounds are always coarticulated with vowels. For example, when the sound of the letter *b* is said alone, it is hard to pronounce it without a following vowel (e.g., as "buh" or "bah"). What we conceptualize as the /b/ sound is really a series of /b/-like consonant sounds, each a little different depending on the vowel it accompanies; that is, the /b/ in *bake* is not quite the same as the /b/ in *bike*. Perhaps because of the coarticulation phenomenon, the medial sounds in words are particularly hard for young children to segment out from a word. Thus, medial vowels are coarticulated with both the initial and final consonants. For example, the medial vowel in *mop* is coarticulated with both the **initial** and **fi-nal** consonants, thus making it hard to segment the word. Kindergarten children tend to segment this word as /m/-/p/ or as /m/-/ŏp/, leaving out the vowel or leaving it attached to the final consonant. Although vowels are especially difficult to segment in words with a **consonant-vowel-consonant (CVC)** structure, vow-els are considerably easier to segment in short words beginning with vowels, such as *age* and *up* (Uhry & Ehri, in press).

Full Segmentation of All Phonemes in Words   Not until about age 6, or the beginning of formal reading instruction, do children usually reach Adams's (1990) fourth level of phonemic awareness in which all phonemes are segmented (e.g., the spoken word "map" segmented as /m/-/ă/-/p/). At this point a child is ready to understand and make use of the alphabetic principle to figure out how to read unfamiliar words on his or her own.

Manipulation of Phonemes   At the fifth and most complex of Adams's (1990) levels of phonemic awareness, children are able to delete or exchange phonemes. They can say *seat* without the /s/ sound as "eat," and they can reverse the sounds in *cat* to say the word *tack*. Children who cannot carry out these phoneme manipulation activities as easily as same-age peers are much more likely to have difficulty with reading and writing. Nonreaders rarely reach this fifth level of phonemic awareness.

At each of these levels of phonemic awareness, there is a wide range of differences in children's abilities. Although variation in performance is expected, children at the low end of the scale do not tend to catch up to peers when they are left on their own. They will continue to have difficulty with both phonemic awareness and the alphabetic principle unless they are provided with direct instruction.

DYSLEXIA

Adams (1994) estimated that roughly 25% of beginning readers fail to grasp the alphabetic principle without direct instruction in phonics and phonological awareness. The percentage is even higher for children from low-income families. About 20% of all elementary school–age children eventually develop symptoms of reading disability (Shaywitz, Fletcher, & Shaywitz, 1996).

Phonological Awareness and Dyslexia

Children with dyslexia, or word-level reading disorder, typically memorize individual words but have difficulty generalizing from one word to another because of deficits in phonological awareness. For example, a child who knows how to read the word *cat* may not generalize to figuring out the sounds for the *c* in *cup*, the *a* in *map*, or the *t* in *nut*. (See Clark & Uhry, 1995, for a detailed description of readers with dyslexia.) Children with dyslexia struggle with unfamiliar words, a characteristic that is often assessed by asking them to read nonwords that are phonetically regular. Children with dyslexia continue to be poorer at reading nonwords than real words relative to proficient readers (Rack, Snowling, & Olson, 1994). Research (DeFries et al., 1997) focused on reading disability and funded by the National Institute of Child Health and Human Development (NICHD) indicated that nonword reading disability is associated with a deficit in phonemic awareness. This deficit runs in families and is believed to be inherited through a specific gene.

Other Phonological Processing Deficits

Phonological awareness is only one of several forms of phonological processing related to reading. Three other forms of phonological processing, all related to dyslexia, are described next. Wagner and Torgesen (1987) provided an overview of research on the relationship between reading and phonological processing deficits. They reviewed literature suggesting that two deficits in addition to the phonological awareness deficit contribute to reading disorder.

Rapid Serial Naming   Wagner and Torgesen's term for one of these phonological processes, *phonological recoding in lexical access*, refers to the process of moving from one code to another, and in the case of reading, moving from letter symbols to a phonological code in terms of retrieving names for letters or words. This process can be measured in prereaders by asking them to name, as quickly as possible, a series of printed color swatches or pictured objects repeated over and over in random order in a matrix. Denckla and Rudel used colors, pictured objects, numbers, and letters in their Rapid Automatized Naming Test (RAN; 1976) to demonstrate that children with dyslexia are much slower at continuous, serial naming than children with typical reading skills. Children who are poor at naming on this test tend to be poor at word reading. Once they learn to read, they read slowly. (See Wolf, 1991, for a detailed description of naming speed deficits and their effects.) A combination of deficits in phonological awareness and **rapid serial naming** is often called a *double deficit.* Uhry (1997) found that in comparison with children who were poor at phonological awareness only, 9-year-old children who had poor phonological awareness and were slow at rapid serial naming made slower progress in reading after 2 years of phonological awareness training. Wood and Felton (1994) found that adults with a childhood history of dyslexia often read accurately following remediation, but those who had had rapid serial naming difficulties as children continued to read quite slowly.

Verbal Short-Term Memory   The other phonological process that Wagner and Torgesen (1987) discussed, *phonetic recoding to maintain information in working memory,* involves verbal short-term memory. This explanation of reading disorder draws on information processing theory, a cognitive model in which there is a limited amount of storage space for holding on to verbal information long enough to carry out an operation using it. Storage involves the use of phonological features. Young readers with difficulty in this type of phonological processing can recode letters to sounds but have difficulty remembering the sounds long enough to blend them into words. Older readers can learn to decode words but have difficulty remembering them long enough to put them together in sentences and to extract meaning.

Articulation Speed   Catts (1989, 1993) described a fourth phonological processing deficit involving speech **articulation.** Some children with dyslexia scramble speech sounds (e.g., saying "aminal" instead of "animal") and produce complex phonological sequences more slowly than children who read typically. One task for measuring articulation speed involves repeating **nonsense syllables** such as "pa-ta-ka" as quickly as possible (Wolff, Michel, & Ovrut, 1990). A slow articulation rate may interfere with the ability to maintain phonological models in verbal short-term memory.

Phonological Awareness as a Predictor of Dyslexia

All four of these phonological processing deficits are associated with dyslexia, both in the research literature and in clinical findings with individual children. Phonological awareness deficit, however, is the only one for which a body of research literature suggests that treatment is effective. Because there is such strong evidence that symptoms of phonological awareness deficit can be remediated, it is critical to identify children with this deficit as early as possible.

Researchers have demonstrated strong correlations between phonemic awareness tasks and later reading ability. Liberman (e.g., Liberman, Shankweiler, Fischer, & Carter, 1974) measured phonemic awareness with a tapping task in which the child was expected to tap once for each syllable (e.g., *elephant* has three taps) or for each phoneme in a word (e.g., *sat* has three taps). Bradley and Bryant (1983) used an initial phoneme oddity task, and Elkonin (1963, 1973) used tiles to represent phonemes. In these studies and in a number of others using phonemic awareness tasks with prereaders, children who were weak on the phonological tasks turned out to be weak readers later on, and children who were good at the tasks turned out to be good readers. This research has demonstrated a strong association between phonological awareness and reading. The following sections discuss the importance of phonological awareness compared with other predictors of reading.

General Development as a Predictor of Reading   Since the 1950s, researchers have investigated factors such as the age of a child relative to others in his or her class, general motor development as well as eye–hand coordination, and cognitive development as measured by IQ tests. Reading was considered to be related to a spectrum of developmental competencies. These competencies did predict how well a child would do in school in general but were not very good predictors of reading ability (Jansky & de Hirsch, 1972). Although children with developmental disabilities (e.g., mental retardation) are usually poor readers, not all poor readers are slow to develop in other ways. At the early stages of reading in which word-level reading is so crucial, cognitive predictors can be particularly misleading. Thus, some very bright children have inordinate difficulty with word reading.

Language Development as a Predictor of Reading   Definitions of literacy focus on the relationships between oral language and written language, and it makes sense that aspects of oral language skill would be good predictors of written language skill (see Chapter 2). Children with language disorders often have difficulty learning to read. Not all children with reading difficulty, however, demonstrate early symptoms of language disorder. Just as children with dyslexia do not have overall developmental delays, they do not have extremely deficient skills in speaking and listening. Their language deficits are subtle and often are not evident until they have trouble with early reading. Catts (1989, 1993), a specialist in language disorders, referred to dyslexia not simply as an oral language deficit but as a deficit specific to phonological awareness rather than to more global language skills.

In the 1960s, Jansky and de Hirsch carried out seminal research in which the range of **reading precursors** was narrowed to focus more on language. Their Screening Index (1972) was developed through a carefully researched narrowing process that started with 50 factors including many of the general developmental characteristics cited previously. Their list of factors was narrowed to a screening with five **assessment** tasks, two of which are visual recognition or visual-motor tasks and three of which are language related: 1) ability to retrieve names of letters in response to visual stimuli, 2) ability to retrieve names of objects in response to visual stimuli, and 3) ability to repeat sentences from memory. As Jansky and de Hirsch reported, the balance among these five factors accounted for reading ability; all five factors did not need to be areas of strength for a child so long as his or her total score was reasonably high. Together these five tasks were quite accurate at predicting successful readers but not so accurate at predicting poor readers. Jansky and de Hirsch's screening, however, did not include a measure of phonological awareness.

Phonological Awareness as a Predictor of Reading   Phonological awareness turns out to be the single best predictor of at-risk status for early reading difficulties. Since the late 1970s, researchers have found consistent and compelling experimental evidence of the importance of phonological awareness in predicting reading ability. For example, Share, Jorm, Maclean, and Matthews (1984) tested 543 Australian children in kindergarten and again in first grade, using 39 measures (e.g., teacher predictions, letter copying, syntax comprehension, the extent of parent–child reading, hours of television watched, IQ scores, preschool attendance). Measures of word reading, spelling, and reading comprehension were administered at the end of first grade, and a reading composite score was developed. The two factors with the highest correlations with this composite were phoneme segmentation (r = .62) and letter naming (r = .58). A statistical procedure called *multiple regression analysis* was then used to determine whether these measures overlapped at all in their contribution or whether they made unique contributions. That is, the analysis checked whether two manifestations of the same underlying factor or different factors were being measured. Again, phoneme segmentation made the largest unique contribution, far surpassing all other predictors. Scores from screening batteries using a variety of phonological and phonemic awareness tasks as well as letter identification tasks are consistently and strongly correlated with later reading skill. Screenings incorporating phonological awareness tasks are quite accurate at identifying children who are at greatest risk of struggling with first-grade reading.

Screening Tests for Phonological Awareness   Several instruments for predicting reading using phonological awareness tasks are commercially available (e.g., Lindamood & Lindamood, 1979; Sawyer, 1987; Torgesen & Bryant, 1994b) or are available through descriptions in journal articles (e.g., Uhry, 1993a; Yopp, 1995b). The group-administered Test of Phonological Awareness (Torgesen & Bryant, 1994b) is intended as a screening tool. Using a workbook format, it presents two tasks similar to those used by Bradley and Bryant (1983). It asks kindergarten children to match pictured words by initial sounds and to identify the odd one out from a group of words. There is also a version for first and second graders in which these two tasks are presented for the final sounds in words. The kindergarten screening is reported by the authors to predict between 30% and 40% of the variance in first-grade word-reading skills. Both versions of the screening provide percentile scores by age.

The other instruments described next all are intended for individual administration. Lindamood and Lindamood's Auditory Conceptualization Test (1979) asks children to use small, wooden cubes to represent sounds in a sequence. For example, the phoneme sequence /d/-/d/-/j/ could be represented by red-red-blue. Next, sounds are analyzed in nonwords (e.g., yellow-blue-red could represent the nonword *vop*). **Criterion-referenced** norms are provided for levels ranging from kindergarten to adult readers. Sawyer's Test of Awareness of Language Segments (1987) also asks children to use colored blocks to represent sounds in words, but it begins at the 4-year-old level and progresses from word segmentation in sentences, to syllable segmentation, to phoneme segmentation. It provides cut-off scores for early literacy benchmarks indicating, for example, prerequisite phonological awareness skills necessary for instruction at the preprimer level. The Yopp-Singer Test of Phoneme Segmentation (Yopp, 1995b) consists of a list of

22 words (i.e., *keep, she*) that children are asked to segment into individual phonemes, with a point credited for each word completely segmented. When the test was administered to kindergarteners, correlations with later reading on the Comprehensive Test of Basic Skills (1974) ranged from .62 in first grade to .74 in sixth grade. The Early Reading Screening (ERS; Uhry, 1993a) includes a subtest with early literacy tasks such as **finger-point reading** and ability to read words found in the children's own kindergarten classrooms (e.g., job-chart words, classmates' names) as well as a subtest with phonological awareness tasks (e.g., matching by rhyme and alliteration, segmenting, blending phonemes). Correlations of the ERS in kindergarten with first-grade reading comprehension scores were .69 for children of middle socioeconomic status (SES) (Uhry, 1993a) and .75 for children of low SES (Uhry, 1994). Thus, schools have a range of available instruments for identifying children at risk for reading difficulties. (See the section on screening for phonological awareness in Appendix B.)

Classroom Observations of Phonological Awareness Indicators   Even before a screening is administered, teachers often are able to spot weaknesses in phonological awareness in preschool and kindergarten children when they are aware of possible indicators. Many of the screening tasks just mentioned can be observed in a natural classroom environment. Three-year-old children who have difficulty learning rhymes or rhyming songs may be at risk for reading difficulties. Four- and five-year-old children should be able to generate rhymes and match classmates' names by initial sounds (e.g., Jim/Jasmine). During kindergarten, children should be able to guess the word that rhymes with the manipulated phoneme in playful songs such as "Willoughby Wallaby Wadeline, the elephant sat on . . . (Madeline)."

Children with phonemic awareness deficits may have difficulty in the early stages of literacy with *finger-point reading,* in which a teacher reads aloud in a shared reading format and children eventually learn the text and read along. This activity teaches children to recognize some words by sight if they are able to match voice and print. Children with phonemic awareness deficits typically cannot segment initial sounds and thus cannot match their voices to initial letters in print (Ehri & Sweet, 1991; Morris, 1993; Uhry, in press). Observations of individual children engaged in this activity can be revealing.

One of the best classroom-based indicators of risk for difficulty with reading is inability to invent spellings for words during kindergarten or early first grade. This activity requires segmenting sounds but also requires matching the sound with a letter to represent it. Invented spelling is popular in whole-language classrooms because it is advantageous to the creative writing process; children are encouraged to think about meaning as they write. The second advantage is that invented spellings reflect a child's level of phonemic awareness. Morris and Perney (1984) found significant correlations between developmental invented spelling scores in September and reading scores in May of first grade. Invented spelling was found to be significantly correlated with word reading skill ($r = .68$) and with reading comprehension scores ($r = .61$) from the Metropolitan Achievement Tests (Durost, 1970). Although only about 9% of the spelling words on the children's tests were spelled conventionally in September, Morris and Perney used a developmental scoring system in which spellings were credited based on the degree to which they reflected the sound structure of the spoken word. For example, for the word *dress,* the spelling *J* received one point, *JS* two points, *JAS* three points, and *DRES* four points, although none provided the conventional spelling. Each of these scores represents a level in the development of spelling skills, ranging from *prephonetic* (i.e., not yet using all sounds) to *transitional* (i.e., nearing conventional spelling). These spellings reflect the degree to which phonemic awareness is developed in a particular child.

Classroom teachers can use invented spellings to identify children who are at risk for later reading difficulties. They can also use them as a diagnostic tool in establishing a starting point for providing more direct instruction for children who appear to have weaknesses in this area. Systematic instruction in letter–sound associations and segmenting provides effective boosts to both early spelling and early reading.

RESEARCH ON PHONOLOGICAL AWARENESS TRAINING

Three sets of European studies (Bradley & Bryant, 1983, 1985; Elkonin, 1963, 1973; Lundberg, Frost, & Petersen, 1988) are often cited as seminal evidence of the effectiveness of phonological awareness training. Lundberg and his Swedish colleagues taught Danish teachers to use games and songs with classrooms of preschoolers, 235 children in all, to increase the children's phonological awareness prior to reading instruction. An English-language version of this program (Adams, Foorman, Lundberg, & Beeler, 1998) is described in detail in the final section of this chapter. Bradley and Bryant used highly directed individual instruction in sorting words by rhyme and alliteration to teach phonological awareness to 4- and 5-year-old British children who were identified either as at risk for reading difficulties or as the lowest performing children in their longitudinal prediction study mentioned previously. In both cases, the group of trained children outperformed an untrained control group in phonological awareness at the end of the training period. They also outperformed them later in print-based tasks, long after the experimental training had ended (Bradley & Bryant, 1995).

Lundberg and his colleagues' study (1988) is often used to make the point that phonological awareness precedes and is causal to reading, as no experiences with print were offered during Lundberg's training of preschoolers. Bradley and Bryant (1983), however, included two phonological awareness training conditions, one with and the other without the use of letters. The training with letters had the most dramatic effect on later reading and spelling, thus indicating that although phonological awareness may be a necessary precursor to reading, the use of letters increases the effectiveness of training and the relationship between the phonological awareness and reading is reciprocal rather than unidirectional. Some researchers make the point that children may be overwhelmed by both sounds and letters and need to learn to listen selectively to phonemes before letters are used in this training. Hohn and Ehri (1983) found the opposite, that letters can actually help young children conceptualize the sound structure of words. The optimal time for introducing letters in phonological awareness training continues to be a point of dispute in the reading field.

Elkonin (1963, 1973) described his Russian colleagues' and his own training studies with young children. The studies were described in scant detail but are important because the teaching method used has been widely incorporated in training programs in the United States. Children were presented with a picture of an object and were asked to say its name aloud and then represent its phonemes with small tiles that slid into a square below the picture as each phoneme was pronounced. It was believed, for example, that presenting three squares for three phonemes helped children conceptualize the sound structure of words. Letters were used instead of blank tiles once phonemes were mastered.

These studies and others that have followed (e.g., Ball & Blachman, 1991; Byrne & Fielding-Barnsley, 1991, 1993; Ehri & Wilce, 1987; Rubin & Eberhardt, 1996; Uhry, 1993b; Uhry & Shepherd, 1993) have demonstrated the effectiveness of teaching children to locate and identify phonemes in spoken words and to represent them with letters. The notion of using phonological awareness training for children with dyslexia, however, emerged in the 1990s.

Phonological Awareness and the Remediation of Dyslexia

Research findings present a model of dyslexia as a reading disorder specific to word reading and associated, for many children, with familial difficulty in phonological processing (Clark & Uhry, 1995; Lyon, 1995). Deficits in phonological awareness are reported as causal to phonological recoding deficits (Rack et al., 1992). That is, children with dyslexia usually have weaknesses in using code-based strategies, a deficit that is often measured through nonword reading. Remediation of this difficulty would allow a child to generalize phonics knowledge to new words, but until the mid-1990s there has been little evidence that this could be done.

For many years, the remedial approach of choice has been to provide children with dyslexia with direct instruction in multisensory phonics (e.g., Black, Oakland, Stanford, Nussbaum, & Balise, 1994; Vickery, Reynolds, & Cochran, 1987). Phonics training alone does not necessarily provide insight into phonological awareness or the alphabetic principle. Researchers have begun to combine phonological awareness training with code-based reading training in the remedial approaches for children with dyslexia.

Alexander, Andersen, Heilman, Voeller, and Torgesen (1991) explored phonological awareness training in nonword reading in 10-year-olds with dyslexia, which effectively increased the ability of these children to read nonwords. This is an important study because it was the first documentation in the research literature of successful remediation of nonword reading. This training was carried out in a tutoring center with one-to-one instruction using a multisensory program developed by Lindamood and Lindamood (1975). The program begins with an emphasis on sensory feedback during the articulation of phonemes. For example, children are encouraged to notice in a mirror the various shapes of the mouth as they utter different phonemes and to feel their vocal cords to experience **voiced** and **unvoiced consonants.** The program also includes training in phoneme segmentation and phonics.

Uhry and Shepherd (1997) found equally dramatic gains in nonword reading with a group of 7-year-old children with dyslexia, also in a tutoring environment. Each session involved phonics, segmentation/spelling using letters to represent phonemes segmented from simple CVC words (see Uhry & Shepherd, 1993), and a chance to read words with these patterns in both phonics-controlled reading books and narrative-controlled storybooks.

In both of these relatively small studies, there was dramatic growth in nonword reading skills following phonological awareness training. Whether increasing ability to use phonology to recode unfamiliar words is sufficient to increase children's reading comprehension is another issue being debated in the field. Phonological awareness training may be necessary but is not sufficient to guarantee long-term progress in skilled reading of connected text and in comprehension.

Phonological Awareness Training for Young Children at Risk for Dyslexia

If phonological awareness training can facilitate the growth of phonological recoding skills in older children with dyslexia and if phonological processing deficits can be identified in young children, then the logical treatment for young children at risk for reading difficulties is early training in phonological awareness. Bradley and Bryant's (1983) seminal study of 4- and 5-year-olds at risk described previously is a model for studies that have followed.

As of 1999, two large-scale longitudinal studies with funding from the NICHD are exploring the longitudinal effects of early phonological awareness training on various aspects of reading in young children at risk because of poor phonological awareness (Foorman, Francis, Beeler, Winikates, & Fletcher, 1997; Torgesen, Wagner, Rashotte, Alexander, & Conway, 1997). In a prevention study in Florida, Torgesen et al. (1997) provided 80 minutes per week of individual supplemental reading instruction to children with phonological awareness deficits beginning in the middle of kindergarten and continuing through fourth grade. Three instructional groups of about 35 children each will eventually be contrasted with typically achieving children and with a classroom control group of children who have poor phonological awareness. One of the three instructional groups received instruction that combined the Lindamood (Lindamood & Lindamood, 1975) method of phonological awareness training with synthetic phonics (PASP) in which phonemic sound production is associated with articulatory gesture prior to training in sound analysis and synthesis of sounds from letters into words. The second instructional group was trained in a method of **embedded phonics** in which phonological awareness and phonics training were taught implicitly through the reading of real words in text. The third group received individual training in whichever method was being employed in the general classroom reading program. By the middle of second grade, all three groups receiving individual support could read words at a level close to that of typical readers, and the PASP group had a significant advantage in nonword reading over the other instructional groups.

The other NICHD-funded longitudinal study (Foorman et al., 1997) is being carried out in Texas. Foorman and her colleagues have used an English-language adaptation of Lundberg's phonological awareness program (Adams et al., 1998) with seven kindergarten classes. Children were given 15 minutes per day of direct instruction in phonological awareness games, songs, and other activities. This program is described in detail in the final section of this chapter. The rate of growth in phonological tasks for these children was significantly greater than that of control groups in kindergarten classes using the school district's standard readiness program.

Phonological Awareness Training for Children of Low Socioeconomic Status

Phonological awareness training has been used with children who are economically disadvantaged. Many of these children have poorly developed phonological awareness, and the same multisensory training programs that improve phonological awareness in children with inherited reading disorders work effectively for these children. Blachman and her colleagues (Blachman, Ball, Black, & Tangel, 1994) have worked with at-risk preschoolers in upstate New York. Blachman trained kindergarten teachers to work for 11 weeks with children from low-income families living in inner cities. Instruction for the children included letter–sound associations, matching words by alliteration, and a segmenting activity called "say-it-and-move-it" (Ball & Blachman, 1991; Blachman, Ball, Black, & Tangel, 2000) in which children slide small disks from a picture, one by one, as they segment phonemes in order. Following this instruction, children were superior to an untrained control group in phoneme segmentation, letter–sound knowledge, inventing spellings, and reading word lists made up of phonetically regular real words and nonwords composed of target sounds from the training. This effect did not carry over to a standardized list of primer-level words. These low–socioeconomic status children were followed into the first grade (Tangel & Blachman, 1995). First-grade training was similar but was embedded in a five-part reading program: 1) letter–sound associations; 2) phonemic awareness training; 3) **sight-word** review (i.e., recognition of printed words), including review of **phonetically regular words;** 4) practice reading both phonetically regular textbooks and storybooks; and 5) writing. The authors reported an advantage over a control group in first grade in regard to ability to represent sounds on a developmentally scored test of invented spelling.

In another NICHD study carried out by Foorman (Foorman, Francis, Fletcher, Schatschneider, & Mehta, 1998), first- and second-grade children eligible for Title I services (i.e., federally funded services for children who are economically disadvantaged) received three forms of phonics and phonological awareness instruction over the course of a school year: direct code instruction (DC) using a synthetic phonics basal series (Adams, Bereiter, Hirshberg, Anderson, & Bernier, 1995), in which letter–sound associations were learned and then combined in words in text limited to the learned patterns; less explicit phonics embedded in controlled text; and implicit code instruction through storybooks. Children who were stronger in phonological awareness prior to the study tended to be stronger in reading by the end of the year regardless of instructional group, but instructional group made a significant difference for those children who initially were weak in phonological awareness. The growth rate and mean scores on word reading were significantly higher for the DC group by the end of the year. In other words, direct instruction in phonics and phonological awareness in the primary grades can help children recover from potentially detrimental effects of low levels of phonological awareness. The DC instruction, Open Court Reading, is described in the section on programs that follows.

INSTRUCTIONAL MATERIALS FOR PHONOLOGICAL AWARENESS

Results of the studies mentioned previously suggest the advantages of direct instruction in phonological awareness. Older children diagnosed as dyslexic, younger children at risk because of poor phonological awareness, and children just learning to read all benefit from this training. Phonological awareness activities are often included in primary classrooms. Yopp described resources including songs and games geared toward developing children's "curiosity about language and their experimentation with it" (1992, p. 702). Many kindergarten and first-grade teachers include phonological awareness training during writing activities in which children are encouraged to sound out invented spellings rather than rely on conventional orthography. There is evidence that phonological awareness plays a role in shared reading and finger-point reading activities in whole-language classrooms (Ehri & Sweet, 1991; Morris, 1993; Uhry, in press). Research suggests that ability to segment phonemes facilitates ability to coordinate memorized text with finger pointing at printed words. To this end, Yopp (1995a) described read-aloud books with rhyme and alliteration that can be used to develop phonemic awareness.

Phonological awareness activities enrich the beginning reading experiences of many young children. Without explicit instruction, however, children with dyslexia may not catch the alliteration or phoneme manipulation in songs and games. They may not learn to read from finger-point reading because often they are not able to segment phonemes. There is evidence in the research literature that children with dyslexia benefit from highly explicit instruction in phonological awareness. In an often-cited study, Iverson and Tunmer (1993) added an explicit phonological awareness and phonics instructional component to the Reading Recovery program for at-risk first graders. All Reading Recovery children in the study were provided with rich experiences with reading text aloud under the one-to-one guidance of a highly trained tutor, but some children also received explicit phonological training, and these children were ready to rejoin peers for general classroom reading instruction sooner than were control children trained in reading recovery alone.

Although there is strong evidence supporting the benefits of phonological awareness instruction, many teachers are not adept at this sort of language analysis. Teachers are mature, capable readers, and most are not conscious of using the alphabetic principle themselves during reading for meaning and do not remember having learned about it in school. Moats (1994) pointed out that many teacher preparation programs neglect phonological awareness as a topic for teacher education. Moats stressed the importance of teachers' having a firm grasp of the structure of spoken and written language to interpret children's miscues and to present solid examples through which patterns can be taught. For example, although a teacher may not use terminology such as *consonant cluster* (e.g., the first two sounds in *clip*) or *consonant digraph* (e.g., the first sound in *chin*) with 6-year-olds, these labels will help the teacher conceptualize for him- or herself the idea of listening for two sounds in one case and just one sound in the other as he or she works with a child trying to sound out and spell a word.

There are a number of commercially available curriculum materials for use with emergent, beginning, and remedial readers. Most curricula provide theoretical information as well as concrete ideas to use with children. Some, such as the Lindamood program (Lindamood & Lindamood, 1975, 1998), have been available for a long time. Others, such as the phonological awareness component of the Open Court Reading series (Adams et al., 1995), are relatively new. The explicit nature of instruction in these materials makes them appropriate for children with dyslexia, but they include activities that could be used in general classrooms as well. These programs all are responsive to research in that they tend to move through a common sequence of activities in which the focus moves toward smaller and smaller segments of sound in oral language and in which the sound structure of words is established through oral activities prior to the introduction of letters. (See Appendix B in this book for a listing of the following curriculum materials.)

The Lindamood Phoneme Sequencing
Program For Reading, Spelling, and Speech

Patricia and Charles Lindamood's Auditory Discrimination in Depth (ADD; 1975) program is based on the authors' backgrounds in linguistics and speech-language pathology. The ADD Program has been revised by Patricia and Phyllis Lindamood and renamed the Lindamood Phoneme Sequencing Program for Reading, Spelling, and Speech (LiPS; 1998). The distinguishing characteristic of the program continues to be its early focus on drawing a student's attention to the oral-motor processes used in articulating phonemes.

Special names describe the multisensory aspects of phoneme production. For example, the voiced and unvoiced **labiodental fricatives** /v/ and /f/ are called *Lip Coolers;* the former is the *Noisy Brother,* or voiced phoneme, and the latter is the *Quiet Brother,* or unvoiced phoneme. Training involves helping students identify phoneme sounds by matching them with photographs of the lips, teeth, and tongue engaged in articulatory gestures. Changes in spoken words are analyzed or tracked as single-phoneme changes occur, first with the mouth pictures and later with colored blocks. For example, the teacher sets up a sequence of colored blocks (blue, red, green) and says, "That's *zab;* show me *zaf.*" The student exchanges the green block for a white one and responds, "The *Lip Popper* is gone and a Lip Cooler took its place" (Lindamood & Lindamood, 1998, p. 12). This involves phoneme manipulation, Adams's (1990) highest level of phonological awareness, and at this point in instruction, letters are not yet associated with phonemes.

In LiPS, once complex word structures such as CCVCC (e.g., *stand*) can be segmented and manipulated, then lettered tiles are introduced for segmenting and spelling real words. Spelling instruction leads into reading instruction using lettered tiles and eventually printed text, consistent with the Lindamoods' (1975, 1998) notion that speech should precede written work. Letter–sound associations are introduced in a carefully sequenced plan, and a set of readers is available for practicing reading. Word reading is done through a careful analysis of letter sounds, in the Orton-Gillingham tradition, with the initial focus on accuracy and later on fluency. Videotapes and a CD-ROM provide support for the teacher.

The Lindamood program (1975) was used by Torgesen et al. (1997) in the NICHD-funded longitudinal intervention study with at-risk first-grade children in Florida. Although long-term effects on reading comprehension are not yet known, there certainly is research evidence that the Lindamood program increases young children's ability in phonetic recoding.

Phonological Awareness Games for Young Children

As mentioned previously, the Lundberg program (Lundberg et al., 1988) was used successfully in research with Danish kindergarten children. An English-language version (Adams et al., 1998) was developed for use in kindergartens in Houston, Texas, where Foorman and her colleagues (1997) have carried out the early intervention portion of her NICHD-funded research. Again, there is strong evidence that this program increases phonological skills.

Adams et al.'s (1998) phonological awareness training program is designed for kindergarten and first-grade classrooms and consists of a carefully sequenced hierarchy of games and activities. The sequence is arranged by chapters that focus on the following:

1. *Listening games*   Children are encouraged to listen selectively to environmental sounds, including the human voice, and to follow directions.
2. *Rhyming*   Children listen to and generate rhymes in order to become sensitive to the sound structure of words.
3. *Sentences and words*   This chapter includes activities for segmenting sentences into words.
4. *Syllables*   Children segment words into syllables and blend syllables into words.
5. *Initial and final sounds*   Initial and then final phonemes are segmented and blended in short, linguistically simple words.
6. *Phonemes*   At this level all of the phonemes in a word are segmented.
7. *Letters*   Phonemes are represented by letters in order to provide support for understanding the alphabetic principle.

Unlike many commercially available collections of ideas, there is sufficient theory throughout to enable a teacher to use the guide to plan his or her own program. A sample daily schedule is included for both kindergarten and first-grade classrooms to help teachers select and repeat activities from the suggested sequence. The theoretical material is an exemplary feature of this program guide.

The activities are playful, child centered, and developmentally appropriate (e.g., clapping, dancing, whispering, tossing balls back and forth). Rhythmic dance and movement activities introduce a kinesthetic element to some of the early listening games. Later, children pull mystery objects from a box and then clap the syllables in the objects' names or guess classmates' names after listening to the teacher say the initial phoneme. Each activity is explained carefully not only in terms of procedures but also in terms of its linguistic features and possible pitfalls. The linguistic features of words are carefully considered in planning instructional sequences, and numerous word lists are included for playing the games at each level. Teachers are provided with clear guidelines for deciding when to move on to harder activities. Most of the games have variations so that children needing additional work at a particular level can be provided with extension activities.

Open Court Reading

The Open Court Reading phonics-based basal-reading series was rewritten in 1995 (Adams et al.) and now includes a phonemic awareness component in the early grades. Segmenting is taught in kindergarten, and both blending and segmenting are taught in first grade. In both cases, instruction at the syllable level precedes instruction at the phoneme level. Activities are game-like and playful and include clapping syllables for classmates' names, talking for a puppet who talks in segments rather than in whole words, singing alliterative songs, and telling riddles (e.g., "What rhymes with *town* but begins with /br/?" p. 304).

In the Open Court program, phonemic awareness instruction precedes phonics instruction (i.e., instruction in letter–sound associations). Phonemic awareness activities are described in red type in the teachers' manuals to differentiate them from reading instruction, and they involve activities that are entirely oral. Teachers are cautioned not to confuse phonemic awareness and phonics and to limit early phonics instruction to just those few patterns that have been taught explicitly. At the point in the first-grade curriculum when letter–sound associations are first introduced, phonemic awareness instruction has already covered many of the sounds.

Phonics lessons reinforce familiarity with phonemes previously taught. For instance, when the letter–sound association for the letter *t* is taught, the teacher uses *timer* as a **key word** and leads the children in an activity in which they make the /t/ /t/ /t/ /t/ /t/ sound of a timer. Repeating consonants rather than stretching them out (e.g., /tuuuuh/) avoids using the schwa vowel sound so that the sound of a letter resembles the sound segmented in earlier oral activities. In addition to cards with letters and key word pictures (e.g., *m* for *monkey*), there are short alliterative rhymes that are read aloud by the teacher while the children listen for the target sound at the beginnings of words. For example, the following is from Lesson 11 in the first-grade program: "For Muzzy the Monkey, bananas are yummy. She munches so many they fill up her tummy. When she eats, she says /m/ /m/ /m/ /m/ /m/" (p. 87).

Early reading activities repeat the structure of earlier phonemic awareness games. Whereas an earlier oral blending activity involved riddles such as "What rhymes with *town* but begins with /br/?" beginning reading instruction involves blending activities such as teaching children to read the word *hamburger* on the chalkboard, then erasing the *h*, replacing it with an *s*, and asking the children to blend and read the new word.

Phonological Awareness Training for Reading

Torgesen and Bryant developed the Phonological Awareness Training for Reading program (PAT; 1994a) out of several research projects seeking to identify those components of phonological awareness that would most effectively increase reading-related skills in beginning readers. Torgesen and his colleagues at Florida State University had carried out one training study in which they demonstrated that both analytic and synthetic skills with phonology were advantageous in learning to read (Torgesen, Morgan, & Davis, 1992). In a second study (Torgesen & Davis, 1993), the revised program was used with minority children at risk for reading difficulties because they lacked phonological awareness skills. These children outperformed a control group on phonological awareness tasks immediately after training in kindergarten and on a second testing early in first grade.

The PAT program uses activities from a number of sources, including classroom teachers, and has been validated by research carried out by Torgesen and others in the field. It is designed for use with individuals or with small groups. It can be used during the second semester of kindergarten or for older at-risk children during first or second grade. The program is planned to last a semester when used in 20–25 sessions, four times per week. There are four phases to the program.

1. *Warm-up activities—rhyming* This short, introductory phase introduces the idea of listening to sounds through rhyming games and activities. The program includes sets of cards to match (e.g., pictures of an egg and a leg). The authors stress that the purpose of the activities should be made clear to the participants.

2. *Phonological training activities—blending* Children begin by blending onsets and rimes (e.g., blending the phoneme /k/ with the rime unit /ăt/) and then later blend all three phonemes in short words (e.g., /k/-/ă/-/t/ blended into "cat"). This leads into segmentation of the initial phoneme in a word.

3. *Phonological training activities—segmenting* Phoneme segmentation activities use a sequence moving from initial to final to medial phonemes in words. Segmentation training also progresses from matching by phoneme to actually segmenting the phoneme in each of the three positions. There is a focus on awareness of the feeling that children experience in the mouth as various sounds are produced, and children are asked to listen for differences between voiced and unvoiced consonants.

4. *Phonological training activities—reading and spelling* Letters are introduced to represent phonemes in the Level 4 activities for both reading and spelling. Letters are used to help children manipulate the sounds in words as in the following sample dialogue from the manual, in which the teacher uses letter cards to spell a word and then asks the child to change the letters to spell a second word: "This is the word *top*, /t/-/ŏ/-/p/. What letter should we change to write the word *mop*?" (Torgesen & Bryant, 1994a, p. 25).

PAT includes a teacher's manual, game parts, and an audiotape. The game parts involve small pictures that can be used to play games that are described in the manual. For example, a child says "cap" while looking at a picture of a cap, and then the teacher points to one of three blocks in a line and asks which sound it is (e.g., /k/ for the first block in *cap*). The audiotape provides sample pronunciations for words segmented into onsets and rimes and into all phonemic segments.

Reading Readiness

The Neuhaus Education Center in Bellaire, Texas, is an educational foundation that offers training in reading instruction to teachers. The center uses Alphabetic Phonics (Cox, 1992; see Clark & Uhry, 1995) both as a remedial program and as the basis of beginning reading and spelling instruction in general education classes. In 1992 Blachman presented a workshop at the center on the importance of phonological awareness, and following this, the center staff developed the Reading Readiness program for younger children (Carreker, 1992).

The Reading Readiness program includes practice in many of the elements of Alphabetic Phonics lessons and, in addition, introduces phonological awareness activities. The manual describes the program as designed for use in the early grades. It begins with daily lessons in letter recognition and sequencing, phonological awareness, and oral language skills. Once letter recognition and phonological awareness are mastered, the lesson is extended from 20 minutes to 30 minutes through the addition of handwriting and sound–symbol activities. Phonological awareness activities are presented in a sequence based on research:

1. Rhyming activities are presented at the initial level (e.g., Do *go* and *top* rhyme? Find a rhyme for *cat*).
2. Awareness of words in sentences and syllables in **compound** and **multisyllabic words** is taught through clapping and counting activities.
3. Phoneme segmentation is taught through a series of activities based on the (Ball & Blachman, 1991; Blachman, Ball, Black, & Tangel, 2000) say-it-and-move-it technique in which markers representing phonemes are moved from a picture down to a line below it in left-to-right order.
4. Segmenting and spelling is taught once students have learned symbol–sound associations. The say-it-and-move-it activity is extended by segmenting and then spelling pictured words with simple CVC constructions, such as *mop*, using lettered markers. Note that this activity is similar to one first introduced by Elkonin (1963, 1973).

Sounds Abound

Sounds Abound (formerly known as Sound Start; Catts & Vartiainen, 1993) was developed by a university researcher and a speech-language pathologist. Catts, a professor who teaches courses in communication disorders and language-based learning disabilities at the University of Kansas, and Vartiainen, a speech-language pathologist in public schools, have written a phonological awareness instructional program for children from ages 4 to 9. The program includes the following five components based on the research literature.

1. Rhyme awareness is encouraged through an extensive list of books of nursery rhymes, songs, poems, and sound play activities. Children listen to these read-aloud activities, join in once they know the rhymes, and ultimately create new verses.
2. Rhyme judgment and rhyme production are taught through activities, games, and songs. Sound sorting activities are similar to Bradley and Bryant's (1983) activities. Reproducible workbook pages provide pictures, and children are directed to mark the ones that rhyme.
3. Segmenting beginning and ending sounds is taught through workbook exercises followed by sound production activities. The authors include activities for songs in which alliteration is used (Yopp, 1992).
4. Full segmentation and blending are taught through oral activities such as the deletion of syllables from compound words (e.g., "Say 'railroad' without 'rail'"). There are workbook pages with Elkonin-type (1963, 1973) tasks using pictured objects and drawings of squares for sliding down a token for each phoneme in the word. There are also pictures to cut into three pieces to use in teaching blending.
5. Explicit instruction in mapping sounds onto letters is taught through the use of letters to represent phonemes in segmenting activities. Activities begin with word families (i.e., rimes such as *-at* for producing the words *sat, fat,* and *mat*). Later, students are taught to spell every segment of a word.

SUMMARY

Research demonstrates a strong link between children's early abilities in phonological awareness and their later reading skills. Children with dyslexia are apt to have phonological processing deficits that are causal to their word-reading deficits. A number of phonological awareness programs are commercially available, and most of these programs share the following principles derived from the research literature:

- Teach phonological awareness explicitly rather than implicitly.
- Teach phonological awareness using a sequence similar to Adams's (1990) research-based hierarchy: 1) rhyming, 2) matching by rhyme and alliteration, 3) syllable splitting, 4) full phoneme segmentation, and 5) manipulation of phonemes.
- Teach letter–sound associations explicitly before using letters to represent phonemic segments.
- Teach phonological awareness using letters to represent sounds. Teach phonological awareness as an oral activity to young children, but work toward using letters to represent sounds as segmentation of initial phonemes is mastered.

Training in phonological awareness can be effectively carried out and can have a positive effect on later word-level reading. A major research issue that may be resolved through findings from longitudinal training studies underway is the long-term effect of phonological awareness training on reading comprehension.

REFERENCES

Adams, M.J. (1990). *Beginning to read: Thinking and learning about print*. Cambridge: The MIT Press.

Adams, M.J. (1994). Phonics and beginning reading instruction. In R. Lehr & J. Osborn (Eds.), *Reading, language, and literacy*. Mahwah, NJ: Lawrence Erlbaum Associates.

Adams, M.J., Bereiter, C., Hirshberg, J., Anderson, V., & Bernier, S.A. (1995). *Framework for effective teaching, grade 1: Thinking and learning about print*. New York: McGraw-Hill.

Adams, M.J., Foorman, B.R., Lundberg, I., & Beeler, T. (1998). *Phonemic awareness in young children: A classroom curriculum*. Baltimore: Paul H. Brookes Publishing Co.

Alexander, A.W., Andersen, H.G., Heilman, P.C., Voeller, K.K.S., & Torgesen, J.K. (1991). Phonological awareness training and remediation of analytic decoding deficits in a group of severe dyslexics. *Annals of Dyslexia, 41,* 193–206.

Ball, E.W., & Blachman, B.A. (1991). Does phoneme segmentation training in kindergarten make a difference in early word recognition and developmental spelling? *Reading Research Quarterly, 26,* 49–66.

Blachman, B.A., Ball, E.W., Black, R., & Tangel, D.M. (2000). *Road to the code: A phonological awareness program for young children*. Baltimore: Paul H. Brookes Publishing Co.

Blachman, B.A., Ball, E.W., Black, R.S., & Tangel, D.M. (1994). Kindergarten teachers develop phoneme awareness in low-income, inner-city classrooms: Does it make a difference? *Reading and Writing: An Interdisciplinary Journal, 6,* 1–18.

Black, J.L., Oakland, T., Stanford, G., Nussbaum, N., & Balise, R.R. (1994). *An evaluation of the Texas Scottish Rite Hospital dyslexia program.* Unpublished report from the Texas Scottish Rite Hospital.

Bradley, L., & Bryant, P.E. (1983). Categorizing sounds and learning to read—a causal connection. *Nature, 301,* 419–421.

Bradley, L., & Bryant, P.E. (1985). *Rhyme and reason in reading and spelling.* Ann Arbor: University of Michigan Press.

Byrne, B., & Fielding-Barnsley, R. (1991). Evaluation of a program to teach phonemic awareness to young children. *Journal of Educational Psychology, 83,* 451–455.

Byrne, B., & Fielding-Barnsley, R. (1993). Evaluation of a program to teach phonemic awareness to young children: A 1-year follow-up. *Journal of Educational Psychology, 83,* 104–111.

Carreker, S. (1992). *Reading readiness.* Bellaire, TX: Neuhaus Education Center.

Catts, H., & Vartiainen, T. (1993). *Sounds abound.* East Moline, IL: LinguiSystems, Inc.

Catts, H.W. (1989). Defining dyslexia as a developmental language disorder. *Annals of Dyslexia, 39,* 50–64.

Catts, H.W. (1993). The relationship between speech-language impairments and reading disabilities. *Journal of Speech and Hearing Research, 36,* 948–958.

Clark, D.B., & Uhry, J.K. (1995). *Dyslexia: Theory and practice of remedial instruction.* Timonium, MD: York Press.

Comprehensive Test of Basic Skills. (1974). New York: McGraw-Hill.

Cox, A.R. (1992). *Foundations for literacy: Structures and techniques for multisensory teaching of basic written English language skills.* Cambridge, MA: Educators Publishing Service.

DeFries, J.C., Filipeck, P.A., Fulker, D.W., Olson, R.K., Pennington, B.F., Smith, S.D., & Wise, B.W. (1997). Colorado Learning Disabilities Center. *Learning Disabilities: A Multidisciplinary Journal, 8,* 7–19.

Denckla, M.B., & Rudel, R.G. (1976). Naming of object-drawings by dyslexic and other learning disabled children. *Brain and Language, 3,* 1–13.

Durost, W. (1970). *Metropolitan Achievement Test.* Orlando, FL: Harcourt Brace & Co.

Ehri, L.C., & Sweet, J. (1991). Fingerpoint-reading of memorized text: What enables beginners to process the print? *Reading Research Quarterly, 26,* 442–462.

Ehri, L.C., & Wilce, L.C. (1987). Does learning to spell help beginners learn to read words? *Reading Research Quarterly, 18,* 47–65.

Elkonin, D.B. (1963). The psychology of mastering the elements of reading. In B. Simon & J. Simon (Eds.), *Educational psychology in the U.S.S.R.* (pp. 165–179). London: Routledge & Kegan Paul.

Elkonin, D.B. (1973). U.S.S.R. In J. Downing (Ed.), *Comparative reading* (pp. 551–579). New York: Macmillan.

Foorman, B.R., Francis, D.J., Beeler, T., Winikates, D., & Fletcher, J.M. (1997). Early interventions for children with reading problems: Study designs and preliminary findings. *Learning Disabilities: A Multidisciplinary Journal, 8,* 63–71.

Foorman, B.R., Francis, D.J., Fletcher, J.M., Schatschneider, C., & Mehta, P. (1998). The role of instruction in learning to read: Preventing reading failure in at-risk children. *Journal of Educational Psychology, 90,* 37–55.

Hohn, W.E., & Ehri, L.C. (1983). Do alphabet letters help prereaders acquire phonemic segmentation skill? *Journal of Educational Psychology, 75,* 752–762.

Iverson, S., & Tunmer, W.E. (1993). Phonological processing skills and the reading recovery program. *Journal of Educational Psychology, 85,* 112–126.

Jansky, J., & de Hirsch, K. (1972). *Preventing reading failure.* New York: Harper-Collins.

Liberman, I.Y., & Liberman, A.M. (1990). Whole language vs. code emphasis: Underlying assumptions and their implications for reading instruction. *Annals of Dyslexia, 40,* 51–76.

Liberman, I.Y., Shankweiler, D., Fischer, F.W., & Carter, B. (1974). Explicit phoneme segmentation in the young child. *Journal of Experimental Child Psychology, 18,* 201–212.

Lindamood, C.H., & Lindamood, P.C. (1975). *The A.D.D. program, Auditory Discrimination in Depth: Books 1 and 2.* Austin, TX: PRO-ED.

Lindamood, C.H., & Lindamood, P.C. (1979). *The LAC Test: Lindamood Auditory Conceptualization Test* (Rev. ed.). Chicago: Riverside.

Lindamood, P., & Lindamood, P. (1998). *The Lindamood sequencing program for reading, spelling, and speech: Teacher's manual for the classroom and clinic.* Austin, TX: PRO-ED.

Lyon, G.R. (1995). Toward a definition of dyslexia. *Annals of Dyslexia, 45,* 3–27.

Lundberg, I., Frost, J., & Petersen, O.P. (1988). Effects of an extensive program for stimulating phonological awareness in preschool children. *Reading Research Quarterly, 23,* 263–284.

Maclean, M., Bryant, P.E., & Bradley, L. (1987). Rhymes, nursery rhymes, and reading in early childhood. *Merrill-Palmer Quarterly, 33,* 255–281.

Moats, L.C. (1994). The missing foundation in teacher education: Knowledge of the structure of spoken and written language. *Annals of Dyslexia, 44,* 81–102.

Moats, L.C. (1995). *Spelling: Development, disability, and instruction.* Timonium, MD: York Press.

Morris, D. (1993). The relationship between children's concept of word in text and phoneme awareness in learning to read: A longitudinal study. *Research in the Teaching of English, 27,* 133–153.

Morris, D., & Perney, J. (1984). Developmental spelling as a predictor of first-grade reading achievement. *The Elementary School Journal, 84,* 441–457.

Rack, J.P., Snowling, M.J., & Olson, R.K. (1992). The nonword reading deficit in developmental dyslexia: A review. *Reading Research Quarterly, 27,* 28–53.

Rubin, H., & Eberhardt, N.C. (1996). Facilitating invented spelling through language analysis instruction: An integrated model. *Reading and Writing: An Interdisciplinary Journal, 8*(1), 27–43.

Sawyer, D.J. (1987). *Test of Awareness of Language Segments.* Austin, TX: PRO-ED.

Share, D., Jorm, A., Maclean, R., & Matthews, R. (1984). Sources of individual differences in reading acquisition. *Journal of Educational Psychology, 76,* 1309–1324.

Shaywitz, S.E., Fletcher, J.M., & Shaywitz, B.A. (1996). A conceptual model and definition of dyslexia: Findings emerging from the Connecticut Longitudinal Study. In J.H. Beitchman, N. Cohen, M.M. Konstantareas, & R. Tannock (Eds.), *Language, learning and behavior disorders* (pp. 199–223). New York: Cambridge University Press.

Stanovich, K.E. (1986). Matthew effects in reading: Some consequences of individual differences in the acquisition of literacy. *Reading Research Quarterly, 21,* 360–406.

Tangel, D.M., & Blachman, B.A. (1995). Effect of phoneme awareness instruction on the invented spelling of first-grade children: A one-year follow-up. *Journal of Reading Behavior, 27,* 153–183.

Torgesen, J.K., & Bryant, B.R. (1994a). *Phonological awareness training for reading.* Austin, TX: PRO-ED.

Torgesen, J.K., & Bryant, B.R. (1994b). *Test of Phonological Awareness.* Austin, TX: PRO-ED.

Torgesen, J.K., & Davis, C. (1993, April). Individual difference variables that predict response to training in phonological awareness. In R. Wagner, Chair, *Does phonological awareness training enhance children's acquisition of written language skills?* Symposium conducted at the annual meeting of the American Educational Research Association in Atlanta, GA.

Torgesen, J.K., Morgan, S., & Davis, C. (1992). The effects of two types of phonological awareness training on word learning in kindergarten children. *Journal of Educational Psychology, 84,* 364–370.

Torgesen, J.K., Wagner, R.K., Rashotte, C.A., Alexander, A.W., & Conway, T. (1997). Preventive and remedial interventions for children with severe reading disabilities. *Learning Disabilities: A Multidisciplinary Journal, 8,* 51–61.

Treiman, R. (1985). Onsets and rimes as units of spoken syllables: Evidence from children. *Journal of Experimental Child Psychiatry, 39,* 161–181.

Uhry, J.K. (1993a). Predicting low reading from phonological awareness and classroom print: An early reading screening. *Educational Assessment, 1,* 349–368.

Uhry, J.K. (1993b). The spelling/reading connection and dyslexia: Can spelling be used to teach the alphabetic strategy? In R.M. Joshi & C.K. Leong (Eds.), *Reading disabilities: Diagnosis and component processes* (pp. 253–266). Dordrecht, Netherlands: Kluwer Academic Publishers.

Uhry, J.K. (1994, April). *Early reading screening: Predicting reading outcomes in low SES urban kindergarten children.* Paper presented at the annual meeting of the American Education Research Association, New Orleans, LA.

Uhry, J.K. (1997). Case studies of dyslexia: Young readers with rapid serial naming deficits. In R.M. Joshi & C.K. Leong (Eds.), *Cross-language studies of learning to read and spell: Phonological and orthographic processing* (pp. 71–88). Dordrecht, Netherlands: Kluwer Academic Publishers.

Uhry, J.K. (in press). Invented spelling in kindergarten: The relationship with finger-point reading. *Reading and Writing: An Interdisciplinary Journal.*

Uhry, J.K., & Ehri, L.C. (in press). Ease of segmenting two- and three-phoneme words in kindergarten: Rime cohesion or vowel salience? *Journal of Educational Psychology.*

Uhry, J.K., & Shepherd, M.J. (1993). Segmentation/spelling instruction as part of a first grade reading program: Effects on several measures of reading. *Reading Research Quarterly, 28,* 218–233.

Uhry, J.K., & Shepherd, M.J. (1997). Teaching phonological recoding to young children with dyslexia: The effect on sight vocabulary acquisition. *Learning Disabilities Quarterly, 20,* 104–125.

Vickery, K.S. Reynolds, V.A., & Cochran, S.W. (1987). Multisensory teaching for reading, spelling, and handwriting, Orton-Gillingham based, in a public school setting. *Annals of Dyslexia, 37,* 189–202.

Wagner, R.K., & Torgesen, J.K. (1987). The nature of phonological processing and its causal role in the acquisition of reading skills. *Psychological Bulletin, 101,* 192–212.

Wolf, M. (1991). Naming speed and reading: The contribution of the cognitive neurosciences. *Reading Research Quarterly, 26,* 123–141.

Wolff, P.H., Michel, G.F., & Ovrut, M. (1990). The timing of syllable repetitions in developmental dyslexia. *Journal of Speech and Hearing Research, 33,* 281–289.

Wood, F.B., & Felton, R.H. (1994). Separate linguistic and attentional factors in the development of reading. *Topics in Language Disorders, 14,* 42–57.

Yopp, H. (1992). Developing phonological awareness in young children. *The Reading Teacher, 45,* 696–703.

Yopp, H.K. (1995a). Read-aloud books for developing phonemic awareness: An annotated bibliography. *The Reading Teacher, 48,* 538–542.

Yopp, H.K. (1995b). A test for assessing phonemic awareness in young children. *The Reading Teacher, 49,* 20–29.

4

Alphabet Knowledge

Letter Recognition, Naming, and Sequencing

Kay A. Allen with Marilyn C. Beckwith

Awareness of the *alphabetic principle,* that letters represent the sounds of spoken language, is an essential component of learning to read an alphabetic language (Chall, 1983; Juel, 1988; Stanovich, 1986). When children can recognize and name the letters of the alphabet, they have a foundation for learning the alphabetic principle (Adams, 1990a; Ehri, 1983). When they learn the sequence of the alphabet, they have access to an organizational system ubiquitous in our culture from the telephone directory to the Internet. They can make efficient use of the dictionary to check spellings, pronunciations, definitions, and usage. This chapter offers a rationale and instruction for 1) the multisensory, structured, and sequential teaching of upper- and lowercase letter recognition and naming and 2) the use of alphabetical order as a sequencing tool, particularly for locating words in the dictionary easily and efficiently. The material presented in this chapter includes principles of effective classroom teaching as well as the instruction, guided practice, and review that dyslexic students require to develop facility in letter recognition and naming skills.

The first section of this chapter discusses the significance of letter identification and naming to the reading process. The second section discusses considerations in teaching these skills, especially to dyslexic students. The third section offers activities for developing accuracy and automaticity in letter identification, letter naming, alphabetizing, and the application of these skills in using the dictionary and other reference materials.

THE ROLE OF LETTER RECOGNITION
AND NAMING WITHIN THE READING PROCESS

The compelling case for teaching letter recognition and naming includes several key points: 1) Letters are the data that make reading possible and are visually processed by every reader (Adams, 1990b); 2) beginning readers who readily recognize individual letters can begin recognizing orthographic patterns (familiar letter sequences), an essential step in becoming a good reader (Ehri, 1980); 3) knowing letter names provides a springboard for learning and remembering letter–sound relationships (Ehri, 1983); 4) the ease or difficulty with which a student acquires letter knowledge reliably predicts how easily and successfully a student will learn to read (Bond & Dykstra, 1967; Chall, 1996); and 5) knowing letter names provides the stable property to which to attach the other variable properties, such as sound and shape (Cox, 1992). These points as well as the significance of letter-naming speed and the relationship of letter recognition to dyslexia are discussed in the sections that follow.

From Recognition of Individual Letters to Recognition of Letter Sequences

As unlikely as it may seem, "skillful readers visually process virtually every individual letter of every word as they read, and this is true whether they are reading isolated words or meaningful, connected text" (Adams, 1990b, p. 18). Although this processing often is not perceived on a conscious level, studies show that misprints of even very familiar words are detected by readers. When the letters *tqe* rather than *the* are embedded in a sentence, the amount of eye fixation time increases (Adams, 1990b).

In a model of word recognition based on work by Seidenberg and McClelland (1989), Adams (1990a) defined the vital role of letter recognition and its relationship to the processing of speech sounds, meaning, and context. Print provides the data that the reader recognizes, recodes (turns into speech sounds), and attaches meaning to in light of the context (e.g., *rose* as flower or action). If a reader has fast, accurate recognition of individual letters, then he or she can locate and learn familiar letter sequences. Through reading many words, the likelihood of letter sequences is learned and reinforced. For fluent reading to develop, a student must learn to recognize frequently occurring orthographic (spelling) patterns in words. The student who must struggle with recognition of individual letters cannot begin to identify frequent letter sequences or recognize letter patterns. Adams described this paradox:

> Ultimately, readers come to look and feel like they recognize words holistically because they have acquired a deep, richly interconnected, and ready knowledge of their spellings, sounds, and meanings. . . . Skillful readers automatically and quite thoroughly process the component letters of text because their visual knowledge of words is from memories of the sequences of letters of which the words are comprised. (1994, p. 9)

From Knowledge of Letter Names to Sound–Symbol Correspondences

In addition to recognizing letter sequences, children must learn how the phonemes of language map onto the letters that represent them. *Phonemes* are the smallest sound segments that make words distinguishable, such as /t/ and /d/

in *time* and *dime.* Learning the alphabetic code is an essential part of learning to read. In an alphabetic language such as English, the alphabet is the bridge from speech to literacy. To travel from the spoken language to the written code, children must acquire the awareness "that all words are specified by an internal phonological structure, the shortest elements of which are the phonemes that the letters of the alphabet represent" (Liberman & Liberman, 1990, p. 60). It is now well understood that beginning readers must come to the same conclusion that the inventors of the alphabet made in their discovery that spoken words differed not holistically "but only in the particulars of their internal structure" (Liberman & Liberman, 1990, p. 61). This discovery led to the invention of the alphabet based on "the idea that if each phonological element were represented by an identifiable, but wholly arbitrary, optical shape, then all could read and write, provided only that they knew the language and were consciously aware of the internal structure of its words" (Liberman & Liberman, 1990, p. 61). An alphabet makes possible a highly efficient writing system that can represent all of the sounds in the language (Logan, 1986).

Alphabetic languages differ in how completely the alphabetic principle is realized (Hanna, Hanna, Hodges, & Rudorf, 1966). English has a less-than-perfect sound–symbol match partly because it is, as Gillingham and Stillman (1960) characterized it, a river of words formed from many tributaries of different languages. Nevertheless, written English shares the advantages of all alphabetic languages: the simplicity of a relatively small number of symbols to be interpreted and written.

Children who know letter names have a foundation for learning the alphabetic principle that children lacking that knowledge do not have. Ehri and Wilce (1979) were successful in teaching letter sounds to kindergarten prereaders who already knew letter names; at the same time, they found that the children who did not know letter names experienced great difficulty in learning letter sounds. Letter knowledge not only helps students infer letter sounds but also helps students remember those sounds. Ehri concluded that letter knowledge aids memory because spellings are "retained as visual symbols preserving the sounds in memory" (1991, p. 68) just as many people can remember a name once they know how it is spelled.

Knowledge of letter names can help students identify unknown words because the phoneme represented by a grapheme (letter or **letter cluster**) is often embedded in the letter's name and can be inferred by students (Ehri, 1987). For example, the sound /m/ is found within the letter name *m*. The spellings of beginning readers (invented or transitional spellings) often reflect use of this knowledge, such as in *PPL* for *people, KAM* for *came,* and *GRL* for *girl,* in which letter names give strong clues to letter sounds. Letter names provide a foundation for learning the alphabetic principle (Ehri, 1987). The previous examples illustrate a beginning understanding of the alphabetic principle in which a grapheme represents a phoneme. Through trying to write it "the way it sounds," students not only learn sound–symbol correspondences but also become aware of the sequences of the sounds and letters, an essential part of the process of learning to read.

Predictive Value of Letter-Name Knowledge

Since the late 1960s, research has shown consistently that ease or difficulty in learning letter recognition and letter names is predictive of reading achievement

(Badian, 1994, 1995; Chall, 1996; Share, Jorm, Maclean, & Matthews, 1984). Bond and Dykstra (1967) found that the ability of prereaders to recognize and name upper- and lowercase letters was the single best predictor of end-of-year reading achievement. Badian (1995) reported results of a study in which 92 students were followed from preschool through sixth grade to determine which prereading skills best predict later reading achievement. Preschool letter-naming ability (speed was not a factor during the letter-naming task) significantly predicted reading vocabulary, reading comprehension, and spelling achievement at each grade level. Letter naming also predicted phonemic awareness ability in first and third grades.

One reason for the strong correlation between letter names and later word recognition is that both require the ability to encode, store, and retrieve lexical labels for abstract symbols. Blachman (1984) reported that for kindergarten students, color-naming speed is correlated with number of letter names learned in kindergarten and that for first graders, letter-naming fluency is correlated with word recognition. She concluded that "the ability to automatize a recently learned set of verbal labels . . . is related to the ability to learn a new set of labels" (p. 619).

Additional Advantages of Letter-Name Knowledge

Knowing letter names helps children recall letter–sound associations. Labeling an item helps store information about that item in long-term memory (Gibson, 1969, and Murray & Lee, 1977, both cited in Walsh, Price, & Gillingham, 1988). Knowing the names of letters also facilitates communication about those letters. Teachers know better when students are confusing letters if students use letter names, and instruction is made easier because there are common referents for letters (Walsh et al., 1988). Sulzby (1983) found that 5-year-olds used letter names in asking their parents questions about word boundaries. Knowing the letter names can make it easier for children to ask for and receive information about the reading process.

There is an advantage to having a constant as well as a common referent for letter shapes. The name of a letter is its most stable property (Cox, 1992). The shape may change (e.g., upper- and lowercase forms, **cursive** and **printed** forms), and the speech sound represented by that letter may change (e.g., **long** and **short vowel** sounds). The name of the letter remains the same, however, as an anchor for its other properties. According to Adams, "research indicates that the provision of a distinctive and uniform label for a concept is especially important—perhaps critically so—for the attainment of concepts whose context and superficial expression varies across occurrences" (1990a, p. 352).

Knowing letter names helps children become sensitive to the differences in individual letter shapes. Gunning (1996) cited the Gibson, Gibson, Pick, and Osser study (1962) that described how children learn letter shapes. They learn to distinguish one letter from another and to identify letters "by noting distinctive features such as whether lines are curved or slanted, open or closed" p. 55).Through many exposures in which children can compare and contrast letters, they can learn these distinctive features.

Some reading programs begin by teaching students to associate a letter with the sound it represents rather than with the letter's name. Because students will eventually need to associate symbols with sounds, some educators ask, "Why not go directly to sound–symbol association and bypass letter names?" According to Adams (1990a), there are some drawbacks to teaching only sound–symbol association without teaching the name of the symbol:

1. Several graphemes in English regularly represent more than one phoneme (e.g., *c* can be pronounced as /k/ as in *cat* or /s/ as in *city*). Learning to recognize letters may take longer if multiple sounds are associated with a letter.
2. When trying to identify an unknown word, new readers are limited to the number of letter–sound correspondences that have been taught, whereas students with letter-name knowledge may be able to use this information to infer or retrieve the sound of the letter and thus identify the word.

Automaticity as a Critical Factor in Reading Success

Durrell (1958) found that the ability to name letters led to successful reading in first grade. Ehri's (1983) critique of studies that failed to show a correlation between instruction in letter naming and subsequent reading ability, however, led Ehri to suggest that letter-name knowledge may well be inseparable from letter–sound knowledge, something that the studies did not consider. She described the role played by letter-name knowledge in the ability of beginning readers to make inferences about the letter–sound system, and she delineated other contributing, perhaps essential factors: phonemic awareness and automaticity in letter recognition.

Walsh and colleagues (1988) supported the vital role of automaticity in letter recognition. In contrast to many of the earlier letter-naming studies, which focused on accuracy, Walsh and colleagues' study pointed to the ease and fluency with which prereaders can name letters as a critical factor in initial reading success. LaBerge and Samuels (1974) suggested that lower-level processing must be automatic in order to free up attention for higher-level processing skills. Single-letter identification must be automatic so that readers learn to associate frequent letter patterns, which in turn leads to rapid word recognition (Ehri, 1992). Word identification skills are significantly correlated with reading comprehension, the next higher level of processing written language (Perfetti, 1985).

Letter-Naming Errors and Dyslexia

Letter reversals and letter transpositions are commonly associated with dyslexic students. Words containing *b*, *d*, or *p* may be read as though those letters were reversed or rotated, such as when *bad* is read as *dad* or *pad*. A transposition of letters results in reading *felt* as *flet*. Beginning readers make both kinds of errors, and the two error patterns appear to be independent of each other.

After looking at letter transpositions and reversals in beginning readers, Liberman, Shankweiler, Orlando, Harris, and Berti (1971) described several important findings: 1) There is no correlation between reversal and transposition errors in low-scoring second-grade readers, and together the two types of errors represented only 25% of misread letters; 2) less-skilled beginning readers make more errors in reading vowels than consonants; and 3) letter reversals are rare when individual letters are presented at rapid exposures. Within the context of words, reversals occur at a much higher frequency, which suggests difficulty "with the rules governing the synthesis of syllables from combinations of letter segments, rather than with strategies for scanning connected text" (Liberman et al., 1971, p. 141).

Liberman and colleagues' (1971) research as well as that of Shankweiler and Liberman (1972) and Vellutino (1979, 1980) is most often credited with dispelling the belief that dyslexia results from deficiencies in the visual-perceptual system (i.e., that dyslexic students perceive letters and words inaccurately). In a study by Vellutino, Smith, Steger, and Kaman (1975), dyslexic and nondyslexic readers who did not know Hebrew were given brief exposure to Hebrew words and letters with which they were not familiar. Then the students were asked to copy the Hebrew symbols from memory. There was no difference in the two groups' ability to accomplish the task and no difference in orientation and sequencing errors. The dyslexic readers actually made fewer orientation errors than the nondyslexic readers did. When linguistic processing was removed from the task of processing symbols, that is, when sounds, verbal labels, and meaning were removed from wordlike symbols, there was no difference in the ability to visually recall and reproduce the symbols. Dyslexics have difficulty when the task requires associating, encoding, storing, and retrieving linguistic material, particularly in conjunction with symbols such as letters. Some of these related reading tasks include the following:

1. Associating a letter name with the letter form (the letter name "b" with the symbol *b*)
2. Mapping sounds onto symbols (the letter *b* represents the phoneme /b/)
3. Learning to associate orthographic patterns with the sounds they represent (*igh* = /ī/ as in *bright*)
4. Recognizing an orthographic pattern as a whole word (*bright* = /brīt/).

When students misidentify *b* as *d* or *p*, visual perception is not the source of the difficulty. They have not made a reliable association between the letter name and letter form (Vellutino, 1979). For many students, it is only through extensive practice that accurate associations are formed. When they read *felt* as *flet*, they demonstrate insufficient knowledge of common orthographic patterns (frequently occurring letter sequences) (Adams, 1990a).

Letter-Naming Speed and Reading

The speed with which young children can name letters, numbers, objects, and colors is a strong predictor of later reading ability, specifically word recognition (Wolf, Bally, & Morris, 1986; Wolf & Obregon, 1992). Rapid automatized naming tasks require students to name 50 items (five common letters, objects, numbers, or colors randomly repeated 10 times on a grid) as rapidly as they can. There is a significant difference between the naming speed of dyslexic readers and the naming speed of nondyslexics (Ackerman & Dykman, 1993), readers whose poor reading skills are commensurate with their IQ scores (Wolf & Obregón, 1992), and students with attention deficit disorder (Felton, Wood, Brown, & Campbell, 1987). This difference in naming speed cannot be attributed to slower articulation speed (Obregón, 1994). Spanning age groups, significantly slower naming speed is present in adult dyslexics (Felton & Wood, 1989) as well as in kindergartners who are eventually classified as having severe reading impairments (Wolf et al., 1986).

Deficits in naming speed may represent a core deficit, distinct from phonological processing deficits, with important implications for reading instruction (Bowers & Wolf, 1993). Wolf (1997) distinguished four groups: average readers without deficits; readers with phonological processing deficits (difficulty encoding, storing, and/or retrieving phonological information); readers with rapid-naming deficits; and those with a *double deficit*, difficulty with both phonological processing and rapid naming. The students with double deficits are most likely to be regarded as classically dyslexic and to have severe reading problems. If these students receive remedial instruction in the area of phonological processing alone, then they are receiving only half of what they need. Wolf, Bowers, and colleagues are studying the feasibility of increasing speed in naming, decoding, orthographic pattern recognition, and word retrieval through intervention programs. Their research has shown that naming speed can be improved through strategies that include vocabulary development and the use of visual mnemonics (retrieving the meaning of *barometer* by previously having visualized a "tall Baron Meter") (Wolf & Segal, 1995, as cited in Wolf, 1997).

An abundance of research points to the importance of letter recognition as a foundation skill in learning to read. Put succinctly, "for children who are lagging behind in development for any environmental or physiological reason or who are at risk for reading failure, the need to develop automatic letter and word recognition skills is critical" (Wolf & Obregón, 1997, p. 200). The clinical experience of practitioners providing letter recognition and naming strategies such as those described later in the chapter provides evidence that at-risk students as well as those who have already experienced difficulty with reading can develop these skills.

TEACHING LETTER IDENTIFICATION, NAMING, AND ALPHABETIZING SKILLS

This section provides information on how students, those with dyslexia in particular, can be helped to develop reliable and more rapid associations of letter names and letter forms through a variety of instructional activities. The clinical experience of many practitioners has shown that these activities can increase both accuracy and speed in letter identification and naming.

Development of Letter Recognition in Nondyslexic Students

It is helpful to view instruction in letter recognition for dyslexic students in the context of how letter recognition develops in most students. Adams (1990a) outlined the process through which the majority of children develop this skill. Long before kindergarten, many children learn letter names before letter shapes through singing the alphabet. Most children can associate letter names with letter shapes for most letters of the alphabet, particularly uppercase letters, before they enter school. They learn the associations through games, puzzles, *Sesame Street,* and attention from interested adults.

Ideally, on entering kindergarten, children are given the chance to develop or consolidate letter identification with uppercase letters before lowercase letters are formally introduced. The same principle is seen in the recommendation that students know letter names well before instruction in sound–symbol association begins (Adams, 1990a). Much confusion among kindergarten and first-grade students can be avoided if letter names are secure before additional information is taught.

Writing plays a role in the beginning reader's ability to recognize letters. Practice in writing letters focuses students' attention on the particular features of the letters and thus helps reinforce letter recognition (Adams, 1990a).

Development of Letter Recognition in Dyslexic Students

Dyslexic students are often not identified until third or fourth grade or later. This means that students already have been exposed to both upper- and lowercase letters and probably to both print and cursive handwriting. In all likelihood, they lack speed and accuracy in letter identification. In their own writing, they may mix together print and cursive and upper- and lowercase letters in the same sentence.

In several programs designed for dyslexics, letter identification is taught or improved through the use of uppercase block capitals because they contain fewer confusing letter shapes. The uppercase forms are more graphically distinct. Letter identification is reinforced through the use of three-dimensional (3-D) letters in alphabetizing activities as part of a comprehensive lesson plan. Alphabet sequencing activities reinforce left-to-right directionality as well, which is essential to the reading process.

Within the same lesson, a lowercase printed letter is introduced through a multisensory procedure in which the letter's name, shape, and the sound it represents are linked (see Chapter 6 for more information on linking). Students practice lowercase letter identification and naming with a letter deck. Handwriting practice within the same lesson provides kinesthetic reinforcement of letter name and shape. The cursive form of the letter is then introduced for writing.

Principles of Effective Instruction

Principles of instruction that make letter identification instruction effective with dyslexic students include the following.

1. *Multisensory teaching*   Because of difficulty with storage and retrieval of lexical labels (including letter names), dyslexic students need the opportunity to learn and practice through simultaneously engaging at least two of the three learning modalities: visual, auditory, and tactile/kinesthetic (involving muscle memory). For example, students say the name of the letter as they locate 3-D plastic letters and place them in alphabetical order.
2. *Sequential presentation*   Information must be presented in a sequence that builds logically on previously taught material.
3. *Guided discovery*   The Socratic method of leading learners to discover information through carefully guided questioning based on information they already possess builds interest and aids memory. When the teacher reviews by starting a sentence and pausing for students to complete it, students are encouraged to participate rather than being placed on the defensive.

4. *Brief instructional segments* Frequent and brief instructional segments are more effective than less frequent segments lasting longer periods of time. Extensive guided practice is required for automaticity.

5. *Teaching to mastery* After presenting the material through **guided discovery,** the teacher models and then provides practice activities, reviews the material on a regular basis, and, when students can be successful, assesses to see whether students have **mastered** the material. Many opportunities for the material to resurface are needed for long-term retention. The teacher should set the students up for success by reviewing the procedure or concept before students are asked to apply it. For example, a quick warm-up of touching and naming the letters on an alphabet strip is strongly recommended before students work on a sequencing, alphabetizing, or dictionary activity.

6. *Teaching proofreading* The teacher guides students through the process of proofreading by which they discover and correct their own errors after completing their work instead of relying on an outside source (teacher or computer).

History of the Alphabet Promotes Interest in Learning Letter Names

The fascinating history of the alphabet can be used to encourage students' interest in developing letter recognition and alphabetizing skills. Students who have difficulty with the two-dimensional symbol system often enjoy learning about the 3-D objects from which the letters of our alphabet are derived. Students can make helpful associations between a letter's history and the letter's name and shape.

The two letters from which we get the very word *alphabet* serve as examples. To the people of Phoenicia, who lived 4,000 years ago, the word for *ox* was *aleph.* When they wanted to send a message about an ox, they drew a simple line drawing of an ox head with two horns and a face in the middle. As time passed, the drawing was turned upside down and began to stand for the first sound of the word. Much later, the Greeks took the sign of the ox's head and called it *alpha,* which became the first letter of their alphabet. The Roman alphabet, which we use today, developed from the Greek letters. The letter we call *A* was the Greek *alpha.* The letter *B* comes down to us from the Phoenician word *beth* meaning *house,* for which they drew a triangle with a base. The Greeks borrowed the word and the sign, called it *beta,* made two triangles, and changed the orientation. Thus, we have our letter *B.*

The final section of this chapter contains references for the history of writing and various alphabets, as well as additional topics to be developed with students. (See Chapter 5 for a history of the English language.) Student interest will be greatly increased by the presentation of pictures and maps to accompany this information.

ACTIVITIES

The following activities and recommended materials are drawn from Cox (1992) and the teaching staff in the Language Laboratory of the Scottish Rite Hospital in Dallas, Texas; the work and writings of Gillingham and Stillman (1960); Hogan and Smith (1987) of EDMAR Educational Associates in Forney, Texas; and the staff of the Neuhaus Education Center in Bellaire, Texas (1998). (See Appendix B at the end of the book for purchasing information on the materials for instruction.)

Materials for Instruction

- Classroom-size alphabet strip, approximately 3" × 48", with alphabet printed in uppercase block letters, without pictures or graphics that can be visually distracting to students; mount at students' eye level
- Set of 3-D plastic uppercase block letters for each student, stored in plastic bags or tubs
- Individual alphabet strip for each student, made of a laminated strip of cardstock, approximately 2" × 17", with uppercase block letters printed in alphabetical order
- For each student, eight sets of words printed in lowercase on cardstock, approximately 1" × 2", 10 cards per set, to be used for alphabetization by 1) first letter; 2) second letter; 3) first and second letters; 4) third letters; 5) second and third letters; 6) fourth letter; 7) third and fourth letters; and 8) first, second, third, and fourth letters
- Container for each student in which to store the individual alphabet strip(s), plastic letters, and word cards to be alphabetized
- Guide-word practice dictionary for each student, purchased or teacher-made
- Dictionary for each student, appropriate to the students' ability level
- *For younger students:* alphabet matching mat made of posterboard or heavy laminated paper, approximately 24" × 18", with the outlines of uppercase block letter shapes arranged alphabetically in an arc (see Figure 4.1). Students can practice matching by placing plastic letters on the mat.
- *For students who do not need to start with a matching activity:* alphabet sequencing mat made of posterboard or heavy laminated paper, approximately 24" × 18", with uppercase block letters in alphabetical order printed across the top and the letters *A, MN,* and *Z* forming an arc (or rainbow) beneath. *M* and *N* are printed at the top of the arc, *A* and *Z* are in the initial and final positions, and space is left for the missing letters to be placed within the arc (see Figure 4.2).
- *For students who have learned uppercase letters:* Lowercase alphabet strip also made of a 2" × 17" strip of laminated cardstock.
- Classroom-size alphabet strip, approximately 3" × 48", with alphabet printed in lowercase block letters

Schedule for Developing Letter
Identification, Naming, and Sequencing Skills

It is suggested that letter recognition and naming activities be a part of each day's structured language lesson, for 5–7 minutes. The letter recognition, naming, and sequencing activities with uppercase letters should be continued until the student can rapidly and accurately identify all uppercase letters in sequence and at random.

Concurrently, the lowercase letters (and letter clusters) should be taught individually through a multisensory procedure often referred to as *linking* (see Chapter 6) in which the letter's name, shape, and the sound it represents are linked in memory. Lowercase letter names should be reviewed daily through the

Figure 4.1. Alphabet matching mat.

use of a *letter deck* or *reading deck*. Students identify the graphemes (letters or letter clusters) on the cards. An additional deck of cards bearing pictures and graphemes from the names of the pictured objects also may be used for students to say the key word and sound. In addition, younger students may need to reinforce speed and accuracy of lowercase letter recognition through the same activities used initially for accurate and rapid recognition and sequencing of uppercase letters. Use 3-D lowercase letters and lowercase alphabet strips if needed.

The activities can be rotated within a weekly lesson plan. A sample plan follows.

Letter Recognition, Naming, and Sequencing Activities
(5–7 minutes in a 50- to 60-minute lesson)

Daily: Touch & name letters on an alphabet strip as a warm-up before the activity. Strip remains in place as a reference.

Monday	**Tuesday**	**Wednesday**	**Thursday**	**Friday**
Naming & Sequencing	Accent & Rhythm	Naming & Sequencing	Before & After	Game

(Missing Letter Deck may be substituted after Naming & Sequencing are secure.)

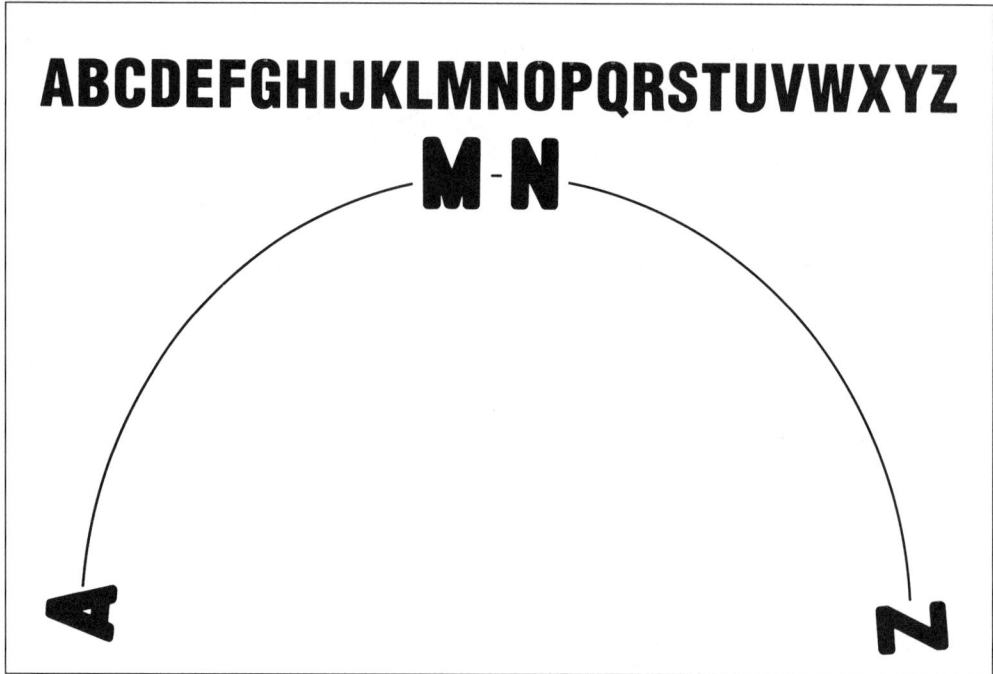

Figure 4.2. Alphabet sequencing mat.

Activities for Developing Letter Identification, Naming, and Sequencing Skills

Matching and Naming Activity

- Set of 3-D letters for each student
- Alphabet matching mat

Students who cannot match 3-D uppercase letters with the outlines of uppercase letters printed on paper should begin with this activity. The teacher has students turn the 3-D plastic letters right-side up and facing the correct direction inside the arc on the alphabet matching mat. The teacher tells students that these are the letters found in the words we read and write. He or she points out the alphabet on the classroom alphabet strip and leads students to discover that an alphabet contains these same letters in a fixed order. The teacher asks students to name each letter before they place the plastic letter on top of the printed form on their individual alphabet matching mats. If all of the letters are not matched within 5 minutes, then the activity is repeated the next day, starting with the letters matched the day before and continuing with additional letters until students can place all of the letters on the mat. The teacher has students check their work each time by touching and naming the letters they have just placed. (Students say "A" and touch the plastic letter sitting on top of the printed letter.)

The teacher leads students to discover the number of letters in the alphabet by pointing to each letter and counting. The teacher leads students in completing the sentence, "The number of letters in the alphabet is _____ [26]."

Students progress from 1) placing the plastic letters on top of the printed forms on the mat for matching, to 2) placing the letters beneath the printed letters on an alphabet strip, to 3) placing the letters in an arc on the mat for sequencing (see Figure 4.2). When students can accurately place plastic letters beneath the letters on an alphabet strip, they are ready for the following activity.

Naming and Sequencing/Discovery of Middle
- Classroom-size alphabet strip
- Individual alphabet strips

Students who do not need to start with a matching activity will start here. If starting here, then the teacher leads students to discover the number of letters in the alphabet (see previous activity).

The teacher asks students to join in naming each letter as he or she points to it in sequential order on a classroom-size alphabet strip. The teacher asks students to touch and name each letter on their individual alphabet strips or mats as he or she leads them in naming the letters together.

The teacher asks younger students to discover the **middle** of the alphabet by putting one index finger on the first letter of the alphabet and one index finger on the last letter and moving in toward the middle. Students discover that the exact middle is between the letters *M* and *N*. The teacher leads students in completing the sentence: "The two middle letters of the alphabet are _____ [*M* and *N*]."

After students can accurately perform this touching and naming activity, any daily alphabet activity should begin with a warm-up in which students touch and name the letters of the alphabet on their strips. This warm-up activity provides the repetition required by dyslexic students to develop automaticity.

Discovery of Vowel and Consonant Sounds
- Mirrors

Before students learn that there are two kinds of *letters* in the alphabet, the teacher introduces the concept of two kinds of *sounds.*

The teacher leads students to discover that we use only two kinds of sounds when we talk: the sounds we form when the mouth is open (vowels) and the sounds we form when the mouth is closed or partially closed (consonants). The teacher illustrates that when we say words, we open and close our mouths. The students try to talk by putting together only closed-mouth sounds, such as /m/, /l/, or /p/. The students try to talk using only open-mouth sounds, such as /ă/, /ĕ/, or /ŭ/. The teacher explains that to form words, we must both open and close our mouths. The teacher illustrates by slowly saying a word, such as *map,* and letting the students see the mouth closing for the consonant, opening for the vowel, and closing for the consonant.

The teacher asks students to look into a mirror as they say /ă/, /ĕ/, /ĭ/, /ŏ/, and /ŭ/ and leads them to discover that their mouths are open when they say these sounds. The shape of the mouth changes, but nothing blocks the air that comes out of the mouth to form these sounds. The teacher explains that vowel sounds open our mouths, and directs students to look in a mirror to see what happens when they say the sound /m/. The teacher explains that their lips close their mouths. Students say /s/, noticing that the teeth and tongue partially close their mouths. Students say /l/ and notice that their tongue partially closes their mouths. These are consonant sounds. The teacher says that consonant sounds close or partially close our mouths. The tongue, teeth, or lips block the air used in making these sounds. The teacher leads the students in saying, "Vowel sounds open our mouths, and consonant sounds close or partially close our mouths." The teacher and students use gestures for *open* (hands open like a crocodile mouth) and *close* (the opposite).

After students are aware of the difference between consonant and vowel *sounds* and have practiced distinguishing between vowel and consonant sounds, they are ready to discover that the *letters* that represent these sounds are classified as vowel letters and consonant letters.

Discovery of Two Kinds of Letters
* Individual alphabet strips (for reference)
* Mirrors

The teacher tells the students that they are going to discover the two kinds of letters in the alphabet. The teacher explains that just as there are two kinds of *sounds* in spoken words, there are two kinds of *letters* in our alphabet. The teacher and students review together, "Vowel sounds open our mouths, and consonant sounds close or partially close our mouths." The names of the letters give clues as to which letters will be called *vowels* and which will be called *consonants*. The teacher directs the students to look in a mirror to see what happens to their mouths when they say the names of the letters *A, E, I, O,* and *U.* Their mouths stay open when they say these letter names. The teacher tells students that these *letters* represent vowel *sounds.* Students use the mirror to discover that when saying the name of the letter *M,* the lips close the mouth. When they say the name of the letter *L,* the mouth is partially closed, with the tongue closing against the roof of the mouth. When they say the name of the letter *F,* the mouth is partially closed by the teeth and lips.

After students are aware that the alphabet is made up of vowel and consonant letters that represent vowel and consonant sounds, the teacher varies the daily warm-up activity of touching and naming the letters by having students whisper or cheer for the vowel letters.

Discovery of Initial, Medial, and Final
* Classroom-size alphabet strip
* Individual alphabet strips

The alphabet can be used to teach students terminology that will be used in other aspects of written language training. For example, in phonemic awareness training, students will be asked whether they hear a specific sound in the initial, medial, or final position in a word. Students can be helped to understand the meaning of the abstract spatial terms *initial, medial,* and *final* by learning them first in relation to picturable space, such as the alphabet arc. The terms *initial, medial,* and *final* can be introduced by teaching the initial, medial, and final letters of the alphabet.

The teacher writes the initials of his or her name on the board and leads students to discover that these letters are the first letters of his or her name. The teacher writes several students' initials on the board and helps students discover that initials are the first letters of names. The teacher explains that *initial* means *first* and that the alphabet also has an initial letter, *A*. The teacher points to the *A* on the classroom alphabet strip, asks students to touch the letter *A* on their alphabet strips, and leads them in saying, "*A* is the _____ [initial] letter of the alphabet."

The teacher touches *Z* on the classroom alphabet strip and asks students to touch *Z* on their strips. The teacher tells students that the last letter of the alphabet is *Z* and that another way of saying *last* is *final*. The teacher leads students in saying, "*Z* is the _____ [final] letter of the alphabet." The teacher tells students that all of the letters between *A* and *Z* are *medial* letters and that there is a difference between *medial* and *middle*. The exact middle of the alphabet is found between the letters *M* and *N*. *Medial* means anything between initial or final. A medial letter is any letter occurring between *A* and *Z*. The teacher asks students to name some of the medial alphabet letters (any letter that is not *A* or *Z*).

The teacher provides kinesthetic reinforcement for this information through gestures. The teacher stands with his or her back to the students, facing the classroom alphabet strip, and raises both arms, fingers pointing above his or her head. The teacher drops his or her left arm horizontally to the left (parallel to the floor) while saying, "*Initial* means *first*." The teacher drops his or her right arm horizontally to the right while saying, "*Final* means *last*." The teacher brings both arms back above his or her head and says, "*Medial* means *anything between initial* (dropping left arm to horizontal) *and final* (dropping right arm to horizontal)."

Sequencing with 3-D Letters
- Individual alphabet strips (for reference)
- Set of 3-D letters
- Alphabet sequencing mats (most older students will place the letters on their desks rather than on the mats)

The teacher writes *A, M, N,* and *Z* in an arc on the chalkboard with *M* and *N* at the top of the arc. The teacher directs students to name and place the initial letter of the alphabet on their alphabet sequencing mats (or desks). They name and place *A* and say, "*A* is the initial letter of the alphabet." Students name and place *Z* and say, "*Z* is the final letter of the alphabet." Students name and place *M* and *N* and say, "*M* and *N* are the two middle letters of the alphabet." The teacher directs students, "Name it, find it, place it," as they fill in the arc with missing letters in alphabetical order. Students say a letter, find it, and place it in the arc until the alphabet is complete. Students then proofread their work by touching and naming each letter, from *A* to *Z*, using the index finger of their writing hand. Soon after beginning this activity, the teacher times students and compares with later timings. The initial goal is accurate naming and placement of all letters in less than 5 minutes, with an ultimate goal of 2 minutes or less. The reason that students place letters in an arc is that often there is not enough space on a desk or a tabletop to place all of the letters in a straight line.

Note for working with younger students: Some very young students may have difficulty crossing the mid-line (moving the right hand and arm into the space to the left of the mid-line of their body or vice versa for left-handed students). These students will want to place the first half of the alphabet letters with their left hand and the second half with their right hand rather than place all of the letters with their writing hand. This is a function of maturation; the teacher will encourage them to work toward the time when they can place all of the letters with their writing hand.

Note for working with older students: Older students may enjoy a variation of this activity. For sequencing, have students use plastic poker chips bearing labels with block capital letters. Older students particularly enjoy the challenge of being timed and having their progress charted. They can compete with themselves to improve their performance.

    Variations:

- Students proofread by returning letters to the storage container in sequence and naming each letter, rather than just touching and naming letters to check.
- After students are able to place the plastic letters in alphabetical order, students may place *A, M, N,* and *Z* as usual and then randomly select a letter and place it in its approximate place in the semicircle.

Discovery of Before and After

- Individual alphabet strips

Dyslexic students often have difficulty with abstract spatial terms such as *before* and *after* and may be confused by directions such as "Look at the consonant after the vowel" or "Listen for the sound before the /k/ sound." To make the abstract terms *before* and *after* more concrete, the teacher directs students to place both hands below their alphabet strips and then models for students with the classroom-size alphabet strip. The teacher asks students to raise the hand that is closer to *A* and tells them that this is their *before* hand. The teacher asks students to raise the hand closer to *Z*, which is their *after* hand.

    Next, the teacher names a letter, such as *E,* and places both index fingers under the letter on the classroom alphabet strip. The teacher moves the index finger of the *after* hand to the letter after *E* and says, "*F* is after *E.*" Students then echo and place their index finger under the chosen letter *(E)* on their individual alphabet strips. With the index finger of their *after* hand, students touch and name the letter that comes after the named letter. Students say the sentence, "*F* is after *E.*" The teacher names several other letters, and students respond appropriately.

    The concept *after* is taught first because it reflects the left-to-right progression of the alphabet. The concept *after* should be practiced in several sessions until it is learned. Then the teacher has students work with the concept *before.* The teacher names a letter, such as *T,* and asks students to tell which letter is before it. Students place both index fingers under *T,* point to *S* with the index finger of their *before* hand, and say, "*S* is before *T.*" Finally, the teacher provides practice with both *before* and *after:* "Find *W.* Tell me what is before and after *W.*"

Missing Letter Decks

- Individual alphabet strips (for reference)
- Missing letter deck

To make a missing letter deck with uppercase block capitals, the teacher prints the alphabet in groups of three letters using a computer or by hand. In the first set, the third letter is missing and is represented by a blank line (AB__, BC__, CD__). In the second set, the entire alphabet is printed in groups of three letters with the middle letter missing (A__C, B__D, C__E). In the third set, the first letter is missing (__BC, __CD, __DE). In the fourth set, the first and third letters are missing (__B__, __C__, __D__).

After students can correctly sequence 3-D letters of the alphabet within 3 minutes, the teacher introduces a teacher-made version of the commercially available Missing Letter Deck, Level 1, printed in uppercase block letters. Only after students can identify all uppercase letters fluently and have been introduced to all lowercase letters should the commercially available deck with lowercase block letters be used.

Students keep their alphabet strips in front of them to refer to if needed. The teacher makes sure the missing letter deck is in alphabetical order and holds up the first card. Students name the two letters on the card and the missing letter: "*AB__ [C], BC ___ [D],*" and so forth. When students can rapidly and accurately name all three letters on each card with the cards in alphabetical sequence (after many practice sessions), the teacher shuffles the cards and presents them in random order. The students then progress to the second, third, and fourth teacher-made sets of the missing letter decks. As with the first set, these are practiced first in sequence, then shuffled. Students should be fluent at each level before progressing to the next level.

Accent and Rhythm
•   Mirrors

Dyslexic students often have difficulty hearing the **accented** syllable in a word. This has consequences for written language skills, for spelling in particular. The following activity provides practice in hearing accented syllables, while also reinforcing alphabetic sequence. The teacher says the names of several students, overemphasizing the accented syllable in their names ("Ja **mal'**, **Sta'** cy, Ta **ke'** sha, **Ja'** son, Jo **sé'''**"). The teacher asks students whether they hear a difference in the way one part of the name is said. The teacher models "robot talk" in which there is no accent. The students discover that we say some parts of spoken words louder than other parts. The teacher explains that when we accent one part of a word, the mouth opens wider, the voice is louder, and the tone is higher. The teacher reinforces each part of the definition with gestures: mouth opens wider (hands open like a crocodile mouth), voice is louder (cupped hand behind ear), tone is higher (flattened hand, palm to floor, is raised above head to designate *higher*).

Some students can learn to "see" accented syllables by using a mirror to notice when their mouths open wider. For students who find perceiving accent particularly difficult, the teacher models laying both hands along the jawline so that students can feel the jaw opening wider on the accented syllable. Students may be better able to discern the change in pitch that occurs with accent if they place their hands over their ears and hum a word rather than say it.

The teacher recites the alphabet in pairs and accents the first letter of each pair: "A' B, C' D, E' F, G' H." The teacher asks students whether the first or the second letter is being accented. The teacher encourages students to use a mirror to see their mouths opening wider and to cup their jaws in their hands to *feel* their mouth opening wider. Using block letters and accenting the first letter in each pair, the teacher writes the first eight letters of the alphabet on the board in pairs: A' B, C' D, E' F, G' H. Stressing the first letter in each pair, the teacher reads the list. With their alphabet strips in view, students say the alphabet and accent the first letter in each pair. Variations include having students clap on the accented letter.

After students are able to accent the first letter of each pair (after many practice sessions), the teacher writes on the board and leads students in accenting the second letter: "A **B'**, C **D'**, E **F'**, G **H'**." Eventually, students practice accenting the first of a group of three letters ("**A'** BC, **D'** EF"), then the second letter ("A **B'** C, D **E'** F"), and finally, the third letter ("AB **C'**, DE **F'''**"). Students will need to apply their knowledge of accenting patterns when reading unfamiliar longer words. In English, multisyllabic words are accented more often on the first syllable (e.g., **bas'** ket), next most often on the second syllable (pa **rade'**, con **ven'** tion), and next most often on the third (guar an **tee'**).

Random Naming of Uppercase Letters
• Classroom-size alphabet strip

To determine an individual student's accuracy and relative speed in naming uppercase letters, the teacher indicates letters in random order on the alphabet strip and the student names them. The teacher notes accuracy and relative speed with which the response is made.
  Variations:
• A student randomly selects and names alphabet letters from 26 plastic letters on his or her desktop.
• A student is presented with all 26 uppercase block letters of the alphabet, printed in random order. The student names the letters. The teacher may time the student and chart progress for motivation.

Naming of Lowercase Letters
• Letter deck

After students have been introduced to all lowercase letters through the multi-sensory procedure known as *linking* (see Chapter 6), students will identify the lowercase letter names daily through use of the letter deck or reading deck.
  If students need additional practice in naming the lowercase letters accurately and rapidly, many of the previous activities for uppercase letters may be adapted. The daily warm-up of touching and naming letters can be done with an alphabet strip of lowercase letters, as can activities such as Discovery of Before and After, Accent and Rhythm, the Missing Letter Deck, and the games Don't Say Z and Twenty Questions (described later).

Random Naming of Lowercase Letters
• Classroom-size lowercase alphabet strip

The same activities to determine the accuracy and relative speed with which students can name the uppercase letters can be used for the lowercase letters: 1) The student names letters designated in random order by the teacher on the lowercase alphabet strip, and 2) the student names lowercase letters printed in a list in random order. The teacher may time the student and chart progress for motivation.

Games to Reinforce Identification, Naming, and Sequencing Skills
Alphabet Battle
• One individual alphabet strip and one set of 3-D letters for each pair of students

Simultaneously, both players draw a letter from the set of 3-D letters without looking at the letters. The players place their letter on the desk and say the name of the letter. The player whose letter is closer in alphabetical order to *Z* wins both letters. The student must say, for example, "*U* is after *G*. I win the letters." The winner is the player with the most letters at the end of the game.

Variation:

- The player whose letter is closer to *A* wins the letters ("*J* is before *T*. I win the letters").

Alphabet Bingo

- Individual alphabet strip and a set of 3-D letters for each student and for the teacher

Each student selects any seven letters from his or her container of letters and places them on the desk in a vertical column on the *before* (left-hand) side. The other letters are put away.

The teacher selects one letter from another container, shows it to the students, and names it. Students repeat the name. If they have the letter on their desk, they move it to the *after* (right-hand) side of the desk to form a second vertical column. The first person to move all seven letters to the *after* side of the desk is the winner. The teacher checks for accuracy by having the winner name the seven letters. For a faster game, start with fewer than seven letters.

Alphabet Dominoes

- One individual alphabet strip and one set of 3-D letters for each pair of students

Students should be proficient in *before* and *after* activities. Each pair of students places the letters *M* and *N* on the desk. Each student draws five letters without looking. The remaining letters become the "bone yard" and are placed inside the storage container on top of the desk. The teacher designates which student in each pair goes first. That student tries to play a letter immediately before *M* or after *N*. The student must have an *L* or an *O* to play initially. If not, then he or she draws a letter from the bone yard without looking. The letters are to be played in alphabetical order to the right of *N* and in reverse alphabetical order to the left of *M*. For example, if the letters placed are *JKLMNOPQ*, then the next player may play an *I* or an *R*. If a player draws a letter from the bone yard that can be played, he or she must wait until the next turn to play it. Each player plays only one letter at a time. As each student places a letter, he or she says, "_____ is before (or after) _____." The winner is the first student to play all of his or her letters.

Alphabet Relay

- One individual alphabet strip and one set of 3-D letters for each team

Divide students into teams of two to four students. Each team receives an alphabet strip and container of letters and places them on a designated desk. At the teacher's signal, the first person on each team goes to the team's desk, picks a letter at random, names it, and places it in its correct position in the alphabet. Each team member places a letter until all of the letters have been played by one team. The last person to play must check the sequence of the letters. If players see a letter out of sequence during play, then they may use a turn to correct one mistake. The first team to place the letters in correct sequence is the winning team.

Guess What?
- One set of 3-D letters for each pair of students

A student, with eyes closed, draws a letter from a container. The student tries to identify the letter by its shape. If successful, the student keeps the letter and his or her opponent takes a turn. If unsuccessful, the student returns the letter to the container and his or her opponent takes a turn. Play continues until all 26 letters have been named or time runs out. The student with the most letters at the end of play is the winner.

Don't Say Z
- One individual alphabet strip for each pair of students

Two players alternate saying letters of the alphabet in sequence. Each player may choose to say two or three letters in one turn. For example, Player 1 may say, "AB," Player 2 says, "CDE," Player 1 says, "FG," or, "FGH," and so forth. The object is to avoid saying Z.
   Variation:
- The game can be changed to Catch the Z in which the object is to be the player who says Z.

Twenty Questions
- Chalkboard and chalk or paper and pencil

The teacher prints the alphabet on the board. The teacher says, "I am thinking of a letter. I want you to try to guess the letter. You can ask me questions about the letter. I can only answer 'yes' or 'no.' See if you can guess the letter in fewer than 20 questions."

Students begin to ask questions about the letter. The teacher encourages students to ask questions that eliminate several letters at a time. Questions such as "Is it a vowel?" or "Is it made of only straight lines?" will eliminate several letters at a time. The teacher helps students to rephrase questions that will require more than an answer of "yes" or "no."

As students eliminate letters, the teacher crosses the letters off the alphabet. The teacher records the number of questions required for students to guess the letter. The teacher can chart the number of questions. Students can compare the number of questions they ask each time the game is played.

Super Sleuth
- One individual alphabet strip and one set of 3-D letters for each pair of students

The students work together in pairs to arrange the letters in an arc. The first student closes his or her eyes while the second student removes one letter and closes the gap left in the arc. The first student then must discover the missing letter. After the missing letter has been identified, it is replaced in the arc and the other student gets the chance to identify a missing letter. Students may keep track of correct guesses to determine the winner. The game continues until time runs out.

Schedule for Developing Alphabetizing Skills

Students are ready to learn to alphabetize words when they show competence with letter recognition, naming, and sequencing. They should be able to place the 3-D plastic letters in an arc within 2 minutes, be fluent with the fourth set of the missing letter deck, and be accurate with random letter naming. Students begin alphabetizing word cards rather than lists of words. Mistakes can be easily corrected by rearranging a card rather than erasing a word in a list. Students move from alphabetizing word cards to alphabetizing lists of words, and then to locating words in the dictionary and other reference materials.

Daily: Touch & name letters on an alphabet strip as a warm-up before the activity. Strip remains in place as a reference.

Monday	Tuesday	Wednesday	Thursday	Friday
Missing Letter Deck	Alphabetizing Word Cards/Lists	Missing Letter Deck	Alphabetizing Word Cards/Lists	Game

Activities for Developing Alphabetizing Skills

The alphabet provides a systematic approach to organizing, classifying, and codifying information in myriad fields, such as science, law, engineering, the social sciences, business, education, communication, and entertainment. The order of the alphabet in turn provides the order of words for every kind of information we seek, in libraries, books, and newspapers and on the Internet. The following activities help develop alphabetizing skills.

Alphabetizing Word Cards by the First Letter
- Pocket chart
- For the teacher, a set of ten 5″ × 7″ cards, each of which bears a word beginning with a different lowercase letter
- For each student, a set of ten 1″× ½″ cards, each of which bears a word beginning with a different lowercase letter
- Individual alphabet strips

The teacher places 10 cards in a vertical column on the *before* side of the pocket chart (or desk, if working with one or two students). In keeping with the principle of having one focus, the words on these cards are for alphabetizing, not for reading. Students name the letters in the word rather than read the word. The teacher asks students whether the first letter of each word is the same as or different from the first letters of the other words. Students respond that they are different. The teacher asks the students which letter will guide them in putting these words into alphabetical order. The teacher explains that the letter used for alphabetizing is called the ***guide letter***. The answer to the question is always an ordinal number ("The first letter is the guide letter").

The teacher points to the first letter of each word as the students recite the alphabet. For example, as students say, "*A,*" the teacher points to the first letter of each word and returns to the first word when students say, "*B.*" If the students see a word beginning with the letter *A* as they are saying, "*A,*" then they say, "Stop!" The teacher forms a second column by placing the word card at the top of the pocket chart on the right side.

The students continue reciting the alphabet and saying, "Stop!" as the cards are aligned in alphabetical order. The students finish saying the alphabet even after all of the cards are placed. Students proofread by saying the alphabet again while the teacher touches the first letter of each card as the students say that letter. The teacher taps the space to the left of the words when students say letters not found at the beginning of one of the words.

Students line up their set of word cards vertically on the *before* side of their desks. The teacher asks students which letter is their guide letter. The students reply, "The first letter is my guide letter." The students recite the alphabet while pointing to the first letter of each word. If students find a word beginning with *A,* they place it in a vertical column on the *after* side of the desk. They follow the same procedures for saying the entire alphabet and then proofread.

Have several different sets of word cards to be alphabetized by the first letter so that the students work with different sets over a period of time. Choose one color of cards for words to be alphabetized by first letter and a different color for words to be alphabetized by second letter (different colors also should be used for words to be alphabetized by third and fourth letters). Word sets can be easily stored in small plastic sandwich bags.

When students can perform this activity easily and efficiently, they are ready to progress to the next level, alphabetizing word cards by the second letter.

Alphabetizing Word Cards by the Second Letter
- Pocket chart
- For the teacher, a set of ten 5" × 7" cards with words that begin with the same first letter followed by a different letter, such as *set, sun, street, six, sled, sand, scout, show, sip, snake,* and *skate*
- For each student, a set of ten 1" × ½" cards with words that begin with the same first letter but are followed by different letter second letters
- Individual alphabet strips

The teacher places 10 cards in a vertical column on the *before* side of the pocket chart. The students discover that the first letter of each of the words is the same. Students respond to the question "What is your guide letter?" by saying, "The second letter is my guide letter." The teacher points to the second letter of each of the words as students follow the procedures detailed in the previous activity for reciting the alphabet, forming a new column on the *after* side, and proofreading.

Students follow the same procedures as they practice with word cards in columns on their desks.

Alphabetizing Word Cards by the First and Second Letters
- Pocket chart

- For the teacher, ten 5″ × 7″ cards with words, some of which have the same first letter and some of which have a different first letter, such as *tent, can, brand, melt, trunk, slant, go, bake, free,* and *luck*
- For each student, ten 1″ × ½″ cards with words, some of which have the same first letter and some of which have a different first letter
- Individual alphabet strips (for reference)

The teacher places 10 cards in a vertical column on the *before* side of the pocket chart. The students discover that some of the first letters are the same and some are different. Students respond to "What is your guide letter?" by saying, "For most of the words, the first letter is the guide letter; for some, the second letter is the guide letter." The teacher points to the second letter of each of the words as students recite the alphabet and say, "Stop!" when they see a word beginning with the letter they are saying. For example, when working the list of words just mentioned, when students reach "*T*," they say, "Stop! Stop!" The teacher moves both *tent* and *trunk* to the column on the right and aligns them side by side, with a space beneath the two words. Students continue reciting the alphabet through *Z.* Students then come back to the two words beginning with *T* and say, "*Te* comes before *Tr.*" The teacher places *trunk* in the empty space below *tent.* Students recite the alphabet again to proofread their work as usual. After saying, "*T*," students say, "*Te* comes before *Tr, U, V, W, X, Y, Z.*" Students follow the same procedures as they practice with word cards on their desks.

After students are proficient at this level, the teacher introduces and students practice alphabetizing by the third letter, then by the second and third letters, then by the fourth letter, and finally, by third and fourth letters.

In typical classrooms, students can apply this procedure by alphabetizing their spelling or vocabulary words written on index cards.

After students can efficiently alphabetize a group of word cards with mixed **guide letters,** students are ready to alphabetize word lists.

Alphabetizing Words in Lists by the First Letter
- Individual alphabet strips (for reference)

The teacher writes a list of words on the board to be alphabetized by the first letter. Students discover that the initial letter is their guide letter, and the teacher underlines it. Students recite the alphabet as the teacher points to the initial letter of each word. Students say, "Stop!" when they say a letter that matches the letter to which the teacher is pointing. The teacher numbers the words to the left of the word list to indicate alphabetical order. The teacher then gives students a list of words on paper to be alphabetized by first letter, and students follow the same procedure in numbering the words. As always, students check their work by reciting the alphabet again.

Alphabetizing a List of Words by First and Second Letters
- Individual alphabet strips (for reference)

The teacher writes on the board a list of words to be alphabetized by the first and second letters. The teacher draws a column of lines to the right of the list labeled *Letter* and a second column of lines labeled *Number.* An example follows.

Word	Letter	Number
track	_____	_____
den	_____	_____
tag	_____	_____
cube	_____	_____
bland	_____	_____
vote	_____	_____
same	_____	_____
gloss	_____	_____
camp	_____	_____
again	_____	_____

The students discover that the first and sometimes second letters are their guide letters. The teacher asks the students to name the initial letter of each word and writes the letter on the line. If a letter is a duplicate, the students name and the teacher writes the second letter of the word beside the initial letter. An example follows:

Word	Letter	Number
track	tr_____	_____
den	d_____	_____
tag	ta_____	_____

Students then recite the alphabet as the teacher points to the letters in the Letter column. The teacher numbers the words when the students say the guide letter(s). When the second letter is the guide letter, as with *track* and *tag*, students say, "*Ta* comes before *tr*." *Tag* is given the next number, and *track* the next.

The teacher gives students a list of words on paper with Letter and Number columns to the right of the list. Students follow the same procedures for numbering their list of words and checking their work.

Students progress to alphabetizing word lists by the third letter, mixed second and third letters, the fourth letter, and mixed third and fourth letters. Eventually students will number mixed word lists without the Letter column.

Schedule for Developing Dictionary Skills

After students are alphabetizing word lists proficiently to the fourth letter, they are ready to develop skill in using the dictionary. A sample weekly lesson plan follows.

Daily: Touch and name letters on individual alphabet strips as a warm-up. Strip remains in place as a reference.

Monday	Tuesday	Wednesday	Thursday	Friday
Quartile Activity or Missing Letter Decks	Guide Word Practice	Alphabetizing Word Cards/Lists	Guide Word Practice	Game

Activities for Developing Dictionary Skills

Discovery of Quartiles
* Dictionary for each student
* Individual alphabet strips (for reference)

The teacher leads students in dividing the dictionary into two parts and marking the location (in the words beginning with *m*) with a 3″×5″ index card. Dividing the first part into halves again, students place a card in the words beginning with *e*. Dividing the second part into halves, students place a card in the words beginning with *s*. The teacher explains that the four parts of a gallon are called *quarts* and that the four parts of a dollar are called *quarters*. The teacher then tells students that the four parts of a dictionary are called *quartiles*. The letters that begin the four quartiles are *A, E, M,* and *S*. Students create a sentence to aid memory, such as "All Eagles Must Soar."

Quartile Practice with 3-D Letters
* Set of 3-D letters for each student
* Individual alphabet strips
* Paper clips

The teacher directs students to place the 3-D letters into the four quartiles:

> ABCD
> EFGHIJKL
> MNOPQR
> STUVWXYZ

The teacher names a letter, such as *q*. Students echo and say the letter's quartile ("*Q* is in the third quartile"). Students practice designating quartiles. After students are proficient with this activity, students may mark the quartiles on their alphabet strips with paper clips and designate the quartile while looking at the strips.

Discovery of Guide Words and Cornering
* Dictionary for each student
* Individual alphabet strips (for reference)

After several practice sessions in which students become proficient with designating quartiles, the teacher directs students to a designated page in their dictionaries. Students discover the two words at the top of the page, called *guide words.* The teacher explains that the guide word on the left is the first *entry word* (in bold print) on the page. The guide word on the right is the last entry word on the page. Just as guide letters are useful when students alphabetize words, guide words at the top of a dictionary page show which words will be on the page according to alphabetical order.

The teacher illustrates the **cornering** technique with the dictionary, an efficient way to focus only on the guide words. When the teacher looks forward in the dictionary (at the right-hand pages), the right hand turns only the corners of the page while the left hand holds the turned pages. When the teacher looks backward in the dictionary (at the left-hand pages), the teacher's left hand "corners" the pages while the right hand holds those pages. Students practice cornering.

Locating a Quartile by Cornering

- Dictionary for each student
- Individual alphabet strips (for reference)

The teacher directs students to find any guide word in the dictionary that begins with a designated letter, such as *r*. Students echo and say, "R is in the third quartile," and turn to the third quartile of their dictionaries. Students corner as they say, "R is after *o*. R is after *q*. Here is *r*." Students then name the letters of any guide word beginning with *r*. This activity is practiced several times until students can proficiently use the cornering technique.

Using Guide Words

- 3" × 5" index cards bearing a target word
- Guide-word practice dictionary
- Individual alphabet strips (for reference)

The teacher writes two guide words from an actual page in the dictionary with a target word between them on the chalkboard. The teacher explains that the target word is the word to be located in the dictionary.

Example: <u>beam   bet</u>
bend

The teacher reviews the definition and purpose of guide words and target words. The guide word on the left is the first entry on the dictionary page; the guide word on the right is the last entry on the page. If the target word is on a particular page, the target word will come after the first guide word and before the second guide word alphabetically.

The teacher models by starting with the target word, *b e n d,* and comparing it with the guide word on the left, *b e a m.* (By naming the letters rather than the word, the teacher keeps the focus on the alphabetizing task rather than on reading.) The teacher asks, "What are your guide letters?" Students should respond, "The third letters are the guide letters because they are different." The teacher emphasizes the importance of starting with the letters of the target word and says, "*B e n* (emphasizing the guide letter) comes after *b e a.* I'll draw an arrow under *beam* that points to the *after* side. My target word may be on this page because it comes after the first guide word."

Example: <u>beam   bet</u>
→bend

The teacher directs students to compare the target word with the guide word on the right and asks for the guide letters. The teacher leads the students in saying, "The third letters are the guide letters. *B e n* comes before *b e t.* I'll draw an arrow to the *before* side. The target word is on this page because it comes after the first guide word and before the second guide word. My arrows meet in the middle and show me that my target word is on this page."

Example: beam   bet
→bend←

The teacher gives each student a 3″ × 5″ index card on which a target word has been written.

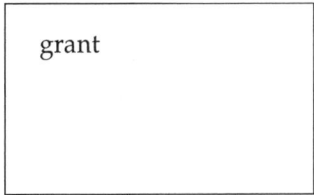

The teacher directs students to a guide-word practice page that contains only two guide words. A sample practice page follows:

glow	green

The teacher leads students in using guide words as detailed previously to discover whether the target word *grant* would be found on this page. (Students discover that the target word comes after the first guide word and before the second. The arrows meet in the middle, so the word is found on this page.) At first, all target words can be found on the page designated by the teacher. Sample guide words and target words for guide-word practice pages include

Guide Words	Target Words
bingo bit	biology, biped, bird, bison
tumbling turboprop	tumult, tuna, tune, turbine
sail scout	saint, same, Saturday, scale

After students have had many practice sessions and are proficient at this level (the teacher sends students to a designated page on which the target word is found), the teacher puts two guide words and a target word on the chalkboard.

tumbling   turboprop
turtle

Comparing the target word with the guide word on the left, the teacher asks which letters are the guide letters. The teacher leads the students in saying, "The third letters are the guide letters. *T u r* is after *t u m.* I'll draw an arrow to the *after* side. The target word may be on this page because it is after the first guide word. In the second guide word, the fourth letters are the guide letters. *T u r t* is after *t u r b.* I'll draw an arrow to the *after* side. The target word cannot be on this page because it is *after* the second guide word on this page. The arrow shows that I need to turn to the page after this one to see whether the target word is on that page." Practice with words found *after* the designated page occurs *first* because it reflects the left-to-right progression of the alphabet.

After students have had many practice sessions and are proficient at this level (target word is after the designated page), the teacher puts two guide words on the board and a target word that comes *before* the guide words. For example:

<u>glean   gluten</u>
glad

The teacher provides practice by sending students to a designated page in their guide-word dictionaries. The students discover that the target word given by the teacher comes before that page. Students progress to locating the written target word without the teacher's designating a page. Students verbalize as they compare the letters of their target word with those of the guide words at the top of the guide-word practice pages ("*G e* is after *g a*")

Using the Column Word
- Guide-word practice dictionary
- Individual alphabet strips (for reference)

After students are proficient at locating the correct page in a guide-word dictionary with designated target words, the teacher writes two guide words and a target word on the chalkboard. The teacher draws a line to indicate the two columns found on a dictionary page. At the top of the second column, the teacher writes a *column word* representing the first entry in that column. Students decide whether their target word will be found in the first or second column on the page by comparing the target word with the column word.

Applying Skills Using a Regular Dictionary
- Dictionary for each student
- Individual alphabet strips (for reference)

After students are proficient at locating the correct page and column for written target words on guide-word practice pages, the teacher leads them in applying the same skills using a regular dictionary. The dictionary should be appropriate for the level of the students, such as an elementary- or junior-level edition, with large print and no tabs. Students work with target words written by the teacher on 3" × 5" cards or on the chalkboard. Students locate the quartile, page, column, and word itself in the dictionary. Locating a word in 60 seconds or less is the goal.

Using Alphabetizing Skills with Other Reference Materials
- A variety of print and Internet reference materials
- Individual alphabet strips (for reference)

Students locate target words in a variety of other reference materials: computer listings, telephone directories, encyclopedias, and indexes in books.

Games to Reinforce Dictionary Skills

Dictionary Relay
- Dictionary Relay Page and dictionary for each team
- Individual alphabet strip for each team (for reference)

Students work in teams of four with one dictionary per team. Each team receives the Dictionary Relay Page of words to be found. The Dictionary Relay Page is a sheet of paper divided into four columns with the following headings: Target Word, Quartile, Page #, and Column #. The first team member locates and records the quartile of the target word, the second team member finds and records the page number, and the third team member determines whether the word falls in the first column or second. The fourth team member locates and records the quartile of the second target word and passes the dictionary back to the first team member, who finds and records the page number. The first team to correctly complete the Dictionary Relay Page is the winning team. If the teacher is working with an individual student, the student can work to improve his or her time completing the page.

Target Word	Quartile	Page #	Column #
trampoline			
parachute			
capitol			
submarine			
elephant			

Dictionary Scavenger Hunt
- Dictionary for each student
- Individual alphabet strips (for reference)

The teacher leads students in discovering sound pictures (phonetic respellings for pronunciation), word origins, parts of speech, and examples of usage in the dictionary. After students are familiar with these aspects of the dictionary, they may apply their knowledge in a Dictionary Scavenger Hunt for information.

Students work individually or in teams to complete a page. A sample Dictionary Scavenger Hunt follows.

1. Look up *telepathy*. What is the first entry word on that page?

   _____

2. What is the sound picture for *doubloon?* _____
   Copy a definition from the dictionary. _____

3. Look up *run*. You may find more than one entry. This word can be used as how many different parts of speech? _____
   Write a sentence that illustrates *run* as a verb and another sentence that illustrates *run* as a noun.

   _____

   _____

4. Give the language of origin of these words or word parts:
   photo _____
   truck _____
   chiro _____
   tomato _____
   biped _____
   bio _____

Variation: Students can complete a Reference Scavenger Hunt using materials such as World Wide Web sites, encyclopedias, telephone books, and indexes in books.

SAMPLE QUESTIONS TO SPARK STUDENTS' INTEREST IN WRITTEN LANGUAGE AND THE HISTORY OF THE ALPHABET

History of Writing

- What are some of the ways people communicated before anyone could read or write?
- What are some hand signals and picture symbols we use today that do not involve words?
- How long ago do you think human beings began to write?
- In what part of the world do you think the oldest writings have been found?
- What were the earliest writing instruments and on what did people write?
- Do you think writing has always gone from left to right and top to bottom on the page?

History of the Alphabet

- What are the differences between writing based on pictures and writing based on an alphabet?
- What group of people are credited with inventing the alphabet?
- How did the English alphabet evolve from the Greek and Roman alphabets?
- From pictures of what objects did our two-dimensional letters evolve?
- What is the history of each of our letters?

CONCLUSION

Knowledge of letters and the phonemes they represent provides students with a foundation for using the alphabetic principle in learning to read. Letter recognition must be automatic as well as accurate. Beginning readers must sequentially process the letters they see in words and the phonemes the letters represent. Practice in sequencing the alphabet provides reinforcement of sequential processing. Facility in using alphabetical order gives students efficient access to information available through reference materials such as dictionaries, encyclopedias, and the Internet. Both research and observation indicate that early, directed experiences with letter names, shapes, and sequencing develop essential skills that students need to become proficient readers.

REFERENCES

Ackerman, P.T., & Dykman, R.A. (1993). Phonological processes, confrontation naming, and immediate memory in dyslexia. *Journal of Learning Disabilities, 26*(9), 597–609.

Adams, M.J. (1990a). *Beginning to read: Thinking and learning about print.* Cambridge: The MIT Press.

Adams, M.J. (1990b). *Beginning to read: Thinking and learning about print* [A summary]. (Prepared by S.A. Stahl, J. Osborn, & F. Lehr). Cambridge: The MIT Press.

Adams, M.J. (1994). Phonics and beginning reading instruction. In F. Lehr & J. Osborn (Eds.), *Reading, language, and literacy* (pp. 3–23). Mahwah, NJ: Lawrence Erlbaum Associates.

Badian, N.A. (1994). Preschool prediction: Orthographic and phonological skills, and reading. *Annals of Dyslexia, 44,* 3–25.

Badian, N.A. (1995). Predicting reading ability over the long term: The changing roles of letter naming, phonological awareness and orthographic processing. *Annals of Dyslexia, 45,* 79–96.

Blachman, B. (1984). Relationship of rapid naming ability and language analysis skills to kindergarten and first-grade reading achievement. *Journal of Educational Psychology, 76,* 610–622.

Bond, G.L., & Dykstra, R. (1967). The cooperative research program in first-grade reading instruction. *Reading Research Quarterly, 2,* 5–142.

Bowers, P.G., & Wolf, M. (1993). Theoretical links among naming speed, precise timing mechanisms and orthographic skill in dyslexia. *Reading and Writing: An Interdisciplinary Journal, 5,* 69–85.

Chall, J.S. (1996). *Learning to read: The great debate* (3rd. ed.). Orlando, FL: Harcourt Brace & Co.

Cox, A.R. (1992). *Foundations for literacy: Structures and techniques for multisensory teaching of basic written English language skills.* Cambridge, MA: Educators Publishing Service.

Durrell, D. (1958). First grade reading success study: A summary. *Journal of Education, 140*(3), 1–24.

Ehri, L.C. (1980). The development of orthographic images. In U. Frith (Ed.), *Cognitive processes in spelling* (pp. 311–338). San Diego: Academic Press.

Ehri, L.C. (1983). A critique of five studies related to letter-name knowledge and learning to read. In L.M. Gentile, M.L. Kamil, & J.S. Blanchard (Eds.), *Reading research revisited* (pp. 143–153). Columbus, OH: Charles E. Merrill.

Ehri, L.C. (1987). Learning to read and spell words. *Journal of Reading Behavior, 19,* 5–31.

Ehri, L.C. (1991). Learning to read and spell words. In L. Rieben & C. Perfetti (Eds.), *Learning to read: Basic research and its implications* (pp. 57–73). Mahwah, NJ: Lawrence Erlbaum Associates.

Ehri, L.C. (1992). Reconceptualizing the development of sight word reading and its relationship to recoding. In P.B. Gough, L.C. Ehri, & R. Treiman (Eds.), *Reading acquisition* (pp. 107–143). Mahwah, NJ: Lawrence Erlbaum Associates.

Ehri, L.C., & Wilce, L.S. (1979). The mnemonic value of orthography among beginning readers. *Journal of Educational Psychology, 71,* 26–40.

Felton, R.H., & Wood, F.B. (1989). Cognitive deficits in reading disability and attention deficit disorder. *Journal of Learning Disabilities, 22,* 3–13.

Felton, R.H., Wood, F.B., Brown, I.S., & Campbell, S.K. (1987). Separate verbal memory and naming deficits in attention deficit disorder and reading disability. *Brain and Language, 31,* 171–184.

Gillingham, A., & Stillman, B. (1960). *Remedial training for children with specific disability in reading, spelling, and penmanship* (6th ed.). Cambridge, MA: Educators Publishing Service.

Gunning, T.G. (1996). *Creating reading instruction for all children* (2nd ed.). Needham Heights, MA: Allyn & Bacon.

Hanna, P.R., Hanna, J.S., Hodges, R.E., & Rudorf, E.H., Jr. (1966). *Phoneme-grapheme correspondences as cues to spelling improvement* (USOE Publication No. 32008). Washington, DC: U.S. Government Printing Office.

Hogan, E.A., & Smith, M.T. (1987). *Alphabet and dictionary skills guide.* Cambridge, MA: Educators Publishing Service.

Juel, C. (1988). Learning to read and write: A longitudinal study of fifty-four children from first through fourth grade. *Journal of Educational Psychology, 80,* 437–447.

LaBerge, D., & Samuels, S.J. (1974). Toward a theory of automatic information processing in reading. *Cognitive Psychology, 6,* 293–323.

Liberman, I.Y., & Liberman, A.M. (1990). Whole language vs. code emphasis: Underlying assumptions and their implications for reading instruction. *Annals of Dyslexia, 40,* 51–76.

Liberman, I.Y., Shankweiler, D., Orlando, C., Harris, H.S., & Berti, F.B. (1971). Letter confusion and reversals of sequence in the beginning reader: Implications for Orton's theory of developmental dyslexia. *Cortex, 7,* 127–142.

Logan, R.K. (1986). *The alphabet effect.* New York: William Morrow and Co.

Neuhaus Education Center. (1998). *Basic language skills: Book 1.* Bellaire, TX: Author.

Obregón, M. (1994). *Exploring naming timing patterns by dyslexic and normal readers on the serial RAN task.* Unpublished master's thesis, Tufts University, Boston.

Perfetti, C.A. (1985). *Reading ability.* New York: Oxford University Press.

Seidenberg, M.S., & McClelland, J.L. (1989). A distributed, developmental model of word recognition and naming. *Psychological Review, 96,* 523–568.

Shankweiler, D., & Liberman, I.Y. (1972). Misreading: A search for causes. In J.F. Kavanagh & I.G. Mattingly (Eds.), *Language by ear and by eye* (pp. 293–317). Cambridge: The MIT Press.

Share, D.L., Jorm, A.F., Maclean, R., & Matthews, R. (1984). Sources of individual differences in reading acquisition. *Journal of Educational Psychology, 76,* 1309–1324.

Stanovich, K.E. (1986). Matthew effects in reading: Some consequences of individual differences in the acquisition of literacy. *Reading Research Quarterly, 21,* 360–406.

Sulzby, E. (1983). A commentary on Ehri's critique of five studies related to letter-name knowledge and learning to read: Broadening the question. In L.M. Gentile, M.L. Kamil, & J.S. Blanchard (Eds.), *Reading research revisited* (pp. 155–161). Columbus, OH: Charles E. Merrill.

Vellutino, F.R. (1979). *Dyslexia: Theory and research.* Cambridge: The MIT Press.

Vellutino, F.R. (1980). Dyslexia—perceptual deficiency or perceptual inefficiency? In J.F. Kavanagh & R.L. Venezky (Eds.), *Orthography, reading, and dyslexia* (pp. 251–270). Baltimore: University Park Press.

Vellutino, F.R., Smith, H., Steger, J.A., & Kaman, M. (1975). Reading disability: Age differences and the perceptual deficit hypothesis. *Child Development, 46,* 487–493.

Walsh, D.J., Price, G.G., & Gillingham, M.G. (1988). The critical but transitory importance of letter naming. *Reading Research Quarterly, 23,* 108–122.

Wolf, M. (1997). A provisional, integrative account of phonological and naming-speed deficits in dyslexia: Implications for diagnosis and intervention. In B. Blachman (Ed.), *Foundation of reading acquisition and dyslexia: Implications for early intervention* (pp. 67–92). Mahwah, NJ: Lawrence Erlbaum Associates.

Wolf, M., Bally, H., & Morris, R. (1986). Automaticity, retrieval processes, and reading: A longitudinal study in average and impaired readers. *Child Development, 57,* 988–1000.

Wolf, M., & Obregón, M. (1992). Early naming deficits, developmental dyslexia, and a specific deficit hypothesis. *Brain and Language, 42,* 219–247.

Wolf, M., & Obregón, M. (1997). The "double-deficit" hypothesis: Implications for diagnosis and practice in reading disabilities. In L. Putnam (Ed.), *Readings on language and literacy* (pp. 177–209). Cambridge, MA: Brookline Books.

5

A Short History of the English Language

Marcia K. Henry

This chapter presents a short history of written English and introduces the reader to the structure of English orthography, the English spelling system. English is a dynamic language, and numerous historical forces shaped the development of written English. The historical perspective is of primary importance to the study of word formation in English. As Nist (1966) and Venezky (1970) have asserted, English orthography begins to make sense when understood from an historical perspective.

An understanding of the historical forces that influenced written English along with a grasp of the structure of the English spelling system provides teachers and their students with a logical basis for the study of English. Students who recognize letter–sound correspondences, **syllable patterns,** and morpheme patterns in words of Anglo-Saxon, Latin, and Greek origin have the strategies necessary to read and spell unfamiliar words. Students begin by learning phonics, the basic orthographic patterns, and their related sounds and then learn **syllable types** and patterns of **syllable division.** They move on to learn Latin and Greek prefixes (beginnings), roots, and suffixes (endings), which are the morpheme, or meaning, units in English. The importance of teaching more than basic phonics cannot be stressed enough. Brown (1947) found that 80% of English words borrowed from other languages came from Latin and Greek. Therefore, teaching relatively few Latin and Greek roots provides students with the key to unlocking hundreds of thousands of words!

HISTORY AND ENGLISH ORTHOGRAPHY

The original inhabitants of the British Isles, the Celts, spoke a language of the **Indo-European** family. They were conquered by Julius Caesar in 54 B.C. The Romans departed to return almost a century later and then stayed for nearly 400 years. Figure 5.1 depicts a time line of important events contributing to the changes in written English over the centuries.

During the 5th century A.D., Germanic groups—the Jutes, Saxons, and Angles—began to settle in different parts of England. They adopted "neither the language nor the religions of their new home" (Balmuth, 1992, p. 75). Rather, Anglo-

Pre-English Period	55 B.C.	The ancient Britons (Celts) defend their land from Julius Caesar and are defeated.
	A.D. 50	Roman Emperor Claudius I colonizes Britain; Celtic and Latin languages coexist.
Period of Old English	450	Romans leave Britain; Teutonic tribes (Jutes, Angles, and Saxons) invade.
	600	England divides into seven kingdoms; Northumbria emerges as the dominant Christian kingdom affiliated with the Roman church.
	700	Christian poetry is exemplified in *Beowulf.*
	800	The Danes (Norsemen) invade England and are defeated by King Alfred in 878.
	900	Old English reaches its literary peak under the West Saxon kings.
	1000	The Danes successfully invade Britain, yet the Anglo-Saxon language continues its dominant role.
	1066	William the Conqueror invades; Norman French becomes the official language of the state, but English remains the language of the people.
Period of Middle English	1350	Edward III takes control; English again becomes the official language of the state.
	1400	Geoffrey Chaucer dies, leaving his classic *The Canterbury Tales.*
	1420	Henry V becomes the first English king to write in Middle English.
	1476	The Renaissance reaches England. English borrows from Latin and Greek; William Caxton sets up his printing press. The English language undergoes a change in pronunciation (the Great Vowel Shift).
Period of Modern English	1603	Queen Elizabeth I and William Shakespeare write in Early Modern English.
	1755	Samuel Johnson compiles the first comprehensive dictionary in English.
	1828	Noah Webster compiles a dictionary of American English.
	1857	The *Oxford English Dictionary* is created and later published in 1927.

Figure 5.1. Events related to development of the English language. (From Henderson, E., *Teaching spelling,* Second Edition. Copyright 1990 by Houghton Mifflin Company. Adapted with permission.)

Saxon became the dominant language, and the vocabulary stressed the people, objects, and events of daily life.

Five major factors shaped the English language during the period of Old English: Teutonic invasion and settlement; the Christianizing of Britain; the creation of a national English culture; Danish–English warfare, political adjustment, and cultural assimilation; and the decline of Old English as a result of the Norman Conquest (Nist, 1966). During this time Germanic, Celtic, Latin, Greek, Anglo-Saxon, Scandinavian, and French words entered Old English. At the end of the period, "that language was no longer the basically Teutonic and highly inflected Old English but the hybrid-becoming, Romance-importing, and inflection-dropping Middle English" (Nist, 1966, p. 107).

The period of Middle English heralded great changes in the native tongue of Britain. It is believed that in the beginning stages, Early Middle English sounded much like present-day German. Claiborne estimated that after the Norman Conquest "more than ten thousand French words passed into the English vocabulary, of which 75 percent are still in use" (1983, p. 112). Anglo-French compounds (e.g., *gentlewomen, gentlemen; faithful, faithfulness*) appeared during this period.

A renewed Latin influence penetrated the language during the period of Mature Middle English in the 14th and 15th centuries, about 115 years in the history of the language. This was the time of the Renaissance, which brought a wave of cultural advancement. Hanna, Hodges, and Hanna observed that "the Latin vocabulary was felt to be more stable and polished and more capable of conveying both abstract and humanistic ideas than was a fledgling language such as English. Further, Latin was something of a lingua franca that leaped across geographical and political boundaries" (1971, p. 47). Many of the words we use today are borrowed from the Latin of this period, including *index, library, medicine,* and *instant.* During the time of Mature Middle English, Latin affixes entered the language in great numbers. Prefixes (e.g., *ad-, pro-*) and suffixes (e.g., *-ent, -al, -ion*) were added to word roots to form words such as *adjacent, prosecution,* and *rational* (Claiborne, 1983).

During the period of Late Middle English (1422–1489), the written word grew in importance. Dutch pressman William Caxton introduced the printing press to England and printed books using the English spoken in London by the well-to-do. Many spelling conventions were set into place at this time, and even more of English orthography was set during the period of Early Modern English (1500–1650).

During the period of Late Middle English and Early Modern English, the sound patterns, especially the vowel sounds, of the language underwent changes. Nist commented that "the changes in the pronunciation from the Mature Middle English of Chaucer to the Early Modern English of Shakespeare, insofar as these tense vowels were concerned, were so dramatic that Jespersen has named their phonemic displacement the Great Vowel Shift" (1966, p. 221; see also Jespersen, 1971). The vowel shift resulted in certain vowel sounds' being articulated in new positions and assured a sharp separation between phonology and spelling. For example, in Chaucer's time, the vowel sound in *bide* was pronounced as we pronounce /ē/ in *bee,* but in Shakespeare's time it shifted to /ā/ as in *bay.* This shift caused problems for spellers "because stabilized spellings now came to represent different sounds" (Hanna et al., 1971, p. 49). Changes continued through the period of Late Modern English to reach the pronunciation of today.

Also during the English Renaissance, Greek- and Romance-based words enriched English enormously. *Romance* refers to the Latin-based languages of Romania, Spain, Italy, Portugal, and France. During the periods of Authoritarian English (1650–1800) and Mature Modern English (1800–1920), vocabulary borrowed from these origins continued to expand, especially in the form of scientific terms that used Greek and Latin morphemes.

English, then, is a **polyglot** language, and Anglo-Saxon, Latin, Greek, and the Romance languages all played a role in establishing the words as they are spoken and written today (Balmuth, 1992; Hanna et al., 1971; Nist, 1966). Claiborne noted,

> The truth is that if borrowing foreign words could destroy a language, English would be dead (borrowed from Old Norse), deceased (from French), defunct (from Latin) and kaput (from German). When it comes to borrowing, English excels (from Latin), surpasses (from French) and eclipses (from Greek) any other tongue, past or present. (1983, p. 4)

FRAMEWORK FOR CURRICULUM AND INSTRUCTION

One framework for teaching a decoding and spelling curriculum is based on word origin and word structure (Henry, 1988a, 1988b). The three origin languages most influential to English are Anglo-Saxon, Latin, and Greek. The major structural categories are letter–sound correspondences, syllables, and morphemes. By teaching all of the components of this framework, teachers can ensure that their students will learn the primary patterns found in English words. Teachers are encouraged to use a multisensory approach for teaching each component so that students will simultaneously link the visual symbol with its corresponding sound and form the pattern accurately. (See Chapter 1 for information on the basic principles of multisensory instruction.)

Teachers who understand the historical origins of words enhance their presentation of reading instruction. Teaching phonics offers a strategy for decoding and spelling that works when the letter–sound correspondence system carries all of the demands of word analysis. When students do not recognize syllabic and morphological patterns, however, they are constrained from using clues to identify long, unfamiliar words. Unfortunately, most decoding instruction largely neglects the instruction of syllable and morpheme patterns, perhaps because these techniques are only useful for the longer words found in literature and subject-matter text beyond second or third grade, at which point decoding instruction becomes virtually nonexistent in most schools.

Students in fourth grade and beyond are expected to read polysyllabic words (words of more than one syllable). Those who know how to use rules for syllable division exhibit strategies for word analysis beyond the use of letter–sound correspondences. Students who recognize meaningful morpheme patterns incorporate still another strategy in word analysis. Yet many students in upper elementary school, secondary school, and adult literacy programs lack the strategies necessary to read and spell longer words. By learning basic syllable and morpheme patterns, they will be able to analyze numerous multisyllabic words of Latin and Greek origin.

Table 5.1 represents the categories in the word origin and word structure framework. Each entry in the matrix corresponds to either Anglo-Saxon–, Latin–,

Table 5.1 Framework for decoding curriculum and instruction: Word-origin by word-structure matrix.

Origin language	Letter–sound correspondences	Syllables	Morphemes
Anglo-Saxon	**Consonants** Single letters Blends Digraphs ___ bid step that **Vowels** Short/long -r Digraphs ___ mad/made barn boat	Closed: băt Open: clōver *Silent e*: māde r-controlled: barn Consonant-*le:* tumble	Compound ___ hardware shipyard Affix ___ like time dislike timely disliking untimely
Latin	Same as Anglo-Saxon but few vowel digraphs Also, use of schwa (ə) as in direction spatial excellent	Closed: spĕct Silent e: scrībe r-controlled: port, form	Affix ___ construction erupting conductor
Greek	Same as Anglo-Saxon but few vowel digraphs Also, unique letter–sound correspondences as in phonograph scholar sympathy	Closed: grăph Open: phōtō Unstable digraph: crēāte	Compound ___ microscope chloroplast physiology

or Greek-based words that are related to letter–sound correspondences, syllables, or morphemes. In the following sections, the major components of the framework are discussed.

ANGLO-SAXON LAYER OF LANGUAGE

Words of Anglo-Saxon origin are characterized as the common, everyday, down-to-earth words that are used frequently in ordinary situations. Nist provided a clever example of Anglo-Saxon words:

> English remains preeminently Anglo-Saxon at its core: in the suprasegmentals of its stress, pitch, and juncture patterns and in its vocabulary. No matter whether a man is American, British, Canadian, Australian, New Zealander, or South African, he still *loves his mother, father, brother, sister, wife, son and daughter; lifts his hand to his head, his cup to his mouth, his eye to heaven and his heart to God; hates his foes, likes his friends, kisses his kin and buries his dead; draws his breath, eats his bread, drinks his water, stands his watch, wipes his sweat, feels his sorrow, weeps his tears and sheds his blood; and all these things he thinks about and calls both good and bad.* (1966, p. 9)

As the Nist example shows, most words of Anglo-Saxon origin consist of one syllable and represent everyday objects, activities, and events. Although consonant letters are fairly regular (i.e., each letter has one sound), vowels are more problematic. Words that are learned early in school are often irregular, and may cause difficulty for students with specific reading disabilities. The spellings of these "weird" or "outlaw" words, such as *rough, does, only, eye, laugh, blood,* and *said,* must be memorized by students because the vowels do not carry the normal "short" or "long" sound. Knowledge of letter–sound correspondences are not much help in either the reading or the spelling of these words.

Letter–Sound Correspondences

Letter–sound correspondences the consonant and vowel letters (graphemes) and their corresponding sounds (phonemes); Anglo-Saxon letter–sound correspondences are the first symbol–sound relationships taught to children learning to read and spell. Consonant letters of the alphabet represent the speech sounds produced by a partial or complete obstruction of the air stream (e.g., *b, c, d, f, m, p, t*). The consonant pairs *gn, kn,* and *wr* are Anglo-Saxon forms. Vowel letters (i.e., *a, e, i, o, u,* and sometimes *y* and *w*) represent the sounds that are created by the relatively free passage of breath through the larynx and oral cavity.

Liberman and her colleagues (Liberman, 1973; Liberman & Liberman, 1990; Liberman & Shankweiler, 1985, 1991; Liberman, Shankweiler, Fischer, & Carter, 1974) noted that children's phonological awareness, or understanding of the role that sounds play in the English language, is extremely important in learning to read. Prior to learning letter–sound correspondences, often called phonics, children benefit from training in phonological awareness tasks such as rhyming, segmentation, and blending (see Chapter 3).

Balmuth (1992), along with Adams (1990), Chall (1983), Chall and Popp (1996), and Richardson (1989), provided insights on the importance of phonics in education since the 19th century. Chall and Popp differentiated between "synthetic" and "analytic" phonics:

> Individual letter–sound correspondences may be taught and then blended to form words (synthetic), or the correspondences may be taught by separating the sounds and letters in known words (analytic). In both cases, some instruction and practice [are] usually given in blending sounds to form words. (p. 6)

When learning phonics, students must link the graphemes and phonemes of English. Table 5.2 represents the primary graphemes (letter configurations) that spell or correspond to each of the approximately 44 speech sounds, or phonemes. Teachers generally use dictionary markings as guides to pronunciation. Linguists and specialists in speech-language disorders tend to use symbols from the International Phonetic Alphabet (IPA). Both ways of marking pronunciation are shown in Table 5.2. (For further information on phonetics (the identification and description of the speech sounds) and specific articulation of sounds, see Chapter 1 of Moats (1995) as well as Chapter 2 in this book.)

Graphemes are organized either in consonant or in vowel patterns. Single-letter consonant spellings seldom vary; each letter stands for a specific sound. The letters *c* and *g,* however, have more than one possible pronunciation: a *hard* and *soft* sound. The letter *c* usually has the sound of /k/ as in *carrot* but becomes soft before *e, i,* and *y* as in *cell, city,* and *cypress.* Likewise, the *g* in *go* or *gas* is hard, whereas *g* before *e, i,* and *y* is hard as in *gem, ginger,* and *Gypsy.* The letter *s* is usually pronounced as /s/ as in *snake*, but sometimes has the /z/ sound as in *dogs*. Note that *x* is omitted from Table 5.2; it represents two possible sounds. A final *x* makes the sound of /ks/ as in *box* but makes the sound of /z/ at the beginning of some words, such as *Xerox*.

Consonant blends (sometimes called consonant clusters), made up of two or three adjacent consonants that retain their individual sounds in a syllable, are common (e.g., *bl* and *mp* in *blimp*; *spl* and *nt* in *splint*). In contrast to blends, *consonant digraphs*, which evolved in Middle English times, often add an *h* to a consonant to form a new sound (e.g., *sh* in *ship*, *ch* in *chump*, *th* in *this*, *wh* in *what*).

Vowel sounds tend to be more difficult to learn than consonant sounds. Single vowels are generally either *short* or *long*. Words often contain clues, referred to as *markers*, which indicate whether the short or long sound should be used. A vowel with a consonant after it in the same syllable carries the short sound (e.g., *cat, let, fit, fox, fun*). In contrast, a vowel at the end of a syllable becomes long or "says its own name" (e.g., *go, baby, pilot*). A silent *e* at the end of a word as in *shape* and *vote* also signals that the word has a long vowel sound. A doubled consonant as in *pinning* and *cutter* marks that the preceding vowel has a short sound. The

Table 5.2.   English spelling correspondences with dictionary (phonic) and phonetic symbols

Consonant graphemes	Examples	American Heritage Dictionary (1991)	International Phonetic Alphabet (IPA)
b	bib	b	b
d	deed	d	d
f, ph, gh	fife, phone, laugh	f	f
g	gag	g	g
h	hat	h	h
j, g, dge	judge, ginger	j	dʒ
k, c, -ck, ch, -que	kick, cat, chorus, unique	k	k
l, -le	lit, needle	l	l, ļ
m	mom	m	m
n	no, sudden	n	n, ņ
p	pop	p	p
r	roar	r	r
s, c	sauce	s	s
t	tot	t	t
v	valve	v	v
w	with	w	w
y	yes	y	j
z, s	zebra, hoses	z	z
-ng	thing	ng	ŋ
ch	church	ch	tʃ
sh	ship	sh	ʃ
th	thin	th	θ
~~th~~	that	*th*	ð
wh	when	hw	hw (ʍ)
si, su, z, ge	vision, treasure, azure, garage	zh	ʒ

(continued)

Table 5.2.   *(continued)*

Vowel graphemes	Examples	*American Heritage Dictionary* (1991)	International Phonetic Alphabet (IPA)
a	pat	ă	æ
a, a-consonant-e, ai, ay, ei, eigh, ey	baby, made, pail, pay, veil, eight, they	ā	e
e	pet	ĕ	ɛ
e, e-consonant-e, ee, ea, ie, y, ey	me, scheme, greet, seat, thief, lady, alley	ē	i
i	bit	ĭ	ɪ
i, i-consonant-e, igh, ie, y,	hi, kite, fight, pie, sky	ī	aɪ
o	hot	ŏ	a
o, o-consonant-e, oa, ow, oe	go, vote, boat, grow, toe	ō	o
u	cut	ŭ	ʌ
a	father	a'	ɑ, a
a, e, i, o, u	alone, item, credible, gallop, circus	ə	ə
au, aw	fault, claw	ô	ɔ
ew, oo	chew, room	o͞o	u
oo	book	o͝o	ʊ
oi, oy	coin, toy	oi	ɔj
ou, ow	cloud, clown	ou	aʊ
ar	car	är	
are	care	âr	ɛr, er
er, ir, ur, or, ear	fern, bird, burn, word, heard	ûr	ɜr
er	butter	ər	ɚ
ier, eer	pier, deer	ir	ɪr, ir

doubled consonant cancels the long-vowel signal that would otherwise be given by the *i* in *ing* and the *e* in *er*.

Students will also read words with a vowel plus *r* or *l* . The vowel sounds are often neither short nor long. These patterns are best taught as combinations, such as *ar* in *star, or* in *corn, er* in *fern, ir* in *bird, ur* in *church*, and *al* in *falter*. (See Appendix A at the end of this chapter for an example of a lesson contrasting *ar* and *or* patterns.)

Vowel digraphs consist of two adjacent vowels occurring in words of Anglo-Saxon origin (e.g., *oa, ee, oi, ou, au*). A vowel digraph usually occurs in the middle of a word. Vowel digraphs are often difficult for students to acquire because of their variability and because of interference from previously learned associations. They can be divided into two sets—those that are fairly consistently linked to a single sound (e.g., *ee, oa, oi, oy*) and those that may have either of two pronunciations (e.g., *ea* in *bead* or *bread, ow* in *show* or *cow*). Balmuth provided the historical origins of vowel digraphs and **diphthongs** and noted that during Middle English times diphthongs were "especially varied in spelling because of the confusions that resulted from the separation of the written *i* and *y* and the introduction of the *w* and other French spelling conventions" (1992, p. 102). (It should be noted that linguists differentiate between the terms *vowel digraph* and *diphthong*. Both contain two adjacent vowels in the same syllable. Diphthongs contain two vowels with a slide or a shift in the middle; they include *oi/oy* and *ou/ow*.)

By the end of the second grade, children should master all of the common letter–sound correspondences and spelling rules relating to these patterns. For example, children need to learn when to use *-ck* rather than *-k* at the end of a one-syllable word. The appendixes at the end of this chapter provide examples of numerous opportunities for reading and writing words containing new target patterns.

Syllables

Syllables are units of spoken language consisting of a single, uninterrupted impulse of voice formed by a vowel or vowel digraph alone or with one or more consonants. Anglo-Saxon–based words have a variety of syllable patterns. Students first learn that each syllable must have a vowel. Children generally have less difficulty with hearing syllables in words than with recognizing written syllables (Balmuth, 1992; Groff, 1971). Therefore, teachers often begin by having children say their own names and counting the number of syllables. Students also begin to listen for accent or stress in words of more than one syllable. Anglo-Saxon–based words (e.g., *sleep, like, time*) tend to retain the accent when affixes are added (e.g., *asleep, likely, timeless*).

Groff (1971) emphasized that syllables are not units of writing, grammar, or structure. He noted that the boundaries of syllables rather than the number of syllables in a word cause difficulty in their analysis. He made the distinction between how linguists divide words based on morphemic boundaries and how dictionaries divide words based on sounds. For example, linguists may prefer to divide the word *disruptive* as dis•rupt•ive (prefix, root, and suffix), whereas dictionaries usually divide the word as dis•rup•tive. Groff wondered whether teaching syllable division is an important part of teaching reading.

Although this argument continues, it is useful for teachers to know the six major syllable types and the predominant syllable-division patterns because children will read multisyllabic words in the primary grades and will find syllable division useful in hyphenating words. The major types of syllables are 1) **closed,** 2) **vowel-consonant-*e*,** 3) **open,** 4) **vowel pair,** 5) **consonant-*le*,** and 6) *r*-**controlled** (see Moats, 1995; Steere, Peck, & Kahn, 1971).

Teachers introduce closed syllables first. In these syllables, the single vowel has a consonant after it and makes a short vowel sound (e.g., *map, sit, cub, stop, bed*). The final *e* in a vowel-consonant-*e* (VCE) syllable makes the vowel long (e.g., *made, time, cute, vote, Pete*). An open syllable contains a vowel at the end of the syllable, and the vowel usually has a long sound. Stanback (1992) found that closed syllables alone make up 43% of syllables in English words. Open syllables and closed syllables together account for almost 75% of English syllables. A vowel pair (or vowel team) syllable contains two adjacent vowels as in *rain, green, coil,* and *pause.* Children learn the long, short, or diphthong sound of each pattern. A syllable ending in *-le* is usually preceded by a consonant that is part of that syllable. For example, *bugle* has a long *u* because the *gle* stays together and makes *bu* a long syllable. *Tumble,* in contrast, contains *tum* and *ble; tum* is a closed syllable. *Little* requires two *t*'s to keep the *i* in *lit* short. As discussed previously, *r*-controlled vowels often lose their identity as long or short and are coarticulated with the *r* as in *star, corn, fern, church,* and *firm.*

Students also need to learn some common rules for syllable division so that multisyllabic words are easier to read and spell. By understanding and practicing the various syllable types in **monosyllables** first, readers will recognize these common syllable types as they learn to divide words into syllables. Understanding how to manage the vowel sounds gives readers an advantage and a more productive grasp of syllable-division rules. Readers may recognize vowel-consonant-consonant-vowel (VC | CV) patterns and other letter combinations (V | CV and VC | CCV) patterns in words such as *napkin, clover,* and *instead.* These are useful separations to know when analyzing unfamiliar words (see Chapter 6).

Morphemes

A *morpheme* is the smallest meaningful linguistic unit. Prefixes (beginnings), suffixes (endings), and roots are the morphemes that are helpful to students learning to read and write because they appear in literally hundreds of thousands of words (Brown, 1947; Henry, 1993).

Anglo-Saxon morphemes are found in both compound (e.g., *football, blackboard*) and affixed words (e.g., *lovely, timeless*). These words tend to be simple because they contain regular orthographic features. Compound words generally comprise two short words joined together to form new, **meaning-based words** (e.g., *blackboard* suggests a black board, *football* refers to a ball for kicking). For example, computer technology is the impetus for many new compound words, such as *software* and *shareware.*

Words can also be expanded by affixing prefixes and suffixes to the base word. These **base words,** or **free morphemes,** can stand alone as words, such as *like* or *hope.* Morpheme affixes have two forms. Inflectional morphemes indicate grammatical features such as number, person, tense, or the comparative forms (e.g., *dog, dogs; wait, waits; walk, walked; small, smaller*). Derivational morphemes, in contrast, change one part of speech to another, chiefly by adding affixes to root words (e.g., *hope, hopeless, hopelessly*). (See Chapter 2 for more on morphemes.)

Students begin learning morpheme patterns by adding suffixes to words requiring no change in the base form (e.g., *help, helpless; time, untimely*). Soon after that they must learn suffix addition rules that affect some base words, such as the rule about when to drop a final *e* or change *y* to *i.*

LATIN LAYER OF LANGUAGE

The Latin layer of the English language consists of words used in more formal settings. Latin-based words, including Romance-based words, are often found in the literature, social studies, and science texts in upper elementary school and later grades.

Letter–Sound Correspondences

Because Latin-based words are longer than Anglo-Saxon–based words, many students expect them to be more complex. Yet, in most cases the words follow simple letter–sound correspondences. Single consonants are identical to those found in Anglo-Saxon–based words, but words of Latin origin contain fewer vowel digraphs. Most Latin roots contain short vowels as in *dict, rupt, script, struct, tract, tens, pend,* and *duct.* The consonant combination *ct* is a signpost for words of Latin origin.

Latin-based digraphs generally appear in suffixes such as *-ion, -ian, -ient,* and *-ial.* When a vowel digraph comes after the letters *c, s,* and *t,* it combines with those letters as the /sh/ sound as in *nation, partial, social,* and *admission* (*-sion* is also pronounced as /zhən/ in words such as *erosion* and *invasion.*)

The schwa (/ə/), or unstressed vowel sound, is often found in words of Latin origin in the unaccented prefixes and/or suffixes and is discussed later in this chapter.

Syllables

The stress patterns in Latin-based words are fairly complex. The schwa (ə) is common in longer words of Latin origin such as *excellent* and *direction.* When one pronounces *excellent,* for example, stress occurs on the first syllable so the initial *e* receives the regular short sound. The following two *e's,* appearing in unstressed syllables, have the schwa sound (/ə/). Listening for the unstressed vowels in open and closed syllables is an advanced skill that students with reading difficulties need to learn. Students who can discover the base word (e.g., *excel*) often will be able to spell the longer word.

Morphemes

Although Anglo-Saxon base words may both compound and become affixed, Latin roots may only become affixed. Nist provided another key example: "So great, in fact, was the penetra*tion* of Latin *af*fixing during the Renais*sance* that it quite *un*did the Anglo-Saxon habit of *com*pounding as the leading means of word form*ation* in English" (1966, p. 11). Words of Latin origin also become affixed with the addition of a prefix and/or a suffix to the root, which rarely stands alone (e.g., *rupt, interrupt; mit, transmitting; vent, prevent*). For example, the prefix *in-* can be added to the bound morpheme *spect* to get *inspect,* and the suffix *-ion* can be added to get *inspection.* (*Note:* Some sources, such as Barnhart, 1988; Gillingham & Stillman, 1997; and *Webster's New Unabridged Dictionary,* 1983, explain *-tion* and *-cian* as noun suffixes. Others teach only *-ion* and *-ian* as suffixes added to roots such as *invent* and *music,* respectively.)

The final consonant of a Latin prefix often changes based on the beginning letter of the root. For example, the prefix *in-* changes to *il-* before roots beginning with *l* (e.g., *illegal, illicit*), to *ir-* before roots beginning with *r* (e.g., *irregular*), and to *im-* before roots beginning with *m, b,* and *p* (e.g., *immobile, imbalance, important*). These **"chameleon" prefixes** are found in several forms (see Henry & Redding, 1996).

Latin word roots form the basis of hundreds of thousands of words (Brown, 1947; Henry, 1993). These roots are useful not only for decoding and spelling words but also for enhancing vocabulary as well. Students can readily observe the prefixes, roots, and suffixes in such words as *prediction, incredible, extracting,* and *reconstructionist.*

Although most of the words with Latin roots follow regular letter–sound correspondences, some do not. *Morphophonemic relations* are the conditions in which certain morphemes keep their written spelling when affixes are added although their phonemic forms change. This concept provides students with a logical reason for many English spellings. For example, in *knowledge,* the morpheme *know* is pronounced differently than the base word *know*. The meaning of *knowledge*, however, is based on the base word *know*. Balmuth noted that

> It can be helpful to readers when the same spelling is kept for the same morpheme, despite variations in pronunciation. Such spellings supply clues to the meanings of words, clues that would be lost if the words were spelled phonemically, as, for example, if *know* and *knowledge* were spelled *noe* and *nollij* in a hypothetical phonemic system. (1992, p. 207)

GREEK LAYER OF LANGUAGE

Greek words, too, entered English by the thousands during the Renaissance to meet the needs of scholars and scientists. In addition, Bodmer noted that "the terminology of modern science, especially in *aeronautics, biochemistry, chemotherapy,* and *genetics,*" (1944, p. 246) is formed from Greek. Greek roots are often called **combining forms** and compound to form words. Words of Greek origin appear largely in science textbooks (e.g., *microscope, hemisphere, physiology*). The following passage from a middle school science text (Cooper, Blackwood, Boeschen, Giddings, & Carin, 1985, p. 20) shows not only how short words of Anglo-Saxon origin mix with longer Romance words but also how the scientific terminology is couched in words of Greek origin.

> Suppose you could examine a green part of a plant under the *microscope*. What would you see? Here are some cells from the green part of a plant. The cells have small green bodies shaped like footballs. They give the plant its green color. They are called *chloroplasts*. A single green plant cell looks like this. *Chloroplasts* are very important to a plant. As you know, plants make their own food. This food-making process is called *photosynthesis*. It is in these *chloroplasts* that *photosynthesis* takes place.

Letter–Sound Correspondences

Greek letter–sound correspondences are similar to those of Anglo-Saxon, but words of Greek origin often use the sounds of /k/, /f/, and /ĭ/ represented by *ch, ph,* and *y,* respectively, such as in *chlorophyll*. These peculiar consonant combinations were introduced by Latin scribes and make words of Greek origin easily recognizable (Bodmer, 1944). Less common Greek letter–sound correspondences, found in only a handful of words, include *mn* in mnemonic, *rh* in *rhododendron, pt* in *pterodactyl, pn* in *pneumonia,* and the more well-known *ps* in *psychology* and *psychiatry.*

Syllables

Syllable types most prevalent in Greek-based words are closed (CVC, as in *graph*) and open (CV, as in *photo*). In addition, a unique type of syllable can be found, that of adjacent vowels in separate syllables, as in *theatre, create,* and *theory*. These "unstable" digraphs appear in distinct syllables and therefore have distinct sounds.

Syllable division in words of Greek origin generally follows the rules given for Anglo-Saxon words, especially the rules for open syllables (e.g., *phono, photo, meter, polis*). For example, the letter *y* sounds like short *i* in closed syllables (e.g., *symphony, gymnasium*), and these syllables are divided after the consonant. The letter *y* sounds like long *i* in open syllables (e.g., *cyclone, gyroscope, hyperbole*), and these syllables are divided immediately after the *y*. Combining forms such as *semi, hemi*, and *micro* do not follow V I CV or VC I CV division. Students rarely need to depend on strategies for syllable division because they learn the patterns as wholes.

Morpheme Patterns

If a person recognizes relatively few Greek roots, then he or she can read and spell many thousands of words. As students learn the common Greek roots that hold specific meaning, such as *micro, scope, bio, graph, helio, meter, phono, photo, auto*, and *tele*, they begin to read, spell, and understand the meaning of words such as *microscope, telescope, phonoreception, telephoto, telescopic, photoheliograph, heliometer, biography*, and *autobiography*. Many Greek roots are often called prefixes because they appear at the beginning of words (e.g., *auto* in *autograph, hyper* in *hyperbole*, and *hemi* in *hemisphere*). Numeral prefixes such as *mono* (1), *di* (2), *tri* (3), *tetra* (4), *penta* (5), *hexa* (6), *hepta* (7), *octa* (8), *nona* (9), *deca* (10), *centi* (100), and *kilo* (1,000) become useful in the study of mathematics and geometry.

Ehrlich (1972); Fifer and Flowers (1989); Fry, Polk, and Fountoukidis (1996); Henry (1990); and Henry and Redding (1996) provided numerous resources for words containing both Latin- and Greek-based words. Specific instructional activities can be found in the last three sources. (See Appendixes B and C at the end of this chapter for examples of lessons for Latin and Greek morpheme patterns, respectively.)

CONCLUSION

Perfetti claimed that "only a reader with skilled decoding processes can be expected to have skilled comprehension processes" (1984, p. 43). When children are able to grasp words important to the gist of a story or to the meaning of text, their understanding will be enhanced.

Teachers who comprehend the origins of the English language along with the primary structural patterns within words can improve their assessment skills, enhance their understanding of reading and spelling curricula, communicate clearly about language issues, and effectively teach useful language strategies to their students. Influences on English orthography stem from the introduction of letters and words from diverse origins. When teachers and their students understand the historical basis and structure of written English, they can better understand the regularities as well as the very few irregularities in English words.

Young students will use these language strategies to decode and spell short, regular words as well as Anglo-Saxon compound words and words using common prefixes and suffixes. Older students and adult learners receiving instruction in more advanced language structure will focus on Latin and Greek roots and affixes.

Finally, students of all ages often greatly enjoy learning about the structure and origins of English words. Students who are learning English as a second language find that English is quite regular after all and is not a language of exceptions. Children with or without specific language disabilities benefit as they learn effective and efficient strategies to read and spell numerous words.

REFERENCES

Adams, M.J. (1990). *Beginning to read: Thinking and learning about print.* Cambridge: The MIT Press.

American heritage dictionary (2nd college ed.). (1991). Boston: Houghton Mifflin.

Balmuth, M. (1992). *The roots of phonics.* Timonium, MD: York Press.

Barnhart, R.K. (1988). *The Barnhart dictionary of etymology.* New York: H.W. Wilson Co.

Bodmer, F. (1944). *The loom of language.* New York: W.W. Norton.

Brown, J.I. (1947). Reading and vocabulary: 14 master words. In M.J. Herzberg (Ed.), *Word study, 1–4.* Springfield, MA: Merriam-Webster.

Chall, J.S. (1983). *Learning to read: The great debate revisited.* New York: McGraw-Hill.

Chall, J.S., & Popp, H.M. (1996). *Teaching and assessing phonics.* Cambridge, MA: Educators Publishing Service.

Claiborne, R. (1983). *Our marvelous native tongue.* New York: Times Books.

Cooper, E.K., Blackwood, P.E., Boeschen, J.A., Giddings, M.G., & Carin, A.A. (1985). *HBJ science* (purple ed.). Orlando, FL: Harcourt Brace & Co.

Ehrlich, I. (1972). *Instant vocabulary.* New York: Pocket Books.

Fifer, N., & Flowers, N. (1989). *Vocabulary from classical roots.* Cambridge, MA: Educators Publishing Service.

Fry, E.B., Polk, J.D., & Fountoukidis, D.L. (1996). *The reading teacher's new book of lists* (3rd ed.). Upper Saddle River, NJ: Prentice-Hall.

Gillingham, A., & Stillman, B.W. (1997). *Remedial training for children with specific disability in reading, spelling and penmanship* (8th ed.). Cambridge, MA: Educators Publishing Service.

Groff, P. (1971). *The syllable: Its nature and pedagogical usefulness.* Portland, OR: Northwest Regional Educational Laboratory.

Hanna, P.R., Hodges, R.E., & Hanna, J.S. (1971). *Spelling: Structure and strategies.* Boston: Houghton Mifflin.

Henderson, E.H. (1990). *Teaching spelling* (2nd ed.). Boston: Houghton Mifflin.

Henry, M.K. (1988a). Beyond phonics: Integrated decoding and spelling instruction based on word origin and structure. *Annals of Dyslexia, 38,* 259–275.

Henry, M.K. (1988b). Understanding English orthography: Assessment and instruction for decoding and spelling (Doctoral dissertation, Stanford University, 1988). *Dissertation Abstracts International, 48,* 2841-A.

Henry, M.K. (1990). *WORDS: Integrated decoding and spelling instruction based on word origin and word structure.* Austin, TX: PRO-ED.

Henry, M.K. (1993). Morphological structure: Latin and Greek roots and affixes as upper grade code strategies. *Reading and Writing, 5*(2), 227–241.

Henry, M.K., & Redding, N.C. (1996). *Patterns for success in reading and spelling.* Austin, TX: PRO-ED.

Jespersen, O. (1971). *Growth and structure of the English language.* New York: The Free Press.

Liberman, I.Y. (1973). Segmentation of the spoken word and reading acquisition. *Bulletin of the Orton Society, 23,* 65–77.

Liberman, I.Y., & Liberman, A.M. (1990). Whole language vs. code emphasis: Underlying assumptions and their implications for reading instruction. *Annals of Dyslexia, 40,* 51–78.

Liberman, I.Y., & Shankweiler, D. (1985). Phonology and the problems of learning to read and write. *Remedial and Special Education, 7,* 8–17.

Liberman, I.Y., & Shankweiler, D. (1991). Phonology and beginning reading: A tutorial. In L. Rieben & C.A. Perfetti (Eds.), *Learning to read: Basic research and its implications* (pp. 3–17). Mahwah, NJ: Lawrence Erlbaum Associates.

Liberman, I.Y., Shankweiler, D., Fischer, F.W., & Carter, B. (1974). Explicit syllable and phoneme segmentation in the young child. *Journal of Experimental Child Psychology, 18,* 201–212.

Moats, L.C. (1995). *Spelling: Development, disability, and instruction.* Timonium, MD: York Press.

Nist, J. (1966). *A structural history of English.* New York: St. Martin's Press.

Perfetti, C. (1984). Reading acquisition and beyond: Decoding includes cognition. *American Journal of Education, 93,* 40–60.

Richardson, S.O. (1989). Specific developmental dyslexia: Retrospective and prospective views. *Annals of Dyslexia, 39,* 3–23.

Stanback, M.L. (1992). Syllable and rime patterns for teaching reading: Analysis of a frequency-based vocabulary of

17,602 words. *Annals of Dyslexia*, 42, 196–221.

Steere, A., Peck, C.Z., & Kahn, L. (1971). *Solving language difficulties*. Cambridge, MA: Educators Publishing Service.

Venezky, R.L. (1970). *The structure of English orthography*. The Hague: Mouton.

Webster's new universal unabridged dictionary (2nd ed.). (1983). New York: Simon & Schuster.

Appendix A

Sample Lesson for Anglo-Saxon Letter–Sound Correspondences: *ar* and *or*

Opening: State that students will review the pattern *ar* and learn a new pattern, *or*.

Review: Have children write the pattern *ar* on their tablets and repeat the sound /ar/. Remind them that the letter *r* with a vowel before it often changes the vowel sound from its typical short or long sound. Ask students whether they remember any words that use the pattern *är* (as in *car*). As children generate words, write them on the chalkboard. Words could include the following:

car	harm	yard
par	harming	arch
jar	harmed	part
star	barn	tarts
scar	farm	partly
park	farmer	discard
lark	start	market
dark	starting	target
stark	started	tarnish
shark	charts	harmless
sharp	mark	harmful
march	marking	garden
starch	marked	harvest
harp	hard	alarm

After you write the words and add some of your own, have children read the words together. You may want to point out prefixes and suffixes if they have been included. Ask children to put their reading papers aside as you dictate a few of the words for spelling.

New: Write *or* on the board, and ask children whether they know what it says (*or* as in *corn*). Have children write *or* on their tablets, first tracing, then copying, then writing while carefully monitoring the letter formation. As children write the pattern four or five times, they repeat the sounds. Have children generate words containing *or*. Words might include the following:

corn	sport	horse
for	storm	order
fort	north	forget
port	scorch	hornet
sort	morn	sordid
pork	morning	record
stork	thorn	report
forth	shorn	border
snort	short	
form	porch	

Again, add words of your own, and have the children read the words. Dictate a few of the words for spelling.

Now ask children to take a piece of paper and fold it in half, lengthwise. Have them write *ar* in the left-hand column and *or* in the right-hand column. Dictate a number of *ar* and *or* words. Children must listen carefully to the vowel sound and spell words in the appropriate column.

Give students sentences containing *ar* and *or* words to read and spell. For example,

Please sort the cards.
They saw a shark jump in the storm.
He played many sports in the park.
The farmer planted corn on his farm.
She sat on the north side of the porch.
Her horse marched by the cars.

Closing: Review the two patterns emphasized in this lesson. Why are they important to learn?

(Adapted from Henry & Redding, 1996)

Appendix B

Sample Lesson for Latin Word Roots

Materials necessary: Students' word work writing book, paper, and pencil or pen

Opening: After an introduction to common Latin prefixes and suffixes, students are now ready to learn many of the common Latin roots. Ask students whether they know what a root word is (the main part of the word, to which prefixes and suffixes are added and which usually receives the accent or stress in Latin-based words). Tell them that roots are valuable not only as patterns for decoding and spelling but also as aids for learning new vocabulary to enhance reading, writing, listening, and speaking.

New: Begin by writing *rupt* on the chalkboard; students write *rupt* in their word booklets. Ask students to generate a number of words with *rupt* as the root. Write these words on the board. Words might include the following:

rupture	corrupt	interrupt
erupt	corruptly	interruption
eruption	bankrupt	interrupted
disrupt	abrupt	disruptive
disrupting	abruptly	irrupt

After students read all of the words that have been generated, see whether they can figure out the root's meaning (*to break*). Next, dictate some of the words for spelling.

Continue giving new Latin word roots in this manner. For each group of words, have students recognize the common roots. Have them note the placement of the root within the word (the beginning if there is no prefix, the end if there is no suffix, the middle if there are prefixes and suffixes). Show them how the root generally cannot stand alone—it is bound to the prefix and/or suffix.

Following are three Latin roots and only a few of the many words containing these roots. Additional suffixes may be added to most of the following words.

port (to carry)	*form* (to shape)	*tract* (to pull)
import	reform	tractor
export	deform	traction
portable	inform	attract
transport	transform	attraction
porter	transformer	attractive
transported	formula	contract
deport	informal	subtract
report	informative	retract
support	conform	protract
deportation	formal	distract
deportment	formality	distraction

Begin dictating sentences that contain the various roots that have been taught. For example,

The contract supported the bankruptcy report.
The exporter interrupted the attractive informant.

Continue teaching common roots such as *spect, scrib/script, stru/struct, dic/dict, flect/flex, mit/miss, cred, duce/duct, vert/vers, pend/pens, jac/jec/ject, tend/tens/tent*, and so forth.

Follow-up: Have students begin looking for Latin-based affixes and roots in their textbooks and in newspapers.

(Adapted from Henry, 1990; Henry & Redding, 1996)

Appendix C

Sample Lesson for Greek Word Roots (or Combining Forms)

Opening: Tell students that many of the Latin word roots just studied were actually borrowed from the Greeks. The Greek roots are often called *combining forms* because the two roots are of equal stress and importance and compound to form a word. Some of the forms appear only at the beginning of a word (and so may be considered prefixes), others come at the end (sometimes thought of as suffixes), and some forms can be used in either position. A few words contain three combining forms (e.g., *photoheliograph*).

Point out that although Greek-based words contain many of the same letter–sound correspondences found in Anglo-Saxon and Latin-based words, they also have unique letter–sound relationships (e.g., *ph* is pronounced as /f/ as in *photograph*; *ch* is pronounced as /k/ as in *chemist*; *y* is either a short or long *i* sound as in *physician* and *typhoon*.)

New: As you introduce the combining forms, have students carefully write each form, along with its meaning.

phon, phono (sound)   *tele* (distant)   *ology* (study; from *logos, logue*
auto (self)   *graph, gram*   [speech, word])
photo (light)   (written/drawn)

Students generate words containing the combining forms. Students read long lists of words containing the previous forms, such as the following:

phone	autograph	telethon
phonics	photograph	automation
phonogram	photography	automatic
phonology	photographer	automobile
phonological	photocopy	photology
phoneme	photoflash	telephotography
phonemic	photogram	monologue
phonograph	telecast	prologue
graphite	telegram	dialogue
graphics	telephone	epilogue
	telephoto	

Have students spell words from dictation. Have students read and spell sentences containing Latin- and Greek-based word parts. For example,

He collected several autographs from the conductors.
The TelePrompTer gave the television broadcaster visual messages.
Phonics instruction is useful in developing reading and writing skills.

Continue adding combining forms, including *micro, meter, therm, bio, scope, hydro, helio, biblio, crat/cracy, geo, metro, polis, dem, derm, hypo, chron, cycl, hyper, chrom,* and so forth.

Follow-up: Have students look for Greek-based words in science and mathematics textbooks.

(Adapted from Henry, 1990; Henry & Redding, 1996)

6

Teaching Reading

Accurate Decoding and Fluency

Suzanne Carreker

THE ROLE OF DECODING

The main goal of reading is comprehension. In order for a person to read, symbols on the printed page must be translated into spoken words (i.e., decoding), and meaning must be connected to those words. Reading is, according to Gough's Simple View of Reading (Gough & Tunmer, 1986; Hoover & Gough, 1990), the product of decoding and comprehension. These two components of reading work together in a delicate, interdependent balance. Inefficiency in one of the components can lead to overall reading failure. The reader who has difficulty with decoding will not be able to derive meaning from the text; conversely, the reader who has difficulty with specific levels of spoken language will receive little reward for his or her decoding efforts. A skilled reader needs to be competent in both decoding and comprehension (Calfee & Chambliss, 1988). For students to become fully literate, especially students with dyslexia, the two components of reading and all other elements of literacy instruction must be explicitly or directly taught in a balanced, comprehensive approach (Adams, 1990; Brady & Moats, 1997). The focus of this chapter is the explicit, systematic, and sequential instruction of decoding and fluency leading to efficient comprehension.

Decoding facilitates the reader's linkage of the printed word to the spoken word (Beck & Juel, 1995). A reader sees a page full of symbols. The reader's success in making sense of these symbols depends on how well he or she understands that the symbols represent spoken language. The extent to which the reader succeeds in establishing the relationship between the symbols and spoken language is dependent on his or her sensitivity to the internal sound structure of language (i.e., phonemic awareness; Adams, 1990). The reader must realize that spoken words have constituent sounds. In addition to recognizing that words have sounds, the reader must realize that printed words consist of letters that correspond to those speech sounds. These insights enable the reader to establish the alphabetic principle or code that is necessary for acquiring decoding skills. The importance of phonemic awareness (Adams, 1990; Bradley & Bryant, 1983; Goswami & Bryant, 1990; Liberman, Shankweiler, & Liberman, 1989; Stanovich, 1991) cannot be overemphasized as it provides the foundation for decoding, enabling the reader to unlock the printed word (see Chapter 3 for further discussion).

Decoding Strategies

Decoding requires knowledge of the phonemic, **graphophonemic,** syllabic, and morphemic structures of the language. The skilled reader uses a variety of strategies for translating the printed word into its spoken equivalent: sound–symbol correspondences, structural analysis, instant word recognition, and **contextual clues.** Although the primary focuses of this chapter are decoding and fluency, the crucial role of oral language in the reading process, as discussed in Chapter 2, must be stressed. Not only is oral language the foundation of comprehension, but it also greatly influences and assists the reader's efficient, effective use of the different decoding strategies.

The appreciation of the relationship between sounds and letters develops through phonemic awareness and instant letter recognition (i.e., **print awareness**; Adams, 1990). This understanding, in turn, develops *sound–symbol correspondences* (i.e., graphophonemic patterns) that enable the reader to sound out unfamiliar words. Initially, the beginning reader recognizes words by associating a word with some visually distinguishing characteristics (e.g., *dog* has a circle in the middle and a tail at the end) (Gough & Hillinger, 1980). As the reader encounters more and more words, the visual characteristics that make words distinguishable diminish. The reader begins to cue recognition by selecting some of the letters in a word, usually the first and last letters (Ehri, 1991). He or she is now better able to distinguish words, but accuracy is limited as many words share the same initial and final letters. When the reader attends to all of the letters, he or she can sound out the correct pronunciation of an unfamiliar word (Gough & Hillinger, 1980).

Both phonological awareness and sound–symbol correspondences are critical co-requisites in reading acquisition (Share & Stanovich, 1995). The reader needs an introduction to a few sound–symbol patterns to begin sounding out words. As the reader sounds out words, he or she reinforces the sound–symbol correspondences that have been introduced and establishes new ones (Adams, 1990). New sound–symbol correspondences are acquired through a "self-teaching mechanism" (Share & Stanovich, 1995, p. 17). By using known sound–symbol correspondences and phonological sensitivity, the reader approximates the pronunciation of the unknown word. This approximate pronunciation combined with available contextual clues enables the reader to determine the correct pronunciation and thereby provides the reader an opportunity to acquire knowledge of the sound–symbol correspondences within the unknown word. With repeated encounters, the reader builds an **orthographic memory** (i.e., memory for patterns of written language) of words so that eventually he or she instantly recognizes the words without having to sound them out (Adams, 1990).

In addition to letters, printed words have syllables (i.e., linguistic units) and morphemes (i.e., the smallest meaningful units of language). *Structural analysis*, the perception of orthographic syllables and morphemes, enables the reader to decode long, unfamiliar words and fosters a decoding process that is less cumbersome and more efficient than sounding out each letter. By recognizing different kinds of syllables, the reader can accurately predict the sound of the vowel in a syllable. With knowledge of morphemes, the reader focuses on units of letters that recur in words (e.g., the reader sees *tract* in *tractor, attractive,* and *subtraction*). The reader does not have to sound out every letter in an unknown word, only the letters that he or she does not recognize as part of a morpheme (Henry, 1988). Morphemes also give clues that allow the reader to infer the meanings of words (Henry, 1988; Moats, 1994). Orthographic patterns established through graphophonemic, syllabic, and morphemic awareness greatly economize the learning of a reader's lexicon (i.e., spoken and written word knowledge). Every word in the reader's lexicon, which may number 50,000 words by the time he or she reaches college, does not have to be stored in memory as 50,000 separate items, and the reader has a way of dealing with the words that he or she may use in speaking but has never seen in print before (Gough & Hillinger, 1980).

The ease and automaticity with which a skilled reader is able to read individual words is known as *instant word recognition*. Instant word recognition is achieved by repeated encounters with words and by **overlearning** (i.e., learning to automaticity) the orthographic and phonological patterns of the language. The ultimate goal of decoding instruction is the immediate, facile translation of a printed word into its spoken equivalent. Automaticity with this translation has a significant impact on the reader's attitude toward reading, comprehension, and overall reading success. Word recognition makes reading effortless, and reading becomes enjoyable. When reading is enjoyable, the reader will read more and, thereby, increase his or her word recognition skills (Beck & Juel, 1995; Juel, 1991). Inadequate word recognition has a negative effect on fluency and comprehension. The reader who does not attain automaticity in word recognition is said to be "glued" to the print (Chall, 1983, p. 17). The reader must focus all of his or her attention on sounding out words and is diverted away from figuring out the meaning (Adams, 1990; Liberman & Liberman, 1990). Evidence suggests that word recognition speed in first graders is predictive of later reading comprehension success (Beck & Juel, 1995; Juel, 1991).

The skilled reader uses *contextual clues* to predict unfamiliar words, but evidence suggests that context is not used as a primary strategy for word recognition (Juel, 1991; Share & Stanovich, 1995). First, the text may prove to be unreliable in yielding clues for accurate prediction. In most cases, context enables the reader to predict accurately one out of four words (Gough & Hillinger, 1980), and the content words that carry meaning are predictable only 10% of the time (Gough, 1983). Therefore, context is not useful when it is needed (Share & Stanovich, 1995). Second, eye-movement research shows that the eyes fixate on a majority of words in a text and do not skip over long words as a heavy reliance on context as a means for predicting words would suggest. Only the short, predictable words are skipped. The duration of a fixation depends on the length, frequency, and predictability of the word as the reader processes its component letters (Rayner & Pollatsek, 1986). The use of context facilitates the recognition of an unfamiliar word only when it is coupled with the reader's orthographic knowledge. When context clues are combined with knowledge of sound–symbol correspondences, the skilled reader should be able to identify words that are part of his or her listening vocabulary (Adams, 1990; Perfetti, 1985).

The skilled reader monitors his or her decoding using syntactic (i.e., sentence structure) and semantic (i.e., meaning of words) cues (Tunmer, Herriman, & Nesdale, 1988). With the use of such cues and sound–symbol correspondences, the reader is able to detect and self-correct a misread word in a sentence. This combination of knowledge used in detecting and self-correcting errors also builds sound–symbol correspondences and word recognition as the reader deals with unfamiliar words. It is a particularly beneficial combination with the reader's discovery of more complex sound–symbol relationships.

The reader does not have to learn all of the possible sound–symbol correspondences before learning about and using structural analysis, and word recognition does not occur only after the reader has learned everything about the letter–sound and structural patterns of the language. The reader's use of a given strategy depends on his or her available knowledge about language patterns, the length and complexity of the words, the frequency of encounters with the words, and/or the availability of useful contextual clues. These decoding strategies provide the reader a means of translating the printed word into spoken language. Decoding is not an end in itself but is a necessary step in getting to the heart of reading: comprehending meaning.

Dyslexic Reader's Difficulty with Decoding

There is considerable agreement that at-risk and dyslexic readers are unable to decode and recognize words automatically and fluently (Adams & Bruck, 1993; Perfetti, 1985; Share & Stanovich, 1995; Stanovich, 1986). Dyslexia stems from a core deficit in phonological processing, not a deficit in visual processing (Adams, 1990; Goswami & Bryant, 1990; Stanovich, 1991; Vellutino, 1980). This difficulty with phonological processing is not a developmental delay. It is a deficit that interferes with reading and spelling development (Foorman, Francis, Shaywitz, Shaywitz, & Fletcher, 1997). Students who have difficulty learning to read have difficulty discovering that spoken words are made up of units of sounds (i.e., phonemic awareness) that relate to letters (Adams, 1990; Adams & Bruck, 1995; Brady & Moats, 1997; Brady & Shankweiler, 1991; Gough, Ehri, & Treiman, 1992; Rack, Hulme, Snowling, & Wightman, 1994). Without this realization, they fail to learn the alphabetic principle. Subsequently, they fail to thrive in reading (Stanovich, 1986). Early intervention is essential.

Teaching Decoding Skills

The English language, a language of approximately 44 speech sounds and 26 letters, operates on an alphabetic principle or code. The speech sounds are represented in print by letters. About 75% of the school population will deduce the alphabetic principle regardless of how they are taught (Liberman & Liberman,

1990). The other 25% of students, including dyslexic students, will not intuit this principle and will require explicit, systematic, and sequential instruction. Failure to receive such instruction can intensify their reading difficulties (Brady & Moats, 1997; Felton, 1993; Foorman, Francis, Beeler, Winikates, & Fletcher, 1997). The beneficial effects of explicit teaching of the alphabetic principle are not limited to students who have difficulty with reading. There is evidence all students benefit from such instruction (Adams & Bruck, 1995; Beck & Juel, 1995; Brady & Moats, 1997; Chall, 1996; Liberman & Liberman, 1990).

Decoding requires knowledge of orthographic patterns of the language that is based on solid phonological processing. Key elements of decoding instruction include the following:

- Phonological awareness training, especially in phonemic awareness
- Instant letter-recognition training
- Introduction of sound–symbol correspondences
- Introduction of the six orthographic types of syllables
- Introduction of common syllable-division patterns
- Introduction of morphemes—prefixes, suffixes, roots, and combining forms
- Training in recognizing and understanding word origins (see Chapter 5)
- Teaching of a procedure for learning to read **irregular words**
- Instruction in the orthographic patterns for encoding (spelling)
- Practice for accuracy and fluency

The teaching of decoding is not an incidental part of reading instruction. It is not done through the use of worksheets or rote learning. Successful decoding instruction is a vital part of reading instruction that engages students in active, reflective, inductive learning. Students learn to be analytic and scientific in their approach to learning the structure of the language. The intensity of instruction will depend on the instructional needs of the students.

MULTISENSORY, STRUCTURED INSTRUCTION

Decoding instruction requires a multisensory, structured presentation within a language content. The characteristics of this instruction are outlined in Chapter 1 of this book. The introductions of decoding concepts and the discussion of instruction presented in this chapter exemplify these characteristics.

Order of Presentation

Students must apprehend phonemic awareness and instant letter recognition (see Chapters 3 and 4) before they are ready for careful instruction in sound–symbol correspondences and structural analysis. For the purpose of introducing the concepts necessary for successful decoding, this chapter presents concepts in concentrated form. It is important, however, to remember that these concepts must be introduced to students according to a systematic order of presentation. A systematic, sequential order of presentation ensures that all important concepts are taught and maximizes the learning of these concepts. To be successful with sound–symbol correspondences, students must understand the concepts of vowels and consonants and the blending of consonant and vowel sounds. Success with structural analysis is dependent on students' knowledge of syllables, syllable-division patterns, prefixes, suffixes, and roots. Information about structural analysis can be introduced when students can read simple words with affixes.

The patterns and structure of the language are taught through a logically ordered presentation that begins with the most basic concepts and progresses to more difficult concepts, with the new learning building on prior knowledge. A systematic order of presentation begins with the establishment of phonemic segmentation and letter recognition. It proceeds to the introduction of the concepts of vowel and consonant sounds (i.e., vowel sounds are open; consonant sounds are blocked or partially blocked by the tongue, teeth, or lips). At first, three or four high-frequency consonants with predictable sounds (see Table 6.1) along with a short vowel (see Table 6.2) are taught. The concept of blending letter sounds together to form words is introduced, and students begin to read words. Students are taught that a vowel in a syllable that ends in at least one consonant (i.e., closed syllable) is short. After a few more consonants and short vowels are taught, one-syllable words in word lists and sentences are presented for students to read. Common suffixes such as -s or -ing are introduced. One-syllable words and **derivatives** are presented for practice. Once they understand closed syllables, students are taught that two-syllable words with two medial consonants are divided between the consonants (e.g., VC I CV syllable-division pattern as in *mascot* or *napkin*), and, subsequently, one- and two-syllable words and derivatives are presented for practice. After letter clusters such as *ck* and *sh* along with additional syllable types such as open, consonant-*le* and vowel-consonant-*e* syllables are taught, many words of various lengths can be read. The introduction of concepts—more letters, letter clusters, syllable types, syllable-division patterns, suffixes, stems, and prefixes—continues, progressing systematically from simple to complex, with each concept building on those previously mastered. As each concept is introduced, it is practiced to mastery, first through **homogeneous practice** and then in **heterogeneous practice.** (See Appendix B at the end of this book for a listing of curricula with systematic orders of presentation.)

Integration with Literature-Based Curriculum

The teaching of decoding is easily incorporated into a literature-based reading curriculum. Of utmost importance is that a logical order of introducing concepts be determined and followed. A new concept should be introduced within the context of the material to be read. The reading text is selected based on the concept that is to be taught, or, without compromising the logical order, a concept is introduced using a predetermined reading text. Before students read the text, previously introduced sound–symbol correspondences are reviewed and the new concept is introduced. Students practice the new concept and/or review previously introduced concepts by reading word lists or sentences containing the new concept and concepts that have been introduced. High-frequency, phonetically irregular words are also introduced and reviewed before the students read the selected text. As students read the text, they are encouraged to use the concepts and strategies that have been taught. After reading the text, students reinforce the new learning with a follow-up activity such as reviewing the text to find words with the new concept, generating lists of words with the new concept, sorting

Table 6.1. Consonants and consonant clusters

Consonants with one frequent, predictable sound

b* = /b/ (*bat*)	k = /k/ (*kite*)	t* = /t/ (*table*)
d* = /d/ (*dog*)	l* = /l/ (*leaf*)	v = /v/ (*valentine*)
f* = /f/ (*fish*)	r = /r/ (*rabbit*)	w = /w/ (*wagon*)
h = /h/ (*house*)	m* = /m/ (*mitten*)	z = /z/ (*zipper*)
j = /j/ (*jam*)	p* = /p/ (*pig*)	

Consonants with more than one sound

c = /k/ (*kite*)—before *a, o, u,* or any consonant
    /s/ (*city*)—before *e, i,* or *y*

g* = /g/ (*goat*)—before *a, o, u,* or any consonant
    /j/ (*gem*)—before *e, i,* or *y*

n* = /n/ (*nest*)
    /ng/ (*sink* or *finger*)—before any letter that says /k/ or /g/

s* = /s/ (*sock*)
    /z/ (*pansy*)

x = /z/ (*xylophone*)—in initial** position
    /ks/ (*exam, box*)—in medial** or final** position

Consonant digraphs with one frequent sound

ck = /k/ (*truck*)	ng = /ng/ (*king*)
sh = /sh/ (*ship*)	wh = /hw/ ***(*whistle*)

Consonant digraphs with more than one sound

ch = /ch/ (*chair*)	th = /th/ (*thimble*)
/k/ (*school*)—in words of Greek origin	/t̶h̶/ (*mother*)
/sh/ (*chef*)—in words of French origin	

Trigraphs with one sound | **Special situations**

dge = /j/ (*badge*)	y = /y/ in initial or medial position as a consonant
tch = /ch/ (*witch*)	qu = /kw/ (*queen*)—q is always followed by *u*

*These are frequently used consonants that are good to use when beginning introduction of sound–symbol correspondences. When these frequent consonants are combined with short *a, i,* and *o,* many simple words can be presented for reading.

**Initial refers to the first position; *final* refers to the last position; and *medial* refers to any position between the first and last positions.

***This exaggerated pronunciation aids in establishing a strong orthographic memory of words that contain *wh*.

word cards by syllable types, or spelling dictated words or phrases with the new concept or previously introduced concepts. A daily reading lesson might follow this format:

1. Daily review previously introduced of sound–symbol correspondences with a letter-sound deck
2. Introduction of a new concept three times per week
3. Daily oral practice using word lists or sentences with the new concept and/or previously introduced concepts
4. Introduction (two times per week) and daily review of high-frequency, phonetically irregular words
5. Daily reading in connected text
6. Daily follow-up reinforcement activity

Table 6.2. Vowels and vowel pairs

Short vowels in closed syllables·		
a* = /ă/ (apple)	i* = /ĭ/ (it)	u = /ŭ/ (up)
e = /ĕ/ (echo)	o* = /ŏ/ (octopus)	
Long vowels in open, accented syllables		
a = /ā/ (apron)	i = /ī/ (iris)	u = /ū/ (unicorn)
e = /ē/ (equal)	o = /ō/ (open)	y = /ī/ (fly)
Vowels in open, unaccented syllables		
a = /ŭ/ (alike)	i = /ĭ/ (divide)	y = /ē/ (penny)
Long vowels in vowel-consonant-e syllables		
a-consonant-e = /ā/ (cake)	i-consonant-e = /ī/ (five)	u-consonant-e = /ū/ (cube)
e-consonant-e = /ē/ (athlete)	o-consonant-e = /ō/ (rope)	y-consonant-e = /ī/ (type)
Vowels in vowel-r syllables		
er = /êr/ (fern)	ar = /âr/ (star)—accented	or = /ôr/ (fork)—accented
ir = /êr/ (bird)	/ēr/ (dollar)—unaccented	/ēr/ (world)—after w
ur = /êr/ (turtle)		/ēr/ (doctor)— unaccented
Vowel pairs with one frequent sound		
ai = /ā/ (sail)	ei = /ē/ (ceiling)	oe = /ō/ (toe)
au = /au/ (August)	eu = /ū/ (Europe)	oi = /oi/ (boil)
aw = /au/ (saw)	ew = /ū/ (few)	oy = /oi/ (toy)
ay = /ā/ (play)	ey = /ē/ (monkey)	ue = /ū/ (rescue)
ee = /ē/ (feet)	ie = /ē/ (chief)	
Vowel pairs with more than one frequent sound		
ea = /ē/ (eat)	ou = /ou/ (out)	
/ĕ/ (head)	/o͞o/ (soup)	
oo = /o͞o/ (food)	ow = /ou/ (cow)	
/o͝o/ (book)	/ō/ (snow)	
Special situations		
a = /ŏ/ (watch)—after w	eigh = /ā/ (eight)	o = /ŭ/ (onion)
a = /au/ (ball)—before l	igh = /ī/ (light)	

·Good concept and letters for beginning reading instruction.

SOUND–SYMBOL CORRESPONDENCES

Generalizations about sound–symbol correspondences are introduced to provide students with a direct link between the printed word and the spoken word and to guide students' attention to the sound–spelling patterns of words. These generalizations are not learned through rote memorization but rather through frequent practice both in and out of context. Once patterns are established, the generalizations are dispensable (Adams, 1990).

Solid Foundation for Solid–Symbol Correspondence

Awareness of the speech sounds of language and awareness of print provide the foundation for sound–symbol correspondences. Phonological awareness involves a sensitivity to the sound structure of language, such as rhyming, counting words in sentences, counting syllables in words, and identifying specific sounds in a word. The key component of phonological awareness is the ability to perceive the constituent sounds of a word (i.e., phonemic awareness) (Adams, 1990; Ball & Blachman, 1988; Liberman, 1987; Lundberg, Frost, & Petersen, 1988; Yopp, 1992). Print awareness involves sensitivity to the conventions of the printed page, such as top to bottom, left to right, punctuation, indentations, spaces between words, and the awareness that words consist of letters. The key component of print awareness is the ability to instantly recognize letters (Adams, 1990).

Instant Letter Recognition A beginning reader's instant recognition of letters is a strong predictor of reading success. Knowledge of the names of the letters can facilitate the learning of the letter sounds as many sounds are embedded in the letter names (e.g., students can hear the /m/ sound in the name of the letter m) (Adams, 1990; Gough & Hillinger, 1980). All letters have four properties: name, sound, shape, and feel (i.e., the sensation of muscle movements while writing the letter or while producing the sound). The name is the only property that does not change. The name of the letter is an anchor to which the reader can attach the other properties of the letter. Automatic letter recognition allows the reader to see words as groups of letters instead of as individual letters that must be identified (Adams, 1990). Activities to reinforce letter recognition are easily incorporated into the classroom routine:

- The teacher writes a letter on the board. All of the students whose names begin with that letter line up.
- The teacher writes a letter on the board and calls on a student, who must name the letter before lining up.
- The teacher writes a letter on the board and calls on a student, who must name the target letter and the letter that comes after (or before) the target letter before lining up.

See Chapter 4 for other suggestions for activities that develop letter recognition.

Phonemic Awareness A beginning reader's ability to segment a word into its phonemes (i.e., phoneme segmentation) is one of the best predictors of reading success. A phoneme is the smallest unit of speech that makes a difference in the utterance of a word. Thus, the reader's awareness of individual sounds in a word increases his or her understanding of the role of the individual letters in words and how the written letters can be mapped onto the sounds. Without these insights, the reader will not successfully learn the code of the language (Adams, 1990; Ball & Blachman, 1988; see also Chapter 3). Because of the importance of phonemic awareness, activities for reinforcing phonemic awareness should be ongoing. They are easily incorporated into the classroom routine:

- The teacher guesses what was for lunch. Students give the teacher rhyming clues so that the teacher can guess what the students ate for lunch (Rubin & Eberhardt, 1996).
- The teacher says a sound. All students whose names begin (or end) with the sound take their place in line (Rubin & Eberhardt, 1996).
- The teacher takes the class roll using blending. The teacher calls out the names slowly. Students guess the name, and the named student indicates his or her presence.

- The teacher says a word with three or four phonemes (e.g., *lap, sit, run, top, dog, jump, stop*). The teacher calls on a student to **unblend** the word (i.e., say the word slowly) before lining up.
- As an attention device, students establish a word of the week. The teacher gains students' attention by saying the word. Students respond by unblending the word.
- After the teacher reads a book, students apply their phonological awareness skills to play with words from the book (Rubin & Eberhardt, 1996; Yopp, 1995). For example, after reading *The Wind Blew* (Hutchins, 1974), students discover that 11 items were blown into the air. Students can play with the names of the items. They say words that rhyme with *wig, hat,* and *flag.* They count the syllables in *balloon, letters, umbrella,* and *newspapers.* They segment the words *kite, shirt,* and *scarf* into their component sounds.

See Chapter 3 for more suggestions of activities to develop phonological awareness.

Orthographic Patterns

As students acquire basic sound–symbol correspondences, they build their knowledge of orthographic patterns in the language and create a scaffold for refining and expanding their knowledge of the spelling–sound system (Share & Stanovich, 1995). Some letters have one frequent sound or a one-to-one correspondence with a sound (e.g., letters such as *d, m, p,* and *v* have one sound). Letter clusters with two adjacent letters in a syllable that represent one speech sound are called *digraphs.* Digraphs that consist of two adjacent consonants are called *consonant digraphs* (e.g., *sh, ng, ck, th*); digraphs that consist of two adjacent vowels are called *vowel digraphs* (e.g., *ai, ea, ee, oa*). Some digraphs have one frequent sound (e.g., *sh* as in ship, *ng* as in *king, ck* as in *truck, oa* as in *boat*). Other digraphs have several sounds (e.g., *th* as in *thimble* and *mother; ea* as in *each, head,* and *steak*). Letter clusters of three adjacent letters in a syllable that represent one speech sound are called **trigraphs** (e.g., *tch, dge*). **Quadrigraphs** consist of four adjacent letters in a syllable that represent one speech sound (e.g., *eigh*). Two adjacent vowels whose sounds blend together are called *diphthongs* (e.g., *ou, ow, oi, oy*). Considerable attention to orthography is needed for readers to deal with letters that have more than one possible sound. The pronunciation of such a letter may depend on its occurrence with other letters (e.g., *c* is pronounced as /k/ before *a, o, u,* or any consonant but as /s/ before *e, i,* or *y*) and/or its position in a word (e.g., *y* is a consonant in initial position pronounced as /y/ or is a vowel in final position pronounced as /ī/ or /ē/). These patterns of language help the reader choose the best pronunciation of a letter with more than one possible sound. In addition, there are constraints to the orthography of English. Some letters and letter clusters may not occur in certain positions in a word (e.g., English base words do not end in *j* or *v*). Some letters may or may not occur adjacent to certain letters (e.g., *q* is almost always followed by *u; scr* occurs, but *skr* does not). Finally, some letters never or rarely double (e.g., *h, j, k, v, w, x, y*) (Moats, 1995; Perfetti, 1985). Careful, reflective study of orthography for reading reinforces information readers need for spelling.

Multisensory Letter Introduction

Sound–symbol correspondences are established via thorough instruction of letters and letter clusters. The three major learning modalities or pathways—auditory, visual, and kinesthetic—are engaged in the introduction of a letter or letter cluster. Students link the look of a letter (visual) with its sound (auditory) and its feel (kinesthetic) to form the letter sound and written shape. The information received through more than one sensory pathway increases the certainty of learning and retrieval. The grouping of the modalities strengthens the weaker pathway(s) as the strongest pathway assumes the lead in learning. The following terms and procedures are helpful in understanding multisensory instruction.

Kinesthetic Awareness   Kinesthetic awareness involves sensitivity to muscle movement. Kinesthetic information heightens students' memory and ability to discriminate speech sounds. Students' awareness of the position of the mouth, tongue, teeth, or lips and the activity of the vocal cords during the production of a sound assists the definitive learning of speech sounds. Kinesthetic information also heightens students' visual memory and ability to discriminate letter shapes. The students' awareness of how a letter feels when written in the air (i.e., sky writing) or on paper connects kinesthetic and visual information so that the letter shapes can be thoroughly learned.

Sounds   The exact individual sounds of letters (i.e., phonemes) are difficult to isolate. Speech sounds do not occur as single units in running speech. In spoken language, sounds in a word are blended together into units with other sounds so that when the speaker says a word, it does not sound as though he or she is spelling the word out loud sound by sound (e.g., *bag* is not pronounced /b/-/ă/-/g/ but rather /bă/-/g/) (Liberman, 1987). The blending of speech sounds into units is termed *coarticulation*. To help students learn the sound–symbol correspondences, it is necessary for them to be able to isolate the sounds as close approximations of the actual sounds that, in running speech, will be coarticulated with other sounds. The following terminology helps build the teacher's understanding of sound–symbol relationships:

- A *voiced speech sound* is a sound in which the vocal cords vibrate during its production.
- An *unvoiced speech sound* is a sound in which the vocal cords do not vibrate during its production.
- A *vowel sound* is an open speech sound, produced by the easy passage of air through a relatively open vocal tract. It is unblocked by the tongue, teeth, or lips and is voiced. (The sound /h/ opens the mouth, but because it is not voiced, it is a consonant sound.)
- A *consonant sound* is a sound that is blocked (e.g., /l/, /s/, /m/) or partially blocked (e.g., /p/, /b/) by the tongue, teeth, or lips and may be voiced (e.g., /m/, /l/, /r/) or unvoiced (e.g., /t/, /s/, /k/). *Note:* The terms *blocked* and *partially blocked* refer to the kinesthetic feel and visual display of the position of the tongue, teeth, or lips during the production of sounds in isolation. *Blocked* refers to the steady position of the tongue, teeth, or lips during the entire production of a sound (e.g., the lips stay together in a steady position as /m/ is pronounced). *Partially blocked* refers to a released position of the tongue or lips during production (e.g., the tongue is released from the ridge

behind the teeth as /t/ is pronounced). These terms are used in decoding instruction because students can easily and clearly feel or see the characteristics that distinguish consonant sounds from vowel sounds.

- *Voiced and unvoiced pairs* (see Table 6.3) are sounds with the same visual display (i.e., the same position of the tongue, teeth, and lips) and kinesthetic feel, but the vocal chords vibrate during the production of one (voiced) and not the other (unvoiced).
- A *continuant speech sound* is prolonged in its production (e.g., /m/, /s/, /f/).
- A *stop consonant* is obstructed at its place of articulation and not prolonged in its production (e.g., /g/, /p/, /t/, /k/). These sounds must be clipped to prevent the addition of the /ŭh/ at the end of the sound (e.g., /p/ not /pŭh/). *Note:* The terms *continuant* and *stop consonant* are linguistic terms. In decoding instruction, continuant consonant sounds are synonymous with blocked consonant sounds. Stop consonant sounds are synonymous with partially blocked consonant sounds.
- A *fricative* is produced by forcing air through a narrow opening between the teeth or lips (e.g., /f/, /v/, /sh/, /s/, /z/).
- A *nasal sound* is produced by forcing air out through the nose (e.g., /n/, /m/, /ng/).

Use of Key Words   Key words serve as a memory device to "unlock" letter sounds and as a trigger for rapid elicitation of letter sounds. A key word illustrates the sound of a letter and provides a connection of that sound to a written symbol (Cox, 1992; Gillingham & Stillman, 1997). A letter–sound deck is used to systematically review key words and sounds. When students are shown a letter card, they name the letter, say a key word and produce the sound (e.g., when shown a card with the letter a, students respond, "*a*, apple, /ă/"). Pictures of the key words may be added to the letter cards.

Coding   The use of **diacritical markings** for the vowels and other code marks provides students with additional visual and kinesthetic information to reinforce the letter sounds. Short vowels are coded with a breve (ă). Long vowels are coded with a **macron** (ā). The obscure *a*, found in the word *along* and pro-

Table 6.3.   Voiced and unvoiced pairs

Unvoiced	Voiced
/p/	/b/
/t/	/d/
/k/	/g/
/f/	/v/
/s/	/z/
/th/	/t̶h̶/
/ch/	/j/
/sh/	/zh/

nounced /ŭ/, is coded with a dot: à. Vowel digraphs (e.g., ai, ea, ee, oa), consonant digraphs (e.g., ch, ng, sh), and trigraphs (e.g., tch, dge) that represent one
speech sound are underlined. Vowel diphthongs that represent two speech
sounds that are blended together are coded with an arc:

$$\underset{\smile}{ou} \quad \underset{\smile}{ow} \quad \underset{\smile}{oi} \quad \underset{\smile}{oy}$$

Silent letters are crossed out:

$$a\cancel{i} \quad \cancel{t}ch$$

Additional codes are introduced later in this chapter.

Sky Writing *Sky writing* involves the engagement of the large "learning"
muscles of the upper arm and shoulder. The movement of these muscles produces a strong neurological imprint of letter shapes (Waites & Cox, 1976). For sky
writing, the arm of the writing hand is fully extended and tensed. Students use
the whole writing arm, with fingers extended, to write large letters in the air, with
a large model in front of them, to develop muscle memory. The nonwriting hand
is placed on the upper arm or shoulder of the writing arm to create tension and
help the students feel the individual strokes more discernibly.

Guided Discovery Teaching The instructional approach called ***guided discovery teaching*** is effective in ensuring that students learn sound–symbol correspondences and other patterns of language. The word *education* comes from the
Latin word *educere*, which means *to lead out*. Discovery teaching uses the Socratic
method of asking questions to lead students to discover new information. When
students make a discovery, they understand and connect the new learning to
prior knowledge.

Students, for example, are led to discover the difference between vowel and
consonant sounds. The teacher asks students to repeat each of the following
sounds one at a time while looking in a mirror: /ă/, /ĕ/, /ĭ/, /ŏ/, /ŭ/. The teacher
asks, "What do you feel happening to your mouth as each sound is pronounced?" (The mouth is open.) The teacher asks students to say the sounds
again while placing their fingers on the vocal cords. The teacher asks, "What do
you feel?" (The vocal cords are activated, or the throat vibrates.) The teacher explains that these sounds are vowel sounds. Students verbalize what they have
learned about vowel sounds through discovery: Vowel sounds are open and
voiced (make the throat vibrate).

When the teacher uses discovery teaching, the students also make discoveries about consonant sounds. When students are asked to repeat consonant
sounds such as /l/, /s/, /m/, /b/, and /p/ while looking in a mirror, they discover that these sounds are blocked (/l/, /s/, /m/) or partially blocked (/b/,
/p/) by the tongue, teeth, or lips. Consonant sounds can be voiced or unvoiced.
Students verbalize what they have learned about consonant sounds through discovery: "Consonant sounds are blocked or partially blocked by the tongue, teeth,
or lips. They may be voiced or unvoiced."

Multisensory Procedure for Introducing a Letter or Letter Cluster
Sound–letter relationships are introduced through discovery teaching and a multisensory, structured procedure (Cox, 1992; Gillingham & Stillman, 1997):

1. The teacher reads five or six **discovery words** that contain the new letter sound.
2. Students repeat each word while looking in a mirror and listening for the sound that is the same in all of the words.
3. While looking in the mirror, students repeat the sound and discover the position of the mouth. Is it opened or is it blocked or partially blocked by the tongue, teeth, or lips?
4. While placing their fingers on their vocal cords, students repeat the sound to discover whether the sound is voiced (i.e., the vocal cords vibrate) or unvoiced (i.e., there is no vibration).
5. Students determine whether the new sound is a vowel or a consonant sound. Vowel sounds are open and voiced. Consonant sounds are blocked or partially blocked by the tongue, teeth, or lips. They may be voiced or unvoiced.
6. Students guess the key word by listening to a riddle or by feeling an object obscured in a container.
7. The teacher writes the discovery words on the board.
8. Students determine the letter that is the same in all of the words.
9. The teacher shows a card with the new letter on it.
10. Students name the letter, say the key word, and give the sound.
11. The teacher names the new letter just before writing a large model of the letter on the board.
12. The teacher names the letter and then demonstrates sky writing. The teacher describes the letter strokes while sky writing the letter.
13. Students stand and sky write, naming the letter before writing.
14. The teacher distributes papers with a large model of the new letter.
15. Students trace the model three times with the pointer finger of the writing hand and three times with a pencil. Students name the letter before writing.
16. Students turn the model over, and the teacher dictates the name of the letter.
17. Students repeat the letter name and write the letter.
18. The teacher shows the letter card again as students name the letter, say the key word, and produce the sound.

During the various steps in this procedure, the four properties of the letter—name, sound, shape, and feel—are being connected through the use of the auditory, visual, and kinesthetic modalities. This multisensory teaching reinforces the discovery information and builds associations in memory.

Blending

Once students have identified the letter–sound relationships of a word, they must meld the sounds to produce a word. The blending of the sounds in a word is a critical component of learning sound–symbol correspondences. Fluid blending of letter sounds aids students in producing recognizable words. Before students begin reading words, they should have opportunities to blend sounds together orally with the use of manipulatives (e.g., buttons, math counters, pennies).

Because of the effects of coarticulation on sounds, letter-by-letter blending in reading does not always produce a recognizable word. Several different strategies, best presented one-to-one or in small groups, are used to promote the skill of blending when reading words. When introducing any of the blending activities for reading, it is desirable to begin blending words that have continuant initial sounds (e.g., /f/, /l/, /m/, /n/, /s/). Continuant sounds are easier to blend than the stop consonant sounds (e.g., /d/, /p/, /k/). The continuant sounds allow the students to slide into the vowel sound. Blending with initial stop consonants is introduced after students have demonstrated facility with the blending of continuant initial sounds.

Say It Slowly   Using one set of letter cards or lettered tiles, the teacher sets out *m, e,* and *t.* The teacher demonstrates how to say the word *met* slowly by blending the sounds together in units—by saying /m/, then /mĕ/, then /mĕt/, not by saying /m/-/ĕ/-/t/ (Beck & Juel, 1995).

Say It Faster/Move It Closer   Using one set of letter cards or lettered tiles, the teacher sets out s and, separated by a wide space, *a.* The teacher points to the first letter. Students say /s/ and hold it until the teacher points to the second letter and students produce /ă/. The letters are moved closer together and the procedure is repeated, with students blending the sounds together faster. The letters are moved closer together and sounds are produced together faster until students can produce the two sounds as a single unit, /să/. A final consonant is added and blended with the unit to produce a word (e.g., *sat, sad, sap;* Blachman, 1987; Englemann, 1969).

Onsets and Rimes   Using letter cards or lettered tiles, the teacher sets out *a* and *t.* Students blend the letter sounds to produce /ăt/. This /ăt/ unit is the *rime,* the combination of the vowel and the consonant(s) that comes after it in a syllable. The teacher places the letter *m* before the rime. This letter is the *onset,* the consonant(s) of a syllable before the vowel. Students blend /m/ and /ăt/ to produce *mat.* The teacher changes the onset to create new words that students blend and read (e.g., *sat, rat, fat, bat*). Other rimes for practice include the following: *in, it, an, am, op, ang, ing,* and *ink* (Adams, 1990; Goswami & Bryant, 1990).

Playing with Sounds   Using one set of letter cards or lettered tiles, the teacher sets out *a* and *t.* Students blend the letter sounds to produce /ăt/. The teacher asks students to change /ăt/ to /săt/. Students add the s and read *sat.* The teacher asks students to read new words by changing or adding new letter sounds (e.g., *sat* to *mat, mat* to *map, map* to *mop, mop* to *top, top* to *stop*) (Beck & Juel, 1995; Blachman, 1987; Blachman, Ball, Black, & Tangel, 2000; Slingerland, 1971).

Tapping Out   The teacher lays out lettered tiles or letter cards to form a word such as *mat.* Using one hand, students quickly tap the pointer finger to the thumb and say the sound of the first letter, /m/. In quick succession, they tap the middle finger to the thumb and say the sound of the second letter, /ă/. Finally, they tap the ring finger to the thumb and say the sound of the final letter, /t/. When all of the letter sounds have been tapped out, they say the word as they tap all of their fingers to the thumb (Wilson, 1988).

Tapping and Sweeping   The teacher lays out letter cards or lettered tiles to form a word such as *mat.* Each student takes a turn. He or she makes a fist and taps under the *m* as he or she says the sound /m/. Next, he or she taps under the *a* and says /ă/. Finally, he or she taps under the *t* and says /t/. After the student has said each sound, he or she sweeps a fist under the letters and says the word (Greene & Enfield, 1985).

Strategies for Accuracy

Accurate reading of words is key to associating pronunciations with correct orthographic patterns as well as facilitating comprehension. The teacher can use the following strategies to guide a student to the accurate decoding of a word or to correct a mistake when he or she is reading:

- *Misreading or skipping letters*   If a student misreads a letter in a word (e.g., *lid* for *lip*) or skips a letter in a word (e.g., *pat* for *past*), then the teacher directs the student to name the letters in the word. The naming of the letters focuses the student's attention on the letters and also serves to strengthen the orthographic identity of the word.
- *Misreading a word*   If a student misreads a word (e.g., *pane* for *plant*), the teacher directs the student to use the "backing-up procedure." The student identifies the syllable type, determines the vowel sound (short or long), and codes the vowel accordingly (i.e., marks it with a breve or a macron). The student produces the appropriate vowel sound and blends it with the consonant sound immediately after the vowel. The reader blends this unit with any remaining consonant sounds after the vowel, adding sounds one at a time. The reader then blends the vowel and all of the consonant sounds after the vowel with the consonant sound immediately before the vowel. Any remaining consonants that precede the vowel are blended on one at a time. The backing-up procedure with the word *plant* looks like this:

Step 1:	Student codes the *a* with a breve and says /ă/	plănt
Step 2:	Student blends /ă/ with /n/	plănt
Step 3:	Student blends /ăn/ with /t/	plănt
Step 4:	Student blends /l/ with /ănt/	plănt
Step 5:	Student blends whole word	plănt

STRUCTURAL ANALYSIS

Knowledge of sound–symbol correspondences enables the reader to successfully read one-syllable base words. Once the reader has established a few sound–symbol correspondences and can blend them together successfully to form words, information about structural analysis is taught concurrently with new sound–symbol correspondences. Structural analysis of the syllabic and morphemic segments of language facilitates the recognition of longer words. Syllables are speech units of language that contain one vowel sound and can be represented in written language as words (e.g., *cat, mop, sad*) or parts of words (e.g., *mu, hin, ter*) with a vowel or a pair of vowels denoting the vowel sound. When a syllable is part of a word, it does not necessarily carry meaning (e.g., *mu* in *museum* or *music*). Awareness of syllables helps the reader perceive the natural divisions of words to aid recognition. Six types of syllables are represented in written English (e.g., a *closed syllable* ends in at least one consonant; an *open syllable* ends in one vowel). (The types of syllables are discussed in detail later in this chapter.) Awareness of the syllable types gives the reader a way to determine how to pronounce the vowel sound in a syllable (e.g., the vowel in a closed syllable is short; the vowel in an open, accented syllable is long). Morphemes are meaning-carrying units of written language (Moats, 1994) such as base words (e.g., *cat, number, salamander*), prefixes (e.g., *un-, re-, mis-*), suffixes (e.g., *-ful, -ness, -ment*), combining forms (e.g., *bio, helio, polis*), and roots (e.g., *vis, struct, vert*). Awareness of morphemes aids recognition as well as word meaning.

Syllables

The teacher leads students to discover the concept of a syllable. Students are asked to repeat words of varying lengths (e.g., *mop, robot, fantastic*), one at time, while looking in a mirror and observing how many times their mouths open when each word is pronounced. They are asked to repeat each word again while cupping their jaws in their hands and feeling how many times their jaws drop or their mouths open. This visual information of seeing the mouth open and kinesthetic information of feeling the mouth open reinforces students' understanding of a syllable. The teacher explains that a syllable is a word or a part of a word made with one opening of the mouth.

The students are asked to think about which kind of letter sounds open the mouth. (Vowel sounds open the mouth.) The teacher explains that a syllable has one vowel sound. When students say a word, they determine the number of syllables by counting the number of times the mouth opens when pronouncing the word. This concept carries over when students look at a printed word; they determine the number of syllables in the word by counting the number of sounded vowels.

Auditory Awareness of Syllables   The following activities promote awareness of syllables in words:

- Syllable awareness begins early with students identifying or generating short words (*farm, feet, fat, fork, food*) and long words (*February, firefighter, fisherman*). The chosen words might begin with a certain sound or pertain to a particular unit of study (*plants, animals, ocean, United States*; Rubin & Eberhardt, 1996).
- Students repeat words dictated by the teacher. They clap or tap out the number of syllables. The teacher starts with compound words (*playground, flashlight, cowboy*), then moves on to two-syllable words (*velvet, plastic, mascot*) and then on to words with three or more syllables (*fantastic, investment, invitation*).
- Students repeat words dictated by the teacher and move a counter (e.g., block, button, penny) for each syllable they hear. The use of the counters provides a visual and kinesthetic anchor for the sounds.
- Students repeat a word with two or more syllables dictated by the teacher. Students are asked to repeat the word again, omitting a designated syllable (Rosner, 1975), as illustrated in the following dialogue:

Teacher: Say *transportation*.
Students: Transportation
Teacher: Say *transportation* without *trans*.
Students: Portation
Teacher: Say *transportation* without *tion*.
Students: Transporta

This activity is effective in helping students with the correct pronunciations of words and becomes important reinforcement for reading and spelling words of more than one syllable.

Awareness of Accent   Correct placement of the accent or stress on a syllable supports students in the pronunciation and subsequent recognition of words. The mouth opens wider, and the voice is louder and higher when the accented syllable is pronounced. The following activities promote awareness of accent:

- Students practice accent by saying the alphabet in pairs, accenting the first letter in the pair: "**A'** B, **C'** D, **E'** F, **G'** H, **I'** J."
- Students practice flexibility in accenting by saying the alphabet in pairs and shifting the accent to the second letter in the pair: "A **B'**, C **D'**, E **F'**, G **H'**, I **J'**." (See Chapter 4 for additional accenting activities.)
- Students practice accenting by saying two-syllable words, first placing an exaggerated accent on the first syllable and then placing it on the second. They then choose the correct accent placement (e.g., **bas'**•ket, not bas•**ket'**; can•**teen'**, not **can'**•teen). Some words have a noun form and a verb form, and the accent may fall on either syllable depending on the form of the word. The nouns are accented on the first syllable, and the verbs are accented on the second (e.g., **con'**•duct, con•**duct'**; **ob'**•ject, ob•**ject'**).

Six Types of Syllables

A complicating factor in learning the sound–symbol correspondences of written English is the instability of the vowels; they have more than one sound (e.g., short sound, long sound, unexpected sound when followed by *r* or in combination with another vowel). There are six orthographic types of syllables: *closed; open; vowel-consonant-e; vowel pair (vowel team); vowel-r (r-controlled); and consonant-le syllable* (see Table 6.4; Steere, Peck, & Kahn, 1984). A high percentage of the more than 600,000 words of English can be categorized as one of the syllable types or as a composite of different syllable types. Knowledge of syllable types is an important organizing tool for decoding unknown words. Students can group letters into known syllable types that give them clues about the sounds of the vowels. Combining this knowledge of syllable types with known morphemes (e.g., suffixes and prefixes) simplifies the decoding of words with more than one syllable.

The closed syllable is the most frequent syllable type in English (Stanback, 1992). Students can be introduced to the closed syllable when they have learned the letter sounds that make up this pattern (i.e., three or four consonants and one short vowel). The remaining sound–symbol correspondences and syllable types

Table 6.4.   Six syllable types

Closed	Open	Vowel-consonant-*e*	Vowel pair (vowel team)	Vowel-*r*	Consonant-*l*-*e*
it	hi	name	each	fern	-dle
bed	no	five	boil	burn	-fle
and	me	slope	sweet	thirst	-tle
lost	she	these	tray	star	-zle

are taught sequentially and cumulatively until all have been introduced and then practiced until all are mastered.

Discovery teaching techniques for the six syllable types are discussed in the sections that follow. The syllable types are introduced in the order that they might be presented to students. Students are led to discover the salient characteristics of each syllable type and the effect of the syllabic pattern on the vowel sound. The teacher pauses after the questions to solicit answers from the students.

Closed Syllable

Teacher:	[Writes discovery words on the board and directs the students' attention to them] Look at these words: *hat, got, hip, mend*. How many vowels are in each word?
Students:	There is only one vowel in each word.
Teacher:	Look at the end of each word. How does each word end?
Students:	They end in at least one consonant.
Teacher:	When the words are read, how are the vowels pronounced? [Reads the words]
Students:	The vowels are pronounced with their short sounds.
Teacher:	Each of these words ends in at least one consonant. What happens to the mouth when a consonant sound is made?
Students:	The tongue, teeth, or lips close the sound.
Teacher:	What would be a good name for a syllable that ends in a consonant?
Students:	A good name is *closed syllable*.
Teacher:	A closed syllable ends in at least one consonant. Therefore, these words are closed syllables. The vowel in a closed syllable is short; the vowel is coded with a *breve* that is written as (˘). [Writes a breve over the vowel in each word] The word *breve* comes from the Latin word *brevis*, which means *short*. What other words might come from the same Latin word?
Students:	*Brief, brevity, abbreviate* also come from the same Latin word.
Teacher:	Let's review what you have discovered about closed syllables. A closed syllable ends in at least one consonant. The vowel is short; code it with a breve.

Note: When reviewing the concept of a closed syllable, or any kind of syllable, a cloze procedure can be used with the students filling in the most salient characteristics of the syllable type. Pausing for students' replies, the teacher says, "A closed syllable ends in at least one _____ (consonant). The vowel is _____ (short); code it with a _____ (breve)."

Students must be sensitive to the fact that accent may affect the sound of a vowel in a syllable. Short vowel sounds in unaccented closed syllables, particularly before *m, n,* or *l,* may be distorted. The resultant vowel sound is schwa. This sound does not build a strong orthographic memory of the words because the schwa sound is not uniquely represented by one letter (Ehri, Wilce, & Taylor, 1987). Students should use an **exaggerated pronunciation,** or spelling-based pronunciation when decoding these words (e.g., students pronounce *ribbon* as /rĭbŏn/). The teacher helps students match the printed word to a familiar word in running speech.

Short vowels before nasal sounds /m/, /n/, or /ng/ are nasalized and may seem distorted (e.g., *jam, ant, drank, thing*). Awareness of this possibility helps students better match the orthographic representation with a known word in their listening and speaking vocabularies. (See Ehri et al., 1987, for more discussion of short vowels.)

Open Syllable

Teacher: [Writes discovery words on the board and directs the students' attention to them] Look at these words: *he, go, hi, me*. How many vowels are in each word?

Students: There is only one vowel in each word.

Teacher: Look at the end of each word. How does each word end?

Students: They end in one vowel.

Teacher: Could these words be called closed syllables?

Students: No, closed syllables end in at least one consonant.

Teacher: When the words are read, how are the vowels pronounced? [Reads the words]

Students: The vowels are pronounced with their long sounds.

Teacher: Each of these words ends in one vowel. What position is the mouth in when a vowel sound is made?

Students: The mouth is open.

Teacher: What would be a good name for a syllable that ends in one vowel?

Students: A good name is *open syllable*.

Teacher: An open syllable ends in one vowel. The vowel in an open, accented syllable is long; the vowel is coded with a *macron*, which is written as (ˉ). [Writes a macron on the board] The word *macron* comes from the Greek word *makros*, which means long. Let's review what you have discovered about an open syllable: An open syllable ends in one vowel. The vowel is long; code it with a macron.

Vowel-Consonant-e

Teacher: [Writes discovery words on the board] Look at these words: *cake, theme, five, rope, cube*. How many vowels are in each word?

Students: There are two vowels in each word.

Teacher: Look at the end of each word. How does each word end?

Students: They end with an *e*.

Teacher: What comes between the vowel and the final *e* in each word?

Students: One consonant.

Teacher: When the words are read, what happens to the final *e*? [Reads the words]

Students: The *e* in final position is silent.

Teacher: How are the vowels pronounced?

Students: They are pronounced with their long sounds.

Teacher: Each of these words ends in one vowel, one consonant, and a final *e*. What would be a good name for this kind of syllable?

Students: A good name is *vowel-consonant-e syllable.*
Teacher: The vowel in a vowel-consonant-*e* syllable is long. How is a long vowel coded?
Students: A macron shows a long vowel.
Teacher: The final *e* in this syllable is silent. How can the *e* be coded?
Students: The silent *e* can be crossed out: ȩ.
Teacher: Let's review what you have discovered about the vowel-consonant-*e* syllable: A vowel-consonant-*e* syllable ends in one vowel, one consonant, and a final *e*. The *e* is silent; cross it out. The vowel is long; code it with a macron.

Vowel-Pair (Vowel-Team) Syllable

Teacher: [Writes discovery words on the board in two columns] Look at these words: *sea, feet, paint, boat, zoo, book, point, head.* How many vowels are in each word?
Students: There are two vowels in each word.
Teacher: Look at the end of each word. How does each word end?
Students: Some words end with at least one consonant.
Teacher: Are they closed syllables?
Students: No, a closed syllable has only one vowel.
Teacher: How about the other words?
Students: They end in a vowel.
Teacher: Are they open syllables?
Students: No, an open syllable has only one vowel.
Teacher: These words are called *vowel-pair syllables* or *vowel-team syllables* because they have two vowels next to each other. Each vowel pair has a different letter combination and sound. Let's review what you have discovered about the vowel-pair syllable: A vowel-pair (or vowel-team) syllable has two vowels next to each other.

Note: The generalization of "when two vowels go walking, the first one does the talking" is reliable about 45% of the time (Adams, 1990). The first four discovery words in this activity follow this generalization; the last four discovery words do not. For accuracy, each pair must be explicitly taught.

Vowel-r (R-Controlled) Syllable

Teacher: [Writes discovery words on the board] Look at these words: *met, red, step, hen, her.* How many vowels are in these words?
Students: There is one vowel in each word.
Teacher: Look at the end of each word. How does each word end?
Students: They end in at least one consonant.
Teacher: What kind of syllable ends in at least one consonant?
Students: A closed syllable ends in at least one consonant.
Teacher: Tell me about the vowel in a closed syllable.
Students: The vowel in a closed syllable is short; code it with a breve.

Teacher: Let's code and read these words. [Students direct the teacher to code each word. Students read each word after it is coded. When students reach the word *her*, they discover they cannot read the word with a short *e* sound.] What happened when you tried to read the word *her*?

Students: The vowel is not short in the word *her*.

Teacher: Something unexpected happens to the vowel in this word. We expect the vowel to be short because it is in a closed syllable. What letter do you see after the vowel?

Students: The letter *r* is after the vowel.

Teacher: In the word *her*, the *r* comes after the vowel. What would be a good name for this syllable?

Students: A good name would be *vowel*-r *syllable*.

Teacher: What happens to the vowel in a vowel-*r* syllable?

Students: The vowel makes an unexpected sound.

Teacher: When an *r* comes after a vowel, the vowel and the *r* are coded with an arc beneath them:

e͜r

The vowel-*r* combination in an accented syllable is also coded with a **circumflex:**

ê͜r

Let's review what you have discovered about a vowel-*r* syllable: A vowel-*r* syllable has an *r* after the vowel. The vowel makes an unexpected sound; in an accented syllable, code the vowel-*r* syllable with an arc and code the vowel with a circumflex.

Note: The vowel before an *r* in an accented syllable is coded with a circumflex (ˆ). In an unaccented syllable, the vowel-*r* combination is coded with an arc and the vowel with a tilde (˜). The vowel-*r* combinations *er, ir,* and *ur* in an accented or unaccented syllable are pronounced /ẹr/. The vowel-*r* combination *ar* in an accented syllable is pronounced /ar/ as in *star*. In an unaccented syllable, *ar* is pronounced /ẹr/ as in *dollar*. The vowel-*r* combination *or* in an accented syllable is pronounced /or/ as in *fork*. In an unaccented syllable, *or* is pronounced /ẹr/ as in *doctor*.

The terms *vowel*-r *syllable* and r-*controlled syllable* are used interchangeably. The term r-*controlled* focuses attention on the influence of the *r* on the vowel, but the term *vowel*-r focuses attention on the orthographic pattern.

Consonant-le Syllable

Teacher: [Writes discovery words on the board] Look at these words: *ramble, uncle, candle, simple, table.* What looks the same in all of these words?

Students: They all have a consonant and *l* and *e* at the end.

Teacher: When these words are pronounced, how many syllables do you hear or feel? [Reads the words one at a time as students echo each word]

Students: There are two syllables.

Teacher: The second syllable in these words is spelled with a consonant, an *l*, and a final *e* and is called a *consonant*-le *syllable*. Tell me about the sound of the *e* in final position.

Students: It is silent.

Teacher: Because the final syllable in each of these words does not have a sounded vowel, these syllables are "rule breakers." The final syllable is coded with a [(half-bracket). The accent falls on the syllable before the final syllable. Let's code the discovery words. [Students verbalize coding of the final syllable and the syllable before the consonant-*le* syllable. Students read words.] Let's review what you have discovered about a consonant-*le* syllable: A consonant-*le* syllable ends in a consonant, an *l*, and a final *e*. Code the syllable with a half-bracket, and accent the syllable before.

Note: The consonant-*le* syllable is one of several syllables that are referred to as *final stable syllables* (Cox, 1992). These syllables appear in the final position in words, and their pronunciations are fairly stable. Advanced final stable syllables, which include syllables such as *ture, age, sion,* and *tion,* are also coded with a half-bracket. Some of the advanced final stable syllables are also identified as suffixes. The advantage of treating these units as final stable syllables is twofold (Cox & Hutcheson, 1988): 1) They serve as an early, interim bridge to reading words of more than one syllable before the introduction of syllable division or advanced morphemes; and 2) they provide predictable identification of the accent, which usually falls on the syllable before the final stable syllable (e.g., **ta'**[ble, as•**sem'**[ble, ex•**plo'**[sion).

Morphology

Morphology comes from the Greek *morphe* meaning *form* and *ology* meaning *study of.* Morphemes are the smallest forms or units of language—base words, prefixes, suffixes, roots, and combining forms—that carry meaning. A word may contain several syllables but represent only one morpheme (e.g., *salamander*) (Moats, 1994), or a word may contain several syllables and represent several morphemes (e.g., *instructor* contains three syllables and the morphemes *in-, struct,* and *-or*). Study of morphemes not only facilitates decoding but also provides a springboard for vocabulary development and spelling (Adams, 1990) and bridges the gap between alphabetic reading (i.e., word-level reading) and comprehension (Foorman & Schatschneider, 1997).

The following definitions are important to the study of morphemes.

- A *base word* is a plain English word with nothing added to it.
- An *affix* is a suffix or a prefix that is added to a base word.
- A *root* is an essential base of letters to which prefixes and suffixes are added (e.g., *audi, vis, struct*). Roots are primarily of Latin origin. A root that stands alone as a word is called a *free morpheme;* a root that requires the addition of an affix(es) to form a word is called a *bound morpheme* (Moats, 1995).
- A *suffix* is a letter or a group of letters added to the end of a base word or root to change its meaning, form, or usage. A suffix that begins with a consonant is called a **consonant suffix** (e.g., *-ful, -less, -ness, -ment, -cian*). A suffix that begins with a vowel is called a **vowel suffix** (e.g., *-en, -ist, -ible*). Some suffixes are grammatical endings called *inflections* (e.g., *-s, -ed, -er, -est, -ing*), which, when added to a base word, change its number, tense, voice, mood, or comparison (Moats, 1995). For the most part, the spelling of a suffix does not change. The

spelling of the base word, however, may change when a vowel suffix is added. In the initial stages of introduction and practice, suffixes are added to base words. The suffix can be coded with a box. This coding visually separates the base word and the suffix, making it easier for students to attend to the base word:

stand $\boxed{ing}$

- A *prefix* is a letter or a group of letters added to the beginning of a base word or root to change its meaning (e.g., *mis-, un-, con-, re-*). A prefix that ends in a consonant is called a ***consonant prefix.*** The spelling of a consonant prefix may change (e.g., *in-* may be spelled *il-, im-,* or *ir-*). A prefix that ends in a vowel is called a ***vowel prefix.*** The spelling of a vowel prefix does not change.
- A *derivative* is a base word or root plus an affix.
- *Combining forms* are similar to roots, but they are combined with equal importance in a word (e.g., *auto* and *graph*, which are neither affixes nor base words, combine to make *autograph*; see Henry, 1990, and Chapter 5 in this book). Combining forms are primarily of Greek origin.

Multisensory Introduction of Affixes   Quite often the means to reading multisyllabic words is identifying affixes (i.e., prefixes and suffixes) that are part of the word. Students may be able to recognize an unfamiliar word simply by identifying the affixes and then the remaining base word or root. Affixes can be introduced using a multisensory, discovery teaching approach:

1. The teacher reads a list of five or six derivatives that have a common trait as students repeat each word (e.g., *joyful, careful, helpful, graceful, cheerful*).
2. Students discover what sounds the same in each word.
3. The teacher writes the derivatives on the board.
4. Students discover which letters are the same in each word and where the letters are found.
5. Students discover whether the same letters (the affix) is a suffix or a prefix, and they discover the meaning of the affix.
6. Students verbalize what they have discovered (e.g., *-ful* is a consonant suffix that means *full of*).
7. The teacher writes the new affix on an index card and adds it to an affix deck that is systematically reviewed. During review, students identify and spell the affix, give a key word and the pronunciation, and give the meaning of the affix (e.g., when looking at the affix card for suffix *-ful*, students say "This is a consonant suffix spelled *f-u-l*. A key word is *hopeful*. The suffix is pronounced as /fŭl/, and it means *full of*").

Syllable Division

Skilled readers are able to perceive where to divide longer words because they have an awareness of syllables, and they have internalized the orthographic patterns of the language so well that they can sense where a longer word might be divided (Adams, 1990). In addition to gaining auditory awareness of syllables and accenting, students begin to have a heightened visual awareness of syllables as they practice syllable division with activities. The teacher does this by presenting words already divided into syllables, by having students manipulate syllables on cards to form multisyllabic words, and by teaching the four major syllable-division patterns of the language.

Separated Syllables   Students identify syllable types of separated syllables, join them into words, and read the words aloud (Gillingham & Stillman, 1997):

cac•tus   mas•cot   ban•dit   nut•meg

mag•net   gob•let   prob•lem   nap•kin

Manipulation of Multisyllabic Words   Students identify syllables written on individual cards, arrange them into words, and read the words aloud (Gillingham & Stillman, 1997):

tas	fan	tic
lan	tic	At
pen	tine	tur

lec	net	e	mag	tro	ic

Scooping the Syllables   As students read multisyllabic words on a worksheet, they call attention to the syllables in the words by scooping the syllables. Using a pencil, students "scoop" (i.e., draw an arc underneath) the syllables from left to right, identify the syllable type, place the syllable code under each syllable (e.g., o for open, r for r-controlled) and code the vowel (Wilson, 1988):

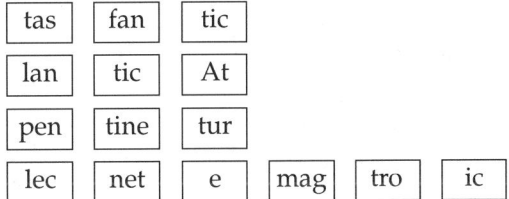

Common Patterns for Dividing Words into Syllables   There are four major patterns in English that indicate that a word will be divided into syllables: VCCV, VCV, VCCCV, and VV. For each of these four patterns, there are different choices for division and accent placement. The best choices for dividing and accenting are listed here in order of frequency. Students must learn to be flexible when they make choices about dividing and accenting multisyllabic words. If the first choice of a pattern does not produce a recognizable word, then they need to try a second choice that usually requires a change in accent placement. If necessary, they may need to try the third choice that usually requires a change in the division of the word. Familiarity and flexibility with syllable-division patterns help students develop strategies for reading multisyllabic words; students do not have to guess or give up when they encounter unfamiliar long words.

VCCV—A pattern with two consonants between two vowels

- **VC′ ❙ CV**—When two consonants stand between two vowels, the word is usually divided between the two consonants. The accent usually falls on the first syllable. Examples include the following: **nap′•kin, vel′•vet, can′•did, cac′•tus, cam′•pus, mag′•net, bas′•ket, in′•sect, op′•tic,** and **mus′•lin.**
  Note: Consonant digraphs such as *ch, ck, sh, ph, th,* and *wh* are treated as single consonants (**ath′•lete, dol′•phin**).

- VC | **CV'**—The word may be divided between the consonants with the accent falling on the second syllable. Examples: un•**til'**, up•**set'**, pas•**tel'**, dis•**cuss'**, can•**teen'**, in•**sist'**
- **V'** | CCV—The word may be divided before both consonants with the accent falling on the first syllable. Examples: **se'**•cret, **fra'**•grant, **ma'**•cron
  Note: Consonant digraphs, two adjacent consonants that represent one sound (e.g., *sh, th, ck, ng*), are never divided. Some consonant clusters contain two adjacent consonants whose sounds flow together. It is not necessary for these clusters to be introduced as separate sound–symbol correspondences because each sound in a consonant cluster is accessible. Visual recognition of consonant clusters is helpful, however, when the reader is determining the division of a word. Consonant clusters that appear in the initial position of one-syllable words may not divide in multisyllabic words. These clusters include the following: *bl, br, cl, cr, dr, fl, fr, gl, gr, pl, pr, sc, sk, sl, sm, sn, sp, st, sw, str,* and *tr.*

VCV—A pattern with one consonant between two vowels

- **V'** | CV—When one consonant stands between two vowels, the word is usually divided before the consonant. The accent usually falls on the first syllable. Examples include the following: **i'**•ris, **o'**•pen, **u'**•nit, **o'**•ver, **ro'**•tate, **a'**•corn, **mu'**•sic, **tu'**•lip, **va'**•cate, **si'**•lent, **su'**•per, and **e'**•ven.
- V | **CV'**—The word may be divided before the consonant, with the accent falling on the second syllable. Examples: re•**quest'**, e•**vent'**, o•**mit'**, u•**nite'**, pa•**rade'**, a•**like'**, a•**lone'**, sa•**lute'**, di•**vine'**.
  Note: The vowels in an open, unaccented syllable require careful attention during syllable division. If students are overly sensitive to sounds in their speech, they may not make the connection between orthography and speech (Ehri et al., 1987). For example, the *e* in the word *elect* sounds more like /ĭ/ in running speech. If students are too sensitive to the /ĭ/ sound, they will not build an orthographic memory of *elect* spelled with an *e*. The *e* in an open, unaccented syllable should be perceived as having a pronunciation that is long (e.g., e•**vent'**) but is shorter than an *e* in an open, accented syllable (e.g., **ze'**•ro). In an open, unaccented syllable, the *o* and the *u* remain long, but their pronunciations are shortened (e.g., o•**mit'**, u•**nite'**). The *e, o,* and *u* are coded with a macron. The *a* in an open, unaccented syllable is obscure and pronounced as /ŭ/ (e.g., a•**long'**). The *a* is coded with a dot. The *i* is short (e.g., di•**vide'**). The *i* is coded with a breve.
- **VC'** | V—The word may be divided after the consonant, with the accent falling on the first syllable. Examples include the following: **rob'**•in, **riv'**•er, **cab'**•in, **trav'**•el, **mag'**•ic, **tim'**•id, **mod'**•ern, **plan'**•et, **sol'**•id, and **sev'**•en.
  Note: Consonant digraphs (i.e., two adjacent consonants that represent one sound) are treated as one consonant. Words with consonant digraphs may be divided before the digraph (e.g., **go'**•pher) or after the digraph (e.g., **rath'**•er).

VCCCV—A pattern with three consonants between two vowels

- **VC'** | CCV—When three consonants stand between two vowels, the word is usually divided after the first consonant. The first syllable is usually accented.

Examples include the following: **pil'**•grim, **chil'**•dren, **pan'**•try, **spec'**•trum, **mon'**•ster, **lob'**•ster, **hun'**•dred, **scoun'**•drel, **ham'**•ster, and **os'**•trich.

- VC | CCV'—The word may be divided after the first consonant with the accent falling on the second syllable. Examples include the following: im•**ply'**, com•**plete'**, sur•**prise'**, in•**trude'**, en•**twine'**, em•**blaze'**, and ex•**treme'**.
- VCC' | CV—The word may be divided after the second consonant or after a final consonant cluster; the accent falls on the first syllable. Examples include the following: **pump'**•kin, **sand'**•wich, **bank'**•rupt, **part'**•ner, **musk'**•rat, and **irk'**•some.

  Note: Consonant clusters that appear in final position of one-syllable words often are not divided in multisyllabic words. These clusters include the following: *ct, ft, lt, nt, pt, rt, st, ld, nd, rd, lp, mp, rp, sp, nb, nk, rk, sk, lb, lf, rb, rf, rm,* and *rn.*

VV—A pattern with two adjacent vowels

- **V'** | V—A word with two adjacent vowels that do not form a vowel pair is divided between the vowels, with the accent falling on the first syllable. Examples include the following: **di'**•al, **cha'**•os, **tru'**•ant, **tri'**•umph, and **li'**•on.
- **V'** | V—A word with two adjacent vowels that form a vowel pair may be divided between the vowels, with the accent falling on the first syllable. Examples: **po'**•em, **qui'**•et, **sto'**•ic, **bo'**•a.

  Note: Adjacent vowels that frequently form digraphs or diphthongs include *ai, ay, au, aw, ea, ee, ei, ey, eu, ew, ie, oa, oe, oi, oo, ou, ow,* and *oy.*
- V | **V'**—The word may be divided between the vowels, with the accent falling on the second syllable. Examples: du•**et'**, cre•**ate'**, co•**erce'**.

  Procedure for Dividing Words   A structured procedure provides readers with a systematic approach for reading long, unfamiliar words and builds an orthographic memory for syllable-division patterns (see Figures 6.1 and 6.2). Dyslexic students may need additional visual and kinesthetic information to build the memory of these patterns. Information helpful to dyslexic and at-risk students (Cox & Hutcheson, 1988) is given in parentheses.

1. *Count the vowels.* To determine the number of syllables in a word, students count the number of sounded vowels from left to right. Vowel pairs count as one sounded vowel. (The vowel pairs can be underlined to call attention to the fact that the two vowels make one sound.) All suffixes are boxed. By boxing suffixes, students may see a base word that requires no further division. Students place half-brackets before any final stable syllables. By bracketing a final stable syllable, students may see that no further division is needed.
2. *Touch the vowels.* Using the index fingers of both hands, students touch the sounded vowels or vowel pairs and identify them. (A line can be drawn over the word from sounded vowel to sounded vowel. The vowels can be labeled by writing a small *v* over each vowel.) Example:

$$\overset{v}{m}a\overset{v}{s}cot$$

The word *mascot* has two syllables because it has two sounded vowels. The vowels are *a* and *o*.

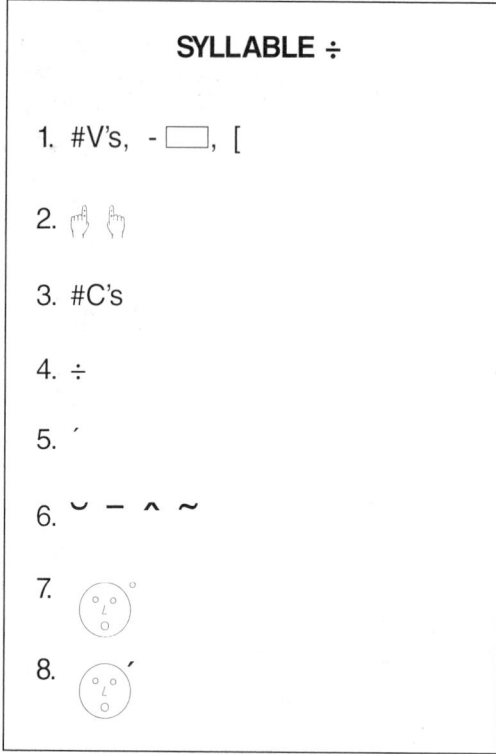

Figure 6.1. The syllable-division procedure provides
ready access to multisyllabic words. Students 1) count
the vowels (box suffixes, and add a half-bracket to
mark a final stable syllable), 2) touch the vowels,
3) count the consonants, 4) draw a vertical line to divide the syllable, 5) mark the accent, 6) code the vowels, 7) read without accent, and 8) read with accent.

3. *Count the consonants.* Students count the number of consonants between the
    two vowels or vowel pairs and identify the division pattern. (Consonant di-
    graphs can be underlined to call attention to the fact that the two consonants
    are treated as one consonant sound. Each consonant can be labeled with a *c*.
    The labeling of the vowels and consonants expedites the orthographic mem-
    ory of the syllable-division patterns.) Example:

$$\text{ma\overset{\text{vccv}}{\text{scot}}}$$

There are two consonants between the vowels in *mascot.* The syllable-division
pattern is VCCV.

4. *Divide.* Students draw a vertical line to divide the word according to the most
    frequent division of this pattern. Example: Because the most common divi-
    sion choice for VCCV is to divide between the consonants, *mascot* is divided
    between *s* and *c*.

5. *Accent.* Students place an accent mark on the appropriate syllable according
    to the most frequent accent of the pattern. Example: With a VC I CV word, the
    is accent is most frequently placed on the first syllable.

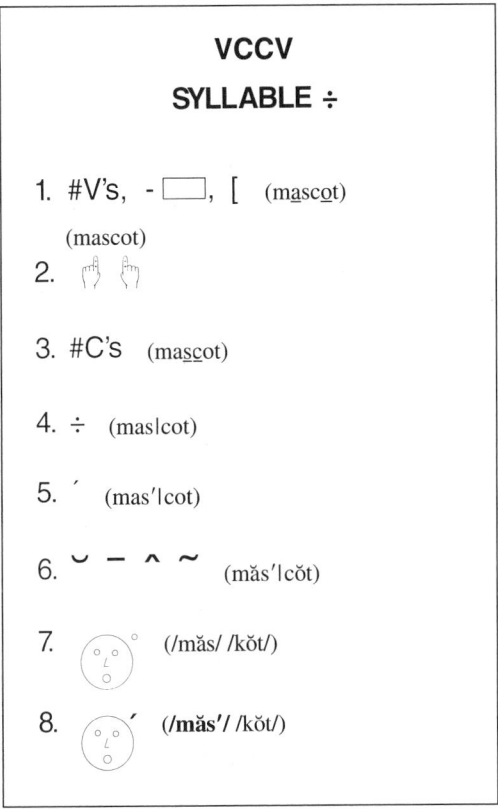

Figure 6.2. The word *mascot* is divided using the syllable-division procedure.

6. *Code.* Students identify each syllable type and code the vowels accordingly. Example: The first syllable of *mascot* is closed. The vowel is short; code it with a breve. The second syllable is closed. The vowel is short; code it with a breve.
7. *Read.* Students read each syllable without accenting either syllable.
8. *Read again.* Students read the syllables together with the appropriate accent.
9. *Adjust.* Students adjust the accent or syllable division if the word is not recognizable. They adjust the coding if necessary. Making adjustments to the accent, the division, or the coding teaches students to be flexible with the language.

Reading Practice   Reading practice to reinforce a syllable-division pattern or any other decoding concepts must be focused. The teacher reviews all information that is pertinent to the reinforcement of the concept. For example, before reviewing a syllable-division pattern, the teacher might review the definition of a suffix, the syllable types that are germane to the pattern, the pattern itself, and the procedure for dividing words into syllables. After a review of relevant information, the teacher models the coding of a word while verbalizing the process and then reads the word. The teacher presents three or four additional words. Students verbalize the coding and/or division of these words and read them. The teacher then presents a homogeneous list of words for students to prepare and read, silently and then aloud. The teacher provides immediate feedback and leads students to self-correct errors so that students connect the correct orthographic patterns and pronunciations (Foorman, 1994). Students use decoded words in complete sentences to ensure they understand the meanings of the words so that, even at the word level, comprehension is attained (Foorman & Schatschnieder, 1997). Closure for the lesson consists of a review of the focused concept. It is important to provide extended practice in connected text that exactly mirrors what students have recently learned. Well-matched reading material extends and reinforces the learning of orthographic patterns and gives relevance to what is being learned (Adams, 1990). (Figure 6.3 shows how reading practice can be incorporated into an intensive, therapeutic reading lesson, with extended reading of text.)

Dividing Words with Three or More Syllables   The same procedure is used for dividing words of three or more syllables. Students choose the most frequent division of a pattern (e.g., VCCV is usually divided between the consonants; VCV is usually divided before the consonant). Choosing accent requires the following considerations: 1) Roots draw the accent; prefixes and suffixes are rarely accented (e.g., in•**vest′**•ment, re•con•**struct′**•ing); 2) the syllable before a final stable syllable is usually accented (e.g., im•mi•**gra′**[tion); 3) a final syllable that ends in a or -ic is not accented, and the accent usually falls on the syllable before the final syllable (e.g., va•**nil′**•la, At•**lan′**•tic); and 4) if there are no clues for accent, try accenting the first syllable (e.g., **cu′**•cum•ber) or the second syllable (e.g., es•**tab′**•lish).

Daily Reading Lesson Plan

1. Review with letter–sound deck

2. Introduction of new concept or review of previously introduced concept

3. Reading practice
   Word lists
   Sentences

4. Spelling practice
   Sound dictation
   Word dictation
   Sentence dictation

5. Introduction of irregular words

6. Reading of connected text

7. Listening to books

Figure 6.3.   A daily reading lesson plan with reading of connected text.

Careful attention to vowels in polysyllabic words is needed. The *a* in an open, unaccented syllable is obscure and is coded with a dot (e.g., al•**fal'**•fà). The *i* in an open, unaccented syllable is short and coded with a breve (e.g., **ar'**•tĭ•chōke). The *i* before a final stable syllable is short and is coded with a breve (e.g., ig•**nĭ'**[tion). The *i* in an open, unaccented syllable before another vowel is pronounced as /ē/ (e.g., **sta'**•di•um).

Advanced Morphemes

In addition to prefixes and suffixes, students benefit from learning about roots and combining forms. These morphemes are predominately of Latin and Greek origins, respectively (see Chapter 5). The ability to instantly recognize roots and combining forms gives students a ready strategy for decoding longer words as well as insight into the meaning of the words.

Common Latin Roots   Words of Latin origin are common in literature and academic writing. Latin words generally are characterized as having a root with affixes. The root carries the base of the meaning:

- *audi* (to hear)—*auditory, audience, audit, auditorium, audible, inaudible, audition*
- *dict* (to say)—*dictate, predict, dictator, edict, contradict, dictation, indict, prediction*
- *ject* (to throw)—*reject, inject, projection, interjection, eject, objection, dejection*
- *port* (to carry)—*transport, transportation, import, export, porter, portable, report, support*
- *rupt* (to break)—*rupture, erupt, eruption, interrupt, interruption, disruption*
- *scrib, script* (to write)—*scribe, describe, manuscript, inscription, transcript, descriptive, prescription*
- *spect* (to watch)—*spectator, inspect, inspector, respect, spectacle, spectacular*
- *struct* (to build)—*structure, construct, construction, instruct, destruction, reconstructionist*
- *tract* (to pull)—*tractor, traction, attract, subtraction, extract, retract, attractive*
- *vis* (to see)—*vision, visual, visit, supervisor, invisible, vista, visualize, visionary*

Common Greek Combining Forms   Words of Greek origin are scientific, medical, and technical terms. They are characterized as having combining forms that carry equal importance in the meaning of the word:

- *auto* (self)—*automatic, autograph, autobiography, automobile, autocracy*
- *bio* (life)—*biology, biosphere, biography, biochemistry, biometrics, biophysics*
- *graph* (write, recording)—*graphite, geography, graphic, photograph, phonograph*
- *hydro* (water)—*anhydrous, dehydration, hydrogen, hydrant, hydrostatic, hydrophobia, hydrotherapy, hydroplane*
- *meter* (measure)—*speedometer, odometer, metronome, thermometer, chronometer, perimeter, hydrometer*
- *ology* (study of)—*geology, theology, zoology, meteorology, phonology*
- *photo* (light)—*photography, photocopy, photosynthesis, phototropism, Photostat, photogenic*
- *scope* (view)—*periscope, stethoscope, telescope, microscope, microscopic*
- *tele* (at a distance)—*telephone, telepathy, telegraph, television*
- *therm* (heat)—*thermos, thermodynamics, thermostat, thermophysics*

Introduction of Roots and Combining Forms   The teacher writes a root or combining form on the board. Students generate derivatives of the word part. The teacher writes the words on the board so that the new word part in each word is aligned. Students determine the meaning of the word part (Henry, 1990):

<u>struct</u>

<u>struct</u>ure

de<u>struct</u>ion

in<u>struct</u>or

recon<u>struct</u>ionist

The teacher writes the new root or combining form on an index card and adds it to a root deck that is systematically reviewed. During a review, students read the root on each card, give the meaning, and generate derivatives of the root (e.g., Students say, "The root is *struct*. It means *to build*. Words that have this root are *construct, structure, instructor,* and *destruction*.").

WORD RECOGNITION OF IRREGULAR WORDS

Knowledge of the orthographic patterns of the language and practice with these patterns develop instant word recognition. But how do readers learn those words with irregular orthographic patterns? Despite claims to the contrary, English is a highly reliable language for reading (Gough & Hillinger, 1980). Approximately 87% of the English language is regular and can be predictably decoded using the orthographic patterns described in this chapter; this leaves only 13% of the language as irregular (Hanna, Hanna, Hodges, & Rudorf, 1966). The irregularities of written English are generally limited to the vowels and silent consonants. For most irregular words, the consonants offer sufficient support so that when an irregular word is encountered in everyday reading, the reader can determine the correct pronunciation of the word with partial decoding (Share & Stanovich, 1995).

Irregular words, particularly high-frequency irregular words (e.g., *the, said, have*), are learned through repeated encounters in text. An understanding of word origins further assists students' orthographic memory of irregular words by giving insight into the spellings of words that do not match their pronunciations. Analyzing irregular words to determine their irregularities reinforces reliable sound–letter relationships, helps students build an orthographic memory of the words, and establishes that the irregularities in English words are not arbitrary (Gough & Hillinger, 1980). Patterns, even if infrequent, can be found in irregular words (e.g., the *gh* may be silent as in *taught*, pronounced /g/ as in *ghost* in initial position, or pronounced /f/ as in *laugh*). When students discover an irregularity in a word, a resounding "Good for you! You found a word that doesn't fit the pattern!" from the teacher confirms that students are thinking about the language and acquiring a flexible understanding of the language.

Procedure for Teaching Irregular Words

A multisensory, structured procedure helps students to achieve permanent memorization of irregular words (Cox, 1992; Gillingham & Stillman, 1997):

1. The teacher writes the irregular word on the board: *said*.
2. Students identify the syllable type and code the word according to the regular patterns of reading. Students read the word and discover it does not follow the reliable patterns of the language: /săĭd/.
3. The teacher erases the coded word and rewrites the word on the board: *said*. Beside the word, the teacher writes the pronunciation in parentheses: (*sĕd*).
4. Students compare the word and the pronunciation. They decide which part is irregular.
5. The teacher circles the irregular part:

s (ai) d

6. The teacher writes the word on the front of a 4″×6″ index card. On the back of the card, the teacher writes the pronunciation. The teacher cuts off the upper left-hand corner of the front of the card.

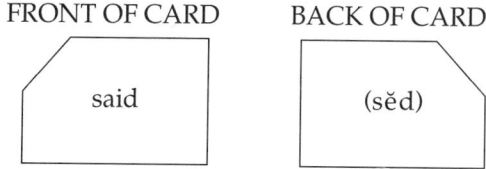

FRONT OF CARD   BACK OF CARD

said   (sĕd)

7. The teacher holds up the card so that students see the front of the card. Students read the word aloud.
8. The teacher turns the card around, and students read the pronunciation aloud.
9. The teacher slowly turns the card from front to back four or five times as students read the word and then read the pronunciation aloud.
10. The new card is added to a deck of irregular words that is reviewed daily.

Review of Irregular Words

Use of a Rapid Word Recognition Chart (RWRC; see Figure 6.4) builds instant recognition of high-frequency irregular words. A transparency is made of the RWRC. The chart contains five rows of six irregular words. Each row contains the same six words in a different order. After placing the transparency on the overhead projector, the teacher points to 8–10 words at random as a warm-up. After the warm-up, students are timed for 1 minute. The teacher points to each square in order on the transparency, starting with the top row and working down across each row. Students read aloud the word in each of the squares. At the end of 1 minute, students count and record the number of words they have successfully read. Progress can be graphed. After students have read all of the words, the teacher points at random to troublesome words to provide further practice and secure the recognition of those words.

Word Origins

A brief overview of word origins helps students develop an understanding of why some words are pronounced in an unexpected way. This understanding al-

RAPID WORD RECOGNITION CHART

pretty	said	who	there	they	what
said	pretty	there	who	what	they
there	who	they	said	pretty	what
who	what	said	they	there	pretty
they	there	pretty	what	who	said

Figure 6.4. The Rapid Word Recognition Chart (RWRC) increases instant word recognition, particularly the recognition of words with phonetically irregular orthography.

lows students to forgive the language for being irregular and, more important, allows them to forgive themselves for having difficulty with the language (Cox, 1992; Gillingham & Stillman, 1997). Words may be pronounced irregularly for four reasons:

1. They are borrowed from another language such as French (*hors d'œuvre*), Dutch (*yacht*), or Greek (*ocean*).
2. They are **eponyms,** or words derived from proper names, such as the German L. Fuchs (*fuchsia*) or the French statesman E. de Silhouette (*silhouette*).
3. They are words from the Anglo-Saxon language whose spellings did not keep pace with their changing pronunciations, such as *laugh, enough, said, through,* and *where*.
4. They are irregular with no easily identifiable reason or "just because," such as *curmudgeon*.

Investigation into the irregularities of words raises students' word consciousness. Becoming more sensitive to the irregular spellings of these words builds students' memory for instant recognition.

THE SPELLING CONNECTION

Noah Webster once wrote, "Spelling is the foundation of reading and the greatest ornament of writing" (as cited in Venezky, 1980b, p. 12). Spelling, by its nature, is a multisensory skill, involving the translation of auditory sounds into visual symbols that are reinforced with the kinesthetic act of writing. The beginning reader's use of invented spelling (Read, 1971) provides the teacher with considerable insight as to how well the reader is learning and internalizing information about the language. The beginning reader applies his or her phonological awareness and acquired knowledge of sounds and patterns to the task of spelling an unfamiliar word. Students who have a sense of how the language works become risk takers. They attempt to sound out and spell words for which they may not have a strong visual image but that are, nevertheless, the best, most appropriate words for their writing (e.g., students attempt *tremendous* or *gigantic* instead of using *big*). In their trials of spelling these unfamiliar words, they reinforce and enhance their reading skills. The use of these more sophisticated words embellishes their writing and better reflects their oral vocabulary. Although it is important for students to become confident risk takers, it is also imperative for them to learn to spell words correctly because their spelling knowledge has a direct impact on their reading proficiency (Adams, 1990). (Chapter 8 provides suggestions for spelling instruction and the use of spelling practice to reinforce reading.)

FLUENCY

Fluency is the rapid, prosodic flow with which a skilled reader reads. When a fluent reader reads aloud, it sounds as though he or she is speaking. His or her reading is fluid and accurate, with adequate speed, appropriate phrasing, and correct intonation. This mirroring of spoken language supports comprehension and facilitates self-monitoring and self-correction. Instant, efficient word recognition greatly facilitates fluency. Automatic word recognition is the result of familiarity with letter–sound correspondences and the spelling patterns (Adams & Bruck, 1995). Lack of fluency is marked by a slow, halting, spasmodic pace; mistakes; poor phrasing; and inadequate intonation (Samuels, 1979). All of these characteristics are the result of inefficient word recognition, and they adversely affect comprehension (Perfetti, 1985) as well as the ability to self-monitor and self-correct. Research suggests that in addition to inefficient decoding skills, deficits in naming speed (i.e., speed in naming colors, numbers, letters, and objects), or rapid serial naming, can interfere with the development of word recognition and fluency (Blachman, 1984; Wolf, 1997; Wolf & Obregón, 1992; see also Chapter 3).

As delineated in Chall's Stages of Reading Development (Chall, 1983), fluency begins in Stage 2 (second or third grade). In Stage 1 (first grade), the reader learns the relationships between letters and sounds and between printed and spoken words. He or she can also read simple text. As Stage 2 begins, he or she is ready to consolidate and automate basic decoding skills and give greater attention to fluency and comprehension. The reader needs to be read to at levels above his or her own **independent level** of reading to develop language and vocabulary that aid word recognition and fluency. The reader also needs wide reading experience with both difficult and easy reading material. Difficult reading material (i.e., instruction-level reading) stretches the reader's knowledge and use of decoding strategies. This reading material forces the reader to reflect on his or her knowledge of language patterns and, thereby, strengthens the memory of those patterns that eventually leads to instant word recognition. The reader should be encouraged to pause and study unknown words instead of to skip or to guess an unfamiliar word (Adams, 1990). Easy reading material (i.e., independent-level reading) that contains a high percentage of decodable words that students readily recognize develops fluency. The focus while reading this material is on the qualities of fluent reading—accuracy, phrasing, intonation, and speed. The reader can vary the rate of reading according to the material, and that rate is built up with gradually harder material. Repeated readings of the same text are beneficial to increasing fluency (Samuels, 1979).

When setting up a fluency practice session using decodable text (i.e., text that contains a high percentage of decodable words), it is helpful for the teacher to read a portion of the text as students look at the text and listen to the teacher. They attend to the teacher's modeling of punctuation, chunking of phrases and clauses, and stressing of important words. This modeling provides a positive framework for the students to strive for when they read. Unknown words or words that contain less-familiar letters or patterns should be previewed. The students need to prepare the selection by reading it silently before reading aloud. Should a reader encounter an unfamiliar word while reading for fluency, the teacher should give some guidance or supply the unknown word in order to preserve the flow of the text. The teacher records any vexing words and reviews them after the practice. The text is too difficult for fluency practice if the reader pauses on too many words or reads with less than 90%–95% accuracy (Adams, 1990).

The reader needs to practice reading both orally and silently. While reading orally, the reader, in addition to decoding words, must attend to the correct articulation of words that can make the use of higher cognitive processes more difficult. Oral reading, however, is an important part of reading instruction as it provides information about how well the reader is generalizing and applying his or her knowledge of language patterns and structures. Oral reading also provides the reader with the best practice for phrasing and intonation. When readers gain accuracy and fluency, silent reading becomes more productive. Silent reading occurs more rapidly and allows the reader to attend to syntactic and semantic structures that provide access to higher levels of comprehension (Venezky, 1980a).

Connection to Spoken Language

Successful decoding requires the reader to translate printed words into their spoken equivalents, whereas successful fluency requires the reader to connect the flow of printed text to the flow of spoken language. It is imperative for the reader to associate the flow of printed text with the flow of spoken language, but he or she must also realize there are significant differences between the two. There are features present in spoken language that are not present in written language (e.g., intonation, phrasing, accent, gestures, facial expressions) and that assist the listener in understanding a given message. Gestures and facial expressions are the result of the social interaction of spoken language (Perfetti, 1985) and cannot be duplicated in written language. Early on children rely on all of these features to understand speech (see Chapter 2 for more information). Lack of these features prevents some readers from learning to group words into meaningful units, especially in the beginning. Oral fluency, which leads to reading fluency, can be taught to readers who do not move from the word level to the phrase level of reading. Phrasing, intonation, and accent can be imitated in written language with oral practice, the study of punctuation, and the study of grammar.

Oral Practice and the Study of Punctuation   Although phrasing and intonation are not conventions of written language, these features can be developed and practiced orally so that students will be able to incorporate them into their reading:

1. *Phrasing*   Phrasing can be taught by using the sequence of the alphabet. Students recite the alphabet in phrases of two or three letters as the teacher draws an arc under each letter grouping. Three possibilities follow:

   AB CDE FG HIJ KL MNO PQ RST UV WXY Z

   ABC DE FGH IJ KLM NO PQR ST UVW XY Z

   ABC DEF GHI JKL MNO PQR STU VWX YZ

2. *Practice with phrases*   The teacher writes phrases of three, four, and five words (e.g., *a little dog, up the steep hill, sat on a green mat*) on the board, and students practice phrasing the words fluently.
3. *Segmented sentences*   The teacher writes five- or six-word sentences on the board in segments that represent the subject and the predicate. Students read the sentences in phrases as the teacher draws an arc under each phrase:

   The mouse   ate the cheese.

   A little dog   ran home.

   When students become fluent in phrasing simple five- or six-word sentences, students can practice with segmented sentences with prepositional phrases:

   The big dog   chased the cat   up the street.

4. *Intonation and punctuation*   Students recite the alphabet as a conversation with appropriate inflection. Students can do this as a group or divided into two halves. The conversation is written on the board or sentence strips. Two possibilities follow:

   ABCD? EFG. HI? JKL. MN! OPQ. RST? UVWX. YZ!
   ABC. DEFGHI? JKL! MN? OPQRS! TUV. WXY? Z.

5. *Intonation and punctuation with sentences*   The teacher writes a two-word sentence three times on the board and punctuates one with a period, one with a question mark, and one with an exclamation point (e.g. *Birds fly. Birds fly? Birds fly!*). The teacher discusses the effect of the different punctuation marks on intonation. Students read each sentence three times, changing their inflection to match the punctuation. The teacher can increase sentence length as students become secure with intonation.
6. *Intonation and stress*   The teacher writes a three-word sentence on the board three times. The teacher underlines the initial word in the first sentence, the second word in the second sentence, and the final word in third sentence

(e.g., I am hungry, I am hungry, I am hungry). Students read the three sentences, stressing the underlined word. They discuss the subtle variations in the meaning of each sentence.

7. *Imitation of spoken language*   The teacher writes a five- or six-word sentence (e.g., *The game will begin at two*) on the board. Students read the sentence once for accuracy. They then read it as though they were talking to a friend. The teacher can add quotation marks to some sentences to reinforce the idea that these marks indicate conversation in written text.

The Study of Grammar   A study of grammar benefits students' use of phrasing and intonation. An understanding of the concepts *subject* and *predicate* aids phrasing because many sentences can be segmented between these two syntactic units of a sentence. Parts of speech such as prepositions and subordinating conjunctions also provide clues for phrasing and intonation. Skilled readers characteristically pause at the end of syntactic units, which aids the flow of their reading (Adams, 1990).

Subject and Predicate   The *subject* is the word or words that tell who or what a sentence is about. The *predicate* tells what the subject is doing or did. An understanding of subject and predicate is taught with simple, two-word sentences such as *Dogs bark*, or *Children sing*. The students study a sentence and determine the word that tells who the sentence is about. The teacher explains that the word is the subject. They study the word that tells what the subject is doing. The teacher explains that the word is the predicate. Students color code the parts of the sentence (e.g., subject is yellow, predicate is orange) (Carreker, 1992) or mark the subject and predicate with a special code (e.g., subject is underlined with a straight line, predicate is underlined with a jagged line) (Greene & Enfield, 1993). Knowledge of subject and predicate provides clues for phrasing. Once students have established the concepts of subject and predicate with two-word sentences, sentences with multiword subjects and predicates are presented. As students read these longer sentences, all of the words in the subject are spoken together as a phrase, and then all of the words in the predicate are spoken together.

Prepositions and Subordinating Conjunctions   Prepositions are the small words (e.g., *in, out, up, down, over, under*) that show the relationship of one noun, pronoun, or proper noun phrase to another element. Students code prepositions with a special color or mark. Because prepositions occur in phrases, students have a signal for reading the words in the prepositional phrase as a unit. When a prepositional phrase of four or more words occurs at the beginning of a sentence, students have a cue that a comma is coming, which will necessitate a pause as they read.

Subordinating conjunctions (e.g., *because, if, while, when*) signal a dependent clause (a group of words with a subject and a predicate that is not a complete sentence) that is spoken together as a unit. Students code subordinating conjunctions with a special color or mark to flag the dependent clause. A subordinating conjunction at the beginning of a sentence cues students that a comma is coming and a pause will be needed as they read.

Developing Fluency

Oral language fluency has been referred to as a neglected goal of reading (Allington, 1983). Most successful beginning readers seem to move from word-level reading to the fluency of phrase reading easily. Their development of fluency is due, in part, to the fact that because successful beginning readers learn the alphabetic code early, they have more time to read (Adams & Bruck, 1995; Juel, 1988) and receive more encouragement to attend to fluency (Allington, 1983). Unsuccessful readers are so focused on learning the code that they receive little time to practice and little encouragement to attend to fluency (Allington, 1983; Chall, 1983). It cannot be assumed, however, that the development of accurate decoding skills guarantees the application of those skills to fluent reading (Torgesen, 1997). Fluency development requires practice. The following activities help students achieve fluency:

1. *Daily practice*   Students benefit from short, daily practice of oral and silent reading at school and home. Both oral and silent reading help increase fluency.
2. *Silent reading*   Prereading the text silently before reading it aloud aids fluency as students can review the text and practice any troublesome words.
3. *Repeated reading*   Students read and reread a text until the reading of the text is fluent. Word recognition, fluency, comprehension, and syntactic sensitivity are improved through repeated reading (Adams, 1990; Samuels, 1979).
4. *Modeling by the teacher*   The teacher reads the text with fluency and expression as students follow along in the text, sliding their pointer finger across the page as the teacher reads. Students join the teacher in reading aloud, or they reread the text incorporating the teacher's techniques of phrasing and intonation (Harris & Sipay, 1984).
5. *Teacher reading with pauses*   The teacher reads the text with expression as the students follow along. The teacher periodically stops at words with particular patterns that are to be emphasized, and the students read the words.
6. *Listening*   Students need opportunities to listen to good models of reading for at least 10–20 minutes daily. Students listen to books at a higher reading level than their own independent reading level to develop skills such as fluency, vocabulary, and syntactic proficiency.
7. *Taped reading*   Students listen to taped text as they follow along in the printed text, sliding their pointer finger across the page as they listen (Harris & Sipay, 1984).
8. *RWRC and flash cards*   Miscues and word-by-word reading indicate a lack of word recognition. Instant word recognition is aided by the use of the RWRC and by flash cards. Reviewing appropriate words before reading a selection keeps the words in memory for the student to refer to. Evidence suggests that an emphasis on the rapid recognition of words benefits poor readers (Tan & Nicholson, 1997).
9. *Use of a marker or pencil*   As students read, they slide a marker or a pencil across and down the page to aid the focus and flow of their reading.

SUMMARY

Reading is a complex process involving decoding, which enables the reader to translate printed symbols into words, and comprehension, which enables the reader to derive meaning from the printed page. With the insight that spoken words consist of sounds and that printed words consist of letters, the beginning reader is able to connect sounds to letters and to read words. Initially the reader is focused on sounding out words. With practice of graphophonemic, syllabic, and morphemic patterns through the use of word lists, sentences, and connected text, the reader's decoding skills become automatic, and he or she is able to give greater attention to fluency. In addition to instant word recognition, attention to phrasing, intonation, punctuation, and grammar further aids fluency. The fluent translation of the flow of print to the flow of spoken language enables the reader to attend to the meaning rather than to the features of the printed text. Fluency is vital to comprehension, which is the main goal of reading.

REFERENCES

Adams, M.J. (1990). *Beginning to read: Thinking and learning about print*. Cambridge: The MIT Press.

Adams, M.J., & Bruck, M. (1993). Word recognition: The interface of educational policies and scientific research. *Reading and Writing: An Interdisciplinary Journal, 5*, 113–139.

Adams, M.J., & Bruck, M. (1995, Summer). Resolving the "great debate." *American Educator, 19*, 7–12.

Allington, R.L. (1983, February). Fluency: The neglected reading goal. *The Reading Teacher*, 556–561.

Ball, E.W., & Blachman, B.A. (1988). Phoneme segmentation training: Effect on reading readiness. *Annals of Dyslexia, 38*, 208–225.

Beck, I., & Juel, C. (1995, Summer). The role of decoding in learning to read. *American Educator, 19*, 8–12.

Blachman, B. (1984). Relationship of rapid naming ability and language analysis skills to kindergarten and first-grade reading achievement. *Journal of Educational Psychology, 76*, 610–622.

Blachman, B.A. (1987). An alternative classroom reading program for learning disabled and other low-achieving children. In R. Bowler (Ed.), *Intimacy with language: A forgotten basic in teacher education* (pp. 49–55). Baltimore: The International Dyslexia Association.

Blachman, B.A., Ball, E.W., Black, R., & Tangel, D.M. (2000). *Road to the code: A phonological awareness program for young children*. Baltimore: Paul H. Brookes Publishing Co.

Bradley, L., & Bryant, P.E. (1983). Categorizing sounds and learning to read: A causal connection. *Nature, 303*, 419–421.

Brady, S., & Moats, L.C. (Eds.). (1997). *Informed instruction for reading success: Foundations for teacher preparation*. Baltimore: The International Dyslexia Association.

Brady, S., & Shankweiler, D. (1991). *Phonological processes in literacy: A tribute to Isabelle Y. Liberman*. Mahwah, NJ: Lawrence Erlbaum Associates.

Calfee, R., & Chambliss, M. (1988). Beyond decoding: Pictures of expository prose. *Annals of Dyslexia, 38*, 243–258.

Carreker, S. (1992). *Multisensory grammar and written composition*. Houston, TX: S.S. Systems.

Chall, J.S. (1983). *Stages of reading development*. New York: McGraw-Hill.

Chall, J.S. (1996). *Learning to read: The great debate revisited* (3rd ed.). Orlando, FL: Harcourt Brace & Co.

Cox, A.R. (1992). *Foundations for literacy: Structures and techniques for multisensory teaching of basic written English skills*. Cambridge, MA: Educators Publishing Service.

Cox, A.R., & Hutcheson, L.M. (1988). Syllable division: A prerequisite of dyslexics' literacy. *Annals of Dyslexia, 38*, 226–242.

Ehri, L.C. (1991). Development of the ability to read words. In R. Barr, M.L. Kamil, P.B. Mosenthal, & P.D. Pearson (Eds.), *Handbook of reading research* (Vol. 2, pp. 383–417). Reading, MA: Addison Wesley Longman.

Ehri, L.C., Wilce, L.S., & Taylor, B.B. (1987). Children's categorization of short vowels in words and the influence of spelling. *Merrill-Palmer Quarterly, 33*, 393–421.

Englemann, S. (1969). *Preventing failure in the primary grades*. Chicago: Science Research Associates.

Felton, R. (1993). Effects of instruction on decoding skills of children with phonological processing problems. *Journal of Learning Disabilities, 26*, 583–589.

Foorman, B.R. (1994). The relevance of a connectionist model for reading for "The Great Debate." *Educational Psychology Review, 6*, 25–47.

Foorman, B.R., Francis, D.J., Beeler, T., Winikates, D., & Fletcher, J.M. (1997). Early intervention for children with reading problems: Study designs and preliminary findings. *Learning Disabilities: A Multidisciplinary Journal, 8*, 63–71.

Foorman, B.R., Francis, D.J., Shaywitz, S.E., Shaywitz, B.A., & Fletcher, J.M. (1997). The case for early reading intervention. In B. Blachman (Ed.), *Foundations of reading acquisition and dyslexia: Implications for early intervention* (pp. 243–264) Mahwah, NJ: Lawrence Erlbaum Associates.

Foorman, B.R., & Schatschneider, C. (1997). Beyond alphabetic reading: Comments on Torgesen's prevention and intervention studies. *Journal of Academic Language Therapy, 1*, 59–65.

Gillingham, A., & Stillman, B. (1997). *The Gillingham manual: Remedial training for children with specific disability in reading, writing, and penmanship* (8th ed.). Cambridge, MA: Educators Publishing Service.

Goswami, U., & Bryant, P. (1990). *Phonological skills and learning to read*. Mahwah, NJ: Lawrence Erlbaum Associates.

Gough, P.B. (1983). Context, form and interaction. In K. Rayner (Ed.), *Eye movements in reading: Conceptual and language processes* (pp. 203–211). San Diego: Academic Press.

Gough, P.B., Ehri, L., & Treiman, R. (Eds.). (1992). *Reading acquisition*. Mahwah, NJ: Lawrence Erlbaum Associates.

Gough, P.B., & Hillinger, M.L. (1980). Learning to read: An unnatural act. *Bulletin of The Orton Society, 30*, 179–196.

Gough, P.B., & Tunmer, W.E. (1986). Decoding, reading and reading disability. *Remedial and Special Education, 7*, 6–10.

Greene, V.E., & Enfield, M.L. (1985). *Project Read reading guide: Phase I*. Bloomington, MN: Bloomington Public Schools.

Greene, V.E., & Enfield, M.L. (1993). *Framing your thoughts*. Bloomington, MN: Language Circle Enterprise.

Hanna, P.R., Hanna, J.S., Hodges, R.E., & Rudorf, E.H. (1966). *Phoneme–grapheme correspondences as cues to spelling improvement*. Washington, DC: U.S. Government Printing Office, U.S. Office of Education.

Harris, A.J., & Sipay, E.R. (1984). *How to increase reading ability: A guide to developmental and remedial methods* (8th ed.). Reading, MA: Addison Wesley Longman.

Henry, M.K. (1988). Beyond phonics: Integrating decoding and spelling instruction based on word origin and structure. *Annals of Dyslexia, 38*, 259–277.

Henry, M.K. (1990). *WORDS: Integrated decoding and spelling instruction based on word origin and word structure*. Austin, TX: PRO-ED.

Hoover, W.A., & Gough, P.B. (1990). The simple view of reading. *Reading and Writing: An Interdisciplinary Journal, 2*, 127–160.

Hutchins, P. (1974). *The wind blew*. New York: Scholastic.

Juel, C. (1988). Learning to read and write: A longitudinal study of 54 children from first to fourth grades. *Journal of Educational Psychology, 80*, 437–447.

Juel, C. (1991). Beginning reading. In R. Barr, M.L. Kamil, P.B. Mosenthal, & P.D. Pearson (Eds.), *Handbook of reading research* (Vol. 2, pp. 759–788). Reading, MA: Addison Wesley Longman.

Liberman, I.Y. (1987). Language and literacy: The obligation of the schools of education. In R. Bowler (Ed.), *Intimacy with language: A forgotten basic in teacher education* (pp. 1–9). Baltimore: The International Dyslexia Association.

Liberman, I.Y., & Liberman, A.M. (1990). Whole language vs. code emphasis: Underlying assumptions and their implications for reading instruction. *Annals of Dyslexia, 40*, 51–76.

Liberman, I.Y., Shankweiler, D., & Liberman, A.M. (1989). The alphabetic principle and learning to read. In D. Shankweiler & I.Y. Liberman (Eds.), *Phonology and reading disabilities: Solving the reading puzzle* (pp. 1–33). Ann Arbor: University of Michigan Press.

Lundberg, I., Frost, J., & Petersen, O.P. (1988). Effects of an extensive program for stimulating phonological awareness in preschool children. *Reading Research Quarterly, 23*, 264–284.

Moats, L.C. (1994). The missing foundation in teacher education: Knowledge of the structure of spoken and written language. *Annals of Dyslexia, 44,* 81–102.

Moats, L.C. (1995). *Spelling: Development, disabilities and instruction.* Timonium, MD: York Press.

Perfetti, C.A. (1985). *Reading ability.* New York: Oxford University Press.

Rack, J., Hulme, C., Snowling, M., & Wightman, J. (1994). The role of phonology in young children learning to read words: The direct-mapping hypothesis. *Journal of Experimental Child Psychology, 57,* 42–71.

Rayner, K., & Pollatsek, A. (1986). *The psychology of reading.* Upper Saddle River, NJ: Prentice-Hall.

Read, C. (1971). Pre-school children's knowledge of English phonology. *Harvard Educational Review, 41,* 1–34.

Rosner, J. (1975). Test of auditory analysis skills. *Helping children overcome learning difficulties.* New York: Walker and Co.

Rubin, H., & Eberhardt, N.C. (1996). Facilitating invented spelling through language analysis instruction: An integrated model. *Reading and Writing: An Interdisciplinary Journal, 8,* 27–43.

Samuels, S.J. (1979, January). The method of repeated readings. *The Reading Teacher, 32,* 403–408.

Share, D.L., & Stanovich, K.E. (1995). Cognitive processes in early reading development: Accommodating individual differences into a model of acquisition. *Issues in Education, 1*(1), 1–57.

Slingerland, B.A. (1971). *A multi-sensory approach to language arts for specific language disability children: A guide for primary teachers.* Cambridge, MA: Educators Publishing Service.

Stanback, M.L. (1992). Analysis of frequency-based vocabulary of 17,602 words. *Annals of Dyslexia, 42,* 196–221.

Stanovich, K.E. (1986). Matthew effects in reading: Some consequences of individual differences in the acquisition of literacy. *Reading Research Quarterly, 21,* 360–407.

Stanovich, K.E. (1991). Cognitive science meets beginning reading. *Psychological Science, 2,* 70–81.

Steere, A., Peck, C.Z., & Kahn, L. (1984). *Solving language difficulties: Remedial routines.* Cambridge, MA: Educators Publishing Service.

Tan, A., & Nicholson, T. (1997). Flashcards revisited: Training poor readers to read words faster improves their comprehension of text. *Journal of Educational Psychology, 89*(2), 276–288.

Torgesen, J.K. (1997). The prevention and remediation of reading disabilities: Evaluating what we know from research. *Journal of Academic Language Therapy, 1,* 11–47.

Tunmer, W.E., Herriman, M.L., & Nesdale, A.R. (1988). Metalinguistic abilities and beginning reading. *Reading Research Quarterly, 23,* 134–158.

Vellutino, F.R. (1980). Perceptual deficiency or perceptual inefficiency. In J. Kavanagh & R. Venezky (Eds.), *Orthography, reading and dyslexia* (pp. 251–270). Baltimore: University Park Press.

Venezky, R.L. (1980a). From Sumer to Leipzig to Bethesda. In J. Kavanagh & R. Venezky (Eds.), *Orthography, reading and dyslexia* (pp. 1–11). Baltimore: University Park Press.

Venezky, R.L. (1980b). From Webster to rice to Roosevelt. In U. Frith (Ed.), *Cognitive processes in spelling* (pp. 9–30). London: Academic Press.

Waites, L., & Cox, A.R. (1976). *Remedial training programs for developmental language disabilities.* Cambridge, MA: Educators Publishing Service.

Wilson, B.A. (1988). *Wilson Reading System: Instructor Manual.* Millbury, MA: Wilson Language Training.

Wolf, M. (1997). A provisional, integrative account of phonological and naming speed deficits in dyslexia: Implications for diagnosis and intervention. In B. Blachman (Ed.), *Foundations of reading acquisition and dyslexia: Implications for early intervention* (pp. 67–92). Mahwah, NJ: Lawrence Erlbaum Associates.

Wolf, M., & Obregón, M. (1992). Early naming deficits, developmental dyslexia, and a specific deficit hypothesis. *Brain and Language, 42,* 219–247.

Yopp, H.K. (1992). Developing phonemic awareness in young children. *The Reading Teacher, 45*(9), 696–703.

Yopp, H.K. (1995). Read-aloud books for developing phonemic awareness: An annotated bibliography. *The Reading Teacher, 48,* 538–542.

7

Teaching Comprehension from a Multisensory Perspective

Margaret Taylor Smith

The ultimate goal of all reading instruction is for readers to understand what they are reading as they are reading. The ability to read and comprehend simultaneously depends largely on completely automatic decoding skills. Comprehension operates on the relations among words in sentences or clauses. The capacity for reading fluently and with comprehension depends on thorough knowledge of spelling–sound correspondences (Adams, 1991; see Chapter 6 for more on teaching decoding skills). The uniqueness of students with dyslexia is that higher-level thinking skills are intact, often at a superior level, but decoding skills are slow to develop. Teachers should consider the following issues:

- Is it possible to teach comprehension skills to students with poor decoding skills?
- Do we wait until their decoding skills become fluent and automatic?
- What kinds of skills should be taught?

This chapter provides some answers to these questions.

Although comprehension and composition (see Chapter 10) are discussed in separate chapters in this book, it is important to note the relationship between understanding what others are saying (comprehension) and expressing oneself clearly so that others can understand (composition). Teachers should make connections between comprehension and composition activities whenever appropriate.

This chapter first provides a brief historical overview of comprehension instruction. Next, various approaches to teaching comprehension are outlined. Following that, features of dyslexia that can affect comprehension are discussed. Next, an explicit instruction model is presented, followed by an outline of basic comprehension teaching techniques. The remainder of the chapter provides specific suggestions to teachers for comprehension instruction, beginning at the sentence level and moving to the **narrative** and **expository** levels. Example lessons are drawn from several published, multisensory programs used successfully by many teachers of students with dyslexia (see Appendix B at the end of this book for specific program information). These examples will help teachers evaluate available materials and select those most appropriate for their students.

HISTORICAL OVERVIEW

Although reading textbooks in the 18th and 19th centuries were concerned with reading for meaning and communication, it was thought that comprehension was a natural result of decoding plus oral language (Fielding & Pearson, 1994). The belief that comprehension occurs naturally after students acquire word-recognition skills persisted even during the 1960s and 1970s. Comprehension was not taught; it was tested via numerous questions about the contents of the text. Very little was done to prepare students for answering the questions in the text (Maria, 1990). Teacher instruction courses did not address how to prepare students for answering the questions in the text (Maria, 1990). Since then, the educational system has moved from virtually no comprehension instruction (Durkin, 1978–1979; Williams, 1987), to teaching isolated **subskills** (May, 1973; Otto & Chester, 1976), to the current practice of teaching a comprehension process that is interactive, constructive, and holistic (Chall, 1983; Maria, 1990; Williams, 1987).

Role of Language in Comprehension

Since the late 1970s, research has examined the role of language and thought as part of reading (Maria, 1990). Although comprehension is only one element of a reading program, it "provides the unifying thread for the integration of instruction in all language processes" (Maria, 1990, p. 203). Fielding and Pearson (1994) described comprehension as being very complex, involving knowledge, experience, and thinking. It involves both inferential and evaluative thinking, and it can be directly taught (Pressley, Brown, El-Dinary, & Afflerbach, 1995). Many dyslexic students have difficulty with both oral and written language processes, which challenge teachers as to how to provide appropriate instruction in all language areas.

"Bottom-Up" versus "Top-Down" Instruction

Although educators recognize the need for direct comprehension instruction, there are differences between what is taught and how it is taught (Anderson, Hiebert, Scott, & Wilkinson, 1984; Calfee, Chambliss, & Beretz, 1991; Williams, 1987). Some view comprehension as a "bottom-up," or **text-driven,** process; students without rapid and automatic decoding skills focus first on words, then on clauses and sentences, and eventually arrive at overall text meaning (Pressley & Rankin, 1994). Others maintain that "top-down," or **concept-driven,** processes are better; in a top-down approach, the focus is on meaning. According to Ekwall and Shanker (1988), students who rely excessively on bottom-up processing are more likely to make comprehension errors because most of their attention is focused on graphic features rather than on meaning; they tend to give verbatim answers from the text rather than rely on what they actually know about the subject. Pressley and Rankin (1994), however, have suggested that bottom-up processing interacts with and is determined in part by top-down processing and that students move back and forth between the two processes. Because students with dyslexia are struggling to decode at the word level, they primarily use bottom-up processing. Students who rely mainly on bottom-up processing are unable to relate pieces of a text, and they do not seek consistent interpretation (Maria, 1990).

What Do Good Readers Do?

We can learn what needs to be taught if we know what good readers do when they are reading. Thinking-aloud reading methods have been used throughout the 20th century. Pressley and colleagues (1995) analyzed studies of thinking-aloud methods used by professors while they read articles in their area of expertise. These readers made predictions based on background knowledge, anticipating what information might be found in the article. They focused on looking forward and backward in the text to find pertinent information. They paraphrased, explained, and summarized information and constructed conclusions. They created a dialogue with the author and reacted on the basis of their prior knowledge. They were very active readers who used diverse monitoring strategies in a flexible manner.

Dyslexic readers need to learn how to apply the same strategies used by accomplished readers, but each strategy must be taught one at a time. After the introduction of a strategy, students must practice applying the strategy with authentic texts. When students demonstrate proficiency using the strategy, another strategy can be presented. Practice activities with authentic texts then include the use of the previously taught strategy as well as the new one. The difference in teaching students with dyslexia and readers without dyslexia is not what is taught but how it is taught. Students with dyslexia require very explicit instruction and need more practice than do readers without dyslexia.

Components of Effective Comprehension Instruction

Fielding and Pearson (1994) described four requirements necessary for successful comprehension instruction.

Ample Time for Reading Authentic Texts   The teacher should provide opportunities for reading widely from a variety of genres and subjects. Because dyslexic students' reading skills often do not permit this kind of independent reading, the teacher should schedule time each day for reading to students. The text selected should contain vocabulary and sentence structure appropriate to students' cognitive level and should not be limited to text the students can read for themselves (Grossen, 1997; Smith & Hogan, 1991). This is primarily a listening activity rather than an instructional activity requiring student response. By listening to stimulating and vocabulary-rich material, students expand both their knowledge base and vocabulary.

Specific Teacher-Directed Instruction in Reading Strategies Specific teacher-directed instruction in reading strategies must be done on the oral level, using authentic texts. The teacher reads the selection to students, then describes the strategy to be taught. The teacher models the strategy first, by talking about his or her thought processes during the modeling. Next, the teacher guides students through the process, involving the group as a whole. The teacher continues to read selections to students.

Cooperative Learning As students begin to assume more responsibility and exhibit confidence during group guided practice, they can begin to work with a partner or small group. After the teacher reads the text, students pair off and carry on dialogues with each other during which they apply the strategies that have been taught. At this point, the teacher is available for guidance when needed.

Time to Talk About Responses to the Text Taking the time to talk about responses to the text is the most important aspect of instruction. Ongoing dialogue about the text happens throughout instruction, not just at a certain point in the instruction. Instead of asking questions implying there is a "correct answer," the teacher should give students the opportunity to explain their reasoning processes to others. It is not just what they know but also explaining how they know it that gives students the opportunity to develop higher-level reasoning processes.

APPROACHES TO TEACHING COMPREHENSION

Since the late 1970s, comprehension instruction has moved away from teaching isolated skills in the form of workbooks or worksheets to teaching how different texts are organized and how to develop comprehension strategies using authentic texts as opposed to workbooks. A number of approaches discussed in this section include teaching cognitive strategies as part of comprehension instruction.

The Specific Skills Approach

Early, direct comprehension instruction involved teaching specific subskills in isolation (May, 1973; Otto & Chester, 1976). Otto and Chester identified six strands that are essential to comprehension (i.e., main idea, sequence, context clues, affixes, reasoning, and reading for detail), and they proposed a sequential hierarchy of subskills for each strand. May listed main idea, sequence, cause and effect, predicting, and recall of important details as necessary comprehension skills. Students generally spent more time on skills workbooks and worksheets than they did on putting skills to work while reading (Fielding & Pearson, 1994). These worksheets were usually assigned as independent practice, with little or no instruction showing students how to complete the task. Often the only students who could complete the worksheet were those students who were experiencing no difficulty with reading and comprehension. Many of the tasks required were not related to comprehension. Ekwall and Shanker (1988) questioned the efficacy of teaching isolated subskills. In spite of countless skills lessons and drills, students' comprehension of authentic text failed to improve.

Gestalt Imagery

Lindamood, Bell, and Lindamood (1997) noted that all comprehension instruction methods have tended to assume that students can assess whether their vocabulary and decoding are accurate. However, Lindamood and colleagues have found individuals, who, in spite of phenomenal decoding skills, have very weak comprehension skills. Bell (1991) stated that imagery is directly related to reading comprehension, recall, and verbal expression. Students with good decoding skills, vocabulary, and background experiences may not be able to comprehend because of their inability to visualize or image thought. Lindamood and colleagues (1997) cited noninvasive brain research (functional magnetic resonance imaging) that indicated that some individuals do not spontaneously associate images with language; therefore, we cannot assume that all individuals will use imagery in association with both spoken and written language. Lindamood and colleagues reported several studies showing that **imagery training** is an important means of improving comprehension. Bell (1991) described imagery as a sensory link that connects incoming language to prior knowledge and experiences. Memory is improved when knowledge structures become internalized in the form of images. Bell suggested that the use of **visual hints** (imaging) may also be a means of processing abstract material; this can be of particular benefit to dyslexics who have difficulty processing abstract language. Bell recommended imagery training, beginning with pictures and progressing to words, sentences, and sentence-by-sentence imaging, as part of comprehension instruction. All imagery training was done on an intensive, one-to-one basis; application of the technique in large-group instruction is difficult.

The Process Approach

The whole-language movement has influenced the way in which comprehension is taught today (Pressley & Rankin, 1994). Previously, comprehension instruction focused primarily on the teacher's asking questions about information in the text that required correct responses. During the 1960s and 1970s, comprehension instruction shifted from the teaching and practicing of only isolated subskills to the teaching of a process for comprehending text passages by focusing on how different kinds of text are organized. For example, narratives have certain common elements: characters, settings, problems/goals/conflicts, rising action, a climax, and resolution. Instruction centered on the elements, and the teacher provided specific skills lessons only as needed. Instructional methods integrated all language areas: listening, speaking, reading, and writing. Teachers related comprehension strategies to composition strategies and taught students how to use writing to improve comprehension (Calfee et al., 1991; Fielding & Pearson, 1994; Maria, 1990; Pressley & Rankin, 1994). Pressley and Rankin described some positive outcomes of the whole-language movement, including a greater emphasis on oral language, higher-quality literature chosen as texts, and an amalgamation of language arts and content-area instruction.

Cognitive Strategies Instruction

Metacognition, the human capacity to think about thought (Calfee et al., 1991), is very helpful in comprehending text (Ekwall & Shanker, 1988). Metacognitive awareness, or an understanding of how we know something, develops through the process of explaining our thoughts to others. Pressley and colleagues (1995) reported that as early as the 1970s, research indicated that students with learning difficulties could benefit from cognitive strategies (metacognitive) instruction for comprehending text. Strategies proven effective in these studies included activating prior knowledge, self-questioning, using mental imagery, and summarizing. By the end of the 1980s, substantial evidence supported instruction in specific **cognitive strategies.** Young students (7–8 years old) and older students (13–14 years old) benefited from instruction in making predictions, generating questions about text, restating difficult text, looking for pertinent information, backtracking as needed, summarizing, analyzing, decision making, seeking clarification when uncertain, analyzing individual words in text for meaning, problem solving by use of reasoning backward, and visualization. Evidence of the benefits of strategies instruction was even stronger by the mid-1990s (Pressley et al., 1995). Fielding and Pearson (1994), maintaining that the strategies taught must be similar to the ones actual readers use when they comprehend the text, reported positive effects when students were taught how to use background knowledge to make inferences or set purposes, how to determine the main idea, how to identify sources needed to find information, and how to focus on typical narrative and expository text structures. They emphasized that strategies should be applied in a flexible rather than a rigidly sequential manner.

Mastropieri, Scruggs, Bakken, and Whedon (1996) did an exhaustive review of all comprehension studies published between 1976 and 1996. They selected 82 studies that were done with students described specifically as having a *learning disability* and did not discuss studies that included students described more generically as *at risk for* or as having a *reading disability*. The selected studies primarily addressed types of comprehension instruction intervention. Mastropieri and colleagues classified interventions as skill training and reinforcement (vocabulary expansion, repeated readings, and fluency practice), text enhancement (use of highlighting, **graphic organizers,** illustrations, mnemonic pictures, and semantic charts), self-questioning (comprehension self-monitoring and questioning, activation of prior knowledge, prediction, summarization, and attribution questioning). The strongest results came from use of some type of self-questioning procedures, followed by use of text-enhancement strategies, and, finally, specific skills training. Mastropieri and colleagues cautioned that generalization of these results is limited because of the small number of studies that employed text enhancement and skills training. They concluded that reading comprehension training has positive effects for students of all ages with learning disabilities and that direct instruction of some type of cognitive or metacognitive strategy was most successful.

Constructively Responsive Reading

Pressley and colleagues (1995) presented a view of reading as more than what traditional reader-response, schema, metacognitive, or bottom-up theorists have suggested. Pressley and colleagues maintained that reading encompasses all of these areas and more. They envisioned reading as an extremely active process affected by complex interactions among text content, prior knowledge, reader's goals, and cognitive and metacognitive processes. Good readers construct their own meaning by exploiting text clues, using prior knowledge, and reflecting on what they have read to determine whether rereading is necessary; in addition, they are constantly monitoring whether they are understanding as they read the text. This process, *constructively responsive reading*, is extremely mindful and purposeful.

Transactional Strategies Instruction

Pressley and colleagues (1995) cited studies that suggested the efficacy of employing *transactional strategies instruction* for both young dyslexic readers and those at middle and high school levels. Use of transactional strategies involves the flexible application of a small repertoire of strategies, such as making predictions, using prior knowledge, creating imagery, questioning when uncertain about meaning, seeking clarification, restating, summarizing, and attempting to decode unfamiliar words. Transactional strategies instruction is designed to help students improve thinking and construct meaning from the text. Strategies are introduced one at a time; the teacher models the process by explaining the strategy and how he or she used it. Students practice applying the strategy in authentic texts, with the teacher providing guidance as needed; as they continue to practice, they are encouraged to model and explain to others their decision-making process and strategies used. Previously taught strategies are eventually coordinated with newly introduced strategies as students acquire facility, again with the teacher modeling and explaining the coordinated use of various strategies. Throughout the process, flexible decision making is emphasized as no two students process the same text the same way. Transactional strategies can be taught in language arts classes but should be applied all day in content areas. Instruction must be intensive; long-term; and include knowledge-rich, interesting material. As students' knowledge of the world increases, their efficient use of strategies also increases. Pressley and colleagues (1995) contended that such instruction leads to high comprehension, expanded world knowledge, and academic success.

THE DYSLEXIC STUDENT: FACTORS AFFECTING COMPREHENSION

Cognition, oral language skills, decoding ability, and background knowledge are essential factors in comprehension for all learners (Chall, 1991). The sections that follow discuss each of these areas briefly as they relate to the dyslexic learner in particular.

Cognition and the Dyslexic Cast of Mind

Bell (1991) defined language comprehension, both oral and written, as *cognition*. This involves connecting to and interpreting language using the ability to reason from what is heard and read. Although Rawson (1988) recognized that all dyslexics are individuals, she spoke of a dyslexic cast of mind; the mind does not work less, it works differently. Some dyslexics have a talent for thinking and working with three-dimensional activities in which they can touch, feel, or manipulate materials, as do surgeons, architects, hair stylists, interior decorators, engineers, and sculptors. For example, Einstein was noted for his ability to envision three-dimensionally his theory of relativity; his difficulty was in finding the words to share his ideas with others (McGee-Cooper, 1982).

Many people with dyslexia are very creative and have exceptional abilities in art, sports, drama, and other "doing" activities. They often have unique ideas and bring a very different approach to problem solving. They sometimes have a tendency to interpret things literally; this literal-mindedness interferes with their comprehension when they encounter idioms or abstract and figurative language

(Smith & Hogan, 1991). Many dyslexics do not automatically make connections or relate parts to the whole easily (Bell, 1991; Maria, 1990); they have difficulty making inferences, predictions, and drawing conclusions (Bell, 1991). These skills must be explicitly taught and practiced extensively.

Oral Language

All language areas—listening, speaking, reading, and writing—are interrelated. They are not skills to be mastered; proficiency with all areas is an ongoing, developmental process. Reading development is only one part of a child's general language development and is not isolated from listening, speaking, and writing (Anderson et al., 1984; Chall, 1991; Ellis, 1991; Maria, 1990; Smith & Hogan, 1991). The word *dyslexia* means *difficulty with language,* and the degree of difficulty ranges from mild to severe. Sometimes only written language ability (reading and writing) is affected; at other times both spoken and written language abilities are involved. Young dyslexics with severe oral language difficulties may require intensive oral language training by speech-language pathologists before they attempt to acquire written language skills. The suggestions in this chapter are designed for students without serious oral language deficits. For more information on the effect of oral language ability on comprehension, see Chapter 2.

Decoding Ability

Most early comprehension studies did not consider decoding as a factor in comprehension. They involved students in fourth grade or above and did not include children with reading disabilities. Reading has come to be viewed as an interaction between decoding and comprehension processes (Chall, 1991). Torgesen (1997) suggested that a delay in the acquisition of fluent, effortless word recognition interferes with the development of a rich reading vocabulary and thus indirectly affects comprehension. The ability to derive meaning from print usually lags behind the ability to understand meaning through other modalities (Chall, 1983; Maria, 1990; May, 1973); this lag is much greater in the case of dyslexic students. When decoding is not automatic, the reader's attention switches between decoding and comprehending. Decoding fluency must be completely automatic, requiring no conscious thought or effort, so that students can apply all of their attention to gaining meaning from the text (Adams, 1991; Samuels & Kamil, 1984). This position echoes Bloom's (1986) explanation that automaticity in a task enables the brain to perform other conscious functions simultaneously. (See Chapter 6 for more on decoding and fluency.)

Background Knowledge

As early as 1917, background knowledge was considered important to comprehension (Chall, 1991; Maria, 1990; May, 1973). Although researchers then recognized the importance of prior knowledge, little was done to show students how to use their knowledge to improve comprehension. Chall (1991) noted that young readers in particular need background knowledge to comprehend expository text. This knowledge helps them make predictions, generate questions, interpret, evaluate, and infer information that is not stated in the text (Pressley et al., 1995).

Students use their unique knowledge, a product of culture, information, and experiences, to construct their own meaning from the text (Chall, 1983; Maria, 1990; Pressley & Rankin, 1994; Williams, 1987). Young readers and poor readers do not consistently see relationships between what they are reading and what they already know (Anderson et al., 1984; Calfee et al., 1991). Because of their poor decoding ability, dyslexic students in middle to upper grades have not had the opportunity to increase their personal lore of world knowledge through reading experiences and thus have a further limitation on their ability to comprehend.

Implications for Instruction

Research with students with learning disabilities at both early and later grade levels indicates that dyslexic students can benefit from explicit instruction in strategies. They do not always perceive relationships or know how to use prior knowledge to understand the text, but they can be taught how to do so. Rawson (1988) expressed the belief that language is caught, not taught; therefore, students need the opportunity to hear and use language interactively to continue developing their oral language facility. The explicit instruction in strategies discussed in the literature provided the rationale for practicing oral language facility. Teacher modeling of thinking-aloud reading methods, followed by ample opportunities for practice, will help dyslexic students develop higher-level thinking skills; they can learn to make the connections between prior knowledge and text information. Use of open-ended questions that have no "right" or "wrong" answers creates an opportunity for using oral language in a nonthreatening, inviting climate. As students contribute their ideas and opinions to a discussion, they have an opportunity to explain their reasons for their viewpoint, thus helping develop important reasoning abilities. Dyslexic students' unique problem-solving abilities enable them to bring to a selection new and different insights that others have not perceived. Class members benefit from hearing the new ideas, and the dyslexic students benefit by gaining the respect and admiration of their peers for their contribution to the discussion. The same principles of instruction that apply to teaching decoding and fluency (see Chapter 6) also apply to teaching comprehension. Dyslexics need systematic, direct instruction with information presented in small, sequential increments; students also must have extensive review and practice that allow them to master each bit of learning before teaching anything new. Dyslexic students learn best from multisensory, structured, explicit instruction presented in a logical sequence, moving from the simplest to increasingly more complex skills. Their tendency to think in concrete rather than abstract terms means that they will benefit from imagery training. Abstract concepts presented in a concrete, experiential manner are also very effective for them.

When to Begin Comprehension Instruction   Beginning and remedial readers cannot learn to decode accurately and comprehend at the same time (Adams, 1991; Samuels & Kamil, 1984; Van Kleeck, 1995); however, Calfee and colleagues (1991) explained that students can be taught to comprehend without reading and taught to compose without writing. Comprehension instruction should not be delayed until students have developed decoding fluency. Because oral comprehension provides the base for written language comprehension, instruction should begin at the oral, or listening, level (Maria, 1990; May, 1973). Students can still experience authentic texts that are stimulating and interesting when the teacher reads the material to them (Cox, 1992; Grossen, 1997). Listening comprehension instruction should take place along with decoding instruction, but the two should be taught in separate activities, using different materials (Grossen, 1997; Smith & Hogan, 1991; Van Kleeck, 1995).

Selecting Appropriate Materials   Beginning or delayed readers can understand and speak many more words than they can read. When teaching comprehension, select materials based on students' listening and speaking vocabulary levels, not on their reading level. By listening to material that is interesting and intellectually challenging, students expand their knowledge and vocabulary (Fielding & Pearson, 1994; Maria, 1990; May, 1973; Smith & Hogan, 1991). When teachers use only material students can read for themselves when teaching comprehension, students are denied this opportunity to gain new knowledge and vocabulary, as the limited vocabulary restricts the kind and amount of information accessible to students. In view of the tremendous influence that background knowledge has on comprehension, it is exciting that the teacher can expose students to a wide variety of literary forms and information by reading the material to their students while they are still at the early decoding stages of reading. As students' background knowledge of the world increases, they can use comprehension strategies more efficiently. Once students have attained effortless decoding, they will be able to apply the comprehension strategies they have learned to the text they are reading.

EXPLICIT INSTRUCTION MODEL

When comprehension instruction consisted of assigning workbooks and worksheets as independent practice, there was little interaction or discussion between teacher and students about their reactions to the text. Students were asked specific questions about text content that required correct answers. In contrast, effective strategies instruction provides ample opportunities for interaction and discussion; students have multiple opportunities to explain their opinions to others.

When teaching a comprehension strategy, the teacher begins by modeling the strategy for students and explains his or her "thinking aloud" process. Students have the opportunity for extensive guided practice, first with the group as a whole. Students practice at this level until they understand the process. The next phase includes teacher modeling, or a review of the process, followed by practice with a partner or a small group in a cooperative learning situation, with the partners or small groups reconvening as a group for discussion of the text. Eventually, students will be able to apply the strategy independently, again reconvening as a whole for group discussion. Ultimately, students will apply the strategy in real reading situations (in which the teacher does the reading) (Fielding & Pearson, 1994; Smith & Hogan, 1991).

Teacher Modeling

After reading a passage to students, the teacher describes his or her own thinking-aloud processes and explains how he or she used clues from the text to understand it (Maria, 1990). In the following example, the teacher models how the setting of the story can be inferred from the text by using background knowledge to interpret clues from the text.

Teacher: We have learned that the time and place in which a story takes place is called the setting. I am going to read a selection to you that doesn't say where or when the story is happening.

The brilliant sun was slowly dipping behind the clouds suspended in the western sky. All was still and quiet, except for the continuous croaking of the frogs. Jimmy and his little brother, Josh, strolled lazily along the path beside a pond, stopping now and then to skim a pebble across the surface of the still water. Jimmy's attention was drawn toward the sky where a flock of starlings were circling high above the tall trees. As his eyes caught sight of the twilight sky, he realized that the sun would be setting soon. Remembering that he promised his mother that he and Josh would be home before dark, he urged Josh along and they both quickened their pace. Suddenly the trail came to an abrupt end. Jimmy and Josh stopped and looked around for familiar landmarks, but there were none. Josh began to cry! (Smith & Hogan, 1991, p. 39)

Nothing in the selection I just read told exactly when or where the events are happening, but I figured it out. I think it happened in the late afternoon because it said that the sun was low in the western sky, and I know that the sun sets in the west. It must have been late afternoon because Jimmy realized that the sun would be setting soon. I also got a clue from the phrase *twilight sky* because I know that *twilight* means just before it gets dark. Although it didn't say where Jimmy and Josh were, I think it was somewhere in the countryside, rather than in a city. The text said that it was still and quiet except for frogs croaking, and it also mentioned a pond and tall trees. It isn't really quiet in a city in late afternoon, and you don't usually hear lots of frogs croaking continuously in a city. It also mentioned that they walked on a path and a trail. I know that cities usually have sidewalks instead of paths and trails. I used things that I knew about to help me decide that this story happened in the countryside, late in the day. When you are reading or listening to a selection, you can figure out information that is not stated explicitly in the text, too. It's a lot like solving a riddle. Listen for clues, and use what you already know to figure out what the text doesn't actually say.

The explicit instruction model is extremely beneficial for dyslexics; however, they may need more teacher modeling and guided practice than some students.

Guided Practice with the Group

After the teacher models and explains a strategy, students need extensive guided practice with the group as a whole, with participation on a volunteer basis. Initially, the teacher continues to provide guidance, modeling again and again as needed. As students are given opportunities to explain their thought processes to others, they will gradually assume more responsibility for explaining their strategy and evaluating their performance. All student responses are honored, and students begin to gain confidence as they explain their reasoning processes to the group. They are also expanding their knowledge base as they listen to others in the class explain their interpretations.

Cooperative Learning

As students gradually take more responsibility for the process during subsequent guided practice, they progress to the next level of guided practice, working with one or more partners. The partners follow the same procedure of explaining their thought processes to each other as they discuss the text. The criterion for success is that students explain things to one another instead of just provide answers with no further explanation (Fielding & Pearson, 1994).

Group Discussion

After partners work together, the group reconvenes for further discussion of the text. As students share and explain their viewpoints, all are broadening their knowledge base and honing their listening, thinking, and speaking skills. Explicit strategies instruction is quite a departure for teachers accustomed to doing most of the talking in a question-and-answer format. To use the strategies instruction model, teachers must be willing to adopt the strategy of guiding student-centered discussions that allow for multiple interpretations and to give students the opportunity to explain the reasons for their unique opinions (Fielding & Pearson, 1994).

TEACHING TECHNIQUES

The following sections discuss the effective techniques for introducing, reviewing, and practicing that Smith and Hogan (1991) described.

Introduction Techniques

Dyslexics benefit from multisensory, experiential learning that actively engages them intellectually. Present abstract concepts, such as parts of speech, in activities that are concrete and experiential in nature. Whenever possible, involve two or more modalities (e.g., visual, auditory, kinesthetic) simultaneously (for an extensive discussion of multisensory techniques, see Chapter 1). Smith and Hogan (1991) also suggested that teachers guide students to discover new concepts, rather than just tell them the information. Questions, clues, concrete materials, and examples should provoke students' curiosity and attention. Conduct lessons in a fun, gamelike manner, and ask questions that focus students' attention on meaningful clues, much like clues to a riddle. When students respond to a question, they are always asked to explain how they arrived at the answer. This technique helps students develop an approach to problem solving. They learn to look at what they already know about a subject, then they determine how things are alike and how they are different and use this knowledge to discover something new. Smith and Hogan (1991) offered the following suggestions for an effective guided discovery minilesson.

1. When applicable, review previously taught, relevant information before presenting new information.
2. Set the stage for guided discovery. Provide appropriate objects, pictures, examples, and/or demonstrations.

3. Ask questions that will help students discover the new learning.
4. Make the presentation lively and fun for students.
5. Limit the amount of new information presented at one time; spend from 3 to a maximum of 10 minutes on the lesson.

The following example lessons illustrate how to incorporate these principles in guided discovery introductions.

Example Lesson: Introducing the Concept of *Nouns*

Use objects, pictures, and/or examples from students' experiences to introduce the idea that a noun is the name of a person, place, or thing. Point to a student in the class, and ask the class, "What do we call this person?" Repeat several times showing pictures of various people known to the students, such as a firefighter or police officer. Each time, ask the class, "What do we call this person?" After several examples, repeat the words (i.e., boy, girl, firefighter, police officer), and tell students that a word that names a person is called a *noun* and that the word *noun* means *name*. Follow a similar procedure to establish the idea that nouns also name places or things.

Example Lesson: Introducing the Concept of *Pronouns*

Introducing the concept of *pronouns* is an instance in which relevant, previously taught concepts should be reviewed first.

Teacher: [Begins by reviewing the concept of *nouns*] We have learned that words that name persons, places, or things are called nouns. Today we will learn about another category of words similar to nouns. [Teacher writes and/or says, "Barry is the new boy in class. He came from a big city"] There are three nouns in the first sentence. Who can name one of them?

Student: *Barry* is a noun.

Teacher: Yes; tell me how you know that.

Student: Because *Barry* is the name of a person.

Teacher: [Repeats the process with *boy* and *class*, each time asking students to explain how they know the word is a noun] The first word in the second sentence is *he*. Who do you think the word *he* is talking about?

Student: *Barry*.

Teacher: The word *he* is not a noun, because it is not the name of a person, place, or thing. In this sentence, *he* is substituting for the noun *Barry*. [Follows the same procedure with several other examples, using various pronouns] We have seen words that can be used to substitute for nouns. This is another category of words called *pronouns*. *Pro* is a word part that means *for*. A pronoun is a word that is used for a noun.

Mary Gilbert, an academic language therapist, used the following example when teaching a lesson introducing pronouns.

Teacher: Pronouns are very useful. Listen to these sentences:

Sally ate Sally's breakfast before Sally went to Sally's school. Sally walked to school with Sally's friend. Sally's teacher welcomed Sally to class.

Could we substitute some other word for Sally? What could we say instead of "Sally ate Sally's breakfast?"

Student: Sally ate her breakfast.
Teacher: [Following the same procedure, asks students to substitute other pronouns in appropriate places]

Mary's student, an 18-year-old high school student, thoroughly enjoyed this lesson. Humor can make the presentation more fun and easier for students to remember.

Example Lesson: Introducing the Concept of *Prepositions*

Teaching the concept of *prepositions* is more challenging, as it is a more abstract concept than *nouns* or *pronouns*. The experiential activities and demonstrations in the following minilesson make abstract concepts more understandable.

Teacher: [Places an object (pen, book, or other) on a table] Where did I place the book?
Student: On the table.
Teacher: What word tells me where the book is?
Student: *On.*
Teacher: [Continues the process by moving the book to different locations, such as under the table, above the table, and over the head, and asks students each time to tell which word showed where the book is] As I moved the book to another location, you used words telling where the book was: on, under, above, and behind. These words showed the relationship of the word *book* to another word, such as *table, floor,* and *head. Book, table, floor,* and *head* are nouns. Words that show the relationship between nouns in a sentence are called prepositions.

Look at these phrases. [Writes a few phrases on the board and reads them to students]

on the table   under the table   above the table

Notice that in each case, the preposition comes before the noun. The word *position* means where something is located. *Pre-* is a word part that means *before.* The word *preposition* means that it comes before the object noun. We simply change the pronunciation of the word part *pre-* when it combines with the word *position* to get *preposition.*

An eighth-grade dyslexic boy's response to this lesson was, "Is that all those things are? I've heard of prepositions all my life, but I never knew what they were. I can't believe it's so simple." When students are actively and intellectually engaged in a guided discovery introduction, they remember what they discover for themselves better than information provided by the teacher in a didactic manner (Cox, 1992). They have the opportunity to use language in a problem-solving situation. The teacher could present the information to students more quickly by just telling them what a preposition is and giving a few examples, but a guided discovery process is a more exciting way to teach and a fun way for students to learn.

Review Techniques

Dyslexics need extensive review of what they have learned. After introducing a concept, such as *nouns*, Cox (1992) suggested that the teacher develop a concept review card. Students and the teacher discuss what to put on the front of a 5" × 7" index card to remind them of the concept. It could be a picture, an abbreviation, or another kind of symbol. After the symbol has been chosen, a student puts it on the front of a card. The teacher writes the definition of the concept on the back. When reviewing the concept, the teacher shows the front of the card to students and reads the information on the back of the card to the students. Students are not asked to memorize or repeat the definition but are asked just to look at the symbol and think about it as the teacher reads the information. The objective for using concept review cards is not to test students' memory but to keep the information at their conscious level of awareness so that they can apply the concept in a practice situation. Figure 7.1 shows Karen's (age 7), Sam's (age 12), and Nancy's (age 15) concept review cards for nouns.

The back of Karen's card reads, *Words that name persons, places, or things are called nouns.* Because Sam and Nancy are older, they are able to grasp the additional idea that nouns also name ideas; hence the back of Sam's and Nancy's cards read, *Words that name persons, places, things, or ideas are called nouns.* In each case, the students made their own drawings on the front of each card. Concept review cards provide a visual reminder for students to look at while the teacher reads the information to students. The objective is not to have students memorize the rule or definition but to implant the information in students' long-term memory so that they can apply the knowledge when they need it.

Independent Practice Activities

The amount of practice needed for mastery varies among students; practice activities must be appropriate to the students' level in terms of kind and amount. The first criterion for determining appropriateness of a practice activity is that students must be able to succeed at it. Vail (1981) warned that before students can practice an activity, they must first learn how to do it successfully. Students learn how to do an activity during group and partner guided practice, with the teacher reviewing, modeling, and demonstrating before each activity. Independent practice is assigned only after students know how to perform the task. Students may need several days, or possibly even weeks, of guided practice before they are ready for independent practice.

Figure 7.1. Concept review cards for nouns for a) Karen, age 7; b) Sam, age 12; and c) Nancy, age 15.

Developing Background Knowledge

Maria (1990) discussed the schema theory, the idea that all of one's knowledge about something is stored in units, called *schemata*. Each person's knowledge about something is based on his or her unique experiences. For example, a small child's schema for a restaurant might be his or her favorite fast-food place. When the child encounters the word *restaurant* in a reading passage, he or she might envision a fast-food restaurant, instead of the restaurant the author had in mind: a quiet place with a maître d', tablecloths on the tables, and five-course meals. Comprehension requires a match between the reader's and the author's schemata. This match can best be accomplished by teachers who know more about their students' background knowledge. Prior to giving the lesson, the teacher prepares by reading the selection and identifying vocabulary or concepts that students may have difficulty understanding or ones that they have heard but do not know the meaning as the author used it. For example, an author of one selection used the word *flat*, meaning *apartment*. Knowing that her students may not know of this usage, the teacher can prepare students by saying, "What do you think of when I say *flat*?" As each student responds, the teacher asks them, "What made you think of that?" If none of the students mentions that *flat* can mean *apartment*, then the teacher says, "In some parts of the world, an apartment is called a *flat*. At the end of the discussion, the teacher asks students, "Have you learned anything new about the word *flat*?" Open-ended questions provide a safe environment, as any reasonable response is appropriate. In this environment, students are using language interactively; they are broadening vocabulary by hearing a number of different meanings for the same word. When they have the opportunity to explain their response, they are developing important reasoning processes, and students' knowledge bases are expanding as they listen to each other.

BASICS OF COMPREHENSION: THE SENTENCE LEVEL

May (1973) found that reading comprehension is significantly related to six basic sentence patterns. He noted that although students might be able to read all of the words in a sentence, they still might not be able to understand it because of sentence-pattern variations, particularly when the sentence includes transitive, intransitive, linking, and *being* verbs as well as adjectives and adverbs. Ekwall and Shanker (1988) suggested that students be taught how to paraphrase, beginning with sentences, then moving to paragraphs. Adams (1991) reported that comprehension operates at the sentence level, not at the level of individual words. Smith and Hogan (1991) recommended that comprehension instruction begin with the study of sentence structure and the names for different parts of sentences, such as *nouns, pronouns, verbs, adverbs, adjectives, prepositions, prepositional phrases, conjunctions,* and *interjections*. Knowing labels of word functions empowers students to manipulate, control, and use all areas of spoken and written language more effectively for higher-level comprehension skills. Familiarity with these terms gives students a language for discussing and learning more about language. For example, after an academic language therapist had taught her adult student these basic concepts, she began introducing the elements of expository text. After she explained that the subject of a selection is who or what the selection is about and that the subject can be identified by watching for repeated words, the student immediately said, "Oh, we're looking for nouns, then." Knowing how to find words that tell how, when, where, or what kind will also help students find important information in text. When students know how to identify nouns, verbs, and descriptors, they can separate important from unimportant information. Similar to good readers, they are able to summarize, paraphrase, and explain what they have read.

It is important to note that teaching the basics of sentence structure is not the primary goal of comprehension instruction. It is best to think of teaching parts of speech and sentence structure more as prerequisite skills that provide a foundation for comprehending paragraphs and then longer selections. Comprehension skills and composition skills are mutually supportive and reinforcing. When students understand the relationships among parts of speech in a written sentence, they can apply this knowledge when they are writing their own sentences. Knowledge of the common elements contained in all stories helps students improve both comprehension and composition.

The following sections contain examples of materials and techniques that provide multisensory structured, sequential, explicit instruction for teaching sentence structure.

Multisensory Grammar and Written Composition

Although Carreker (1993) taught grammar from the standpoint of composition, it has application to comprehension as well. She suggested using a color-coding process for analyzing sentence parts, in which yellow is assigned to nouns and pronouns, red to noun markers (articles), orange to verbs, blue to adjectives, green to prepositions, purple to adverbs, and brown to conjunctions. Interjections are not assigned a color because of their relative unimportance to meaning. Each part of speech and its color code is taught and practiced one at a time. Practice activities involve only parts of speech that have been previously taught; for example, after students have been taught nouns and verbs, each practice sentence contains only a noun and verb. Students underline the noun in yellow and the verb in orange.

<u>Birds</u> <u>sing.</u>

When noun markers have been taught, the practices include noun markers as well as nouns and verbs. The noun marker is underlined in red, and a red arrow is drawn from the noun marker to the noun.

<u>The</u>   <u>boy</u> swims.

After students have learned about complete subjects and predicates, they highlight the complete subject in yellow and the complete predicate in orange. Students begin by underlining each word in the sentence in the color assigned to it before highlighting the complete subject and predicate. As additional components are taught, each practice session includes practice with the newest information as well as previously introduced concepts. Lessons are sequenced logically, beginning with nouns and progressing to action verbs, noun markers, completer or complement nouns, adjectives, proper nouns, prepositions, pronouns, linking verbs, verb tenses, adverbs, conjunctions, and interjections. Practice pages for the student are black line duplicating masters.

Framing Your Thoughts

Greene and Enfield (1993) proposed that grammar be taught through a system of diagramming, using unique graphic symbols to represent sentence parts. The subject, which names a person, place, thing, or idea, is represented by a line:

<u>Flowers</u> bloom.

The action verb, described as the action of the subject, is depicted with a jagged line:

<u>Flowers</u> bloom.

Greene and Enfield represented the definition of a sentence as a formula: The <u>subject</u> + action of the subject expressing a complete thought = a sentence.

Adverbs are encased in triangles, with how, when, where, or why written on the left-hand side of the triangle:

The man played ╱well.╲

Adjectives are encased in rectangular boxes:

The | cunning | | red | fox

Adverb phrases are encased in triangles and labeled how, when, where.

Flowers bloom <u>in mountain meadows</u> in late July and early August.

Greene and Enfield's (1993) exercises concentrate not just on labeling the parts of speech within a sentence but also marking them according to their function in the sentence. Pronouns and nouns are marked according to their function in the sentence. Subjects are underlined once:

The <u>girl</u> sat.

<u>He</u> sat.

Direct objects are coded as follows:

Whom
The <u>dog</u> bit (Jack)

Whom
The <u>dog</u> bit (him)

Connectives are coded as follows:

both <u>boys</u> and <u>girls</u>

The lessons progress from simple to complex, teaching one new part at a time, and incorporating the new with previously taught concepts. A wide variety of interesting and enjoyable practice activities give students the necessary practice and reinforcement.

Winston Grammar Program

Erwin (1982) developed a system of teaching grammar, called the Winston Grammar Program, which uses color-coded cards. Article cards are red, noun cards are white, verb cards are blue, helping verb cards are pale blue, possessive pronoun cards are gray with a red border, adjective cards are orange, adverb cards are green, preposition cards are yellow, conjunction cards are tan, and interjection cards are pale lavender. The front of the card bears the name of the part of speech and its code; the back of the card bears a clue (a picture, example sentence, or list of words):

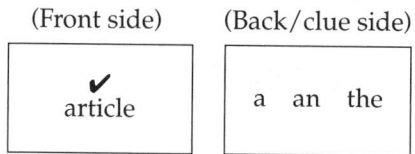

The checkmark on the article card indicates that students are to code articles in a sentence with a checkmark.

Parts of speech are taught one at a time, using the cards. The clue side of the card for the part of speech being introduced is shown. After the introduction, the teacher shows students an example sentence containing the newly introduced part of speech. In the example that follows, students have been taught articles and nouns.

The boy and the girl saw a man eat an apple.

The teacher models how to break the sentence down into its component parts of speech, placing the cards that correspond with the words in the sentence and showing how to check each part of speech by using the question/clues on the cards. Students are given multiple sets of article and noun cards, clue side up, plus several black "mystery" cards that can be used as blanks for grammatical forms not yet taught. At first, the teacher dictates all sentences. Sentences for the practice sessions are provided in the teacher materials. The teacher dictates a sentence to the students. They repeat the sentences and place the cards for each part of speech in sequence, using black cards for parts of speech that have not been introduced. Students then "read" the sentence back to doublecheck the syntactical relationships in the sentence. Students think of this activity as a game, yet they are learning more and more complex elements of grammar.

When using this or any of the other grammar programs with a group, a pocket chart allows versatility and easy visibility in manipulating the sentences and cards. Students can participate and can check their peers' work. Information on pocket charts and other teaching materials can be found in Appendix B at the end of this book.

Multisensory Teaching Approach:
Teaching a Process for Comprehension and Composition

As discussed previously, Smith and Hogan (1991) recommended the use of a guided discovery process to introduce each part of speech and a concept review card to review the concepts before practice. In the Multisensory Teaching Approach (MTA), practice activities are provided in the form of black line duplicating masters. They involve both comprehension (identifying the part of speech in the context of a sentence) and composition (making a sentence using the part of speech) in a sentence. Practice exercises consist of students' explaining sentences that teachers read to the students. After a student identifies a certain part of speech, the teacher asks him or her to explain how he or she knew. For example, if a student identifies a word in a sentence as a noun, the student explains, "I know that *tree* is a noun in this sentence because it is the name of a thing."

AFTER THE BASICS: WHAT NEXT?

Knowledge of grammar and parts of speech is only the beginning of comprehension. After students have developed a basic understanding of the parts of speech and sentence structure, they are ready to begin a study of the elements of narrative text and expository (informational) text. Just as a study of parts of speech shows students the relationship between words in sentences, a study of the elements of text and how they relate to each other will help students identify the important aspects of written material. Once they know these important aspects, they will be able to summarize and restate information and analyze, discuss, and evaluate texts. Although these activities have been presented as aids to improving comprehension, they will also help improve composition skills.

Making Inferences: A Vital Prerequisite

The ability to make inferences is a basic skill for making predictions, drawing conclusions, determining cause and effect, categorizing information, and using context clues to comprehend the meaning of an unknown word. The ability to make inferences is extremely important and should be taught early. Using the explicit instruction model, begin by reading a short selection that contains a few explicitly stated facts. After identifying explicitly stated facts, explain to students that sometimes they can figure out something that is not clearly stated by playing detective and using clues to figure out the new information. Maria (1990) said that teaching and practicing a comprehension skill or strategy is not enough; we cannot assume students will apply it automatically when they are reading. The teacher must *tell* students that they can apply it whenever they need to by saying, "This is what you can do when. . . . "

Example Lesson: Introducing Inferences

Teacher: [Reads two sentences to students] The man is entering the store. The woman is leaving the store.

Teacher: What two pieces of information do we know?

Student: A man is entering the store, and a woman is leaving the store.

Teacher: Yes. The text told us exactly that. What if someone asked you which one has finished shopping? Did the sentences say anything about that?

Student: No.

Teacher: I am going to show you how you can use clues to figure out the answer. I think the woman has finished shopping because she is leaving the store. The man is just going inside the store, so he hasn't

had a chance to do his shopping yet. Using clues to figure out
something that isn't stated is called *making an inference*. The word *in-*
fer has two parts: *in-* means *in* or *into*; *-fer* means to carry. When you
infer something, you are using clues to carry into the text meaning
that was not explicitly stated. When you are reading or listening to
a selection and someone asks you a question that is not answered
in the selection, you can make an inference by using clues to figure
out information that isn't directly stated.

After the concept has been introduced, students need additional practice, first
with short selections, then increasingly longer selections; students should always
explain their reasoning process as they perform the task. Once students have
learned how to make an inference, continue to reinforce the inferential skill at
every opportunity. (See the Teacher Modeling section in this chapter for another
example of teaching students how to make inferences.)

Graphic Organizers

A graphic organizer is a way of organizing critical information in a logical manner. Graphic organizers enhance comprehension and recall. The matrix shown in
Figure 7.2 is a form of organizer that is helpful for making comparisons. The
structure provided by each column helps students find important information related to each disease listed. The blank spaces indicate that the text does not provide all of the necessary information, and the students must go to other sources
to find the missing information. Once the matrix has been completed, students
can compare how the diseases are alike as well as how they are different. This
kind of graphic organizer can be used as a study guide, sometimes called an *ad-*
vanced organizer, for students. As a study guide, the teacher lists the diseases to be
compared in the first column and the areas to be compared on the top row. As
students read (or listen to the text read by the teacher), they can fill in specific information.

Semantic mapping and webbing are other kinds of graphic organizers. Figure 7.3 shows one kind of graphic organizer for a narrative. The organizer, pat-
terned after Greene and Enfield (1994), provides a place for all of the elements of
a narrative: characters, time, and place; important events; the characters'
goals/problems/conflict; the climax; and the resolution. The important events
are sometimes called *rising action;* they capture and increase the reader's interest
in finding out what will happen. The descending line for resolution represents
the "winding down," or ending, of the story. The graphic organizer provides visual reference so that students can focus on the most important information. (See
Chapter 13 for more on semantic maps and webbing.)

The graphic organizer for an outline in Figure 7.4 is a way of organizing the
elements of expository text. Expository text is about a subject; information is organized in paragraphs. Each paragraph provides an important piece of information about the subject, with supporting details about that bit of information. Students write the title, then the subject of the selection on the organizer. The widest
bands are for the main idea of each paragraph. The narrower bands beneath provide space for listing important supporting details. The outline format can be introduced with this kind of graphic organizer.

Infectious Diseases

Disease	Symptoms	Cause	Affects	Treatment
Encephalitis	headache fever drowsiness	virus mosquito	nerves in brain	none available
Rabies		animal bite	brain spinal cord	vaccine
Influenza	cold sick to stomach	virus		
Tuberculosis	fever coughing loss of appetite	germs	lungs	anti-TB drug

Figure 7.2. Example of a matrix used for comparisons.

Graphic organizers can take many forms; the completed organizer in Figure 7.5 shows an alternative to outlining. This organizer is more succinct than the outline graphic organizer. It can be used to show the main idea of a paragraph with supporting details. In this instance, it shows the main variables that affect the climate of a region. This kind of organizer can also be used as a study guide. The teacher fills in the first block. The three blank spaces below that let students know that they are looking for three variables that affect climate.

Once a graphic organizer has been completed, it provides the basis for summarizing, analyzing, discussing, and evaluating a selection (Smith & Hogan, 1991). After students have been exposed to different kinds of graphic organizers, encourage them to invent their own.

COMPREHENDING LONGER SELECTIONS OF TEXT

When dealing with longer selections, how do students know what is important and what is of lesser importance? How can they condense and summarize the information into its barest essentials? Knowledge of the elements of narrative and expository texts provides students with a framework for organizing such important aspects of a selection. A graphic organizer showing the elements of a selection helps them decide what kind of information to focus on. Knowledge of the elements of text also helps students understand relationships between the parts, something that dyslexics are unable to intuit for themselves (Smith & Hogan,

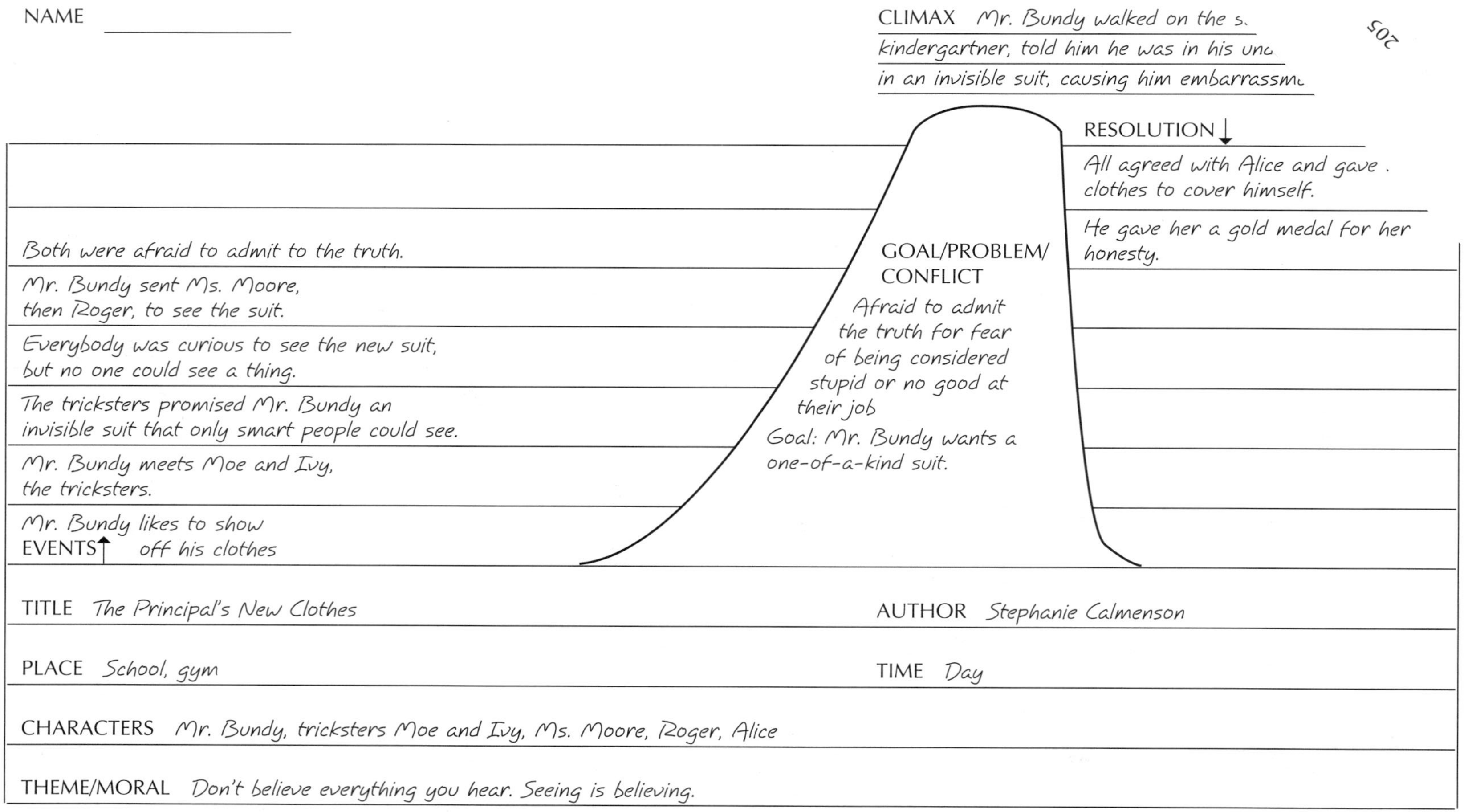

NAME _____

CLIMAX Mr. Bundy walked on the s.
kindergartner, told him he was in his und
in an invisible suit, causing him embarrassme.

RESOLUTION →

All agreed with Alice and gave
clothes to cover himself.

He gave her a gold medal for her
honesty.

GOAL/PROBLEM/
CONFLICT

Afraid to admit
the truth for fear
of being considered
stupid or no good at
their job

Goal: Mr. Bundy wants a
one-of-a-kind suit.

Both were afraid to admit to the truth.

Mr. Bundy sent Ms. Moore,
then Roger, to see the suit.

Everybody was curious to see the new suit,
but no one could see a thing.

The tricksters promised Mr. Bundy an
invisible suit that only smart people could see.

Mr. Bundy meets Moe and Ivy,
the tricksters.

EVENTS ← Mr. Bundy likes to show
off his clothes

TITLE The Principal's New Clothes

PLACE School, gym

AUTHOR Stephanie Calmenson

TIME Day

CHARACTERS Mr. Bundy, tricksters Moe and Ivy, Ms. Moore, Roger, Alice

THEME/MORAL Don't believe everything you hear. Seeing is believing.

Figure 7.3. Graphic organizer for a narrative. (Based on Greene, V.E., & Enfield, M.L. (1994)). Arrows indicate direction in which entries should be added.

Figure 7.4.   Graphic organizer for expository text (outline format).

1991). The elements of text should be explicitly taught, one at a time. As each new element is added, the practices should include all previously taught elements, not just the newest one taught. Younger students can begin studying elements of narratives first because they have often been exposed to stories and most early reading material is in story form. Students in fourth grade and above should learn the elements of expository text first so they are better able to deal with their content-area subjects.

Elements of Narratives

The elements of narratives include a title, characters, a setting (time and place), goal/problem/conflict, a series of important events (rising action), a climax, and then resolution. Sometimes the author has a moral, a theme, or a message in mind.

- The *title* is the author's way of telling who or what the story is about; it can be directly or indirectly stated. A directly stated title, such as "The Moon," tells who or what the subject of the selection is. Authors sometimes use an indirectly stated title to pique the reader's interest. An indirectly stated title, such as "Nocturnal Glow" or "Nightlight," draws on a unique feature of or about the subject (Greene & Enfield, 1994a).

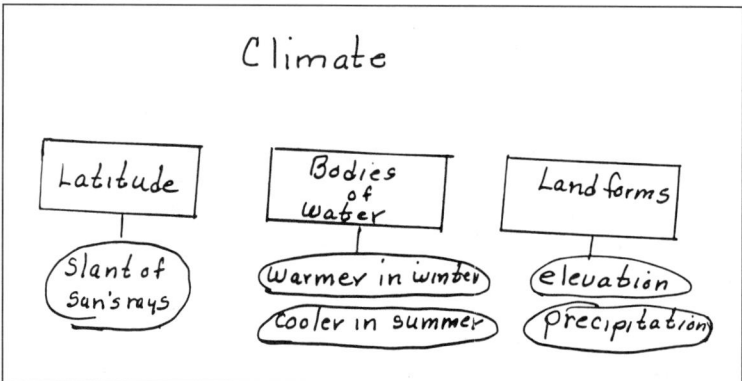

Figure 7.5. Alternative graphic organizer for expository text (web format).

- *Characters* are who or what the story is about.
- Characters exist in settings. The *setting* is where and when the story takes place. It could be one or more locations and one or more time periods.
- Characters usually have *goals;* they encounter *problems* or engage in *conflict* while trying to achieve their goals. The problems and/or conflict can be caused by the physical setting, such as when the main character attempts to rescue someone in a mountainous area in a snowstorm; this is called a *man-against-nature conflict*. Sometimes the problem or conflict is between characters; this is called a *man-against-man conflict*.
- As a story progresses, a series of important events (*rising action*) holds the reader's interest.
- The *climax* is the highest point of interest, and the reader can predict the outcome. The climax tells whether and how the conflict will be resolved.
- Falling action, or *resolution,* brings the story to a close, as does the classic fairy-tale ending, "They lived happily ever after." Readers like to know what happens to the characters before they leave the story. The teacher could explain that the resolution is sometimes called the *denouement,* a French word that means *untying*.

Greene and Enfield (1994b) explained that an *inciting force* is an event that triggers the conflict; they described rising action as a series of events that stem from the conflict, beginning with the inciting force and ending with the climax. The *crisis* is when the conflict becomes most intense, and can occur before or at the same time as the climax. Greene and Enfield developed a system of graphic symbols to depict each element. Characters are represented by a rough outline of a figure. The setting is depicted by a rectangular box. Conflict is represented by a circle, and the inciting force is represented with an arrow that starts outside the circle and ends within the circle.

Smith and Hogan (1991) recommended an explicit instruction model for introducing each element, and whenever appropriate, for relating the information to parts of speech that students have been taught. Characters are who or what the selection is about. Students know that nouns name the "who" or the "what"; when the teacher asks them to identify the characters of a selection, they know they are listening/looking for nouns that name people or things. Determining the setting of a story often requires the ability to make inferences because the setting is not always explicitly stated. The time period can be explicit, such as a specific time of day, night, or year, or it can be general, such as "long, long ago," "before John was born," or "in ancient times." Teach students to look and/or listen for adverbs or time signal words, such as *before, after, during, later, while,* and *when.* The place is where the story is happening. Because nouns name places, students know to look/listen for nouns that name places.

In keeping with the general recommendations for presenting information in small increments and building knowledge cumulatively, the elements of narratives should be introduced one at a time. After one element has been taught and students have had practice applying it, they are ready to learn the next element. The practice or application of the knowledge should include previously taught elements.

Elements of Expository (Informational) Text

An understanding of the structure of expository text is invaluable for comprehending content-area material. The elements of expository text are the *title, subject,* and *paragraphs* (which have *main ideas with supporting details*).

- As in narratives, expository material usually has a *title* that is directly or indirectly stated.
- An expository selection is about a *subject.*
- The information about the subject is organized in a series of *paragraphs.*
- Each paragraph usually has a *main idea* with supporting details that gives an important piece of information about the subject. Sometimes the main idea is explicitly stated in a topic sentence; other times it is not expressed in a topic sentence and must be inferred. In some selections, the first and/or last paragraphs have no one main idea. The first paragraph serves as an introduction; the last paragraph summarizes or explains the author's viewpoints (Greene & Enfield, 1994a).

Title If the title of an expository text is indirectly stated and mentions something unique about the subject, then prediction can be brought into play after the title is read. Smith and Hogan (1991) suggested several ways of teaching and helping students practice the concept of directly and indirectly stated titles. Using a picture, students can describe what they see in the picture, then take turns making up titles for an expository text about the picture. The teacher asks students to explain why they chose a title, then the students identify whether the title is directly or indirectly stated. The same process can be followed by reading a short selection to students and asking students to think of a title. Another approach is for the teacher to write a group of words on the board and read them to students, such as *helicopter, balloon, glider, jet, monoplane,* and *dirigible.* Students take turns identifying how all of the words are alike, then how they are different. Next, the teacher asks them to make up a title for a selection about the items; once again students must explain why they chose a particular title. Other students can identify the title as directly or indirectly stated.

Identifying the Subject   Greene and Enfield (1994b) suggested that students should learn to identify the subject of a selection by listening to or looking for frequently repeated words or substitutes for those words, such as pronouns or synonyms. After reading the indirectly stated title to students and letting them predict what they think the selection is about, give them a copy of the selection and read it to them. They underline repeated and substituted words on their copy of the selection.

Paragraphs   Give students a copy of a selection containing two or three paragraphs, and explain the concept of a paragraph while tracing the left side of the text and each paragraph indentation. Tell students that each time a line is indented, it is the beginning of a paragraph. A paragraph usually tells one important fact about the subject. Ask students to count the indentations and tell how many important facts the text will give about the subject (Greene & Enfield, 1994a).

Main Idea of a Paragraph   Smith and Hogan (1991) have used a task-analysis approach for teaching the concept of main ideas. The analysis begins with an examination of the relationships among a group of words, then among words in a sentence, and finally among groups of related sentences. Students are shown a group of words, such as *exciting, game,* and *difficult.* After reading the words to students, explain that in this group of words, the main word is *game* because *exciting* and *difficult* give more information about *game.* After modeling, provide other groups of words to students. Read the words to them, then ask them to tell which word they think is the main word and why. Gradually increase the number of words in the group to four or five, each time asking students to explain how they decided which word was the main word. As soon as students perform the task independently and accurately, extend the task to finding the main idea in a sentence, once again modeling first until students understand the concept.

Example Lesson: Introducing the Main Idea of a Paragraph

Teacher: [Writes then reads a sentence to students] *The pretty, colorful wildflowers covered the roadside.*
What is this sentence about?

Student: Pretty, colorful wildflowers

Teacher: What is the main word in that group of words?

Student: Wildflowers, because pretty and colorful tell more about wildflowers.

The next level of practice is working with three or more sentences, one that expresses the main idea of the paragraph and the others that supply supporting details.

Teacher: [Arranges three sentence strips in random order on the chalkboard and reads them to the students]
Water can be used to put out fires.
Water has many uses.
Water is used for drinking and cooking also.
We have learned to identify the main word in a group of words and the main word in a sentence. One of these sentences is the main sentence. All of the sentences are about uses of water. I think the

main sentence is *Water has many uses* because the other two sentences tell ways water is used. [Rearranges strips so that the main idea comes first]

After teacher modeling, students can work with a partner and practice identifying the main sentence. Each time, students must explain their choice. Students will eventually work up to groups of five or six sentences. As students develop confidence in identifying the topic sentence, they can arrange the remaining sentences as supporting details into a meaningful sequence. Eventually they are able to find the topic sentence within a paragraph.

Greene and Enfield (1994a) used the outline of a key to represent the "key fact" in a paragraph. When students identify the key fact, they write it inside the outline of a key. After the key fact has been identified, students work with sentence strips to arrange the supporting details into a meaningful paragraph. Students learn the format for outlining by putting a Roman numeral beside the key fact and capital letters beside each supporting detail.

One of the most difficult tasks for students is to find the main idea of a paragraph when it is not directly stated within a topic sentence. Teach students to underline important bits of information in a paragraph, such as nouns, verbs, and descriptive words and phrases (Greene & Enfield, 1994a). Students then write the abbreviated bits of information down and label each one, as follows:

Subject: Raccoons
Has ring around eyes (description)
Long, grayish hair with brown undercoat (description)
Sharp nose like a fox (description)
32 inches long (description)
Weighs 25–30 pounds (description)

As each bit of information (key fact) is labeled, students know that the this paragraph provides a description of raccoons.

DO WE EVER NEED TO TEACH SPECIFIC SKILLS?

Although the main focus of comprehension instruction is on teaching the elements of text, the previous exercise illustrates how the ability to categorize information is invaluable as students try to comprehend longer selections. Dyslexics in particular need direct instruction in understanding figurative language and idioms, classifying, determining cause and effect, drawing conclusions, using time signal words, and making predictions. These specific skills need not be taught in a particular sequence and can be taught as the need arises in mini-lessons that require only a small amount of time. Students can be taught to recognize signal words and phrases for determining cause and effect and drawing conclusions, such as *then, because, due to, so that, thus, therefore, as a result of, hence,* and *in conclusion.* Some words and phrases, such as *however, although, nevertheless, on the other hand, contrary to, still, but,* and *yet,* signal a contrasting opinion or contradiction. Analogies are helpful in teaching students how to perceive relationships. The ability to recognize broad categories and analyze relationships within categories helps students grasp main points (Vail, 1981). After the ideas have been taught in a minilesson, subsequent applications should take place in the context of the passage under study, rather than as a separate, isolated activity.

Carlisle's (1982a, 1982b, 1982c) *Reasoning and Reading* workbooks are another proven resource for specific skills minilessons. The series includes books for word meaning, sentence meaning, paragraph meaning, and reasoning skills. The books are organized in grade-level intervals of grades 3–5 (Level I), grades 6–7 (Level II), and grades 8–9 (Level III). Word-meaning activities teach multiple word meanings, classification, categorization, synonyms, antonyms, analogies, and syllogisms. All of the exercises in the books involve some kind of reasoning process. Practice activities also teach students to read sentences in phrases, rather than word by word. Composition activities that complement the comprehension activities are also included. Although the exercises are designed as workbook activities, the teacher can read the information to students and involve the whole class in the activities.

PLANNING INSTRUCTION

Maria (1990) described activities that take place in three stages of instruction: before instruction begins, during reading, and after reading.

Before Instruction Begins

Teacher Preparation   Prepare by reading the selection while keeping your students in mind. As you read, list vocabulary or concepts that students may not understand if they are not explained in the text. Complete a graphic organizer as you read. After reading, review the information on the graphic organizer. If you used certain strategies as you read, then note what they were. Did you make an inference? Did you draw a conclusion? What led you to that conclusion? Label each strategy you used during the reading so that you will be able to model it for students and be able to tell them which strategy was involved. After the graphic organizer is completed, prepare two lists of possible questions; one for use in activating the students' schemata (described previously in the Developing Background Knowledge section of this chapter), the other for discussion after the selection has been read.

Student Preparation   Investigate the students' schema for unknown meanings of vocabulary and/or concepts, then read the title and involve students in predicting what the selection is going to be about. If the selection is informative material, ask students, "What do you know about . . . ?" "What do you want to know about . . . ?"

During Reading

When reading the selection to students, provide them with a graphic organizer, and guide them in completing it, pausing for discussion when appropriate. Ask for comments from students, model the use of a strategy, or lead students in applying the strategy. Take care not to interrupt the reading so much that it detracts from the students' purpose or enjoyment.

After Reading

After students have read (or heard) the text, engage them in discussing, analyzing, and sharing opinions about the material. Always ask students to explain their reasoning. You can honor all responses, even those comments that seem "off the wall" or totally unrelated by saying something similar to "I never thought of it that way." As stated previously, it is essential that teachers refrain from asking specific questions requiring only one right answer. This is particularly true when the author appears to have had a moral or theme in mind. Students derive their own meaning from text, and they may see a different lesson or theme than what the author had in mind. Allow them to explain their thinking; in many cases the student's interpretation is accurate for him or her.

Lesson Plan Format

Divide the comprehension instruction time period into several parts.

- *Review of previously taught concepts*   When appropriate, review concepts related to the day's activity first, using concept review cards described in the Review Techniques section of this chapter.
- *Minilessons*   Set aside a few minutes for direct instruction when something new needs to be introduced. You do not need to teach something new every day.
- *Application*   Apply the concepts under study in connected text. Relate comprehension to composition whenever possible.
- *Listening Activity*   Early on, spend a few minutes each day reading to students to expose them to a variety of different literary forms. Although some incidental instruction or reinforcement can take place during the listening activity, keep the emphasis on enjoyment and appreciation of well-written material.

WHAT ABOUT GRADES?

The ideal world would not require teachers to put a "grade" on students' comprehension skills. When grading is required, it is important to remember not to devise a grading system that discourages students from participating. A point system that rewards participation can be part of a grading system. If a test is necessary, then teach students how to study with their graphic organizers and concept review cards. Administer oral tests to students whose reading and writing skills are insufficient. Develop ways of documenting how students have progressed, not how they compare with each other. Whatever grading system is used, make certain that both students and parents understand it.

SUMMARY AND GENERAL RECOMMENDATIONS

Researchers now agree that comprehension is a very complex, interactive process. Students must be able to use their background knowledge, make predictions, summarize, restate, ask themselves questions, explain, monitor whether they understand as they read the text, analyze, evaluate, and draw conclusions. Students must learn how to interact with the text, using cognitive and metacognitive processing strategies. Dyslexic students benefit from direct instruction in these processes and how they are applied with authentic texts over a prolonged period of time. Most dyslexics use bottom-up processing while they read, so instruction should begin at the sentence level and gradually move to longer selections.

- Teach the students, not the curriculum. Rather than try to cover material in the text quickly, within a certain time frame, ensure that students are mastering what you are teaching by providing enough practice with one aspect before introducing new skills or strategies. Avoid trying to keep a time schedule. Take as long as students need for each aspect of instruction; comprehension is an ongoing, lifetime process, and it is taught in every grade level.
- Honor your students' learning styles, but do not lower expectations. Teach to their intellect, not to their reading ability.
- Teach so that your students will be successful in the activity.
- Be a facilitator. Plan your lessons so that students are doing most of the talking; think of yourself more as a guide than as a lecturer.
- Use an explicit instruction model. Model and demonstrate the process, and verbalize how you performed the task as many times as necessary. Provide ample guided practice, first with the group as a whole, then with students working in pairs. Encourage students' active participation in the discussion, and always ask them to explain their reasoning processes.
- Make the learning process enjoyable for students, and have fun!

REFERENCES

Adams, M.J. (1991). Why not phonics and whole language? In W. Ellis (Ed.), *All language and the creation of literacy* (pp. 40–53). Baltimore: The International Dyslexia Association.

Anderson, R.C., Hiebert, E.H., Scott, J.A., & Wilkinson, I.A.G. (1984). *Becoming a nation of readers: The report of the Commission on Reading.* Pittsburgh: The National Academy of Education.

Bell, N. (1991). Gestalt imagery: A critical factor in language comprehension. *Annals of Dyslexia, 41,* 242–260. Baltimore: The International Dyslexia Association.

Bloom, B. (1986, February). Automaticity: The hands and feet of genius. *Educational Leadership,* 70–77.

Calfee, R., Chambliss, M., & Beretz, M. (1991). Organizing for comprehension and composition. In W. Ellis (Ed.), *All language and the creation of literacy* (pp. 79–93). Baltimore: The International Dyslexia Association.

Carlisle, J. (1982a). *Reasoning and reading, level I.* Cambridge, MA: Educators Publishing Service.

Carlisle, J. (1982b). *Reasoning and reading, level II.* Cambridge, MA: Educators Publishing Service.

Carlisle, J. (1982c). *Reasoning and reading, level III.* Cambridge, MA: Educators Publishing Service.

Carreker, S. (1993). *Multisensory grammar and written composition.* Houston, TX: S.S. Systems.

Chall, J. (1983). *Stages of reading development.* New York: McGraw-Hill.

Chall, J. (1991). American reading instruction: Science, art, and ideology. In W. Ellis (Ed.), *All language and the creation of literacy* (pp. 20–26). Baltimore: The International Dyslexia Association.

Cox, A.R. (1992). *Foundations for literacy: Structures and techniques for multisensory teaching of basic written English language skills.* Cambridge, MA: Educators Publishing Service.

Durkin, D. (1978–1979). What classroom observations reveal about reading comprehension instruction. *Reading Research Quarterly, 13,* 481–533.

Ekwall, E.E., & Shanker, J.L. (1988). *Diagnosis and remediation of the disabled reader.* Needham Heights, MA: Allyn & Bacon.

Ellis, W. (Ed.). (1991). *All language and the creation of literacy.* Baltimore: The International Dyslexia Association.

Erwin, P. (1982). *Winston grammar program.* Washougal, WA: Hewitt Research Foundation.

Fielding, L.G., & Pearson, P.D. (1994, February). Reading comprehension: What works. *Educational Leadership,* 62–68.

Galloway, C. (1976). *Psychology for learning and teaching.* New York: McGraw-Hill.

Greene, V.E., & Enfield, M.L. (1993). *Framing your thoughts: The basic structure of written expression.* Bloomington, MN: Language Circle Enterprise.

Greene, V.E., & Enfield, M.L. (1994a). *Report form comprehension guide* (Rev. ed.). Bloomington, MN: Language Circle Enterprise.

Greene, V.E., & Enfield, M.L. (1994b). *Story form comprehension guide* (Rev. ed.). Bloomington, MN: Language Circle Enterprise.

Grossen, B. (1997). *30 years of NICHD research: What we now know about how children learn to read.* Santa Cruz, CA: Center for the Future of Teaching and Learning.

Lindamood, P., Bell, N., & Lindamood, P. (1997). Sensory-cognitive factors in the controversy over reading instruction. *Journal of Developmental and Learning Disorders, 1*(1), 143–182.

Maria, K. (1990). *Reading comprehension instruction: Issues and strategies.* Timonium, MD: York Press.

Mastropieri, M., Scruggs, T., Bakken, J., & Whedon, C. (1996). Reading comprehension: A synthesis of research in learning disabilities. *Advances in Learning and Behavioral Disabilities, 10B,* 201–227.

May, F.B. (1973). *To help children read: Mastery performance modules for teachers in training.* Columbus, OH: Charles E. Merrill.

McGee-Cooper, A. (1982). *Building brain power.* Dallas: Author.

Otto, W., & Chester, R.D. (1976). *Objective-based reading.* Reading, MA: Addison Wesley Longman.

Pressley, M., Brown, R., El-Dinary, P., & Afflerbach, P. (1995). The comprehension instruction that students need: Instruction fostering constructively responsive reading. *Learning Disabilities Research & Practice, 10*(4), 215–224.

Pressley, M., & Rankin, J. (1994). More about whole language methods of reading instruction for students at risk for early reading failure. *Learning Disabilities Research and Practice, 9*(3), 157–168.

Rawson, M.B. (1988). *The many faces of dyslexia.* Baltimore: The International Dyslexia Association.

Samuels, S.J., & Kamil, M.L. (1984). Models of the reading process. In P.D. Pearson (Ed.), *Handbook of reading research* (pp. 185–224). Reading, MA: Addison Wesley Longman.

Smith, M.T., & Hogan, E.A. (1991). *MTA: Teaching a process for comprehension and composition.* Forney, TX: EDMAR Educational Associates.

Torgesen, J. (1987). The prevention and remediation of reading disabilities: Evaluating what we know from research. *Journal of Academic Language Therapy, 1,* 11–47.

Vail, P.L. (1981). *Clear and lively writing.* New York: Walker & Co.

Van Kleeck, A. (1995). Emphasizing form and meaning separately in prereading and early reading instruction. *Topics in Language Disorders, 16*(1), 27–49.

Williams, J. (1987). Educational treatments for dyslexia at the elementary and secondary levels. In R. Bowler (Ed.), *Intimacy with language: A forgotten basic in teacher education* (pp. 24–32). Baltimore: The International Dyslexia Association.

8

Teaching Spelling

Suzanne Carreker

In many classrooms spelling instruction is treated as an afterthought to or as a by-product of reading. The assumption is that if students learn to read, they learn to spell; therefore, spelling instruction is given little importance and minimal attention during the instructional day. Frequently, it is confined to irrelevant spelling exercises (Cronnell & Humes, 1980) or relegated to the memorization of word lists with little or no instruction (Peters, 1985; Treiman, 1998). The prevailing philosophy in whole-language classrooms (Goodman, 1986) is that if students are immersed in print and given opportunities to write, then they will learn to spell without formal instruction. These views fail to recognize the integral role spelling instruction plays in learning to read. Spelling is the foundation of reading and, until the 20th century, was the primary method of teaching reading (Venezky, 1980). Spelling instruction enhances reading proficiency through the reinforcement of letter patterns (Adams, 1990). Spelling is a more difficult skill to learn than reading (Frith, 1980; Johnson & Myklebust, 1967). Learning to spell requires explicit instruction (Brady & Moats, 1997; Moats, 1995), which is the focus of this chapter.

THE DISTINCTIVENESS OF SPELLING

In order to decode text, the reader must translate symbols on a printed page that represent spoken words (see Chapter 6 for more on decoding). To each letter in a printed word, the reader must attach a speech sound. In this manner the reader can sound out or pronounce the word that is represented by printed symbols. In order to spell, the speller must translate spoken words into printed symbols. To each speech sound in a spoken word, the speller must attach a written letter or letters. In this manner the speller can represent spoken words with printed symbols. It would appear from these simple descriptions that decoding and spelling are simply inverse operations that require knowledge of sound–symbol correspondences and are performed in opposite order. Following this logic, it could be assumed that if a student can read a word, then he or she can also spell it. Although both decoding and spelling require phonological and orthographic knowledge, they are not simply inverse operations (Frith, 1980). First, sound-to-spelling translations are less dependable than spelling-to-sound translations (Adams, 1990). Second, decoding requires recognition of words, whereas spelling requires complete, accurate recall of letter patterns and words (Frith & Frith, 1980; Fulk & Stormont-Spurgin, 1995).

Orthography refers to how spoken words are represented in written language. When the reader has the decoding skills discussed in Chapter 6, English orthography is 87% reliable (regular) for reading (Hanna, Hanna, Hodges, & Rudorf, 1966). The reader needs to memorize or infer from the context only about 13% of the words he or she will encounter. The rest of the words that are not instantly recognized can be sounded out. To sound out an unfamiliar word, the reader assigns known sounds to known letters in the word. With the assistance of phonological awareness, approximate pronunciations, and contextual clues, the reader can accurately pronounce the unfamiliar word (Share & Stanovich, 1995). When a letter or group of letters has more than one possible pronunciation (e.g., *ea* can be pronounced /ĕ/, /ē/, or /ā/), the reader affirms his or her pronunciation choice by determining whether the chosen word makes sense in the sentence (e.g., one nods one's /hĕd/, not one's /hēd/ or /hād/). The more the reader knows about decoding, the easier it is for him or her to recognize words, but even with partial decoding, a reader can read unfamiliar words.

The 87% reliability of English orthography (Hanna et al., 1966) is deceiving when the speller tries to spell an unfamiliar word, even if he or she can read it. The speller must rely on phonological awareness to segment the unfamiliar word into its constituent sounds and then determine how those sounds are best represented in print. But because many speech sounds in English are represented by **multiple spellings** (e.g., initial or medial /ā/ in a one-syllable word can be spelled *a*-consonant-*e* cake, *ai* as in *rain*, *ei* as in *vein*, *eigh* as in *eight*, *ea* as in *steak*), making the correct choice can be confusing to the speller. Contextual clues do not affirm the speller's choice of spelling (Fulk & Stormont-Spurgin, 1995). After all, the word that is pronounced /tām/ (*tame*), spelled incorrectly as *taim*, *teim*, *teighm*, or *team*, would share the same context. The speller's only confirmation of a correct spelling is to compare the spelled word with a word held in memory. If the word is not held in memory or if the speller has a poor memory for letters and words (i.e., poor orthographic memory), it is difficult for the speller to independently confirm that the spelling choice is correct. Spelling requires an awareness of and exact memory for letter patterns and words that reading does not require.

In addition to the need for exact recall and the ambiguities of the sound-to-spelling translations, spelling is a complex linguistic skill that demands simultaneous integration of syntactic (see Bryant, Nunes, & Bindman, 1997, for a discussion), phonological, morphological, semantic, and orthographic knowledge (Frith, 1980; Moats, 1995; Smith, 1980). This integration can be illustrated as the speller attempts to spell /jŭmpt/. Phonological awareness enables the speller to hear all of the sounds and play with the idea that /jŭmpt/ without /t/ is /jŭmp/. Syntactic awareness alerts the speller that /jŭmp/ can be used as a verb and that verbs have tenses. Morphological awareness helps the speller realize that /jŭmpt/ consists of two meaningful units—base word /jŭmp/ and suffix /t/. Semantic awareness provides the speller with the understanding that /t/ represents the past tense. Finally, using orthographic knowledge, the speller apprehends that /t/ will be spelled *ed* and not *t*. Spelling obligates the speller to attend to multiple layers of language concurrently.

Knowing how to read a word does not guarantee that a person can spell the word correctly. If this were true, then there would be no individuals who read quite well but are poor spellers, and spelling development would not lag behind reading development. Spelling instruction should be intimately integrated with the teaching of reading, but because spelling has its own distinctive characteristics and demands, it also must be distinct from reading and explicitly taught. Spellers must be taught in a manner that will increase their awareness and memory of letter patterns and words. Sequential multisensory structured spelling instruction is essential.

SPELLING DEVELOPMENT

To understand the vital role spelling plays in learning to read and the spelling errors students make, it is important to understand how spelling develops. Evidence suggests that spelling is a unitary, interactive process that requires both phonological and orthographic knowledge (Lennox & Siegel, 1998). Beginning spellers take advantage of both phonological and visual strategies (Bryant & Bradley, 1980; Treiman, Cassar, & Zukowski, 1994).

A young child's first writing experience is usually in the form of drawing. As the child is exposed to print, he or she begins to differentiate writing from drawing and begins to imitate the print he or she has seen, using letterlike or numberlike forms (Cassar & Treiman, 1997). In this precommunicative stage (Moats, 1995), the child's writing shows a lack of understanding of the **concept of a word,** the alphabetic principle, or the conventions of print such as spaces between words and the left-to-right progression of writing. The organization of the child's writing may be described as "willy-nilly" (Bear, Invernizzi, Templeton, & Johnston, 1996, p. 16). At age 3 or 4, the child may think that the length of the word reflects the size of the object it names instead of the sounds of language (e.g., *cow* should have more letters than *chicken* because a cow is bigger than a chicken) (Treiman, 1997). To the 3- or 4-year-old child, meaning takes precedence over spelling. Only when the child becomes aware that meaning is irrelevant and that print is related to speech does he or she come to understand that letters represent speech sounds.

A grasp of the alphabetic principle emerges with the child's realization that spoken words are made of sounds that can be represented in print. He or she will first attempt to connect speech to print at the level of the syllable instead of at the level of the phoneme and will write a symbol for each syllable, for example, *b* for *be* or *nf* for *enough* (Ferreiro & Teberosky, 1982). As the child becomes more aware that individual letters represent individual sounds, he or she enters a **semiphonetic stage** (Moats, 1995) and uses incomplete but reasonable phonetic representations of words. The child usually uses the initial or salient consonants of a word, such as *s*, *c*, or *sd* for *seed* (Rubin & Eberhardt, 1996), or the child may use letter names, such as *lft* for *elephant* (Adams, 1990; Treiman, 1994). At this semiphonetic stage, the child demonstrates awareness of left-to-right progression, but he or she tends to run letters together with little or no sense of wordness (e.g., *RUDF* for *Are you deaf?*) (Moats, 1995).

Further experiences with print and writing move the child to a stage of complete phonetic representations, or the **phonetic stage** (Moats, 1995). Every sound in a word is represented, but the child does not demonstrate knowledge of conventional spelling patterns. The child may spell *same* as *sam*, thus neglecting the final silent *e* (Treiman, Zukowski, & Richmond-Welty, 1995). The inflection *-ed* may be represented as *t* as in *askt* or *d* as in *hugd* (Read, 1971). At this phonetic stage, the child is aware not only of sounds but also of mouth positions used to make sounds. The child may seem to be "spelling by mouth" (Moats, 1995, p. 37). For example, the child may use *y* to spell /w/ because not only does the letter name contain /w/, but the mouth position to say the letter name *y* is also the same as to say /w/. Other odd but linguistically understandable spelling choices may be observed at this stage, such as spelling /t/ before /r/ as *ch* as in *chrie* for *try* or /d/ before /r/ as *j* as in *jragin* for *dragon* (Read, 1971). Phonetically, /t/ or /d/ would not be spelled with *ch* or *j*, but when /t/ or /d/ occur before /r/, the **place of articulation** (i.e., where the sound is obstructed in the mouth during production) matches the place of articulation for /ch/ and /j/, respectively (Treiman, 1998). Consistent spelling anomalies may occur, such as /r/ overwhelming the vowel *hr* for *her* or the omission of nasal (i.e., /m/, /n/, /ng/) and liquid sounds (i.e., /l/, /r/) *drik* for *drink, jup* for *jump, od* for *old* (Treiman, 1998; Treiman et al., 1995).

In these early stages of spelling development, a child is literal in his or her spelling of words (e.g., /k/ is almost always spelled *k*). As the child begins to read more, he or she becomes more sensitive to the letter patterns in words. Without being taught, he or she may discover an orthographic pattern and sense its constraints. The child may discover that /k/ can be spelled *ck* and sense that it does not occur in the initial position of a word. He or she is more likely to spell *cake* as *kack* than *ckak* (Treiman, 1997). In this transitional stage of spelling, as the child becomes more aware of letter patterns in words, his or her spelling may seem "off-base" (Moats, 1995, p. 40). From exact phonetic representations of every sound, the child's spelling may become a mixture of phonetic components and salient visual features in words. This change in spelling usually signals a heightened awareness of letter patterns.

Through their early spelling experiences, children build a foundation for reading as they begin to establish sound–symbol correspondences and develop a sensitivity to letter patterns. But just as beginning readers need explicit teaching to become good readers, beginning spellers need explicit teaching to become good spellers. Without this formal instruction, beginning spellers will not establish the awareness and memory of letter patterns that will make them good spellers.

GOOD AND POOR SPELLERS

Good spelling ability is contingent on the speller's sensitivity to letter patterns (Adams, 1990). Research has shown that good and poor spellers do not differ greatly in their visual memory abilities (Lennox & Siegel, 1996). What differs in good spellers is that they possess well-developed phonological processing skills that not only make them aware of the sounds in words but also support the learning of letter patterns in words (Lennox & Siegel, 1998; Moats, 1995). Good spellers possess an orthographic memory. This orthographic memory is a more specific memory than visual memory; it is specific to remembering letter patterns and words. The development of this memory is dependent on well-developed phonological processing skills. Good spellers know not only how sounds are represented in language but also how words should look (Adams, 1990). They are able to deal with the ambiguities of the orthography (e.g., the multiple spellings of /ā/) by weighting the variable spellings by their frequency or exposure in reading (e.g., the good speller weights *a*-consonant-*e* as a more frequent or stronger connection to /ā/ than *eigh* because he or she sees it more frequently) (Adams, 1990; Foorman, 1994; Seidenberg & McClelland, 1989). In addition to possessing phonological and orthographic knowledge, good spellers are able to simultaneously draw support from their awareness of syntax, morphology, and semantics. Because good spellers possess the very skills that are needed for good decoding, good spellers are good readers. It is unusual to find a good speller who is a poor reader.

The Orton Dyslexia Society's definition of dyslexia (as cited in Lyon, 1995) includes individuals who have reading disabilities as well as specific spelling disabilities. As noted in Chapter 6, dyslexic students have difficulty learning to decode because of a core deficit in phonological processing (Adams, 1990; Bradley & Bryant, 1983; Goswami & Bryant, 1990). It is rare for dyslexic students who have difficulty with reading not to have difficulty with spelling. It is possible, however, for students to be fairly good readers but poor spellers. Moats (1995) made these observations about poor spellers. Good readers who are poor spellers have problems with the exact recall of letter sequences and subtle difficulties with complex spelling patterns and aspects of language structure, but they do not have a deficit in phonological processing. Poor readers who are poor spellers have a deficit in phonological processing that interferes with their mastery of spelling. They also have a specific problem with memory of letter patterns, which is rooted in their poor phonological processing. In addition, poor spellers do not possess the ability to deal with several layers of language simultaneously. With proper instruction, poor spellers who are poor readers will improve their decoding skills, but they seldom master spelling (Moats, 1994; Oakland, Black, Stanford, Nussbaum, & Balise, 1998).

Roberts and Mather (1997) characterized poor spelling as the result of difficulties in both phonological and orthographic processing. Difficulties with phonological processing may include poor sequencing of sounds, omission or addition of sounds, confusion with similar-sounding phonemes (e.g., /f/ and /th/, /p/ and /b/), and limited knowledge of spelling rules. Orthographic processing difficulties are manifested as poor sequencing of nonphonetic patterns, confusion with graphemes that look similar (e.g., *b* and *d*, *n* and *u*), transposition of letters (e.g., *fro* instead of *for*), overgeneralization of rules, and overreliance on auditory features (e.g., *becuz* for *because*).

Poor spellers may be perceived as "free-spirit" spellers who spell words the way they sound without regard to conventional letter patterns. They may spell *does* as *duz*, *dress* as *dres*, or *girl* as *gerl*. They may spell the same word several different ways within the same paragraph, such as *thay*, *tha*, and *thai* for *they*. The true dyslexic spellers may appear to be "bizarre" spellers. They struggle with the conventional letter patterns of words and use inappropriate letter sequences, such as *oridr* for *order;* transpositions, such as *gril* for *girl;* letter reversals, such as *dady for* baby; or incomplete letter patterns, such as *boht* for *bought.* Not only do dyslexic spellers lack the ability to use conventional letter patterns, but they also are unable to fully or correctly translate the sounds in words. They may have difficulty hearing the word correctly (e.g., hearing "fan" instead of "van"), hearing all of the sounds in a word (e.g., hearing "butful" for "beautiful"), or keeping the sounds in sequence (e.g., using *slpit* for "split"). They may have difficulty discriminating similar sounds as (e.g., hearing "baf" for "bath" or "wint" for "went").

Problems with spelling persist in dyslexic adolescents and adults. Moats (1996) found that dyslexic adolescents showed lingering, subtle signs of phonological difficulty, primarily in segmenting words into their phonemic and morphemic units, as evidenced by their consistent omissions, substitutions, and misrepresentations of inflected morphemes (e.g., *-ed* spelled as *t* or *d*). Their errors in spelling high-frequency words suggested that their underdeveloped phonological and linguistic awareness compromised the development of orthographic memory. When comparing the writing samples of dyslexic and nondyslexic adults, Sterling, Farmer, Riddick, Morgan, and Matthews (1998) found that the sentences of dyslexic adults were no shorter or longer than those of their peers but that there was a conspicuous use of monosyllabic words and misuse of **homophones.** Spelling errors suggested specific phonological impairment as well as problems with the complexities of English. Adolescents and adults who are poor spellers demonstrate the tenacious nature of a phonological processing deficit and its chronic effect on spelling development. Phonological awareness along with morphemic and orthographic awareness must be considered significant elements of spelling instruction.

It is important to note that spelling ability and IQ scores are not related. Poor spelling does not reflect a lack of intelligence (West, 1991). Take, for example, the spelling errors of neurosurgeon Harvey Cushing: *swoolen* for *swollen, neybour* for *neighbor,* and *quire* for *choir.* He was a brilliant man who was a *mediocher* speller.

KNOWLEDGE NECESSARY FOR SPELLING

Traditional spelling instruction that involves the repetitious copying of words or the memorization of word lists does not promote active, reflective thought about language. Informal spelling instruction that assumes that spelling will develop through writing experiences does not provide students with the necessary knowledge of language structure they need to become correct spellers. Students must be explicitly taught about language structure for spelling, and they must be actively engaged in thinking about language. The teacher must assume an active role in spelling instruction. It is imperative that the teacher have and be able to impart knowledge about the sounds of the language; the most frequent and reliable letter patterns; and rules of English orthography, morphology, and word origins (Brady & Moats, 1997; see Chapter 5 for a discussion of English word origins).

Phonetics, Phonology, and Phonics

Phonetics is the study of the characteristics of individual speech sounds (i.e., phonemes) that occur in all languages. There are approximately 44 speech sounds in English with some variants of these sounds (i.e., allophones) that are not considered separate speech sounds (e.g., the *a* in the word *sank* is different from the *a* in *sack* but is not a separate speech sound). Phonetics involves the categorization or description of the articulation of each speech sound—where the sound is produced, the way in which air stream flows through the mouth and nose, and the activity of the vocal cords during production.

Spoken words are made up of the speech sounds. Every language has its own set of rules and patterns that governs the utterance of these sounds and the sound patterns that are allowed. This system of rules and patterns that determine how sounds are used in spoken language is called *phonology* (Moats, 1995). There are constraints about sound sequences in spoken language based on what humans are capable of producing easily (e.g., /np/ rarely occurs in spoken English, hence the pronunciation /ĭm•pôrt/ rather than /ĭn•pôrt/). Pronunciation variations may occur because of a phoneme's position in a word (e.g., /p/ in *pot* is different from the /p/ in *spot* or *top*) or because of surrounding sounds (e.g., the *a* in *sank* is nasalized before nasal /ng/). These perfunctory pronunciation differences do not affect meaning (Treiman et al., 1994). Accent may vary pronunciations as well as the meanings of words (e.g., /ŏb'•jĕkt/ is a noun, and /ŏb•jĕkt'/ is a verb). No one is taught the rules and patterns that govern the use of speech sounds (Read, 1971); they are unconscious rules and patterns that automatically occur in spoken language.

Phonics is an instructional method that teaches the use of written symbols to represent speech sounds for reading and spelling. Phonics provides a visual representation of the phonology of spoken language (e.g., the *a* in *sank* is nasalized because it comes before *n*, which is pronounced /ng/ instead of /n/ before any letter pronounced /k/ or /g/). In order for students to be successful with phonics, they must be aware of the sounds in spoken words.

Brady and Moats (1997) contended that knowledge of phonetics and phonology assists the teacher in understanding the reading and spelling errors of students, increases his or her ability to provide **corrective feedback,** and enables him or her to plan instruction that is linguistically informed. Knowledge of phonetics heightens the teacher's awareness of speech sounds and how they are produced so that he or she can provide correct models for the students. Knowledge of phonology gives the teacher insight into why students might have difficulty unblending or spelling words. For example, a nasalized vowel plus a nasal consonant sound is pronounced as a unit. Therefore, students may have difficulty hearing that /jŭmp/ consists of four separate sounds. They may unblend it as three sounds: /j/, /ŭm/, and /p/. When spelling, students may hear /t/ before /r/ as /ch/ and spell it accordingly. As mentioned previously, /t/ before /r/ has a place of articulation in the mouth that is similar to /ch/, so the use of *ch* is not outrageous but instead is "reasonable and well motivated" (Treiman et al., 1994, p. 1336) and worthy of recognition (Read, 1971). The teacher need not be a linguist but rather should have phonemic awareness and a working knowledge of the sound structure of English.

Production of Speech Sounds Correct pronunciation of speech sounds is encouraged through an understanding of the descriptions of the individual speech sounds (Moats, 1995). When students understand the kinesthetic feel and the visual display of the mouth as a sound is pronounced, they are better able to determine sounds.

In decoding instruction, students learn that vowel sounds are open and voiced. (See Table 2.3 for the place of articulation of each vowel sound.) The short vowels are most difficult to discriminate. Figure 8.1 (Cox, 1992) illustrates the mouth positions of the short vowel sounds. The teacher should study and share this figure with students. Visual awareness of the mouth positions for the production of vowel sounds heightens students' ability to discriminate the vowel sounds. Awareness of the distinctive, kinesthetic feel of sounds as they are produced also assists in discriminating easily confused vowel sounds (e.g., /ĭ/ makes you grin, /ĕ/ drops your chin).

To be able to provide correct models of consonant sounds, the teacher should study the sound production of consonant sounds in three categories: the place of articulation, the flow of the air stream, and the activity of the vocal cords. Table 8.1 provides information about the place of articulation of the consonant sounds, using the phonic spellings that often are used in reading and spelling instruction. Table 8.2 provides information on the kinesthetic feel of the mouth and how the air stream flows from the mouth or nose during production of consonant sounds. Table 8.3 presents information about voiced and unvoiced consonant sounds. With awareness of each aspect of consonant sounds, the teacher will be better able to provide correct models for students.

Phonemic Awareness   The importance of phonemic awareness in learning to read and spell has been well documented (Adams, 1990; Bradley & Bryant, 1983; Goswami & Bryant, 1990; Liberman, Shankweiler, & Liberman, 1989). Spelling begins with the speller's awareness that spoken words are made up of sounds that are represented in print by letters. For the speller to represent those sounds in print accurately, he or she must be able to pronounce them correctly and discriminate them clearly.

Activities that promote phonological awareness, especially phonemic awareness, are outlined in Chapter 3 and must be included in beginning reading and spelling instruction. As students prepare to spell words, they need to engage in activities that promote the recognition or discrimination of specific sounds in words:

- *To heighten sensitivity to a particular sound in a word:* The teacher says a word and asks students to listen for a certain sound. Students repeat the word, lis-

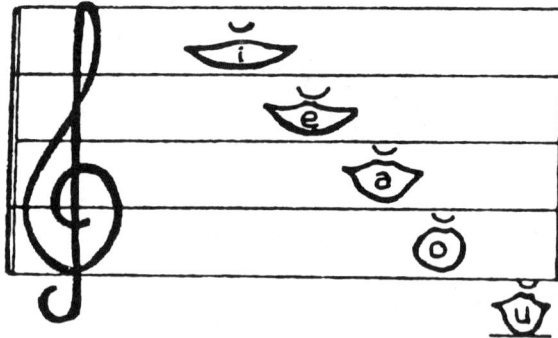

Figure 8.1.   Mouth position for the short vowel sounds. (From Cox, A.R. [1992]. *Foundations for literacy: Structures and techniques for multisensory teaching of basic written English language skills* [p. 129]. Cambridge, MA: Educators Publishing Service, Inc.; reprinted by permission.)

Table 8.1.   Places of articulation of consonant sounds

Both lips	Teeth and lower lip	Between the teeth	Ridge behind teeth	Roof of mouth	Back of mouth	From the throat
/b/	/f/	/th/	/d/	/ch/	/g/	/h/
/m/	/v/	/t̶h̶/	/l/	/j/	/k/	/hw/
/p/			/n/	/sh/	/ks/	
			/r/	/y/	/kw/	
			/s/	/zh/	/ng/	
			/t/		/w/	
			/z/			

tening for the sound. If they hear the sound, then they say the sound. If they do not hear the sound, then they say, "No."

- *To heighten sensitivity to the position of a particular sound in a word:* The teacher says a word and asks students to listen for the position of a particular sound in the word. Students repeat the word, listening for the position of the sound. Students indicate the position: initial, medial, or final (see Chapter 4 for activities that explore the concepts *initial, medial,* and *final*).

- *To promote spelling by analogy (Goswami, 1988; Nation & Hulme, 1998):* The teacher says a word, and students repeat it. The teacher tells students to change a sound (not a letter name) in the word. Students pronounce the new word (e.g., change /s/ in *sat* to /m/ and pronounce the new word or change /t/ in *bat* to /g/ and pronounce the new word).

Orthography

Orthography refers to the rules that govern how words are represented in writing. Chapter 6 contains information that assists the student in managing English orthography for reading. With this information, the reader knows how to translate the orthography into its spoken equivalents. The speller's task is to determine how the phonemes of oral language are transcribed into the graphemes (i.e., letters or letter clusters) of written language. There are constraints in English orthography; for example, certain letters never double (e.g., *j, y, w*), certain letters do not occur in sequence (e.g., *skr*), and words do not end in certain letters (e.g., *v, j*). Formal spelling instruction calls attention to these constraints and helps students manage English orthography for spelling by establishing a sense of the frequency and reliability of letter patterns (Brady & Moats, 1997).

Twenty-four speech sounds can be established as having a one-to-one correspondence with written letters (see Table 8.4). These sounds have only one spelling (e.g., /m/ is spelled *m*, /p/ is spelled *p*), or they have one spelling that is far more frequent than any other spelling (e.g., /f/ is spelled *f* much more often than *ph* or *gh*, /ĕ/ is spelled *e* much more often than *ea*) (Hanna et al., 1966). This information will enable students to spell more than half of the phonemes of English.

The other speech sounds of English have a more precarious link to orthography (see Table 8.4). The transcriptions of each of these sounds depends not only on frequency but also on the position of the sound in a word, the length of the

Table 8.2. Flow of air during production of consonant sounds

Partially blocked[a] and clipped	Totally blocked[a] and continuous	Unblocked[a] and aspirated	Through the nose, blocked, and continuous
/b/	/f/	/h/	/m/
/ch/	/hw/		/n/
/d/	/ks/		/ng/
/g/	/kw/		
/j/	/l/		
/k/	/r/		
/p/	/s/		
/t/	/sh/		
/y/	/~~th~~/		
	/th/		
	/v/		
	/w/		
	/z/		
	/zh/		

[a]The terms *blocked, partially blocked,* and *unblocked* are used in spelling instruction to refer to the kinesthetic feel of the position of the tongue, teeth, or lips during the production of sounds in isolation. *Blocked* refers to the steady position of the tongue, teeth, or lips during the entire production of a sound. *Partially blocked* refers to a released position of the tongue or lips during the production of a sound. *Unblocked* refers to no obstruction of the sound by the tongue, teeth, or lips during the production of a sound. These terms are used to aid students in clearly feeling and distinguishing sounds for spelling.

word, the accent, or the influence of surrounding sounds. To make sense of spelling choices, students must realize there is a difference between decoding and spelling. When decoding, students look at the printed symbols and translate those graphemes into phonemes. Students have no difficulty reading *gate* because they know that *a*-consonant-*e* is pronounced as /ā/. They can read *bait* because they know that *ai* is pronounced /ā/. Knowing that *eigh* is pronounced /ā/ enables readers to pronounce the word *weight*. All of these words follow frequent, reliable patterns for reading.

Spelling a word starts with sounds, not letter sequences. For spelling, students hear /gāt/, /bāt/, and /wāt/. Except for the initial phonemes, these words sound similar. They all are one-syllable words with medial /ā/ that end in /t/. Students will have little trouble spelling the initial or final sounds, but spelling the medial sounds may be problematic. Without the memory of letter patterns, either because of lack of exposure to print or because of poor orthographic memory, spellers have difficulty knowing whether to use *a*-consonant-*e*, *ai*, or *eigh*. They must be taught that when they hear /ā/ in medial position of a one-syllable base word, it is most frequently represented with *a*-consonant-*e*. With this information, students will be able to spell correctly a high percentage of one-syllable words with /ā/ (Hanna et al., 1966). Not only does their spelling accuracy increase but the focus on one spelling also establishes that pattern well and actually heightens awareness of other possible spellings of /ā/. If all of the possible spellings of /ā/ are taught, however, beginning spellers and poor spellers in particular will be overwhelmed with choices.

This problem exists with most published spelling series. The weekly spelling lists confuse students with multiple choices and seldom offer direction in terms

Table 8.3. Unvoiced and voiced consonant sounds

Unvoiced	Voiced
Pairs (read across)	
/p/	/b/
/t/	/d/
/k/	/g/
/f/	/v/
/s/	/z/
/th/	/t̶h̶/
/ch/	/j/
/sh/	/zh/
Nonpairs (read down)	
/h/	/kw/
/hw/	/l/
/ks/	/m/
	/n/
	/ng/
	/r/
	/w/
	/y/

of establishing frequency or reliability, as in the following example (Cook, Farnum, Gabrielson, & Temple, 1998, p. 28):

Words with /ū/ and /o͞o/

1.	bloom	8.	loose	15.	avenue
2.	ruler	9.	whose	16.	dew
3.	broom	10.	glue	17.	flute
4.	usual	11.	clue	18.	due
5.	roof	12.	rescue	19.	tune
6.	few	13.	movie	20.	beautiful
7.	used	14.	human		

This list has two sounds, /ū/ *use* and /o͞o/*moon.* These two sounds are auditorily similar with similar visual displays. The only noticeable difference is in the production of the two sounds. The tongue is tensed when pronouncing /ū/. But because /ū/ is often pronounced /o͞o/in running speech, it will be difficult for students to clearly discriminate the sounds. The other problem with this list is the number of spelling choices (7) for these two sounds: *u*-consonant-*e, ue, u, oo, o, ew,* and *eau.* Some of the choices are extremely infrequent (see Table 8.5). Few words have the /o͞o/or /ū/ sound spelled with *o* as in *move* or the letter patterns *ew* as in *dew* or *eau* as in *beautiful.* Helpful information for students includes the following: /ū/ is best spelled with *u*-consonant-*e* in one-syllable words *use* or *cube*; /ū/ at the end of a syllable is spelled *u* as in *human* or *ue* at the end of a word as in *statue* (Cox, 1977). Good spellers, who of course are good readers, begin to weight the frequency of these spellings as they read (Adams, 1990; Foorman, 1994; Seiden-

Table 8.4. Sound-to-spelling translations of speech sounds based on frequency

Vowel sounds with one frequent spelling	Consonant sounds with one frequent spelling	Vowel sounds with more than one frequent spelling	Consonant sounds with more than one frequent spelling
/ă/ = a (apple)	/b/ = b (bat)	/ŏ/ = o (octopus), a (watch)	/ch/ = ch (cheek)
/ĕ/ = e (echo)	/f/ = f (fish)	/ŭ/ = u (cup), a (banana)	ch (lunch, speech)
/ĭ/ = i (itch)	/g/ = g (goat)	/ā/ = a-consonant-e (cake)	tch (catch)
/ŏŏ/ = oo (book)	/h/ = h (house)	a (apron)	/d/ = d (dog), ed (smelled)
/ōō/ = oo (moon)	/l/ = l (leaf)	ay (tray)	/j/ = j (jam)
/är/ = ar (star)	/m/ = m (mitten)	/ē/ = ee (feet)	g (gentle, giant, biology)
/ôr/ = or (fork)	/n/ = n (nest)	e-consonant-e (athlete)	dge (edge), ge (hinge)
	/p/ = p (pig)	e (equal)	/k/ = c (cat, cot, cut, clam, crab)
	/kw/ = qu (queen)	ee (three)	k (keep, kite, sky)
	/r/ = r (rabbit)	y (penny)	ck (pocket)
	/w/ = w (wish)	/ī/ = i-consonant-e (five)	ck (back)
	/ks/ = x (box)	i (iris)	k (book, milk)
	/y/ = y (yarn)	y (fly)	ke (make), c (music)
	/th/ = th (rather)	/ō/ = o-consonant-e (rope)	/ng/ = ng (king)
	/th/ = th (thimble)	o (open)	n (sink, angle)
	/hw/ = wh (whistle)	ow (snow)	/s/ = s (sock)
	/sh/ = sh (ship)	/ū/ = u-consonant-e (cube)	c (grocery, icicle)
	/zh/ = si (erosion)	u (unicorn)	ss (kiss, discuss), s (cactus)
		ue (statue)	ce (mice)
			se (horse, mouse)
		/er/ = er (fern), or (world)	/t/ = t (table), ed (jumped)
		/au/ = au (saucer), aw (saw)	/v/ = v (valentine)
		a (ball)	ve (nave)
		/oi/ = oi (boil), oy (boy)	/z/ = z (zipper)
		/ou/ = ou (out), ow (cow)	s (pansy)
			s (has)
			se (cheese)

Table 8.5. Infrequent spellings of vowel sounds

/ă/ = pl<u>ai</u>d, l<u>augh</u>
/ā/ = r<u>ai</u>n, caf<u>é</u>, st<u>ea</u>k, matin<u>ee</u>, v<u>ei</u>n, <u>eigh</u>t, th<u>e</u>re, th<u>ey</u>, ball<u>et</u>
/au/ = c<u>augh</u>t, br<u>ough</u>t, br<u>oa</u>d
/ĕ/ = h<u>ea</u>d, s<u>ai</u>d, <u>a</u>ny
/ē/ = b<u>ea</u>ch, c<u>ei</u>ling, monk<u>ey</u>, sk<u>i</u>, pr<u>ie</u>st, (i-consonant-e) petit<u>e</u>
/er/ = doll<u>ar</u>, b<u>ir</u>d, anch<u>or</u>, b<u>ur</u>n, s<u>ear</u>ch, j<u>our</u>nal
/ĭ/ = capt<u>ai</u>n, (a-consonant-e) clim<u>ate</u>, forf<u>ei</u>t, (i-consonant-e) capt<u>ive</u>, g<u>y</u>m
/ī/ = <u>ai</u>sle, k<u>ay</u>ak, h<u>eigh</u>t, t<u>ie</u>, l<u>igh</u>t, n<u>y</u>lon, (y-consonant-e) st<u>yle</u>, d<u>ye</u>, b<u>uy</u>
/ō/ = b<u>eau</u>, b<u>oa</u>t, t<u>oe</u>, d<u>ough</u>
/ŏŏ/ = p<u>u</u>sh
/ōō/ = s<u>ou</u>p, d<u>o</u>, sh<u>oe</u>, thr<u>ough</u>
/ou/ = pl<u>ough</u>
/ŭ/ = s<u>o</u>n, bl<u>oo</u>d, t<u>ou</u>ch
/ū/ = b<u>eau</u>ty, <u>Eu</u>rope, n<u>ew</u>, fr<u>ui</u>t

berg & McClelland, 1989) and are better able to deal with a list that has multiple spellings of one sound. Poor spellers who are poor readers do not receive sufficient exposure to these patterns to weight them. Poor spellers who are good readers do not have adequate sensitivity to letter patterns to determine frequency. The goal of effective spelling instruction is to make the reliability of English orthography obvious to all students by teaching the most frequent, reliable orthographic patterns of English.

Morphology

Morphology refers to morphemes, the smallest units of language that carry meaning (prefixes, suffixes, roots, and combining forms; see Chapters 5 and 6 for more information on morphemes). Morphemic knowledge advances students from the spelling of one-syllable base words to the spelling of one-syllable base words with suffixes and eventually to the spelling of other derivatives (i.e., a base word plus one or more affixes) and multisyllabic words. Knowledge of suffixes and inflectional morphemes signals to students that /pĭnz/ contains two morphemes or meaningful units: the base word /pĭn/ and the suffix /z/, which makes the word plural; therefore, /z/ is spelled *s* not *z*. Without the understanding of suffixes and inflectional morphemes, students remain literal in their spellings and write /jŭmpt/ as *jumpt* and /băngd/ as *bangd* because that is what they hear. The understanding that a suffix that begins with a consonant is a consonant suffix and a suffix that begins with a vowel is vowel suffix helps students when they add suffixes to base words to spell derivatives. The final letter of a base word may be doubled or dropped, but this is true only when adding a vowel suffix (e.g., *starring* but not *starrless*, *hoping* but not *hopful*).

Knowledge of prefixes and roots facilitates students' spelling of multisyllabic words (Adams, 1990; Brady & Moats, 1997; Henry, 1988). For example, the word *attraction* contains three morphemes. These morphemes serve not only as meaning-filled units but also as spelling units. The word *attraction* can be spelled in chunks instead of sound by sound. Knowing that some consonant prefixes change their spellings for **euphony** (i.e., to ease pronunciation; see Table 8.6), students know to spell a word such as *attraction* with two *t*'s because the *at-* in *attraction* represents a spelling deviation of the prefix *ad-*. The prefix changes the final letter to match the initial letter of the root *tract*. With knowledge of morphology, students can clarify spelling choices and contend with more complex levels of orthography.

Word Origins

Chapter 5 outlines the Anglo-Saxon, Latin, and Greek layers of language in English. These languages and others have shaped the orthography of English as evidenced in the spelling of /sh/. Fourteen different spellings have been noted in English (Bryson, 1990): *sh ship; ch chef; ti nation; si discussion; ci special; xi anxious; sci conscious; sch schnauzer; ce ocean; se nauseous; s sugar; ss tissue; psh pshaw;* and *chsi fuchsia.* These spellings represent different layers of language within English: *sh* from Anglo-Saxon; *ch* from French; *ti, ci, si, xi,* and *sci* from Latin; *sch* and *chsi* from German; and *ce* from Greek. The layers of other languages make English a rich tapestry of words, but they create a confusing orthography, thus compounding the difficulties poor spellers have with spelling. It would seem logical to change orthography to make it less confusing and to make words easier to spell.

There have been many attempts to reform English orthography but to no avail (Venezky, 1980). Benjamin Franklin proposed a phonetic alphabet with a better one-to-one correspondence, which in the end did not gain much favor. Noah Webster, who advocated educational reform and America's own form of spelling to complement its unique form of government, proposed changes such as *bred* for *bread, laf* for *laugh,* and *crum* for *crumb.* Although these changes were not accepted, Webster was successful in changing the spellings of words such as *honour* to *honor, centre* to *center,* and *publick* to *public.* An organization dedicated to spelling reform, the American Philological Association, made concerted efforts to change the orthography of English in the late 1800s and early 1900s but had little success. In the 1930s, *The Chicago Tribune,* in an effort to increase readership by making words easier to read, used these spellings in their newspaper: *thru, tho,* and *thoro.* Although it seems reasonable to simplify and unify orthography, such attempts have failed. Perhaps this is because changing the orthography of English would mask its rich, interesting history.

Rather than bemoan the inconsistencies of English, students can take advantage of information about word origins to refine their spelling knowledge. Ini-

Table 8.6. Prefixes that change spelling for euphony

Prefix	Prefix changed for euphony
ab-	a-, abs-
ad-	a-, ac-, af-, ag-, al-, an-, ap-, ar-, as-, at-
con-	co-, col-, com-, cor-
en-	em-
ex-	e-, ec-, ef-
in-	il-, im-, ir-
ob-	oc-, of-, op-
sub-	suc-, suf-, sup-, sur-, sus-

tially, students are taught that the most frequent, though not the only, spelling of /f/ is *f*. This information serves them well for spelling most words. With the knowledge that long, scientific terms are usually of Greek origin and that Greek words containing /f/ are spelled with *ph*, students have information that will help them to spell words such as *chlorophyll* and *photosynthesis*. Students will also note that words of Greek origin containing /k/ are often spelled with *ch* and those containing /ĭ/ are often spelled with *y*. With knowledge of word origins, students come to understand why some words are spelled in unexpected ways, and, more important, they can determine the appropriate spellings for these words. (See Henry, 1988, for more on spellings according to word origin.)

FORMAL SPELLING INSTRUCTION

Spelling is a skill that must be formally taught. In preschool and kindergarten, the use of invented spelling should be encouraged and supported with phonological awareness training (Blachman, Ball, Black, & Tangel, 1994, 2000; Castle, Riach, & Nicholson, 1994; Rubin & Eberhardt, 1996). (See Chapter 3 for activities that can be incorporated into the classroom routine; see also Adams, Foorman, Lundberg, & Beeler, 1998.) Through the use of invented spellings, students learn the essence of spelling: translating sounds to symbols. Good spelling, however, requires more than translating sounds to symbols; it also demands a sensitivity to letter patterns in words. Although invented spelling reinforces sound–symbol correspondences, it does not provide the correct models that students need to build orthographic knowledge. Students must be formally taught the patterns and rules of English orthography, beginning in the middle of first grade. Learning the patterns and rules cannot be left to chance. Correct spelling has a direct impact on students' reading proficiency (Adams, 1990).

Formal spelling instruction should include the following:

- Phonological awareness training
- Opportunities for kindergarteners and students beginning in first grade to experiment with writing using invented spelling
- Multisensory, discovery teaching introductions to the sounds, sound–symbol correspondences, patterns, rules, and morphemes of English, beginning in the middle of first grade and using a systematic, sequential, cumulative order of presentation
- Opportunities to analyze and sort words
- Practice using multisensory, structured procedures
- A multisensory procedure for learning irregular words
- Opportunities to use the words in writing through dictation and personal writing

Invented Spelling

Students' use of invented spelling provides the teacher with information about how well students have learned and internalized information about language structure. When students use invented spelling, they are not reinventing the spelling of words. They are applying their acquired knowledge of sounds, symbols, and letter patterns to the task of spelling an unfamiliar word (Read, 1971).

As students learn more about language structure, their knowledge is reflected in the spelling. The development of invented spelling should follow the definite stages of spelling development. These stages match students' acquisition of language knowledge (Rubin & Eberhardt, 1996): 1) Students spell words that represent partial phonetic patterns (e.g., *s, c,* or *sd* for *seed*), 2) students spell words that represent complete phonetic patterns (e.g., *sed, ced,* or *cd* for *seed*), and 3) students spell words that represent complete phonetic patterns and use conventional orthographic patterns (e.g., *sead, ceed, sede,* or *cede* for *seed*). Children who demonstrate progression through these stages in their invented spelling are gaining a solid foundation for spelling as well as reading. When children can use word structure to spell phonetically, they are better able to learn more complex spellings; they also make rapid progress in learning to read (Moats, 1995). The teacher must be alert to the children who are not moving through this sequence and give them guidance to ensure they will have the necessary foundation for reading and spelling.

Formal spelling instruction extends the spelling information students gain through invented spelling and teaches the structure of the language for spelling, thus enabling students to move from invented spelling to conventional spelling. Words can be categorized as regular, rule, and irregular (Carreker, 1992). It will be helpful to introduce information for spelling instruction in these same categories.

Regular Words

Regular words are spelled the way they sound. They follow the frequent, reliable sound-to-letter translations or patterns of the language (see Table 8.4). Some regular words are transparent in their spellings, such as *in, rag,* or *help.* There is only one spelling or only one predominant spelling of the sounds; hence there is no confusion about how to spell the sounds in these words. Not all regular words are as transparent in their spellings. Some regular words contain sounds with indefinite spellings, such as /k/, which can be spelled *k, c,* or *ck.* One spelling is not overwhelmingly apparent as the best choice. Students need to be taught generalizations about the use and frequency of letter patterns in English (Cox, 1977; Hanna et al., 1966).

Sounds with Multiple Spelling or Letter Patterns When there is more than one frequent spelling or letter pattern for a sound, the best choice of the pattern is based on the frequency and the **situation** of the sound in a word. The situation (i.e., the particular circumstances of how a sound occurs in a word) of the sound may be based on the position of the sound in a word, the placement of accent (see Chapters 4 and 6 for activities that promote awareness of accent), the length of the word, the influence of surrounding sounds, or a combination of these factors. Awareness of sounds and syllables in words is important in determining the best choice of letters or letter patterns (see Chapter 6 for activities that promote awareness of syllables). The terms that are introduced in decoding to express the positions of letters in words—*initial, medial,* and *final*—are also used to describe the positions of sounds in words.

Students need not guess or give up when dealing with the sounds that have more than one frequent spelling or letter pattern. Instead, they consider the situation of the sound that may be represented by more than one spelling. The situation provides clues that will help students in their decision-making process. For example, in considering the spelling of /măch/, students think about possible, frequent spellings of /ch/ (*ch* or *tch*). To decide which spelling is the best choice, they determine the situation of the sound in the word. The sound is in the final position of a one-syllable word, and it comes after a short vowel. On the basis of this situation, students know that *tch* is the best choice for spelling /ch/ in the word *match*. The following examples of spelling patterns show the best choices for spelling sounds according to their situations. Each pattern should be introduced one at a time and practiced to mastery. A suggested order of introducing these patterns is mentioned later in this chapter.

Spelling Choices with Situations Based on Position

1. When is /oi/ spelled *oi*, and when is it spelled *oy*?

oil	boy
ointment	toy
boil	joy
coin	enjoy
joint	employ
In initial or medial position, /oi/ is spelled *oi*.	In final position, /oi/ is spelled *oy*. (A less frequent but reliable spelling choice for /oi/ at the end of a syllable is *oy* as in *royal* or *voyage*.)

2. When is /ou/ spelled *ou*, and when is it spelled *ow*?

out	cow
ouch	how
found	plow
shout	meow
ground	In final position, /ou/ is spelled *ow*.
In initial or medial position, /ou/ is spelled *ou*.	

(Less frequent but reliable spelling choices that could be introduced later as refinement include the following: /ou/ is spelled *ow* in a one-syllable word before final /l/ or /n/ *owl* or *down*, and /ou/ is spelled *ow* before /er/ as in *shower* or *flower*.)

Spelling Choices with Situations Based on Surrounding Sounds

1. When is /k/ spelled *k*, and when is it spelled *c*?

keep	cat
kit	cost
sky	cup
Before any sound represented by *e, i,* or *y,* /k/ is spelled *k*.	clasp
	cramp
	Before everything else, /k/ is spelled *c*.

2. When is /j/ spelled *g*, and when is it spelled *j*?

gem	jam
giant	jot
biology	just
Before any sound represented by *e, i,* or *y,* /j/ is spelled *g*.	Before everything else, /j/ is spelled *j*.

Spelling Choices with Situations Based on Position, Length, and Surrounding Sounds

1. When is final /ch/ spelled *tch,* and when is it spelled *ch?*

catch	speech
sketch	porch
pitch	pouch
blotch	belch
Dutch	sandwich

   Final /ch/ in a one-syllable base word after a short vowel is spelled *tch.*

   Final /ch/ after two vowels or a consonant or in a word of more than one syllable is spelled *ch.*

2. When is final /j/ spelled *dge?*

   badge
   edge
   ridge
   dodge
   fudge
   Final /j/ in a one-syllable base word after a short vowel is spelled *dge.*

3. When is final /k/ spelled *ck,* and when is it spelled *c?*

back	picnic
peck	music
sick	lilac
block	Final /k/ in a multisyllabic base
stuck	word after a short vowel is spelled *c.*

   Final /k/ in a one-syllable base word after a short vowel is spelled *ck.*

Spelling Choices of Vowels

1. What are the best choices for spelling /ŏ/?

odd	want
hot	wash
top	wand
lost	wasp
spot	wall

   The sound /ŏ/ is spelled *o,* except after /w/, when /ŏ/ is spelled *a.*

2. What are the best choices for spelling /ŭ/?

up	alike
us	along
cup	parade
rust	tuba
shut	sofa

   The sound /ŭ/ is spelled *u,* except at the end of an unaccented syllable, when /ŭ/ is spelled *a.*

3. What are the best choices for spelling /ā/?

ate	table
ape	baby
made	lady

same

pale

Initial or medial /ā/ in a one-syllable word is spelled *a*-consonant-*e*.

basic

paper

At the end of a syllable, /ā/ is spelled *a*.

day

say

play

delay

repay

Final /ā/ is spelled *ay*.

4. What are the best spelling choices for /ē/?

eel

feet

green

need

Initial or medial /ē/ in a one-syllable word is spelled *ee*.

stampede

complete

compete

extreme

In medial position of a final syllable, /ē/ is spelled *e*-consonant-*e*.

meter

fever

even

evil

At the end of a syllable, /ē/ is spelled *e*.

bee

see

free

three

In final position of a one-syllable word, /ē/ is spelled *ee*.

tardy

sixty

ugly

candy

In final position of a word with two or more syllables, /ē/ is spelled *y*.

5. What are the best choices for spelling /ī/?

ice

five

time

kite

Initial or medial /ī/ in a one-syllable word is spelled *i*-consonant-*e*.

iris

fiber

tiger

lilac

At the end of a syllable, /ī/ is spelled *i*.

fly

try

sky

shy

At the end of a word, /ī/ is spelled *y*.

6. What are the best ways to spell /ō/?

rope

home

open

over

smoke
slope
Initial or medial /ō/ in a one-syllable word is spelled *o*-consonant-*e*.

robot
polite
At the end of a syllable, /ō/ is spelled *o*.

show
slow
window
yellow
Final /ō/ is spelled *ow*.

7. What are the best ways to spell /ū/?

use
cube
fuse
cute
Initial or medial /ū/ in a one-syllable word is spelled *u*-consonant-*e*.

unit
tunic
music
tuna
At the end of a syllable, /ū/ is spelled *u*.

sue
cue
rescue
continue
Final /ū/ is spelled *ue*.

These spelling patterns offer students a way to manage English orthography for spelling. There will be exceptions to these patterns. It is exciting when students discover the exceptions. To find an exception, students must understand the pattern when it is introduced and remember it. They must compare that pattern with words they hold in memory and realize that there are words that share the same sound but have different spelling patterns. That is active reflection on language. An enthusiastic "Good for you! You found a word that doesn't fit the pattern!" from the teacher affirms that students are thinking about language.

The patterns are not to be memorized. They will be established in memory through multisensory, discovery introductions; multisensory practice; and opportunities to write through spelling dictation and personal writing. The teacher should direct students' attention to spelling patterns as they occur in the reading. The teacher should refrain from describing the patterns as *rules*. The term *rule* should be reserved for situations in which a letter in a base word is doubled, dropped, or changed.

Order of Presentation of Spelling Patterns   When students are deciding the best-choice spelling of a sound, the situation of the sound and the frequency of possible letter patterns are important determiners. When a teacher is deciding the order of introduction of letter patterns, he or she should follow the order of introduction of reading concepts, which is based on frequency of occurrence in English. Students first learn the letter patterns that occur with greater frequency so that they can spell many words. Less frequent patterns are taught later. In considering the patterns just delineated, which represent a sampling of patterns, the approximate order of introduction is as follows (Cox, 1977, 1992):

/ŏ/ = *o* as in *octopus*   /ī/ = *i* as in *iris*
/ŭ/ = *u* as in *up*   /ō/ = *o* as in *open*
/k/ = *k* as in *kit*   /ū/ = *u* as in *unit*
/k/ = *c* as in *cup*   /k/ = *c* as in *music*
/k/ = *ck* as in *truck*   /oi/ = *oi* as in *oil*
/j/ = *j* as in *just*   /oi/ = *oy* as in *boy*
/ē/ = *ee* as in *feet* and *three*   /ch/ = *ch* as in *chip*
/ā/ = *a*-consonant-*e* as in *cake*   /ch/ = *tch* as in *witch*
/ī/ = *i*-consonant-*e* as in *five*   /ou/ = *ou* as in *out*
/ō/ = *o*-consonant-*e* as in *rope*   /ou/ = *ow* as in *cow*
/ū/ = *u*-consonant-*e* as in *cube*   /ŭ/ = *a* as in *along* or *sofa*
/ē/ = *e*-consonant-*e* as in *athlete*   /ō/ = *ow* as in *snow*
/ī/ = *y* as in *fly*   /j/ = *g* as in *giant*
/ē/ = *y* as in *penny*   /j/ = *dge* as in *badge*
/ā/ = *ay* as in *tray*   /ū/ = *ue* as in *statue*
/ā/ = *a* as in *apron*   /ŏ/ = *a* as in *watch*
/ē/ = *e* as in *even*

The introductions of the multiple spelling patterns of a sound should be widely separated to allow time and practice to master one possible pattern before another is introduced. It is important to note that all of the possible spellings of a sound are not introduced at one time and that other spelling patterns not delineated previously will be interspersed in the order of introduction.

   Introduction of Spelling Patterns with Discovery Teaching   The patterns of spelling are introduced using a discovery teaching procedure, similar to that used in the introduction of reading concepts. The discovery teaching procedure uses a Socratic method in which the teacher asks questions to lead students to discover a new spelling pattern. This procedure heightens students' awareness of sounds in words; encourages students to think about how sounds are represented in words; and gives them the opportunity to notice letters in words, thereby heightening their sensitivity to letter patterns.

1. *Auditory discovery*   The teacher reads five to seven discovery words one by one, which contain the same sound and spelling pattern. Students repeat each word after the teacher. Students discover the sound that is the same in all of the discovery words. It is helpful for students to look in small mirrors as they repeat the words. The visual display on the mouth helps students discriminate the sound. Attention to the kinesthetic feel of the mouth also helps students discriminate the sound. **Auditory discovery** heightens students' awareness of a particular sound in words.

2. *Prediction*   After students have discovered the sound, they predict how the sound might be spelled. The sound students are discovering has been previously introduced for reading. This step encourages students to reflect on their language knowledge.

3. *Visual discovery*   After the students have made their predictions, the teacher writes the discovery words on the board. The students carefully look at all of

the words and decide which letter or letters are the same and where the letter or letters are located in the words. They also notice any other common features about the words, such as number of syllables, accent, or surrounding sounds. This step heightens awareness of letter patterns.

4. *Verbalization of the pattern*   With the discovery of the sound and its spelling, students verbalize the pattern (e.g., /ch/ in final position of a one-syllable word after a short vowel is spelled *tch*). Students are encourage to verbalize the pattern in their own words. Students then apply this information by spelling five to seven new words with the pattern.

Introducing a Spelling Pattern

Teacher:	Listen as I read some words. I want you to repeat each word after me. Listen for the sound that is the same in all of the words. [The teacher reads the words *pick, sack, luck, clock,* and *peck* one at a time as students repeat.] What *sound* (not letter name) do you *hear* in all of the words?
Students:	/k/
Teacher:	Where do you hear the sound? In what position(s)?
Students:	The sound is in the final position.
Teacher:	Make a prediction about how this sound might be spelled. Think about what you know about the language. How might this sound be spelled? [Students might predict *c, k,* or *ck.*] Watch carefully as I write the discovery words on the board. What letter or letters are the same?
Students:	All of the words have the letters *ck.*
Teacher:	In what position(s) do you see the letter(s)?
Students:	The letters *ck* are in final position.
Teacher:	Is there anything else that is similar about these words?
Students:	All of the words have short vowel sounds and have one syllable.
Teacher:	What does the pattern seem to be?
Students:	Final /k/ after a short vowel in a one-syllable word is spelled *ck.*
Teacher:	I want you to apply what you have discovered. I will dictate some words for you to spell. [The teacher dictates five to seven words with the pattern one at a time as students write them on paper. The **Simultaneous Oral Spelling (S.O.S.)** procedure described later in this chapter is a helpful tool in word dictation.]

Multisensory Practice of Sounds and Patterns   Spelling sounds and patterns are practiced daily using multisensory, structured procedures.

Sound Dictation   Daily review with a sound or spelling deck develops automaticity in translating sounds to spellings (Cox, 1992). Each introduced sound is written on the front of a separate index card. The sounds are represented with parentheses or slash marks; for example, (t) or /t/. The possible spellings of the sound are written on the front of each card. Key words that unlock the spellings of each sound are also written on the fronts of the cards.

While looking at a card that is not shown to the students, the teacher dictates the sound written on the card. Students repeat the sound and name the letter or letters that spell the sound as they write them. If students hesitate about the spelling of a sound, the teacher cues students with the appropriate key word.

(See Appendix B at the end of this book for multisensory, structured reading programs with spelling components. Several of these programs have commercially produced spelling decks that provide daily review of sounds that have been taught through a multisensory procedure for reading.)

When students are spelling sounds with multiple spellings, they repeat the sound and name and write the frequent, reliable spelling choices. For example, the teacher dictates /ā/. Students repeat /ā/ and say, "*a*-consonant-*e*, *a*; final, *ay*." In this abbreviated response, the best spelling choices for /ā/ are recognized. Students write this information in shorthand: *a*-consonant-*e*, *a* // *ay*. The double slash marks (//) define the spellings according to their positions in words. Everything to the left of the slash marks represents possible spellings of a sound in initial or medial position. Everything to the right represents possible spellings of a sound in final position.

The media that students use to write their responses can be varied daily to provide different kinesthetic reinforcement. Students may write responses on unlined paper, on the chalkboard, on their desktops, on carpet squares, or in salt trays.

Word Dictation   As each new spelling pattern is introduced, it is practiced to mastery first through the use of homogenous practice sessions in which every word contains the new pattern. When students demonstrate success in spelling the new pattern, heterogeneous practice sessions that contain the new pattern and previously introduced patterns are used. The words used for these practice sessions are not words that students have memorized or will need to memorize. At first, the words for heterogeneous practice should be one-syllable words that progress from two to three sounds to five to six sounds. When students are ready, they start with the spelling of one-syllable base words with suffixes, then move on to multisyllabic words, and finally, to multisyllabic derivatives. Word dictation practices provide review of sounds and patterns and instills a thinking process for spelling.

To establish this thinking process for spelling, a structured procedure is used for word dictation practice. S.O.S. was introduced by Gillingham and Stillman (1960) and adapted by Cox (1992; see Figure 8.2). At each step the teacher provides the necessary corrective feedback. The steps and rationale are as follows:

1. *Look and listen.*   Students look at the teacher and focus on his or her mouth as he or she dictates the word. By focusing on the teacher's mouth, students use the visual display to clarify the sounds in the dictated word. For example, /f/ will be visually displayed with the upper teeth resting on the lower lip, whereas /th/ will be displayed with the tip of the tongue protruding between the teeth.

2. *Echo and think.*   Students echo, or repeat, the word while looking in a small mirror. The use of a mirror provides visual cues such as the position of the mouth or the placement of the tongue, teeth, or lips. The repetition of the word affirms that students heard the word correctly and gives them additional auditory input and kinesthetic feedback. The kinesthetic feedback clarifies the sounds in the dictated word. For example, with /f/, students feel the upper teeth resting on the lower lip, and with /th/, they feel the tip of the tongue protruding through the teeth.

Figure 8.2. Simultaneous oral spelling (S.O.S.) procedure. 1) Look and listen, 2) echo and think, 3) name the letters, 4) name and write, and 5) read to check. (Used by permission of Neuhaus Education Center, Bellaire, TX.)

The thinking part of this step depends on the kind of word students are spelling. A monosyllabic word should be unblended into its constituent sounds. A derivative should be orally separated into morphemic units (e.g., /jŭmpt/ is base word /jŭmp/ plus suffix /t/). A multisyllabic word should be unblended into its component syllables.

When unblending a word into two to five sounds or syllables, the students may use a fist to mark the sounds (or syllables). Beginning with the thumb of their nonwriting hand (left palm up for right-handers; right palm down for left-handers) and moving in a left-to-right progression, students extend a finger for each sound (or syllable) that they hear as they unblend the word. Students may also move counters such as buttons or pennies for each sound (or syllable) they hear as they unblend the word.

3. *Name the letters.* Before writing the word on paper, students spell the word aloud. This is a rehearsal step for writing. The teacher can guide students to the correct spelling before they write. The naming of letters impresses letter sequences in memory (Gillingham & Stillman, 1997).

If students have unblended the word using their fingers or counters, then they may want to touch each finger or counter as they spell, thereby reinforcing the sound–letter connection and sequence.

4. *Name and write.* Students write the word while naming the letters (Cox, 1992; Gillingham & Stillman, 1997). The rationale for this step is that naming letters builds the visual sequence of letters in the word through auditory and kinesthetic input. It is important for the students to see the word they have spelled orally. If handwriting is not fluent, students could use plastic letters or letter cards to spell the words, or the teacher could serve as an **amanuensis** by writing for the students on paper or the board.

5. *Read to check.* After students have written the word, they read the word silently, using their decoding information. Knowledge of syllable types and syllable-division patterns will aid students' accurate reading of the word

and confirmation of the spelling (see Chapter 6). This final step is intended to build independence in knowing that the word is spelled correctly and to teach proofreading skills. To monitor a large group in a class environment, the teacher may have students read the word aloud together and then touch and name the letters of this word. The teacher gives appropriate corrective feedback.

The S.O.S. procedure provides a structure for teaching students how to think about the process of spelling a word. Instead of impulsively writing a word on paper, students think about the sounds in the word and how those sounds can be spelled. They also impress the letter sequence in memory by naming the letters, they monitor the spelling of the word by naming the letters while writing, and they check the spelling by reading the word. In the initial stages of spelling instruction with dyslexic students, it may be necessary to build an understanding and memory of the five steps gradually by breaking the procedure down into smaller parts. Students may begin with Steps 1 and 2. The teacher says the word, and the students repeat the word and unblend it into its constituent sounds. Students may use this abbreviated procedure for several days or weeks. When students are secure with these two steps, Step 3 may be added, in which they spell the word aloud. When these three steps are secure, students can add Steps 4 and 5, with the teacher serving as the amanuensis. When the teacher writes the word, students can better attend to the letter sequence in the word and do not have to worry about the formation of the letters. Eventually, students will complete all five steps of the S.O.S. procedure independently.

Sentence Dictation   When students' handwriting is fluent and they have demonstrated success with word dictation, the dictation of phrases and sentences can begin. The dictation practice sessions are designed to review previously introduced spelling patterns in context. Only three or four phrases or simple sentences are used for a dictation session. A structured procedure for dictation (Cox, 1992; Gillingham & Stillman, 1997; see Figure 8.3) aids this process. The steps and rationale of the procedure are as follows:

1. *Look and listen.*   Students look at the teacher and listen as the teacher dictates a sentence. As with S.O.S., students look at the teacher's mouth to clarify the sounds in the words.
2. *Echo.*   Students repeat the sentence. Using a nonverbal cue, the teacher signals that students should repeat the sentence. Students continue to repeat the sentence until it is secure.
3. *Write.*   When the teacher believes that the sentence is secure, he or she indicates that students should begin writing the sentence. The teacher again uses a nonverbal cue to indicate that students should begin to write. The use of nonverbal cues does not interrupt the students' auditory memory of the sentence sequence.
4. *Proofread.*   When students have finished writing the sentence, the teacher dictates it three times as students check for missing words, for capitalization and punctuation, and for spelling errors. As students check each item, they place a checkmark at the end of the sentence. Three checkmarks after the sentence indicates that all three items have been checked. This method of checking can be extended to their written composition. After writing a paragraph,

DICTATION

Figure 8.3. Dictation procedure. 1) Look and listen, 2) echo, 3) write, and 4) proofread. (Used by permission of Neuhaus Education Center, Bellaire, TX.)

they should check it three times for these same items. Three checkmarks in the top margin of a paper indicate that all three items have been checked.

It is suggested that students be given one more opportunity on another day to check the dictation paper for spelling errors. A freshly completed dictation paper is considered "hot" (Cox, 1992). It is difficult to see errors in a "hot" dictation paper. When students have the opportunity to review the dictation sentences at another time, they are better able to see errors.

With knowledge of the frequent, reliable patterns in English, orthography is no longer a conundrum to students. They have a means of organizing and managing the language for spelling.

Rule Words

Rule words are spelled the way they sound, but certain information needs to be considered before the word is written. There are five major rules that indicate when a letter should be doubled, dropped, or changed. Two of these rules are used for doubling consonants within a base word. The other three major rules deal with spelling derivatives. They involve a change to the spelling of a base word (i.e., a letter is doubled, dropped, or changed) when adding a suffix. All of the rules are introduced through multisensory discovery teaching procedures.

Major Spelling Rules   The five major rules include the Rule for Doubling the Final Consonant (the Floss Rule), the Rule for Doubling a Medial Consonant (the Rabbit Rule), the Doubling Rule, the Dropping Rule, and the Changing Rule. Each rule has a set of **checkpoints.** These checkpoints signal students that a letter may be doubled, dropped, or changed. All of the salient checkpoints must be present for a letter to be doubled, dropped, or changed.

1. *The Rule for Doubling the Final Consonant (the Floss Rule)*
    Discovery words:

tiff	tell	toss
puff	doll	pass
staff	hill	mess

    In a one-syllable base word after a short vowel, final /f/, /l/, and /s/ are spelled *ff*, *ll*, and *ss*, respectively. When deciding whether to apply this rule, students must think about these checkpoints: 1) one syllable; 2) short vowel; and 3) final /f/, /l/, or /s/. If all three checkpoints are present, then the final consonant is doubled. If any one of the checkpoints is missing, then the final consonant will not be doubled.
    Note: The term *floss* is a mnemonic device that reminds students that *f, l,* or *s* will double in a one-syllable base word after a short vowel.

2. *The Rule for Doubling the Medial Consonant (the Rabbit Rule)*
    Discovery words:

    ballot

    tennis

    mitten

    pollen

    muffin

    In a two-syllable base word with one medial consonant sound after a short vowel, the medial consonant is doubled. The three checkpoints for this rule are 1) two syllables, 2) one medial consonant sound, and 3) a short vowel in the first syllable. If all of the checkpoints are present, then the medial consonant is doubled. If any checkpoint is missing, then the medial consonant will not be doubled.
    Note: The term *rabbit* is a mnemonic device that reminds students that a medial consonant doubles in a two-syllable base word after a short vowel.

3. *The Doubling Rule*
    Discovery words:

hop + ed = hopped	star + ing = starring
red + ish = reddish	begin + er = beginner

    When a word ends in one vowel and one consonant and the final syllable is accented (all one-syllable words are accented), and a vowel suffix is being added, the final consonant is doubled before the suffix is added. There are four checkpoints for consideration: 1) one vowel in the final syllable, 2) one consonant after that vowel, 3) final syllable accented, and 4) a vowel suffix that is being added. If all four checkpoints are present, then the final consonant is doubled. If one checkpoint is missing, then the suffix is just added on. Seven letters in English orthography never or rarely double. Knowing these seven letters assists students in deciding whether to double a letter. These letters can be taught as a cheer:

    h, k
    y, j
    v, w, x

    Never or rarely double in English words.

With this bit of information students will understand why the *x* in *faxing* does not double or why the *v* in *river* does not double.

The doubling rule is an extremely important rule for students to know for writing, as it is used often in spelling participles and the past tense of verbs. Figure 8.4 (Carreker, 1992) shows a visual aid that students can use to remember the four checkpoints of this rule. The four-leaf clover can be reproduced on green cardstock and cut apart for each student. As students search for the checkpoints in a word, they build the four-leaf clover. If all four leaves of the clover are used, they are lucky. The stem is added to the clover, and students know they must double the final consonant. If any leaf is missing, they will not double the final consonant.

4. *The Dropping Rule*
    Discovery words:

> bake + er = baker
> solve + ed = solved
> blue + ish = bluish
> house + ing = housing
> complete + ed = completed

When a base word ends in final *e* and a vowel suffix is being added, the final *e* is dropped before the suffix is added. The two checkpoints are 1) final *e* and 2) a vowel suffix that is being added. If a consonant suffix is being added, then the final *e* is not dropped.

5. *The Changing Rule*
    Discovery words:

> try + ed = tried
> silly + est = silliest
> penny + less = penniless
> happy + ness = happiness

When a base word ends in a consonant before a final *y* and a suffix that does not begin with *i* is added, the final *y* changes to *i* before the suffix is added. The checkpoints for this rule are 1) a consonant before a final *y*, 2) final *y*, and 3) a suffix that does not begin with *i*. If the base word has a vowel before the final *y*, the *y* does not change to *i* (e.g., *boys, enjoying, stayed*). If a suffix that begins with *i* is added, the *y* does not change to *i* (e.g., *crying, babyish, lobbyist*). The teacher can explain to students that the *y* does not change when adding a suffix that begins with *i* because "two *i*'s are unwise." Of course, when students discover the word *skiing*, the teacher will say, "Good for you!"

Introduction of the Spelling Rules   As mentioned previously, the introduction of the spelling patterns begins with an auditory discovery procedure to get students to focus on the sound. The goal of teaching the patterns is that when students hear a particular sound in a word, they will know the most frequent, reliable way to spell the sound. Spelling rules are introduced differently. **Visual discovery** is used to introduce the spelling rules because students must learn to recognize and remember not a sound but a distinguishing visual feature of the rule words.

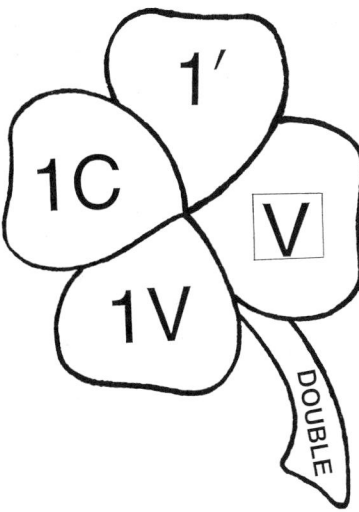

Figure 8.4. Manipulative four-leaf clover indicating checkpoints for the doubling rule: one vowel (1V), one consonant (1C), one accent (1´), and a vowel suffix (a boxed V). When a word has these checkpoints, students add the clover stem indicating that the final consonant of the base word should be doubled. (From Carreker, S. [1992]. *Scientific spelling.* Bellaire, TX: Neuhaus Education Center; reprinted by permission).

Introducing the Rules with Doubled Consonants (the Floss Rule and the Rabbit Rule)

Teacher: Watch carefully as I write some words on the board. [When introducing the Rabbit Rule, for example, the teacher writes discovery words such as *rabbit, pollen, tennis, mitten,* and *sudden* on the board in a column as students watch.] What looks the same in all of these words? [Students notice doubled letters and the position of the doubled letters.] Do you notice anything else? [Teacher leads the students to discover the other checkpoints of the rule.] Let's review the checkpoints and state the rule. [After students have reviewed the checkpoints and stated the rule, they spell five to seven new words that follow the rule.]

Introducing the Rules for Spelling Derivatives (the Doubling Rule, the Dropping Rule, and the Changing Rule)

Teacher: Watch carefully as I write some words on the board. [When introducing the Doubling Rule, for example, the teacher writes a list of discovery words on the board in formula format, such as *run + er = runner, shop + ing = shopping,* and *stop + ed = stopped*] The first column of words contains base words. The second column contains suffixes. The third column contains derivatives. Look at the column of base words. How are all of the base words the same?

Students: They each have one vowel, one final consonant, and an accented final syllable.

Teacher: Look at the column of suffixes. How are all of the suffixes the same?

Students: All of the suffixes are vowel suffixes.

Teacher: Look at the derivatives. How are all of the derivatives the same?

Students: The final consonant of each base word is doubled.
Teacher: Let's review the checkpoints and state the rule. [After students have reviewed the checkpoints and stated the rule, they spell five to seven new derivatives that follow the rule.]

Importance of Awareness of Language Layers   As mentioned previously, spelling requires attention to several layers of language structure at once. If these different layers are taught as part of or concurrently with formal spelling instruction, the necessity of teaching many traditional spelling rules is eliminated. For example, the teacher could state the following spelling rule: "After the sibilant sounds /s/, /z/, /sh/, and /ch/, the plural form of a noun is spelled by adding -es." This rule would help students spell the word *wishes*, but students might be able to spell the word correctly without knowing the rule. Students could do so with phonemic awareness (the word ends in /ĕz/) supported by awareness of syntax (a plural form is needed), morphology (the word has two meaningful units—/wĭsh/ and /ĕz/), semantics (/ĕz/ means *more than one*), and orthographic knowledge (suffix /ĕz/ is spelled *es*). Therefore, careful instruction with all language structures is important to support spelling. Learning too many rules is burdensome. Many rules are superfluous when instruction with all language structures is provided. Only the rules that aid in the memory of words by drawing attention to visual features (e.g., doubled letters) need to be introduced. These visual features cannot be accessed through awareness of any other language structure or system and must be taught through spelling rules.

Irregular Words

Irregular words have unexpected spellings. A word may be irregular for one of two reasons: 1) Its orthographic representation does not match its pronunciation (e.g., *should, enough, colonel*), or 2) it contains an infrequent orthographic representation of a speech sound (e.g., the spellings of the vowel sounds in *beach, train,* and *soap;* see Table 8.5). Words whose orthographic representations do not match their pronunciations are usually also irregular for reading. Words with infrequent orthographic representations are usually regular for reading, but because they contain less frequent representations of sounds, they are classified for spelling as irregular. Different procedures can be used to establish irregular words in memory. Various mnemonic strategies help students to learn words that contain less frequent patterns. A more structured and multisensory procedure (Cox, 1992; Fernald, 1943; Gillingham & Stillman, 1997) is needed to ensure the learning of some irregular words. The introduction of irregular words should be kept to a minimum when working with dyslexic students. They must establish a sense of the regular, reliable patterns of English before working extensively with irregular words.

Irregular Word Procedure   The following procedure uses visual, auditory, and kinesthetic input to assist in the permanent memorization of those words with truly atypical spellings. It is an involved but effective procedure that must be directed by the teacher. The efficacy of the procedure depends on students' naming the letters. This naming of letters as they trace or write is more effective than writing or copying words over and over again because it focuses students' attention on the letter sequence in the word. The steps and rationale for each step follow:

1. *Circle the irregular part.* The teacher provides students with a large model of the irregular word on a sheet of paper. Students circle the part of the word that does not conform to the frequent, reliable patterns or rules. Analyzing the irregular part engages students in active reflection of the language. Circling the irregular part draws their attention to the letter patterns in the word.

    Because many irregular words are Anglo-Saxon or are borrowed from other languages, a discussion of the **etymology** can provide insight into the unexpected spelling of the word (see Chapter 5 for a discussion of words from Anglo-Saxon, Latin, and Greek). Over time students may begin to recognize patterns in irregular words (e.g., words from Anglo-Saxon are short, common, everyday words with the sound /f/ occasionally spelled as *gh* *enough* or *laugh*).

2. *Trace a model.* Students trace the model word three times, saying the word before they write and naming the letters as they write. Tracing the word while naming the letters provides the consummate multisensory experience. The students reinforce the letter sequence in the word through the visual, auditory, and kinesthetic modalities.

3. *Make copies.* Students make three copies of the word with the model in view, saying the word and naming the letters of the word as they write. This step extends the multisensory impressing of the letter sequence of the word in memory.

4. *Spell the word with eyes closed.* Students close their eyes and spell the word, imagining the word as they spell. They open their eyes and check the model. They close their eyes and spell the word two more times in this manner.

5. *Write from memory.* Students turn their papers over or fold them so that the model does not show. They write the word three times, saying the word before they write and naming the letters of the word as they write. Because students no longer have a model to rely on, they must call on their memory of the letter sequence of the word that was established through the multisensory input.

Other Procedures for Learning Irregular Words Some irregular words do not require the intensity of the irregular word procedure just outlined. Instead, the use of exaggerated or spelling-based pronunciation builds a strong orthographic memory of these irregular words (Cox, 1992; Ehri, Wilce, & Taylor, 1987). Silent consonants will often mark that a word will be irregular for spelling. When practicing irregular words, students may pronounce the silent *k* in words such as *knee, knife,* and *knock* or the silent *b* in words such as *comb, limb,* and *crumb* so that they will remember to write the silent *k* or *b* when they spell. They might exaggerate the pronunciation of *i* as /ī/ in *fragile* so that they will remember to spell the word with an *e* at the end. Schwa is not uniquely represented in English and therefore is difficult to spell. It is best managed with the use of the exaggerated or spelling-based pronunciation (e.g., students say /rĭbŏn/ instead of /rĭbŭn/) (Ehri, Wilce, & Taylor, 1987).

To remember the spellings of certain irregular words, students could use a mnemonic association: "There is *a rat* in *separate*," "The *capitol* has a *dome*," or "The *principal* is your *pal*" (Moats, 1995). Students could group words in whimsical sentences as a mnemonic device to remember the infrequent spelling patterns that words share: "*Which rich* people have so *much* money and *such* big houses?" or "I am *ready* to *spread* the *bread*" (Cox, 1992).

Spelling Homophones   *Homophones* are words that share the same pronunciation but differ in their orthographic representations (e.g., *plane/plain*, *to/too/two*, *red/read*). Published spelling series are notorious for presenting lists of homophones for students to learn. Students often find these words difficult to learn. The problem usually is not the spelling of homophones but rather their usage. Students are not sure when to use which spelling. To alleviate this confusion, homophones should not be introduced in pairs. Often one word in a pair of homophones is regular for spelling (e.g., *plane*) and the other word is not (e.g., *plain*). Students first should be introduced to the homophone with the regular spelling. When they are secure with the spelling of that word and are clear about its usage, the other homophone can be introduced. If both homophones are irregular for spelling (e.g., *there/their*), the word with the most frequent usage should be introduced first, followed by the other.

SPELLING LESSONS

This section discusses spelling lessons in general classrooms as well as in therapeutic environments (one-to-one or small-group) with dyslexic students. In any environment, it is important to remember that spelling is an interactive process that involves phonological and orthographic knowledge. Spelling instruction enhances this knowledge through synthetic and analytic teaching. Synthetic teaching (i.e., sounds to whole words) systematically builds awareness of sound–letter correspondences and provides a foundation for phonological knowledge and reinforcement of orthographic knowledge. Analytic teaching (i.e., whole words to sounds) builds awareness of letter patterns and provides the foundation for orthographic knowledge and reinforcement of phonological knowledge. Effective lesson planning employs both teaching strategies to provide opportunities for students to develop both phonological and orthographic knowledge. Appendix B at the end of this book lists programs for spelling and resources for planning spelling lessons.

Spelling Lessons for Dyslexic Students

Teaching dyslexic students to spell is a long, tedious process that requires careful lesson planning. The teacher must plan for success as success builds confidence and confidence builds independence. Dyslexic students need spelling instruction that is closely integrated with reading instruction. Because of the exacting demands of spelling on complete and accurate recall of letter patterns, dyslexic students need to spell words with sounds and patterns that have previously been introduced for reading and practiced. Reading words before spelling them heightens students' awareness of orthographic patterns. The number and choices of activities for a spelling lesson will depend on the readiness and needs of the student or students. The teacher will want to plan a rotation of activities that ensures that all areas of spelling are covered regularly. The teacher also will want to discuss the meanings and usages of spelling words to ensure that all of the different layers of language structure are covered in a lesson.

Because dyslexic students' primary deficit is in phonological processing, spelling instruction must be designed to address this deficit. Without phonemic awareness, dyslexic students will not be able to develop facility in reading or spelling. Initially, spelling instruction for dyslexic students should build phonemic awareness. Students should engage in activities that require the unblending of words into sounds. As they prepare to spell words, they need to engage in activities that heighten the recognition or discrimination of specific sounds, such as listening for a specific sound in a word or listening for the position of a specific sound in a word. After letter–sound correspondences have been introduced for reading, they can be introduced for spelling. These spelling associations are reviewed daily using a sound or spelling deck. Students spell words and derivatives with regular spellings using these sounds. Students should use the previously described S.O.S. procedure when spelling words. New spelling patterns or rules are introduced as needed. As described in previous sections, multisensory, structured discovery teaching is used to introduce the new pattern or rule.

When students are ready, the lesson plan is extended. Students begin dictation practice, first with phrases and then with sentences. High-frequency irregular words can be introduced as needed, and students can use the irregular word procedure discussed previously. Analyzing and sorting activities focus students' attention on letter patterns in words, reinforce letter–sound correspondences, and help students generalize patterns and rules. Students can analyze and sort words written on individual index cards by sounds or letter patterns. As they gain greater knowledge of letter patterns, they may analyze and sort words as regular words, rule words, or irregular words. Students can develop a spelling notebook in which they record information about spelling (Cox, 1992). The notebooks could contain a section for spelling patterns, with one page for each speech sound. Students enter the sound, a picture of the key word, the reliable spelling(s) of the sound, and words that follow that pattern (see Figure 8.5). Students may also have a section for rules, with one page for each rule, and a section for irregular words, with one page for each letter of the alphabet so that irregular words can be recorded on pages by first letter. Once per week during a spelling lesson, students may record information in their spelling notebooks. On other days students may simply read information from the notebooks as a means of reviewing spelling information.

Initial Lesson Plan for Spelling
1. *Phonological awareness activities*   The teacher chooses one or two of the following activities:
   - Students repeat words dictated by the teacher and listen for a specific sound.
   - Students repeat words dictated by the teacher and identify the position of a specific sound.
   - Students repeat and unblend words dictated by the teacher.
   - Students repeat words dictated by the teacher and change a sound in a word as designated by the teacher to create a new word.
   - Students repeat words dictated by the teacher and say them again, leaving out a syllable designated by the teacher.

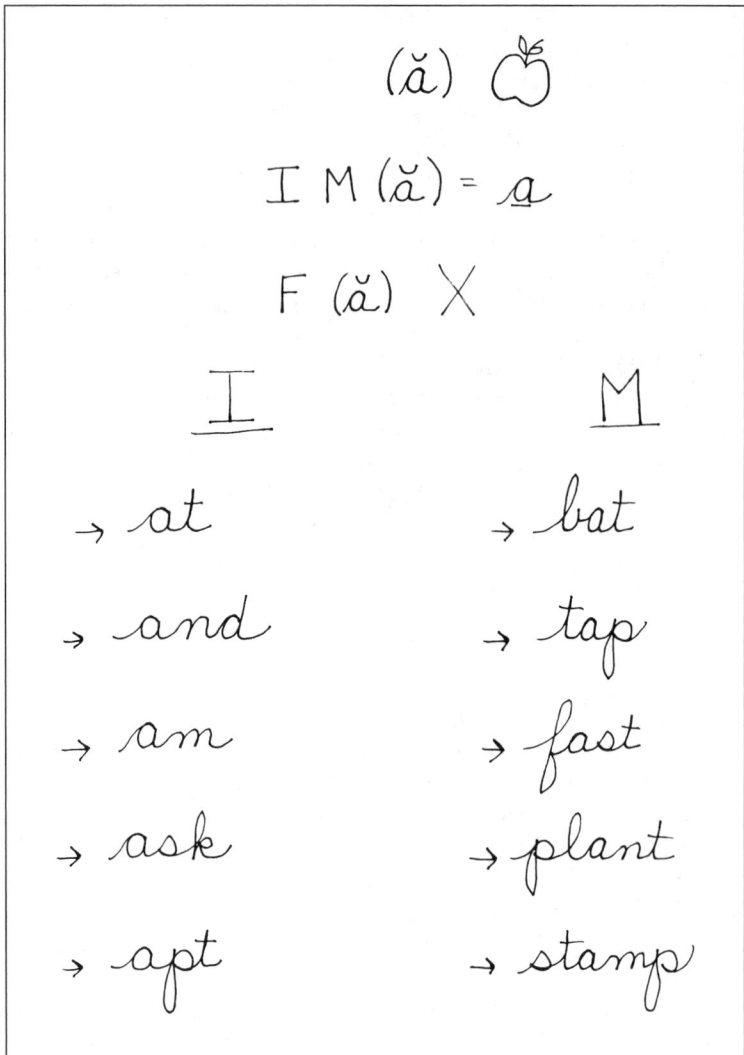

Figure 8.5. Spelling notebook page that reviews the initial and medial spelling of /ă/, spelled *a*. The *X* indicates that /ă/ does not occur in final position.

2. *Sound dictation*
   - The teacher dictates the sounds one at a time.
   - Students echo the sounds, then name and write the letter or letters that spell each sound.
   - A mirror is available for students who are unable to discriminate the sounds.
   - The teacher cues students with a key word if they cannot remember the spelling.
   - The teacher varies the media for the response daily (e.g., unlined paper, chalkboard, desktop).

3. *Word dictation*
    - Before students spell words, the teacher reviews the patterns or rules that are germane to the practice session.
    - The teacher reviews the appropriate steps of S.O.S.
    - The teacher dictates the words (as few as 3–4 but no more than 10–12) as students spell using S.O.S. The words should be homogeneous when students are practicing a new spelling concept and then heterogeneous when students demonstrate mastery of the concept. The teacher should be careful to plan a lesson rotation that includes the spelling of regular words on one day and the spelling of rule words on another day.
    - The teacher provides immediate corrective feedback as needed.
4. *Introduction of new spelling concept (synthetic teaching)*
    - The teacher introduces a new spelling pattern or rule following a sequential, cumulative order that allows time for concepts to be practiced to mastery.
    - The teacher uses discovery teaching techniques.
    - It is extremely helpful for students to use mirrors when discovering the new sound.
    - After the new pattern or rule has been introduced, students apply the concept by spelling three to five words with the pattern or rule.

Extended Lesson Plan for Spelling   This extended lesson plan for spelling includes the four activities of the initial lesson plan plus three additional activities. The word dictation activity is expanded to include the dictation of phrases and simple sentences. This new lesson plan can be used after students have been introduced to 10–12 spelling patterns and the Floss Rule and are spelling words with these concepts with relative ease and accuracy.

1. Phonological awareness activities
2. **Sound dictation**
3. Word dictation and/or sentence dictation
4. Introduction of a new concept (synthetic teaching)
5. Introduction of a high-frequency irregular word
6. Analyzing or sorting spelling words (analytic teaching)
7. Use of spelling notebook

Technology Available to Spellers   Although complete mastery of spelling for dyslexic students is a rather elusive goal (Oakland et al., 1998), the teacher must be tenacious in pursuing this goal. The technology of computer and hand-held spell checkers greatly aids dyslexic students with the accuracy of their spelling when writing compositions and reports, but it is not a substitute for systematic instruction of spelling patterns and rules. Knowledge of the structure of the language for spelling increases the effectiveness and efficiency of this technology. If students' spelling attempts do not match the probable patterns in English, then the spell checker will not be able to choose the correct word, or it may overwhelm students with too many choices. Such technology is not a replacement for explicit instruction for dyslexic students but instead serves as a complement to this instruction.

Spelling Lessons for the Classroom

Spelling instruction that requires the copying of words or the memorization of lists is dull and uninspiring. Spelling instruction that engages students in active, reflective thought about language is exciting. The goal of spelling instruction is to teach the reliable patterns and rules of English for spelling, thereby creating enthusiasm for language. Effective spelling instruction provides students with meaningful lists of words they will use in their academic work.

Order of Presentation   The order of presentation of spelling concepts should follow the order of presentation of reading concepts (see Chapter 6 for order of presentation of reading concepts). Because of the demands of spelling, the introduction of spelling concepts will lag behind the introduction of reading concepts.

Weekly Lesson Plan   The following weekly lesson plan systematically teaches the patterns and rules of English for spelling and provides opportunities for students to generalize and apply this information. The plan allows for modification to meet the needs of dyslexic students in the general classroom. These activities could also be incorporated into therapy lessons with dyslexic students.

Monday (15 minutes)   A new spelling pattern (e.g., initial or medial /ou/ is spelled ou) or rule is introduced through multisensory, discovery teaching. Students spell five to seven words with the new pattern or rule, using S.O.S. This synthetic teaching ensures that students are systematically learning information about the structure of language for spelling. The words that students practice on Monday become the first words of the weekly spelling list.

Tuesday (15–20 minutes)   The rest of the words for the weekly spelling list come from the content area (e.g., words from a map skills unit in social studies). The number of words presented depends on the age or the needs of the students. Because the words are selected from the content area, students will need to know and use them. The need for and use of the words increases the likelihood that students will learn the words. Arbitrary lists of words from published spelling series seldom present words commensurate with students' classwork.

Students must analyze the words on the weekly spelling list and decide whether the words are regular words, rule words, or irregular words. To be successful with analyzing, students must disengage what they have learned about decoding. It is true that they will be able to read a word such as *east*, but for spelling purposes, it is considered irregular because *ea* is not the most frequent spelling of /ē/ in initial or medial position of a one-syllable base word. Words such as *eel* or *street* follow the frequent, reliable patterns of the language and would be analyzed as regular words.

The Tuesday lesson provides analytic teaching that ensures that students will look carefully at words to notice how they are spelled. It helps them generalize the patterns and rules they have learned. It engages students in active reflective thought about language. Students cannot decide the category of a word without thinking about all of the aspects of the word.

When students have finished analyzing and sorting the words, they have strategies for learning them. The regular words are spelled just the way they sound and can be sounded out. The rule words can be sounded out, but students must remember there is a letter that must be doubled, dropped, or changed before they write it. Irregular words have unexpected spellings. They cannot be sounded out and must be memorized (see Table 8.7). No more than three or four irregular words should be included in the Tuesday lesson.

The weekly spelling list is easily modified for dyslexic students in the classroom. Rather than require these students to learn all of the words in the list, the teacher may ask them to be responsible for only the discovery words from the Monday lesson (e.g., all of the words with /ou/ that are spelled *ou*), or if they are ready, the teacher may ask them to be responsible for all of the regular words in the weekly list. The addition of the daily use of a spelling deck and phonological awareness activities for these students creates a pattern of covering all areas of the spelling curriculum routinely and intensively.

Wednesday (15 minutes)   Students practice the irregular words that were sorted in the Tuesday lesson. They decide the best way to learn them: using the irregular word procedure, a mnemonic device, or a spelling-based pronunciation. If time permits, they use the dictionary to determine why each word is irregular: 1) They are Anglo-Saxon; 2) they are borrowed from another language; 3) they are slang or an abbreviated form of a word; 4) they are borrowed from a proper name; or 5) they are spelled that way "just because," with no apparent reason listed in the dictionary.

Thursday (15 minutes)   The teacher uses the spelling words in various phonological awareness activities: unblending words into sounds, counting syllables, omitting syllables, and changing sounds in words. Students also practice words through word or sentence dictation.

Friday (15 minutes)   Throughout the week students have had the opportunity to analyze, play with, read, and write the spelling words. On Friday, students are tested on the words through word and/or sentence dictation.

Table 8.7.   Weekly spelling list with 5 discovery words from the Monday lesson and 10 words from content areas

Regular	Rule	Irregular
found	mapping	ocean
mouth		country
ouch		east
count		
shout		
north		
south		
west		
globe		
river[a]		
continent		

[a]Note the inclusion of *river* shows an example of how *v* usually is not doubled in English.

Effective Spelling Instruction

Effective spelling instruction does not teach students how to spell individual words. It teaches students how to think about spelling. An old adage says that if you give a man a fish, he eats for a day. If you teach a man how to fish, he eats for a lifetime. So it is with effective spelling instruction. Effective spelling instruction teaches students to think about language so that they know how to spell the words they need.

SUMMARY

Spelling serves as a foundation for reading; provides a means of communication; and, even if not rightly or fairly, is used by society to judge one's level of literacy and intelligence. Spelling is a valuable skill, yet it receives a modicum of attention and respect in schools. It has been reduced to mindless busywork or has been subjugated by the content in writing. Perhaps this has happened because of the belief that English orthography is impossibly irregular and that there is no way to teach it or because of the perception that spelling is a rote, mechanical skill that does not promote cognition. The time has come to view spelling instruction in a different light.

The orthography of English is not hopeless. There are frequent, reliable patterns and rules that can be taught, which thus equip students with a system for managing the orthography of English for spelling. These patterns and rules are not taught through passive, rote memorization. Spelling instruction is deeply ensconced in a rich study of language structures and takes place in a manner that promotes active, reflective thought. Spelling instruction does not distract from the content of writing but rather enhances it by enabling students to choose the words that best express their thoughts instead of those words that are easy to spell. Effective spelling instruction is engaging, thought-provoking, and exciting.

REFERENCES

Adams, M.J. (1990). *Beginning to read: Thinking and learning about print.* Cambridge: The MIT Press.

Adams, M.J., Foorman, B.R., Lundberg, I., & Beeler, T. (1998). *Phonemic awareness in young children: A classroom curriculum.* Baltimore: Paul H. Brookes Publishing Co.

Bear, D.R., Invernizzi, M., Templeton, S., & Johnston, F. (1996). *Words their way: Word study for phonics, vocabulary, and spelling instruction.* Upper Saddle River, NJ: Prentice-Hall.

Blachman, B.A., Ball, E.W., Black, R., & Tangel, D.M. (2000). *Road to the code: A phonological awareness program for young children.* Baltimore: Paul H. Brookes Publishing Co.

Blachman, B.A., Ball, E.W., Black, R.S., & Tangel, D.M. (1994). Kindergarten teachers develop phoneme awareness in low-income, inner-city classrooms: Does it make a difference? *Reading and Writing: An Interdisciplinary Journal, 6*(1), 1–18.

Bradley, L., & Bryant, P.E. (1983). Categorizing sounds and learning to read: A causal connection. *Nature, 303,* 419–421.

Brady, S., & Moats, L.C. (1997). *Informed instruction for reading success: Foundations for teacher preparation.* Baltimore: The International Dyslexia Association.

Bryant, P.E., & Bradley, L. (1980). Why children sometimes write words which they do not read. In U. Frith (Ed.), *Cog-*

nitive processes in spelling (pp. 355–370). London: Academic Press.

Bryant, P.E., Nunes, T., & Bindman, M. (1994). Children's understanding of the connection between grammar and spelling. In B. Blachman (Ed.), *Foundations of reading acquisition and dyslexia: Implications for early intervention* (pp. 219–240). Mahwah, NJ: Lawrence Erlbaum Associates.

Bryson, B. (1990). *The mother tongue and how it got that way.* New York: Avon Books.

Carreker, S. (1992). *Scientific spelling.* Bellaire, TX: Neuhaus Education Center.

Cassar, M., & Treiman, R. (1997). The beginnings of orthographic knowledge: Children's knowledge of double letters in words. *Journal of Educational Psychology, 89*(4), 631–644.

Castle, J.M., Riach, J., & Nicholson, T. (1994). Getting off to a better start in reading and spelling: The effects of phonemic awareness instruction within a whole language program. *Journal of Educational Psychology, 86*(3), 350–359.

Cook, G.E., Farnum, M., Gabrielson, T., & Temple, C. (1998). *McGraw-Hill spelling.* New York: McGraw-Hill School Division.

Cox, A.R. (1977). *Situation spelling: Formulas and equations for spelling the sounds of spoken English.* Cambridge, MA: Educators Publishing Service.

Cox, A.R. (1992). *Foundations for literacy: Structures and techniques for multisensory teaching of basic written English language skills.* Cambridge, MA: Educators Publishing Service.

Cronnell, B., & Humes, A. (1980). Elementary spelling: What's really taught? *Elementary School Journal, 81,* 59–64.

Ehri, L.C., Wilce, L.S., & Taylor, B.B. (1987). Children's categorization of short vowels in words and the influence of spelling. *Merrill-Palmer Quarterly, 33,* 393–421.

Fernald, G. (1943). *Remedial techniques in basic school subjects.* New York: McGraw-Hill.

Ferreiro, E., & Teberosky, A. (1982). *Literacy before schooling.* Portsmouth, NH: Heinemann.

Foorman, B.R. (1994). The relevance of a connectionist model for reading for "The Great Debate." *Educational Psychology Review, 6,* 25–47.

Frith, U. (1980). Unexpected spelling problems. In U. Frith (Ed.), *Cognitive processes in spelling* (pp. 495–515). London: Academic Press.

Frith, U., & Frith, C. (1980). Relationships between reading and spelling. In J.P. Kavanagh & R.L. Venezky (Eds.), *Orthography, reading, and dyslexia* (pp. 287–295). Baltimore: University Park Press.

Fulk, B.M., & Stormont-Spurgin, M. (1995). Spelling interventions for students with disabilities: A review. *Journal of Special Education, 28*(4), 488–513.

Gillingham, A., & Stillman, B.W. (1960). *Remedial training for children with specific disability in reading, writing, and penmanship.* Cambridge, MA: Educators Publishing Service.

Gillingham, A., & Stillman, B.W. (1997). *The Gillingham manual: Remedial training for children with specific disability in reading, writing, and penmanship* (8th ed.). Cambridge, MA: Educators Publishing Service.

Goodman, K. (1986). *What's whole in whole language: A parent–teacher guide.* Portsmouth, NH: Heinemann.

Goswami, U. (1988). Children's use of analogy in learning to spell. *British Journal of Developmental Psychology, 6,* 21–23.

Goswami, U., & Bryant, P. (1990). *Phonological skills and learning to read.* Mahwah, NJ: Lawrence Erlbaum Associates.

Hanna, P.R., Hanna, J.S., Hodges, R.E., & Rudorf, E.H. (1966). *Phoneme–grapheme correspondences as cues to spelling improvement.* Washington, DC: U.S. Government Printing Office, U.S. Office of Education.

Henry, M. (1988). Beyond phonics: Integrating decoding and spelling instruction based on word origin and structure. *Annals of Dyslexia, 38,* 259–277.

Johnson, D., & Myklebust, H.R. (1967). *Learning disabilities: Educational principles and practices.* New York: Grune & Stratton.

Lennox, C., & Siegel, L.S. (1996). The development of phonological rules and visual strategies in average and poor spellers. *Journal of Experimental Child Psychology, 62,* 60–83.

Lennox, C., & Siegel, L.S. (1998). Phonological and orthographic processes in good and poor spellers. In C. Hulme & R.M. Joshi (Eds.), *Reading and spelling development and disorders* (pp. 395–404). Mahwah, NJ: Lawrence Erlbaum Associates.

Liberman, I.Y., Shankweiler, D., & Liberman, A.M. (1989). The alphabetic principle and learning to read. In D.

Shankweiler & I.Y. Liberman (Eds.), *Phonology and reading disabilities: Solving the reading puzzle* (pp. 1–33). Ann Arbor: University of Michigan Press.

Lyon, G.R. (1995). Toward a definition of dyslexia. *Annals of Dyslexia, 45,* 3–27.

Moats, L.C. (1994). Assessment of spelling in learning disabilities research. In G.R. Lyon (Ed.), *Frames of reference for the assessment of learning disabilities: New views on measurement issues* (pp. 333–349). Baltimore: Paul H. Brookes Publishing Co.

Moats, L.C. (1995). *Spelling: Development, disabilities, and instruction.* Timonium, MD: York Press.

Moats, L.C. (1996). Phonological spelling errors in the writing of dyslexic adolescents. *Reading and Writing, 8*(1), 105–119.

Nation, K., & Hulme, C. (1998). The role of analogy in early spelling development. In C. Hulme & R.M. Joshi (Eds.), *Reading and spelling development and disorders* (pp. 433–445). Mahwah, NJ: Lawrence Erlbaum Associates.

Oakland, T., Black, J.L., Stanford, G., Nussbaum, N., & Balise, R.R. (1998). An evaluation of the dyslexia training program: A multisensory method for promoting reading in students with reading disabilities. *Journal of Learning Disabilities, 31*(2), 140–147.

Peters, M.L. (1985). *Spelling, caught or taught?* London: Routledge & Kegan Paul.

Read, C. (1971). Pre-school children's knowledge of English phonology. *Harvard Educational Review, 41*(1), 1–34.

Roberts, R., & Mather, N. (1997). Orthographic dyslexia: The neglected subtype. *Learning Disabilities Research & Practice, 12*(4), 236–250.

Rubin, H., & Eberhardt, N.C. (1996). Facilitating invented spelling through language analysis instruction: An integrated model. *Reading and Writing: An Interdisciplinary Journal, 8,* 27–43.

Seidenberg, M., & McClelland, J. (1989). A distributed developmental model of word recognition and naming. *Psychological Review, 96,* 523–568.

Share, D.L., & Stanovich, K.E. (1995). Cognitive processes in early reading development: Accommodating individual differences into a model of acquisition. *Issues in Education, 1*(1), 1–57.

Smith, P.T. (1980). Linguistic information in spelling. In U. Frith (Ed.), *Cognitive processes in spelling* (pp. 33–49). London: Academic Press.

Sterling, C., Farmer, M., Riddick, B., Morgan, S., & Matthews, C. (1998). Adult dyslexic writing. *Dyslexia: An International Journal of Research and Practice, 4*(1), 1–15.

Treiman, R. (1994). Use of consonant letter names in beginning spelling. *Developmental Psychology, 30*(4), 567–580.

Treiman, R. (1997). Spelling in normal children and dyslexia. In B. Blachman (Ed.), *Foundations of reading acquisition and dyslexia: Implications for early intervention* (pp. 191–218). Mahwah, NJ: Lawrence Erlbaum Associates.

Treiman, R. (1998). Beginning to spell in English. In C. Hulme & R.M. Joshi (Eds.), *Reading and spelling development and disorders.* Mahwah, NJ: Lawrence Erlbaum Associates.

Treiman, R., Cassar, M., & Zukowski, A. (1994). What types of linguistic information do children use in spelling? The case of flaps. *Child Development, 65,* 1318–1337.

Treiman, R., Zukowski, A., & Richmond-Welty, D.A. (1995). What happened to the "n" in sink? Children's spelling of final consonant clusters. *Cognition, 55,* 1–38.

Venezky, R.L. (1980). From Webster to rice to Roosevelt. In U. Frith (Ed.), *Cognitive processes in spelling* (pp. 9–30). London: Academic Press.

West, T.G. (1991). *In the mind's eye.* Buffalo, NY: Prometheus Books.

9

Teaching Handwriting

Lynn Stempel-Mathey and Beverly J. Wolf

In many textbooks on teaching reading, handwriting is classified as one of the mechanics along with spelling, punctuation, and grammar. Rarely is handwriting given the importance it deserves in the overall language arts program for typical students or even in intervention programs for students with learning disabilities. This chapter gives the rationale for placing handwriting as a vital component of the multisensory teaching of literacy skills.

This chapter 1) highlights the importance of handwriting instruction in early education and in remediation, 2) provides a brief history of handwriting instruction, 3) discusses some of the syndromes related to difficulties with handwriting, 4) reports research evidence of the efficacy of direct teaching of handwriting to dyslexic students, and 5) presents specific information on how to teach print and cursive handwriting using a multisensory framework that integrates handwriting instruction with reading and spelling instruction.

THE IMPORTANCE OF HANDWRITING INSTRUCTION IN EARLY EDUCATION AND REMEDIATION

Writing has been credited by some as being the most practical invention of all time. It has added a timeless dimension to oral communication, thus expanding communicative capabilities the way mathematics did to counting on fingers and toes, and made possible our modern world (vos Savant, 1988). Handwriting is the last of the four language skills to develop, following listening, speaking, and reading (Vail, 1981). The ability to write legibly has often been presumed to be a characteristic of a literate person. As early as the 1960s, educators bemoaned the attitude of indifference to the importance of penmanship and called to task those who indicated lack of respect for readers who had to decipher carelessly executed script (Myers, 1963).

The use of handwriting to organize one's thinking and improve health has been documented by journal keepers and reports of research studies such as the one conducted by a university professor who showed that students who wrote about their feelings paid fewer visits to health care professionals than did their peers (Smith, 1987). Even though the computer is a revolutionary tool for writers that facilitates the act of writing and increases the volume of written material, it is not always as readily available as the pencil and pen, which are easily carried in the pocket or left waiting on the bedside table.

Etiquette experts, such as Judith Martin, who writes the "Miss Manners" newspaper etiquette column, still advise people to use handwritten notes (preferably in cursive) for formal invitations, thank-you notes, and messages of condolence (Phelps & Stempel, 1987). Other situations calling for legible handwriting include filling out job applications, taking notes, taking tests, writing prescriptions, addressing envelopes, and leaving instructions for employees. Even so, Carole Kennedy, former president of the National Association of Elementary School Principals, said that the teaching of handwriting, with drills to ensure accurate letter formation, is no longer widely stressed (Tabor, 1996). In support of content-based learning, many teachers encourage their students to write journal entries as a way of practicing letter formation but do not give them an appropriate model and accept either print or cursive as long as it is legible. They appear to be by-passing the use of formal instructional material (Tabor, 1996). Research conducted in the United Kingdom, however, suggested that teachers who are not taught to produce letter forms accurately inculcate their own writing forms in their pupils, so small idiosyncrasies in teachers' writing become magnified in that of the children's (Sassoon, 1991). The company Zaner-Bloser addressed this problem by providing correct letter forms on an electronic speller that shows the correct cursive letter joinings.

McMenamin and Martin (1980) explained that lack of time is often given as one of the arguments against using practice drills in formal writing programs, and they disputed the validity of this argument. After initial training, they stated, the teacher will find that time is saved. Myers (1963) made a similar assertion, saying that time spent on handwriting practice to improve legibility and develop fluency saves time for both the teacher, who spends less time deciphering the writing, and the pupil, who completes written assignments in less time. An additional bonus is the pride the student will have in a product that is neat, legible, and attractive and is a sample of "everyone's art" (Phelps & Stempel, 1987, p. 237).

Writing about the development of handwriting and its connection to reading, Adams said that the activities of letter tracing and copying "may contribute valuably toward the development of those **fine motor skills** that determine the willingness as well as the ability to write" and help in "developing necessary skills for reading as well as writing" (1990, p. 357). Adams also pointed out that Montessori (1966) encouraged writing before reading and that Durkin (1966) found in her studies of children who read early that many wrote and spelled before they could read. Instruction in writing and spelling often comes before instruction in reading; efforts to promote phonemic awareness through the teaching of letter names and sounds and phonemic segmentation begin while children are in kindergarten (Rubin & Eberhardt, 1996).

Alphabet wall cards provide easy reference for children. They may be made by the teacher or purchased. Some teachers prefer to use cards with key word pictures that also serve to help children recall the sounds of the letters. Prepared materials used in the Alphabetic Phonics (Cox, 1992), Gillingham (Gillingham & Stillman, 1997), and Slingerland (Slingerland, 1976; Slingerland & Aho, 1985) approaches are available from Educators Publishing Service (see Appendix B at the end of the book). The cards should be visible so that children can refer to them easily at any time. Most classroom teachers display them above the chalkboard at the front of the classroom.

Naming the letters aloud while tracing or copying them is not just a remedial technique. Adams pointed out that children often say the name or the sound naturally as they write, a process that helps to "bind the visual, motor, and phonological images of the letter together at once" (1990, p. 355).

By establishing that the goal of a handwritten text is to be aesthetic and give satisfaction to both reader and writer, the government of Finland reorganized the alphabet style taught in schools in 1986 by training all teachers and emphasizing their role as adult models. They were taught letter forms that were easy to learn, remember, and read and were internationally understandable. Emphasis was placed on both rate and legibility so that increased speed did not detract from appearance (Odman, 1989).

There is evidence that penmanship as a useful art form is being recognized in this country as well. School districts in Texas and Kentucky reported studies showing the effects of implementing specific writing programs. In Houston, Texas, the focus was on using handwriting as a starting point for student achievement in other areas of the curriculum, and parents and others outside the school recognized and complimented the handwriting skills of the students ("A Penchant for Penmanship," 1996). Bridge, Compton-Hall, and Cantrell (1997) described the effects of statewide reform on writing instruction in a school district in Kentucky. They found that in 1995 teachers spent twice as much time teaching writing as in 1982 and that students were engaged in higher-level writing activities two to three times as often while not changing the amount of time spent teaching handwriting skills. Researchers at the Educational Testing Service (1994), who analyzed essays of a sample of 32 college students participating in a pilot study of a new teacher's licensing exam, found that handwritten essays received slightly higher scores than did the same essays written on a computer; the researchers said possible reasons were that the computer-produced work had a shorter appearance and that mistakes were easier to identify.

Handwriting practice counts, according to a teacher who organized a contest at her school that produced a state champion in a national penmanship contest cosponsored by Parker Pens and Zaner-Bloser. Students practiced for 20 minutes daily, and the winner reported that she practiced on her own as well. The school principal said, "Some people argue [penmanship is] a lost art and it ought to stay lost, but we think that for students, the ability to produce something aesthetically pleasing is important" (Flick, 1996, p. A26).

Individuals need to be able to write for others to have something to read. For most students, motor skills such as those used in handwriting can be improved with drills once proper models are shown, and many models are made available. Young children usually become aware of the concept of groups of letters as symbols with meaning (i.e., the alphabetic principle) through their most personal possessions, their names. This introduction is commonly presented by parents or teachers who show children their names are written with printed letters. Whether a child's name is written in upper- or lowercase letters, it becomes a symbol of self.

Clinicians and teachers who work to remedy difficulties with handwriting have often given anecdotal reports. Strickling (1974) noted that spelling improves when legibility increases. The writer can discover errors more easily with fewer ambiguously formed letters, which interfere with proofreading, and a greater amount of reinforcement of correct word patterns becomes available. Kinesthetic memory, the earliest, strongest, and most reliable form of memory, may aid spellers in remembering orthographic patterns. Automaticity and fluency in handwriting are also important because they give individuals the freedom to concentrate on spelling, higher-level thought processes, and written expression. Last, students need to be aware that teachers often judge students' abilities and grade them based on the appearance of their written work.

A BRIEF HISTORY OF HANDWRITING INSTRUCTION

In a comprehensive review of research in reading, writing, and math disorders for the U.S. Interagency Committee on Learning Disabilities, Johnson (1988) described a shift in the teaching of penmanship: In the late 1800s and early 1900s, penmanship was taught as a separate subject with copying drills that focused on the form of the letter itself and appropriate posture, but after the 1940s changes in the curriculum led to a broader emphasis on language arts and resulted in less time devoted to handwriting instruction in schools. This reordering of priorities led to a debate about whether teachers should provide direct instruction in skills and processes or allow children to engage in extensive reading, writing, and speaking experiences without explicit input on component language subskills such as handwriting.

Richardson (1995) described the use of models in the early stages of handwriting instruction and expressed her support for the kinesthetic method of teaching handwriting. She noted that Plato (428 B.C.–348 B.C.), Horace (65 B.C.–9 B.C.), and Seneca (4 B.C. to A.D. 65) were specific in their instructions to those who taught handwriting. Plato instructed the master to draw lines (letters) for the student to copy, Horace incorporated the idea of using pastry formed in the shape of letters, and Seneca had the teacher guide the student's hand as the letters were traced. In addition, Quintilian (A.D. 35–A.D. 100) suggested using a board with letters cut into it so that the child could confine the pen in the letters and make letter forms accurately. Quintilian recommended that the student learn the sound and shape of the letter simultaneously.

Cursive letters have evolved over time from the highly ornamental and calligraphic forms used by medieval monasteries. Each monastery developed and used its own alphabet until a common alphabet was established during the 9th century. Today the more simplified styles of Palmer and Zaner-Bloser and the even simpler D'Nealian method are taught (Phelps & Stempel, 1987).

Most public school districts use print form when introducing handwriting to young children, perhaps because it is most consistent with preschool learning. Print writing introduces children to the letter forms they will need to recognize as they begin to learn to read. The typeface used in the basic readers is more like print writing than cursive in appearance. The use of print by the teacher allows primary-grade children to see the same symbol forms used for reading, writing, and spelling, thereby lessening confusion. Slingerland (1976) explained,

> Children may fail to recall the sequence of movement necessary for speech and/or for letter formation, and it is this recollection which triggers reliable voluntary motor function to pull the muscles and tendons for speech and hand mechanisms . . . lack of kinesthetic recall for word pronunciation and/or for letter formation may interfere with fluency in speech or with penmanship.

Kinesthetic performance with the use of visual symbols and their letter names forms a multisensory association that helps strengthen recall for both reading and writing (Clark, 1988; Slingerland, 1971). The addition of this kinesthetic component is especially valuable for children with confusions between commonly reversed letters such as *b, d, g, p, q,* and *s*. Some school districts have devised their own handwriting curriculum by analyzing letters and developing directions for making them easily and legibly (Wessel, 1984). Self-help workbooks for students and adults have been developed, and it has been suggested that the main cause of poor legibility is writing too fast (Precker, 1994). College students, however, have difficulty with lecture comprehension when their note taking is too slow (Blalock, 1985). People of any age suffer embarrassment when they feel that their writing is inadequate. In most school districts formal training in handwriting appears to be limited to the first three or four grades, and some poor handwriting may be caused by the students' not having had enough training to form letters automatically when rapid writing is needed as a tool to perform assigned writing tasks (Hamstra-Bletz & Blöte,1990).

SYNDROMES RELATED TO DIFFICULTIES WITH HANDWRITING

Research on poor handwriting suggests that it stems from disorders of visuospatial processing; revisualization to recall letters and correct spellings of words; visual-motor integration factors in the coordination of eye and hand movements plus smooth coordination of the arm, hand, and finger muscles; motor planning; and production of movement for output, ongoing feedback, and regulation especially in children with **finger agnosia** (a kinesthetic feedback disorder in which the fingers do not report their location to the brain). Another difficulty seen in children with poor handwriting is an inability to copy from the far point, such as a chalkboard, to a near point, such as a piece of paper. Another factor contributing to poor handwriting is poor instruction in the early stages of learning handwriting.

Children and adults who have difficulty with handwriting often have impaired spelling abilities as well. Yet it is possible to know how to spell words correctly but not be able to write them by hand. This condition in which letter shapes, letter sequences, and motor patterns are impaired is called *specific agraphia* (Goodman & Caramazza, 1986). Moats (1995) pointed out that there is little research on the relationship between handwriting and spelling. In S.T. Orton's research on reading problems, he considered poor handwriting both as an interrelated and a separate language function (as cited in J.L. Orton, 1966). According to S.T. Orton, poor handwriting could result in poor visual reinforcement of word patterns and thus a weakened circuit between visual memory for printed words and their writing, reading, and spelling and auditory memory for words in speech, spelling, and writing. He recognized, too, that slow, messy handwriting could constitute a specific language disability itself.

Researchers and educators often ask, "Are writing and drawing related skills?" Neuropsychologist Louisa Moats offered an interesting answer:

> Drawing is nonlinguistic. It's nonverbal. It taps areas in the brain, probably in the right hemisphere, primarily that are dissociated from language areas. But letter formation is a linguistic activity. And many dyslexic people are in fact quite dysgraphic or have real trouble with letter formation, and those people may be very good at graphic art. (in Potts & Potts, 1997)

Some students have enough difficulty producing legible writing that they are diagnosed with **dysgraphia** (difficulty with handwriting). Many children, according to Levine (1994), have fine motor problems that affect only their writing. Their writing is slow and laborious as well as sometimes illegible. There are three common forms of this graphomotor dysfunction. The first is motor memory dysfunction, in which there is trouble integrating motor output with memory input. Children with this condition have difficulty in recalling the sequence of motor engrams (muscle movements) that are needed to form a specific letter. The second is graphomotor production deficit, in which the larger muscles of the wrist and forearm are used during letter formation because they are under better control than the small muscles of the fingers; this results in laborious and slow but legible writing. The third is a motor feedback problem (sometimes referred to as *finger agnosia*), which results in the child's having to visually monitor the location of the pencil point as the fingers do not "report" (Levine, 1994, p. 187) their location to the brain. The child with agnosia may use an awkward, fistlike pencil grip in which he or she places the thumb over the other fingers, preventing the fingers from moving the pencil efficiently and causing writing to be exhausting and painfully slow, to such an extent that it interferes with fluency.

Some improvement can be achieved through formal handwriting programs that provide practice with appropriate models. School occupational therapists are often involved in providing the instruction (Reisman, 1991). The bypass strategy of learning keyboarding and using a computer is usually recommended for older students, who are encouraged to utilize either print or cursive, whichever is their preference (Black, 1996). (See Appendix B at the end of this book for recommended keyboarding programs and handwriting programs.)

EVIDENCE FOR EFFICACY FOR THE DIRECT
TEACHING OF HANDWRITING TO DYSLEXIC STUDENTS

There are proponents for teaching either print or cursive at all ages (Phelps & Stempel, 1987), although customarily print is taught to first and second graders and cursive is taught to third graders. Proponents, such as Cox (1992), have cited a number of advantages of cursive handwriting, especially for students with dyslexia. The letters are connected and continuous for each word, and students find it easier to write cursive than to make the discrete forms required in writing print. They simultaneously assimilate the whole word more easily. There are no look-alike letters and only one starting point (on the line at the beginning of the word). There are only half as many initial strokes and one final stroke compared with six and eight strokes, respectively, for print. All cursive letters are curved, whereas print letters are both straight and curved (Phelps & Stempel, 1987). The rationale for teaching cursive handwriting given to teachers of dyslexics at the Texas Scottish Rite Hospital for Children (TSRHC; 1996) includes the following:

- To eliminate the student's need to decide where each cursive letter should begin because all cursive letter shapes begin on the baseline
- To provide directional movement from left to right
- To reduce reversals by eliminating the need to raise the pencil during the process of writing a single letter or series of letters in a word
- To provide unique letter shapes
- To promote flowing, rhythmic movements
- To eliminate the need to learn two different writing skills
- To teach the four basic approach strokes for producing cursive lowercase letters

Developmental Stages for Learning Handwriting

Levine (1987) suggested that the acquisition of the skills needed for writing occurs in six stages with variation in the rate of progress of even typically achieving children.

1. *Imitation—preschool to first grade*   Children pretend to write by mimicking actual writing while acquiring skill in letter and number formation but lack precise graphomotor skill. Early warning signs of potential problems may be observed in children who have fine motor weaknesses and become frustrated and self-conscious as they notice their peers' proficiency. Hand preference is shown although not fully established in all children.

2. *Graphic presentation—first and second grades*   Children become more aware of spatial planning as they learn to form both lower- and uppercase letters and recognize the need for more space between words than letters. Letter reversals are common, sometimes because of confusion over directionality and **laterality** and at other times because the need to concentrate and remember the configuration of the letter causes the child to overlook directionality. Fine motor control becomes better developed, and the child relies increasingly on **proprioceptive** and kinesthetic feedback (an inner sense of where the fingers are on the page). Letters become smaller to fit the lines on the paper.

3. *Progressive incorporation—late second to fourth grades*   Children produce print letters with less conscious effort, are less preoccupied with spatial and aesthetic appearance of their writing, and are ready to accept cursive writing as a more efficient system. Rules of capitalization, punctuation, syntax, and grammar are incorporated.

4. *Automatization—fourth through seventh grades*   Writing rate and efficiency become significant as children are expected to communicate in writing using correct grammar, spelling, punctuation, capitalization, and vocabulary while automatically recalling and producing legible letter forms.

5. *Elaboration—seventh through ninth grades*   Writing is used to establish and express a viewpoint. In proficient writers, written language exceeds everyday speech in complexity.

6. *Personalization-diversification—ninth grade and beyond*   Individual style and talent for writing, if any, develops. Students who find writing too difficult may never reach this stage.

Luria (1973), a neuropsychologist, described the process of learning to write as initially depending on memorization of the graphic forms of every letter. It takes place through a chain of isolated motor impulses, each of which is responsible for the performance of only one element of the graphic structure. With practice this structure of the process is radically altered, and writing is converted into a single "kinetic melody."

The child with learning disabilities apparently experiences a breakdown in the development continuum described by Luria (1973). Handwriting, according to Hagin (1983), should be taught at a level appropriate to the child's motor mastery and as a task that involves visual, motor, kinesthetic, temporal, and spatial skills. Getman (1984) cited research that showed that the most productive arm and hand movements that produced the least physiological and cognitive stress came from the shoulder with the full arm involved in the movements required for the formation of letters. The completion of the motor patterns eventually allows handwriting to become such a habitual skill that the mind is free to think while the arm and hand automatically produce the words chosen by the mind. A student experiencing a problem with the motor act of handwriting will often resist writing anything at all because it is tiring or will at best write as little as possible (Cicci, 1995).

Rationale for Multisensory Teaching

Although it is not a handwriting program per se, the Fernald (1943) method is a special remedial approach to teaching reading and spelling that involves handwriting directly (see Table 1.1 for more on the Fernald method). The tracing of words to be learned involves all four sensory pathways: visual, auditory, kinesthetic, and tactile. For reading, the student traces the word the teacher has written (a process involving visual, kinesthetic, and tactile senses) while saying the word (a process using the auditory sense). When the student can write the word correctly without looking at the sample, the word is stored in a file box and the student is asked to write a story using the words in the box. After that the student just says the words to him- or herself while looking at them. Note that there is no naming of letters or sounds in the process of learning words for reading or spelling. For spelling, the student selects a word to learn. The teacher writes the word on a large piece of paper, saying the word as the student observes. This next step is the most important: The student traces the word on the large piece of paper while saying it several times and then writes it on a separate piece of paper while saying the word. If the student can correctly write the word from memory without referring to the original word, it goes into the file box. The elements of tracing, repetition, and saying the word aloud have been adapted by other multisensory approaches but mainly for use as students are learning to read and spell words with irregular orthographic patterns. (See Appendix B at the end of this book for a listing of other programs utilizing multisensory approaches for teaching handwriting.)

Cox (1980, 1985, 1992), who evolved the Alphabetic Phonics system of teaching for children with dyslexia from the Orton (1937) and Gillingham (Gillingham & Stillman, 1960) methods, stressed the multisensory aspects of teaching handwriting and, as mentioned previously, insisted on the use of cursive. Cox suggested that "a strong kinesthetic memory may reinforce the visual memory of letter shapes for reading" (1992, p. 19). Some students who have better kinesthetic memory than visual memory learn to write more easily than they learn to read; thus, writing training may take the lead in multisensory language training as the student's strongest pathway to learning (Cox, 1992). Retrieval of letter symbols from visual memory, typically weak in dyslexics, is a major deterrent to rapid, automatic production of alphabet letters, which is a lower-order writing skill that is most important in the beginning stages of writing (Berninger, Mizokowa, & Bragg, 1991).

In the Dyslexia Laboratory at the TSRHC, students are given multisensory training in cursive writing from the beginning of instruction. The need for careful instruction from the outset with continuous supervision is recognized. Staff members also believe that reading, writing, and spelling are naturally interrelated skills that reinforce each other. Students with weaknesses in one area can use their strengths to achieve success in another.

General Principles in the Multisensory Teaching of Handwriting

Good Posture   Poor body position can significantly interfere with ease of coordinating the hand movements in writing (Kurtz, 1994). The student should use a chair with a flat back and a seat that allows his or her feet to rest flat on the floor with hips, knees, and ankles all at 90° angles. The desk should be 2 inches higher than the child's bent elbows (Benbow, 1988, cited in Kurtz, 1994). A desk that is too high will cause the child to elevate his or her shoulders, which will restrict freedom of movement, whereas a desk that is too low could cause the child to slouch. The nonwriting hand and arm should be on the desk to hold the paper in place.

Proper Pencil Grasp   The child should use a normal tripod pencil grip (see Figure 9.1 for correct and incorrect writing grips). The pencil rests on the first joint of the middle finger with the thumb and index fingers holding the pencil in place and the pencil held at a 45° angle to the page. An awkward pencil grip can indicate finger agnosia. The use of an auxiliary plastic pencil grip or a metal writing frame can aid in changing the fatiguing grip to a normal, less tiring one. The pencil should point toward the shoulder of the writing arm for both left- and right-handed students (Phelps & Stempel, 1985; TSRHC, 1990).

An alert, diligent teacher *can* help a student change pencil position, but this requires consistency and patience. At any time that incorrect position is noted, the teacher can instruct the class as follows:

Teacher:	Stop.
Students:	[Students place their pencils on the desk with the point toward them.]
Teacher:	Pinch.
Students:	[With the index finger and thumb in a "pinch" position, students lightly grasp their pencils where the paint begins (approximately 1 inch from the point).]
Teacher:	Lift.
Students:	[As the children lift the pencil, it will fall back to correct writing position and rest on the first joint of the middle finger.]

After a few practice sessions, this teacher interruption of the writing process is brief; students only need to hear, "Stop, pinch, lift," to adjust their pencil positions. Teacher perseverance will help students become accustomed to the feel of the new position and to use it consistently. After a time, only the one or two children who have continued difficulty will need reminders. The older the child, the more difficulty he or she will have with changing the pencil position.

Writing Implement   A No. 2 pencil should be used. "The complex motor action of writing is overwhelmingly dependent upon accurate, ongoing kinesthetic [reafferent] feedback" (Levine, 1987, p. 226). While the child is writing, he or she is receiving feedback in the form of pressure and the pull of the pencil against the paper. Pencils with soft lead require less pressure from the child, thereby reducing fatigue. Children with impaired kinesthetic feedback will benefit from the use of softer leads that will not break as they press firmly in an attempt to receive that feedback when writing (Levine, 1987). It is preferable to use pencils without erasers. Instead, teach children to bracket mistakes: *I [wahsed] washed my dog.* This reduces time spent erasing and allows teachers to see the errors children have made and incorporate reteaching into lesson planning.

Paper   Handwriting instruction begins with activities that involve gross motor movement so that children may feel the movement in the shoulder and arm and improve their kinesthetic memory. Tracing at the chalkboard is the first step. Paper patterns also should be large and gradually become smaller as children become proficient with letter forms. Children of any age should be introduced to folded newsprint or lined paper with the widest spaces available. Reduce the size of lines as children's formation of letters becomes automatic.

Initially, letter forms should be taught using a chalkboard or dry marker board, unlined paper, then wide-lined 11" × 17" size paper, next primary-grade lined paper, and finally regular lined notebook paper. Additional practice utilizing other media such as carpet squares, Jell-O, salt trays, sand, tabletops, and varying styles of columned paper (newspaper want ads, telephone books, computer paper) can be beneficial and gamelike.

Paper Position   To achieve the consistent slant that is needed in cursive writing, the edge of the paper should be parallel to the writing arm (at about a 45° angle to the edge of the desk) and anchored at the top by the nonwriting hand. A slant guide (a piece of paper with slanted lines that is positioned beneath the writing paper) can be helpful after the child forms all lowercase letters automatically and after the child's writing is small enough to permit him or her to use regular notebook paper. Some instructors prefer that a left-handed student write with a backward slant with the paper parallel to the left arm; others teach a for-

Recognized Correct
and Incorrect Writing Grips

Correct

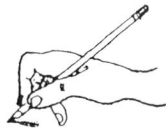

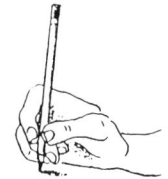

1. The pencil rests on the first joint of the middle finger with the thumb and index fingers holding the pencil in place.

2. Same as figure 1 except the fingers are closer to the pencil point.

3. Same as figure 1 except the pencil is held perpendicular to table.

Incorrect

4. Thumb and index finger holding pencil, with the index finger overlapping the thumb.

5. Pencil held by tips of fingers. Thumb on one side, middle and index finger on the other.

6. Thumb wraps around pencil, with the index and middle fingers pressing pencil to ring finger.

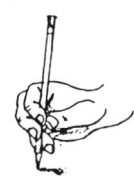
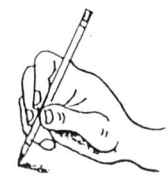

7. Index, middle and ring finger tips hold one side of pencil, the thumb holds the other.

8. Pencil is held between the index and middle fingers, pressing pencil to the thumb.

9. Thumb on one side, index and middle fingers on the other, all pressing the pencil to ring finger.

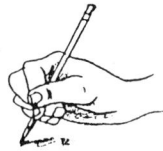
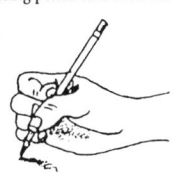

10. Index finger holds pencil to middle finger, with the thumb overlapping the index finger.

11. The thumb holds the pencil along the first joints of the rest of the fingers.

12. The pencil is grasped in the fist, and held up against the thumb.

Thē Pencil Grip

P.O. Box 67096 Los Angeles, CA 90067   (310)788-9485   Fax (310) 788-0644

Figure 9.1.   Recognized correct and incorrect writing grips. (Reprinted by permission of Thē Pencil Grip.)

ward slant to both left- and right-handed students (see Figure 9.2 for sample slant guides). It has been suggested that left-handers who write with a hook (the "curled wrist" method) were taught by teachers who insisted all students place their papers in the right-handed position. To avoid smudging the paper and to see what they have written, they curl their wrists while writing. Athenes and Guiard asked, "Is the inverted handwriting posture really so bad for left handers?" By comparing rate of writing of noninverters with that of inverters in left-handed adults and children, they concluded that "the handwriting performance of inverters was just as good as that of noninverters" (1991, p. 149). Bertin and Perlman, authors of Preventing Academic Failure (1991), a multisensory curriculum for teaching phonics, spelling, and reading, have developed a handwriting program for teaching cursive to left-handers that is available commercially. See the Watch our Writing (W.O.W.) chart (Figure 9.3) for illustrations of proper posture, pencil grasp, and paper position.

Importance of Motivation   Students will be motivated to improve their handwriting if they take part in deciding which areas need help. Pre- and posttesting, using a standardized measure such as the Children's Handwriting Evaluation Scale (CHES; Phelps, Stempel, & Speck, 1984), can help students discover the qualities needing remediation and can provide a measure of progress. If a standardized measure is not available, then have students copy a 200-letter paragraph printed on unlined paper. Time them for 2 minutes, and count the number of letters written. Compare the total with what a published test such as the CHES lists as the average number of letters. Then help students analyze the quality of their writing, using the generally accepted criteria: correct letter forms,

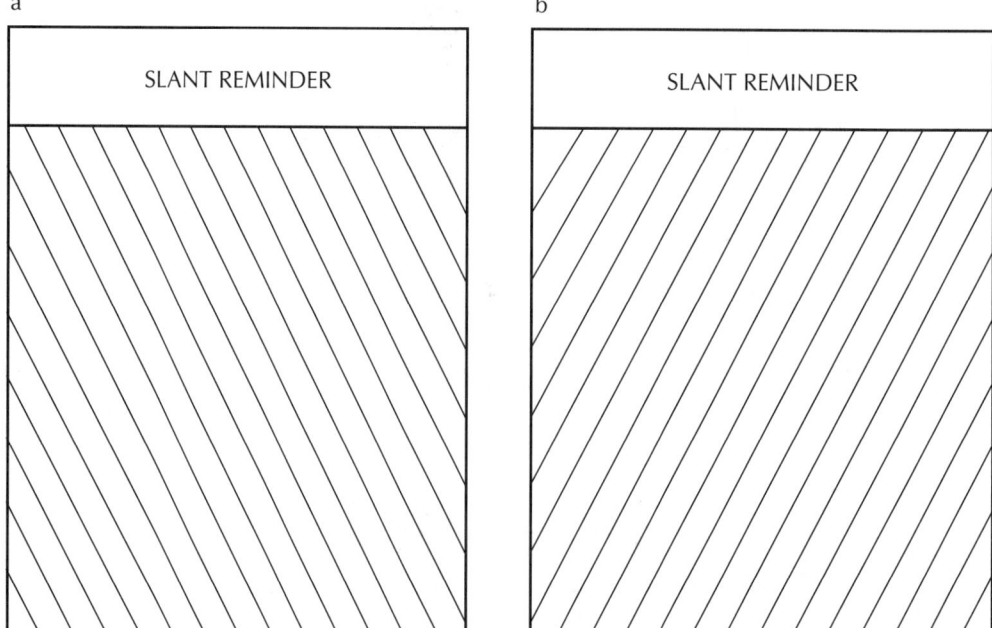

Figure 9.2.   Slant reminders for a) left-handers and b) right-handers. (From Texas Scottish Rite Hospital for Children, Child Development Division. [1996]. *Teaching cursive writing* [Brochure]. Dallas: Author; reprinted by permission.)

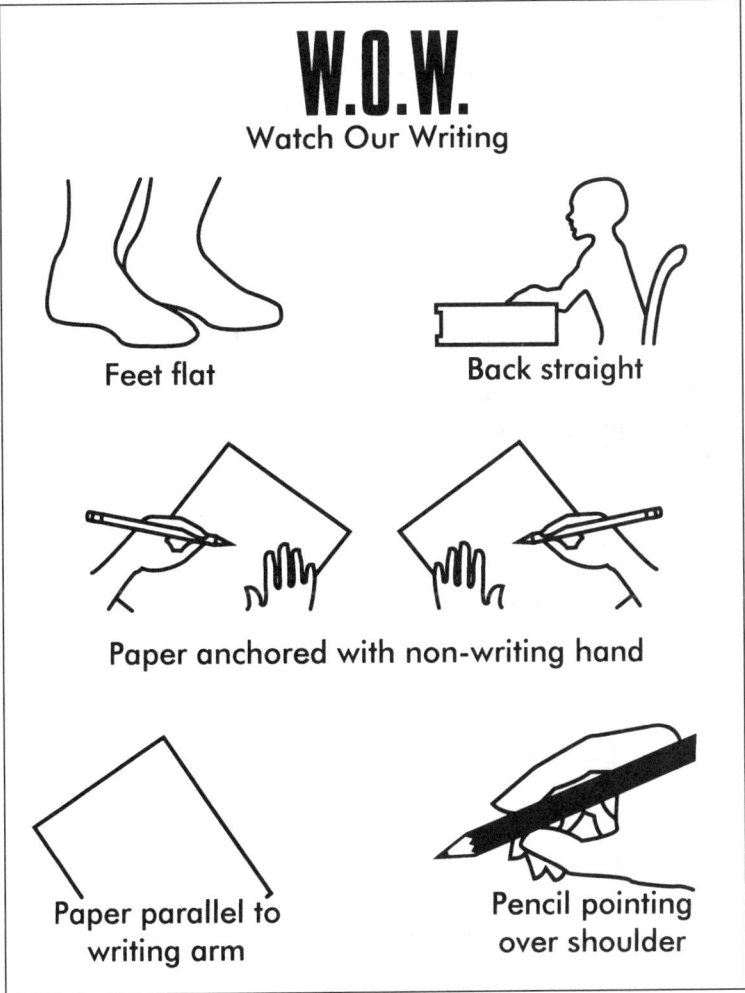

Figure 9.3. Watch Our Writing (W.O.W.) chart. (From Phelps, J., & Stempel, L. [1985]. *CHES's handwriting improvement program* [CHIP]. Dallas: Children's Handwriting Evaluation Scale; reprinted by permission of Jamie Williams.)

rhythm (fluency), consistent slant, good use of space within and between words and lines, and general appearance (copy is free of excessive strikeovers or erasures). Cursive writing is an acquired skill that requires good training in order to write legibly and rapidly. Although not all individuals have superior handwriting, many can achieve legibility with effort and practice (TSRHC, 1996).

HOW TO TEACH PRINT HANDWRITING USING A MULTISENSORY FRAMEWORK

Print handwriting introduces primary-grade children to the symbol forms used in printed text. Through multisensory association of sight, sound, and feel, children integrate the letter name with its visual form and the feel of how the letter is written, strengthening intersensory associations.

There are many forms of print writing, but the one most often recommended for dyslexic children is one that utilizes a continuous stroke whenever possible (Beery, 1982; Slingerland, 1971). A continuous stroke letter is most similar to cursive writing in that lines are retraced whenever possible and the pencil is lifted only when necessary, for example, to cross a *t* or dot an *i*. This helps prepare the child for a natural transition to cursive writing. Continuous stroke letters also reduce the opportunities for reversals that may occur each time that the child lifts the pencil. (Figure 9.4 shows lower- and uppercase print alphabets that use continuous strokes when possible; Figure 9.5 shows descriptions for writing print letters using continuous strokes.)

When a letter such as *h* is taught first, it introduces children to the idea of using a continuous stroke to form a letter because the child starts at the top of the letter, pulls down to the baseline, slides up almost to the midline, curves out and down without lifting the pencil. When a letter such as *t* is taught first, the student must lift the pencil to cross the downstroke line, children have more difficulty ad-

Lowercase Manuscript Letter Forms

All lower case manuscript letters are made with a continuous line with the exception of *f, k, t,* and *x.*

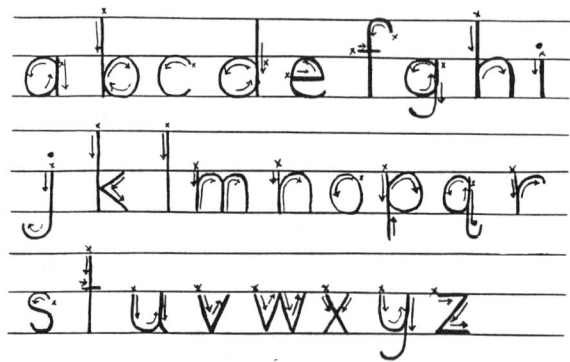

Uppercase Manuscript Letter Forms

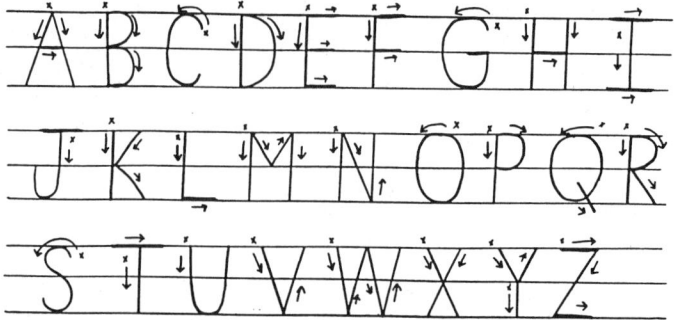

Figure 9.4.   Print letters using a continuous stroke (when possible). (Developed by the Renton School District, Renton, WA; reprinted by permission; versions taught in local school districts may vary slightly.)

<u>a</u>	Around, down.	<u>n</u>	Down, hump.
<u>b</u>	Down, up, around.	<u>o</u>	Around, close.
<u>c</u>	Around, stop.	<u>p</u>	Down, up, around.
<u>d</u>	Around, up, down.	<u>q</u>	Around, down, flag.
<u>e</u>	Across, around, stop.	<u>r</u>	Down, up, over.
<u>f</u>	Curve, down, cross.	<u>s</u>	Curve, slant, curve.
<u>g</u>	Around, down, hook.	<u>t</u>	Down, cross.
<u>h</u>	Down, hump.	<u>u</u>	Down, curve up, down.
<u>i</u>	Down, dot.	<u>v</u>	Slant down, up.
<u>j</u>	Down, hook, dot.	<u>w</u>	Slant down, up, down, up.
<u>k</u>	Down, slant in, out.	<u>x</u>	Slant right. Slant left.
<u>l</u>	Down.	<u>y</u>	Slant right. Slant left.
<u>m</u>	Down, hump, hump.	<u>z</u>	Across, slant, across.

Figure 9.5. Continuous stroke descriptions of print letters. (Reprinted by permission of Neuhaus Education Center, Bellaire, TX.)

justing to moving their arms without lifting the pencil from the paper when *h* is presented later.

It is neither necessary nor desirable to teach the alphabet in sequence. When planning the presentation of print letters, the following should be considered:

- Ease of production of the letter
- Continuity of stroke
- Similarity of strokes to those letters previously taught
- Ease of perception and production of the sound associated with the letter

Although sounds are not taught during handwriting class, their associations with letter forms are part of the multisensory experience. For example, the letter *l* is the simplest to write, but its sound is more difficult for young children, so it is a poor choice as the first letter to be introduced. It may be taught more easily after a few letters and their sounds have been presented.

The h Group   The sound of the letter h is easy to hear and reproduce. The letter form introduces the idea of continuous stroke. Its basic arm movement is also used in such letters as *b, m, n, r,* and *p.*

Be prepared to spend considerable time on the letter *b* because of the confusions between *b* and *d.* Slingerland (1971) recommended preparing students for the introduction of the letter *b* with an auditory-motor activity in which students stand and hold their writing arms in front of their bodies. The teacher then separates right- and left-handed students and helps them understand that to move in the direction that handwriting should go, right-handed students move their arms away from their bodies, whereas left-handed students move their arms across their bodies. Then, when patterns are introduced at the chalkboard, the teacher verbalizes, "Away from my body if I'm right-handed," and, "Across my body if I'm left-handed," to help both right- and left-handed students understand and remember the direction of the letter.

The a Group   The a group consists of letters that start with the same movement as the a. It includes *a, c, d, g, o, q,* and *s.* These letters begin at the "2 o'clock" position just below the mid-line. As children begin to form these letters, they should move their pencils at approximately a 45° angle toward the mid-line, curving around toward the baseline. The exaggerated slant typical of beginning writers' letters will become more rounded as children's writing becomes automatic. The angle of the pencil will eliminate a nearly vertical upward stroke and produce a rounded letter.

HOW TO TEACH CURSIVE
HANDWRITING USING A MULTISENSORY FRAMEWORK

The following lesson is an excerpt from the TSRHC *Teaching Cursive Writing* brochure (1996) and CHES's Handwriting Improvement Program (CHIP; Phelps & Stempel, 1985). Lessons are appropriate for one-to-one therapy, small groups, or general education classrooms. As with teaching print handwriting, it is not necessary to keep the alphabet in sequence while teaching cursive, although it is preferable for children to recognize all of the letters of the alphabet by name before attempting cursive writing. The TSRHC Luke Waites Child Development Center Dyslexia Therapy Program teaches the reading, spelling, and writing of sounds and letters in a sequence that is not alphabetic but reflects ease of learning and frequency in English. Other multisensory curricula follow the same procedure.

Lowercase cursive letters are taught first. A new letter is introduced each day, and previously learned letters are reviewed and practiced after the new one has been learned. A lowercase cursive alphabet strip should be in full view at all times during the lessons (see Figure 9.6). After all lowercase letters are learned and can be written legibly, students should practice writing the alphabet in sequence in connected cursive, giving extra attention to the bridge strokes used to connect *b, o, v,* and *w* with the next letter. Extra practice should be provided for frequent combinations such as *br, oa, vi,* and *wh* (see Figure 9.7 for examples).

Because cursive uppercase letters are used in only about 2% of writing, they should be introduced only after students write all lowercase letters automatically and legibly. See Figure 9.8 for a version of simplified uppercase letters.

It is beneficial to follow the order and grouping of cursive letters by the four basic approach strokes (see Figures 9.9–9.12). The students learn the four approach strokes as they learn new letters. The approach stroke always begins on the baseline and moves from left to right. An arrow is provided to establish a baseline when the student practices on the chalkboard or on unlined paper. The drop stroke follows the approach stroke and ties the letter to the baseline. The remaining shape is added to form the letter, which is then finished by a release stroke. The release stroke is an important part of every letter because it allows for uniform spacing between letters and promotes rhythmic writing.

Students appear to recall the sequence of movements of a given letter better if the instructor verbalizes consistent, precise directions for each letter (see Fig-

Figure 9.6. Cursive alphabet letters. (From Texas Scottish Rite Hospital for Children, Child Development Division. [1996]. *Teaching cursive writing* [Brochure]. Dallas: Author; reprinted by permission.)

Figure 9.7. Lowercase cursive bridge strokes between common letter combinations. (From Texas Scottish Rite Hospital for Children, Child Development Division. [1996]. Teaching cursive writing [Brochure]. Dallas: Author; reprinted by permission of Betty Muse.)

ures 9.10–9.12). The descriptive phrases should be repeated each time the letter is traced or written until the letter shape is automatic.

The teacher should encourage students to repeat the phrases as they write the letter shape to reinforce motor memory (TSRHC, 1996). Each time the student starts to write the letter, it is important for him or her to name it as he or she writes. This is an adaptation of Gillingham's Simultaneous Oral Spelling (Gillingham & Stillman, 1960) that provides kinesthetic reinforcement in which movements of the speech organs help the memory for letter name, sound, and shape.

To introduce a letter, the instructor prints a large letter (1–2 feet high) on the board, naming the letter and drawing a cursive letter on the print letter while describing the strokes used. The teacher writes a new, large model of the cursive letter. The student stands in front of the written letter and traces it with his or her hand in the air several times, always naming the letter before he or she begins the approach stroke. When the student completes the **air writing** (also called *sky writing*) reasonably well, he or she practices writing the letter on the board, on wide-lined 11″× 17″ paper, and then on primary lined paper. If the student is unable to write the letter satisfactorily, then he or she should return to the air writing step. This procedure should be followed meticulously with each letter until all have been learned and written legibly and automatically.

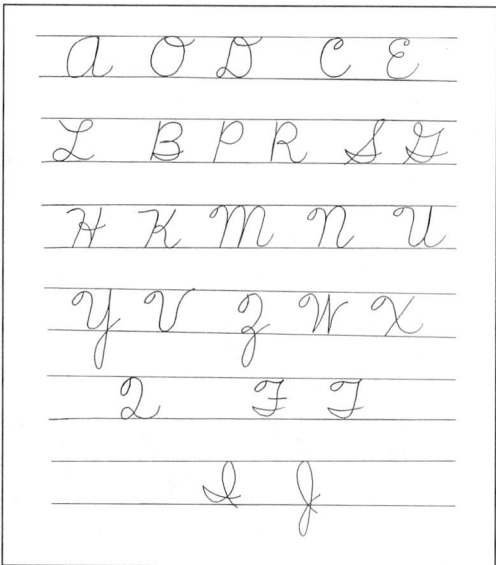

Figure 9.8. Uppercase cursive letters. (From Texas
Scottish Rite Hospital for Children, Child Development
Division. [1996]. *Teaching cursive writing* [Brochure].
Dallas: Author; reprinted by permission of Betty Muse.)

During the handwriting part of the daily lesson, students can practice at different levels. Each practice session should establish a single focus. The focus can be practicing a selected approach stroke; exercising rhythm and control when writing by naming letters before writing; writing cursive over print to reinforce a letter shape; regulating letter proportion, especially of tall letters; or repeating individual strokes such as "pull down straight" strokes, circles, release strokes, and lower loops. For each activity, the teacher follows a hierarchy of modeling for the students, giving them specific wording to help them monitor their visual-motor responses, and having the students air write, trace, copy, and write on their own. It is a good idea to vary the media from day to day to include the chalkboard; large, unlined newsprint; newspaper want ads; sand trays; and/or a dry-erase marker board.

Classroom teachers should plan to spend 20–30 minutes per day teaching handwriting. When all letter forms are taught, a 5- to 10-minute daily review of difficult letter forms or those that confuse students will maintain standards and automatic performance.

Handwriting instruction should be done in a structured way with attention to posture, pencil grip, position of the writing surface, and emphasis on naming the letters before writing them. This daily attention to handwriting using a multisensory process helps students learn the letter shapes, increases their automaticity for writing, and facilitates the connection between the letters and the sounds they represent for reading and spelling.

Sample Lesson #1—Cursive Letter *a*

Teacher: [Prints lowercase letter *a* (1–2 feet high) on board with arrow indicating baseline and direction *a*; superimposes cursive letter; as let-

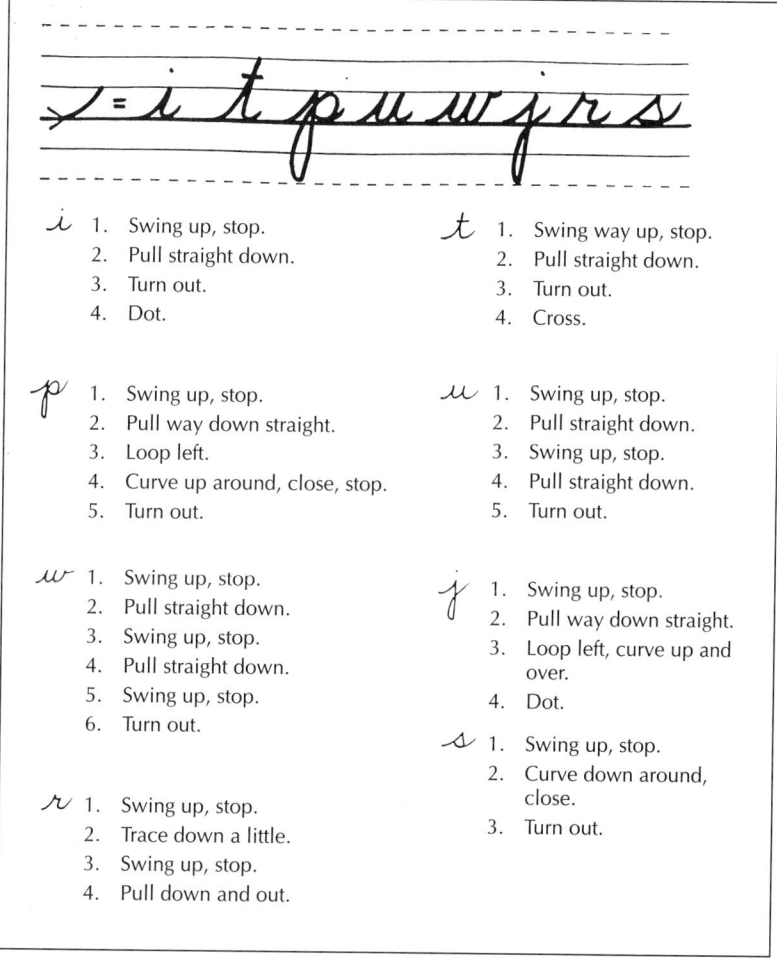

Figure 9.9. Approach stroke: "Swing up, stop." (From Texas Scottish Rite Hospital for Children, Child Development Division. [1996]. *Teaching cursive writing* [Brochure]. Dallas: Author; reprinted by permission.)

ter is drawn, describes the strokes] This letter is *a*. Curve up and over, stop. Trace back, down around, and close. Pull straight down. Turn out. [Erases letters and writes cursive letter, 1–2 feet high, again repeating name of letter and descriptive words]

Student: [Names letter and traces model in air three times with arm extended, elbow straight and index finger pointing, using waist as baseline]

Teacher: [As the student writes in the air, teacher repeats description of letter] This is letter *a*. Curve up and over, stop. Trace back, down around, and close. Pull straight down. Turn out.

Student: [Traces letter on the board, naming letter first and repeating descriptive phrase if able. Continues tracing at least three times until strokes are smooth. Writes letter on the board three times, using model as guide. Names letter each time. Writes the letter on the board with eyes closed as a final check that the letter has been

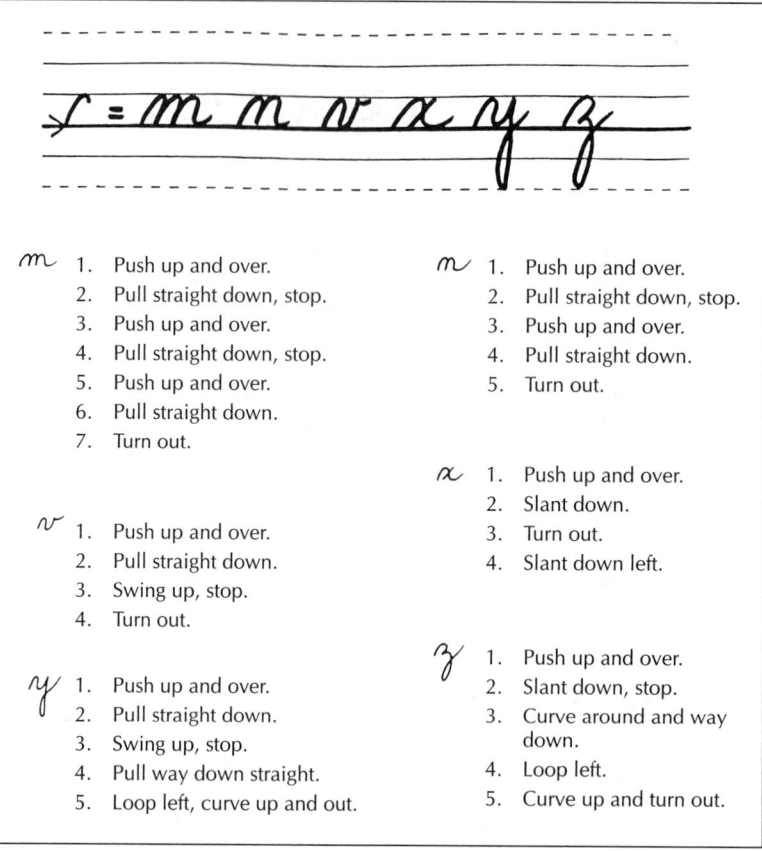

Figure 9.10.   Approach stroke: "Push up and over." (From Texas Scottish Rite Hospital for Children, Child Development Division. [1996]. *Teaching cursive writing* [Brochure]. Dallas: Author; reprinted by permission.)

learned and to promote motor memory. Puts pencil grip on pencil and traces model on wide-lined practice sheet. Names letter and practices writing it until writing becomes smooth and automatic. Writes letter on primary practice sheet several times. Practices 5 minutes per day. At the conclusion of the group using the same approach stroke, practices all letters learned to that point.]

CONCLUSION

This chapter has presented a specific technique for teaching handwriting that utilizes a multisensory framework and integrates the teaching of print and cursive handwriting with reading and spelling. The importance of handwriting instruction in early education and in remediation, a brief history of the teaching of handwriting and techniques used to teach it in schools now, some syndromes related to difficulties with handwriting, and research evidence of the efficacy of direct teaching of handwriting to dyslexic students have been discussed.

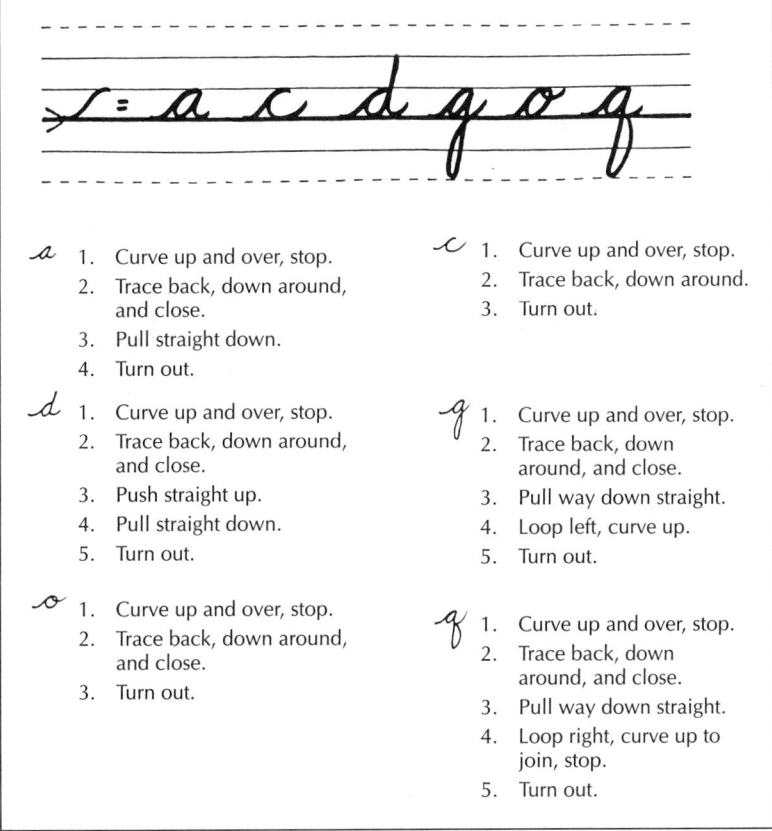

1. Curve up and over, stop.
2. Trace back, down around, and close.
3. Pull straight down.
4. Turn out.

1. Curve up and over, stop.
2. Trace back, down around.
3. Turn out.

1. Curve up and over, stop.
2. Trace back, down around, and close.
3. Push straight up.
4. Pull straight down.
5. Turn out.

1. Curve up and over, stop.
2. Trace back, down around, and close.
3. Pull way down straight.
4. Loop left, curve up.
5. Turn out.

1. Curve up and over, stop.
2. Trace back, down around, and close.
3. Turn out.

1. Curve up and over, stop.
2. Trace back, down around, and close.
3. Pull way down straight.
4. Loop right, curve up to join, stop.
5. Turn out.

Figure 9.11. Approach stroke: "Curve under, over, stop." (From Texas Scottish Rite Hospital for Children, Child Development Division. [1996]. *Teaching cursive writing* [Brochure]. Dallas: Author; reprinted by permission.)

Emphasis is placed on a hierarchy of skills—utilizing large-muscle movements at first, providing a model of cursive over print to tie how the letter is written to how it appears in printed reading material, practicing individual strokes within letters, and connecting letters. Spacing, proportion of single letter shapes (one letter to another and individually), rhythm, and fluency are emphasized, leading to instant writing and writing from memory. All is done in a structured way in correct position, with models to refer to, with students naming the letters before writing to utilize the visual, auditory, kinesthetic, and tactile senses. The teacher does not hurry the student to reduce the size of the letter shapes prematurely but demands automaticity at each level of air writing, tracing, copying, and writing from memory large letters before allowing smaller letters to be practiced.

A number of programs have been specifically developed to emphasize the proper formation of letters treating handwriting as a basic skill to be taught systematically. All of the programs direct the writer's attention to the distinctive features of each letter. Letters are grouped by beginning strokes; by the number of spaces above and below the lines; and by stopping points, vertical lines, loops, and curves. The main feature of these programs is consistent motor patterns supported by explicit verbalization of the proper order and direction of making the

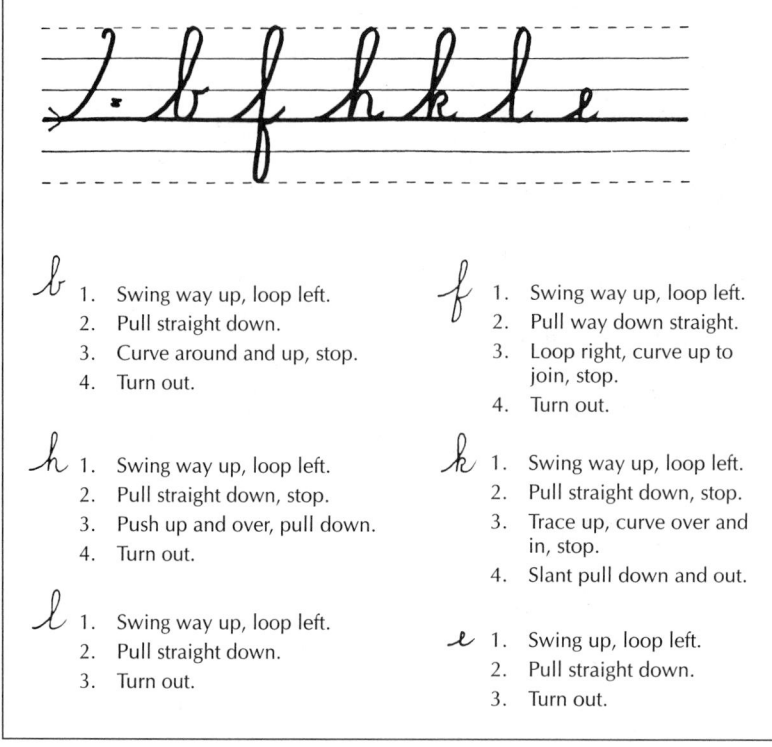

Figure 9.12. Approach stroke: "Curve way up, loop left." (From Texas Scottish Rite Hospital for Children, Child Development Division. [1996]. *Teaching cursive writing* [Brochure]. Dallas: Author; reprinted by permission.)

strokes as the letters are learned and practiced. Verbal descriptions have been developed for all 26 lowercase cursive and print letters. Uppercase cursive letters are usually taught later. (See Appendix B at the end of this book for a list of published multisensory, structured language programs that deal directly and explicitly with handwriting as a remedial adjunct to reading and spelling.)

Research has shown that students who are unable to take notes and write papers at an efficient level fall behind not only in notation but also in comprehension (Phelps, Stempel, & Browne, 1989). Because the basic skill areas appear closely linked, handwriting should be integrated into curricula designed to help students who have academic difficulties. Very often the focus in language arts education is on spelling and reading to the exclusion of the technique of handwriting. This vital omission can lower overall achievement and affect the child's attitude toward all school learning (Askov & Peck, 1982).

REFERENCES

Adams, M.J. (1990). *Beginning to read: Thinking and learning about print.* Cambridge: The MIT Press.

Askov, E., & Peck, M. (1982). Handwriting. In *Encyclopedia of educational research* (5th ed., Vol. 2, pp. 764–766) New York: Free Press.

Athenes, S., & Guiard, Y. (1991). The development of handwriting posture: A comparison between left-handers and right-handers. In J. Wann, M. Wing, & N. Sovik (Eds.), *Development of graphic skills*. London: Academic Press.

Beery, K. (1982). *Administration, scoring, and teaching manual for the Developmental Test of Visual–Motor Integration* (Rev. ed.). Cleveland, OH: Modern Curriculum Press.

Berninger, V., Mizokowa, D., & Bragg, R. (1991). Scientific practitioner. Theory-based diagnosis and remediation of writing disabilities. *Journal of School Psychology, 29*, 57–79.

Bertin, P., & Perlman, E. (1991). *Preventing academic failure*. Cambridge, MA: Educators Publishing Service.

Black, J. (1996). *The clumsy child*. Unpublished manuscript, Texas Scottish Rite Hospital for Children, Dallas.

Blalock, J.W. (1985, November 13). *Oral language problems of learning-disabled adolescents and adults*. Paper presented at the 36th Annual Conference of the Orton Dyslexia Society, Chicago.

Bridge, C.A., Compton-Hall, M., & Cantrell, S.C. (1997, November). Classroom writing practices revisited: The effects of statewide reform on writing instruction. *Elementary School Journal, 98*, 151–170.

Cicci, R. (1995). *What's wrong with me? Learning disabilities at home and in school*. Timonium, MD: York Press.

Clark, D. (1988). *Dyslexia: Theory and practice of remedial instruction*. Timonium, MD: York Press.

Cox, A. (1980). *Structures and techniques: Multisensory teaching of basic language skills*. Cambridge, MA: Educators Publishing Service.

Cox, A. (1985). Alphabet phonics: An organization and expansion of Orton-Gillingham. *Annals of Dyslexia, 35*, 187–198.

Cox, A.R. (1992). *Foundations for oral literacy: Structures and techniques for multisensory teaching of basic written English language skills*. Cambridge, MA: Educators Publishing Service.

Durkin, D. (1966). *Children who read early: Two longitudinal studies*. New York: Teachers College Press.

Educational Testing Service. (1994, November). Handwritten essays score higher, study shows. *American Teacher, 79*, 2.

Fernald, G. (1943). *Remedial techniques in basic school subjects*. New York: McGraw-Hill.

Flick, D. (1996, April 27). Minding her Q's, girl is a textbook study in cursive expertise. *The Dallas Morning News*, pp. A1, A26.

Getman, G.N. (1984). About handwriting. *Academic Therapy, 19*, 139–140.

Gillingham, A., & Stillman, B.W. (1960). *Remedial training for children with specific disability in reading, spelling, and penmanship*. Cambridge, MA: Educators Publishing Service.

Gillingham, A., & Stillman, B.W. (1997). *The Gillingham manual: Remedial training for children with specific disability in reading, writing, and penmanship* (8th ed.). Cambridge, MA: Educators Publishing Service.

Goodman, R., & Caramazza, A. (1986). Dissociation of spelling errors in written and oral spelling: The role of allographic conversion in writing. *Cognitive Neuropsychology, 3*, 179–206.

Hagin, R.A. (1983). Write right or left—a practical approach to handwriting. *Journal of Learning Disabilities, 16*, 266–271.

Hamstra-Bletz, L., & Blöte, A. (1990). Development of handwriting in primary school: A longitudinal study. *Perceptual and Motor Skills, 70*, 759–770.

Johnson, D.J. (1988). Review of research on specific reading, writing, and mathematics disorders. In J.F. Kavanagh & T.J. Truss (Eds.), *Learning disabilities: Proceedings of the national conference*. Timonium, MD: York Press.

Kurtz, L. (1994, Fall). Helpful handwriting hints. *Teaching Exceptional Children*, 58.

Levine, M. (1987). *Developmental variations and learning disorders*. Cambridge, MA: Educators Publishing Service.

Levine, M. (1994). *Educational care: A system for understanding and helping children with learning problems at home and in school*. Cambridge, MA: Educators Publishing Service.

Luria, A.R. (1973). *The working brain*. London: Penguin Books., Ltd.

McMenamin, B., & Martin, M. (1980). *Right writing*. Spring Valley, CA: Cursive Writing Associates.

Moats, L.C. (1995). *Spelling: Development, disability, and instruction*. Timonium, MD: York Press.

Montessori, M. (1966). *The secret of childhood*. New York: Ballantine Books.

Myers, E.H. (1963). *The whys and hows of teaching handwriting*. Columbus, OH: Zaner-Bloser.

Odman, A. (1989, July). *Reorganization of handwriting in Finland*. Paper presented at the Fourth Conference of the International Graphonomic Society, Development of Graphic Skills, University of Trondheim, Norway.

Orton, J.L. (1966). The Orton-Gillingham approach. In J. Money (Ed.), *The disabled reader: Education of the dyslexic child*. Baltimore: The Johns Hopkins University Press.

Orton, S.T. (1937). *Reading, writing, and speech problems in children*. New York: W.W. Norton.

A penchant for penmanship. (1996, November–December). *Learning, 25*, 72–74.

Phelps, J., & Stempel, L. (1985). *CHES's handwriting improvement program* (CHIP). Dallas: CHES. (Available from the publisher, Post Office Box 25254, Dallas, TX 75225)

Phelps, J., & Stempel, L. (1987). Handwriting: Evolution and evaluation. *Annals of Dyslexia, 37*, 228–239.

Phelps, J., Stempel, L., & Browne, R. (1989). *Children's handwriting and school achievement*. Unpublished manuscript, Texas Scottish Rite Hospital for Children, Dallas.

Phelps, J., Stempel, L., & Speck, G. (1984). *Children's Handwriting Evaluation Scale*. Dallas, TX: CHES. (Available from the publisher, Post Office Box 25254, Dallas, TX 75225)

Precker, M. (1994, January 29). Written off: Penmanship is becoming a lost art in our high-tech, hurry-up world. *Dallas Morning News*, p. C1.

Reisman, J. (1991, September). Poor handwriting: Who is referred? *American Journal of Occupational Therapy, 45*(9), 849–852.

Richardson, S. (1995). Specific developmental dyslexia: Retrospective and prospective views. In C.W. McIntyre & J. Pickering (Eds.), *Clinical studies of multisensory structured language education*. Salem, OR: IMSLEC.

Rubin, H., & Eberhardt, N. (1996). Facilitating invented spelling through language analysis instruction: An integrated model. *Reading and Writing: An Interdisciplinary Journal, 8*, 27–43.

Sassoon, R. (1991). The effect of teachers' personal handwriting on their reproduction of school handwriting models. In J. Wann, A.M. Wing, & N. Sovik (Eds.), *Development of graphic skills* (pp. 151–161). London: Academic Press Inc.

Slingerland, B. (1976). *Basics in scope and sequence of* A multisensory approach to language arts, book II. Cambridge, MA: Educators Publishing Service.

Slingerland, B.H. (1971). *A multisensory approach to language arts, book I*. Cambridge, MA: Educators Publishing Service.

Slingerland, B., & Aho, M. (1985). *Manual for* Learning to use manuscript handwriting. Cambridge, MA: Educators Publishing Service.

Smith, M. (1987, September 27). Capital letters: Writers of the lost art keep missives flowing. *Dallas Times Herald*, pp. D1, D7.

Strickling, C.A. (1974). The effect of handwriting and related skills upon the spelling scores above average and below average readers in the fifth grade. *Dissertation Abstracts International, 34*(07), 3717A.

Tabor, M. (1996, May 8). Penmanship: Fine art to lost art. *The New York Times*, pp. B1, B12.

Texas Scottish Rite Hospital for Children: Child Development Division. (1990). *Dyslexia training program developed in the Dyslexia Laboratory, Texas Scottish Rite Hospital* [Videotape]. Cambridge, MA: Educators Publishing Service.

Texas Scottish Rite Hospital for Children: Child Development Division. (1996). *Teaching cursive writing* [Brochure]. Dallas: Author.

Vail, P.L. (1981). *Clear and lively writing*. New York: Walker & Co.

vos Savant, M. (1988, June 5). Ask Marilyn. *Parade*, 8.

Wessel, D. (1984, June 27). Pupils are minding their P's and Q's and other letters. *The Wall Street Journal*, p. 1.

Zaner-Bloser. (1968). *Expressional growth through handwriting*. Columbus, OH: Author.

10

Composition

Expressive Language and Writing

Judith C. Hochman

Written language is considered by many to be the most challenging skill to teach and to learn. Some proponents of multisensory instruction believe that the teaching of written language skills should be delayed until students have achieved proficiency in decoding, spelling, and handwriting (Clark & Uhry, 1995). It is feared that dyslexic children will be overwhelmed if they are exposed to additional language training before they reach middle school. There is reason to believe, however, that there are large numbers of oral and written activities that teachers should use in the primary grades concurrently with the beginning of instruction in reading, spelling, and handwriting.

Many individuals with excellent reading and speaking skills have problems generating written language. Even for typical learners, mastering the skills associated with good writing is a daunting task, but those with learning and language problems face especially formidable obstacles. Students with learning and language disabilities have difficulties with decoding, spelling, word retrieval, and syntax that are often exacerbated by a limited vocabulary. As a result, understanding what others say and expressing oneself with clarity and accuracy are significantly compromised. In addition, weak organizational skills often accompany learning and language problems. The inability to distinguish essential from nonessential information and to set forth facts or ideas in logical order can impede students as they try to formulate outlines or generate well-organized paragraphs and compositions.

Writing problems remain a persistent learning disability personally, vocationally, and academically for many adults who were not taught specific strategies as young students (Scott, 1989). Because reading disabilities receive far more attention in school than do writing problems, many students receive little, if any, explicit instruction in written language (Scott, 1989). Too often it is assumed that mastery of the conventions of written language will naturally follow fluent decoding and good reading comprehension.

Competent writers are able to focus on meaning, purpose, and audience as they plan and organize information. These tasks require simultaneous processing at higher cognitive levels than are required in other areas of skills acquisition. Moreover, older students are often required to demonstrate in writing assignments their understanding of subject matter by paraphrasing or summarizing texts that are linguistically complex or densely loaded with factual information.

The development of narrative skills and sound expository writing abilities, discussing ideas or explaining processes, should be the primary aims of a written language curriculum. Given the limited time teachers have to provide instruction in writing, the goal should be to help students develop a solid foundation in those writing skills that are required most often in academic tasks and assignments. Writing and thinking are inextricably linked. Therefore, primary instructional goals should be to enhance clarity and precision in both process and product. Although mechanics such as spelling and handwriting (see Chapters 8 and 9, respectively) are important and should not be ignored, they should be addressed separately whenever possible so that students can focus on developing the higher-level skills required for written language.

Creative writing activities, which center on self-expression rather than on communication with the reader, are frequently the major focus of elementary school writing programs. Imaginative stories, poems, journal writing, and descriptions involving personal perceptions are assigned in many classes, often with little or no guidance from the teacher. These activities are not the same as those used during direct instruction in how to write. Students with and without learning and language disabilities should be given opportunities to experiment with a variety of forms and styles only after they learn how to write sentences and paragraphs competently.

Although writing lessons should take place daily, tasks involving paper and pencil are not always necessary. For example, many sentence and paragraph activities can and should be done orally. Activities for longer compositions should include carefully orchestrated discussions dealing with the identification of the audience, selection of a topic, and description of the purpose of the assignment. The teacher must provide explicit demonstrations of what is expected. Independent writing should not take place until students have been well prepared.

Because many students have difficulty applying the writing principles learned in one class to the subject matter of another, reinforcement is important. For teachers to achieve the best results, writing instruction should be integrated into every content area and at all grade levels through secondary school. Students with a wide range of abilities will then have a chance of becoming better writers in all academic areas.

This chapter describes activities for writing sentences, paragraphs, and compositions. Most of them should take place concurrently. Sentence activities are the foundation for revising and editing skills, which are crucial in developing competency in writing. Activities for paragraphs and compositions are necessary to develop the thinking and study skills students need.

SENTENCES

Sentence activities have two primary purposes. The first goal is to enable students to write compound and complex sentences rather than only simple, active, declarative forms. This will enhance reading comprehension (Maria, 1990). The second goal is to improve revision and editing skills, which benefit critical thinking skills. The importance of allocating a great deal of time working with sentences cannot be emphasized enough.

Teachers may use many sentence activities, most of which can be performed both orally and in writing. They should provide as many opportunities as possible to practice developing sentence skills. These activities can be adapted to be made more challenging or easier, depending on the age and ability levels of the students.

Sentences and Fragments

Teacher: A sentence is a complete thought. Tell me whether groups of words you hear (or read) are sentences or not: Jane gave me her book.
Student: *Sentence*
Teacher: Into the forest
Student: *Not a sentence*
Teacher: A fragment is a piece of a sentence. Change this fragment into a sentence: At night
Student: *The deer ran at night.*

Note: Students often use fragments (incomplete sentences) in spoken language, and they do the same when they write. The teacher must explain that far more precision is necessary in writing than in speaking. Students should be able to identify a fragment in a selection read aloud to them before attempting to correct them in their own work.

Scrambled Sentences

Teacher: Rearrange words into sentences, and add the correct punctuation and capitalization. [Some students may need to be given the first word of the sentence.] live did where tim
Student: *Where did Tim live?*

Sentence Types: Statements, Questions, Exclamations, and Commands

Teacher: Add the correct punctuation and capitalization to these sentences. Write this as a statement: john stayed at home
Student: *John stayed at home.*
Teacher: Write this as a command: give that to me immediately
Student: *Give that to me immediately!*
Teacher: Write this as a question: where are you going
Student: *Where are you going?*
Teacher: Write this as an exclamation: my father hates cauliflower

Student: *My father hates cauliflower!*
Teacher: [Asks students to write on worksheets or on the chalkboard an example of each of the four sentence types using a particular spelling or vocabulary word] Write a statement, a command, a question, and exclamation using the word *retract*.
Student: *The teacher retracted what she said.*
               Retract that statement
               Will he retract that remark?
               I want you to retract that statement!
Teacher: [Asks students to change statements to questions (and vice versa)] He is the governor.
Student: *Is he the governor?*
Teacher: [Asks students to generate a question from an answer; students can do this orally or in writing] Albany
Student: *What is the capital of New York?*
Teacher: [Asks students to help develop essay questions for social studies, science, or literature tests]
Student: *Discuss the events leading up to the War of 1812.*
               Describe the process of photosynthesis.
               Explain the great and continuing public interest in The Diary of Anne Frank.

Sentence Expansion

The teacher should display the question words *who, what, when, where, why,* and *how* and then give students sentence kernels (a simple sentence without modifiers), such as *Jane ran* or *Candidates debate.* The teacher should ask the class to expand the kernels by using one, two, three, or more of the question words. When introducing this strategy, it is best for the teacher to begin with *when, where,* or *why* because they are easier than *who, what,* and *how.* (Figure 10.1 shows an example of a **sentence expansion** worksheet.) Reading comprehension or knowledge in any content area can be assessed using sentence kernels, such as *Colonists fled. Where? Why?* Students often assume that the reader has more prior knowledge than is actually the case; sentence expansion enables them to provide information with greater precision.

Conjunctions

Conjunctions (also called *connectives*) are uninflected words that join words, phrases, or clauses. Their purpose is to link or relate parts of a sentence. Table 10.1 lists conjunctions that teachers may use as a reference and insert in students' notebooks to aid them in independent writing. Students should write sentences starting with conjunctions to construct linguistically complex sentences. Consider having students embed spelling or vocabulary words in their sentences or write about their experiences.

Teacher: Use the three following sentence starters, and write three sentences about the ice skating trip for each sentence starter.
Student: **Whenever** *we go ice skating, we have a great time.*
               Since *we are going ice skating, I am going to get my skates sharpened.*

Name:_____Date:_____

SENTENCE EXPANSION

Expand the following kernels using three of the following question words: where, when, why, how.

Kernel: The boys ran.

when   Tuesday

how   quickly

where   in the park

Expanded Sentence: Last Tuesday the boys ran quickly in the park.

_____

_____

Kernel: Rose entered.

when   yesterday

how   cautiously

why   scared

Expanded Sentence: Yesterday Rose entered cautiously because she was scared.

_____

_____

Figure 10.1.   Sentence expansion worksheet.

After we go ice skating, we will write about it in school.

Teacher:	[Asks students to combine short, active declarative sentences using conjunctions and explains that repetition can be avoided by using pronouns] Combine this sentence using a conjunction: John was at the bus stop. John's car was being repaired.
Student:	*John was at the bus stop because his car was being repaired.*
Teacher:	[Asks students to use conjunctions to complete given sentences] Mother was happy because. . .
Student:	*Mother was happy because we cleaned our room.*
Teacher:	Mother was happy, but. . .
Student:	*Mother was happy, but she saw clothes on the floor.*
Teacher:	Mother was happy, so. . .
Student:	*Mother was happy, so she let us go to the movies.*

This activity is useful in assessing students' understanding of literature, social studies, or current events, as shown in the following examples:

Table 10.1.   Conjunctions for use in independent writing

after	however	than
although	if	that
and	if . . . then	then
as if	in order that	though
as soon as	neither . . . nor	till
as though	nevertheless	unless
because	nonetheless	until
before	or	when
but	rather than	whenever
either . . . or	regardless of	where
even if	since	wherever
even though	so	while
for (meaning because)	so that	yet
how		

Teacher: Andrew Jackson was a popular president, but. . .
Student: *Andrew Jackson was a popular president, but there were many critics of his "kitchen cabinet" and the "spoils system."*
Teacher: Andrew Jackson was a popular president because. . .
Student: *Andrew Jackson was a popular president because he was a champion of the common people.*
Teacher: Andrew Jackson was a popular president, so. . .
Student: *Andrew Jackson was a popular president, so he won the election of 1828 easily.*
Teacher: Anne Frank and her family were hidden in the attic; however. . .
Student: *Anne Frank and her family were hidden in the attic; however, they were discovered by the Nazis.*

Grammar

The parts of speech and usage should be taught within the writing program. Teaching grammar during sentence activities helps students gain an understanding of how parts of speech are used in context, which proves especially useful when they are expected to revise and edit their own work or assigned passages.

Teacher: [Asks students to change nouns to pronouns] Mary danced.
Student: *She danced.*
Teacher: [Asks the class to change tenses from present to past (or from present to future or vice versa)] The car races.
Student: *The car raced.*
            The car will race.
Teacher: [Asks students to insert an adjective, an adverb, and a prepositional phrase] The runner won.
Student: *The amazing runner won easily in spite of keen competition.*
Teacher: [Asks students to use an **appositive** after a proper noun (an appositive is a second noun, placed beside the first noun to explain it more fully; it usually has modifiers)] George Washington was a brilliant general.
Student: *George Washington, our first president, was a brilliant general.*

Topic Sentences

Teach students to generate topic sentences for given topics. Have students brain-storm sentences about a given topic. For example, if the topic is *hiking,* a range of topic sentences can emerge: *Hiking can be dangerous. My favorite weekend activity is hiking. Hiking is a great way to enjoy nature. Try hiking this summer!* Encourage students to experiment using different sentence types, and remind them that topic sentences do not necessarily have to begin with the topic word.

Teacher: Topic: New York City
Student: *I love New York City.*
          Have you a favorite place to visit in New York City?
          Visit New York City!
          New York City is a study in contrasts.

Make sure that students can distinguish between topic sentences and supporting details. *Visiting the Metropolitan Museum of Art is a wonderful experience* supports but does not convey the main idea, *New York City.* Selecting the topic sentence from a group of sentences is a beneficial activity.

Teacher: I'm going to read you several sentences. One is a topic sentence. The others are supporting details. Listen for the topic sentence, and tell me which one you think it is. Remember, the topic sentence might not be the first one I read to you.
          The western frontier closed.
          European nations were competing for resources and markets.
          There were several causes for the United States' expansion overseas.
          Businesses were seeking raw materials and new markets.
Student: *The topic sentence was the third one, "There were several causes for the United States' expansion overseas."*

PARAGRAPHS AND COMPOSITIONS

Very little has been written on the developmental stages of writing for children with language disabilities (Clark & Uhry, 1995). Narratives setting forth a sequence of events are the form of composition taught most frequently to younger or less skilled writers (Alley & Deshler, 1979). Narrative writing relates events in chronological order, and sentences can be sequenced using transition words, such as *first, next, then,* and *finally* (see Table 10.2). Written in either the first person (as a participant) or third person (as an observer), this type of composition is most beneficial when it is based on a personal or a class experience.

In contrast with narratives, expository writing explains or informs. Typically, students are asked to define, discuss, criticize, list, compare, contrast, explain, and summarize. Expository writing is also used to provide an example or describe a process. The topic sentence of a paragraph or thesis statement of a composition should clearly state the writer's objective, and the product should contain sufficient support for the writer's position. Because this type of assignment is required most frequently in school in fourth grade and beyond, teachers should

Table 10.2.   Transition words and phrases

Group 1 Time and sequence	Group 2 Conclusion	Group 3 Illustration
first	in conclusion	for example
second	consequently	for instance
then	in closing	specifically
next	in summary	as an illustration
also	to conclude	
after	therefore	
later on	as a result	
in addition	thus	
before		
last of all		
finally		

Group 4 Change of direction	Group 5 Emphasis	
but	keep in mind	furthermore
however	remember that	undoubtedly
yet	a major concern	certainly
in contrast	the best thing	above all
otherwise	the biggest advantage	most importantly
still	it is valuable to note	primarily
on the other hand	obviously	
on the contrary		

spend the most time on it (Alley & Deshler, 1979). Several common types of expository writing are described next.

Persuasive writing presents a point of view to a specific audience, such as parents, fellow students, teachers, or the editor of a newspaper. Facts are gathered in order to convince the reader of the validity of the writer's position. The conclusion usually proposes the action that the writer would like the reader to take.

Descriptive writing taps the five senses in order to effectively transmit experiences about people, places, things, and thoughts. Varied and vivid vocabulary is especially important when developing a descriptive passage. Brainstorming and generating lists of adjectives and adverbs or more precise nouns and verbs are appropriate activities to use in conjunction with descriptive writing lessons.

The *compare-and-contrast composition* is usually the most difficult type of expository writing for students to master. This form of writing highlights the similarities (comparisons) and differences (contrasts) among two or more people, places, things, ideas, or experiences. A conclusion must be developed from the facts presented. When presenting this type of writing assignment, teachers should be aware that organizing compare-and-contrast essays can be particularly challenging for the less skillful writer. Teachers should explain that it is easier to compare and contrast two subjects in a composition with several paragraphs than in one paragraph.

A great deal of time must be spent teaching students how to develop a single good paragraph before moving on to longer compositions. Many teachers are eager to encourage their students to write at length about a topic, thus confusing quantity with quality. The chances are that if students write too much too soon, they may not stick to the topic and will not proofread and improve their writing effectively.

The following four steps are involved in most writing assignments. A lesson can end after any one of them, except that it is not a good idea to have students end an assignment with an uncorrected draft.

- Planning and outlining
- Drafting
- Revising and editing
- Writing a final copy

The first step, planning and outlining, and the third step, revising and editing, are the most important to master. Therefore, they should be given far more instructional time than drafting or producing final copies, which can be done independently by some students.

Planning and Outlining

Planning requires a great deal of instructional time. This is the point at which students begin to organize their assignments and thoughts systematically and sequentially. Class discussions that establish the topic, type, purpose, and audience of the paragraph or composition are extremely important. During the planning phase, information is gathered and shared. Students are guided to distinguish between relevant and nonessential material. Ideas and supporting details are categorized and sequenced in outline form. Topic sentences and, for older students, thesis statements can be developed at this time. Initially, all of these activities can be done as a class with teacher demonstrations and guidance. When students become more proficient, they can begin to work independently.

Initial lessons in how to develop outlines are done with the teacher guiding the development of a model for the class. By providing an overall view of the finished product, the outline serves as a map that allows students to visualize the project as a cohesive whole that has a beginning, middle, and end. Outlines help students to distinguish essential from nonessential material and to sequence information. As students become more proficient through practice and group work, they can develop their outlines independently.

Three useful outline forms are as follows (Hochman, 1995):

- The *Quick Outline* is used for developing a single paragraph and is intended to help the students discern the basic structure of the paragraph: topic sentence, supporting details, and concluding sentence.
- The *Transitional Outline* is useful when students are beginning to write compositions of two or three paragraphs.
- The *Multiple Paragraph Outline* (MPO) is for developing compositions of three or more paragraphs.

After students have mastered a particular outlining format, they should be encouraged to proceed to writing drafts. When teaching outlining, teachers should use topics that require no special prior knowledge unless something that has just been taught or experienced by the class is being reviewed or reinforced. The emphasis should be on the skills required to outline, not on the material to be learned or reviewed.

Quick Outlines   Students must master several preliminary skills before they can develop a Quick Outline (see Figure 10.2) independently (Hochman, 1995). Several activities for developing and improving outlines are helpful in providing practice for students. First, the student must be able to produce a topic sentence for a given topic. (e.g., if the topic was the Industrial Revolution, a topic sentence might be *There were several major causes and effects of the Industrial Revolution*). Second, the student has to learn to write supporting details using key words or phrases (e.g., *Eli Whitney/cotton gin/interchangeable parts*). This skill is an important one and is a precursor to note taking. A great deal of practice is needed for students to convert sentences into phrases. Complete sentences should not be used on the outline except for the topic and concluding sentences. Third, the students have to understand that the concluding sentence is either a restatement of the topic sentence or a summary of the paragraph's main point (e.g., *The Industrial Revolution was a time of great change*). Topics can be easier or more challenging depending on the age and abilities of the students. The skills used in the creation of Quick Outlines will require a great deal of teacher demonstration and group work.

Many activities focus on just one segment of the Quick Outline. These activities can be done before or concurrently with completing a full Quick Outline. An overhead projector is useful when working as a class. The students should have a copy of the overhead text so they can work along with the teacher.

Teacher: Provide the details for this topic sentence: Thanksgiving is a wonderful traditional holiday.
Student: *Pilgrims, Indians*
            preparation, fun
            family reunion
            wonderful food
Teacher: Generate a topic sentence from the following phrases:
            pilgrims and Indians
            family gets together
            turkey, trimmings, desserts
            football
Student: *Thanksgiving is my favorite holiday.*
Teacher: Identify the topic sentence and sequence the others.
            I ate too much candy. [4]
            My sister and I selected our costumes. [2]
            Sheila was a princess and I was a witch. [3]
            Last Halloween was great! [Topic Sentence]
            The next day we were exhausted. [5]
Student: *The topic sentence is Last Halloween was great! The others should be in this order:*
            My sister and I selected our costumes.
            Sheila was a princess and I was a witch.
            I ate too much candy.
            The next day we were exhausted.

BASIC WRITING SKILLS
Quick Outline

Name _____   Date _____

T.S. _David is a wonderful friend._

_____

_____

1. _loyal_ ....

2. _smart_ ....

3. _lots of fun_ ....

4. _things in common_ ....

C.S. _We have great times together and I hope_

we always will!

_____

Figure 10.2. Quick Outline.

Teacher: Identify the topic sentence, and write the others in phrases and key words.
Texas was perfect for raising cattle and growing cotton.
There was fertile land in Oregon.
Americans believed in Manifest Destiny.
There were many causes of the westward expansion in the United States.
Mormons wanted a safe haven.
Gold was discovered in California.

Student: *The topic sentence is There were many causes of the westward expansion in the United States. Key words are:*
perfect/cattle/cotton
Oregon/fertile
belief in Manifest Destiny
Mormons/safe haven

California/gold

Teacher: Here is a topic sentence: Autumn is my favorite season. Eliminate irrelevant phrases and those that do not relate directly to the topic sentence.
go for a drive/changing colors
buy cider/doughnuts/pumpkin
watch a video
carve a jack-o'-lantern
Concluding sentence: Some of my best memories take place in autumn.

Student: *Watch a video is the irrelevant phrase.*

Teacher: Convert the following paragraph into a Quick Outline:

Autumn is my favorite season. I love to drive through the country and look at the changing colors of the leaves. It's fun to stop for cider and doughnuts and to buy a pumpkin. Later, at home, we carve the jack-o'-lantern. Some of my best memories are of autumn.

Student: *Topic sentence: Autumn is my favorite season.*
go for a drive/changing colors
buy cider/doughnuts/pumpkin
carve a jack-o'-lantern
Concluding sentence: Some of my best memories are of autumn.

To develop a complete Quick Outline with the class, the following sequence is suggested:

- Introduce and discuss a topic.
- Identify audience and discuss purpose.
- Present a topic sentence to the students, or have them generate one as a group. (Eventually students should do this independently.)
- Elicit as many supporting details as possible from the class, and write them on the chalkboard or a flipchart. If the details are stated as complete sentences, convert them into phrases or key words.
- Depending on the topic and number of details, either select three or four of the most important ones or, whenever possible, group the details in categories for the outline.

Distribute a blank Quick Outline to each student.

- Ask the students to write their preferred topic sentence (if more than one was generated) and to select details for the outline.
- Generate a concluding sentence as a class. If students are able, they can do this independently.

Transitional Outline   The Transitional Outline (see Figure 10.3) is used after the students have had experience writing paragraphs and are ready to attempt longer compositions. Students should be comfortable with the format of the Quick Outline before moving on to the Transitional Outline, and this generally does not occur before fourth or fifth grade. The Transitional Outline provides an overview of the whole composition, including topic sentences and details for

---

BASIC WRITING SKILLS
Transitional Outline

Name _____ Date _____

Title ___Immigration_____

T.S. Immigrants from all over the world came to the U.S. between
1880 and 1920.

　1. steerage / lowest fares / bad food + conditions................................
　2. arrived in NYC / Statue of Liberty...
　3. shouting / passengers pushed and pulled................................

T.S. Many immigrants viewed Ellis Island as a place of hope
and fear.

　1. Great Hall / lines / confusion..
　2. Med. exam / diseases ⟶ sent back.....................................
　3. Inspectors' question / name changes / $ exchange..................

T.S. Life after Ellis Island was filled with many different
experiences.

　1. English language / customs / religions..................................
　2. NYC / big cities / neighborhoods.......................................
　3. melting pot / children blend together..................................

C.S. Adjustment to the U.S. was not easy but it was worth it for
most immigrants.

Figure 10.3. Transitional Outline.

every paragraph. A concluding sentence is not necessary for any paragraph other than the last one.

Multiple Paragraph Outline   The MPO (see Figure 10.4) is designed for students who are ready to develop unified, coherent compositions of three or more paragraphs. This type of outline poses a number of challenges for students with learning disabilities. They must be careful not to select topics that are either too broad or too narrow. A specific purpose for writing as well as the audience must be identified. The thesis statement should be clear and succinct.

In order to develop an MPO, students must be able to construct a good paragraph. Unlike the Quick Outline, the main idea of each paragraph is not written as a topic sentence but as a category on the left side of the MPO (e.g., pro, con; cause, effect; similarities, differences; 1st reason, 2nd reason). Supporting details should be written as brief, clear phrases or key words. The MPO helps students

BASIC WRITING SKILLS
Multiple Paragraph Outline

Name _____ Date _____

Title *Pets*

Thesis Statement *Dogs make wonderful companions.*

Main Idea	Details
Introduction ¶1 Dogs/People/Pets	many reasons long history of pets filled many needs
Reason #1 Devotion ¶2	especially for elderly/children obedient not judgmental loyal prevents loneliness
Conclusion Reason #2 Protection ¶3	guards territory defends owners better than alarm system saves lives consider owning a dog

Figure 10.4. Multiple Paragraph Outline.

learn to construct an introduction; a body, which can consist of several paragraphs; and a conclusion. It guides students to stay with a consistent topic, purpose, and point of view by providing a clear visual diagram of the entire work.
As with the other outlines, students will need group work and teacher modeling
before they can develop an MPO independently.

The teacher does not need to move in sequence from three- to four- to five-
paragraph compositions, because the number of paragraphs usually depends on
the topic. For example, a book report may require three paragraphs with categories such as *introduction, plot summary,* and *opinion.* A topic such as *pollution*

might have four categories: *introduction, causes, effects,* and *possible solutions.* A biographical essay about Andrew Jackson may require five categories, such as *introduction, early life, military career, presidency,* and *conclusion.*

Depending on the topic, most MPOs require a thesis statement, which can be presented as follows:

- A personal judgment on a topic
- Advice or directions
- Consequences
- An argument for or against an issue
- An interpretation (usually when writing about fiction or poetry)

At this point older or more advanced students can be taught that it is not necessary for the topic sentence to be the first one in a paragraph. The teacher should explain that the last few words in a paragraph or composition will have the most impact on the reader, and, therefore, the points the writer wishes to emphasize should be at the end. The last sentence of a selection is as important as the first one.

To develop a complete MPO, the following sequence is suggested:

- Select the topic that will be the basis for the title when writing the draft.
- Discuss purpose and audience.
- Develop the thesis statement.
- Write the main idea as a phrase or a category for each paragraph in the left-hand column. This prevents repetition and enables the student to plan the entire composition more effectively. Each paragraph must relate to the overall theme.
- After determining the main idea for each paragraph, write the supporting details in the right-hand column and tell the students that it is acceptable to include more items than they may eventually include in their draft. Remind students that each supporting detail should relate directly to the main idea of its paragraph.

Writing the introduction and the conclusion requires the ability to summarize information. Students should be given plenty of oral practice summarizing news stories, chapters, or plots in one or two sentences. The sentence expansion strategy (*who, what, when, where, why*) and conjunctions (especially *but, because,* and *so*) are helpful aids when summarizing. Because many writers have difficulty with summarizing, it is a good idea to provide lessons that focus exclusively on introductions and conclusions of given topics.

Drafting

Drafting begins with writing paragraphs or compositions based on Quick Outlines, Transitional Outlines, or MPOs. Inexperienced or less competent writers should limit their writing to one paragraph of five or six sentences because longer papers tend to discourage attempts to revise and edit. The teacher should tell students that a draft can never be left uncorrected or unimproved. Revisions and editing will always be expected. In order to provide room for improving their work, students must skip lines when writing drafts or leave sufficient space when working on a computer. A teacher may decide to end an activity with a corrected draft instead of moving on to a final copy if the objectives of the lesson have been met.

Even after a final copy is produced, drafts should not be discarded because they can be helpful in assessing how much the students have improved and the areas in which they need further work. They also provide students with graphic examples of their progress.

Revising and Editing

The importance of revising and editing must be stressed when teaching writing skills to students. *Revision* refers to the clarification or alteration of the meaning or structure of a draft. This is in contrast to *editing*, which involves proofreading and correcting errors in grammar, punctuation, syntax, and spelling. Highly competent writers spend the most time on revision, and consequently, it is the area in which the largest amount of instructional time should be invested. The sentence activities presented previously provide the foundation for developing the skills to improve written work. In order to teach students to refine their own or others' writing, remind them that there are several ways to improve the quality of written language. The five fundamental techniques for revising and editing are as follows:

- Adding words
- Deleting words
- Substituting words, phrases, or clauses
- Rearranging words, phrases, clauses, and sentences
- Proofreading for errors

All too frequently, students are given credit for the quantity of their written work rather than for the quality. They should be reminded regularly that clarity and accuracy, not length, are their goals. Assignments should be kept brief.

The teacher should provide students with checklists for revising and editing. Typical items include the following, with variations for age and ability:

- Does your draft follow your outline?
- Is your topic sentence clearly stated?
- Are your supporting details clear and in order?
- Do the details support the topic sentence?
- Did you use different types of sentences?
- Do your sentences vary in length?
- Are there sentences that should be combined or expanded?
- Did you use transition words or phrases?
- Are your word choices repetitive? vivid? accurate?
- Have you checked for run-ons? fragments? spelling, punctuation, or capitalization errors?
- Have you checked tense and number agreement?

Initially, only a few items should be selected from the checklist to provide a focus for the students as they improve and correct their work. As they become more adept, more checklist items can be added. Students will need reminders to revise style first, then edit the mechanics.

In addition to listing specific items on the checklist, it is often helpful for the teacher to give younger or less advanced students explicit instructions that will add flair to their compositions, such as *Add two adjectives, Insert more transition words*, or *Use sentence starters*. At first, the teacher will have to show students exactly where to place the words and phrases. In time, they will be able to see where to insert them independently. Much attention should also be given to the selection of strong and varied nouns and verbs as well as modifiers. Time and sequence transitions should be taught first, followed by conclusions, and then illustration transitions. The remaining two groups can be taught in any order. (See Table 10.2 for examples of transition words and phrases.) The teacher should encourage students to use transitions even at the beginning stages of paragraph development. Together with the use of sentence starters and conjunctions, the application of these skills will raise the level of linguistic complexity and quality of the students' written work. The teacher should stress that a draft can be reworked at least two or three times and that the better the writer, the more often the draft will be rewritten.

Students will require a great deal of direct instruction, demonstrations, and group participation as they correct and improve their work. They have to understand that their goals should be compositions that flow smoothly, are properly organized, and maintain the reader's interest. Sentences should vary in length and style. Although short, simple, active, declarative sentences are useful for emphasis, too often they are the only forms used by less skillful writers. It should be noted that teachers' comments and feedback should be explicit and plentiful during drafting and during revising and editing.

Students should routinely read their work aloud as an important component of any writing program. This can take place during sentence activities and the drafting or revising and editing stages. Students can read to a partner, to a small group, or to the entire class. One purpose of oral reading is to sharpen proofreading capabilities. Many students are able to correct their errors more accurately and effectively when they read their written work aloud. Another goal is to enhance critical listening skills. The reader's classmates can contribute suggestions based on the checklist explained previously, which will improve proficiency in revision and editing.

Writing a Final Copy

It is not advisable for students to spend a great deal of time recopying written work for final copies. Certainly, this type of activity should not be done during instructional time. Therefore, teachers must be selective as to which activities should be developed to this stage. If final copies are produced, every effort should be made to display them. Students should be given opportunities to see their written work on bulletin boards or published in a class journal, school or local newspaper, or parent bulletin. Writing letters that will accomplish a purpose or elicit a reply can also be rewarding.

CONCLUSION

Explicit instruction of narrative and expository writing skills is given very little time in most schools, although students are routinely given independent writing assignments. Because writing is the most difficult skill to teach and learn, teachers may need to use a writing program with clear guidelines and goals that will enable students to succeed. The key to helping all students, but especially those with learning and language disabilities, to develop proficiency in written language is to provide them with the structure and strategies for building acceptable sentences, paragraphs, and compositions. Goals should be established carefully but should not be overly ambitious. If a teacher of children in primary or elementary grades teaches strategies for sentence expansion and the use of sentence starters as well as activities for developing Quick Outlines in the course of a year, that can be considered a great accomplishment. If students move more quickly than anticipated, then the activities can be easily made more challenging. Composition skills do not develop automatically. Students need carefully sequenced direct instruction, teacher demonstrations, and a great deal of practice in order to succeed.

REFERENCES

Alley, G.R., & Deshler, D.D. (1979). *Teaching the learning disabled adolescent: Strategies and methods.* Denver, CO: Love Publishing Co.

Clark, D.B., & Uhry, J.K. (1995). *Dyslexia: Theory and practice of remedial instruction* (2nd ed.). Timonium, MD: York Press.

Hochman, J.C. (1995). *Basic writing skills.* New York: GSL Publications.

Maria, K. (1990). *Reading comprehension instruction, issues, and strategies.* Timonium, MD: York Press.

Scott, C.M. (1989). In A.G. Kamhi & H.W. Catts (Eds.), *Reading disabilities: A developmental language perspective* (pp. 261–302). Boston: Little, Brown.

11

Multisensory Mathematics Instruction

Margaret B. Stern

This chapter is devoted to the description of the *Structural Arithmetic* (Stern & Stern, 1971) method of teaching mathematical concepts, in which multisensory materials are used. Thus, children achieve mastery of arithmetic without being forced to learn only by memorization and parroting. These materials are designed to enable children to learn on their own; after giving such materials to her students, one first-grade teacher cried, "They teach themselves!"

A structured, multisensory teaching approach is of special importance to children with learning disabilities. These children have difficulty with language concepts and associations and memory. They are usually struggling with a combination of these deficits and may also have difficulties with attention. To understand concepts, students with learning disabilities must learn to receive and integrate information from as many different senses as possible. They often have difficulty in "getting things" from books; however, they begin to trust their ability to learn when they have real experiences with multisensory materials. Because Structural Arithmetic is a multisensory approach, it enables children to develop concepts through experimenting with materials on their own.

The materials described in this chapter convey concepts through structures that are true to the mathematical relationships being taught. To understand these relationships, children pick up the materials and measure and compare them. A concept or a quantity is not presented in isolation but in context so that children can explore and discover the many different mathematical relationships that are possible. Good multisensory materials not only will stimulate such activities but also should present concepts so vividly and clearly that children can visualize them later. More than 100 sequenced activities and games have been gathered together in teacher's guides titled *Experimenting with Numbers: A Guide for Preschool,*

Kindergarten, and First Grade Teachers (Stern, 1988) and *Structural Arithmetic Workbooks 1–3 and Teachers' Guides* (Stern & Gould, 1988–1992). They are the result of the further development of the original work published in *Children Discover Arithmetic: An Introduction to Structural Arithmetic* (Stern & Stern, 1971). These materials have been used successfully in classrooms for more than 45 years. Teachers also have expressed their appreciation for the illustrated directions that make teaching with multisensory structured materials much easier.

What is involved in the formation of concepts? Children seem to reason with mental pictures. Therefore, when teaching children to think, we must develop their ability to form images. Multisensory materials will have fulfilled their purpose when the children can visualize the concepts presented. It is not sufficient, however, for them to visualize a quantity in isolation; they must be able to visualize it in relation to other numbers and turn it around in their minds, and they must understand the actions that can be performed on it. For example, a teacher turned face down a pattern board with blanks for eight cubes and asked Sean to build the cube pattern he thinks will fit into it. When Sean built the 8-pattern correctly, he explained, "I imagined it in my brain, then I built it, then I turned the board over, and the cubes all fit!"

In addition to mental pictures, language plays a crucial role in the formation of concepts. The best way to teach children the meaning of spoken language is to give them the opportunity to see and touch what the words describe and, thus, work out for themselves what the words mean. In many of the math games in this chapter, children are asked to carry out spoken directions. This develops both their receptive language and their auditory memory. It is especially important for children with language deficits to develop these abilities.

In mathematics, as in any other subject, language is a vehicle for thought; therefore, students need many opportunities to put newly discovered concepts into their own words. Parroting the words of teachers is not a sign of true learning. Instead, the teacher should often encourage students to talk about concepts by asking them, "How did you figure out your answer?"

In the Structural Arithmetic approach, the children progress from activities and games with concrete materials that help them form basic concepts to the final steps of recording addition and subtraction facts with number symbols, or *numerals*. Here are the steps of Structural Arithmetic, stated as goals and objectives, to be followed in the first years of mathematics instruction:

- *Level I*   To discover size relationships between amounts from 1 to 10, to know where each comes in the sequence from 1 to 10, to recognize odd and even numbers built as cube patterns, and to form number combinations with sums ranging from 1 to 10 using number blocks
- *Level II*   To learn number names and how to count from 1 to 10, to understand terms such as *bigger than* and *smaller than*, and to recite the addition facts with sums of 10 or less that have been discovered with the materials
- *Level III*   To identify and write the numerals 1–10 and 0, to understand the amount each numeral stands for, to understand the meaning of addition or subtraction equations, to write the answers to addition facts with sums of 10 or less and the answers to their related subtraction facts, and to demonstrate with materials the solution of a word problem and then record the addition or subtraction equation used to solve it

At Levels I and II the amounts from 1 to 10 are introduced in two different ways: with groups of *cubes* to be counted and with *number blocks.* For example, the amount of 4 is introduced both with 4 single cubes and by a number block called a *4-block,* which looks like four cubes glued together in a straight line. Number symbols or numerals are introduced later on. Children realize that they can name a small number block of 2 or 3 units at a glance but that they need to verify the name of a longer number block of 8 or 9 units by counting its units. They soon realize that each number block is easily recognized by its relative size, its position in the sequence from 1 to 10, and its color (a peripheral characteristic that is not mathematical). For example, children learn that the 10-block is the biggest number block, stands last in the sequence from 1 to 10, and is blue. The 9-block thus is the "next-to-biggest" number block, comes just before the last number block, and is black. These characteristics enable children to identify each number and study its changing role in different situations.

FIRST EXPERIMENTS: THE COUNTING BOARD

Children begin their explorations of number concepts by fitting cubes or number blocks into grooves of the *counting board* (see Figure 11.1). Using the board, they carry out many experiments on their own. Concrete materials alone, however, do not lead to the development of mathematical thinking. The number blocks or cubes must be looked at, picked up, compared, and fit into activities that have been fashioned so as to make clear the structure of our base-10 number system. Teachers as well as children must put discoveries and relationships into words. Once the students understand these concepts, the teacher will introduce the symbols that stand for them (see Number Symbols and Signs: Level III).

Number Concepts and Language: Levels I and II

By experimenting with materials, children discover the many things they can do with numbers. Soon they are impatient to tell each other about their discoveries.

Figure 11.1.   The counting board: matching number markers to numerals on the number guide.

Once they have learned the number names of the blocks, they begin to express their thoughts in language that comes to them naturally. (For example, Sumi might point to a 5-block and a 3-block and say, "I am 5, but my brother is only 3.") When children express ideas about numbers in their own words, they will have a more secure understanding of the language of mathematics when they hear it later. Teachers who listen to their students' words are often alerted to difficulties in comprehension and are able to give help before the problems cause even more trouble. In more formal environments, teachers give children orders to carry out. In doing so, children show whether they understand new vocabulary. For instance, a teacher might say, "Add 3 and 2, and tell me what 3 plus 2 equals." Students respond by adding together a 3-block and a 2-block and placing them alongside the 5-block. They see that 3 and 2 are "the same size as 5," which they learn is expressed by the words "equals 5." The relationship among the blocks enables them to gain this insight. In contrast, the piecemeal act of counting single cubes often camouflages the meaning of the word *equal*.

Number Symbols and Signs: Level III

The teacher should introduce number symbols (numerals) after number concepts have been explored. The teacher fits the number guide into a slot at the top of the counting board (see Figure 11.1). When attached, it shows where each numeral comes in the sequence from 1 to 10. Each numeral appears above the groove that holds the number of cubes or the number block for which it stands (e.g., the 10 on the number guide appears above the groove that can hold 10 cubes or a 10-block). Between the number guide and the grooves are empty spaces for number markers bearing the numerals 1–10. On each number marker a line beneath the numeral indicates the correct orientation of that numeral (e.g., 6 indicates the marker is for 6, not 9). Having children match the numerals on the markers to the numerals on the number guide is an excellent check of the children's ability to perceive symbols and to position them correctly. This step prevents errors that might arise when they try to read or write numerals.

The teacher then lets the numerals "call back" the number blocks, an activity the children enjoy. The teacher says, "Pick a number. Where does it go?" The child selects a numeral such as 3, matches it to the 3 on the number guide, then finds the 3-block and fits it into the 3-groove.

Building Basic Concepts

Children who don't know math facts (e.g., 4 + 4 = 8) will have had difficulty learning them by rote and will resort to counting them out over and over again because they have become rigidly attached to the "counting song." Such children profit from remedial work with basic math concepts. When they realize they can learn basic concepts by playing exciting games with the counting board, they respond with improved concentration. One such game follows.

The Snake Game   The object of the Snake Game is to build the longest snake of number blocks. The teacher fills a counting board with number blocks and divides students into two teams of six to eight players. The teams take turns selecting a number marker from the face-down number markers that are scattered on the table. Each number marker indicates which number block the team may add to their snake of blocks. Children give up counting individual units on the number blocks when they realize it is quicker to name and select the number block below the number on the guide that matches the marker drawn. The winning team will have the longer snake of blocks.

The Snake Game prepares students to see and remember number combinations that they will discover when they later fill a number box with blocks (discussed later in this chapter). It is more impressive to note that working with counting board materials will enable children to move easily from addition to subtraction. But first they must be able to name the numbers and understand the concepts for which the number symbols stand.

DEVELOPING A NUMBER SENSE: PATTERN BOARDS

Each *pattern board* provides between 1 and 10 empty blanks in a set pattern into which cubes may be inserted (see Figure 11.2). Children show that they recognize a number pattern by building it with cubes. They then check the pattern they have built by placing the cubes into the blanks of the correct pattern board. To learn the name of each number pattern, they count the cubes.

Even and Odd Numbers

The characteristics of evenness and oddness cannot be taught with number blocks, but they can be taught with cubes and pattern boards. Even numbers are formed by pairs of cube partners so that the pattern ends evenly. Children see that even numbers are made with 1 + 1, 2 + 2, 3 + 3, 4 + 4, and 5 + 5 (math facts that are taught later). When one cube is added to an even number pattern, it becomes odd. Children learn that "one cube all alone" distinguishes an odd number and that odd numbers are named 1, 3, 5, 7, and 9. A stick or pencil can be used to split an odd number pattern down the center to yield two consecutive

Figure 11.2.   Pattern boards: matching cube patterns.

numbers that form it. These odd number patterns are $1 + 0, 2 + 1, 3 + 2, 4 + 3$, and $5 + 4$. When building the sequence from 1 to 10, the odd number patterns are positioned between the even patterns. These facts are studied later under the name Doubles and Neighbors (discussed later in this chapter). The structure of these patterns makes the relationships visible and easy to recall later as addition facts.

Introduction to Word Problems

Acting out word problems with multisensory materials will prepare children to analyze complex word problems later. It is important for children to learn how to demonstrate word problems of their own creation. Pattern boards and cubes are excellent materials with which to begin. Each child in the group selects a different pattern board. For example, Laura selected the pattern board for the number 6, filled it with cubes, and then acted out her problem, saying, "My dog had 6 puppies. I gave 4 away. How many are left?" Even though she had subtracted 4 cubes, the children could still see the original number she started with because she chose a pattern board with 6 blanks. The pattern board allowed Laura's classmates to see at the same time the 4 subtracted cubes, the remaining 2 cubes, and their relationship to the original total of 6 cubes. Teachers know that some children, when taking 4 loose cubes away from 6 loose cubes, cannot visualize the original amount and wonder just how much they began with. They lose any sense of the relationship of 4 to 6 and of the remaining 2 to the 6 they began with. Well-planned lessons in which children act out word problems with multisensory materials such as pattern boards will help build strong foundations for later learning.

ADDITION AND SUBTRACTION WITH THE 10-BOX

Discovering Combinations that Make 10

As a first step, children fill the 10-box with pairs of number blocks as though they were working on a puzzle. The *10-box,* a square measuring 10 units by 10 units, has a frame around the edge that tells children when the total units of the block-partners is 10 (see Figure 11.3). Kindergartners often know which blocks go together in the 10-box before they can name them or designate them with number symbols. Each time they put a number block in the 10-box, they measure with their eyes to judge the size of the block that will fit with it. Thus they systematically study the relationship between each separate number block and the total, which is 10 units long. When they make a mistake, they can see and feel how the block does not fit. The teacher does not need to say, "Wrong!" The emphasis is on experimenting. When the children find pairs of blocks that fit, they feel a satisfaction that is unforgettable. This success with filling the 10-box helps them remember the block combinations that total 10 units. Once the children have learned the names of the blocks, they will find it easy to name the block partners that make 10 (see Figure 11.3).

The combination in the middle of the 10-box is a double, a 5-block and a 5-block. A double, children will discover, can be found in the center of every even

Figure 11.3. Filling the 10-box with number blocks.

number. In addition, students will understand the *zero fact* even before it is recorded; they can put the 10-block in the 10-box and say, "10 needs no other block to make 10." The children can show they understand the concept of equality when they place two number blocks next to the 10-block and say, for example, "8 and 2 are just as big as 10." This concept will be recorded later with the equal sign.

Building the Stair from 1 to 10 in the 10-Box

The teacher scatters number blocks 1–10 next to the 10-box and begins to build the stair in the lower left corner with the 1-, 2-, and 3-blocks. The teacher asks the children to complete the stair. When they put in a block that is too long (e.g., placing the 5-block after the 3-block), they realize that the structure is wrong and look for the correct block (e.g., the 4-block). The choices they make are guided by how the stair looks. The teacher can also challenge the children by removing one step of the completed stair while they are not looking and asking them to name the missing step.

Recording the Story of 10: Writing Equations

The goal is for students to record from memory the "Story of 10," the pairs of numbers that equal 10, but first they must learn how to record an equation after they fill a column in the 10-box. The teacher places the empty 10-box and two sets of number blocks before the children and sets to one side the number markers 1–10 and the plus and equal signs. The children put two number blocks (**addends**) into the 10-box and name them, for example, "6 and 4." The teacher records this by arranging the symbols 6 + 4 next to the 10-box. The students continue by saying, "equal 10," and the teacher records this by putting the appropriate symbols last, yielding *6 + 4 = 10*. When the children later write equations, they understand the process from having recorded the combinations of blocks as they placed them in the box. Using the 10-box while recording equations also enables students to understand an equation when they read it.

For many children, the **missing addend** form of an equation (e.g., 6 + ___ = 10) is difficult to deal with as they do not understand what it means. When the children put a 10-block in the box and place a 6-block next to it, however, they find it natural to ask, "6 needs what to make 10?" They then record what they have just said with the number markers and symbols: *6 + ___ = 10.* Students discover that the missing symbol is the numeral that stands for the missing block, which they know is the 4-block. Teachers often find that using the 10-box is the first time they have had an easy way of teaching equations with missing addends.

Subtraction and Its Relation to Addition

An addition example contains two or more addends, and students are asked for the sum or total; subtraction can easily be shown to have the opposite character. The children place a 6-block and a 4-block into the first column of the 10-box and note that they measure 10. The teacher states the addition fact 6 + 4 = 10. The teacher's next step is to explain how this addition fact will yield two subtraction facts. To demonstrate the first fact, the children realize that they begin with the total, 10, from which they subtract the 4-block; the 6-block remains. This demonstration gives meaning to the words, "10 take away 4 leaves 6," which students record as *10 − 4 = 6.* The teacher then asks someone to demonstrate the other subtraction fact, 10 − 6 = 4, and to record it below the first. The structure of the materials makes it obvious that the smaller number is always subtracted from the larger number.

Combinations that Make 10

Playing the Hiding Game (described next) gives children more than practice in remembering the combinations that make 10. To discover which combination has been hidden, they must first figure out how the block combinations have been organized; they then find a strategy for identifying the missing combination. Afterward, it is interesting to ask students, "How did you do that?"

The Hiding Game   The teacher displays the 10-box filled with number block combinations in sequence from 1 + 9, 2 + 8, 3 + 7, and so forth up to 10 + 0. When the children's eyes are closed, the teacher removes one combination, such as 4 + 6, and says, "Open your eyes. What did I hide?" A child answers, "4 + 6," and says while pointing to the blocks in the lower stair, "I counted each step, 1, 2, 3, and found 4 was missing, so I knew 4 and 6 were missing."

ADDITION AND SUBTRACTION: OTHER NUMBER BOXES

Children are delighted to find there are more number boxes smaller than the 10-box and enjoy fitting them inside one another to form a pyramid. On finding that the peak of the pyramid would be the 1-box, a precocious kindergartner called out, "I have the pièce de résistance!"

When asking the children to fill one of the smaller boxes, such as the 8-box, the teacher presents two sets of blocks as well as the box to be filled. Students will respond by rejecting the blocks that are too big (the 9- and 10-blocks) and finding the block combinations that exactly fit the 8-box. They realize that this task has the same features as filling the 10-box and adjust their performance accordingly. This adjustment comes about as a result of learning through insight, not by rote. Students enjoy playing the same addition and subtraction games in each box as they played in the 10-box. They later write the number story for each box and give each a title, such as the "Story of 8."

Different Roles a Number Can Play

Students will be excited when they become aware that a number plays a different role in each number box. Each number block's distinctive size and color enables children to observe how a number changes its role as it comprises the total of each different box. For example, consider the changes in the role of the 5-block. When filling the 5-box, a kindergarten child said, "5 is the control of this box!" When discovering the combinations while filling the 6-box, another child ran to his teacher and said, "Look! 5 is the 9 of this box." He had noticed that the 5-block plays the same role in the 6-box as the 9-block does in the 10-box: Both are the next-to-biggest block and thus join with a 1-block to fill a column in the box.

In addition, when putting together the combinations to make 9, an odd number, children find that there are two sets of consecutive numbers that make 9; they see that a 5-block joins a 4-block to make 9, and next to these blocks, a 4-block joins a 5-block to make 9. And finally, they discover that doubles are found only in the even numbers. Thus, when filling the 8 box, they find a pair of 4-blocks in the center.

SOLVING WORD PROBLEMS

It is easy for children to understand when to solve a word problem by addition: There are two or more addends, and the total is being asked for. Children have greater difficulty identifying problems that are to be solved by subtraction. When a total is stated and a smaller amount is lost, it is relatively easy for children to decide to solve the problem by subtraction. Children, however, are more confused when trying to solve problems that say nothing about an amount being lost or taken away. In this type of problem a total and one amount are given, and children must figure out the other amount (e.g., The book costs $10. Tobias has $3. How much does he need to earn?). The children have to learn that the way to solve this type of word problem, a missing addend problem, is to subtract. Teachers usually start with problems in which the numbers are small, as in the previous example. Unfortunately, the use of small numbers makes it difficult for children to understand why they must subtract because they can so easily solve this kind of problem in their heads: "3 needs what to make 10? 7." This type of problem is especially difficult for children to solve later when the problems deal with big numbers (e.g., The television set costs $225. Tobias has $37. How much does he need to earn?) Children cannot solve $37 + \_\_\_ = 225$ in their heads. The teacher must show them how to think about this type of problem by setting up a model so that when the numbers are big, it will make sense to subtract. For example, the teacher can put 10 cubes in a *number track* (a grooved track with numerals on one side that holds cubes or number blocks in sections of 10 units, or *decades;*

308 Stern

see Figure 11.4) and say, "The book costs $10. Tobias doesn't need to earn all $10; he already has $3." The teacher covers 3 cubes with a scarf and says, "I covered 3 cubes to show that Tobias doesn't need to earn those $3; he already has them. I've taken 3 away from 10." The teacher writes $10 - 3 =$ ___ and says, "Tobias needs to earn the rest." The children conclude in a full sentence, "Tobias needs to earn $7." The children now have a model of how to solve missing addend problems. Later, they will be able to substitute big numbers in this model. For example, "Ted wants $225. He has $37. He doesn't need to earn it, so I'll take it away! He needs to earn the rest!" They will understand that missing addend problems are solved by subtraction and will set them up correctly.

TEEN NUMBERS

It is important for the teacher to show mathematical concepts such as teen numbers in more than one way. The teen numbers are the numbers above 10 through 19, composed of a 10-block and a number of ones (the rest of the number). They will be shown first in the *20-tray* (a square tray similar to a 10-box, which measures 20 units by 20 units), then in the number track (see Figure 11.4), and also in the *dual board* (see Figure 11.5).

Building the Stair from 1 to 20

In the 20-tray, children begin by building the familiar stair from 1 to 10. On reaching 10, they discover they must piece together the next numbers using a 10-block and another number block (e.g., 1 ten and a 1-block to make 11, 1 ten and a 2-block to make 12, 1 ten and a 3-block to make 13). Students will be surprised when they see that the stair from 1 to 10 repeats itself in the teen numbers on a base of 10-blocks. They name each number in the 20-tray by naming the steps from 1 to 20. To make certain that the students understand the structure of teen numbers, the teacher says, "Close your eyes," and hides the blocks composing a teen number such as 14. When the children look at the stair of teen numbers, they see which step is missing and cry, "14!" As the teacher replaces the number blocks in the missing step, the students name them: "10 and 4." After this activity they will think of the number 14 as the teacher has built it, with 1 ten and 4 ones (a 4-block). Visualizing the structure and naming the blocks enables students from the start to write the digits in the correct order as 14, not as the number is pronounced, "Four-teen."

Measuring Teen Numbers in a Number Track

When the number blocks for a teen number are placed in the number track, the numerals on the side of the track record the total. Children need to be familiar

Figure 11.4. Building 14 in the number track.

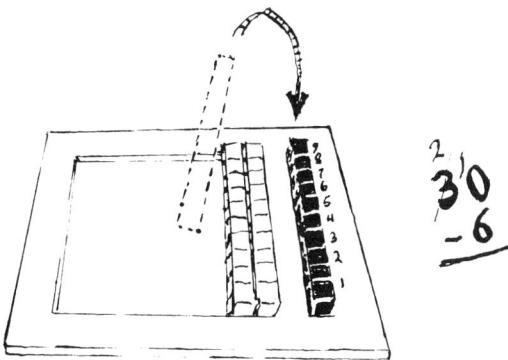

Figure 11.5. A dual board. The example 30 − 6 is worked out by carrying back 1 ten to the ones compartment, exchanging it for 10 ones, and subtracting 6.

with the structure of a teen number in the number track. Operating from this base, they will easily understand the next step, that of adding to 9, in which they first add a number block, such as a 3-block, to a 10-block and then to a 9-block. They can see that the 10-block and the 3-block reach 13 but that the 9-block and the 3-block only reach 12.

Building Teen Numbers in the Dual Board

The dual board has two compartments, a large "tens" compartment the same size as a 10-box, and a small "ones" compartment that holds a column of ten 1-blocks. Before using the dual board for purposes such as subtracting from 2-place numbers (see Figure 11.5), it is important for children to construct the teen numbers in the dual board.

When children first look at a written number such as *12*, they see two numerals that seem to stand for numbers of about the same size. By building a number in the dual board, they gain insight into the important role that the *place*, or the position, of each numeral plays. The teacher builds a number, such as 12, in the dual board by placing 1 ten in the tens compartment and a 2-block in the ones compartment. To record this number, the number marker 1 is put below the tens compartment and the number marker 2 is put below the ones compartment. This shows the meaning of each symbol in the written number 12. To make the term *place value* clear, the teacher can change the places of the number markers 2 and 1 and have children show the new value of each symbol, that is, 2 tens and a 1-block.

ADDITION FACTS WITH ANSWERS IN THE TEENS

There are 36 addition facts with answers in the teens (e.g., 9 + 2 = 11 to 9 + 9 = 18). These facts can be categorized into different groups of structurally related facts: Adding 9, Adding to 9, Combinations that Make 11 and 12, and Doubles and Neighbors. Children master them by understanding the general rules for each group.

Adding 9

There are eight facts in the Adding 9 group (2 + 9, 3 + 9, 4 + 9, 5 + 9, 6 + 9, 7 + 9, 8 + 9, 9 + 9). Children can master these eight facts at once by learning only one general rule. First they add a 10-block to any number, such as 3, in the number track and realize that the digit in the ones place of the total, 13, is the same (e.g., 3 + 10 = 13). Students then add a 9-block to a 3-block and discover that they only reach 12, a number that is 1 less than if they had added a 10-block to the number they started with (e.g., 3 + 10 = 13, but 3 + 9 = 12). Students demonstrate that they understand these facts by adding a 9-block to each number block from 2 to 9.

Adding to 9

Seven addition facts result from adding a number *to* 9. To learn these Adding to 9 facts, which are the reverse of the Adding 9 facts, children add blocks to a 9-block. This time, the teacher places a 9-block in the number track, holds a 3-block above the track, and asks, "What do you think 9 + 3 equals?" The children have time to answer before the teacher places the 3-block after the 9-block in the number track. When the blocks are joined end to end, the children can see that the 3-block had to move down one unit to fill the gap between 9 and 10; thus, adding 3 to 9 reaches the number 12 (i.e., 10 + 3 = 13, but 9 + 3 = 12). They figure out all of the Adding to 9 facts adding the numbers 2 through 8 to 9.

Combinations that Make 11 and 12

The children begin by building a stair from 1 to 10 in the 10-box. They then add the top stair of blocks to this stair so that each column in the 10-box is filled. Now they move the whole top stair up one step. This results in combinations that make 11. The children know the combinations that make 10, so when making combinations that total 11, they realize that one of the component parts will be one unit bigger. For example, 5 + 5 = 10, but 5 needs 6 to make 11; 7 + 3 = 10, but 7 needs 4 to make 11.

To build combinations that make 12, students again move the blocks of the top stair up one step. This time 2 units must be added to one of the component parts that totaled 10; for example, 5 + 5 = 10, but 5 needs 7 to make 12. The teacher can now use the clock on the wall as an unforgettable way to show the combinations making 12. The numbers that stand across from each other on the clock face add up to 12. For example, 9 is across from 3, and 9 + 3 = 12; 8 is across from 4, and 8 + 4 = 12; and 7 is across from 5, and 7 + 5 = 12. Once the children have learned Adding 9, Adding to 9, and Combinations that Make 11 and 12, they have studied two thirds of the addition facts with sums that are teen numbers.

Doubles and Neighbors in the Teens

The next group of structurally related addition facts is called Doubles and Neighbors in the Teens and consists of six new facts. Children usually find the doubles (6 + 6 = 12; 7 + 7 = 14; 8 + 8 = 16; 9 + 9 = 18; 10 + 10 = 20) easy to learn. To illustrate the doubles, the teacher places pairs of like blocks side by side and explains that the sum of each pair is an even number. For practice in learning doubles, children should play a game such as Stop and Go (described later in this chapter). To illustrate the facts that are neighbors of the doubles ($5 + 6 = 11, 6 + 7 = 13, 7 + 8 = 15, 8 + 9 = 17, 9 + 10 = 19$), the teacher places the pair of 6-blocks (12) next to the pair of 7-blocks (14) and leaves a space between the pairs. The teacher points to this empty space. To make the neighbor between 12 and 14, a child takes a 6-block from the pair that totals 12 and a 7-block from the pair that totals 14. This produces the number 13, built from the consecutive numbers 6 and 7. The teacher demonstrates how each odd teen number can be formed from two consecutive numbers. Once students have mastered Doubles and Neighbors in the Teens, there are only four final addition facts with answers in the teens to be learned: $8 + 5$ and $8 + 6$ and the reverse facts, $5 + 8$ and $6 + 8$.

Addition and Subtraction Facts in the Teens

Teachers often must work with children who find math especially difficult to comprehend. The teacher must first discover which concepts these students do not understand. Looking at students' final answers to math problems does not indicate their level of understanding. For example, if the teacher sees that a student wrote $15 - 9 = 6$, then the teacher still does not know how the student figured out the answer to this example. If the teacher, however, sees that the student made 15 dashes, crossed off 9 of them, and counted the remaining dashes, then the teacher has gained valuable information. Students who have difficulty with math concepts need to work with materials structured so as to give them the foundation they never had to understand computation with answers that are teen numbers.

First, they must build the stair of teen numbers in the 20-tray using 10-blocks and unit blocks to construct the numbers 11–20. Second, they must build a teen number such as 15 in the number track using a 10-block and a 5-block. Then by substituting the 9-block and the 1-block for the 10-block, they should conclude that the result of taking 9 from a teen number such as 15 is easy to figure out. When the 9-block is removed, the 1-block remains in the number track with the 5-block to yield the answer, 6. Children find it easy to demonstrate similar examples with the same structure: $17 - 9 = 8$ or $16 - 9 = 7$. This kind of insight gives children confidence in their ability to answer difficult math problems without the endless counting of dots or dashes. In particular, children with learning disabilities profit most from such experiences. They need to realize that they can think and that they can do arithmetic.

Games with Teen Numbers

It is important for all children to learn the concepts about teen numbers and to practice them by playing games that they find challenging.

The Hard Snake Game   The Hard Snake Game may be played by two teams or two children. On each of 10 cards, the teacher writes a teen number and turns it face down. One member of Team A then selects a card and announces the number written on it. The player must form this total by adding two blocks, one of which must be a 9-block. Thus, if the card said 15, then the player must build 15 using a 9-block and a 6-block. If the player forms the correct total, the blocks are then added to Team A's snake of blocks. The winner is the team with the longest snake of blocks. This game reinforces the students' learning of these difficult teen number facts.

The Probe Game   To prepare for the Probe Game, the teacher displays the number track from 1 to 20 and covers the numbers 1–10 with a cardboard box. The teacher has the children close their eyes and then hides a number block, perhaps the 5-block, under the cardboard box. The teacher lets the students open their eyes and asks a child to discover the size of the hidden block by using the 9-block as a probe. As he or she pushes the 9-block down the track and under the box, the children wait expectantly until it stops and shows that the sum is 14. The child must reason, "If this were the 10-block, then the hidden block would be the 4-block, but it is only the 9-block, so the hidden block has to be one bigger than 4: it must be the 5-block." At this point the teacher verifies the answer by lifting the cardboard box to reveal that the hidden block is indeed the 5-block.

PLACE VALUE OR POSITIONAL NOTATION

Giving up dealing with ones and grouping them into tens as the new unit of measure is one of the most ingenious ideas of mankind. Here is an experiment that will show the children how the use of place value, or *positional notation*, helps us deal with big numbers. The teacher throws only a few cubes on the table and explains that it is easy to say how many are in a small group of cubes. Next, the teacher throws more than 50 cubes onto the table and writes down a few of the children's estimates of the amount. To determine the exact number, the teacher arranges the cubes in rows of 10 in the tens compartment of the dual board and places any leftover cubes in the ones compartment. Students can see at a glance that the amount of cubes is 5 tens plus the 4 leftover cubes in the ones compartment (i.e., 54). The teacher can explain that grouping objects in tens and ones is one advantage of the structure of our number system.

Recording Teen Numbers and Understanding the Numeral 0

When students built the teen numbers, they discovered that the composition of each number corresponded exactly with its numerals: 1 ten and 1 one were recorded as *11*, 1 ten and 2 as *12*, and so forth up to 1 ten and 9 as *19*. The teacher asks the children to put two 10-blocks in the dual board and record it by placing the number marker for 2 below the tens compartment. The teacher then places the marker for 0 below the empty ones compartment and explains why 0 is called a *place holder*: "If we write the numeral 2 and let it stand alone, it would mean 2 ones. So we write 0 in the ones place to tell us that this time the digit 2 stands for 2 tens and that there isn't anything in the ones place. Moreover, in 20, the 0 is also holding a place for another numeral. If we replace 0 with 1, we must also put 1 cube in the ones compartment." The teacher explains that the numeral is now 21, records the amount in the dual board, and says, "2 tens, 1 one."

Building 2-Place Numbers in the Dual Board and the Number Track

Children are now ready to discover the meaning behind the structure of the 2-place, or 2-digit, numerals between 10 and 100. They first build a number such as 25 with 2 tens and 5 ones, then they reverse the digits and build 52, using 5 tens and 2 ones. They are now ready to play an interesting game.

Build Your Guess   The game Build Your Guess gives children practice building 2-place numbers in the dual board and then measuring them in the long number track to note where they come in the sequence of 1 to 100. To begin, the teacher writes a 2-place number on a piece of paper and hides it. The student who comes closest to guessing the teacher's number is the winner. Each child should guess a different number and must then build his or her guess in the dual board. For example, Erin decides to guess 39, so she puts 3 tens in the tens compartment and a 9-block in the ones compartment and records it with number markers for 3 and 9. She then measures her blocks in the number track; they reach 39. She places her number markers, 39, next to the track to show her guess. Then the teacher shows the hidden number, 36. Erin finds that her guess, 39, is 3 units bigger than 36, whereas Toshi's guess, 32, is 4 units smaller than 36. The others were even further away. Erin concludes she is the winner.

In this game and the other Structural Arithmetic activities, the children have been expressing their ideas by building numbers with blocks and recording them with numerals. This solid foundation in understanding 2-digit numbers will make regrouping in addition and subtraction (i.e., carrying and borrowing) easier for them to understand.

REGROUPING IN ADDITION

The procedure called **regrouping** is known to previous generations as *carrying* and *borrowing*. The teacher explains that in our system of positional notation, when the amount in one column exceeds 9, it can only be expressed by a 2-digit numeral that has a tens digit and a ones digit; therefore, the amount must be regrouped. For example, when dealing with an amount in the ones column such as 12 ones, 10 ones must be exchanged for or regrouped as 1 ten and carried to the tens column. That leaves 2 in the ones place. The numeral that records 1 ten and 2 ones is 12. When children work with the blocks in the dual board, these procedures will have meaning from the very start.

Students learn addition with regrouping step by step using the dual board. The first step in adding two numbers, such as 39 and 1, is to build the 2-place number in the dual board. The children place 3 tens in the tens compartment and 9 ones in the ones compartment and say the name of the number, "Thirty-nine." The teacher adds 1 cube to the 9 cubes that are already in the ones compartment and explains, "We cannot record the 10 cubes in the ones compartment with a single numeral; we must regroup!" Students exchange the 10 cubes for 1 ten, carry it to the tens compartment, and add it to the 3 tens already there, resulting in a total of 4 tens.

Once the children have understood regrouping, they record each step on paper; writing on paper lined in half-inch squares is a great help. The children write *39*, then they write *+ 1* below the *9* in the ones column, draw a horizontal line beneath it, and say, "9 plus 1 equals 10. I must regroup." They reenact the carrying of 1 ten to the tens compartment and record this move by writing a small figure *1* above the *3* in the tens column of their example. They write *0* in the ones place below the horizontal line (because there are no ones left). Next they add the digits in the tens column and say, "3 plus 1 equals 4." They write *4* in the tens place in their answer. The sum is written as *40*, which accurately records the 4 tens in the dual board.

Next, the students add a bigger number, perhaps 3, to 39. When they add three cubes to the 9 that are already in the ones compartment, they see that they have twelve cubes and must regroup. They exchange ten cubes for 1 ten and carry it to the tens compartment to join the 3 tens. That move leaves 2 cubes in the ones compartment. The students record each step on paper and get the answer, 42, which they see accurately records the 4 tens and 2 ones in the dual board.

Money and Regrouping

To make clear the value of different coins, the teacher tapes a dime to each of several 10-blocks, a nickel to each of several 5-blocks, and a penny to each of about 20 cubes. Children are now able to see the relationship among the values of the different coins. The nickels are taped to blocks that are half the size of the blocks to which the dimes are taped. Students can see that nickels, which are larger in size than dimes, are worth less than dimes and that it takes 10 pennies (also larger in size than dimes) to equal a dime, or 10 cents. The children will enjoy using the money on blocks in a store game. They can also use the money on blocks in other games.

Score 1 If You Carry   This game is played with the dual board, money on blocks, and a die. The teams take turns tossing the die and placing pennies in the ones compartment of the dual board. For example, Team A tosses the die, gets 3, and places 3 pennies in the ones compartment. Team B tosses a 4 and adds 4 pennies, bringing the total to 7. Team A tosses the die and gets 5, which, when added to 7, yields 12 pennies. Team A must regroup; it exchanges 10 pennies for 1 dime and carries it to the tens compartment. The team puts the 2 remaining cents in the ones column. Team A "scores 1" because it got the chance to regroup, or "carry 1." The game continues. The game could end when one team's score is 5.

REGROUPING IN SUBTRACTION

The process of regrouping in subtraction has also been known as *borrowing*. The children again work in the dual board. They write *30* on their papers and build it with 3 tens. The teacher dictates, "Subtract 6." The children write − 6 below the 0 in *30* and draw a horizontal line below the subtraction example. The teacher explains that the students cannot take 6 cubes away from the ones compartment of the dual board because there are no cubes there and that they must regroup. They carry back 1 ten from the tens compartment and exchange it for 10 ones. On their papers they cross out the 3 and write a small 2 above it to indicate that there are only 2 tens left. The students write a small figure *1* above and to the left of the 0 in the ones place to indicate they now have 10 cubes in the ones column (see Figure 11.5). Now they can subtract 6 cubes, which leaves 4 cubes. The final amount is 2 tens and 4 ones, which matches the written answer, *24.*

Regrouping with the Dual Board

After working with the blocks in the dual board, the children need to practice regrouping in a more exciting situation, such as a game.

Your Answer Is Your Score   During each turn in the game Your Answer Is Your Score, one player selects two face-down number markers and uses them to build a two-digit number with number blocks in the dual board. He or she must then subtract from this number an amount that is large enough to require regrouping. The player's score is the number that remains after this subtraction operation; the player with the highest score wins. For example, Robert, who has selected the markers 6 and 3, understands that the goal is to get a big score, so he explains, "I don't want to build 36; I'll build 63, of course!" The teacher asks, "How much will you subtract from 63 so that you must regroup?" Robert reasons, "I have only 3 cubes in the ones compartment, so I think I'll subtract 4 from 63." He exchanges 1 ten for 10 ones and puts them into the ones compartment; he now has a total of 13 single cubes. He subtracts 4 cubes from the 13, and this leaves 9 cubes. Robert sees that there are now 5 tens and 9 ones in the dual board and exclaims, "My score is 59!" He writes 59 on the chalkboard. The rest of the players will try to beat his score.

MULTIPLICATION

To most people, *multiplication* still means the memorization of 100 facts such as $7 \times 6 = 42$, which are repeated again and again until they have been learned by heart. Actually multiplication and division are fascinating operations that, when studied with the Structural Arithmetic materials, allow children to discover new relationships among numbers. They come to realize that they are viewing the same facts from opposite sides when they discover that the relationship between multiplication and division is one of doing and undoing, just as it is between addition and subtraction. Students will not only grasp this interrelationship but also understand, through their experiments with the materials, just how division is the opposite of multiplication.

The operation of multiplication can, of course, be taught by the addition of equal addends. For example, the answer to 5×2 can be figured out by addition: $2 + 2 = 4, 4 + 2 = 6, 6 + 2 = 8$, and $8 + 2 = 10$. In Structural Arithmetic, however, children produce an amount a given number of times, and by measuring it in the number track, they discover how this total is expressed in our base-10 system, that is, with tens and ones.

Discovery of What a Multiplication Table Is

The children will discover that multiplication is a new way of expressing number relationships. The essence of multiplication is that an amount is taken not once but several times. Therefore, to find the answer to 5×2, the children take a 2-block five times. The number 5 is not represented by a block but is the **operator** and plays a different role from the 2; it indicates how many times 2 is to be produced.

Multiplication tables are often recited by saying, for example, "5 times 1 equals 5, 5 times 2 equals 10, 5 times 3 equals 15," and so forth. To represent these facts with materials would mean changing the size of the number blocks used each time: five 1-blocks, then five 2-blocks, then five 3-blocks, and so forth. It makes more sense to demonstrate the multiplication table using the same size number block each time: one 5-block, then two 5-blocks, then three 5-blocks, and so forth (see Figure 13.6). By following this procedure children will be able to discover the products of any multiplication table by themselves. They can take a block a certain number of times and measure the total in the number track. They can find, for example, the way that three 5s are expressed in our base-10 number system: 1 ten and 5 ones, or 15 (see Figure 11.6). Students discover not only the interrelationship among the facts within one multiplication table (e.g., $1 \times 5, 2 \times 5$,

3×5, and so forth up to 10×5) but also the interrelationship among the facts of different tables, such as the multiples that two or three tables have in common.

One approach used to teach children to represent a multiplication fact is to have them draw circles and stars. To demonstrate 3×4, they make three circles and put four stars in each circle. This arrangement shows the role of the operator, or **multiplier,** 3, and the size, 4, but does not show how the total is expressed in the denominations of our number system, tens and ones. There is no visible connection between the fact 3×4 and the product 12, which can only be found by counting. The same is true when children create arrays, such as 4 rows of 5 dots each.

Sequence of Teaching the Multiplication Tables

Children begin by studying the 10-table because our number system is built on base 10. When the **multiplicand** is 10, each product can be expressed immediately. The product of 3×10, 30, does not have to be calculated but can be shown by writing 3 in the tens place of the numeral and adding a 0 as a placeholder; the multiple is already expressed in tens and ones. The need for multiplication tables arises because for any multiplicand other than 10, the products must be expressed in tens and ones.

The multiplication facts in the 1-table can be shown by producing the 1-block a certain number of times (5×1) or each number block one time (e.g., to show 1×5, a student produces a 5-block); the answer is the quantity the number block itself represents. The 2-table is studied next because its characteristic feature is that a given number of 2s is the same as the double of that given number (e.g., $6 \times 2 = 12$ and the double of 6 is 12). Because the children know the doubles, they easily master the 2-table . The 5-table is studied next because of the special relationship of 5 to 10 (5 is half of 10), followed by the 9-table because of the closeness of 9 to 10 (9 is 1 less than 10).

To teach the 9-table, the teacher puts one 10-block in the number track and writes *$1 \times 10 = 10$*. The 10-block is then replaced by a 9-block and a 1-block. The

Figure 11.6.   Discovering what 3 times 5 equals.

teacher then subtracts the 1-block and writes *1 × 9 = 10 − 1*; beneath that he or she writes, *1 × 9 = 9*. To show the second multiple of 9, the teacher places two 10-blocks in the track and writes *2 × 10 = 20*. Next, the teacher replaces the 10-blocks with two sets of 9-blocks and 1-blocks. Both 1-blocks are subtracted, and the two 9-blocks are shoved together; they reach 18. The teacher writes *2 × 9 = 20 − 2*. Below that he or she writes *2 × 9 = ___* ; the children copy the fact and write 18 in the blank. By following this procedure the teacher and the children continue to demonstrate and record the 9-table and finish with *10 × 9 = 100 − 10; 10 × 9 = 90*.

Multiplication Games

Stop and Go   Stop and Go is one of several exciting games that children can play to reinforce their understanding of a multiplication table. To play Stop and Go with the 5-table, the teacher fills the number track with 10 of the 5-blocks. He or she assigns a red cube to the Red Team and a blue cube to the Blue Team and places them at the beginning of the track. The stop-and-go cube has two red "Stop" sides and four green "Go" sides. The Red Team drops the stop-and-go cube and gets Go. The Red Team places its cube on the end of the first 5-block above the number 5 on the track, and one of the Red Team's players says, "1 times 5 equals 5." The Blue Team also gets Go, so it places its blue cube piggyback on top of the red cube. Here are the two possible moves for the Red Team: If Red gets Go, it must carry the Blue Team's cube, move both cubes up to the end of the number 10 on the number track, and say, "2 times 5 equals 10." If the Red Team gets Stop, however, both teams' cubes remain on 5. If the Blue Team gets Go at the next turn, it will move off of the red cube. In this way, they race each other up the track landing on each multiple of 5 until one team reach the 10th multiple, 50.

When studying the multiples of the 5-table in the number track, as with Stop and Go, the children will discover that each decade in the number track holds 2 fives. Therefore, when the multiplier is even, the product ends in 0 because it equals a number of 10s; when the multiplier is an odd number, the product has 5 in the ones place because an odd number of 5s reaches the middle of a decade: *1 × 5 = 5, 3 × 5 = 15, 5 × 5 = 25, 7 × 5 = 35, 9 × 5 = 45*.

Capture Peaks   Capture Peaks is another favorite game. First, the children choose a multiplication table and place 10 of the appropriate blocks in the number track. For example, the children decide on the 4-table and place ten 4-blocks successively in the number track. Then they dictate each fact for the teacher to write on the chalkboard. On each of 10 dominoes a fact is printed in this form: 1 × 4 = ___. The Red and Blue Teams each get 10 cubes of their respective color, which thus limits each team to 10 turns. A member of the Red Team turns up one of the face-down dominoes and reads it aloud: "3 times 4 equals 12." Then the team places its red cube on 12 in the number track. The domino is then returned to the pool so that each multiple in the number track can have more than one cube on it. After several more turns a member of the Blue Team might get 3 × 4 = ___ and say, "3 times 4 equals 12! I'm on top of the Red Team!" At the end of the game, the color cube on top of each peak or multiple determines which team claims the entire tower of cubes beneath it. The team with the most cubes wins.

The Screen Game   The Screen Game, which focuses on the use of words in math, builds a foundation that will enable students to understand similar wording when they encounter it later in algebra problems. Children who have had difficulty understanding the meaning of words sometimes mistake the words "3 times as big" to mean "3 times bigger than" and thus produce an amount "3 times as big" as the original and then add this tripled amount to the original amount. The result is an amount that is 4 times as big as the original. For children who make similar mistakes, the Screen Game is an important activity.

To begin, the teacher suggests that the children watch the Screen Game carefully so that they can invent similar problems of their own. Then the teacher writes a few math expressions on the chalkboard, such as *times as big as, times as long as, times as much as, times as heavy as,* and *times as old as.* The children then invent their own problems in which they use one of the expressions.

The teacher gives the children a pile of number blocks and stands a screen on a table. He or she places a 6-block in front of the screen and says, "This represents a stick 6 feet long—perhaps 6 doll-feet! In back of the screen is a stick 3 times as long. Show me with the blocks how long the hidden stick is." If the children have understood the words "3 times as long," they will build a stick with 3 of the 6-blocks. The hidden stick is then revealed for comparison. The children write their equations on paper ($3 \times 6 = 18$) and say, "The stick is 18 feet long." The teacher then asks several children to demonstrate a problem of their own.

For example, Chan invented this problem: "My dog weighs 20 pounds. I weigh 3 times as much. How much do I weigh?" The teacher had to help another student, Jim, to come up with the wording of his problem: "My father is 4 times as old as I am. I am 10 years old. How old is my father?"

After having students come up with their own problems, such as in the Screen Game, teachers often reflect that they have been too interested in leading every activity themselves. They realize that they must learn to stand back and encourage the children to develop and use their own powers of creation.

THE RELATIONSHIP BETWEEN MULTIPLICATION AND DIVISION

Students who have learned multiplication with the Structural Arithmetic materials have experienced for themselves how different the role is that each number in an equation plays.

In a multiplication example, such as $3 \times 5 = \underline{\quad}$, the multiplier, 3, and the multiplicand, 5, are given; the product is to be found. In one of the related division examples, the total, called the **dividend,** is given and has to be divided into a given number of parts. The question is "What is the size of each part?" ($15 \div 3 = \underline{\quad}$). This is the *partition aspect* of division. In contrast, when the total and the size of the part are given, the question is "How many times is the size, or part [5] contained in the dividend?"

$$5\overline{)15}$$

The answer, 3, is called the **quotient.** This is the *containing aspect* of division.

Students can take the idea that three 5s make 15, turn it around to answer the new question, "How many 5s are in 15?" and immediately answer, "3." By contrast, children who learn the 100 multiplication facts by rote acquire a habit of absent-minded mechanical activity that does not allow them to see the relationship between multiplication and division.

The Partition Aspect of Division

Most children experience the partition aspect of division at home whenever food or toys are divided among a few children. For example, a total, such as 15 cookies, is divided among 3 children; the answer to the question "How many cookies will each child receive?" (5) is the answer to the division problem 15 ÷ 3. The children can carry out many such problems and record them (e.g., *15 ÷ 3 = 5*).

The Containing Aspect of Division

When considering the partition aspect of division, the total and the number of shares are stated, and the question is to find the size of the share. In contrast, when considering the containing aspect of division, the total and the size of the part are given. The question is to find the number of shares (e.g., "How many times is the part contained in the total?"). For example, the previous problem changed to demonstrate the containing aspect of division would be stated like this: "Mother has 15 cookies. She wants to give 5 cookies to each child. How many children can she give cookies to?"

The containing aspect of division is taught first because it makes the structure of the division algorithm so clear. Children find they can solve a division example as soon as they understand multiplication.

The *division radical* looks like this: $\overline{)}$ and can be presented so as to make sense to students. The teacher places a small paper division radical on the number track over a multiple, such as 15. By doing this the teacher shows how the number 15 changes roles from being the product in a multiplication example to being the **dividend** in a division example. When the children see a division example, such as

$$5\overline{)15}$$

the teacher explains that this asks, "How many 5s are in 15?" To answer this question, students lay their pencils across 15 on the number track and find it takes 3 of the 5-blocks to reach 15, thus 3 tells them "how many times" the **divisor** (5) are contained in the dividend (15). The children then place the number marker for 3 on top of the number track above the number 15. This placement reminds them to write the quotient above the division radical when they record the answer to a division example (see Figure 11.7). By demonstrating examples such as this one, the children begin to understand the relationship between multiplication and division.

Under the Box   The game called Under the Box helps children remember which number in a division example is written "under the box" (under the division radical). When children hear words such as "24 divided by 4," they often write the numbers in the order in which they hear them, like this:

$$24\overline{)4}$$

The teacher hides several number blocks of the same size under a box, such as four 5-blocks, writes the total on a card, and says, "The blocks under the box make 20." The children write *20* "under the box" on their papers, like this:

$$\overline{)20}$$

The teacher continues, "The blocks under the box are 5-blocks. How many 5s are there?" The students ask themselves, "How many 5s are in 20?" and write

$$5\overline{)20}$$

They answer, "4," and lift the box, which reveals the four 5-blocks. They write *4* above the division radical:

$$5\overline{)20}^{4}$$

Division with Remainder

When long division is presented with the Structural Arithmetic materials, children can see that each step of the process makes sense. The teacher dictates a division example that will have an answer with a remainder, such as "How many 5s are in 14?" (see Figure 11.7). The children place two 5-blocks in the number track plus 4 cubes to reach 14, and write

$$5\overline{)14}$$

on their papers. The children see that there are 2 fives in 14, so they write *2* above the division radical, but they know that 2×5 is only 10. The teacher explains that now the students should find the number of cubes left, so he or she takes the 2 fives out of the track. The children say, "Subtract 10 from 14," and they write – *10* below *14* in their examples:

$$
\begin{array}{r}
2 \\
5\overline{)14} \\
-10
\end{array}
$$

Figure 11.7. Division with remainder.

Because 10 has been subtracted from 14, 4 cubes remain in the number track. Thus, the expression "remainder of 4" makes sense to the students. They complete their work by writing the remainder in their answers:

$$
\begin{array}{r}
2\,R4 \\
5\overline{)14} \\
-10 \\
\hline
4
\end{array}
$$

Division Word Problems

Division (Containing Aspect)   15 children want to go on boat rides (total). One boat holds 5 children (size of part). Question: How many boats will they need? We want to find how many 5s are contained in 15, so we write

$$5\overline{)15}$$

They will need 3 boats. We can check this: $3 \times 5 = 15$.

Division (Partition Aspect)   15 children want to go on boat rides (total). There are only 3 boats. Question: If there are an equal number of children in each boat, how many children are in each boat? We want to know the size of the part or the number of children in each boat. [To show that the students are finding the size of the part this time, the teacher can use a different way of writing the example, such as *15 ÷ 3 = 5.*] There will be 5 children in each boat.

CONCLUSION

This chapter shows how the multisensory Structural Arithmetic materials enable children to discover mathematical concepts and relationships that they could not have discovered through counting procedures and memorization alone. Children often respond appreciatively when a demonstration gives them insight into a new concept by exclaiming, "How neat!" Such enthusiasm is quickly responded to by the other children and gives the teacher special pleasure in working with these materials.

Piaget (1952) explained that children develop an understanding of mathematical concepts as a result of the actions they perform with objects, not as a result of the objects themselves. This makes clear why pictures in workbooks do not teach children. The Structural Arithmetic blocks invite children to handle them and perform actions at every step. By the time students reach the level of writing in workbooks, they are free to focus on how to write numbers and equations; they have already worked out the concepts with the multisensory materials and are ready to record them.

By using these structured materials, children, especially children with learning disabilities, learn to trust their intelligence; they come to feel pleased with themselves and proud of their ability to think. This feeling of self-confidence increases their self-esteem and often spreads to their work in other fields. Furthermore, they have developed a reliable understanding of number concepts from the very beginning. They will not have to discard these early formulations as deceptively simple but can carry them forward as the building blocks of algebra.

When we teach mathematical truths and facts by rote, we take away from children not only the joy of using their minds but also their sense of independence. They feel manipulated, and the result is unimaginative mechanical work. In some cases this causes students to be bored; in other cases, this leads students to turn off their minds, to withdraw, or to fail. What children crave is freedom to carry out their own experiments and draw their own conclusions. When they are permitted to do this to the degree that they can, their work will be fulfilling.

REFERENCES

Piaget, J. (1952). *The child's concept of number.* London: Routledge & Kegan Paul.

Stern, C., & Stern, M. (1971). *Children discover arithmetic: An introduction to Structural Arithmetic.* New York: Harper-Collins.

Stern, M. (1988). *Experimenting with numbers: A guide for preschool, kindergarten, and first grade teachers.* Cambridge, MA: Educators Publishing Service.

Stern, M., & Gould, T. (1988–1992). *Structural arithmetic workbooks 1–3 and teachers' guides.* Cambridge, MA: Educators Publishing Service.

12

Applying Multisensory Techniques to Interdisciplinary Studies

Cecily Selling and Dorothy Flanagan

Interdisciplinary studies may be known by other names. *Thematic units, theme cycles, central subject curriculum, central study,* and *integrated curriculum* are all names for the in-depth study of a topic, often in science or social studies. Within an interdisciplinary unit, students are able to connect subject areas and avoid fragmented learning. Students may find connections among history, geography, math, art, and music while studying Native Americans or among reading, writing, math, science, and social studies while studying weather. Interdisciplinary studies reflect the world in its complexity and interrelatedness. Very few adults do all of the math for a project at once, followed by all of the reading and then all of the writing. Life is not broken into segments but is a web of interconnected manmade and natural systems. During interdisciplinary studies units, children learn through a series of experiences around a given theme that life is complex and that it can be explored in many ways.

A thematic, interdisciplinary approach to learning must include multisensory teaching and learning. Many students with learning disabilities learn best by doing, and they acquire meaning through different senses. Children retain facts, concepts, skills, and vocabulary best when they have multisensory experiences. Those who have well-developed skills in areas other than reading and writing can use those skills in the study of a theme. Children with dyslexia or other learning disabilities are often concrete thinkers who do best with material presented in the context of real-life situations rather than in abstract textbook descriptions. For some students who struggle with school, a multisensory approach to thematic learning keeps learning alive and exciting and can be a significant confidence builder.

GOALS FOR INTERDISCIPLINARY STUDIES

The goals of interdisciplinary studies are similar to those of a good liberal arts college. Students should learn problem solving, research skills, and how to present what they have learned to others. They should be able to see and make connections among subjects such as history, geography, and science. The studies should be presented in such a way that students learn to make decisions, both individually and as a group, based on facts and concepts learned during thematic study. They need to see and value the connections between what they study in school and what they see in the world.

Students should be able to see similarities among other cultures and our own as well as value the differences among cultures. Learning to respect each other's unique experiences, understanding different cultural backgrounds, and finding ways to make bridges between them are crucial goals for interdisciplinary studies. The world is a complicated, wonderful, sometimes dangerous, and often chaotic place. Children need to see themselves as creators and shapers of this reality and not as overwhelmed spectators. Children with learning disabilities often feel powerless and confused when presented with facts or concepts in isolation. If such students have a theme within which they can organize their own learning, they will be more likely to remember facts, make connections, and feel in control of their learning.

MULTISENSORY ACTIVITIES

Children with language-learning disabilities will benefit from saying what they know about a subject, hearing what others know about the same subject, watching as the teacher writes lists, and writing their own questions during the introduction of a unit. If they have a chance to see, hear, speak, and write the words that connect them to the subject, they are more likely to remember and connect the subsequent learning to those words. Children's literature provides a wealth of stories that can add to any unit of study. Students who have trouble remembering isolated facts may find that the structure of a story helps them to remember facts.

There are senses other than those of hearing and sight. Most interdisciplinary studies units lend themselves very well to experiences involving tactile and kinesthetic senses and the sense of smell. Teachers must be sure to connect these multisensory activities with language so that students have a way of communicating their knowledge and connecting it to other areas of experience. It is not enough for a child to smell the spices of India. Each sensory experience should be connected to the language that we use to express that experience. While smelling cloves, a dyslexic student might look at a label with the word *cloves* written on it. A follow-up activity could include smelling a mystery spice and matching the name of the spice with the scent. After hearing and reading the name, students might write a shopping list in preparation for cooking an Indian dish. The experiences with the spices should be combined with an understanding of the climate of the country and, for older children, some discussion of the role of spices in the European desire to explore the world.

CHOOSING TOPICS

Several organizational models for thematic units have been used successfully in schools. The number and type of subjects are unending. The organization works best when it fits with the style of the school; the expectations of the community; and, above all, the needs of the teachers. Interdisciplinary studies succeed or fail depending on the enthusiasm and interest of the teachers involved.

The theme or themes to be studied can be chosen each year by the teachers. In one school some effort is made to balance the curriculum to include the study of a culture, a physical science, a natural science, a theme based on the values of the school, and a theme that would lend itself to a performance. The teachers brainstorm a long list of possible themes and eliminate those that are not popular or that are problematic. Then they advocate various themes, negotiating and convincing each other of the value of each theme. After this fairly long process, four or five themes are chosen that are of interest to all teachers.

Themes in some schools are relatively permanent. The second grade may study Native Americans, the fourth grade may study ancient Greece, and the fifth grade may study colonial America, for example. This type of organization has its advantages. The teacher becomes an expert and has less research to do each year. The students leave the school with specific bodies of knowledge. Disadvantages are that after several years the teachers do not learn along with the students and that their presentation of subject matter might be less than fresh.

A school that uses a central subject curriculum has several criteria for choosing that central subject. The subject must inspire the teachers. It needs to offer possibilities for instruction in many disciplines, such as history, geography, math, science, music, and art. It should include the diversity and commonality of human experience. Each theme for this school must include the possibility of metaphor. One school's themes have included Walls and Bridges, Journeys, Childhood, and Rivers. In the fall of the year that classes studied Walls and Bridges, one student wrote a paper on Nelson Mandela and his prison cell walls.

Another idea for a thematic unit, found in Boyer's (1995) book *Basic Schools: A Community for Learning* centers around the question, "What does it mean to be human?" Topics for study and discussion can include the following:

- The use of symbols
- Aesthetics
- Rites of passage and life cycles
- Connections to nature
- Community groups and organization
- A sense of time and place (history and geography)
- Working to live (producing and consuming)
- Values and the meaning of life

If all of the themes for a school year can be grouped under an "umbrella theme," then a subject can be presented in many modes. Each time the subject is reintroduced from the point of view of another discipline, another dimension of the concept is added. An example of such an umbrella theme is the year-long study of water that took place at Stratford Friends School from 1994 to 1995. The opening theme was simply Water, followed by Immigration, a study of those who came over the water. The next theme was Australia, a land surrounded by water, whose geography and culture are profoundly affected by water and the lack of it. A unit on storytelling gave children the chance to notice how water is used in stories. The final theme, Farms and Food, included the study of how important clean water is to crops and farming. By the end of a year of studying water, the students had learned about water as an element, as part of weather and climate, as a barrier to be conquered, as a human need, and as a resource to be protected.

In some schools the teachers begin the year by asking the students what they would like to study. If students are used to making choices, this question could generate 200–300 ideas, as Dockstader-Anderson reported. "The next day we categorized the ideas based on commonalities. We came up with five major topics of study: animals, astronomy, electricity, toys, and geology" (1994, p. 26). Dockstader-Anderson's class spent a day discussing issues, lobbying for favorites, and generating curriculum ideas. They then voted on the topics and started with the topic that got the most votes.

This way of selecting subjects for study may be difficult if students are not used to having a choice. Ramirez reported that she got blank looks when she asked her students what they would like to study:

> I realized that for these students, learning meant open your books, read the chapter, and answer the questions at the end. I knew I was going to have a very difficult time bringing about change. Eventually, with my guidance, the students did select such themes as Sports, Countries, and Inventions. Tapping the collective knowledge and generating and posing problems or questions was very difficult for them. They were only used to answering questions, not asking them! (1994, p. 33)

Students with learning disabilities may have difficulty in choosing topics to study on their own, but it is important that all students' interests be taken into consideration when themes are chosen. A reluctant student may turn into a dedicated student if the class is studying a topic of interest to him or her. Many teachers know students who cannot remember how to spell *said* but who can spell *triceratops* and *diplodocus*.

GETTING STARTED

Children often know more than teachers think. It is very useful to begin a study of a theme by making a list of what students already know. It is important that the teacher include everyone's ideas on the list. Students need to be able to take the risk of being wrong in their ideas about a subject. It may be necessary to go back to the list at a later point and correct any inaccuracies. Figure 12.1 is a "What We Know About Africa" list generated by a group of 11- and 12-year-olds at Stratford Friends School in the spring of 1996. This list of beginning knowledge should be saved until the end of the interdisciplinary unit so that the students can have a visual display of how much they learned during the unit.

To help the students become interested in the unit to be studied, it is good for the class to also make a "What We Want to Know About _____" list. This list

What We Know About Africa

It is very big.
The people there live in tribes.
There are lots of wild animals there.
Laura's father lives there.
Slaves came from Africa.
They carry things on their heads.
People go on safari there.
They eat bugs like grasshoppers.
It is very hot in Africa.
The Nile is a long river in Africa.
Egypt is there. They have pyramids.
The Africans believe that there are gods everywhere.
The people go barefoot and don't wear much.

Figure 12.1. "What We Know About Africa" list created by 11- and 12-year-olds at the beginning of a thematic unit.

of questions can be a jumping-off point for study within the unit. The list can also be another gauge of the students' current knowledge of a subject. If the questions are relevant to the goals that the teacher has for the unit, they can be used to get started. If the questions are far off the mark for the topic, it may mean that the teacher must do some background work before starting the thematic unit. Figure 12.2 shows the questions about Africa that the class of 11- to 12-year-olds asked. Their teacher also saved this list and used it as a review at the end of the thematic unit.

EXAMPLES OF MULTISENSORY ACTIVITIES: WATER

A unit of interdisciplinary studies can be taught at many different levels. Children as young as 5 or 6 years of age can learn about the same topic as students in upper elementary grades, middle school, or high school. The approach would be

Questions About Africa

What language do they speak?
What kind of food do they eat?
Why did they sell slaves?
How can they stand to eat bugs?
Who is in charge in Africa?
Is it hot everywhere in Africa?
Who is Nelson Mandela? Why is he a hero?
Is Africa bigger than our country?
What time zone is Africa in?
Are all people in Africa black? Why?
Is it true that civilization began in Africa?
Why are there wars in Africa?

Figure 12.2. "Questions About Africa" list generated by 11- and 12-year-olds during a thematic unit.

different, of course, depending on the age and reading level of the students. Students of all ages can benefit from multisensory activities, often called *hands-on activities*. The following sections give examples of how to present the theme *water* in multisensory ways appropriate to various age levels. The students in the examples all are students with learning disabilities.

Water for Young Children

A group of 6- and 7-year-old children began their study of water with a game of charades. They acted out ways in which people and animals use water. The ways of using water included filling a water balloon, making orange juice, washing toes, and going scuba diving. The children discussed how water is essential for nearly every part of our lives.

This group went on to look at living things and learn about how all living things need water. The children cut up fruits and vegetables to see how plants get and use water. Then they made a collage from magazine pictures of how living things use water. They measured water used to cook, wash, and drink and made a graph of water use in math class.

Another important concept about water is that it can be in three forms: solid, liquid, and gas. The students added water to orange juice concentrate and put it in Popsicle containers in the freezer. They measured the juice level before and after freezing. They learned that there has to be room for the Popsicle stick and for the ice to expand. As the children ate the juice Popsicles, they talked about solids and liquids and the ideas of expanding and contracting. A mirror for each child helped demonstrate the idea of water as a gas. The children breathed on the mirrors and noticed that they fogged up. As they wondered out loud about where the fog came from, their teachers were able to take this moment to explain water vapor. The students watched the mirrors become less foggy and finally clear and were introduced to the concept of evaporation.

For many 6- and 7-year-olds, water is for swimming in or playing in. These children learned about floating and sinking and a bit about the scientific process by making a list of things that float in water and things that sink in water. After some initial experiences with items that sink and float, the students were asked to make predictions before testing items. They finished this experience by making some generalizations based on their data about which types of items sink and which types float.

Water for Older Children

The teachers of a group of third, fourth, and fifth graders chose to focus their study of water on the concept of water as the most precious resource. Their goals included the following: understanding how the water cycle works; learning how water is purified for human use and comes to schools and homes; learning about the history of human impact on a river ecosystem; learning about various fresh- and saltwater ecosystems, their locations in the world, and the plants and animals in each; and using a science notebook for recording information, research, wonderings, and questions.

This class began with a group of charts called *AQUA charts*. The *A* chart was for the things the students *a*lready knew about water. The *QU* chart was for *ques-*

tions they had about water, and the final *A* chart was for *a*nswers they found. The first two charts were made during the opening activity, and the final chart was filled in as the students learned about water.

The teacher read *The Magic School Bus at the Waterworks* (Cole, 1986) as an introduction to the water cycle. The students began using their science notebooks by writing two facts that they learned from the book. Fact versus fiction was included as part of the discussion following the book.

The students made boxes to demonstrate the water cycle. They took transparent plastic sweater storage boxes and made a hill at one end of each box using modeling clay. At the other end of the box, they placed a small bowl of water to represent the ocean. A desk lamp placed close to the bowl of water outside the box represented the sun. The lid to the plastic box was placed on top, and a bag of ice cubes was put on top of the box above the clay hill. As the lamp (sun) heated the water, some of it evaporated and rose to the top of the box. The vapor over the land met the cold air from the ice cubes and condensed, causing rain. The students were very excited over their power to "make it rain." They followed up on this activity by drawing a diagram of the weather cycle in their notebooks and labeling the parts that represented the following: solid, liquid, gas, ice, water, water vapor, precipitation, condensation, and evaporation. With the experience of making rain so fresh in their minds, these words meant much more to the students than if they had been presented in isolation or even as pictures in a book.

Transferring knowledge from experience and oral language to diagrams and written language can be difficult for students with learning disabilities. They may resist or say, "I can't draw." An atmosphere of acceptance in the classroom is the most important way of dealing with this reluctance. In addition, teachers can provide assistance by drawing a model on the chalkboard with correctly spelled vocabulary. Alternatively, students might be asked to do their best at spelling and write with pencil so that the issues of spelling can be separated from getting the language down on paper.

The next step in making the water cycle become real to the third, fourth, and fifth graders was to visit a water treatment plant. The students were able to see the reservoir near their homes where water is stored. They toured the plant and saw scientists at work taking dirty water from the reservoir and turning it into clean, drinkable water. The scent of chlorine was strong and may have reminded students after the visit of all that goes into making water clean. The guide told the most active child in the class how many gallons of water were held in the reservoir. The student was pleased to remember the eight-digit number and recite it at various points during the tour. This experience with such a large number enriched a math activity about place value with large numbers.

The students took the knowledge gained from the experiment with water cycle in a box and from the trip to the water treatment plant and made a mural of how water gets from rain to homes and buildings. The students worked in pairs to draw the steps in order. Sequencing is often a difficult task for students with learning disabilities, and this mural helped those who may not have remembered whether the water treatment plant filters the water first or puts the chlorine in first.

The class then turned to exploring the bodies of water in the larger world. They used globes, atlases, and wall maps to locate the world's continents, oceans, polar regions, and major rivers. They labeled them on outline maps of the world.

Literature was again brought in when the teacher read aloud from *A River Ran Wild* (Cherry, 1992). The students located the places in the story on maps and the globe. They followed up on the theme of keeping rivers clean by making a game called Dream a Clean River. Each child wrote a game card for something that is good for a river (with instructions to go ahead a certain number of spaces) and something that is bad for a river (with instructions to go back a certain number of spaces). As they played the game, they were reviewing some important concepts about pollution and the care of our water resources.

The class came back to a local river and made a class book about the development and settlement of a local river based on the format of *A River Ran Wild*. They worked in pairs, and each pair was responsible for a two-page spread in the book. Sharing this book with younger children was another way of reviewing what had been learned.

This unit continued with the creation of a class riddle book about plants and animals that live in a river ecosystem. They also created an information chart of water ecosystems. For each of five ecosystems (freshwater lake, Everglades wetlands, coral reef, Antarctic oceans, and rocky shoreline tidal pool), they made a list of one fact they already knew, three facts they learned, and questions they still had. The unit culminated with a trip to a local aquarium, where the children used their notebooks to research answers to "I wonder" questions they had written.

Middle School Water Activities

A group of 11- and 12-year-olds began their study of water by listening to a storyteller tell a Native American creation story. They discussed the importance of water in myths and legends and its importance in the lives of all people.

This group also learned about the water cycle but approached it from a more kinesthetic angle. The students acted out the water cycle. One child was the sun and put a pan of water on a heater. A second child was a cold air mass and held a glass with ice in it high in the air on a tray. A third child was the wind and blew the air from above the heated water over to the ice on the tray. The water vapor condensed on the cold tray and fell as rain. The students vied for a chance to be one of the characters in the play, and the process was repeated. These students followed up their activities with worksheets that helped them turn the activity into a vocabulary lesson as well.

The science teacher worked with this group on the molecular structure of water and had the students act out the various parts of a water molecule. They learned just what H_2O means and how elements such as water are based on combinations of chemicals. He also explained that the molecules of water that are around now are the same molecules of water that were around in the time of the dinosaurs. This view of the history of water was fascinating to the students when the teacher announced that the molecules of water in a glass on the table could be the same molecules that were in dinosaur urine!

Math was brought into this thematic unit by exploring the amount of water on the earth. The classes were working on the meaning of *percent* and used the statistic that 97% of the world's water is saltwater to explore what this really means. They filled 10 gallon jugs with water and used that amount to represent the total amount of water in the world. They then figured out that only three tenths of one of the jugs of water represented freshwater. They learned that of that amount of water, only about 1 tablespoonful is available to humans and that much of the rest is frozen in the polar ice caps. This physical example of an abstract statistic helped the students to understand how limited our freshwater resources really are.

This group did research into topics of interest, including animals that live in or near water, oceans, and seas and water pollution. The students did reports on their topics and displayed their knowledge in a pop-up book about water. Each student needed to think of a three-dimensional way to display some of the facts he or she had found.

A trip to a water treatment plant helped with further understanding of the water cycle and pollution issues. A camping trip near the ocean that included a swamp walk to discover insect-eating plants and a guided tour of a salt marsh led by a retired biology teacher helped these students bring to life their work on water. The students used a seine (a large fishing net) to collect and examine the living things in a tidal pool near a salt marsh.

High School Water Studies

Most high schools are very departmentalized, and teachers are not used to the idea of interdisciplinary studies. Concepts at the high school level, however, can be taught in a multisensory way, and teachers can cooperate to teach an interdisciplinary theme.

For example, a history teacher and an ecology teacher may collaborate on a study of the history and science of a local creek. Because the history of a body of water is closely tied to the way people have treated that body, students can come to understand the links between history and science. They can see the need to know both subjects in order to make decisions about the use of resources. A trip to the stream may include an exploration of an abandoned paper mill as well as water tests to see which pollutants are in the water around the mill.

CULMINATION

There are many multisensory ways to wrap up a thematic unit. Usually the culmination of a unit is a way to present what students have learned and to let them share that knowledge with others who may or may not have been studying the same theme. The advantage of a whole school's studying the same theme is that younger students are able to understand what older students are presenting because they have been studying the same theme.

A play is one multisensory way of presenting information. Students must read, listen, speak, and perhaps write. They use motions to act and express emotions. Students who might have trouble with memory in an isolated context sometimes find that they can memorize their lines quite easily. Some plays that are already written for children may be appropriate for the culmination of a theme, but more often the teacher will write the play with the help of the students. Students and teachers in classes that study water could write a play as the culmination of the water theme. Each class could present a skit about one part of the water cycle and sing a water-related song. Students could act as water molecules, pollutants, and clumping substances to show how water is treated. Music teachers can assist in finding water-related songs or in writing new lyrics for familiar tunes.

Almost any topic can be presented with song, though some are easier to conceive of than others. A group of teachers at Stratford Friends School spent many lunchtime hours planning a musical to end the 2-month study of astronomy. Creating *1996: A Space Odyssey* was a large task, but all of the teachers agreed that it had been a success for the students involved. They remembered what they had learned much better after it had been set to music.

Another way to present the information learned in a unit is to turn the classroom into another place. A study of the Middle Ages may culminate in a festival in which one classroom is a cathedral, another a castle complete with knights and ladies, and another a village house with tools from the Middle Ages. Students can demonstrate what they have learned by doing activities that would have been done in that location. Scribes could copy religious tracts with homemade quill pens in the cathedral, while knights and ladies dance in the castle. The village folk could card wool and serve homemade bread.

A trip can be a good culmination if the students are well prepared for what they will see. A trip to Ellis Island after studying immigration can bring to life all of the ideas presented. It is important that there be activities because students with dyslexia or other learning disabilities will probably not get as much out of displays unless some response is required.

Another type of culmination is a reenactment. Putting together a reenactment takes a great deal of organization and some special resources but can be a very powerful tool. Students who have been taken out to the country after dark for a reenactment of the Underground Railroad will keep powerful images. They will remember having to stay quiet for fear of a large man on a horse who is trying to take them back to slavery. They will remember the anxiety of waiting in a small closet as a Quaker couple assures the man on a horse that there are no slaves in their house. Reenactments are multisensory learning at its most powerful, but they must be followed by discussion. Children can get very skewed impressions from an activity such as the Underground Railroad simulation and must have time to talk about their feelings and their experiences. One child might worry about bounty hunters coming in the night and will need to be assured that in the United States, slavery ended more than 100 years ago. Another child might see the activity as an enjoyable game and might express the wish that he or she lived "back in slavery times." This child needs to be reminded that the Underground Railroad was not fun for those involved.

There are other possibilities for culminating a thematic unit. A class may write a book together, put on an art show, have a science fair, display dioramas, or create any other type of display that seems appropriate. What is important is that the students be involved in the final display and that the language and vocabulary of the unit being studied be used while planning and carrying out the culmination.

EVALUATION

Teachers do need to have some way of knowing what their students have learned. In an interdisciplinary studies unit, it is important to make it clear to the students that there are concepts, vocabulary, and information to be learned. There are as many ways to evaluate what has been learned as there are ways to teach. A teacher can always prepare the students for a pencil-and-paper test. This is a skill that they will need all the way through school. If students are being taught using multisensory methods, however, it makes sense to use multisensory ways of evaluating them.

One alternative way of evaluating students is to have a hands-on activity as part of a test. If students have been studying about the classification of animals, they could take pictures of animals on cards and sort them into groups of mammals, reptiles, fish, birds, and amphibians. The third, fourth, and fifth graders discussed previously finished their unit on water with a River Puzzle (see Figure 12.3). This puzzle consisted of a piece of paper with 20 different parts of a river, including a farm, a forest, a park, a paper mill, a large city, a power plant, a dam, the source, the mouth, and other places. The students were asked to cut the pieces apart and put them together in a way that made sense to them. Each student had to think about what he or she had learned about water and sources of pollution and had to make some decisions based on that knowledge. The activity was a simple cut-and-paste activity, but the students had to be able to explain their choices to the class.

Another evaluation technique is to play a game in which students have to answer questions orally. A version of the television game show *Jeopardy!*, in which the contestant is given an answer and must respond with a question, is popular among students. It is much more motivating to be told, "The answer is the chemical name for water," and to respond, "What is H_2O?" than it is to answer that same question on paper. This game-show format is also a good way to help a class review for a test because everyone hears the answers and the questions. Students with different abilities can participate as a team, with cooperation among teammates as a goal.

It has been said that if one really wants to learn a subject well, one should try to teach it to someone else. Teachers who teach interdisciplinary studies can attest to this, and they can also use it as a way of teaching or evaluating their students. Older students who are given a group of facts or concepts and asked to come up with a way of teaching those concepts to others will certainly work harder and most probably learn more than if they were told to learn the information for themselves.

SUPPORT FOR TEACHING INTERDISCIPLINARY STUDIES

The use of thematic or interdisciplinary approaches to teaching is not easy. As with most powerful ways of teaching, it requires work on the part of the teacher, support from school administrators, and help from parents and other members of the community.

Creative teachers with enough planning time can do an excellent job of teaching multisensory interdisciplinary studies. Most teachers who have seen the success of this method would not want to go back to textbook or worksheet teaching alone. Multisensory teaching of thematic units does require more time for planning and preparing materials than do more traditional ways of teaching. It also requires a sense of adventure on the part of the teacher. He or she must

Directions for the River Puzzle

1. Pretend that your group is a regional planning commission. Together decide what can be built where along the river so that the water will not become polluted.

2. Cut out the squares on the puzzle sheet, and decide how they will be placed, starting from the source of the river in the mountains and ending with the mouth of the river flowing into an ocean. Decorate the squares (before or after Step 3).

3. When your group has decided where each square should go, glue them onto a long strip of paper, matching the sides of the river as much as you can.

Remember, there is no one correct answer, but you will be asked to defend your choices in a Town Meeting of the citizens (class meeting).

Figure 12.3.   River Puzzle used by third, fourth, and fifth graders at the end of a thematic unit on water.

have the ability to look at a subject or theme, set goals for the students, find materials or make them, try activities, and risk failure. A teacher who can plan an activity that does *not* work and model to the class how to solve the problems of the activity gives students with learning disabilities the message that failure is part of life and that problem solving is something we all do.

In order for teachers to be able to take the risks involved in multisensory thematic teaching, they must have the support of the school administration. Administrators need to understand the curriculum well enough to provide time for planning and flexibility in scheduling for the teachers. Administrators will also have to provide explanations (e.g., by sending a friendly note, by having students display classwork at home, by inviting parents to class presentations) to parents who want to know why students aren't studying traditional subjects in traditional ways. A supportive administrator can help teachers plan together and can help find resources at school and in the community.

Teachers or administrators who are interested in using multisensory methods to teach interdisciplinary studies might begin on a small scale. One project or theme during a school year would give the school a taste of how interdisciplinary studies can work. A visit to another school that is doing thematic teaching can provide inspiration as well as advice on issues that may arise and day-to-day procedures. Thematic teaching with multisensory techniques is not a method to be imposed on teachers who do not understand or support it. Working at getting everyone to agree to give it a try will lead to a much greater chance of success.

CONCLUSION

For many students with dyslexia or other learning disabilities as well as for typical students, multisensory presentation of interdisciplinary studies is the way to keep learning alive, to connect subjects, and to show students that learning is a lifelong adventure. As students become immersed in a subject, they understand why they need to learn to read and write. As activities increase students' curiosity about the world, they come back to reading and writing classes refreshed and with a greater willingness to tackle the hard work of learning to read and write.

REFERENCES

Boyer, E. (1995). *Basic schools: A community for learning*. Princeton, NJ: Carnegie Foundation for the Advancement of Teaching.

Cherry, L. (1992). *A river ran wild*. Orlando, FL: Harcourt Brace & Co.

Cole, J. (1986). *The magic school bus at the waterworks*. New York: Scholastic.

Dockstader-Anderson, K. (1994). Democracy in action: Negotiating the curriculum beyond the classroom. *Primary Voices, 2*(1), 26–31.

Ramirez, L. (1994). Reflections. *Primary Voices, 2*(1), 33–34.

13

Organization and Study Skills

Claire Nissenbaum

It is not the smartest student who gets the highest marks; it is the student who knows how to study (Tonjes & Zintz, 1981). Students of high intellectual ability may be among the lowest-ranking students in the class. Too often, low-achieving students are struggling because of unrecognized language-based learning disabilities (dyslexia), especially if they have not received training in efficient, effective learning strategies and study skills (Deshler, Ellis, & Lenz, 1996; Strichart & Mangrum, 1993; Wiig & Semel, 1990).

Deshler and colleagues stated, "An individual's approach to a task is called a strategy. Strategies include how a person thinks and acts when planning, executing and evaluating performance on a task and its subsequent outcomes" (1996, p. 12). In contrast, "Study skills are those competencies associated with acquiring, recording, organizing, synthesizing, remembering and using information and ideas found in school . . . [the ones] more or less indispensable for school success" (Devine, 1981, p. 4).

Systematic instruction in study skills may or may not be provided in the upper elementary grades or secondary school. Study skills training may not be provided by an instructor with adequate knowledge and expertise (Tonjes & Zintz, 1981). Even when study skills are well taught, there may or may not be sufficient time allotted for dyslexic students to develop adequate facility in using them

---

The term *dyslexia* is used here to refer to language-based specific learning difficulties in receptive and expressive language skills, including conceptualization, oral expression, decoding, listening and reading comprehension, written English (spelling, mechanics, syntax, and grammar), memory (storage and retrieval), time management and organization, and—even among the mathematically talented—difficulty with concepts and problem-solving. No student has all of these difficulties; some have just a few. (It should be noted that very bright dyslexic students will *appear* to have little or no difficulty in reading.) Dyslexic students who have deficiencies in language skills, memory, and conceptual thinking may have difficulties with social, as well as academic, skills (Deshler et al., 1996; Wiig & Semel, 1990).

(Deshler et al., 1996). Furthermore, even when ample time has been allotted to teaching study skills, the process of transferring those skills successfully to the content subject classroom may have received little or no attention (Deshler et al., 1996; Wiig & Semel, 1990).

The failure to provide good training in study skills handicaps all students in their ability to learn efficiently and to achieve academically at the level of their potential intelligence.[1] For students with language-based learning difficulties, particularly those who are included in the general classroom for part or all of the day, and for any student with poor reading skills, lack of good training in study skills is a serious omission. When this happens, such students are left to a demeaning and unrewarding struggle to survive in school; to the probability of life-long physical and/or mental health problems; to narrowly limited college and vocational options; and, for too many, to self-abasement and despair (Kamhi & Catts, 1989). A few students with dyslexia may develop self-destructive or anti-social behaviors (Levine, 1987).

Given the demands of the modern school curriculum, the pressures on teachers' time, and the typical characteristics of preadolescent and adolescent dyslexic students, training in learning strategies and study skills must be as efficacious as possible. It must be accomplished in the shortest possible time and must be immediately and broadly applicable to all of the student's subject classes with minimal additional training from the classroom teachers. Most important, for the dyslexic student, the training in study skills must facilitate the transition from passive, indifferent involvement to proactive and productive participation in learning (Deshler et al., 1996).

OVERVIEW

This chapter discusses techniques for training students in using *unconventional* (adapted) learning strategies and study skills. The strategies described facilitate improvement in the performance of *all* students in general classes, even when they are taught to an entire class as a single group. For dyslexic students, training in learning strategies and study skills may make the critical difference between passing and failing and may mean the difference between grades of Ds and Bs or Cs and As for some students. The student who masters the strategies and skills *and uses them routinely* will be able to adapt and translate them from secondary school to college and beyond, to the adult world of work. The goal for the student is self-knowledge, self-management, and self-advocacy (i.e., independence). No assumptions are made about student motivation or commitment. Rather, the operative assumptions are 1) that the student has little interest, motivation, or commitment to learning and 2) that study skills training will elicit all three in the student. Clinical experience has shown that failure to achieve this motivational change occurs in three instances: when there is no true commitment from the teacher; when there is a significant health problem, such as a severe anemia; or, in some cases, when there is a disabling psychiatric illness.

This chapter details the typical difficulties of dyslexic adolescents and the negative impact of these difficulties on learning and academic success, and presents considerations for working with preadolescent and adolescent dyslexic stu-

---

[1]The IQ scores of dyslexic students are reliable indicators of current functioning in school; however, because of the language difficulties of dyslexic students', their IQ scores understate their actual cognitive ability.

dents. After the discussion of considerations, details of the actual strategies and skills training follow. Such skills training begins with fast-working "Quick Tricks" that have been designed to do the following:

- Engage students' attention and cooperation
- Reduce high-frequency errors and common teacher irritants in written work
- Begin systematic memory training
- Provide students with certain emergency strategies for dealing with text

Simultaneously, organization and time-management strategies and skills are discussed as the indispensable foundation of academic success, including strategies for dealing with homework assignments and for self-monitoring and self-evaluation. The first phase of study skills training usually results in improved performance and reawakened motivation in the student. The second phase focuses on strategies and techniques for mastering content, including ways to effect rapid improvement in vocabulary and conceptual thinking and techniques for studying for tests. Strategies and techniques to improve critical and evaluative thinking, develop higher-level oral and written language skills, and improve self-confidence are presented.

Written English skills are taught incrementally, beginning with the mechanics of English, proofreading, accurate spelling, sentence patterns, and syntax, and moving on to extension of vocabulary, summary writing, **précis** writing,[2] and mastery of nonliteral language forms (e.g., idioms, puns). The emphasis on concept formation, on explication of abstract terms, and on expansion of oral language skills contributes to improved writing skills. More extensive training in written English is not feasible simply because of time limitations. As Deshler and colleagues (1996) stressed, requiring student mastery of each learning strategy taught is crucial. Therefore, the study skills instructor who devotes substantial time to developing writing skills cannot move students to mastery levels in the fundamental learning strategies and study skills and ends up doing a poor job of teaching both writing skills and study skills.

DYSLEXIC STUDENTS AND ACADEMIC ACHIEVEMENT: CONVENTION, PERCEPTION, AND REALITY

The problem with conventional study skills training is that there is too much "study" and too little "skill." One explanation for this situation is that teachers cannot teach what they themselves have not been taught (Askov & Kamm, 1982). In general, teachers were not trained in efficient and effective study skills as young students. College and university education departments do not offer undergraduate or graduate courses in teaching study skills, not even to secondary or college teachers (Deshler et al., 1996) or to teachers of students with reading and learning problems. Nevertheless, for many American students, study skills courses are now required in the upper elementary school, middle school, and high school years. As in other classes, teachers lecture, provide practice exercises in discrete skills (e.g., identifying the main idea), test students' knowledge, and assign grades. Students are expected to pay attention, listen, understand, take

---

[2]The French term *précis* (pronounced "pray-**see**") means a *cut-down statement*. It is merely the essence—the pith—of a paragraph or even of a whole essay.

good notes, remember, adapt the information to other school subjects, and transfer and apply the techniques effectively to get better grades. These areas, however, are precisely the areas in which dyslexic students have significant difficulties, difficulties that make success problematic, despite long hours of study and intense effort.

Many adults believe that academic achievement is a critical marker of adult success. This belief is not supported by research or by common experience in our culture. For example, Winston Churchill was a poor student and was much reproached by his father for this. To compound the problem, parents typically believe that academic success is a function of the amount of time and energy the student spends on school work. The assumption is that there is a direct relationship between the time spent and the grades earned. Both teachers and parents tend to characterize the low-achieving student as unwilling to work hard enough to do well. School and clinical experience confirms that teachers often view parents of bright, low-achieving students as part of the problem, and believe that parents are unwilling or unable to make the student do the work required. But teaching and clinical experience shows that "students *who are able to make the most of their minds* like to work and . . . generally do quite well" (Wittenberg, 1965, p. 15, emphasis added).

The reality is that some preadolescent and adolescent dyslexic students fail to do well academically because they have not had effective training in learning strategies and study skills to compensate for their significant deficits in cognitive operations. These deficits are caused by underlying neurological differences in brain architecture and function (Cruikshank, 1967; Gaddes & Edgell, 1994) and can result in difficulties in the following areas:

- *Understanding, acquiring, and interpreting verbal symbols, such as apostrophes; sounds; letters; and suprasegmentals (Orton, 1937; Wiig & Semel, 1990)*   Such difficulties with verbal symbols can affect speaking, reading, and writing skills; learning foreign languages; and social skills. Students typically develop an aversion to reading.
- *Receptive and expressive language, including vocabulary, grammar, and syntax*   These language difficulties can affect all verbal communication skills and personal relationships (Tomatis, 1960).
- *Processing rapidly presented spoken information, including discrimination of discrete sound units (e.g., syllables, phonemes) in words*   Impaired language processing may affect listening skills, vocabulary, concept development, ability to follow directions, memory, and note-taking skills. As Johnson and Myklebust explained, "A perceptual disorder by reciprocation disturbs all levels of experience that fall above it" (1967, p. 33).
- *Selective and sustained attention,[3] difficulties resulting from both innate and environmental influences**   Difficulty with attention may affect all aspects of intellectual and social functioning.

---

[3]Several of these deficits (marked by an asterisk) are characterized by Goldstein (1939) as resulting in part from central nervous system disturbances in *figure–ground perception*. The *ground* is the continuous, nonspecific activity of the entire nervous system. The *figure* is any change in the activity—a burp, an ache, a birdsong, a ray of sunlight, a thought. Goldstein's observations of the cognitive difficulties of World War I veterans with brain injuries are suggestive of the typical difficulties of dyslexic students. He explained these functional deficits as a consequence in part of the isolation of individual brain cells. Autopsy studies of brains of people who had dyslexia appeared to confirm Goldstein's explanation (Galaburda, 1993). Although it is challenging reading, Goldstein's classic study is well worth the effort.

- *Memory—storage and retrieval, functions of selection and association, and language ability* Memory problems affect a student's ability to understand (Neisser, 1976), to learn, and to use skills and information.
- *Freedom from anxiety* Dyslexic students typically experience a generalized ever-present anxiety, which arises from linguistic, cognitive, and temporal-spatial deficits. This is compounded by anxiety caused by stress in specific situations, such as social introductions, class recitations, oral reading, and tests. Anxiety may affect all areas, especially memory (Cruikshank, 1967), class recitation, and test-taking.
- *Categorizing, classifying, abstracting, generalizing, and making analogies* Such difficulties affect concept development, abstract thought (Lakoff & Johnson, 1980), comprehension, and understanding of logical relations (Wiig & Semel, 1990). Tomatis explained that "conceptual systems are organized in terms of categories . . . categorization is the main way we make sense of experience" (1969, p. 32).
- *Understanding, remembering, and correctly following directions* Problems with directions affect the quality of classwork, homework, test-taking, and interpersonal relationships (Wiig & Semel, 1990).
- *Accurate and fluent silent reading* Difficulty with silent reading has an impact on reading rate, memory, and comprehension (Levine, 1987; Maria, 1990; Orton, 1937; Wiig & Semel, 1990).
- *Accurate and adequate comprehension of text* Comprehension problems affect performance in all academic subjects (Maria, 1990).
- *Writing skills—legible and fluent handwriting, accurate spelling, note-taking, cohesion, syntax, expository or discursive writing, and mechanics* Difficulty with writing skills affects lecture notes, written assignments, and test-taking.
- *Orientation in space and time—directional sense, ability to tell time, and sense of duration of time* Difficulty with orientation in space and time affects a student's ability to estimate lapsed time (duration), such as time remaining on a test, and time needed to accomplish tasks (time projection); punctuality; planning; assignments; and interpersonal relationships.
- ***Figure–ground perception****—discrimination of figure from ground, discrimination of relevant from irrelevant stimuli, pattern recognition* Difficulties with figure and ground have pervasive effects on perception, attention, and recognition of saliency, and can cause perseveration and difficulty with closure (Goldstein, 1939). (For the best simulated experience of these difficulties, see *Magic Eye 3D Illusions*, Hyperion, 1993, and *Magic Eye 3D Optical Illusion Cards*, Hyperion, 1995, which offer the perfect way to understand the frustration and confusion of the student who cannot see the forest for the trees.)
- *Integration (related to figure–ground discrimination)*—*recognizing and understanding whole–part relationships and the ability to deconstruct wholes into parts and to reconstruct wholes from constituent parts* Difficulties with integration have a pervasive impact on handwriting, reading, subtraction and division, outlining and summarizing, and comprehension of complex subject matter, such as science or economics (Cruickshank, 1967; Tomatis, 1969).
- *Organization (perceiving and effecting structure in space and time and discriminating essential components of structure), hierarchical relationships, and logical sequences* Organizational difficulties affect a student's ability to plan and function efficiently, including planning of time, materials, and work (McNeil, 1992).

- *Simultaneous intersensory integration of verbal symbolic data with motor output (visual, auditory, kinesthetic, and tactile [VAKT] motor output)*   Difficulties with integrating verbal symbolic data and motor output have an impact on attention, memory, spelling, note-taking, and handwriting (Orton, 1937).
- *Stimulus-free behavior*—*freedom from concrete thinking, from the tangible, the "here and now"*   Concrete thinking results in difficulty with temporal and spatial terms (e.g., *the day before yesterday, every other one, beside, among*) and with understanding idioms, metaphors, proverbs, and other nonliteral and abstract language (Cruikshank, 1967; Wiig & Semel, 1990).
- *Ability to shift the frame of reference,* *such as making transitions, starting, stopping, and changing a routine or procedure*   Trouble with shifting the frame of reference results in rigidity; perseveration; inability to assimilate multiple word meanings, such as *post the mail* and *post the notice;* and other difficulties (Cruikshank, 1967; Wiig & Semel, 1990).
- *Ability to take risks*   Avoidance of risk can result in nonparticipation in class discussions and can affect selection of easier courses over harder but more appropriate courses, of less challenging jobs, of less competitive schools, and of friends (Deshler et al., 1996; Levine, 1987).

WORKING WITH DYSLEXIC STUDENTS

Students who have experienced continual failure inevitably have low self-esteem. It is difficult to restore self-esteem once it has been eroded, even in achieving adults. For example, Nobel Laureate and professor Seymour Martin Lipset (1986) referred to himself as the man whose wife had to write his thank-you notes. Prevention of failure is the strongest argument for aggressive intervention in the earliest school years. In 1984, de Hirsch stated that the teacher of a student with language deficits sometimes must function as the student's ego until the student begins to experience success and a renewal of hope and self-confidence. Cruikshank held that a student with a learning disability "needs every stable external support possible to assist him in developing a strong ego" (1967, p. 9). To do this, the instructor must assume the role of coach, mentor, personal cheerleader, and unflagging optimist. His or her faith in the student's ability to overcome his or her learning difficulties must be unshakable. To win the student, the instructor must continually communicate honest respect and a positive regard and forego all negative feedback, criticism, ad hominem comments, and punitive action. Tonjes and Zintz (1981) stated that teachers must make learning a process of communication, hope, and trust for dyslexic students. The instructor must not voice the kinds of questions put to dyslexic students so frequently: "What's the matter with you?" "Don't you care?" "Why don't you do your work?" "When are you going to wake up?" and the like.

The study skills instructor should have unflagging patience, a sense of humor, a high energy level, flexibility, a wide repertoire of strategies and varied applications, and total commitment to the success of each student. He or she also must be willing and able to work collaboratively with other teachers. All of these qualities together will be of no avail, however, unless the instructor has a thorough command of the subject and a thorough knowledge of each student; unless he or she can teach in ways so that the student can learn; and, most important, unless there is tangible payoff for the student in the form of better grades in his or her other subject classes and an easing of tensions with teachers and parents. Thus, the study skills instructor must be extremely well-organized, structured, and overly prepared, both in general and for every session. He or she is "a manager, an instructional leader, and a mediator of learning who demonstrates how to think about a task, apply strategies, and problem-solve in novel situations" (Deshler et al., 1996, pp. 463–464). The study skills instructor should also honor Torgesen's Law: "Know your stuff. Know who you are stuffing. Stuff them every chance you get" (personal communication, 1998).

The rewards for the committed instructor are great. There can be no deeper satisfaction than helping a discouraged and failing student to become an enthusiastic and successful learner, and there is no greater reward than to be the vehicle for the student's journey from hopelessness to confidence.

In the general experience of special teachers and academic coaches, the odds are strongly against the teacher's success in getting the dyslexic student to use learning strategies and study skills consistently and effectively in subject classes. Obstacles come from persisting skills deficits in areas such as accurate and rapid decoding, handwriting, and spelling; from lack of adequate teaching time; from lack of coordination with other teachers who have different expectations and demands; from lack of sufficient time for practice in transferring and applying the techniques; and from the resulting student resistance to using the techniques in other classes.

The student, classroom teachers, and parents must understand the goals for study skills training and the strategies used. Everyone must agree in advance to the ground rules. Everyone needs to understand that it takes much time to establish effective study skills. Deshler and colleagues suggested that "the full benefits of effective programming . . . are realized only . . . over a period of years" (1996, p. iii). The reward for patience is that once the student has learned effective study skills, his or her performance in every area will be significantly improved, and he or she will have the skills for life. The instructor plays the role of an expert guide who coaches students to successfully acquire and use learning strategies and study skills by providing instruction, adequate practice, and supervision. A good metaphor for this role is that of the personal trainer; the job of personal trainer involves the same levels of personal interaction and commitment as does the job of study skills instructor. To avoid misunderstandings and negative fallout for the student, everyone, including the student, must understand that the strategies and techniques are *unconventional.*

Everyone involved should understand that the training is designed to teach strategies and skills that can be used for every subject and that the instructor's role is not that of a homework aide. Aspects of assignments in other classes can serve as a vehicle for applying a technique such as mnemonics, but helping students to complete those assignments or memorize information for tests is not a legitimate function of the study skills teacher. For best results, other teachers should work closely with the study skills instructor to reinforce certain skills by requiring, cuing, and monitoring the student's use of the techniques and strategies outside study skills classes, especially with regard to use of the notebook, spelling, vocabulary development, note-taking, mnemonics, and handling assignments. Students must understand that study skills training is a cooperative effort toward a common goal. In this relationship the student and the instructor are partners, although it is understood that the instructor has the expertise and the ability to help the student acquire skills—more important, to acquire the necessary *self-discipline* to use the skills consistently. It is essential to the success of the training that the student set his or her own priorities for the use of time and for the desired outcomes. The student does not need to work for an A in every subject. It is sufficient for the student to bring to the training sessions his or her perennial September optimism and to be willing to give the new teacher and the new strategies a fair trial.

Catch Them While You Can

From late spring to early fall, the adolescent dyslexic is a "pie-eyed" optimist. No matter how many past years have ended in disaster, he or she always has the expectation that with the new year, new teachers, and/or a new school, all of his or her academic problems will disappear. It takes only 6 weeks in the fall, from the start of school to the end of the first marking period, for the student to resign him- or herself to another year of frustration, misery, and resentment. Dr. Helen Hall was expert in turning around the failing adolescent. "If you are going to catch them," she said, "you have 6 weeks to do it" (personal communication, 1977). The dyslexic student must quickly come to believe that something *is* changing for the better this time. Students, teachers, and parents need to know that it really is possible for dyslexic students to get As and Bs and good SAT scores. This is the rationale for the Quick Tricks, described later in this chapter, which are the first set of strategies taught.

Structured Procedures

The importance of a high degree of structure when working with dyslexic students cannot be overemphasized. Strichart and Mangrum (1993) explained that students with learning disabilities typically experience disorganization. Thus, they may have trouble perceiving and using information as it is structured in their texts and may have trouble creating structure in their own work. However hampered by personal inclination, ability, or professional training, study skills instructors must impose and require maximum structure daily in all aspects of the work (Cruickshank, 1967). This is done through the use of structured procedures for acquiring skills and applying techniques, from time management to summarizing, from proofreading to outlining. "Structured teaching . . . unites the teacher and student in a learning partnership by providing informed, explicit, and *interactive* instruction" (Deshler et al., 1996, p. 459). It is often overwhelming to a student, even threatening, to have to function in an unstructured environment (Cruikshank, 1967). This can be seen in the difficulties experienced in the transition to the first year of high school or college.

Materials: A Fatal Attraction

During the first study skills session, the student receives the basic equipment, a set of *two* 3-ring binders equipped as described in the following section. One is the student's *only* notebook for other subjects; it is critical to the student's success in all other classes (Williams, 1984). Use of a single binder for all school subjects will require the prior agreement of other teachers. The second is the study skills notebook, which is organized for the student *in advance*. It is designed to be a continually expanding resource book that accompanies the student throughout secondary school and college. For the period of training, the study skills notebook always remains in the possession of the instructor; the student does not take it home or to other classes. Using the study skills notebook as a model, the student sets up the general subject notebook *with the guidance of the study skills instructor* at the start of the academic year.

If another teacher insists on the use of a spiral notebook, it should be thin, perforated so that pages can be removed cleanly, and hole-punched so that it can be bound into the appropriate section of the general subject notebook and replaced as needed. The study skills instructor, however, should exert every effort to discourage the use of spiral notebooks because using "a sturdy, well constructed three-ring binder as a central organizing system for students will eliminate most problems caused by fragmentation" (Williams, 1984, p. 12).

Most students are intrigued and delighted when presented with their ring-binders, more so if the binder is colorful. The binder cover should be plain, with no design or printing. A *large* label reading *STUDY SKILLS* should be affixed to the spine or the cover. One of the first tasks for the teacher is to model and to have the student practice opening and closing the rings of the binder by using the levers at either end, not the rings, to avoid breakage. The student's name, address, and telephone number should be displayed prominently on a label affixed to the notebook with strong glue.

Fittings for the Binders   Both binders should be equipped with the following:

- A large ($8\frac{1}{2}$" $\times$ 11") three-hole punched plastic zipper case containing two pens and two sharpened pencils; a set of colored felt-tip pens; a small, flat pencil sharpener; an art gum eraser; a few rubber bands and paper clips; a small pad of yellow sticky notes; three or four *very* roughly textured, flat, double-fold paper towels (the sort found in gas stations); and four sets of 3" $\times$ 5" index cards in different colors (about six cards in each color). The zipper case is inserted in the front of the binder.
- Two sturdy double-pocket dividers, one placed after the zipper case and one placed just inside the back cover
- Self-tabbed colored or color-coded dividers, of heavy stock (Tabs should be extensions of the stock itself, not insertable plastic holders. Dividers and subdividers should be labeled in pencil or *erasable* pen; color coordination is a plus.)
- Self-tabbed white or cream subdividers, of lighter stock
- Flat hole-punch, clipped into the *middle* of the ring-binder (to prevent breakage)
- *Transparent* plastic sheet protector, $8\frac{1}{2}$" $\times$ 11", inserted in the binder after the first double-pocket divider. A 12-month calendar is inserted on one side; the school calendar is inserted on the other side
- A supply of *wide-ruled* loose-leaf paper inserted in the binder in front of the second double-pocket divider

In addition to the general subject notebook and its fittings, students should carry in their backpacks a good pocket dictionary. The most recent paperback edition of

Webster's New World Dictionary is recommended. If possible, secondary school students, who must write extensively, should carry with them *Roget's Thesaurus* (1992; a paperback edition is available).

Table of Contents The Table of Contents page (see Figure 13.1) is placed in the study skills notebook after the front pocket divider. Instructors may wish to defer insertion of the subdividers until they are needed.

The general subject notebook is equipped in the same way as the study skills notebook. In the general subject notebook, the student's class schedule is inserted in the front side of the plastic sheet protector. The annual calendar may be taped to the inside front of the binder. The Table of Contents is organized *at the discretion of the student,* alphabetically by subject or however he or she deems most useful. (The instructor may have to revise this order with the student later, should it prove unworkable.) Titles for subdividers in each section are added at the discretion of the subject teacher or may be devised by the study skills instructor and the student.

The student should file all papers and handouts from other classes in the pocket of the back cover of the binder, then file them in the appropriate section of the notebook as soon as possible on the same day, preferably before the student leaves the building. The final study skills session of each week should be devoted to checking and organizing the general subject notebook.

ORGANIZATION, TIME MANAGEMENT, AND SELF-MONITORING

Structure is the first and most imperative need of the dyslexic student. Through structure, the student is enabled to manage him- or herself and his or her work and world. No other aspect of study skills training is more fundamental or more critical to success than training in being systematic; organizing time, space, materials, and equipment; and using structured procedures to perform these tasks. This organization is essential because the dyslexic student needs additional time and far greater efficiency to achieve mastery. It is also essential to reduce the free-floating anxiety and sense of general confusion that typically impair memory and impede progress.

Teacher tardiness, inadequate teacher preparation, forgotten instructional materials, or "winging" the design and content of the teaching session are practices that send a powerful message to the student: Don't do as I say, do as I do. The instructor who must struggle to achieve and maintain organized performance will have more empathy with the student—a plus—but will need to exercise greater vigilance to maintain standards.

Time Management

The student is first introduced to structure through the organization and maintenance of the notebooks. Next, the student must begin to learn how to organize and monitor his or her time. The notebooks contain a set of coordinated calendars, schedules, and worksheets that the student consults monthly, weekly, and daily. They include the following:

- Annual calendar
- School calendar

I   Time Management
    Monthly Calendar
    Weekly Schedule
    60-Day Calendar [for high school and college students]
    Self-Monitoring Form
    Notes

II   Quick Tricks
    Level One
    Level Two
    Level Three

III   Memory—Spelling
    Mechanical (Kinesthetic)
    Syllable Spelling
    Spelling Patterns
    Etymological Spelling

IV   **SkORE** for Mastery of Subject Content
    Preparing the Text
    Cue Cards
    Mapping (Webbing)
    Abstracting
    Note Taking
    Note Taking from Lectures
    Outlining and Summarizing
    Précis Writing
    Note Taking on Fiction

V   Memory—General
    Mnemonics
    Graphics
    Cartoons
    Use of White Space, Borders, Color

VI   Vocabulary
    14 Master Words
    Lexicons by Geometric Progression
    Nonliteral Language

VII   Syntax
    Sentence Patterns
    Paragraph Development

IX   Test-Taking
    Preparation
    General
    Specifics
    Semantics

Figure 13.1. Study skills notebook Table of Contents page.

- Monthly calendar (for high school and college students, a 60-day calendar), kept in the Time Management section of the study skills notebook *and* in a sheet protector in the general notebook
- Weekly schedule sheet
- Daily schedule sheet
- Daily assignment sheet(s)

The study skills instructor should keep a supply of blank weekly and daily schedules and daily assignment sheets.

Step One: Monthly Calendar   On a blank monthly calendar form, the student fills in any holidays, school holidays, school half-days, and special events in the proper spaces. Then, standing commitments are filled in, such as daily classes, soccer practice, scheduled meetings or appointments, music or other lessons, volunteer work, regular time spent with parents or other relatives, and so forth. After that, nonroutine commitments are filled in, such as dental and medical appointments, trips away, soccer games, and so forth. Finally, deadlines for long-range assignments are written in. Each entry is filled in according to the time of day of the event; for example, an afternoon commitment is posted in the middle of the square for that date. For the first several months, this task should be done under the guidance of the study skills instructor. Later, the instructor should monitor this when checking the notebook.

Step Two: Weekly Calendar   Using the monthly calendar as a reference, the student blocks out (literally, colors in) the time needed for each commitment listed for the week. For example, if Saturday morning is committed to a soccer game, then the time from waking up to returning home is colored in. The student should also record deadlines for long-range assignments due that week. Finally, the student should write in the appropriate space all quizzes, tests, or other assignments due. It is advisable to set up calendars for 2 weeks at a time. *The white space remaining is the time available to the student to work on all short- and long-term assignments and to study.*

To complete Step Two, the student must next estimate *and schedule in* the time needed for completing assignments, for studying for quizzes and tests, and for working on long-range assignments. Dyslexic students may lack adequate "time sense" to plan and schedule realistically, or they may have only a global, vague notion of what is really required to accomplish the task (Williams, 1984). *Students invariably underestimate the time needed.* The instructor must work with the student to break down every task into its smallest steps and to estimate the time needed for each. For example, the steps and time needed to complete an assignment for a book report might be as follows:

- Visit the school or public library   30 minutes
- Select the book   20 minutes
- Preview (scan, skim) the book   20 minutes
- Read the book (can be read in several sittings)   3 hours
- Outline (brainstorm) the report   15 minutes
- Complete the first draft   60 minutes
- Proofread and correct the draft   20 minutes
- Consult with a teacher or other adult   15 minutes
- Write or type the revised draft   30 minutes
- Proofread and correct the revised draft   15 minutes

- Hand in the assignment *on time*
  Total time needed: 6 hours, 45 minutes

This 6¾ hours must now be scheduled across the week, with each task noted specifically and the estimated time blocked out on the weekly calendar. The student must follow this procedure for every assignment.

Long-range assignments require special attention. Working with the instructor, the student should break the assignment into manageable tasks, similar to the plan just mentioned. The student should build in extra time in case of illness, unexpected events, or difficulty with the assignment. The subject teacher should be involved or consulted during the scheduling of long-range assignments and should sign off on the schedule. The study skills instructor has a special obligation to see that the student actually does the scheduled work and that the work is appropriate and acceptable (up to the teacher's standards). It helps for the student to have a separate worksheet for each long-range project on which the student can check off completed components.

Step Three: Daily Schedule Sheet   At the end of each week, the student should fill out daily schedule sheets for each day of the following week, beginning with morning time at home and listing in chronological order every class, appointment, and task for the day and evening. For every class for which homework is due, the student should place an asterisk in red ink before the subject. A double asterisk is used to indicate a quiz or weekly test. A circled double asterisk can be used to indicate a major test or exam. Figure 13.2 shows a sample daily schedule sheet. The instructor has the responsibility to help the student understand that he or she must spend more time on assignments than other students to achieve similar grades.

Step Four: Self-Monitoring Time Use   In the last session of each week, the instructor should review with the student his or her use of time and skill in scheduling by comparing time actually spent completing tasks with the estimated time. The schedule for the following week should be planned, including times for submitting first drafts to classroom teachers for review and approval before rewriting. *The use of schedules and self-monitoring are the first steps to enabling the student to develop a more objective view of him- or herself as a learner.*

A useful self-monitoring strategy is the maintenance of a monthly record sheet to track time spent on assignments and time spent preparing for each class in relation to the grades received in that class. Such a record sheet might look like the one shown in Figure 13.3. A version of such a record sheet might also include the number of assignments completed *and handed in* for each subject; the number not completed or not handed in, or both; the grades for each; and the grades for quizzes and tests. A column might be included that rates the student's relationship with the subject teacher, say on a scale of 0 to 2 (2, *good*; 1, *fair*; 0, *poor*).

Although it is very difficult for teachers to accept, the reality is that many dyslexic students truly do not understand the connection between their (academic) behavior and their grades. It is not unusual for the first review of such a record to be an *"aha"* experience for a student.

Organizing Space

The study skills instructor must work with the student to organize three areas: the locker, the book bag or backpack, and the home study area.

Wednesday, September 30   **RETURN LIBRARY BOOKS**

  7:00   Review notes for math test
  7:15   Leave. Take LIBRARY BOOKS
  7:30   Spanish
  8:40   *Social Studies
  9:30   Math
 10:20   Free. RETURN LIBRARY BOOKS. Work on math
 11:30   Lunch—Sit with Guy; discuss science project
 12:00   *Science
 12:50   Phys. Ed. SEE MR. HASKINS ABOUT EQUIPMENT ROOM
  1:45   **English—Make appointment with Mrs. G to go over book report draft
  2:45   Meet Reshad to get math book
  3:00   Soccer practice
  5:30   Nap
  6:00   Dinner
  6:45   Science project—Work with Guy, my house
  8:15   Read novel for book report, due 10/5, Chaps 6, 7 (30 pages; 67 to go)
  9:00   Spanish assignment
  9:20   Math assignment
  9:45   Pack backpack, check off assignments

Figure 13.2.   Sample daily schedule sheet. An asterisk indicates that homework is due; double asterisks indicate a quiz.

Space in the Locker   The student's locker should be structured in an orderly way, with assigned places for books, clothing, a gym bag, and other belongings. Books may be stored with reference to A.M. and P.M. classes or according to the exact order of classes during the day. The locker should be inspected weekly until the structure is set; it should be cleaned out no less than once a month. For fuller details, see Williams (1984).

Space in the Book Bag or Backpack   The student's book bag or backpack should be even more organized, with a section for the general subject binder, texts, and other books, including a pocket dictionary and thesaurus. The student should never be permitted to keep loose papers in the book bag or backpack.

Space at Home   Organizing the student's study space at home presents a challenge for the instructor as it is difficult to influence. Three aspects must be addressed: 1) location and environment, 2) furniture and equipment, and 3) materials and supplies. The cooperation of the student and parents is essential.

Location and Environment   Ideally, schoolwork should be done in the same place at the same time each night, or, if a fixed time is not possible, on a flexible schedule (e.g., Monday, 7:00–9:30 P.M.; Tuesday, 5:30–8:30 P.M.). The study area may be anywhere so long as it is free from noise and other distractions. Despite students' protests to the contrary, music is a distraction; studies show that students alternate between listening and studying, thereby lengthening the time needed to do their work, interrupting concentration, and interfering with memory storage. The study location should facilitate the orderly and permanent storage of books and materials needed within arm's reach, on convenient over-the-

Subject	Hrs spent preparing				Total hrs	Hrs to date	Grade
	Wk 1	Wk 2	Wk 3	Wk 4			
Social Studies	3	2	4	1	10	23	B-
Spanish	2	2	2.5	1	7.5	12.5	F
Math	4	5	4.5	7	20.5	36.5	A

Figure 13.3. Monthly record sheet for self-monitoring.

desk shelves or on adjacent wall shelves. Good lighting is very important to prevent eye fatigue and drowsiness.

Furniture and Equipment   The student should work at a desk or a well-lighted, proportionately sized work table, in a sturdy chair designed for comfortable *upright* posture. The chair should support the back. A low footstool can relieve back strain. To prevent fatigue, the table should be neither too high nor too low; the student's arms, when bent at right angles, should just rest on the surface of the desk. Ideally, equipment should include a clock; a typewriter or a computer with a printer; a filing drawer or cabinet; an electric pencil sharpener; a stapler; and, if the student makes audiotapes of class lectures, a good-quality audiotape player. Every student should have training in keyboarding.

Materials and Supplies   Desk reference books should include the following:

- A good collegiate dictionary, such as the most recent edition of *Merriam Webster's Collegiate Dictionary*
- *Roget's Thesaurus* (or a dictionary and thesaurus together in a single volume, such as *The Oxford Dictionary and Thesaurus*, 1996)
- An etymological dictionary (for secondary and college students, *The Oxford Dictionary of English Etymology*, 1983)
- A handbook of essential English idioms, such as Makkai, Boatner, and Gates's (1995) *A Dictionary of American Idioms*
- Dictionaries of literary and historical allusions, such as *Brewer's Dictionary of Phrase and Fable* (Evans, 1981)
- A reference book of English composition and grammar, such as Warriner (1988)
- A handbook on English usage, such as Fowler (1983) or Partridge (1966)
- General reference books, such as *The New York Public Library Desk Reference* (Gold, 1993)
- *Optional:* computer manuals, world atlas, books of historical time lines

Materials should include the following: at least two packages of *wide-ruled,* hole-punched loose-leaf paper; 8½" × 11", 8½" × 14", and 11" × 17" unlined paper; graph paper; pencils; pens; colored felt-tip pens; paper clips; spring clips; cellophane tape; sticky notes; tape flags; scissors; 6" and 12" rulers; 100-card packs of white and colored index cards—at least three colors; rubber bands and "scratch paper." Materials should be checked and replenished at fixed times—weekly or biweekly.

The most effective way to dramatize the attractiveness and utility of this approach is for the instructor to set up his or her desk and maintain it in an orderly manner according to these suggestions.

QUICK TRICKS: STRATEGIES FOR CHANGING THE STUDY CLIMATE

As soon as possible, preferably at the first session, the student is coached to use Quick Tricks strategies. These are presented to students as strategies that can change teachers' attitudes and grading habits to the student's advantage—which, in fact, is true. (Some students will need to be cautioned about disclosing this to the subject teachers. The study skills instructor should take care to speak positively about other teachers at all times.) Although they may seem simplistic, Quick Tricks almost always result in perceptible changes for the better, which students themselves report with obvious satisfaction. The intent is to begin the process of moving the student into a more conscious, proactive, and responsible mode of behavior in other classrooms, especially to bring him or her into better relationships with other teachers, thereby gradually reducing whatever tensions may exist. The student should have opportunities to role-play the Quick Tricks with the study skills instructor before trying them in subject classes.

With the right "sell" by the study skills instructor—enthusiasm mixed with confident assurances—the Quick Tricks get results in a short time. Invariably, after a few weeks a student will come in and say incredulously, for example, "Guess what! My science teacher smiled at me today!" Around the same time, another student will report a better grade than ever before in one class. It is not unusual for a student to shout gleefully when reporting these gains. Teachers do notice and usually make positive comments to the student, increasing the student's motivation to use the Quick Tricks more often. Also, because they perceive the student as making more effort and displaying a better attitude, teachers sometimes comment positively to parents, thus helping to defuse tensions at home. Teachers may even respond by giving a slightly better grade to reward the behavior, thereby further reinforcing in the student's eyes the effectiveness of the Quick Tricks. Students assume that the teacher's behavior has changed. At this point, however, students are not apt to make the connection that the change is in their own behavior, and the study skills instructor must forego any comments to that effect or risk aborting the process.

Quick Tricks are presented to the student in three sets; each set requires slightly more investment (and risk taking) than the one before it. The student may be given the handouts for the first two sets at the same time, but only the first set should be undertaken until the student is comfortably into the routine. Then the second set of Quick Tricks is put into practice, *while the student continues to use the first,* and so forth.

Level One

The instructor should take pains to inform the student that the first set of Quick Tricks requires no extra time and a minimum of effort.

1. Look directly at the teacher when he or she is speaking. If making eye contact is uncomfortable, then look at the teacher's forehead, ear, tip of the nose, or chin. The teacher cannot detect the difference.
2. Use the teacher's name at least once a day.
3. At least once in every class session, ask a question or make a comment. It can be as simple as asking the teacher to repeat a definition or repeating what has been said to get confirmation that you heard it correctly.

4. Arrive to class on time. Better yet, arrive 1–2 minutes before the bell.
5. Leave only after the bell has rung. Pack up *after* the bell has started to ring but only if the teacher has finished speaking. Never slam a book shut, slam it on the desk, or slam the seat up.
6. Say, "Thank you," at least once a week as you leave (can be combined with Quick Trick #2 or #3).

Level Two

The second set of Quick Tricks requires no more time or work and only a little more efforts but has a bigger payoff than the first group. When asked for proof, the study skills instructor should say only, "You will see that I am right."

1. Always hand in assignments on time, no matter what you think of them and whether or not you have completed them. Ask the teacher to give you the opportunity to complete the assignment later that day, *even if it has already been graded*.
2. Always use the heading and format the teacher has requested. (Ideally there is a uniform heading for the whole school.) Be sure that every paper is dated.
3. Draw only *one* line through an error (two at most). Never erase or cross out.
4. Ask the teacher to explain anything you do not understand and to use different words and different examples than he or she used the first time.
5. Type or have someone else type your papers and reports.
6. Proofread your work, looking for only one kind of error at a time—check capitalization (at beginning of sentence), return to the start, then check ending punctuation, and so forth (discussed later in this chapter). Use your index finger to **track** while proofreading.

Level Three

For the last group of Quick Tricks, the instructor must explain that although it requires a little extra time, it saves time in the long run. Similarly, a little more effort is required, but using these Quick Tricks saves much greater effort later on. As with the first two sets of Quick Tricks, no more knowledge or academic work is required.

1. Go to the teacher after class for help with anything you still do not understand.
2. Ask a different teacher for help if the first teacher does not explain satisfactorily.
3. Ask a counselor or a school librarian for help if that does not work.
4. Trade with a classmate who is good in the subject. For his or her help, you can trade your help in fixing a bike, playing chess, learning to use the Internet, or playing the guitar.
5. Ask the librarian at the public library for help. Reference librarians are especially glad to be helpful.
6. Don't give up. *Keep asking* until you get the help you need.

Advanced Quick Tricks

The presentation of the study skills notebook, the organization of the general notebook, and discussion of the Quick Tricks will take the first two or three sessions, but this is time that is well invested. The novelty and the pristine condition of the notebook are attractive to the student, but the greater attraction is in its explicit order and structure, an attraction that is so strong as to be irresistible to almost every student (including adults). This is the rationale for presenting the study skills binder to the student fully indexed, organized, and equipped. Instruction must result in optimal learning with a minimum of effort by both the teacher and the student.

With this beginning, the instructor has earned the student's attention and a dawning respect for the instructor's savvy. To capitalize on initial gains, the instructor must move the student beyond Quick Tricks to the next set of strategies and techniques. New gains must be more tangible and must come quickly. If not, earlier gains will be lost, the student will revert to old ways, and it will be difficult to regain his or her attention. Although still preliminary to actual studies skills training, the next step is important because the strategies and techniques can soon result in better grades. As Askov and Kamm explained, "Early success can have a very positive effect on students' attitudes about learning" (1982, p. 3).

This second phase of strategies and techniques involves training in the following, which can be presented as advanced Quick Tricks:

- Structured procedures for completing assignments
- Emergency techniques for handling long reading assignments
- Structured procedures to reduce spelling errors
- Structured procedures to reduce errors in mechanics
- Spelling by geometric progression

Structured Procedures for Completing Assignments   Homework assignments represent one of the most frustrating, contentious, and divisive issues for everyone concerned: teachers, parents, and especially dyslexic students. The impact on family life can be dramatic and severe. Students who do well during class and on tests nevertheless may receive a failing grade in a course because of missing homework assignments.

As part of the Quick Tricks, students have been encouraged to hand in assignments on time (no easy task for dyslexic students) even if they have not completed the assignments, and they have been encouraged to ask for the opportunity to complete them later. As soon as possible, the instructor must train the student to complete assignments *before* handing them in; this is done by providing training in structured procedures for time management, for managing the papers involved, and for self-monitoring and tracking.

Techniques for handling assignments are part of the structured procedures (steps performed in fixed, graded sequences) for using the notebook. It is vital that the student observe these procedures. No deviation is to be permitted. The student follows the same procedures in every subject class.

1. All handouts or worksheets regarding assignments are filed in the front side of the pocket divider inside the front cover of the general subject binder. This ensures that the student can locate them easily after class. This pocket is labeled *ASSIGNMENTS*.
2. All assignments that have been worked on but not completed are filed in the reverse side of the same pocket divider. This side is labeled *WORK IN PROGRESS*.

3. Completed assignments are filed in the reverse side of the pocket divider inside the back cover of the notebook so that they are easy to locate when completed and ready to be handed in. This side of the pocket divider should be labeled *COMPLETED ASSIGNMENTS*.
4. Papers that have been graded and returned to the student are filed in the *front* side of the pocket divider at the back of the notebook. The label is *CONSULTATION*.

The student must take any paper with errors to the teacher at the first opportunity to discuss the errors and to ask for the opportunity to correct them for a better grade. *This practice is extremely important to ensure a continual improvement in grades.* It also furthers improved student–teacher and parent–child relationships. It motivates the subject teacher to go the extra mile to give the student the assistance that he or she needs. Most important, it is another step in developing the student's ability to assess his or her own learning style, characteristic error patterns, strengths, and deficits. Asking for the chance to discuss and correct errors continues the student's process of self-monitoring and self-evaluation.

Papers with no errors or omissions are clipped to the inside front cover of the general subject binder with a large spring clip and filed in the appropriate subject section as soon as possible. For middle school and secondary students, the instructor should work out with subject teachers a consistent system for recording assignments. If this is a problem, then the student should not be permitted to leave the room before the subject teacher has checked to see that the student has recorded the assignment accurately. Assignments may be recorded on a specially designed form that can be filed in the front side of the pocket divider in the front of the general subject binder atop the day's worksheets or may be recorded on a sheet of notepaper placed at the beginning of each subject section in the binder. Small assignment pads are undesirable as they are easily misplaced and lost (Williams, 1984); if used, they should be kept in the plastic zipper case in the binder. Younger students should have a single form for listing all daily assignments.

Dyslexic students often have difficulty remembering to bring home the books and materials that they need to do their assignments. They also have difficulty remembering to bring the books and the completed assignments back to school. When this is the case, the study skills teacher, student, subject teacher, and parent must work out a cooperative plan and a structured routine whereby the student's book bag can be checked before he or she leaves home and before he or she leaves school. A form should be designed and a careful record should be kept of the student's ability to come to school and go home prepared. It is best if the student and a parent organize and pack the book bag the night before, using a checklist to make sure that nothing has been forgotten. If all else fails, the only solution is to arrange for the student to be issued two sets of textbooks, one for home and one for school.

Emergency Techniques for Handling Long Reading Assignments   No prospect is more daunting or frustrating for a dyslexic student than an assignment to read and remember information from a long passage or text, such as chapters in a social studies or history textbook. Too often the student puts off this task until the last minute, when he or she usually has too little time and too little energy to do the job right; this procrastination can become an entrenched habit. The anxiety and distress generated by the fear of the consequences of this behavior compound the problem. While the student is being taught scheduling, he or she should learn emergency techniques to compensate when the reading has not been done and to deal with long reading assignments more effectively.

Before beginning, the student should "psych" him- or herself up to be as focused and attentive as possible and form an active *intention* to hold as much as possible in memory. Using a structured procedure, he or she should be coached to go through the text as follows.

First, he or she should complete these three steps at the same time:

1. Read the introduction, advance organizer (or first three paragraphs), and the summary and questions at the end of the chapter, if any.
2. Read the text headings and subheadings in order.
3. Read all uppercase, boldface, and italic type *in the order in which they appear* in the selection.

Next, the student should return to the beginning of the text and complete these steps:

4. Read the first and last sentence of every paragraph.
5. Read the captions under all graphics, and read any charts or tables.
6. Copy on 3″ × 5″ index cards all definitions set apart in the text. (If time permits, the student should read through or scan the text rapidly without stopping and discuss the highlights of the text with a friend before class.)

This strategy lays the groundwork for later techniques to master subject course content. When the strategy works, it has the advantage of increasing confidence in the instructor, bolstering the student's self-confidence, and renewing motivation.

Structured Procedures to Reduce Spelling Errors (Stage 1): VAKT Solutions
Misspellings account for the most frequent errors made by college freshmen (Deshler et al., 1996). When dyslexic students have poor memories for auditory or visual sequential patterns or both, spelling is "The Last Skill Acquired" (Tomkins, 1963, p. 127). In the initial stages of training, memory is facilitated by the work on organizing, scheduling, and managing time; by the daily attention to scheduling and the weekly evaluation sessions; by the organization of the notebooks; and by the introduction of structured procedures, for example, for proofreading (described later).

Systematic memory training begins with instruction in the use of structured procedures for improving spelling. Success with these techniques fosters confidence and a dawning awareness in the student that academic skills need not depend only on good ability to memorize. At this stage, training to correct spelling weaknesses is physical, relying principally on repetition and **kinesthetic memory**—which is the most enduring sense memory—but this spelling training does not involve memorizing or learning spelling rules. Structured procedures and multisensory techniques for *internalizing* orthographic (writing) patterns are employed, involving simultaneous seeing, saying, hearing, and writing or tracing (VAKT). (See Chapter 8 for more on spelling instruction.) Except when printing is specified, students should use cursive handwriting.[4] The techniques of copying, the cloze procedure, and tracing can be used simultaneously. Although the tech-

---

[4]Many students will need systematic instruction in cursive writing. Such systematic training is highly advantageous to dyslexic students and helps to reinforce left–right directionality, to simplify the writing task, and to prevent reversals and inversions. For more on handwriting instruction, see Chapter 9.

niques are mechanical and physical, requiring no knowledge of spelling rules, clinical experience shows that they result in rapid and significant improvement in spelling when used daily, and they eliminate at least 50% of the student's frequent spelling errors.

Copying On wide-ruled paper, the student writes (or is given) a model *in cursive writing* to copy. The teacher must check the student's model for accuracy before the student begins to copy. Copying should be done in a column *under* the model, with the letters aligned directly under each other, not across the line. The student copies the word directly under the word above, then carefully checks *letter by letter* by "fingerproofing" to be sure that the copy is identical to the model. To fingerproof, the student says the name of each letter aloud while touching the index fingers of each hand to the same letter in the model and the copied word. Only the student can determine how many times he or she must copy a word to retain it in long-term memory. About 7–10 copyings per practice session is usually effective. Copying for each word should be practiced over time—days or weeks.

If a student is unable to master the word with that many copyings, the cloze technique may be more effective. Some students are willing to practice spelling the word many more times on the computer; this must be monitored very closely so that the student does not practice errors.

Cloze Technique When a student uses the cloze technique, he or she again does the copying in a column, with the letters *printed* in the same space on each successive line as on the one above. First, the student *prints* the word in full. On the next line, the student omits the letter that he or she thinks will be easiest for him or her to recall. Next, the student omits that letter and one other that he or she can easily recall. An additional letter is omitted on each new line until only blanks remain. (Two letters forming a digraph, such as *sh*, may be omitted together.) Memory is strengthened if the student spells the word aloud as he or she creates each line.

```
p   r   i   n   t   e   d
_   r   i   n   t   e   d
_   r   i   n   _   e   d
_   r   i   n   _   e   _
_   _   i   n   _   e   _
_   _   i   _   _   e   _
_   _   _   _   _   e   _
_   _   _   _   _   _   _
```

Then the student covers all but the second line of writing. Beginning with the first letter, he or she says each one aloud in turn and writes the missing letter in the blank that was left for it, thereby spelling the word. Next, only the third line is exposed; the process is repeated until all of the lines have been exposed and all of the missing letters are correctly filled in. By the time the student reaches the last line, he or she usually can spell the entire word from memory. At each step, the student checks the newly finished line with the line above for accuracy by fingerproofing as described previously.

It is important for the student to maintain vigilant attention while practicing this technique. To achieve the best results, he or she must actively *intend* to attend closely to spelling aloud, to writing the letters, and to checking for accuracy. He or she must understand that being on automatic pilot will not do the trick. The cloze technique is extremely effective. Occasionally, however, a student may display great agitation if asked to use it. In that case, the student should not be forced, although the instructor might try gently to ease him or her into using it.

Tracing   Almost all dyslexic students will have to use tracing to learn the spellings of irregular words they cannot master by copying or by using the cloze technique, such as *their, llama, unique,* and *rough.* For this technique, the student will need a black felt-tip pen and double-fold coarse paper towels, the kind used in service stations—the rougher and scratchier the better. The student can work on three words in one class or session and later, five per session. No more than five words should be attempted during one session.

With the paper towel folded up and the open edge at the top:

1. The student (or teacher) writes the model in large, evenly spaced *cursive* letters, centered on the panel.
2. Using the fleshy ends of the index and middle fingers of the writing hand, the student traces the word three times without lifting the fingers, *naming each letter aloud as the fingers trace over it, and saying the word.*
3. The bottom edge of the towel is lifted, exposing the center panel (the top panel is now behind the rest of the towel). The student writes the word in cursive on the center panel while saying each letter aloud and compares it with the model on the top panel by fingerproofing.
4. If correct, the student folds up the bottom panel to cover the center panel and repeats Step 3, again saying each letter aloud and comparing with the model for accuracy.

If at any point the student makes an error, then he or she returns to Step 1. At each return, he or she must trace and spell the word aloud *three* times. Only two "retries" are permitted for each word. If there is still an error, then the word is put away until the next day. In this case, consideration should be given to whether the word is too advanced for the student at the time. If a student spells a word correctly 3 days in succession, the word may be put away and reviewed once a week for 3 weeks. If the student still makes no errors, he or she should review it monthly for 3 months for storage in long-term memory. After that, the word should be reviewed periodically with other similarly spelled words.

Structured Procedures to Reduce Spelling Errors (Stage Two)   When the VAKT spelling techniques just mentioned have been mastered and are used daily, the student can turn his or her attention to phonically regular words, words spelled exactly as they sound. Only two kinds of words can be spelled "by ear": words built on the closed syllable, or vowel-consonant (VC), pattern (*that, chant, swinging, impish, unintended*) and words built on the open syllable, or vowel (V), pattern (*be, no, spry*). The student must have mastered at least the basic sound–symbol correspondences of English. For example, the student must know the spellings for the most frequent consonant sounds and for the short and long sounds of the five vowels. The student who does not know these spellings should be given intensive instruction in a structured multisensory approach to phonics, such as an Orton-Gillingham–based approach (Gillingham & Stillman, 1997).[5] Students who have difficulty discriminating and spelling sounds should receive intensive short-term instruction in phonemic awareness by a method such as Auditory Discrimination in Depth (Lindamood & Lindamood, 1975), now renamed the Lindamood Phoneme Sequencing Program for Reading, Spelling, and Speech (LiPS; Lindamood & Lindamood, 1998); Slingerland (1971); or the Association Method (DuBard & Martin, 1994). (See Chapters 3 and 8.)

If the student has reasonable skill in spelling words with open and closed syllables by ear, he or she is taught the structured procedure called *Simultaneous Oral Spelling* (S.O.S.; Gillingham & Stillman, 1997): listen, echo, tap the sounds, spell the word aloud, then write the word on paper using cursive writing. Words of three, four, and more closed syllables can be spelled securely this way, such as *intended, extending, unextended.* Words combining the two patterns (VC, V) can be practiced, such as *open, remit, unit, events, unrepentant.* The S.O.S. technique has a very big payoff in improved decoding and contributes to greater accuracy, speed, and fluency in reading. Because the closed syllable is by far the most common syllable in English words, the impact of this bonus on reading is not to be underestimated.

Structured Proofreading to Reduce Errors in Mechanics The habit of proofreading written work must become automatic for the dyslexic student. Teachers regard the "carelessness" of mechanical errors as clear evidence of indifference at best and of low intellectual ability at worst. Spotting spelling errors is problematic for dyslexic students because of their difficulties with focusing and sustaining attention, figure–ground constancy, systematic scanning, rapid processing, and visual sequential memory. A structured procedure is the solution to the difficulty. At the outset, it is necessary to *preclude* the student from making a general survey of the written work and to train the student to check for only one specific kind of error at a time (Askov & Kamm, 1982).

Beginning with the first sentence and moving sentence by sentence to the end, the student should search systematically for one kind of error at a time:

1. Check capital letters at the start of each sentence *only;* return to the beginning.
2. Look at end punctuation; again, return to the beginning.
3. Proofread capitalization of proper nouns; go back again.
4. Look for sentence fragments and run-on sentences. Run-on sentences are found in the written work of 50% of freshman college students (Deshler et al., 1996). Fragments and run-on sentences are corrected by a four-step process— first, check for and eliminate every *and;* then immediately insert a period and change the first letter of the next word to a capital. Next, read each group of words *aloud* to determine whether it is a complete sentence. Restore the *and*'s and eliminate the capital and period where a group of words is correctly written as a phrase or clause.
5. Repeat this four-step procedure for every comma found.

---

[5]Orton-Gillingham–based approaches include Alphabetic Phonics (see Clark & Uhry, 1995), Hardman, Herman (n.d.), MTA (Smith & Hogan, 1991), Project Read (Enfield & Greene, n.d.), Reconstructive Language, Sequential English Education (Pickering, n.d.), Slingerland (1971), the Sonday System (1997), Spalding (1990), Starting Over (Knight, 1986), and the Wilson Reading System (n.d.), among others.

The student must practice proofreading daily until this procedure is firmly established and he or she is able to locate and correct the errors specified at mastery level (95%–100% accuracy) without cuing or prompting. Training to avoid run-on sentences is especially important.

Spelling by Geometric Progression   Dyslexic students are at a disadvantage whenever teachers expect them to derive information inferentially or indirectly. Many dyslexic students do not see what is obvious. Often, they do not perceive or translate verbal patterns to other, similar situations unless these patterns are highlighted, explicated, clearly delineated, and dramatized, such as by color coding. This is true even for the spelling of inflected forms of the same word. To bring orthographic patterns into sharp focus, the student should be given practice, first in extending, then in *creating*, related arrays such as the one shown in Figure 13.4. Students should not be asked to memorize the spellings; they should be guided to analyze the *patterns* of the affixes, many of which are spelled just as they sound. The roots, prefixes, and suffixes in the array should be coded with three different colors. Further gains in spelling (and reading speed and fluency) are made through the mastery of roots and affixes, especially those of the Fourteen Master Words: *detain, non-extended, insist, indisposed, oversufficient, intermittent, offer, precept, uncomplicated, aspect, reproduction, mistranscribe, monograph,* and *epilogue* (Brown, 1947).

MEMORY

With strategies and techniques in place for time management and organization, Quick Tricks, and advanced Quick Tricks for completing assignments, handling long reading assignments, improving spelling and vocabulary, and strengthening mechanics, the student is ready to begin to learn techniques for mastering subject content. The next focus in study skills instruction is on broader memory training.

Generally speaking, dyslexic students have problems with memory, have variable memory (memory that is alternately available and unavailable) or, in very serious cases, have virtually no memory for linguistic material (Deshler et al., 1996). Research has cited many contributing variables: lack of focus and attention, absence of intention, inability to sustain attention, lack of attention to detail, lack of filtering or screening mechanisms for irrelevant stimuli, problems with figure–ground perception, inability to organize and categorize, inadequate prior

Anglo-Saxon		Latin	
stand	**sew**	**friend**	**human**
stand s	**sew** s	**friend** s	**human** ness
stand ing	**sew** ed	**friend** ly	in **human** ness
un der **stand** ing	**sew** ing	**friend** ship	in **human** ity
un der **stand** ing s	**sew** er	be **friend**	**human** ize
mis un der **stand** ing	**sew** n	be **friend** ed	**human** iz ed
up **stand** ing	un **sew** n		**human** iz ing
out **stand** ing			

Figure 13.4.   Spelling by geometric progression.

knowledge, inability to visualize, anxiety, situational stress, attitude, expectation of failure, and others.

The study skills instructor should keep in mind that the dyslexic student's difficulties are based in the neurophysiology of the brain, with resulting differences or deficits in the brain systems for meaning, association, classification, storage, and recall of verbal information. But memory is inseparable from learning and is related to productivity, and "severe problems in memory equate to severe problems in school" (Brown, 1979). Therefore, dyslexic students must be taught techniques to internalize and remember information (i.e., *mnemonics*; from *mnemon*, Greek for *mindful*). In the process of developing mnemonics, the student works at forming associations that do not exist naturally in the content, a necessary condition for remembering (Trudeau, 1995). The use of mnemonics help students to change, store, and retrieve information in long-term memory by creating connections to otherwise unconnected data.

Mnemonic Devices

Most students are aware of the simple mnemonic devices: *acronyms*, which are names made up of the initial letters of the words, such as *HOMES* for the Great Lakes, and *acrostics*, which are groups of words that start with the initial letters of the words to be recalled, such as *Every Good Boy Does Fine* for the lines of the musical staff. Some other mnemonic devices include the following:

- *The key word strategy*, changing the unfamiliar word to a familiar word or words to serve as a cue for the meaning of new word (e.g., *aberrant*; cue words, *Abner ran crazy*)
- *The mnemonic sentence or story*, linking the words to be recalled in a narrative coherent sentence or story (e.g., a shopping list of bread, milk, party plates, and fabric softener dryer sheets: *Brad milked the company dry*)
- *Chunking*, separating the material into manageable sets (e.g., memorizing the alphabet as *abc, def, ghi . . .*)
- *Creating rhymes* (e.g., *Columbus sailed the ocean blue in fourteen hundred and ninety-two*)
- *Visualizing* (e.g., calling up a mental image of a cityscape)

(For mnemonic techniques, see the resources in Appendix B at the end of the book.)

For the dyslexic student, long-term memory storage is secured by use of the Skills for Organizing and Reading Efficiently (SkORE) procedures, especially the techniques for organizing material, elaborating, and deep processing; mapping (or webbing); summarizing; and writing précis. In all of these operations, the effect of the kinesthetic (motor) reinforcement is key.

The author has omitted a discussion of *schemata*, from *schema*—literally, information pickup—as a factor in learning and memory, for lack of space. The term refers to the student's prior experience and knowledge relevant to the new topic, insofar as it constitutes a frame of reference, factual and attitudinal, for the new information, creating links or structures through which the new information can be assimilated. For an excellent discussion of schemata, see Neisser (1976); see also Deshler et al. (1996), Maria (1990), and McNeil (1992).

STRUCTURED PROCEDURES FOR
MASTERING SUBJECT CONTENT: SkORE[6]

The key focus in secondary school classes is on *memorizing* information and demonstrating knowledge on tests that are graded to indicate relative mastery— or the lack of it. Most dyslexic students, however, have difficulty with learning by rote; they may also have difficulty retrieving information on demand, such as answering questions in class. In addition, students with learning disabilities have particular difficulty with semantic memory, that is, memory in the form of words that consists of interrelated information, theories, and generalizations (Deshler et al., 1996).

Dyslexic students are at a particular disadvantage when the text (or the teacher) is not well structured or well organized. This is especially true when they come to the subject with less background and information in the subject (usually the case) because they have read less and remember less than the other students. In addition, "organization plays an important role in memory and concentration" (Devine, 1981, p. 287).

Unless the student processes the information to be learned at a deep cognitive level, it is not stored in long-term, so-called permanent, memory. Dyslexic students, however, are rarely taught the techniques for deep processing that are effective for them (Deshler et al., 1996; Levine, 1987; Maria, 1990; McNeil, 1992) and often resort to rereading what they have read, which is not the best method for learning content (Deshler et al., 1996). The study skills instructor must offer dyslexic students quicker, more reliable, and more effective alternatives.

The SkORE strategies are an integrated system of multisensory, structured procedures that facilitate memory, comprehension, logical thinking and written expression. Whenever possible, work proceeds from the simple to the complex, from the concrete to the abstract, and from the specific to the general. Articulated and cumulative skills sequences are built systematically through explicit, direct instruction (especially for extracting meaning), modeling, demonstration, rehearsal, guided practice, systematic transfer, and application to other subjects. The 36-hour SkORE course has been called a CRAP course; the approach is cognitive, repetitive, active, and physical. SkORE techniques require deep cognitive processing by the student. The student is trained to use both analysis and synthesis as techniques for mastering subject content. The SkORE approach fits the definition of a *teaching device*, which helps

> To make abstract information more concrete, connect new knowledge with familiar knowledge, enable students who cannot spell well to take useful notes, highlight relationships and organizational structures within the information to be presented, and draw unmotivated learners' attention to the information (Deshler et al., 1996, p. 445)

SkORE is designed to produce noticeable differences in academic performance over the course of 1 school year. Students need at least 1 year to fully mas-

----
[6]SKORE is a study skills approach developed in the late 1970s at the TRI-Services Center for Children and Adults with Learning Disabilities, Rockville, Maryland. The author gratefully acknowledges the writings of S.T. Orton (1925, 1937), Gillingham and Stillman (1956), Cruikshank (1967), and Alley and Deshler (1979); and the modeling and direct training of TRI-Services Founder and Former Director Betty S. Levinson, Ph.D., and Alice A. Koontz, M.A., Jemicy School, Owings Mills, Maryland, as influential in the development of SkORE.

ter the strategies and techniques and to learn to apply them in subject classes. It should be noted that SkORE training can be started when students are in the third or fourth grade. The first two phases of SkORE training, which include preparation and organization of information, are critical to the dyslexic student's mastery of the material to be learned. The rationale for the first two phases is found in Deshler and colleagues' description of the characteristics of poor readers with memory problems. Such students

> Start reading without preparation . . . read without considering how to approach the task . . . are easily distracted . . . do not know they do not understand . . . do not know what to do when they lack understanding . . . do not recognize important vocabulary . . . do not see any organization . . . [and] add on rather than integrate information. (1996, p. 68)

In addition, the first two phases of SkORE help students with learning disabilities understand what, when, and how they need to study (Strichart & Mangrum, 1993; Wiig & Semel 1990; Williams, 1984).

Ellis and Colvert criticized instruction in which the student is left alone to make discoveries because such teaching is not usually efficacious among students who have learning disabilities. Research does not demonstrate the effectiveness of such methods but has shown the effectiveness of more explicit teaching strategies (Ellis & Colvert, 1996, as cited in Deshler, et al., 1996). Study skills instruction for dyslexic students is effective only when it is direct and explicit, with techniques continually demonstrated and modeled for the student.

SkORE strategies and techniques help dyslexic students compensate for their difficulties with attention, scanning, memory, vocabulary, reading comprehension, abstract and nonliteral language, association and categorization, outlining, comprehension, summarizing and paraphrasing, evaluative thinking, and selected social skills relating to interactions with teachers.

By design, SkORE requires the following of the student:

- Continuous, active involvement, mental and physical
- Continual consultation with subject teachers
- Continual self-questioning
- Repeated and varied manipulation of the material
- Elaboration and extension of the material
- Frequent use of reference books, especially dictionaries and *Roget's Thesaurus*
- Systematic extensions of the text vocabulary
- Systematic explication of abstract and nonliteral language
- Systematic explication and elaboration of important concepts
- Systematic use of mnemonic devices
- Routine conversion of verbal symbolic material to graphic displays
- Routine conversion of graphic material to verbal material, including paraphrasing
- Critical and evaluative thinking
- Frequent monitoring by both student and teacher, with teacher feedback
- Ongoing and periodic self-evaluation

There is little similarity between SkORE and Robinson's **SQ3R** (survey, question, read, recite, and review; 1946) technique, which rely primarily on reading, mental rehearsal, and rote memory—weak areas for most dyslexic students. The SkORE student is trained to deal with textual material in progressive sequences (note-taking from lectures is taught separately). The five sequences are

(Phase One)
- Preparing the text and setting up a skeleton web, or mindmap, and cue cards
- Selecting, noting, and organizing salient information and completing the map

(Phase Two)
- Generating graphic displays and mnemonics

(Phase Three)
- Extending text vocabulary
- Summarizing, making conventional outlines, and writing précis

The SkORE procedure is equally effective for whole-class, small-group, or one-to-one study skills instruction. In the case of whole-class or small-group instruction, the teacher simply models on the overhead projector what is to be done, and the class follows exactly what the teacher does. Guided practice is carried out in the same way.

Materials Needed

The following materials must be ready and available *before beginning:* assignment sheet and textbook(s) or worksheets, four sets of unlined index cards of different colors (e.g., white, yellow, gold, orange), a small manila envelope (6" × 3¼"), sharpened pencils, pens, a set of colored felt-tip pens, 11" × 17" and 8½" × 11" unlined white paper, an art gum eraser, a pack of wide-ruled loose-leaf paper, 6- and 12-inch rulers, dictionaries, and *Roget's Thesaurus.*

The Instructor's Role

The instructor must *demonstrate* SkORE procedures for the student, beginning with short samples of text and proceeding to longer, more complex text. When the student shows clear understanding of the process, the instructor and the student together work through several brief rehearsals to give the student a comfort level with the process. Then the instructor guides and supervises the student through independent exercises. Separate but concurrent instruction should be provided to train the student in the use of the dictionaries (see Chapter 4) and the thesaurus, and in the techniques for abstracting, note-taking, creating cue cards and mnemonics, mindmapping (webbing), and writing précis.

Phase One: Preparing the Text

The first phase of SkORE training is designed to train the student to familiarize him- or herself *in advance* with the information, the vocabulary, and the important concepts and to begin the process of organizing and structuring the material. Specific tasks involve 1) surveying and scanning the text; 2) setting up the basic framework of the mindmap; and 3) preparing rehearsal or cue cards for learning and reviewing vocabulary, definitions, major concepts, and spelling.

Surveying and Scanning   Beginning with the title and subtitles, if any, the student goes through the text and reads only what *sticks up, stands out, or in some other way is different from the body of the text.* This survey includes boldface and italic type, subheadings, marginal glosses (printed commentary in the margins), boxed text, diagrams, photos, drawings, charts, and other graphics with captions. (Footnotes should be omitted.) Some students will gain from reading aloud or subvocalizing, but others may lose comprehension; the student should try both at first to determine what works best. Before going on, the student should formulate in one to three sentences what he or she believes is the important information or theme of the text.

Then, the student does a cursory reading of the text (scanning), beginning with the introductory questions, concepts, and/or summary (or the first three paragraphs), *the first sentence of each subsequent paragraph,* and the concluding summary and questions, if any.

Setting Up the Mindmap   After this cursory reading, the student sets up a mindmap, using one to three words *printed in block capital letters* to designate the topic. A word or a brief phrase to correspond with the sub-heads in the text serve as the main "branches" of the map. (Skill building in mapping can start with brainstorming familiar topics.)

Preparing Cue Cards   Next, the student reads through the entire text rapidly but at a comfortable rate, making no effort to memorize or remember as he or she goes. During the reading, the student uses coded symbols to mark unfamiliar vocabulary, definitions, important concepts, and, separately, vocabulary words that he or she does not know how to spell. The code symbols are arbitrary.

- *Underline* unfamiliar words.
- *Circle* unknown or difficult words for spelling practice.
- Place a *single asterisk* in the margin next to definitions.
- Place *double asterisks* in the margin for important concepts and abstract terms.

After the student has marked the text, he or she writes vocabulary words on cue cards using the following procedure (the colors of the cards are arbitrary):

- On white index cards, *print* each vocabulary word in the upper left-hand corner.
- On yellow index cards, using a medium-point black felt-tip pen, write the spelling words *in cursive,* centered on the cards. Write as large as possible in the space. Doublecheck accuracy by fingerproofing, or have someone check the spelling for accuracy. (Tracing the spelling words is useful for acquiring cursive handwriting skill if the model is a good model of cursive writing.)
- On gold cards, copy the definitions *exactly as they appear* in the text. Start with the term being defined, and print it in block capital letters.
- On orange cards, write the concept words or phrases on one side. (It may be necessary to use 4" × 6" cards for concepts. Fold these cards to place them in the manila envelope.)

Next, the student adds definitions to the cue cards:

- From the most recent edition of *Webster's New World Dictionary,* copy onto the reverse side of the vocabulary cards the first *two* definitions given, and number the definitions. Younger students should begin with just one definition. On the same side, write a sentence that makes the meaning of the word very clear. *Earth is a planet* will not do.

- On the front of each vocabulary card, right next to the word, copy from the dictionary the part of speech (e.g., *n., adj.*). In the upper right-hand corner, place an abbreviation for the language of origin—Anglo-Saxon (*A.S.*), Latin (*L.*), or Greek (*G.*). Later, the student can add inflected forms and extensions of the word on this side of the card—*planet-s, planet-ary, planet-ari-um, planet-oid*—which show the base word and affixes separately.
- The student should *trace* the spelling words daily by using the fleshy ends of the index and middle fingers, naming aloud each letter as the finger traces over it, and finally saying the whole word. Each word should be traced three or more times at each rehearsal.
- On the reverse side of the orange concept cards, print the detailed aspects of the concept according to the related features semantic map (described later in this chapter) or in a similar manner (see Chapter 9 in Deshler et al., 1996, and Chapter 5 in Maria, 1990).

After the cards are prepared, they are banded together by color and kept in the manila envelope in the plastic zipper case at the front of the student's general subject notebook. Students are encouraged to review the cards daily at odd moments, such as in class, during lunch, on the bus, while waiting for class to begin, and so forth.

Phase Two: Selecting and Organizing the Information

As an adjunct to the SkORE process, separate but concurrent systematic training in related subskills is necessary for the student to gain facility in the component techniques. To self-monitor attention and concentration—or the extent of his or her distractibility—the student can be asked to complete a brief reading or exercise and to check a form or ring a bell each time his or her attention wanders. Exercises in abstracting (by underlining the most salient information) should be given, beginning with simple sentences and paragraphs and working up to a selection of several paragraphs and brief chapters (see Lehmann, 1960a, 1960b). The student should mindmap or web first by filling in major details under the topic lines, then by creating topic words and phrases for subsections with details filled in (see Buzan, 1983, and Wycoff, 1991). (For students with more severe dyslexia who have difficulty with abstracting, note-taking, and webbing, the instructor is referred to the *Reading and Thinking in English* series edited by Moore & Widdowson, 1981, especially the first volume, *Concepts in Use*, written by Moore & Munévar. This resource should be used in conjunction with the SkORE process.) The dyslexic student needs practice in categorizing and classifying, as well as practice in detecting and verbalizing relationships between and among concepts and terms.

The instructor should encourage the student to verbalize his or her thinking as he or she works. This gives the instructor the opportunity to help the student to clarify his or her thinking and the chance to model spoken English by repeating what the student says, in complete, grammatically correct, coherent sentences. More important, the student's verbalizations give the instructor a window on the student's thought processes.

In Phase Two of SkORE, the student must make the conscious decision to maintain attention and concentration to the best of his or her ability throughout each step. The tasks involve 1) abstracting the text, 2) note-taking on the mindmap, 3) consulting with the instructor to correct and complete the mindmap, 4) completing and enhancing the mindmap by color-coding and creating graphics, and 5) developing mnemonics.

Abstracting by Underlining: An Example   The process of abstracting (condensing) text forces the student to determine the essential information. The abstract extracts the most important information from the paragraph or text. The goal is to reduce the text at least by half, later by as much as two thirds. To do this, the student must ask him- or herself questions. The technique of questioning should be taught concurrently, with the teacher using both Socratic questioning (to get the correct answer) (see Murdoch, 1987; out of print but still available in many libraries) and open-ended questioning (to provoke the student to think; see Maria, 1990). For lengthy text, such as a chapter in a social studies, history, or science textbook, structured group discussion is a useful tool; in this type of discussion, the questions originate from the students (see Chapter 6 of Christensen, Garvin, & Sweet, 1991). An example of a text marked (underlined) for abstracting follows:

> The student returns to the beginning of the text and, reading paragraph by paragraph, abstracts the text by underlining only the salient parts. (Because dyslexic students have significant difficulty determining saliency (relative importance, from *L. salio*, leap, i.e., to be "over" others), this will be quite difficult.) The finished abstract should be in complete, grammatically correct sentences, keeping the author's own words. Paraphrasing is not permitted. Minor changes are permitted for smooth transitions and correct syntax; including transitional words and changes in tense or number. The instructor must approve the final product.

The previous paragraph (92 words) has been abstracted (42 words) to read as follows:

> The student returns to the beginning and abstracts the text. This will be difficult. The finished abstract should be in grammatically correct sentences [in] the author's words. Paraphrasing is not permitted; minor changes are permitted. The instructor must approve the final product.

For the dyslexic student, who has difficulty processing large volumes of language, it is vital that the text be reduced in this manner (Deshler et al., 1996). The advantages of abstracting are as follows: The student is not so overwhelmed by the task, his or her storage capacity is less taxed by the task (dyslexic students often think it is necessary to memorize everything), comprehension is improved because the essential information is "laid bare," and the student can see the focus of the lesson more clearly. Maria (1990) stated that in "many texts . . . the real point of the lesson is often obscured." Once the abstract is approved by the instructor, the original text is put aside and is *never referred to again.*

Note-Taking on the Mindmap   Working from the abstract only, not from the original text, the student next fills in the details on the mindmap, beginning at 12 o'clock and working clockwise. It is best to use unlined 11″ × 17″ paper. Single words or brief phrases should be printed in *block capital letters* (Buzan, 1983) to serve as cues for retrieving information. The student must not be permitted to print long phrases, clauses, or sentences or to write in cursive. Unless the sub-heads of the text provide a clear structure for the web, the student usually must reorganize the map by grouping related details in narrower categories. With the instructor's guidance, the student should reexamine each cluster to determine whether details belong under that subtopic label, whether the heading should be reworded, and whether one cluster should be merged with another or, conversely, made into two clusters.

It is expected that full mastery of the mapping technique will take time and much practice. Both instructor and student should regard the time invested as normal and productive in the learning curve. For a full treatment of mindmapping, see Buzan (1983) and Wycoff (1991). (*Note:* Buzan's system of note-taking is not recommended for dyslexic students.)

Reexamining the details of the web, the student should next try to identify concepts and details that are grouped separately but somehow related. Connections can be shown by dotted lines ending in arrows. The relationships—the basis of the associations—should be verbalized by the student.

Consultation with the Instructor   When the student has finished the mindmap, he or she should ask the study skills instructor to review the map with him or her to determine whether important information has been omitted and whether unimportant information has been included. (Later, the student will ask the subject teacher to review the map.) Appropriate corrections are made. *This is an important step in facilitating the student's ability to assess his or her own work and monitor the outcomes.*

Color-Coding and Adding Graphics   After consulting with the instructor, the student color-codes the web by "washing" (shading in) each module with a different *pale pastel* color, by circling the modules in different colors, or by underlining the branches and "twigs" of separate modules with different colors. (Students must not be permitted to print the words in each block using different colors; this is time consuming, and the visual result is disorganized.) Color differentiation further structures the material by establishing boundaries, and enhances the graphic display by helping the student to focus on modules of information. Also, it adds to the sensorially *pleasing quality* of the mindmap, which should not be underestimated as an additional reinforcer. Students often produce maps that are beautiful and creative enough to display as graphic art.

Developing Mnemonics   The student devises mnemonics as aids to remember specific data on the map, such as lists, and creates cartoons, graphs, sketches, diagrams, maps, and other visual aids to illustrate the material to be learned. These are added to the map. All material is written on the same (front) side of the paper. (*Note:* Dyslexic students do better with mnemonics that are provided by the instructor, rather than ones they make up themselves [Deshler et al., 1996].)

Students often are amazed and shocked when, after completing the map, they are asked to recreate it without referring to the original. Invariably, they find that they already know 60%–80% of the material *without having memorized it.* This outcome has a dramatic effect because students typically protest throughout the mindmapping process that they do not have time to "do all this" because they need the time *to memorize* the material. After recreating the mindmap without referring to it, however, *they know what they know and they know what they do not know.* Instead of having to memorize the whole map, they only have to review the portion that has not already gone into working memory.

The colored mindmap and cue cards should be reviewed and redrawn daily during the first week until the student can complete the entire map accurately without referring to the original. Thereafter, the mindmap should be reviewed weekly, then monthly, to maintain it in long-term memory. The mindmap should be reviewed together with the summary and précis of the material, described in the sections that follow.

Phase Three: Summarizing, Outlining, and Writing Précis

In the final phase of the SkORE process, the student uses the mindmap to write a summary of the information on the map, create an outline, and write a précis of the abstract.

Summarizing   After having converted the text into a visual display, the student now converts the visual display back to discursive English. This transformation is at first a mechanical process. Beginning at 12 o'clock on the map and moving clockwise, the student labels each main branch with a Roman numeral—I, II, III, and so forth—to set up the order of the paragraphs in the summary.

The first branch should be introductory. The details noted on subbranches under each main branch can be assigned letters—A, B, C, and so forth. If the subbranches are further modified by subbranches, then the details are numbered with Arabic numerals—1, 2, 3, and so forth.

When the student has labeled all of the branches of the mindmap, he or she returns to the branch labeled with the Roman numeral I and begins to create the summary using the notation on the main branch as the topic sentence of the first paragraph. The word or phrase that appears at the "heart" of the mindmap, which states the general topic to be discussed, should be included in the topic sentence of the first paragraph. The student then makes the details on the subbranches into full sentences; these are the supporting detail sentences. The student follows this procedure for each main branch around the clock. Finally, the student creates a closing paragraph by either stressing the main point or reemphasizing the import of the author's point(s). The précis can be used as a final paragraph. The habit of proofreading for errors has been established as an automatic practice long before this, beginning at Level Two of the Quick Tricks, and has been reinforced during the abstracting procedure.

Writing Skills   The study skills instructor should inform students that teachers require at least three sentences in a paragraph and at least three paragraphs in a theme or composition. If students follow this recipe, then their work will be accepted. This formulaic approach to devising summaries gives students an initial approach to expository writing that appears to reduce their characteristic resistance to writing by eliminating what they perceive as the vagueness of the process. To go beyond the mechanical, formulaic method of summarizing, students should receive instruction in sentence patterns (see Helson, 1971). They should be given practice in elaborating sentences, first with adjectives and adjective phrases, next with adverbs and adverb phrases, and then with clauses. Subjunctive clauses present a particular difficulty for dyslexic students. Until they can read and understand them easily, the use of the subjunctive in writing should be delayed. If the student uses the subjunctive, however, the instructor should enforce the use of the proper verb. For example, *If I was rich, I'd be happy* is not correct; the correct form is *If I were rich, I'd be happy.* (See Chapter 7 for more on writing composition.)

Automaticity in handwriting skills is an absolute prerequisite for facility in written English. Students will be far less apt to want to write if they have not mastered automatic letter formation and connected writing, if their inappropriate grip causes unnecessary fatigue, or if they write with an uncorrected, obstructive hooking of the writing hand. (For an excellent handwriting program, see King, 1985; see Chapter 9 in this book for more on multisensory handwriting instruction.)

There is no good substitute for reading widely and deeply as the best way to learn to write. The study skills instructor can entice students in two ways into reading for information as well as for pleasure. After determining a student's interest or ambition (e.g., soccer, gymnastics, inventing, computers, space travel, dance), the instructor can get good, well-illustrated trade books, including biographies, in large, clear type from the public library. The first group of books should be written *many* years below the student's reading ability. For example, when working with a seventh grader, books written for fourth graders can be very useful. As the student gains facility in reading because of study skills training, more difficult texts can be used. The books should never be used for instruction; they are sources of information and pleasure. The instructor should also take a few minutes of every period to read aloud from works of fiction, biographies, essays, and poems of literary worth. These can be tied to classwork in English, science, history, mathematics, and even physical education.

Some dyslexic students have a talent for writing and intend to be journalists or authors despite their difficulties with written language. Notable authors who have experienced such difficulties include W. Somerset Maugham, Beatrix Potter, Agatha Christie, Winston Churchill, and John Updike. These people, along with mediamen Fred Friendly, Richard Cohen (formerly of *The Washington Post*), Richard Scheer of *The Los Angeles Times*, and others have demonstrated that dyslexics can be very successful writers. Students who desire to be writers should be encouraged.

Writing Précis   Unlike the abstract, which must keep to the author's words, the précis is a condensation of the material in the student's own words. The goal is to state the author's essential message, the main thrust of the selection, the author's underlying thesis, or a combination of these in a highly condensed form. A précis of a chapter or even a book might consist of just a few sentences or paragraphs. As an example, the moral that follows one of Aesop's fables can be considered a précis (e.g., *Slow and steady wins the race*); a proverb also can serve as a précis (e.g., *Pride goeth before a fall*). The practice of précis writing is an invaluable aid to comprehension, as it requires "the student to choose with discrimination his words, thoughts, and ideas, and to restrict his final version to a terse, smoothly-worded statement in his own phraseology" (Brown, 1965). The précis should be no more than one third to one fourth as long as the abstract and may be much shorter. The best technique for formulating a good précis is a group discussion of the essence of the abstract. (See Christensen and colleagues, 1991, for excellent discussion techniques focused on problem solving. For the subskills prerequisite to précis writing, see Lehmann, 1960a.)

Outlining   Ideally, subject teachers will agree to accept the mindmap in lieu of traditional, linear outlines from students with dyslexia. Nevertheless, some will not. In this case, it is a simple matter to convert the mindmap to outline form. Using the numbers assigned for developing the summary, the student simply copies the Roman numerals, letters, and Arabic numerals onto a template provided by the study skills instructor. The words and phrases on the main branches and subbranches can be copied next to the appropriate number or letter. The outline should be checked by both the study skills instructor and the subject teacher before being put into final form. The study skills instructor should exert every effort, however, to have the mindmap accepted by classroom teachers because there is nothing to be gained from this redundant activity, and—more important to the student—it uses valuable time.

Note-Taking from Works of Fiction   To retain information about works of fiction, the student should take notes on 3″ × 5″ index cards, using the following structured procedure. Information is entered onto the cards according to a preset pattern. When completed, the cards are arranged in vertical columns of one, two, or three cards, with each column representing one paragraph. The student may need 20 or more cards when taking notes on one work of fiction. The information is written on the front side of the card only.

Data relevant to one topic, such as characters, may require more than one card. The information should be added to the cards in the order shown, and the cards should be numbered. When writing paragraphs, the student should keep the three-sentence rule in mind.

1. Title, author, illustrator (if any), publisher, date of publication
2. Setting: time (or times), place
3a. Major characters
3b. Major characters' traits
4. Story type (e.g., action story, romance, historical account, fable)
5a. Content: theme or main idea
5b. The point at which the theme is expressed most clearly*
    How often the theme is expressed*
    Through which characters it is most clearly expressed*
5c. Conflict(s)
6. Author's purpose
7. Actions that take place
8a. Technique: how the text is organized*
8b. Kinds of characters, incidents, or images used
    Why these were used instead of others*
8c. Style of writing used (e.g., realistic, formal, informal)
(Starred items are for use with older students.)

Note-Taking from Lectures   Taking notes from lectures is very difficult for the dyslexic student because it requires competency in attention and concentration, processing and remembering rapid speech, rapid and accurate handwriting, vocabulary, determining saliency, prioritization, and proficiency in written English, among others. Instruction in note-taking must be the most direct, explicit, supported, and sustained of all of the study skills to be learned. This training should not be attempted until the student has gained proficiency in handwriting (see Chapter 9) and note-taking from text. These skills are prerequisites to taking notes from lectures because, as Deshler and colleagues explained,

> Notetaking skills and subskills must be applied at the same time and at a rapid rate if the lecture is fast. The student must attend to a lecture idea, process the meaning of the idea by associating or integrating it with prior learning, extract the important information from the lecture idea, retain the meaning in memory, use a framework for recording notes, and write the idea using sufficient speed and abbreviations while simultaneously listening to additional lecture information. (1996, p. 271)

These are formidable obstacles for the dyslexic student. He or she, however, will have addressed many of these areas during SkORE training.

The study skills instructor should begin by arranging for the student to receive lecture notes or a study guide from the subject teacher or from a fellow student by means of carbonless reproduction paper. According to federal, state, and local regulations (e.g., the Individuals with Disabilities Education Act Amendments of 1997, PL 105-17), students with language and learning disabilities have a legal right to this accommodation. The subject teacher(s) working cooperatively with the study skills instructor can be kept informed of the student's progress in the subskills for note-taking. It is important for subject teachers to know that the accommodation is temporary but may extend throughout the school year.

To assess processing and memory, the instructor can read aloud *very brief* passages of three or four sentences; then the instructor should ask the student to repeat orally as much of the information as possible in his or her own words. If the student performs reasonably well, then the instructor can use other passages and ask the student to *record on a simple web* only a word or a phrase to cue memory of important information. This cuing system of simple webbing should be made without concern for classification or organization. The branches should simply be spokes radiating from the topic word or phrase in the center. *It is critical to work at this level until the student has mastered the cuing system—recording a word or a phrase to call up the data—with about 80% accuracy.* The length of the passage can be increased gradually as the student gains mastery.

The instructor can also offer direct, systematic instruction in simple shorthand symbols for common words:

⌐   for *the*
•   for *a*
ʃ   for *if*

Other symbols can be taught: & for *and*, w/ for *with*, % for *percent*, and @ for *at*. Some students will do better with vowel-less writing: *Sm stdnts wl do bttr w/vwllss wrtng;* the instructor must check carefully, however, to determine whether the student can retranslate the notes accurately.

When the student is ready, the study skills instructor and the classroom teacher can monitor the notes that the student takes in class. As with notes taken during training, notes should be merely single words or phrases on spokes radiating from a wheel, recorded without regard to organization or classification. The student should be monitored for accuracy, completeness, and the ability to read back and translate the notes.

Once the radial web has been approved by the study skills instructor (later, by the classroom teacher), the student proceeds in the same fashion as with taking notes from the mindmap by reordering and reorganizing the web according to classification, categorization, and associated ideas. Cue cards, concept and semantic maps (explained later in this chapter), mnemonics and graphics are included as when working with text. Two advantages of taking notes from lectures this way is that lecture and reading notes can be merged into a single web later, and webs that are made on large enough paper can be amended and extended.

Key Words   The cue words on the simple webs developed by the student while taking notes from lectures are like the key words that are used in more conventional two- or three-column note-taking systems. Therefore, once the student has mastered the note-taking process just described, he or she will be able to use conventional systems well with a little guided practice. (See Chapter 6 of Deshler et al., 1996, for more on note-taking and dyslexic students.)

COMPREHENSION

Good groundwork for improved comprehension has been laid by the training in "mechanical" spelling, vocabulary development, and the SkORE processes for mastering content course information, especially techniques for abstracting and webbing with graphics. Some of the advantages of this instruction are as follows:

- The improvement in spelling results in improved decoding and therefore greater speed and accuracy in reading, which facilitates comprehension.
- The practice of having the student identify and define unfamiliar words and explicate concepts and abstractions *before reading the text* improves comprehension.
- The process of abstracting forces the student to weigh and consider by asking questions about the relevance and relative importance of every part of the text. Abstracting also clarifies the structure and development of the information, thereby greatly increasing comprehension.
- The process of webbing—which involves note taking, categorizing, identifying related concepts and details, and creating graphics and mnemonics—requires the deep processing and manipulation that is requisite to deriving meaning and storing information in long-term memory.

As this list demonstrates, students can significantly improve comprehension just by using SkORE strategies and techniques. To improve comprehension for all students, however, additional techniques are required, such as semantic mapping; concept mapping; creating lexicons by geometric progression; and systematically studying nonliteral language, especially idioms and metaphors. For dyslexic students, these collateral activities are critical to improvement in comprehension, writing, and higher-order thinking skills.

For an excellent discussion of the specific comprehension problems of dyslexic learners, the reader is referred to Wiig and Semel (1990), who noted that students with learning disabilities have problems with syntax, semantics, and memory that may cause them to have difficulty with comprehending complex texts. Kamhi and Catts (1989) commented that such problems with reading means reduced exposure to new vocabulary words, and Maria stated that "the reader's level of vocabulary is the best predictor of his or her ability to understand the text" (1990, p. 111). Therefore, as stated previously, the best tool to improve the reading comprehension of dyslexic students rapidly is discussion.

Semantic Mapping

In addition to vocabulary limitations that result from a combination of language problems, the dyslexic student typically has poor decoding ability (tends to skip unknown words), has very limited reading experience (hates to read), and has a general distaste for multisyllabic words and specific terms (prefers to use words such as *stuff, things*, other contentless nouns, and when all else fails, *y'know*).

To aid in comprehension, three kinds of semantic maps are recommended: *synonym–antonym map, related features map,* and *multiple meanings map.* These maps are best developed through group discussion, with Socratic-type questioning from the teacher as the stimulus. By this process, the teacher asks questions designed to elicit the desired answers, such as "What is the missing word in 'Jack fell down and broke his _____?'"

Creating synonym–antonym maps (see Figure 13.5) benefits students' oral and written language ability by expanding vocabulary, offering the opportunity to discuss nuances of meaning (see Hayakawa, 1968), and facilitating the mastery of classification of parts of speech. Resources to use include synonym–antonym dictionaries, *Roget's Thesaurus,* and *The Oxford Dictionary and Thesaurus* (1996). In order to "take possession" of the words on the map, students must have extensive practice in using the words in sentences, both orally and in writing.

The related features map (see Figure 13.6) is a simple version of the concept map (explained in the next section); it is a good place to start with younger students, by brainstorming. The related features map can be organized to show different categories as the main entry, such as *weather, animals,* or *plants.*

Multiple meanings, many different meanings for the same word, is a characteristic of English that makes it very difficult for non-English speakers to learn the language. Similarly, the concept of multiple meanings causes great problems for dyslexic learners in both oral and reading comprehension. This is all the more true of words that have metaphorical meanings, such as *foot, head, place, arm,* and *bloom,* or words that are part of an idiomatic expression. It is important for the student to have practice with the different meanings of such words from the very beginning of study skills training. This practice begins when more than one definition is written on a vocabulary cue card that is made in preparation for webbing. That step is a good introduction, but it is an inadequate way to teach the numerous English words that have multiple meanings. Creation of multiple meaning maps similar to the one shown in Figure 13.7 is a good second stage. For further development, see the section in this chapter called Creating Lexicons by Geometric Progression.

These semantic maps are not to be memorized; students achieve better command by discussing the words on the maps and debating the nuances of meaning (e.g., "What is the same about seeing to a guest, seeing the waiter, and seeing someone home?") and by illustrating the meanings. (For more on semantic mapping, see Chapter 7 of McNeil, 1992.)

JOY, L. n.	
Synonyms	**Antonyms**
(*name for same*)	(*name for what is opposite*)
delight	sorrow
gladness	sadness
elation	depression
lightheartedness	downheartedness
ecstasy	despair
happiness	joylessness

Figure 13.5.   Synonym–antonym map. L., Latin; n., noun.

```
┌─────────────────────────────────────────┐
│            DESERT, L. n.                 │
│   sand                  lizards          │
│   dry                   tents            │
│   oasis                 no rain          │
│   camel                 palm trees       │
│   cactus                mirages          │
│   sun                   sandstorms       │
└─────────────────────────────────────────┘
```

Figure 13.6.   Related features map. L., Latin; n., noun.

Concept Mapping

Dyslexic students may have significant difficulty understanding abstract terms; this difficulty can be a great barrier to comprehension for secondary and postsecondary students. Noting that their understanding of words is too concrete and literal, Levine (1987) pointed out that bright dyslexic students are able to get by with a very partial understanding (a corner) of an abstract concept (e.g., *democracy, latitude, empathy*). This literal understanding of the language, however, results in an imperfect, perhaps distorted, grasp of meanings and implications. Levine stressed that

> The ability to derive concepts is crucial. Several steps are involved: recognizing the salient properties of objects, actions, or events; categorizing those objects, actions, or events by identifying their common properties; forming a superordinate concept to other instances or settings. *The entire process can be viewed as a system of testing hypotheses by making careful decisions to accept or reject formulated hypotheses about problems.* (1987, p. 177, emphasis added)

The study skills instructor must train the student to understand concepts and abstract terms through the systematic creation of concept maps similar to the one in Figure 13.8 to accompany the cue cards for vocabulary. (For more detailed concept maps, see Deshler et al., 1996; Maria, 1990; and McNeil, 1992.)

Creating Lexicons by Geometric Progression

Because they come to the task of comprehension with a smaller personal lexicon than other students, dyslexic students must be enabled to enlarge their vocabulary very quickly and efficiently *without memorization*. Also, because of difficulties with pattern recognition, making associations, seeing relationships, and memorizing, dyslexic students need very explicit instruction, in which patterns are highlighted, extensions (e.g., affixes) are easy, and meaning is revealed in a logical and *dramatic* fashion. This training is best done using *graphic arrays,* or *lexicons by geometric progression,* that convey the morphological (Greek, shape or form of units of meaning) structure of the language, such as roots and affixes. Bywaters (1998) and Murray and Munro (1989) are good resources for lexicons by geometric progression. Partridge (1966; out of print but in libraries) is the best reference for study skills instructors.

The lexicon work should begin with short, easy exercises, such as the one shown in Figure 13.9. It is very important to observe the spacing as indicated, to highlight the root in color (printed in Figure 13.9 in bold type), to include idioms,

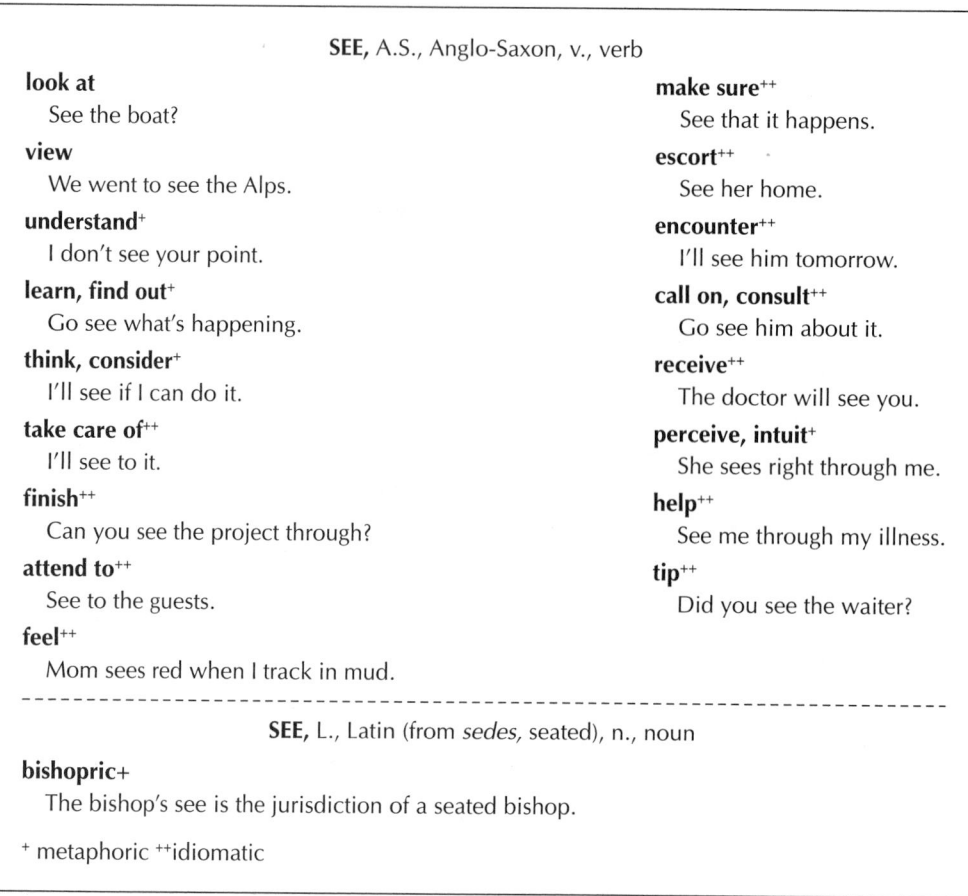

Figure 13.7. Multiple meanings map. Definitions from *The Oxford Dictionary and Thesaurus* (1996).

and to ask the student to generate short paragraphs using both literal and nonliteral words from the array.

Nonliteral Language: Idioms, Metaphors, Proverbs, Puns, and Jargon

Dyslexic people commonly have difficulty with nonliteral language (Kamhi & Catts, 1989; Maria, 1990; Wiig & Semel, 1990), language that uses words in an atypical way to convey meaning that is different from the standard usage, such as *a raging torrent, out of the mouths of babes, he got the axe, she's a peach, his crimes caught up with him, get off my back,* and *an ounce of prevention is worth a pound of cure.* It is important for the instructor to appreciate the vast amount of figurative language, especially idioms and metaphors, used in reading materials for even the youngest children. Moreover, metaphor appears every day in conversations and print media (Lakoff & Johnson, 1980). Although they may not voice their difficulties, dyslexic children are confused by figurative language.

The dyslexic student does not achieve comprehension of nonliteral language incidentally. He or she needs direct, systematic presentation and explication of the language. A good resource to begin with is Makkai and colleagues (1995), but

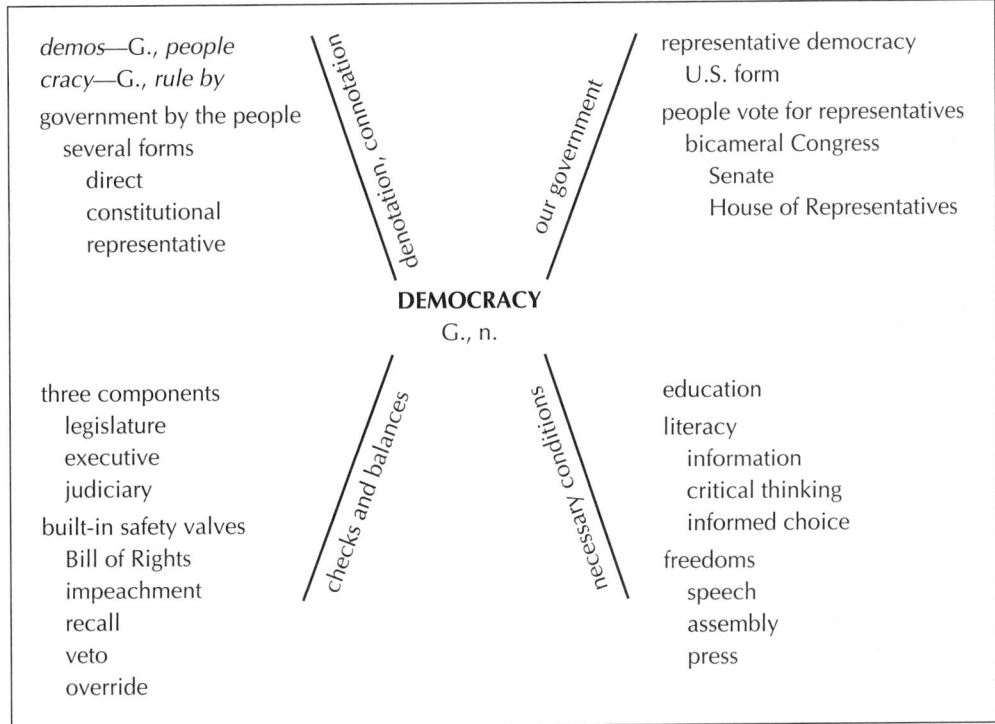

Figure 13.8. Concept map. G., Greek; n., noun

the instructor must simultaneously search out, list, and teach all nonliteral language in the student's required reading. Students enjoy acting out some of the expressions (e.g., *His eyes are bigger than his stomach*) and creating stories and scenarios to illustrate meaning (e.g., *He did that to save face*). These exercises can take just a few minutes and can provide pleasant relief in the midst of hard work. All lexical arrays should include figurative uses of some of the words developed (see Figure 13.8).

TAKING TESTS

The goal of teaching study strategies and skills is for students to solve problems. Although study skills instruction focuses on learning how to learn—not on learning how to cram for tests—tests cannot be avoided in the academic setting. Study skills instruction should address test-taking issues in the following ways:

- *Training in organizing and scheduling time*, given at the outset of training, deals with the issue of time in preparing for tests and final exams.
- *Training in semantics* should include the distinctions in the vocabulary of testing: *define, discuss, detail, compare, contrast, list, explain, justify*, and so forth.
- *The abstracts, mindmaps, and summaries developed by the student in the SkORE process are the materials used for study;* the student *should not* refer back to the original text.
- *The periodic reviews are what constitute "studying for tests and exams."* This ongoing process is designed to retain and strengthen the information in the stu-

---

Root   *dict* (from Latin, *dicere, dictus—to show, point out, tell, say, proclaim*)

dic tate	**dic** tion ar y	pre **dict**
dic tate s	**dic** tion ar ies	pre **dic** tive
dic ta ted		pre **dic** tion
dic ta tion		contra **dict**
dic ta tor		contra **dic** tory
dic ta tor s		contra **dic** tion
dic ta tor ship		
dit to (from Italian, *the same as [was said] before*)		

Idiomatic: He can't dictate what I do.   Metaphor: He's a little dictator.

Figure 13.9.   A lexicon by geometric progression.

dent's long-term memory. In this way, the student comes to know the material; he or she does not need to struggle to remember and recall it. Thus, the stress and anxiety typically accompanying cramming and test taking are much abated, and the negative impact of stress on retrieval (memory) is avoided. In short, the student has a far better chance of doing his or her best on the test.

- *Training in self-monitoring for attention* should enable the student to sustain concentration during tests better than he or she could before the start of study skills training.

At this point in training, what remains is for the instructor to give the student test-taking savvy by coaching him or her on how to apportion time for each section; to read directions carefully and highlight critical words or phrases; to avoid guessing unless only correct answers are scored (i.e., points are not deducted for wrong answers); to eliminate answers in multiple-choice tests; and to proofread carefully at the conclusion, not only for the usual errors in writing but also to ensure that no question was overlooked.

Dyslexic students need to learn specific strategies for tracking during tests (following along with the text of the test). For example, when doing matching exercises, students may need to number the items on the left, letter those on the right, and cross out the words they have already matched as they work. Other specific strategies for test-taking can be found in Deshler and colleagues (1996), Millman and Pauk (1969), and Strichart and Mangrum (1993).

CONCLUSION: STUDY SKILLS TRAINING AND METACOGNITION

Metacognition has been described as the individual's conscious awareness of his or her functioning *and the ability to verbalize that awareness.* Wiig and Semel (1990) and others have called metacognition the ability to use language as a tool. Deshler and colleagues wrote that the term "convey[s] the idea that the learner uses . . . processes to provide [him- or herself] with feedback on learning" (1996, p. 13). *Meta,* from Greek, means *beyond, above,* or *higher.* For the dyslexic student, the objective of study skills training is to develop higher-level thinking, objective judgment, and serious reflection, all of which the student can use to assess him- or herself as a learner.

The strategies and techniques discussed in this chapter build in from the beginning techniques for self-monitoring and self-evaluation to the methods for taking notes from texts and lectures, and call for frequent interaction with supportive adults who offer feedback and guidance. During study skills training, the student emerges from randomness and confusion to deliberate and focused behavior and develops the capacity to relate his or her habits and actions to achievements. All the study skills activities contribute to metacognition. They demand more from the student, not less. The procedures take time, discipline, and the will to win. The study skills instructor is the mentor and supporter of the student while he or she acquires the necessary skills. Instructor and student have a formidable task, which is well articulated by Dr. Baruj Benacerraf, recipient of the 1980 Nobel Prize in Physiology and former president of Harvard's Dana Farber Cancer Research Center:

> Dyslexia is a challenge to overcome, rather than a deficiency to be sorry about. To achieve excellence, I found that I needed to always examine my own work with a merciless, critical eye. It is far better to be more severe and demanding of oneself than others can be. (personal communication, 1988)

This advice must be balanced, however, by the revision of Torgesen's Law: "Know your stuff. Know who you are stuffing. *Stuff them as explicitly, as systematically, and as supportively as you possibly can*" (personal communication, June 19, 1998, emphasis added).

REFERENCES

Alley, G.R., & Deshler, D.D. (1979). *Teaching the learning disabled adolescent: Strategies and methods.* Denver, CO: Love Publishing.

Askov, E.N., & Kamm, K. (1982). *Study skills in the content areas.* Needham Heights, MA: Allyn & Bacon.

Brown, A.L. (1979). The development of memory. In H.W. Reese (Ed.), *Advances in child development and behavior.* New York: Academic Press.

Brown, J.I. (1947). Reading and vocabulary: 14 master words. In M.J. Herzberg (Ed.), *Word study, 1–4.* Springfield, MA: Merriam Webster.

Buzan, T. (1983). *Use both sides of your brain.* New York: Dutton/Plume. [*Note:* The note-taking system is *not* recommended; for mindmap design and enhancement only.]

Bywaters, D. (1998). *Affix and root cards.* Cambridge, MA: Educators Publishing Service.

Christensen, C.R., Garvin, D.A., & Sweet, A. (1991). *Education for judgment: The artistry of discussion leadership.* Boston: Harvard Business School Press.

Clark, D.B., & Uhry, J.K. (1995). *Dyslexia: Theory and practice of remedial instruction.* Timonium, MD: York Press.

Cruickshank, W.M. (1967). *The brain-injured child in home, school, and community.* Syracuse, NY: Syracuse University Press.

de Hirsch, K. (1984). Language and the developing child. *The Orton Society Monographs, 4.* Timonium, MD: York Press.

Deshler, D.D., Ellis, E., & Lenz, B.K. (1996). *Teaching adolescents with learning disabilities: Strategies and methods* (2nd ed.). Denver, CO: Love Publishing.

Devine, T.G. (1981). *Teaching study skills: A guide for teachers.* Needham Heights, MA: Allyn & Bacon.

DuBard, N.E., & Martin, M. (1994). *Teaching language-deficient children: Theory and application of the Association Method for multisensory teaching.* Cambridge, MA: Educators Publishing Service.

Enfield, M.L., & Greene, V. (n.d.) *Project read*. Bloomington, MN: Language Circle Enterprise.

Evans, H. (Ed.). (1981). *Brewer's dictionary of phrase and fable* (Centenary rev. ed.). New York: HarperCollins.

Fowler, H. (1983). *A dictionary of modern English usage*. New York: Oxford University Press.

Gaddes, W.H., & Edgell, D. (1994). *Learning disabilities and brain function: A neuropsychological approach* (3rd ed.). New York: Springer-Verlag.

Galaburda, A. (Ed.). (1993). *Dyslexia and development: Neurobiological aspects of extraordinary brains*. Cambridge, MA: Harvard University Press.

Gillingham, A., & Stillman, B.W. (1956). *Remedial training for students with specific disability in reading, spelling and penmanship*. Cambridge, MA: Educators Publishing Service.

Gold, S. (Ed.). (1993). *The New York Public Library desk reference* (2nd ed.). Upper Saddle River, NJ: Prentice-Hall.

Goldstein, K. (1939). *The organism*. Houston, TX: American Book Company.

Hayakawa, S.I. (1968). *Choose the right word: A modern guide to synonyms*. New York: HarperCollins.

Helson, L.G. (1971). *Basic English sentence patterns*. Cambridge, MA: Educators Publishing Service.

Herman, R.D. (n.d.). *The Herman method*. (Available from R.D. Herman, Herman Method Institute, 4700 Tyrone Avenue, Sherman Oaks, CA 91423)

Hyperion. (1993). *Magic eye 3D illusions*. Kansas City: Author.

Hyperion. (1995). *Magic eye 3D optical illusion cards*. Kansas City: Author.

Johnson, D.J., & Myklebust, H.R., (1967). *Learning disabilities: Educational principles and practices*. New York: Grune & Stratton.

Kamhi, A.G., & Catts, H.W. (1989). *Reading disabilities: A developmental perspective*. Boston: Little, Brown.

Kellett, M. (1977). *The memory and concentration guide book: A comprehensive program for study skills and review*. Rockaway, NJ: Creative Learning Services.

King, D.H. (1985). *Writing skills for the adolescent*. Cambridge, MA: Educators Publishing Service.

Knight, J.R. (1986). *Starting Over: A combined teaching manual and student textbook for reading, writing, spelling, vocabulary, and handwriting*. Cambridge, MA: Educators Publishing Service.

Lakoff, G., & Johnson, M. (1980). *Metaphors we live by*. Chicago: University of Chicago Press.

Lehmann, P.W. (1960a). *The junior précis practice pad*. Cambridge, MA: Educators Publishing Service.

Lehmann, P.W. (1960b). *The senior précis practice pad*. Cambridge, MA: Educators Publishing Service.

Levine, M. (1987). *Developmental variation and learning disorders* (2nd ed.). Cambridge, MA: Educators Publishing Service.

Lindamood, C.H., & Lindamood, P.C. (1975). *The A.D.D. program: Auditory Discrimination in Depth. Books 1 and 2*. Austin, TX: PRO-ED.

Lindamood, P.C., & Lindamood, P. (1998). *LiPS: Lindamood Phoneme Sequencing*. San Luis Obispo, CA: Gander Publishing.

Makkai, A., Boatner, M.T., & Gates, J.E. (1995). *A dictionary of American idioms*. Hauppage, NY: Barron's Educational Series.

Maria, K. (1990). *Reading comprehension instruction, issues, and strategies*. Timonium, MD: York Press.

McNeil, J.D. (1992). *Reading comprehension: New directions for classroom practice*. New York: HarperCollins.

Millman, J., & Pauk, W. (1969). *How to take tests*. New York: McGraw-Hill.

Moore, J., & Munévar, T. (1981). *Reading and thinking in English series: Vol. 1. Concepts in use*. New York: Oxford University Press.

Moore, J., & Widdowson, H. (Eds.). (1981). *Reading and thinking in English* [Series]. New York: Oxford University Press.

Murdoch, I. (1987). *Acastos*. New York: Viking Penguin.

Murray, C., & Munro, J. (1989). *30 roots to grow on*. Cambridge, MA: Educators Publishing Service.

Neisser, U. (1976). *Cognition and reality: Principles and implications of cognitive psychology*. San Francisco: W.H. Freeman.

Orton, S.T. (1937). *Reading, writing and speech problems in children*. New York: W.W. Norton.

Partridge, E. (1966). *Origins: A short etymological dictionary of modern English*. New York: Greenwich House.

Pickering, J.S. (n.d.). *Sequential English education*. Dallas, TX: The June Shelton

School. (Available from Joyce Shelton, Executive Director, The June Shelton School, 5002 West Lovers Lane, Dallas, TX 75209)

Robinson, F.P. (1946). *Effective study*. New York: HarperCollins.

Roget's thesaurus (5th ed.). (1992). New York: HarperCollins. [*Note:* Only this version is recommended.]

Shaywitz, S.E. (1998). Current concepts in dyslexia. *New England Journal of Medicine, 338*, 307–312.

Slingerland, B.H. (1971). *A multisensory approach to language arts for specific language disability children: A guide for primary teachers*. Cambridge, MA: Educators Publishing Service.

Smith, M.T., & Hogan, E.A. (1991). *MTA: Teaching a process for comprehension and composition*. Forney, TX: MTS Publications.

Sonday, A. (1997). *The Sonday system: Learning to read*. Cambridge, MA: Educators Publishing Service.

Spalding, R.B., with Spalding, W.T. (1990). *The writing road to reading: The Spalding method of phonics for teaching speech, writing, and reading* (4th rev. ed.). New York: Quill.

Strichart, S.S., & Mangrum, C.T., II. (1993). *Teaching study strategies to students with learning disabilities*. Needham Heights, MA: Allyn & Bacon.

The Oxford dictionary and thesaurus (American ed.). (1996). New York: Oxford University Press.

The Oxford dictionary of English etymology. (1983). New York: Oxford University Press.

Tomatis, A. (1969). *Dyslexia*. Ottawa, Ontario, Canada: University of Ottawa Press.

Tomkins, C. (1963, September 14). The last skill acquired. *The New Yorker,* 127–133.

Tonjes, M.J., & Zintz, M.V., (1981). *Teaching reading/thinking/study skills in content classrooms*. Dubuque, IA: William C. Brown.

Trudeau, K. (1995). *Megamemory*. New York: William Morrow & Co.

Warriner, J.E. (1988). *English composition and grammar: Complete course*. Orlando, FL: Harcourt Brace & Co.

Wiig, E.H., & Semel, E. (1990). *Language assessment and intervention for the learning disabled*. Columbus, OH: Charles E. Merrill.

Williams, J. (1984). *The organization of study skills*. Dallas, TX: The Polished Apple.

Wilson reading system. (n.d.). Millbury, MA: Wilson Language Training Corp. (Available from the publisher, 162 West Main Street, Milbury, MA 01527)

Wittenberg, L. (1965). *A study manual: Methods and habits*. Cambridge, MA: Educators Publishing Service.

Wycoff, J. (1991). *Mindmapping: Your personal guide to exploring creativity and problem-solving*. New York: Berkley Books.

14

Assessment of Progress

Margaret Jo Shepherd

Assessment, as educators and psychologists use the term, is the process of collecting information to make decisions about people's lives (Salvia & Ysseldyke, 1998). Assessment activities are guided by specific questions. Information relevant to the questions is collected, organized, and interpreted. Answers to the questions are formulated, leading to decisions. If the questions and decisions are about learning and school, the process is called *educational assessment.*

When a parent or teacher sees an intelligent child struggle to read and spell, three questions come to mind: "Is this child's struggle with reading and spelling best described as dyslexia?" "What remedial plan will facilitate learning to read and spell?" and "Is the remedial plan effective?" These questions are related to each other but have distinct answers. The first question seeks an explanation for the struggle with reading and spelling and requires information that compares the child's performance with the performance of other children of the same age. The second and third questions require detailed descriptions of the child's reading and spelling skills. The child's development is evaluated relative to knowledge attained and knowledge yet to be mastered. Direct comparisons with other children are less important. Assessment designed to answer the first two questions typically occurs during one, two, or three sessions. Assessment of the effectiveness of the remedial plan, or *assessment of progress,* is ongoing.

Assessment is supposed to be a reasonably objective process. Data collection is organized and sequential, and there are checks and balances in the process because data is obtained from multiple sources, such as children's school records, interviews with their teachers, and tests. Although assessment is organized as an objective endeavor, it is not a neutral enterprise. Assessments are made by people, and people have perspectives and opinions on the problems they are asked to assess. The assessors' perspectives influence the way questions are constructed and which procedures are used to collect data.

The subjective influence of the assessors' perspective is a particularly important consideration when children with reading and spelling problems are being assessed. Professionals have differing opinions about the value of sorting children with reading problems into diagnostic categories. Specifically, professionals have differing opinions about the efficacy of placing children into diagnostic categories based on IQ scores. Because dyslexia is a diagnosis reserved for children whose IQ scores are average or higher, opinion is divided about the legitimacy of this diagnosis. Obviously, such differing views influence assessment questions. People who believe that the diagnosis of dyslexia is legitimate will ask, "Is this child dyslexic?" Others who are concerned that dyslexia is an unproven idea prefer to skip this question and focus assessment on questions about appropriate instruction and progress (see Siegel, 1999, for a full treatment of this perspective). Again, the way reading and spelling problems are assessed depends on the way the problem is perceived.

This chapter is based on the presumption that the diagnosis of dyslexia is a useful way to characterize the struggle that some children with average or above-average intelligence have with reading. The chapter, presuming that the diagnosis is legitimate, focuses on the question, "Is this child, described as dyslexic, learning to read and spell?" This chapter is organized in three sections. First, dyslexia is defined and discussed with regard to how diagnosing dyslexia justifies particular goals for assessment of progress.[1] Next is a description of the data sources that are used to answer assessment questions, with emphasis on the point that the data that assessors collect depend on the assessment questions. The third section of the chapter discusses some of the data that are useful when assessing progress.

DYSLEXIA

The word *dyslexia* has origins in both Latin and Greek. *Dys,* from the Greek, signifies *difficulty with.* The Latin *legere* means *to read.* The Greek *lexis* means *speech* or *to speak.* Thus, we can define *dyslexia* as "difficulty with reading and speaking" (Hornsby, Atkinson, & Howard, 1997, p. 37). A dual emphasis on difficulty with reading and speaking is consistent with the historical perspective (Orton, 1937) and reflects contemporary definitions of dyslexia. Consider, for example, the definition created in 1994 by the Research Committee of the Orton Dyslexia Society (ODS), which is now known as the International Dyslexia Association:

> Dyslexia is one of several distinct learning disabilities. It is a specific language-based disorder of constitutional origin characterized by difficulties in single word decoding, usually reflecting insufficient phonological processing abilities. These difficulties in single word decoding are often unexpected in relation to age and other cognitive and academic abilities; they are not the result of generalized developmental disability or sensory impairment. Dyslexia is manifested by variable difficulty with different

---

[1]Assessment designed to identify dyslexia is discussed in several other sources (Clark & Uhry, 1995; Farnham-Diggory, 1992; Pennington, 1991; Shaywitz, 1996, 1998; Shepherd, Charnow, & Silver, 1989; Shepherd & Uhry, 1993). Several chapters in this book address remedial programs that facilitate students' learning to read (Chapters 6 and 7), spell (Chapters 4 and 8), and write (Chapters 7 and 9). Good information about procedures for assessing reading progress is available (Barr, Blachowicz, & Wogman-Sadow, 1995; Chall, 1994; Cohen & Spenciner, 1998; Miller, 1995; Rhodes & Shanklin, 1993). This information is a part of the literature about reading but is less frequently considered a part of the literature about dyslexia.

forms of language, often including, in addition to problems reading, a conspicuous problem with acquiring proficiency in writing and spelling. (as cited in Lyon, 1995, p. 9)

This definition represents a significant departure from previous definitions of dyslexia. The definition accepted in 1968 by the World Federation of Neurology illustrates the difference:

> "Specific developmental dyslexia" is a disorder manifested by difficulty in learning to read despite conventional instruction, adequate intelligence and socio-cultural opportunity [which is] dependent upon fundamental cognitive disabilities which are frequently of constitutional origin. (as cited in Critchley, 1970, p. 11)

Notice that although both definitions referred to a biological etiology, they list different symptoms. The World Federation of Neurology described symptoms as "difficulty learning to read," whereas the ODS described symptoms as "difficulties with single word decoding." Note also that the World Federation of Neurology omitted references to writing and spelling disabilities. Statements about symptoms are more precise in the ODS definition. Also, the ODS named a cognitive deficit (insufficient phonological processing abilities) thought to be the cause of dyslexia, whereas the World Federation of Neurology definition named no cognitive deficit.

The Controversy

Differences between definitions of dyslexia reflect knowledge about the disorder that has accrued from research conducted between 1968 and 1994. This research has pointed to difficulty with single-word reading and spelling as the primary symptoms of dyslexia and has suggested that the cognitive deficit underlying these symptoms is a phonological processing disorder. The phonological processing disorder makes it difficult for an individual to segment spoken words into constituent sounds, to hold verbal information briefly in memory, and to retrieve words easily from long-term memory. (Research supporting these changes in definition is vast. For syntheses, see Clark & Uhry, 1995, and Sternberg & Spear-Swerling, 1999.) Despite evidence supporting the more recent definition, diagnosing dyslexia remains controversial.

Although historic and contemporary definitions of dyslexia are not explicit on this point, the diagnosis is intended to separate poor readers with average or above-average intelligence from poor readers with below-average intelligence. When diagnosing a reading and spelling problem as dyslexia, one must presume, among other things, that the cognitive skills required for learning to read can be selectively impaired but that other cognitive skills are left intact. Furthermore, one must presume that the specific cognitive impairment, which is not severe enough to result in below-average intelligence, derives from neurological impairment. These inferences draw support from the fact that individuals who incur injury to specific areas of the brain after they learn to read do experience impairment to reading without necessarily losing other learned skills. Dyslexia acquired after an individual learns to read is presumed to be analogous to dyslexia present at the time an individual is learning to read.

Some critics challenge the presumption that poor readers with average or above-average intelligence are qualitatively different from poor readers with below-average intelligence (see Siegel, 1999, in particular). The most significant challenge to this presumption comes from the finding (Fletcher et al., 1994; Pennington, Gilger, Olson, & DeFries, 1992; Stanovich & Siegel, 1994) that all poor readers have phonological processing deficits and difficulty acquiring the alphabetic skills that are required for word recognition and spelling. This finding means that the phonological processing deficits referred to in the ODS (1994) definition are not unique to poor readers with average or above-average intelligence. Other critics acknowledge interesting neurological research with individuals described as dyslexic but contend that the results of that research are inconclusive (see Coles, 1998, in particular). Thus, the use of dyslexia as an explanation for reading and spelling problems is controversial because it has been difficult to find cognitive characteristics that are unique to children with average or above-average intelligence who are poor readers and to find a neurological cause for their reading problems. The diagnosis stays alive, despite controversy, because clinicians and teachers continue to find individuals who present with the problem. Careful clinical descriptions of individuals with average or above-average intelligence and poor reading are the one stable indicator that developmental dyslexia is a valid diagnosis.

Clinical Portraits of Dyslexia

The first accounts of developmental dyslexia appeared in British medical journals more than 100 years ago (Kerr, 1897; Morgan, 1896). These accounts described children who were intelligent but, mysteriously, could not learn to read. Contemporary examples of developmental dyslexia are remarkably similar to the original descriptions published by Kerr and by Morgan. Because the clinical portrait is stable, case studies of individuals with good intelligence alongside reading and spelling disability verify the importance of diagnosing dyslexia. The following anecdotes from the lives of three university students bring dyslexia to our attention in a way that is not captured in definitions or by research findings. These students were identified as dyslexic when they were 7 years old. They received special instruction in reading, spelling, and writing from that age until they finished high school. Although there was variation in their school experiences and in the amount and kind of remedial instruction they received, each of these students received the best remedial instruction that their parents could provide. Their families did not anticipate their reading and spelling problems and did not understand them at first. Indirectly, these students' stories suggest which skills should be assessed when monitoring dyslexic students' progress.

> When perusing a paper she had written recently, Laura and her professor found an interesting spelling error. Laura's attention was drawn to the switch from *comprehension* to *compression* in her paper. She said that she knows how to spell *comprehension* but that she has to concentrate to spell it correctly. She must concentrate constantly to spell words with several syllables correctly. She claimed that the way she spells *college* (as *colage*) is a different matter. *Colage* is the only spelling she knows, though she has read the word many times. She told her professor, "I spell it the way it sounds to me when I say it." A pensive look crossed her face, and she said, "I wonder if I switched from saying *comprehension* to saying *compression* as I wrote my paper about dyslexia?"

> Michael searched unsuccessfully through the dormitory for a friend and left a note taped to the door of her room: *Im nextor*. When Michael's friend found the

note, she was stunned by his spelling but knew that difficulty with spelling is part of a larger struggle for him. They are enrolled in the same political science course and study together. He leads their study sessions because he understands the course material better than she does. In return, she gives him feedback on his papers. His grades on these papers are better than hers. Essay tests taken in class are a different story. Because she is the better writer, her grades are higher than his. She is puzzled by the fact that he speaks so well but has such difficulty writing.

While writing a paper about hearing impairments, Shawna repeatedly wrote *death* and *interruptor* when she meant *deaf* and *interpreter*. She did, however, spell *hearing impairments* correctly. Because Shawna's professor was curious about her spelling errors, he asked her to read parts of the paper to him. She said "deaf" when she encountered *death* and "interpreter" when she encountered *interruptor*. In response to her instructor's query as to why she spelled those words one way and read them another, she responded that she did not see or hear the difference. Shawna's professor assumed that the spelling program she used had directed her to spell *hearing impairments* correctly, so he asked her to spell the phrase. To his surprise, she knew the correct spelling. She told him that she, too, was puzzled by seeming inconsistencies in the way she spells. She said that she often finds simple words difficult to learn yet has little difficulty with words that represent more complicated spelling patterns.

Laura, Michael, and Shawna are obviously intelligent. They have been chosen for admission to graduate programs (in counseling psychology, political science, and special education, respectively) at a university known for selecting graduate students carefully. Their struggle with written language extends far beyond a few misspelled words. Their compositions are replete with spelling errors, including errors with words that they have read and written hundreds of times, such as *college*. They need assistance to write papers, and they have friends and tutors who help them. Sentence structure and text organization are as difficult for them as spelling. They read with reasonable accuracy, but they read slowly. If they were asked to read **pseudowords** (words that represent English spelling patterns but are not English words), then they would have readily apparent difficulties.

On the basis of the fact that they are in graduate school and of the careers they have chosen, it can be assumed that these three students are competent speakers. Their difficulties with written language illustrate the profound contrast between competence with oral language and difficulty with written language that is a primary characteristic of dyslexia. Their lives also illustrate the persistent nature of dyslexia. Dyslexia has been a challenge for these students and their teachers since they entered kindergarten and will remain a challenge for them as long as they choose to read and write.[2]

Developmental Story of Dyslexia

Laura's, Michael's, and Shawna's lives attest to the fact that although dyslexia is diagnosed in childhood, the problem is not specific to childhood. Remedial teach-

---

[2]There is other evidence that symptoms of dyslexia persist despite remedial instruction (Felton, 1998; Olson, Wise, Ring, & Johnson, 1997; Snowling & Hulme, 1989).

ing ameliorates the symptoms, and compensation occurs, but the reading difficulties remain similar from childhood to adulthood (Bruck, 1998). As children, they have difficulty learning and using letter–sound associations to read and spell. As they progress through school and are tested for reading ability, they typically earn the lowest scores on tests that measure skill at reading pseudowords. (Pseudowords are a relatively unbiased test of the ability to decode letters back to speech because they can be read only by decoding, unlike real words, which can be read with the help of other cues.) Children who have difficulties with letter–sound associations try to memorize words by shape and rely heavily on the meaning of the text to help them guess at words as they read. Learning to spell is more difficult for them than learning to read. These children's spelling errors reflect their difficulty memorizing letter sequences and tendency to spell words as they pronounce them. Often, they use an imprecise pronunciation as the basis for spelling. Their listening comprehension exceeds reading comprehension; the latter is often limited by slow, inaccurate word recognition. Their writing skills are limited, in part, by poor spelling ability.

The profile of adults with dyslexia, documented by Bruck (1998), Farnham-Diggory (1992), Fink (1996), Goldsmith-Phillips (1994), and Turner (1997), resembles the profile of children with dyslexia in that adults earn particularly low scores on tests of pseudoword reading and spelling. Clearly, tasks that require fluent use of alphabetic knowledge remain difficult for them. Adults with dyslexia typically read slowly and write with great effort. Compensation for weak word recognition skills is evident because these adults earn higher scores on tests of reading comprehension than they earn on tests of single-word reading. The typical pattern is that reading comprehension scores are higher than single-word reading scores, which are higher than scores on tests of pseudoword reading. Scores on spelling tests are usually similar to scores earned on tests of pseudoword reading. Reading and spelling skills improve as people with dyslexia reach adulthood, but their learning problems do not disappear, and they continue to interfere with reading and writing proficiency.

Pennington (1991) and Stanovich (1986) suggested another perspective on dyslexia and development. As children described as dyslexic grow, secondary symptoms may emerge as a consequence of slow reading development. Stanovich suggested the following developmental pattern. Children who are dyslexic begin school with a specific linguistic deficit that impairs, singly or in combination, their ability to segment speech, hold verbal sequences in memory, and retrieve from a verbal memory store the pronunciation of familiar words. In turn, these phonological deficits impair these children's ability to learn the alphabetic code and their ability to acquire accurate, automatic word recognition and spelling skills. Reading and spelling development are slow. Certain language skills, such as vocabulary, are influenced by reading. If reading development is slow, then the development of these oral language skills may also be slow. Following this line of reasoning, vocabulary limitations would emerge as a consequence of poor reading and as a secondary symptom of dyslexia.

Pennington (1991) classified problems with reading comprehension as secondary symptoms of dyslexia. By definition, individuals described as dyslexic have average or above-average aptitude for language comprehension. When reading comprehension is compromised, the problem is a consequence of limitations imposed by inaccurate, slow word recognition skills. If secondary symptoms develop, then they could alter the pattern of reading development that is frequently observed in adults: reading comprehension that is better than word recognition, which is better than pseudoword recognition and spelling.

In summary, dyslexia is a controversial diagnosis that is easier to describe than to explain. Case studies keep alive an idea that has been difficult to verify, namely, that children with average or above-average intelligence who struggle with reading are different from children with below-average intelligence who struggle with reading. Although both groups of children share problems with phonological processing and difficulty mastering the alphabetic code, for poor readers with average or above-average intelligence, the impact of the learning disability is at least initially restricted to word recognition and spelling. These students can comprehend printed text when they can decode it. Wondrously, some of them manage to comprehend text even when they do not decode it very well. Although the relationship between dyslexia and development has not been fully substantiated, the primary symptoms of dyslexia—problems with word recognition, reading fluency, and spelling—persist in adulthood. Thus, although achievement levels are obviously different, reading profiles of children and adults with dyslexia are remarkably similar. Secondary symptoms may become important characteristics of dyslexia as children grow toward adulthood.

Which Skills Do We Assess?

When assessing dyslexic students' progress in literacy, it is essential to determine which skills to assess. This determination is made using knowledge about dyslexia and development (described previously), incomplete as it may be. Students' progress in mastering the skills with which they have difficulty should be documented. In other words, teachers should be particularly attentive to the effects of instruction on the persistent, primary symptoms of dyslexia. Assessment of progress, viewed from this perspective, emphasizes the following: the acquisition and use of graphophonemic knowledge (letter–sound associations), accuracy and speed of printed word recognition in lists and in text, and accuracy and speed of spelling from dictated lists and from text. The assessment of such skills is consistent with the traditions of multisensory instruction, which emphasizes the acquisition of these skills. Teachers should also be watchful for the emergence of secondary symptoms and, in particular, should monitor vocabulary development. If teachers find evidence that students are not acquiring knowledge of the meanings of words at the expected rate, then they can plan instruction accordingly.

It may seem shortsighted, or even wrongheaded, to emphasize skills assessment when others are advocating assessment goals based on a view of reading and writing as the construction and communication of meaning (Falk, 1998).[3] The skills that dyslexic students struggle to learn are tools for constructing meaning from and through text. Their learning disability is resistant to remediation, and they are inclined to compensate for the consequences of the disability. Although compensation is a strength, compensatory strategies may also interfere with the

---

[3]As the entries for this chapter in Appendix B at the end of this book indicate, the means for assessing progress are similar regardless of the specific goals one specifies for assessment.

acquisition of fluent word reading and spelling. With careful attention to students' progress, focused specifically on accurate, automatic word recognition and spelling, we can modify instruction so that it is more effective. More effective, in the final analysis, means that students have the tools to obtain meaning from text and to construct text that conveys meaning effectively. There is ample evidence of increases in achievement in particular skills when teachers assess students' progress with these skills on a regular schedule (Fuchs, 1986).

SOURCES OF ASSESSMENT DATA

In the minds of many people, *assessment* and *testing* are synonyms. People who believe this, however, miss an important point. Tests are procedures for collecting data. In contrast, assessment is an *ongoing process*. Testing is subsumed within the process of assessment and is only one source of assessment data. Educators and psychologists who conduct educational assessments use several sources of data, including the following: family, developmental, medical, and educational histories; school records and examples of schoolwork; interviews; observations; both formal and informal tests; rating scales; structured presentations of reading, spelling, and writing tasks; and sample lessons, which are called *trial teaching*. Depending on the purpose of the assessment and particularly in the case of identifying dyslexia, examinations will be requested from other people such as speech-language pathologists and physicians. Data collection is comprehensive and extends far beyond the information provided by a test.

Types of Tests

Even though assessment does not depend exclusively on information obtained from tests, it is important to understand that different types of tests are used during assessment. Tests can be classified as *formal* (**standardized**) or *informal.* Standardized tests must always be administered and scored following procedures that are prescribed in the manual accompanying the test. Unless people who give a standardized test follow the prescribed procedures exactly, the interpretation of test scores will be compromised. Such tests are standardized using a carefully selected sample of people who are representative of the larger group of people for whom the test was created. Informal tests, in contrast, are structured but not standardized. Typically, informal tests use the format of a standardized test, but the person giving the test can modify the presentation of test items and probe the student's responses in ways that are not permissible during the administration of standardized tests.

Tests can also be classified as *norm referenced, criterion referenced,* or *curriculum referenced.* Norm-referenced tests produce scores that permit comparisons among people. These tests allow a child's command of the knowledge measured by the test to be compared with that of other children of the same age. Standards for judging the performance of the child taking a norm-referenced test have been determined by the performance of a group of children who took the test when it was standardized. The children whose performance created the norms, or standards, against which the test taker's performance is compared have been selected to be comparable to all children who might take the test with regard to characteristics that influence test performance (e.g., age, gender, ethnicity, socioeconomic status, geographic region of residence). Norm-referenced tests, then, give information about a child's development relative to the development of other children of the same age. All norm-referenced tests are standardized.

The difference between criterion-referenced tests and norm-referenced tests is the standard used for judging performance. Norm-referenced tests produce an index (score) of one child's development relative to the development of other children, whereas criterion-referenced tests produce descriptions of one child's knowledge within the domain of knowledge represented in the test. Criterion-referenced tests allow the test administrators to generate an item-by-item description of knowledge attained and knowledge yet to be acquired. Curriculum-referenced tests are a variation on criterion-referenced tests; questions included in a curriculum-referenced test are taken from the curriculum in use in the child's classroom.[4] Curriculum-referenced tests avoid the error of testing a child on content that he or she has not had the opportunity to learn. Thus, curriculum-referenced tests allow for a good match between assessment and instruction; children are only tested on material that they have been taught. Criterion- and curriculum-referenced tests can be standardized or informal. The important point about these two kinds of tests is that they allow comparisons to be made between a child's present performance and that child's immediate past performance. Thus, the child's previous performance (rather than other children's performance) is the standard for judging progress. Criterion- and curriculum-referenced tests were designed to guide teaching decisions.

An Important Assessment Principle

People who conduct educational assessments have at their disposal several procedures for collecting data. The overriding principle governing assessment is that the procedures that are selected from among these options depend on the assessment questions that have been chosen. The question "Is this child dyslexic?" obligates those conducting the assessment to look for word recognition, decoding, and spelling deficits. Such an assessment must also verify language competence alongside the reading deficits. If the child being assessed is 8 years old or younger, then the assessment must also verify the presence of a phonological processing deficit. These are all reasonably objective judgments. People making such an assessment would determine that a child has weak word recognition skills by comparing his or her performance on a word recognition test with the performance of other children of the same age, using norm-referenced tests. In contrast, when the assessment question is "What remedial plan will facilitate learning to read and spell?" criterion- and curriculum-referenced tests dominate the assessment process. The people making the assessment examine the knowledge/skill descriptions that these tests provide and determine goals for the remedial plan.

Formative versus Summative Data

There is another way to classify data collection procedures that is particularly important when the assessment question is about progress or learning. Data collection can be *formative* or *summative*. Formative data collection applies to imme-

---

[4]Curriculum-referenced tests may be norm referenced but they are more commonly constructed and used as criterion-referenced tests.

diate or short-term instructional goals and yields information about a child's progress acquiring particular skills or knowledge. Summative data collection applies to long-term, comprehensive teaching goals and yields information about the accumulation and integration of knowledge. In the context of assessment of progress in literacy, formative procedures can be used to track the acquisition of word recognition skills, whereas summative procedures can provide information about reading comprehension. Formative procedures include criterion- and curriculum-referenced tests (including tests constructed by teachers), checklists, anecdotal reports, examples of schoolwork, and records from trial teaching procedures. Formative procedures create an intimate record of progress. Summative procedures are typically norm-referenced tests. For example, a formative assessment might evaluate the students' knowledge of the *r*-controlled phonics rule using a list of *r*-controlled words as the assessment task; a summative assessment would evaluate reading comprehension and, perhaps, reading fluency using a norm-referenced test.

Criterion- and curriculum-referenced tests can be used to collect summative data, but norm-referenced tests do not work well for formative data collection. Many norm-referenced tests are only available in one form and, therefore, cannot be given repeatedly to the same child because the child will learn the test and it will cease to be a reliable indicator of performance. A second limitation is the probability of a mismatch between the content of the test and the instruction the child has received, as is the case, for example, when the words on a norm-referenced test of word recognition are different from those words included in the lessons given to the child taking the test. Finally, norm-referenced test scores are, at best, gross indicators of progress. It is hard to recover from those scores detailed information about the knowledge a child has acquired since the last test was administered. Progress should be documented in smaller increments and in greater detail. Assessment of progress depends on both summative and formative procedures. The details of progress, however, are provided by formative procedures.

INFORMATION NEEDED FOR ASSESSMENT OF PROGRESS

Building on Traditions of Multisensory Education

This section discusses the specific information needed to assess students' progress. Some multisensory programs include information on how to make formative assessments of progress. For example, Alphabetic Phonics (Cox, 1992) and the Dyslexia Training Program (Peckham & Biddle, 1988) use curriculum-referenced tasks called Bench Mark Measures (Cox, 1986) and Progress Measurements (Rumsey, 1992), respectively, to assess progress in letter-knowledge acquisition and alphabetizing skills and to assess reading, spelling, and handwriting. Teachers who use the Recipe for Reading approach (Traub & Bloom, 1975) maintain an assessment folder for each student that includes a record of words the student has learned to read and spell. A list of books that the student has read is also included in the folder. Entries to the folder are dated and arranged chronologically to facilitate evaluation of progress. The Wilson Reading System (Wilson, 1995) includes tests to evaluate mastery of knowledge taught in one curriculum unit before the student moves to the next curriculum unit. Assessment of progress in these programs does focus on students' mastery of word recognition and spelling skills.

To build on this tradition of assessing progress in multisensory programs, educators can identify the classes of data needed to assess progress and identify some sources for methods of data collection. When assessing children who have failed to learn to read despite instruction, assessment of progress may focus on nine classes of data.[5] The following skills should be tracked: the acquisition and use of graphophonemic knowledge (letter–sound associations), accuracy and speed of printed word recognition out of context (word lists) and in context, word recognition strategies, accuracy and speed of spelling in dictated lists and in text, and oral vocabulary. There are several sources of information about procedures for assessing these skills (see footnote 1 on p. 384). In addition to these sources, spelling assessment should be used as a means for assessing phonics knowledge, and informal reading inventories should be used during assessment.

Although it is useful to directly assess children's knowledge of letter–sound associations using checklists of phonics knowledge (e.g., Blachowicz, 1980), children's spellings also provide a window on their knowledge of letter–sound relationships. By examining children's spellings, teachers can gain insight into children's phonics knowledge (Treiman, 1998). Use of spelling to assess phonics knowledge requires a spelling curriculum, that is, an outline of the content domain of English spelling, knowledge of the developmental sequence for acquiring English spellings, and a method for scoring spellings that evaluates spelling elements within words rather than simply marking words as correct or incorrect. Reading and spelling are usually taught as separate subjects; consequently, teachers might not think to use spelling to assess reading.

Although not intended for this purpose, Spellmaster (Greenbaum, 1987) is a criterion-referenced assessment procedure that is organized to allow the simultaneous assessment of spelling and phonics knowledge. (For more information about spelling assessment, see Moats, 1995, and Mosely, 1997.) Spellmaster is composed of tests that assess knowledge of spelling rules, patterns, and generalizations, as well as knowledge of homonyms and irregular words.

Informal reading inventories (see Leslie & Caldwell, 1995, and Woods & Moe, 1999) typically are used to obtain the data needed to plan remedial programs. The structure of these inventories could provide a model for teachers to use for ongoing assessment. Informal reading inventories are used to establish reading levels for individual students on the basis of accuracy reading single words, accuracy reading words in text, and accuracy answering comprehension questions. These inventories include conventions for marking reading errors (insertions, hesitations, mispronunciations, omissions, regressions, substitutions, self-corrections, pauses, and repetitions) and, more important, provide classifica-

---

[5]The author of this chapter acknowledges the importance of print awareness, print knowledge, and phonological skills in early literacy and also acknowledges that comprehension and composition are the goals of literacy instruction. This chapter, however, argues for an emphasis on formative data collection. For an assessment procedure that includes structured observation of print concepts, letter knowledge, and writing as well as running records of oral reading proficiency, see Clay (1995). To learn about the assessment of phonological skills, see Clark and Uhry (1995). Procedures for assessing comprehension are described in Barr et al. (1995). Writing assessment is described in Cohen and Spenciner (1998) and Rhodes and Shanklin (1993).

tion systems for word reading errors, commonly called *miscues.* Mispronounced words (words read incorrectly) are classified as graphically similar, semantically acceptable, or syntactically correct. This classification allows the teacher to make some inferences about the word recognition strategies students are using. Given the view that word recognition accuracy and fluency depend on the coordinated use of graphophonemic, semantic, and syntactic cues for word recognition (Ehri & McCormick, 1998), the analysis of miscues is important. Some informal reading inventories (e.g., Leslie & Caldwell, 1995) provide procedures for assessing reading rate for words and text and give standards for evaluating a student's fluency with word lists and text. In all informal reading inventories, comprehension is assessed by observing students thinking aloud as they read, retelling stories they have read, and answering questions about the text. Background knowledge is assessed by observing students making predictions about the text before they read based on the title and the first few sentences of the text. Vocabulary is assessed by observing students defining words encountered in the text.

Most inventories are organized to permit comparisons between a student's skills (i.e., fluency and comprehension) with narrative text and his or her skills with expository text. Comparisons can be made between a student's reading performance (i.e., accuracy and fluency) with word lists and his or her performance with text and between reading and listening comprehension. Although the authors of informal reading inventories may not view the inventories from this perspective, they are criterion-referenced tests. As indicated previously, data obtained from these inventories are used to construct remedial programs. The rules included in these inventories for marking reading errors, classifying miscues, and assessing reading rate can be used to create curriculum-referenced assessments based on the texts used for instruction. These structured observations of reading of texts that students use for reading instruction can also be used to assess comprehension, vocabulary, and use of background knowledge. It is easy to imagine an assessment folder that includes records of such observations made on a regular basis. These records would be similar to the running assessment records recommended by Clay (1995). To repeat, the text is from the students' reading lessons; the structure for assessing reading is borrowed from informal reading inventories.

Teachers and Parents Learn, Too

Teachers assess progress for two related reasons. First, teachers use data about students' progress to evaluate the effects of instruction. A teacher will decide that a particular lesson is too easy or too hard based on students' responses. Or, a teacher will decide that a particular student needs more practice based on that student's responses during a lesson. These decisions and others like them are made within a lesson or over a series of lessons. Assessment of students' progress, then, is a learning experience for the teacher. It provides information that the teacher uses to modify instruction. Second, a teacher assesses learning to give information to students and their parents. Information given to students is specific, meaningful and immediate (i.e., provided during the lesson) and cumulative (e.g., collected in folders that are either kept by or easily accessible to the student). The same repositories of information that are available to students also provide information to parents. When parents need to know about their child's progress, the teacher can respond immediately.

For example, Laura's and Michael's teachers may or may not have kept careful documentation of Laura's and Michael's progress when they were learning to read, spell, and write. Imagine, though, a conference between Laura's teacher and parents. Laura's teacher might open a folder containing compositions, spelling tests, structured observations of reading as described previously, lists of books that Laura has read, checklists of phonics knowledge, and other documents of progress; pulls out two records of Laura's oral reading abilities; and says to Laura's parents, "This is a record of what Laura read aloud to me 3 weeks ago, and this is a record of her reading that Laura and I made together yesterday. When you look at each document, you will see that I recorded the word recognition errors she made, the time it took her to read the text, the story as she retold it to me, and her answers to questions I asked about the story. Let's look at both records, and see whether we can see changes that show she is making progress with reading." Later Laura's teacher says, "These are the spelling words that Laura studied this month. As you can see from the spelling test and a story she wrote last week, she spelled the words correctly on the test and in the story. I think that we can trust that she knows how to spell these words."

Michael's parents might have heard from his teacher, "As you can see from the date, Michael wrote this story last month. Yesterday we read it together, and then I dictated it for him to rewrite. After he rewrote his story from dictation, I removed it from view and asked him to write a new version of the original story. Notice the differences among the three texts. Every sentence in the dictated version and the new edition begins with a capital letter. Four of the words that he misspelled in the original story are correct both in the dictation and in the new text. He corrected a verb tense in one dictated sentence and maintained that correction when he wrote the new version of the story. We don't yet know whether these changes mean that Michael has acquired this knowledge and will not forget it, but we certainly can see evidence of change in punctuation and grammar across these three compositions."

CONCLUSION

At the beginning of this chapter, *assessment* is defined as an information-gathering process that is guided by questions and that culminates in decisions that have an effect on an individual's life. The author of this chapter stands by that definition. Assessment of progress, however, is a special type of assessment and warrants a second definition. The English word *assess* derives from the Latin word *assidere* which means *to sit by one's side* (Wiggins, 1993). With this definition in mind, one can imagine a student and teacher sitting side by side and collecting evidence of learning to include in the student's assessment folder. One can also imagine this assessment folder sitting beside the student so that it is easily accessible to anyone who is interested and has a right to gain access to the information. Assessment of progress is a learning experience for all involved. As a result of assessment of progress, a student's reading and spelling may improve, and the teacher's instruction may improve. In addition, the student, his or her parents, and the teacher gain a better understanding of the student's learning and his or her strengths and areas of need.

REFERENCES

Barr, R., Blachowicz, C.L.Z., & Wogman-Sadow, M. (1995). *Reading diagnosis for teachers: An instructional approach* (3rd ed.). Reading, MA: Addison Wesley Longman.

Blachowicz, C.L.Z. (1980). [Blachowicz informal phonics survey.] Evanston, IL: National College of Education. Unpublished assessment device.

Bruck, M. (1998). Outcomes of adults with childhood histories of dyslexia. In C. Hulme & R.M. Joshi (Eds.), *Reading and spelling: Development and disorders* (pp. 179–200). Mahwah, NJ: Lawrence Erlbaum Associates.

Chall, J.S. (1994). Testing linked to teaching. In N.C. Jordan & J. Goldsmith-Phillips (Eds.), *Learning disabilities: New directions for assessment and intervention* (pp. 163–176). Needham Heights, MA: Allyn & Bacon.

Clark, D.R., & Uhry, J.K. (1995). *Dyslexia: Theory and practice of remedial instruction* (2nd ed.). Timonium, MD: York Press.

Clay, M.M. (1995). *An observation survey of early literacy attainment* (Rev. ed.). Portsmouth, NH: Heinemann.

Cohen, L.G., & Spenciner, L.J. (1998). *Assessment of children and youth*. Reading, MA: Addison Wesley Longman.

Coles, G. (1998). *Reading lessons: The debate over literacy*. New York: Hill and Wang.

Cox, A.R. (1986). *Bench Mark Measures*. Cambridge, MA: Educators Publishing Service.

Cox, A.R. (1992). *Foundations for literacy: Structures and techniques for multisensory teaching of basic written English language skills*. Cambridge, MA: Educators Publishing Service.

Critchley, M. (1970). *The dyslexic child*. Springfield, IL: Charles C Thomas.

Ehri, L.C., & McCormick, S. (1998). Phases of word learning: Implications for instruction with delayed and disabled readers. *Reading and Writing Quarterly, 14*, 135–163.

Falk, B. (1998). Testing the way children learn: Principles for valid literacy assessments. *Language Arts, 76*, 57–66.

Farnham-Diggory, S. (1992). *The learning disabled child*. Cambridge, MA: Harvard University Press.

Felton, R.H. (1998). The development of reading skills in poor readers: Educational implications. In C. Hulme & R.M. Joshi (Eds.), *Reading and spelling: Development and disorders* (pp. 219–233). Mahwah, NJ: Lawrence Erlbaum Associates.

Fink, R.P. (1996). Successful dyslexics: A constructivist study of passionate interest in reading. *Journal of Adolescent and Adult Literacy, 39*, 268–280.

Fletcher, J.M., Shaywitz, S.E., Shankweiler, D.P., Katz, L., Liberman, I.Y., Steubing, K.K., Francis, D.J., Fowler, A.D., & Shaywitz, B.A. (1994). Cognitive profiles of reading disability: Comparisons of discrepancy and low achievement definitions. *Journal of Educational Psychology, 86*, 6–23.

Fuchs, L.S. (1986). Monitoring progress among mildly handicapped pupils: Review of current practice and research. *Remedial and Special Education, 7*, 5–12.

Goldsmith-Phillips, J. (1994). Toward a research-based dyslexia assessment: Case study of a young adult. In N.C. Jordan & J. Goldsmith-Phillips (Eds.), *Learning disabilities: New directions for assessment and intervention* (pp. 85–100). Needham Heights, MA: Allyn & Bacon.

Greenbaum, C.R. (1987). *Spellmaster*. Austin, TX: PRO-ED.

Hornsby, G., Atkinson, M., & Howard, J. (1997). *Controversial issues in special education*. London: David Fulton, Publishers.

Kerr, J. (1897). School hygiene in its mental, moral and physical aspects. *Journal of the Royal Statistical Society, 60*, 613–680.

Leslie, L., & Caldwell, J. (1995). *Qualitative reading inventory* (2nd ed.). New York: HarperCollins.

Lyon, G.R. (1995). Toward a definition of dyslexia. *Annals of Dyslexia, 45*, 3–27.

Miller, W.H. (1995). *Alternative assessment techniques for reading and writing*. West Nyack: NY: The Center for Applied Research in Education.

Moats, L.C. (1995). *Spelling: Development, disability, and instruction*. Timonium, MD: York Press.

Morgan, W.P. (1896). A case of congenital word-blindness. *British Medical Journal, 2*, 1378.

Mosely, D.V. (1997). Assessment of spelling and related aspects of written expression. In J.R. Beech & C. Singleton (Eds.), *The psychological assessment of reading* (pp. 204–223). London: Routledge.

Olson, R.K., Wise, B., Ring, J., & Johnson, M. (1997). Computer-based remedial reading training in phoneme awareness and phonological decoding: Effects on the post-training development of word recognition. *Scientific Studies of Reading, 1,* 235–253.

Orton, S.T. (1937). *Reading, writing and speech problems in children.* New York: W.W. Norton.

Peckham, B., & Biddle, M.L. (1988). *Dyslexia training program.* Cambridge, MA: Educators Publishing Service.

Pennington, B. F. (1991). *Diagnosing learning disorders: A neuropsychological perspective.* New York: The Guilford Press.

Pennington, B.F., Gilger, J.W., Olson, R.K., & DeFries, J.C. (1992). The external validity of age-versus IQ-discrepancy definitions of reading disability: Lessons from a twin study. *Journal of Learning Disabilities, 25,* 562–573.

Rhodes, L.K., & Shanklin, N.L. (1993). *Windows into literacy.* Portsmouth, NH: Heinemann.

Rumsey, M.B. (1992). *Dyslexia Training Program Progress Measurements* (Schedules I–III). Cambridge, MA: Educators Publishing Service.

Salvia, J., & Ysseldyke, J.E. (1998). *Assessment* (7th ed.). Boston: Houghton Mifflin.

Shaywitz, S.E. (1996). Dyslexia. *Scientific American, 275,* 98–104.

Shaywitz, S.E. (1998). Dyslexia. *New England Journal of Medicine, 338,* 207–312.

Shepherd, M.J., Charnow, D.A., & Silver, L.B. (1989). Development of reading disorder. In H. Kaplan & B. Sadow (Eds.), *Comprehensive textbook of psychiatry* (5th ed., Vol. 2, pp. 1790–1800). Baltimore: Lippincott Williams & Wilkins.

Shepherd, M.J., & Uhry, J.K. (1993). Reading disorder. *Child and Adolescent Clinics of North America, 2,* 193–208.

Siegel, L.S. (1999). Learning disabilities: The roads we have traveled and the path to the future. In R.J. Sternberg & L. Spear-Swerling (Eds.), *Perspectives on learning disabilities: Biological, cognitive, contextual* (pp. 159–175). Boulder, CO: Westview Press.

Snowling, M., & Hulme, C. (1989). A longitudinal case study of developmental phonological dyslexia. *Cognitive Neuropsychology, 6,* 379–401.

Stanovich, K.E. (1986). Matthew effects in reading: Some consequences of individual differences in the acquisition of literacy. *Reading Research Quarterly, 21,* 360–406.

Stanovich, K.E., & Siegel, L.S. (1994). The phenotypic performance profile of reading-disabled children: A regression-based test of the phonological-core variable-difference model. *Journal of Educational Psychology, 86,* 24–53.

Sternberg, R.J., & Spear-Swerling, L. (1999). *Perspectives on learning disabilities: Biological, cognitive, contextual.* Boulder, CO: Westview Press.

Traub, N., & Bloom, F. (1975). *Recipe for reading.* Cambridge, MA: Educators Publishing Service.

Treiman, R. (1998). Why spelling? The benefits of incorporating spelling into beginning reading instruction. In J.L. Metsala & L.C. Ehri (Eds.), *Word recognition in beginning literacy* (pp. 289–313). Mahwah, NJ: Lawrence Erlbaum Associates.

Turner, M. (1997). *Psychological assessment of dyslexia.* San Diego: Singular Publishing Group.

Wiggins, G. (1993). *Assessing student performance: Exploring the purpose and limits of testing.* San Francisco: Jossey-Bass.

Wilson, B.A. (1995). *Wilson reading system.* Unpublished manuscript.

Woods, M.L., & Moe, A. (1999). *Analytic reading inventory* (6th ed.). Upper Saddle River, NJ: Prentice-Hall.

15

Transition to the General Classroom and Content Areas

Shary Maskel

Schools must begin to focus on educating a wide range of students with diverse backgrounds, abilities, and styles of learning. Students bring different learning styles and strengths to the classroom, which means that not every student learns in the same manner (Gardner, 1985). To successfully teach students who have such a wide range of abilities and talents, educators must become more accepting of learning differences, be more willing to make accommodations, and be able to teach to a wide range of students (Liberman, 1992). Reaching and teaching a diverse student population not only is expected in educational circles but also is mandated by law.

According to federal mandates, all students with disabilities, including students with learning disabilities, are entitled to a free and appropriate public education in the least restrictive environment (Individuals with Disabilities Education Act [IDEA] Amendments of 1997, PL 105-17). A continuum of placement alternatives must be available to each identified student. These alternatives may range from instruction in general education classrooms, to inclusive classes, to special classes, to special schools, to hospitals or institutions, or even to the student's home. To provide equal access to all educational programs, the necessary modifications, **accommodations,** transition plans, and supplementary services must be provided. The Orton Dyslexia Society (ODS), now called the International Dyslexia Association, made the strong statement that "no single type of placement option will meet the needs of all students with specific learning disabilities" ("ODS Position Statement on Inclusion," 1992, pp. 2–3). The ODS cautioned educators to consider that full **inclusion,** in which all students receive services within the context of the general education classroom, must not be the only placement option. Furthermore, they contended that

> Students with specific learning disabilities require individualized and/or differential instruction that includes systematic multisensory instruction in reading, writing, and spelling which emphasizes phonemic awareness and the structure of the language. These students must be provided services that will match the severity and intensity of their disability. Each student's individual educational program defines the services needed. The decision as to where these services are provided must be based upon the specific needs of the individual. These services must be student centered and provided in the least restrictive environment that includes regular education, special classes, or a combination of the two. (pp. 2–3)

The trend in school reform since the early 1990s has been to serve children with learning disabilities in general classrooms as an alternative to providing services in **self-contained classrooms** or pull-out programs. Although this approach may be appropriate for students who can perform in the general classroom with accommodations, other students need intensive remediation beyond what can be offered in general classrooms. Because of the nature and severity of their disability, these students need intensive, systematic instruction that may not be available in general classrooms. This chapter explains transition planning for students who have learning disabilities and the role that multisensory structured language education (MSLE) plays in transition plans. First, however, the inclusion and placement policies that are integral to transition planning are explained.

In general, students who are 2 or more years behind their expected level of achievement are candidates for the specialized techniques and strategies offered by MSLE approaches, although most students would benefit from these types of approaches. Students for whom this approach is most recommended have been diagnosed by a licensed psychologist or a trained learning disabilities specialist as having a specific learning disability in the area of reading or as having dyslexia. They have failed to learn to read or have had extreme difficulty in doing so using standard classroom practices that usually are based on the sight-word approach or utilize whole-language applications. In general, these students demonstrate a weakness in phonological awareness, have difficulty remembering the consistent patterns of the language, and are slow to learn sight words. In many cases, these students also demonstrate accompanying difficulties with written language, including spelling, mechanics, and composition skills.

Students with learning disabilities in general classrooms who participate in MSLE programs usually need instructional accommodations to keep pace with the other students in the classroom. These students' programs should be substantive and should not be a watered-down version of the classroom curriculum. These students need to be exposed to the material presented in the content area classes, especially science and social studies, and they also need to participate fully and appropriately in typical classroom activities even if they are in the general classroom for only a portion of the day. Classroom teachers must work effectively with these students even if the students also are receiving remedial help in an alternative environment. For this to happen, general classroom teachers need to understand how MSLE programs work and how to work effectively with students with learning disabilities in the general classroom. By receiving appropriate accommodations and a modified curriculum, these students can achieve success in general classrooms. Once a child has demonstrated an acceptable level of competence in reading and written language, certain instructional strategies can be implemented in the general classroom that may further improve the student's reading skills and ensure a successful transition to full-time education in the general classroom. Teachers can implement numerous strategies that have a foundation in MSLE.

Once a student is ready to make the transition into the general classroom on a full-time basis, the teacher can incorporate some multisensory strategies in instruction. Direct teaching, mastery learning, overlearning, prompts, cues, and mnemonics are some of the strategies that the classroom teacher could employ to make the transition smoother and more effective. In addition, students should be encouraged to practice the word-attack skills that they have learned, such as dividing unfamiliar words into syllables to figure out pronunciation. Using the knowledge of the morphology of the language as clues to discovering the meaning of new vocabulary words can help students improve word identification skills. Other strategies that the teacher might employ include using a weekly syllabus, teaching semantic and syntactic variations, giving prereading questions to guide comprehension, extending time spent on assignments, and other such accommodations as may be appropriate.

It is important for the multidisciplinary team to work cooperatively in exploring placement options during the early stages of the transition process. Classroom teachers who are prepared for the challenges of teaching diverse learners are equipped to handle the special needs of students with learning disabilities. Attention also should be given to students who need help in understanding their learning differences so that they can be self-advocates and have the confidence to suggest modifications to their academic program.

The successful transition of students with learning disabilities into general classrooms requires careful planning and is influenced by the degree of support given to classroom teachers and students. Teachers need training in applying MSLE strategies in general classrooms, integrating study skills, and making the appropriate accommodations for students. Unfortunately, because the majority of school districts experience financial difficulties, many teachers do not receive the necessary training and support from administrators when students with learning disabilities are included in general classrooms (Learning Disabilities Association of America, 1993; Silver, 1991). In general, teachers and administrators do not always have the benefit of the intensive preparation, manageable classroom size, state-of-the-art technology, or increased educational support that is needed (Liberman, 1992). This has profound implications when the transition team is considering how to make transition effective once the student returns to the general classroom on a full-time basis.

INCLUSION AND MULTISENSORY
PROGRAMS IN THE GENERAL CLASSROOM

The major problem faced by students in need of the specialized techniques offered by MSLE program is that this type of instruction may not be available. The special techniques for remediation used in resource classrooms vary. There is no agreement on what the instructional content should be in resource classrooms

(Haight, 1985). Deshler, Lowrey, and Alley (1979) surveyed 98 secondary school teachers from 48 states to identify the curricular content in resource classrooms. The most prevalent instruction, found in 45% of the classrooms, was remediation that emphasized basic skills. None of the teachers surveyed, however, reported using multisensory approaches that utilize specialized materials and strategies and can best be described as basic-skills remediation that relies on a specific theoretical philosophy and techniques adapted from the Orton-Gillingham approach (Gillingham & Stillman, 1997). The Orton-Gillingham approach, which is useful for all types of learners, has been particularly successful for students who need stronger decoding skills to unlock the code structures of words. Content area teachers can use strategies from this approach to strengthen reading skills. The second most prevalent resource room approach, found in 24% of the classrooms, was the use of tutorials in which teachers assisted students in subject areas that complemented the general classroom curriculum. An approach that focused on functional or survival skills, such as completing a job application or mastering driver's education competencies, was used in 17% of the classes. A small percentage of resource room programs used a **learning strategies model** as the instructional approach. For purposes of this discussion, a resource room program that uses MSLE strategies based on the Orton-Gillingham approach is proposed as the means of helping students with severe reading/written language problems.

A student who participates in MSLE programs may be placed in a general classroom if the classroom teacher has had training, but usually classroom teachers do not have the required expertise in teaching language structure (Moats, 1994). It is hoped, though, that this type of training will eventually be added to teacher education programs. In most cases, MSLE instruction occurs in an alternative environment. Usually, the student either is pulled out of the general classroom for a portion of the day to receive instruction in a resource environment or attends a one-to-one or small-group tutorial after regular school hours. In any case, the general classroom teacher must make appropriate accommodations that do not include watered-down content or limitations in substance in the general classroom for the student who has reading and written language difficulties.

Federal laws mandate academic accommodations that ensure a student's progress and success while receiving remedial help and while making the transition to the general classroom on a full time basis. Vital pieces of legislation for individuals seeking accommodations include the following: Section 504 of the Rehabilitation Act of 1973 (PL 93-112), which was reauthorized in 1986 (PL 99-506) and 1992 (PL 102-569); the Education for All Handicapped Children Act of 1975 (PL 94-142), which later became IDEA of 1990 (PL 101-476), which was amended in 1991 (PL 102-119) and was reauthorized and amended in 1997 (PL 105-17); and the Americans with Disabilities Act of 1990 (ADA; PL 101-336).

School systems have individuals who are responsible for translating federal guidelines into operational plans at their own schools. It is important for educators to be aware of the mandates that affect their own teaching situations. Appropriate accommodations in general education environments are important not only for students with disabilities who remain in general education classrooms but also for students who receive intensive help in basic skills outside the classroom and are included in general classrooms for specific content area classes.

There are residential schools for students with learning disabilities who need intensive remedial instruction, such as Landmark in Prides Crossing, Massachusetts, which has designed its own MSLE program, and there are day schools such as the Carroll School in Waltham, Massachusetts, and the Churchill School in St. Louis, Missouri. The Churchill School actually offers a specialized 1- to 2-year transitional program for students preparing to be included in the general classroom on a full-time basis. In Durham, North Carolina, kindergartners through 12th graders attend a unique half-day MSLE program at the Hill Center. For the remainder of the day, these students attend another public or private school, where they take science, social studies, art, music, and physical education classes.

When a student is pulled out of general classroom activities during key instructional times or when the student is not able to perform alongside peers as a result of his or her academic performance, every effort should be made to keep this student involved and engaged in the instructional program and activities of the general classroom even though he or she is receiving specialized help during part of the school day. An example of this type of instructional model is included in the following case study of the Hill Center's MSLE program.

Case Study: The Relationship Between an MSLE Program and a General Classroom

The Hill Center, which is one division of Durham Academy, an independent day school with 1,000 students in North Carolina, offers a program that can serve as a model for public and private schools that are interested in providing intensive remedial instruction using MSLE approaches to students with learning disabilities who are included in general education classes. Students attend the Hill Center only during the morning or afternoon and attend another public or independent school for the remainder of the day. This arrangement allows the students to remain in general classrooms for part of the day and receive the intensive remediation that they need to improve academic performance. In general, students take science, social studies, physical education, and elective classes at their other schools.

The Hill Center offers small-group instruction in reading, written language, and mathematics for students in grades K–8 and, at the high school level, adds Spanish courses along with literature, advanced composition, and upper-level math courses including precalculus and discrete math. High school students can take one to three classes depending on the level of their difficulties and how close they are to making a full transition from the program to the general classroom.

The Hill Center's teachers work closely with the classroom teachers at the other schools. School visits and observations, joint individualized education program (IEP) and individualized transition plan (ITP) meetings, and contact with parents all take place. Periodic written progress reports, grades, and standardized test data are shared with the other schools and with the parents. The Hill Center's teachers work cooperatively with the other schools, the parents, and outside professionals so that there is a team approach to dealing with the diverse needs of the student. For example, a psychologist or counselor who is seeing a student may be asked to join that student's intervention team. When a student is ready to be included in the general classroom on a full-time basis, the Hill Center coordinates the transition plan with the other school and the parents. For students who need continued support after leaving the program, the Hill Center offers after-school tutoring. For students ages 14 and older who plan to enter the job market after high school, the Hill Center works with the school's transition committee and parents to establish goals and make decision to carry out a well-thought transition plan (LDA Postsecondary Education Committee, 1999).

The Hill Center provides services to students in the other divisions of Durham Academy who have been diagnosed with learning disabilities and/or attention-deficit/hyperactivity disorder (ADHD). Such services include making recommendations for psychological testing, helping to interpret test results, and making recommendations for placement, as well as consulting with teachers about appropriate classroom accommodations and monitoring academic performance. This relationship could be replicated by other schools that serve students with diverse learning needs.

In addition, the Hill Center acts as a community resource for teachers, administrators, parents, and students who are interested in finding out more about learning disabilities and the techniques found to be successful in remediating learning difficulties. The Hill Center provides in-service training to teachers in the community and across the country.

One of the Hill Center's week-long summer institutes addressed the following issues, which are also key concerns when working with students with learning disabilities who are making the transition to general classrooms:

- Overview of learning disabilities and ADHD
- Recognizing students with learning disabilities
- Diagnosis: psychological and educational assessment
- Instructional models for meeting individual students' needs
- The teacher: supporting parents and acting as an advocate for students
- Successful instructional methods for working with students who have learning disabilities and/or ADHD
- Implementing a study skills program within the curriculum
- Accommodating students with learning difficulties in general classrooms
- Adapting new instructional techniques to the classroom
- Developing a schoolwide plan for improving academic performance

When schools are able to address these concerns, they focus not only on providing new instructional techniques and strategies but also on the teachers' ability to discover what they are already doing that works and on offering them the opportunity to share this information. Emphasis is on improving classroom instruction and discovering teaching techniques that are not necessarily labor-intensive for the teacher and are beneficial to most students, such as teaching students to decode words by applying syllabification rules.

ADAPTING MULTISENSORY
STRATEGIES FOR USE IN GENERAL CLASSROOMS

In 1996 Moats stated the following:

> Students with learning disabilities in general education classes may be able to pass courses because their assignments are modified, they are read to, or someone writes for them, but often they are not learning how to read, write, calculate, solve problems, and study. (p. 89)

The use of multisensory teaching strategies in general classrooms offers some alternative approaches to daily classroom instruction that may help to reach students with diverse learning needs.

Haring and Bateman (1977) noted that dyslexic students need direct, intensive, and systematic instruction (see also Chapter 1). In general, professional organizations that advocate for students with learning disabilities assert that "students with learning disabilities sometimes require an intensity and systematicity of instruction uncommon to general education classrooms" (Fuchs & Fuchs, 1994, p. 304). Direct instruction, which is both planned and controlled by the teacher, has proven to be a useful way to teach academic skills to students with disabilities (Winograd & Hare, 1988). An important consideration in direct instruction is the amount of active learning time in whole-class instruction, which, according to Karweit (1985), varies widely with the size and diversity of the class and the procedural demands on the teacher. A key classroom management issue, then, is the amount of engaged time that a dyslexic student spends on-task.

Another important principle in remedial instruction is aiming for mastery learning. This teaching goal is based on the premise that a student must master the specific subskills of one task to learn a new task. Lerner (1993) likened mastery learning to climbing rungs on a ladder. Each rung must be touched while the learner is climbing to the top; the learner who misses some rungs may fall off. Lerner offered this detailed description of mastery learning:

> First, a sequence of skills in a subject area (reading, arithmetic, spelling, and so forth) is established. The teacher attempts to determine how far the student has gone along that sequence, what the student does not know within the sequence, and where in the sequence teaching should begin. The skill of reading, for example, is presumed to be composed of many skills and subskills; by mastering the component skills, the student should master the skill of reading. Teachers must have a thorough understanding of the skills sequence in each subject area. (1993, p. 122)

According to Rosenshine (1983), to ensure retention, student mastery needs to be at the 70%–80% level when new information is to be learned and at the 100% level during independent practice. An important aspect of mastery learning is the student's automatic recall of basic information, or automaticity. For example, automatic recall of words frees up working memory to allow for more efficient processing of a written passage and thus aids comprehension (Stanovich, 1984). Overlearning (Bateman, 1979), in which students perform skills automatically, such as decoding words, stresses the need for repetition and practice in learning a new concept. The systematic review and practice of previously learned skills ensure retention of this information and prevent gaps or holes in the hierarchy of basic skills to be mastered.

Wood (1992) explained how to adapt mastery learning techniques for general classrooms. Using mastery learning units, students are tested, graded, and given additional instruction and practice if they do not meet a specified level of performance. If they demonstrate mastery, then students can move on to the next unit. According to Guskey (1981), mastery learning actually facilitates **cooperative learning** rather than competitive learning in classrooms. (For more on cooperative learning, see Putnam, 1998.) To successfully implement a mastery learning program, the teacher must implement specific procedures for teaching and reinforcing concepts and skills, and a wide variety of materials appropriate to the level of the skills being taught must be available.

Prompts, cues, mnemonic devices, and learning strategies are often utilized in programs that incorporate multisensory instructional strategies. Prompting a student to respond is just another way of giving that student encouragement. A cue gives a student an extra nudge or hint when he or she has problems retrieving specific information. Sometimes just a single word or a nonverbal signal will help a student who has retrieval problems come up with the correct response. Pictures or objects can also serve as memory aids in remedial instruction (Bryant et al., 1980). Explicit instruction on using keyword strategies for facilitating retrieval of information is another technique used for helping students memorize material (Fulk, 1994). Learning strategies involving the memorization of acronyms help students to structure inner language. These strategies were initially associated with the University of Kansas Learning Disabilities Institute under the direction of Deshler (Clark, Deshler, Schumaker, Alley & Warner, 1984; Deshler, Alley, Warner, & Schumaker, 1981; Deshler, Schumaker, Lenz, & Ellis, 1984). Learning strategies exist for reading paragraphs, completing multiple-choice test questions, reading chapters in a subject-area text, studying captions under pictures in a textbook, and many other academic tasks. A sample learning strategy is the COPS strategy (Schumaker, Nolan, & Deshler, 1985), which is intended to improve students' proofreading skills.

COPS: The Most Common Mistakes in Writing

Capitalization

Overall Appearance

Punctuation

Spelling

In math, teachers often use the mnemonic **P**lease **E**xcuse **M**y **D**ear **A**unt **S**ally (parentheses, exponents, multiplication, division, addition, subtraction) to help students remember the order of operations in a math problem such as [43 − 5 (8 + 2)] ÷ 7 + 3 • 4 − 1, and teachers use the mnemonic **FOIL** (multiply the first, outer, inner, and last numbers) to help students remember how to find binomial products such as (x+3)(x+2).

The use of feedback that is both immediate and specific is another helpful tool for working with dyslexic students. Most established programs that adhere to the notion of *learning to mastery* include some type of feedback system. Immediate feedback from the teacher is one of the five most important contributive factors to academic achievement (Rosenshine & Stevens, 1984). Students take on more responsibility for learning and are better monitors of their progress when they are given standards that measure their performance (Bandura, 1982). Older students appear to be more motivated when their performance is monitored frequently, and they thus have a gauge for measuring their progress (Zigmond & Miller, 1986).

ACCOMMODATING THE NEEDS OF
DIVERSE LEARNERS IN GENERAL CLASSROOMS

With the trend toward inclusive education—including alternative administrative arrangements such as "mainstreaming"; regular education initiatives, "which in spirit attempt to extend the rights and resources of EHA [Education of the Handicapped Act of 1970; PL 91-230] to all students" (Skrtic, 1992, p. 204); and full inclusion—students who need specialized instruction may not get the intensive help they need unless there is some commitment to providing a continuum of educational program alternatives (Lerner, 1993). Evidence suggests that students with learning disabilities do not fare well in general education classrooms in which undifferentiated, large-group instruction is the norm (Baker & Zigmond, 1990; McIntosh, Vaughn, Schumm, Haager, & Lee, 1993). For example, a classroom teacher must have all of the skills and time necessary to successfully teach students with severe reading difficulties in the context of their general classroom. These students need intensive instruction beyond what usually takes place in most general classrooms; specifically, they need to participate in an MSLE program that has been found to improve academic performance (Maskel & Felton, 1995).

Some discouraging research shows that general education teachers do not modify their teaching when children with learning disabilities are placed in their classrooms (Baker & Zigmond, 1990). Possible modifications might include extending time on assignments, adapting grading criteria, or developing a contract for completing classwork and homework. Schumm and Vaughn reported that their 5-year study that addressed teacher and student perceptions of instructional adaptations for students with diverse learning needs indicated that "classroom teachers feel they lack preparedness to teach students with disabilities, lack opportunities to collaborate with special education teachers, and make infrequent and unsystematic use of adaptations" (1995, p. 169). Some of the study's other findings, which have implications for teachers involved in modifying daily instructional programs for students with learning disabilities, suggested that, in general, teachers do not prepare written individualized lesson plans; that students with learning disabilities are expected to be responsible for the same content as general education students; and that adaptations and modifications to content, materials, assignments, and evaluations are made on a whole-class basis instead of in terms of accommodating individual differences. Teachers need training in how to make appropriate accommodations in the classroom, as well as the necessary resources to address the needs of a diverse student population and, perhaps most important, time to collaborate with special education teachers.

Students who participate in MSLE programs usually do so for only part of their school day, and they are expected to participate in general classroom activities as much as possible for the remainder of the day. In order to keep pace with fellow students, their assignments may need to be modified, they may need to be read to, or they may need to have someone write for them. PL 105-17 clearly addresses the fact that modifications should be made within general classrooms for students who are identified as unable to keep up with the general education program. Even when students participate in a multisensory program, they still need to be able to maintain an active level of participation in their general classrooms—especially in content area courses. These students can be successful in academic classes provided that modifications are made. Even once the student makes the transition to full-time attendance in the general classroom, certain accommodations may still be warranted.

General educators interested in modifying their programs may make any of the following commonly used adaptations:

- Seat dyslexic students close to the front of the classroom
- Extend time on assignments
- Reduce length of assignments
- Break long-term assignments into manageable parts
- Monitor students' understanding of directions and assigned tasks
- Adapt evaluations, scoring, and grading criteria
- Match a student with learning disabilities with a classmate
- Always give a purpose for reading, and structure postreading activities to increase retention of content
- Develop a study guide or study outline
- Introduce key vocabulary before a specific unit of study
- Pair oral and written directions
- Use books on tape, or read textbooks aloud to students
- Place students in cooperative learning groups
- Develop a contract for classwork and homework completion
- Teach learning strategies approaches
- Have students use technology (e.g., computers, calculators, tape recorders) whenever possible

Now emerging within professional publications is a collection of ideas and strategies on how to successfully accommodate dyslexic students in general classrooms. For example, math teachers could provide graph paper for students having difficulty lining up columns of numbers; student scribes could take notes in social studies classes, and audiotapes of chapters of a biology textbook could be made available for listening. Suggestions for helping students cope with dyslexia (McCoy, 1988) include providing frequent drill and reinforcement on previously learned concepts, reviewing math equations with students before implementing them in scientific calculations, offering numerous practical examples during instruction, giving students an outline of notes keyed to the structure of the text, providing weekly homework assignment sheets, and varying teaching styles to match learning styles. In addition, students could be required to use a notebook system with color-coded spiral notebooks and pocket folders in which to keep homework, review sheets, and tests for each class (see Chapter 13).

Ideally, a dyslexic student would participate in an MSLE program that addresses his or her need for remedial help while allowing that student to stay engaged in the academic and social activities of the general classroom. This is accomplished through thoughtful and planned modifications to the general curriculum and instructional plan.

There is a growing amount of information available on how to make accommodations within each of the content areas—English, science, social studies, math, and technology. There is also some very useful information available on how to adapt the socioemotional, behavioral, and physical environment as well as on how to adapt lesson plans, teaching techniques, content, media, and evaluation/grading techniques (Wood, 1992). General classroom teachers need to have access to this information, which is beginning to emerge more frequently in professional books and journals. For teachers to feel comfortable in making adaptations in the classroom, there has to be administrative support, more time allotted to incorporate these ideas, and guidance from trained professionals on how to implement these strategies in the daily operations of the classroom.

Vallecorsa, Ledford, and Parnell (1991) described how to teach composition skills to students with learning disabilities by elaborating on a writing process that has three stages: 1) a planning stage in which ideas are developed, the audience is considered, and the purpose of writing is formulated; 2) a drafting stage in which ideas are elaborated without attention to mechanics and perfection; and 3) an evaluation and revision stage in which proofreading skills are emphasized and whether the paper reflects the author's intent is determined. Specific strategies at this final stage of writing include proofreading each other's papers, using a thesaurus, referring to a list of transition words, and reading one's work aloud. An evaluation guide is useful to some students so they become aware of specific areas that need scrutiny such as organization, style, spelling, handwriting, capitalization, and punctuation.

Directly teaching story elements (main character, setting, problem, plan, ending) and showing students how to use self-monitoring checklists is useful in improving coherence and organization in students' writings. Various writing formats, such as the *hamburger paragraph* (topic sentence, three supporting details, and conclusion), the *relationship planner paragraph* (topic, fact, and their relationship), and the *comparison/contrast jot list* (separate lists of similarities and differences, followed by a conclusion), are also helpful to students when they are organizing and formulating written exercises.

Graphic organizers help students form a mental image of what they have read. Graphic organizers that have been found to be effective in helping students visualize concepts include the following: story boards (the student draws or writes story events in sequence), character webs (a character's name is put in the center of a web with traits and descriptions stemming from the center), Venn diagrams (two similar pieces of literature or characters are compared and/or contrasted in a diagram of overlapping circles), and **prediction charts** (students make initial predictions and modify the chart as the story is being read). Creative projects can also help students expand their understanding of concepts. Students can pantomime scenes from a book, create a book jacket, videotape a book scene, design costumes for characters, or produce a commercial that promotes a favorite book. Creative opportunities for students to expand concepts and build mental images are limited only by the teacher's and students' imaginations.

In order to promote an in-depth understanding of science terms and concepts for students with disabilities, the American Association for the Advancement of Science suggested several principles for instruction, including promoting the study of common themes, highlighting the interrelationships of various science disciplines, and organizing content by aspects of the world rather than by traditional disciplines (McFarland & Shepard, 1992). In general, a "hands-on" approach that utilizes models, charts, and diagrams, as well as careful attention to lab activities and step-by-step explanations, will help students who have difficulty with abstract scientific concepts.

In content area courses such as science and social studies, the note-taking demands may become overwhelming for students with written language difficulties. These students would find a weekly or daily outline of material to be covered in class to be invaluable. The outline provides a structure for recording essential information. It is also helpful for the teacher to use **boldface** for particularly significant topics in the outline. The student could then make notecards concerning the boldfaced topics and use these notecards to study for subsequent tests. For example, if a student made notecards of the boldfaced items in his or her outline and made the effort to study those notecards nightly for 10–15 minutes, then the material would be familiar to the student during an exam. Waiting to the last minute to cram information into short-term memory is rarely a successful technique for students with learning disabilities. Following is a sample of preparation strategy used in a general education classroom.

Sample Preparation Strategy for an Eighth-Grade British History Class

First, the teacher gives students an outline of the week's lesson with important terms in boldface (see Figure 15.1). The teacher and the class define each of the boldfaced words on notecards, with term on one side and definitions on the other side, as shown in Figure 15.2.

Next, the teacher labels a recipe box SOCIAL STUDIES, then divides the box into sections according to material to be covered on each test (e.g., Cromwell, the Glorious Revolution, William and Mary). The teacher encourages students to study the cards nightly and to divide the cards into material they know well, material they need to review, and unfamiliar material. They can even color-code this material: red for *know well*; yellow for *review*; and green for *unfamiliar*. When a teacher does not provide students with an outline, the students can construct notecards based on class notes, handouts, old tests, boldfaced or italic words in textbooks, items on lists (e.g., causes of the English Civil War), or vocabulary.

The National Council of Teachers of Mathematics has offered a number of recommendations on how to help teach algebra and other math subjects to students with learning disabilities (Manheimer & Fleischner, 1995). A number of suggestions have been made as to how to help students with learning disabilities solve word problems (Marzano, 1992; see also Chapter 11 in this book). Some teachers have used checklists, key word/phrase charts, and illustrations (Karrison & Carroll, 1991). Others have suggested cognitive strategy training to help students solve math problems (Montague & Box, 1986).

Students with spatial difficulties may need to work math problems on graph paper or may need to divide their paper into fourths, sixths, or eighths and place one problem in each box. Teachers should introduce concepts using manipulatives (see Chapter 11), encourage students to highlight key words in the problem, or use a basic problem-solving sequence such as the following:

- Read the problem.
- Identify key words.
- Identify the operation.
- Write the number sentence.
- Solve the problem.

It would be helpful for the teacher to model these techniques for the students. Some students could be permitted to draw pictures to illustrate word problems. To ensure success, a teacher could reduce the number of problems per assignment and ask students to work one or two problems on a page as a group before they complete the page independently.

OLIVER CROMWELL

   I. Oliver Cromwell
      1. New Model Army: defeat of the King
      2. Second Civil War: defeat of the Royalists at Preston
   II. Pride's Purge (December 1648)
      1. Creation of the Rump
      2. Trial of the King
      3. Execution of the King (January 1649)
      4. Creation of the Republic
   III. The Republic Period
      1. Subduing of the Scots
         a. Defeat of the forces of Charles I at Worcester
         b. The "Royal Oak"
      2. Navigation Acts of 1650
      3. War with the Dutch
      4. Dissolution of the Rump, 1653
   IV. Commonwealth Period (1653–1658)
      1. Cromwell as Lord Protector
      2. Religious toleration
      3. Major generals
      4. Concluding the Dutch War
   V. End of Cromwell's Rule
      1. Ineffective rule of Richard Cromwell
      2. General Monck's discussions with Charles II
      3. Declaration of Breda
      4. Restoration of the monarchy

Figure 15.1 Weekly outline for an eighth-grade British history class.

Teachers have recognized the computer as an important tool for dyslexic students. Using a word processor helps reduce the frustration felt by many students who struggle with paper-and-pencil writing (Chalmers & Wasson, 1993). Teachers have found that word processors do not actually increase the quality of students' language and use but often encourage students to write more and to experiment with words, so they may have an indirect effect in improving writing (Keefe & Chandler, 1989). Computers have also been found to aid a classroom instructor in teaching students with learning disabilities or ADHD by providing opportunities for direct instruction, mastery learning, overlearning, cooperative learning, and monitoring student progress (Vockell & Mihail, 1993). There are programs that turn a student's mapping of ideas into an outline and vice versa.

Modifying how a student with learning disabilities is evaluated does not have to mean that the content of a course is compromised. Many students with learning disabilities will need extended time on assignments or tests or possibly shortened assignments. They would also benefit from teacher–student conferences after tests. Another useful adaptation is breaking long-term writing assignments into manageable parts, that is, grading separately the research process, cards for data collection, the outline, the rough draft, and the final product.

| Lord Protector | Title chosen by Oliver Cromwell when he ruled England. Cromwell would not accept the title of King because he had fought to depose the monarchy. |

Figure 15.2.   Notecard with definition.

The construction of tests is an extremely important consideration for teachers who work with students who have language processing and memory problems. All questions should be stated clearly and succinctly. The choices for multiple-choice questions should be limited to three, and questions that have more than one possible correct choice should be avoided. Matching questions should be limited to 10, with questions on the left and answers on the right. It also helps for the teacher to put possible answers to matching questions in some kind of logical order, such as alphabetical order. With fill-in-the-blank questions, a set or word bank of possible choices helps students with memory retrieval problems. Teachers should avoid tricky and long, wordy true/false questions, and they should avoid asking students to change false statements to ones that are true. Essay questions can be given ahead of time, or the teacher can accept an essay question written in outline form. The amount of credit earned for a test can be based on the sources available to a student for reference. For example, a student can earn a maximum of 100% on the test if they use no outside sources, 90% if they use their notes, and 80% if they use notes plus the textbook. There are a number of ways to evaluate students' performance by modifying tests or offering alternative methods of evaluation, such as having students construct posters, draw cartoons, make oral presentations, or devise a computer-generated product.

HOW TO HELP A STUDENT MAKE AN EFFECTIVE TRANSITION TO A GENERAL CLASSROOM

An important component of the IEP required by PL 105-17 is the monitoring and yearly review of a student's progress. In fact, PL 105-17 places greater emphasis on evaluating the child's involvement and progress in the general curriculum. This information is used in determining whether a student is ready to make the transition into the general classroom on a full-time basis. Typically at the end of each school year, a specified evaluation procedure is used to determine whether long-term goals (to be accomplished in 1 year) and short-term objectives (specific, measurable steps toward long-term goals) have been met. This information, the recommendations of the multidisciplinary team, and standardized evaluation outcomes are used to determine placement options. All of this information is vital when developing a transition plan for the student who no longer needs the intensive instruction offered through participation in a multisensory program that takes place outside the general classroom.

To ensure that the best possible placement decisions are made, the multidisciplinary team must work together in an atmosphere of collaboration and trust.

The National Joint Committee on Learning Disabilities (1993) specified that general and special education teachers must work together in equal partnership. The committee further contended that "successful collaboration requires…[a] willingness to collaborate, good communication skills, cooperation among participating teachers, adequate planning time, and administrative support" (pp. 3–4). PL 105-17 requires that multidisciplinary teams be composed of a special education teacher with expertise in the identified disability, a classroom teacher, a member of the school district who can commit resources (typically an administrator), the student, and one or more parents. Other members may include support personnel from inside or outside the school district (e.g., counselor, social worker, medical personnel); all team members work cooperatively.

The special educator, who is often the case manager or service coordinator, is usually responsible for monitoring the student's progress by gathering assessment data (see Chapter 14), modifying the curriculum, acting as a liaison with other professionals, and providing insights into the unique needs of the student. If the student is in a general classroom for part of the day, then the classroom teacher provides information on the student's performance and describes how well the student is performing in relation to grade-level peers vis-à-vis his or her ability to handle the general curriculum. The administrator sets the tone for providing the most appropriate, least restrictive educational environment for students with special needs and gives teachers permission and resources to adapt the curriculum while providing them with recognition, appreciation, and encouragement for their efforts. The parents are extremely important in this process because they know their child better than anyone else. They can provide much-needed follow-up and support and can help generate solutions and interventions. The student, too, has a role on the IEP team, especially when the student is an adolescent. Some of responsibilities a student needs to assume to become an independent learner include coming to class on time with the necessary materials, completing assignments in a timely manner, initiating questions, recognizing when extra help is needed, and eventually becoming a self-advocate in the learning process.

Some of the roadblocks to developing a successful transition plan appear to be gaining administrative support from school personnel, having time to plan and implement appropriate accommodations/modifications, and securing the necessary training to learn the specific instructional strategies that have been found to be successful. The continued growth and development of students with learning disabilities in general classrooms is dependent on a sound educational environment that nurtures these students.

WHEN THE TRANSITION SHOULD BE MADE

Factors that influence the successful transition of the student to the general classroom on a full-time basis include the following: 1) the student's level of proficiency as compared with his or her classmates while taking into consideration the expectations for that student; 2) the general classroom teacher's understanding of the student's unique instructional needs and the willingness to provide appropriate accommodations in the classroom; 3) the general classroom teacher's ability to incorporate specific multisensory strategies to enhance the student's program; 4) the type of learning environment in which the student will be placed; and, finally, 5) the student's ability to articulate specific requests for help by demonstrating appropriate self-advocacy skills and the student's understanding of his or her strengths and weaknesses in learning.

SUCCESSFUL PLANNING BEFORE TRANSITION

That multidisciplinary teams are responsible for placing a student in the least restrictive learning environment fuels the need for monitoring and evaluation of student progress at least on a yearly basis. When determining whether a student is ready to spend more time in the general classroom, a number of factors should be considered: a student's performance on assessment instruments (see Chapter 14), teacher recommendations, and the student's level of motivation. Whether the classroom teacher knows how to make appropriate accommodations and is willing to do so should be investigated. Other important factors from the standpoint of the teacher are time considerations and resource allocations. Does the teacher have adequate time to plan for modifications and collaborate with the specialists? Are help and support available from specialists and administrators? If a student has been instructed in the use of multisensory strategies, then the classroom teacher's ability to incorporate some of these strategies in the student's daily instructional program is an important consideration. The type of learning environment into which the student would make the transition should be considered. Can the student participate successfully in the general classroom on a full-time basis with modifications? Is part-time placement an option? Would a new school with a different curricular emphasis, such as a magnet school, be warranted? Last, is the student prepared to be a self-advocate? That is, does he or she understand his or her style of learning? All of these factors should be considered when determining whether a student is ready to make the transition to the general classroom on a part- or full-time basis.

Coping with Learning Differences in the Classroom

Observations of students with learning disabilities in general education classrooms have demonstrated that these students are less adept at handling their learning environment than their peers without disabilities are. For example, a study that looked at students with learning disabilities in general classrooms found them to be less likely to 1) seek help in the classroom, 2) volunteer to ask questions, and 3) engage in class discussions (McIntosh et al., 1993). The same study also found that students with learning disabilities and/or ADHD tended to interact less with the teacher and other students and also participated less in classroom activities. Another study highlighted that students with learning disabilities or attentional problems experience "labeling, stigmatization, and gatekeeping" (Barga, 1996, pp. 414, 416). These barriers serve to maintain the status quo of an organization but are often hurtful to students who are shunned or excluded throughout their school years.

When considering the adversities and ensuing struggles that challenge these students, the transition team should note how students respond to the expectations of others, including the barriers and obstacles that they face. Barga (1996) proposed that students with learning disabilities or attentional problems use two types of coping mechanisms: positive techniques and negative techniques. She further divided positive techniques into three subcategories: finding benefactors, using self-improvement techniques, and using study skills and management strategies. Benefactors provide emotional support and understanding and act as a sounding board for personal problems. Self-improvement techniques include taking extended breaks, seeking help, using positive affirmations for motivation, and seeking situations that would be growth producing. Study skills and management strategies were the most frequently employed techniques and included using technology such as computers; utilizing time-management skills; performing relaxation techniques before tests; taping classes; maintaining a personal calendar, utilizing tutorial assistance, test readers, and setting aside time each night to study. Negative coping techniques, which did not benefit or help students, fell under the category of "passing" either to avoid disclosure of their disability or to just make it through school.

HELPING STUDENTS UNDERSTAND THEIR LEARNING STYLE

Although standardized assessment instruments provide useful information about students' strengths and weaknesses with regard to how they learn, it would be helpful for students to get firsthand experience about their learning style. A number of informal assessments can be used with students that gauge learning style based on the preferred modality for learning. (See Chapter 14 for more on standardized and informal assessment.) In Soper's (1993) *Crash Course for Study Skills,* students complete a number of activities in the Learning Style section, which demonstrates whether they are primarily an auditory, visual, kinesthetic, or tactile learner. Another similar resource is presented in Frender's (1990) *Learning to Learn.* She included a section called Self-Assessment of Modality Strengths (pp. 22–24) that is simple to complete and appears to provide useful information about one's preferred learning style.

This learning style material is not intended to provide definitive data on how a student learns but does serve to heighten a student's awareness of differences in learning styles and how he or she best processes information. For example, after finding out more about learning style, a student might explain to a teacher that when he is learning vocabulary that is presented orally, he also needs to see it at the same time because he is a visual learner. Another student may need to take notes to follow the content of a lecture and to structure the speaker's ideas into his or her own frame of understanding, whereas another student may have great difficulty doing this and may be distracted by the process of notetaking. This student may need a scribe for notetaking. Using knowledge about learning style helps a student to become a self-advocate in and out of the classroom. The goal, of course, is for a student to take responsibility for his or her own learning.

HELPING STUDENTS TO DEVELOP SELF-ADVOCACY SKILLS

For students to develop the skills necessary to become independent learners, they should not only be aware of their own style of learning but also be able to articulate how their strengths and weaknesses affect them in the learning process. Using the student's psychological test results, the school psychologist or counselor could explain to the student, in general terms, his or her strengths and weaknesses in the learning process. For example, a psychologist could suggest to a student that he or she would benefit from extra time on assignments because assessment data demonstrated that his or her speed of processing information was somewhat slow. Information derived from informal learning-style inventories and teacher observations could also be shared to add to the student's repertoire of information.

Becoming a self-advocate depends not only on the student's understanding of his or her learning style and learning differences but also on that student's confidence to communicate this information. Through self-evaluation and self-reflection activities designed to tap the student's perception of his or her abilities, a student would have a better understanding of how to articulate his or her learning differences. For example, a student could keep a journal of the type of instructional activities, teaching scenarios, learning strategies, and study techniques that were helpful when learning new information. These journals could be used individually or shared in a group situation. A culminating activity would be a goal-setting exercise in which students are responsible for setting specific goals for developing self-advocacy skills. These goals might include how to appropriately bring an issue to a teacher or how to explain one's learning style and the need for specific accommodations.

SUMMARY AND RECOMMENDATIONS

Teachers must be prepared to meet the challenge of educating a diverse student population with a wide range of abilities and learning styles. Research in instructional practices that promote learning for all students must be the focus of the future. Even with the growing body of literature on the instructional adaptations that teachers can make in general classrooms, few teachers are actually prepared to implement such accommodations, and when they are, such implementations seem to be incidental and inconsistent (Schumm & Vaughn, 1995). Classroom teachers need in-service training on how to plan and make adaptations for students with learning disabilities within the framework of planning and instructing the entire class. Students whose skills are well below grade level should be given the opportunity to participate in an MSLE program so that they may receive the intensive remediation they need to improve academic performance. From the standpoint of time, resources, and training required, it does not seem feasible to expect the classroom teacher to offer this kind of specialized instruction. Such intensive instruction should be provided by a trained specialist working in collaboration with the classroom teacher. Perhaps as more teacher education programs incorporate MSLE strategies in their programs, classroom teachers will be better prepared to address the diverse learning needs of students.

The classroom teacher does have the responsibility of adapting the instructional program when a student is enrolled in both an MSLE program and the general classroom or when the student makes the transition to the general classroom. Because most adaptations for students with disabilities occur during the lesson (Schumm & Vaughn, 1995), it appears that making adaptations is an area in which teachers would need help in developing proficiency. Preparing to make such adaptations has been termed *interactive planning,* in which teachers actually make adaptations on their feet, such as adjusting the pace of a lesson, monitoring student understanding, and providing peer support. Situation-driven teaching, which allows the teacher to monitor students' understanding of the material and make adjustments when they do not understand, increases the teacher's ability to deal directly and spontaneously with the instructional needs of their students.

Teachers need to be skilled at interactive planning. They must structure content area instruction that meets the educational needs of all of their students, but if a student's skills are so weak as to limit his or her ability to learn in the classroom even with adaptations, then alternative instructional approaches should be offered as a part of that student's program. Because MSLE programs have been found to be effective in improving the academic performance of students with learning difficulties, placement in such a program would be an acceptable option for the student who needs intense help to perform in the general classroom. Dual enrollment in an MSLE program and a general classroom takes careful planning, sufficient time for collaboration, and appropriate resources.

REFERENCES

Americans with Disabilities (ADA) Act of 1990, PL 101-336, 42, U.S.C. §§ 12101 *et seq.*

Baker, J.M., & Zigmond, N. (1990). Are regular education classes equipped to accommodate students with learning disabilities? *Exceptional Children, 56,* 515–526.

Bandura, A. (1982). Self-efficiency mechanism in human agency. *American Psychologist, 37*(2), 122–147.

Barga, N.K. (1996, July). Students with learning disabilities in education: Managing a disability. *Journal of Learning Disabilities, 29*(4), 413–421.

Bateman, B. (1979). Teaching reading to learning disabled and other hard-to-teach children. In L.B. Resnick & P.A. Weaver (Eds.), *Theory and practice of early reading* (Vol. 1., pp. 227–259). Mahwah, NJ: Lawrence Erlbaum Associates.

Bryant, N.D., et al. (1980). The effects of some instructional variables on the learning of handicapped and non handicapped populations: A review. In *Integrative reviews of research* (Vol. 1, 10–70). New York: Columbia Teachers College, Institute for the Study of Learning Disabilities.

Chalmers, L., & Wasson, B. (1993). *Successful inclusion: Assistance for teachers of adolescents with mild disabilities.* Moorhead, MN: Practical Press.

Clark, F.L., Deshler, D.D., Schumaker, J.B., Alley, G.R., & Warner, M.M. (1984). Visual imagery and self-questioning strategies to improve comprehension of written material. *Journal of Learning Disabilities, 17,* 145–149.

Deshler, D.D., Alley, G.R., Warner, M.M., & Schumaker, J.B. (1981). Instructional practices for promoting skill acquisition and generalization in severely learning disabled adolescents. *Learning Disability Quarterly, 4,* 415–421.

Deshler, D.D., Lowrey, N., & Alley, G.R. (1979). Programming alternatives for LD adolescents: A nationwide survey. *Academic Therapy, 14,* 389–397.

Deshler, D.D., Schumaker, J.B., Lenz, B.K., & Ellis, E.S. (1984). Academic and cognitive interventions for LD adolescents: Part II. *Journal for Learning Disabilities, 17,* 170–187.

Education for All Handicapped Children Act of 1975, PL 94-142, 20 U.S.C. §§ 1400 *et seq.*

Education of the Handicapped Act (EHA) of 1970, PL 91-230 U.S.C. §§ 1400 *et seq.*

Frender, G. (1990). *Learning to learn.* Nashville, TN: Incentive Publications, Inc.

Fuchs, D., & Fuchs, L.S. (1994). Inclusive schools movement and the radicalization of special education reform. *Exceptional Children, 60,* 294–309.

Fulk, B.M. (1994). Mnemonic keyword strategy training for students with learning disabilities. *Learning Disabilities Research & Practice, 9*(3), 179−185.

Gardner, H. (1985). *Frames of mind: The theory of multiple intelligences.* New York: Basic Books.

Gillingham, A., & Stillman, B.W. (1997). *The Gillingham manual: Remedial training for children with specific disability in reading, writing, and penmanship* (8th ed.). Cambridge, MA: Educators Publishing Service.

Guskey, T. (1981). Individualizing instruction in the mainstream classroom: A mastery learning approach. In *Toward a research base for a least restrictive environment: A collection of papers* (pp. 32−46). Lexington: University of Kentucky.

Haight, S.L. (1985). Learning disabilities resource room teachers and students: Competent for what? *Journal of Learning Disabilities, 18,* 442−448.

Haring, N.G., & Bateman, B. (1977). *Teaching the learning disabled child.* Upper Saddle River, NJ: Prentice-Hall.

Individuals with Disabilities Education Act (IDEA) of 1990, PL 101-476, 20 U.S.C. §§ 1400 *et seq.*

Individuals with Disabilities Education Act Amendments of 1991, PL 102-119, 20 U.S.C. §§ 1400 *et seq.*

Individuals with Disabilities Act Amendments of 1997, PL 105-17, 20 U.S.C. §§ 1400 *et seq.*

Karrison, J., & Carroll, M.K. (1991, Summer). Solving word problems. *Teaching Exceptional Children,* 55−56.

Karweit, N. (1985). Time spent, time needed, and adaptive instruction. In M.C. Wang & H.I. Walberg (Eds.), *Adapting instruction to individual differences* (pp. 281−297). Berkeley, CA: McCutchan.

Keefe, C.H., & Chandler, A.C. (1989). LD students and word processors: Questions and answers. *Learning Disabilities Focus, 4*(2), 78−83.

LDA Postsecondary Education Subcommittee. (1999, March−April). Transition planning: Preparing for postsecondary employment for students with learning disabilities and/or attention disorders. *LDA Newsbriefs,* 12−13.

Learning Disabilities Association of America. (1993, January−February). Position paper on "Full inclusion of ALL students with learning disabilities in the regular education classroom." *LDA Newsbriefs, 28*(2), 1.

Learning disabilities: Preservice preparation of general and special education teachers. (1998, January−February). *LDA Newsbriefs,* 3−7.

Lerner, J.W. (1993). *Learning disabilities: Theories, diagnosis, and teaching strategies* (6th ed.). Boston: Houghton Mifflin.

Liberman, L.M. (1992, October). *Preventing and preserving special education...for those who do and do not need it.* Paper presented at the Washington Association of School Administrator's fall conference, Seattle, WA.

Manheimer, M.A., & Fleischner, J.E. (1995). Helping students with learning disabilities to meet the new math standards. In *Secondary education and beyond: Providing opportunities for students with learning disabilities.* Pittsburgh: Learning Disabilities Association of America.

Marzano, R.J. (1992). *Dimensions of learning.* Colorado: McRel Institute.

Maskel, S., & Felton, R. (1995). Analysis of achievement at the Hill Learning Development Center: 1990–1994. In C.W. McIntyre & J.S. Pickering (Eds.), *Clinical studies of multisensory structured language education* (pp. 129−137). Poughkeepsie, NY: Hamco Corp.

McCoy, L. (1988, November). Coping with dyslexia. *The Science Teacher, 25*−27.

McFarland, J., & Shepard, T. (1992). Oral and written compositions of students with learning disabilities in the content area of science. *Learning Disabilities, 6,* 13−18.

McIntosh, R., Vaughn, S., Schumm, J.S., Haager, D., & Lee, O. (1993). Observations of students with learning disabilities in general education classrooms. *Exceptional Children, 60,* 249−261.

Moats, L.C. (1994). The missing foundation in teacher education: Knowledge of the structure of spoken and written language. *Annals of Dyslexia, 44,* 81−102.

Moats, L.C. (1996). Implementing effective instruction. In S.C. Cramer & W. Ellis (Eds.), *Learning disabilities: Lifelong issues* (pp. 87−93). Baltimore: Paul H. Brookes Publishing Co.

Montague, M., & Box, C.S. (1986). The effect of cognitive strategy training on verbal math problem solving performance of learning disabled adolescents. *Journal of Learning Disabilities, 19*(1), 26–33.

National Joint Committee on Learning Disabilities. (1993). Providing appropriate education for students with learning disabilities in regular education classrooms. *Journal of Learning Disabilities, 26*(5), 330–332.

ODS position statement on inclusion. (1994, Fall). *Perspectives on Inclusion, 20*(4), p. 2–3.

Putnam, J.W. (1998). *Cooperative learning and strategies for inclusion: Celebrating diversity in the classroom* (2nd ed.). Baltimore: Paul H. Brookes Publishing Co.

Rehabilitation Act Amendments of 1986, PL 99-506, 29 U.S.C. §§ 701 *et seq.*

Rehabilitation Act Amendments of 1992, PL 102-569, 29 U.S.C. §§ 701 *et seq.*

Rehabilitation Act of 1973, PL 93-112, 29 U.S.C. §§ 701 *et seq.*

Rosenshine, B. (1983). Teaching functions in instructional programs. *Elementary School Journal, 83,* 335–340.

Rosenshine, B., & Stevens, R. (1984). Classroom instruction in reading. In P.D. Pearson (Ed.), *Handbook of reading research* (Chap. 23). New York: Walker and Co.

Schumaker, J.B., Nolan, S.M., & Deshler, D.D. (1985). *The error monitoring strategy.* Lawrence: The University of Kansas.

Schumm, J.S., & Vaughn, S. (1995). Getting ready for inclusion: Is the stage set? *Learning Disabilities Research & Practice, 10*(3), 169–179.

Silver, L.B. (1991). The regular education initiative: A déjà vu remembered with sadness and concern. *Journal of Learning Disabilities, 24,* 389–390.

Skrtic, T.M. (1992). The special education paradox: Equity as the way to excellence. In T. Hehir & T. Latus (Eds.), *Special education at the century's end: Evolution of theory and practice* (pp. 203–272). Cambridge, MA: Harvard Educational Review.

Soper, M. (1993). *Crash course for study skills.* East Moline, IL: LinguiSystems.

Stanovich, K.E. (1984). The interactive-compensatory model of reading: A confluence of developmental, experimental, and educational psychology. *Remedial and Special Education, 5,* 11–19.

Vallecorsa, A.L., Ledford, R.R., & Parnell, G.G. (1991, Winter). Strategies for teaching composition skills to students with learning disabilities. *Teaching Exceptional Children,* 52–55.

Vockell, E.L., & Mihail, T. (1993, Spring). Instructional principles behind computerized instruction for students with exceptionalities. *Teaching Exceptional Children,* 38–43.

Wood, J.W. (1992). *Adapting instruction for mainstreaming and at-risk students* (2nd ed.). Upper Saddle River, NJ: Prentice-Hall.

Winograd, P., & Hare, V. (1988). Direct instruction of reading comprehension strategies: The nature of teacher explanation. In C. Weinstein, E. Goetz, & P. Alexander (Eds.), *Learning and study strategies: Issues in assessment, instruction, and evaluation* (pp. 121–140). San Diego: Academic Press.

Zigmond, N., & Miller, S.E. (1986). Assessment for instructional planning. *Exceptional Children, 52,* 501–509.

16

Reading and Writing Instruction in Adult Basic Education

Joan R. Knight

During the 20th century the United States has moved slowly toward an understanding of the adult literacy problem. In the 1960s then-President John F. Kennedy recognized the large number of adults with poor literacy skills and the harm it caused to the independence, security, and productivity of individuals and the nation. Not until the 1990s, however, did research from the National Institutes of Health (NIH) provide valuable information that led to the identification of learning disabilities, including dyslexia, in children and adults with poor literacy skills. Since then, interest in finding answers to puzzling questions that surround adult literacy issues has increased. Research has helped to develop specific approaches to Adult Basic Education (ABE) and to shed new light on the diagnosis and treatment of the learning disabilities that have prevented so many Americans from achieving basic educational goals.

Individuals who did not learn to read in the early grades were and still are students with complex learning needs who require the expertise of a specialist. They lack information in a variety of areas, such as history, geography, biology, politics, physics, economics, psychology, and the arts. Their capacity for learning and curiosity about the world are years beyond their reading level. Often the damage done to their self-esteem is devastating.

Research from the NIH indicates that many reading problems among children have a constitutional (genetic) basis and that the core characteristic is inadequate phonological processing ability. Phonology, the science of speech sounds, includes phonetics, the study of how sounds are produced anatomically through the action or involvement of various body parts such as the tongue, teeth, lips, or facial orifices, and phonemics, the study of phonemes, the smallest units of sound that distinguish one sound from another (e.g., the /f/ of *fin*, the /p/ of *pin*) (see

Adams, Foorman, Lundberg, & Beeler, 1998, pp. 1–4). Lyon explained, "It is phonological awareness that appears to be the most deficient linguistic skill in disabled readers" (1995, p. 11). Wise and Olson explained phoneme awareness as "the ability to segment and manipulate sounds within a syllable (1995, p. 100). Stone and Brady described phonological awareness as the reader's "becoming consciously aware of the sound structure of words, [which] has proven to be a necessary requirement for learning to read" (1995, p. 52). According to Shaywitz et al. (1996), of the approximately 20% of children in the United States who have difficulties with basic reading skills, 80%–90% have phonological processing difficulties. Ample evidence has indicated that "phonological deficits appear to impede the development of basic reading abilities (decoding and word recognition) regardless of the level of general intelligence" (Lyon, 1996, p. 34) and that the "co-occurrence of poor phonological awareness and poor reading is a relationship that is, in fact, a causal one, with deficits in phonological awareness impeding the acquisition of reading skills (Lyon, 1995, p. 11). (For more on phonological processing, see Chapter 4.)

Research also has indicated that when children do not receive remedial instruction in childhood, they grow up to have the same inadequate phonological awareness and poor decoding skills in adulthood (Banks, Guyer, & Guyer, 1995; Bat-Hayim, 1996; Elbro, Nielsen, & Petersen, 1994; Knight & Randell, 1995; Shaywitz & Shaywitz, 1996).

Dyslexia is one area that researchers have begun to explore as a possible cause of entrenched poor reading in adults. The core characteristic of dyslexia is poor phonological processing ability that requires specific educational methods for remediation (Pennington, 1991; Truch, 1994; Yancey Padget, Knight, & Sawyer, 1996). According to Lyon, "reading disability reflects a persistent deficit rather than a developmental lag" (1996, p. 33), and Pennington said that "most dyslexic children are still measurably dyslexic as adults" (1991, p. 63). Ellis and Cramer reported that "estimates suggest that 30%–50% of illiterate adults in Adult Basic Education and literacy programs may be learning disabled" (1996, p. xxx). Tests to measure phonological awareness and decoding facility, however, are rarely administered in ABE programs, and multisensory, structured language education (MSLE) methods are seldom practiced in these programs. For these reasons, adult educators may make testing, curriculum, and methodology decisions that do not maximize research on learning and memory and on the best ways to teach adults who have inordinate difficulty learning to read, write, and spell.

An outgrowth of research in phonological processing and reading disabilities was the collaboration of NIH and the Orton Dyslexia Society (ODS, which is now known as the International Dyslexia Association). In 1994 the ODS published a new definition of *dyslexia* (also referred to as *reading disorder* or *reading disability*).[1] The new definition departed from previous attempts by narrowing the list of skills difficulties and describing what dyslexia is rather than what it is

---

[1] "Dyslexia is one of several distinct learning disabilities. It is a specific language-based disorder of constitutional origin characterized by difficulties in single word decoding, usually reflecting insufficient phonological processing abilities. These difficulties in single word decoding are often unexpected in relation to age and other cognitive and academic abilities; they are not the result of generalized developmental disability or sensory impairment. Dyslexia is manifested by variable difficulty with different forms of language, often including, in addition to problems reading, a conspicuous problem with acquiring proficiency in writing and spelling." (ODS, as cited in Lyon, 1995, p. 9)

not. The definition identified poor phonological processing ability with its resultant poor decoding skills as the core characteristic.

Many people in ABE and literacy programs also exhibit self-defeating behaviors in areas that are not academic yet have an impact on learning. These adults frequently complain of an inability to attend to or focus on information that is presented orally or read silently. Some of these adults have attention-deficit/hyperactivity disorder (ADHD). Considered a disorder of behavior, its main characteristics are difficulties with attention, impulsivity, and/or hyperactivity (American Psychiatric Association, 1994). It should not be subsumed under learning disabilities, the constituents of which include difficulties with reading, written expression, listening and speaking, math, and handwriting. Social skills or social competence difficulties also can interfere with the pursuit of learning by disturbing social interactions, thus causing individuals to be alienated, depriving them of a network of helping acquaintances and in some cases leading to criminality.

Substantial evidence from laboratory studies of brains of deceased individuals (Galaburda, Sherman, Rosen, Aboitiz, & Geschwind, 1985) and from neuroimaging studies of the brains of living individuals points to the constitutional origin of learning disabilities, including dyslexia; of ADHD; and of social skills disabilities (Denckla, 1994; Lyon, 1995; Pennington, 1995; Shaywitz et al., 1996; Voeller, 1994). An individual can have one or more of these disorders, but they are separate from one another and one does not cause the other. When the term *learning disability* is used as a catch-all phrase for an undifferentiated condition, an effective course of remediation is nullified. Diagnosis leads to accurate identification of an individual's specific learning difficulty that dictates the method of instruction.

A diagnosis, conducted by a teacher who has had in-depth training in diagnosis and remediation, will disclose whether the problem is a learning disability such as dyslexia, a behavioral disorder such as ADHD, a social skills disorder, several co-occurring disorders, or something other than a learning disability. A diagnosis of dyslexia leads to a course of intervention using an MSLE approach with emphasis on improving phonological awareness and mastering sound–symbol correspondences, as well as instruction in all of the other related language areas, including vocabulary, spelling, writing, handwriting, and comprehension. When two adults score at the same grade level on a silent reading comprehension test, it is important that they not be placed in the same class until both are thoroughly diagnosed. If one adult has dyslexia and the other does not, then they will need different curricula. The student with dyslexia will need intensive instruction in phonological awareness and word attack in an accepting, respectful atmosphere. The nondyslexic individual will not need such detailed instruction and often will blurt out answers impatiently when forced to sit through repetitive, slow-paced, step-by-step teaching. Conversely, without a diagnosis, dyslexic adults may be placed in a class that teaches only comprehension development; they need such instruction but cannot make full use of it without also learning how to read the words (Knight, 1997).

MULTISENSORY STRUCTURED LANGUAGE EDUCATION

In a strictly phonic approach, one that teaches sound–symbol correspondences only, the student would see or hear a letter name and utter its sound and would rely on visual and auditory memory. The student with a reading disability needs to involve many of the senses. MSLE teaches the student how to connect the visual, auditory, kinesthetic, and tactile channels simultaneously to learn sounds and other language elements. Memory is further enhanced by associating a sound with words, stories, and drawings because more of the brain is involved in learning. The term *structured* means that the order in which elements are introduced proceeds from simple to complex with frequent repetitions and that there is never a random presentation. Regularities and anomalies of the language are explained and explicitly taught.

Many multisensory methods have been developed as a result of the theories and practices of S.T. Orton, a neuropsychiatrist, and Gillingham, an educator and psychologist. Other practitioners also developed multisensory methods independently as a result of observing that certain students could learn to read only with such an approach.

Teaching phonics is but one strand of MSLE. In every teaching session, MSLE methods cover most aspects of language learning, including the following:

- Phonological awareness (see Chapter 4)
- Decoding (see Chapter 6)
- Spelling (see Chapter 8)
- Writing (see Chapter 10)
- Grammar
- Handwriting (see Chapter 9)
- Comprehension (see Chapter 7)

STARTING OVER

Many ABE students fit the profile of individuals with dyslexia. MSLE programs have helped many of these students overcome poor literacy and achieve educational goals that foster new levels of productivity and independence. Starting Over (Knight, 1986) is an example of a successful MSLE program.

Starting Over (Knight, 1986) was designed to diagnose children and adults with reading difficulties, with an emphasis on dyslexia, and provide them with remedial instruction. Using instruments that assess students' facility with sounds and related language areas, the program identifies students with inadequate phonological awareness and decoding skills and teaches them to read using MSLE methods.

The next sections contain a description of the procedures used to evaluate and instruct adults with dyslexia in the following government-funded Starting Over programs:

1. *Starting Over classes for dyslexic union members of District Council 37 (DC 37), American Federation of State, County, and Municipal Employees* These classes have been funded by the New York State Department of Education for Workplace Literacy. A local union president who had been diagnosed with dyslexia in adulthood urged the union to establish a program for dyslexic members. The classes began in 1988 and are ongoing as of 1999.

2. *Starting Over for dyslexic adults who are in residential treatment for alcoholism or other substance abuse (Knight & Randell, 1995)* This Starting Over program was funded by the New York State Office of Alcoholism and Substance Abuse

Services (OASAS). Starting Over of New York, Inc., designed a diagnostic and instructional reading program for dyslexic adults in residential treatment for substance abuse as a means of helping them to move from welfare to work. The students were high school dropouts who had attended ABE classes at their therapeutic communities but had made very little progress. The classes began in 1987 and continued through 1995.

DIAGNOSIS

The Starting Over diagnosis serves two purposes: 1) It specifies the language learning problem for the student, and 2) it serves as a screening device for placement in a Starting Over class. Individuals who exhibit the phonological processing problems that are characteristic of dyslexia will enroll in class and will complete the pretests on the first day of class. Individuals who do not exhibit such characteristics are referred to other classes in the union, therapeutic community, or school.

Diagnosis consists of an interview and six tests from the Starting Over textbook (Knight, 1986), the reading subtest of the Wide Range Achievement Test (WRAT; Jastak & Jastak, 1978) and the Word Discrimination Test (Huelsman, 1958). The tests are administered based on the assumption that reading and writing abilities are made up of component parts or discrete skills, which once identified, can be taught. Each test assesses the student's competence with either the end product or a component part such as phonological awareness, alphabetizing, decoding, spelling, and sentence structure. Testing is preceded by an explanation of the relationship of the contents of the test to dyslexia. After completion of each test, the notated protocol is shown to the student, and the teacher points out possible evidence of dyslexia in incorrect responses. The teacher proceeds to use the Starting Over method to correct one error (discussed later in the Teaching During Pretesting section) and to demonstrate that the adult is capable of learning when using a method that is specifically designed for individuals with dyslexia.

The Interview   The diagnosis begins with an interview in a private setting (Knight, 1986). Questions encompass early schooling, previous diagnoses and tutoring, family history and attitudes, health factors, work history, appraisal of self, strengths and weaknesses in academic subjects, and the specific academic skills the learner hopes to acquire on completion of the Starting Over program (Knight, 1998a). The student's answers to each question are written verbatim and interpreted by the teacher; these interpretations are explained to the student.

For example, if a student answers, "Yes, I was held back in the first grade," then the teacher interprets what being held back may indicate. The student can be told that children entering first grade expect to have attained the magic of reading by the time they finish the school year. If this did not happen, they may not have verbalized their great disappointment at the time but may have experienced emotional distress. The interviewer can also explain that when a child is held back instead of promoted to the next grade, it usually means that the student had a learning difficulty that went undiagnosed. Thus, by giving enlightening feedback after each question, the interviewer helps to alleviate students' feelings of guilt from mistaken beliefs that their childhood behavior caused their reading problems. Because failure to keep up in school is a red flag, the interview helps to expose factors in the school and home history that may point to a learning disability. The tests that follow the interview will confirm or negate that possibility.

Six Starting Over Tests   The diagnosis continues with the following six tests from the Starting Over program (Knight, 1986).

1. *Segmenting and Counting Sounds in Words*   This test of phonemic awareness asks the student to manipulate the sounds in words and nonwords by counting them, saying each sound separately in sequence, isolating the vowel, and saying the word parts that remain after manipulating designated consonants. For example, when the nonword *dats* is given, the student should respond that there are four sounds: /d/, /ă/, /t/, and /s/. When asked to remove the first sound, the student should respond with /ăts/; when the last sound is removed, /dăt/ remains; the vowel sound is /ă/; and when the third sound is moved to the end, the new word is *dast*.

2. *Recognizing Sounded Letters*   This test of phonological awareness asks the student to identify vowel and consonant sounds produced by the teacher. For example, when the teacher says the first sound in *eddy*, the student should respond that the sound is the letter *e*.

3. *Spelling Words and Numbers*   This test reveals problems with spelling, rhyming, and handwriting by asking the student to think of and write words that end with four different letters that individuals with dyslexia frequently have difficulty controlling: *r, l, b,* and *n*. To do so, students must be able to hear the consonant sound internally, place a vowel before it, hear the two as a word family, and use rhyme or another language device to come up with four more words that end the same way. Some individuals with dyslexia unwittingly interchange the letters *b* and *d* and the letters *m* and *n*. After the student completes the spelling test, the teacher corrects it and shows the notated protocol to the student, pointing out any of these errors as possible evidence of dyslexia.

    Good spelling depends on three factors: auditory memory, linguistic knowledge, and visual memory. *Auditory memory,* related to phonological awareness, means the ability to recognize sounds within a word, separate them into single entities, and know their corresponding written symbols. An example of auditory memory at work would be distinguishing, isolating, uttering and naming the five sounds of the word *grand* after hearing it as one unit. *Linguistic knowledge* is the knowledge that certain parts of a word sound one way but are regularly spelled another way. For example, the sound of /sh/ in *mention* and other *-tion* words is spelled differently than how one would expect it to be spelled. *Visual memory* means memory of the spelling of sounds that are unclear, such as the schwa (represented by *e* in *correspond*); letters that are silent, such as the *b* in *lamb* or the final *e* in *little;* or sounds that can be spelled more than one way, such as the /s/ in *city* and *silly.* These various spellings have to be remembered as "looking right."

    In addition, the word *mention* requires all three spelling factors to work harmoniously: 1) auditory memory to hear and spell /men/ and /shŭn/, 2) linguistic knowledge to know that because /sh/ is part of a regular ending, it is rarely spelled *sh,* and 3) visual memory to remember whether the sound /shŭ/ in this word is spelled *ti, si, ci, ce, sh* or *xi* (*mention, dimension, magician, ocean, fashion, anxious*). The test also requires writing 20 numbers as words, a skill that is rarely assessed but needs to be mastered for writing a report or a check.

4. *Writing a Sentence*   This test reveals spelling, creativity, grammar, syntax, and handwriting problems by asking students to write a sentence telling what they would like to accomplish after 1 year of remedial instruction. Students often express their aspirations and feelings in this task. An adult wrote the following sentence: *In the Dark of my mine I can not writ or reed and **sum** day the spark will **egnite** in to a flame of **knowledge**.*

5. *Reading One-Syllable Words and Word Parts*   This test reveals decoding ability by asking the student to read 20 one-syllable words and 20 word parts that have consonants surrounding a medial short vowel in three-letter patterns (e.g., *lax, bev*). Each short vowel appears eight times; most consonants appear at least four times, twice at the beginning and twice at the end of words. After completing the test, the student is shown the notated protocol and is helped to analyze the reading problem. The greatest number of errors is usually with vowels. As for consonants, more errors are observed at the end than at the beginning of a word. The student realizes that knowing an initial consonant sound does not ensure that he or she will be able to control its placement elsewhere in the word. Most students with decoding problems do well with initial consonants but poorly with final consonants and short vowel sounds anywhere in the word. This test will specify decoding strengths and weaknesses precisely and enable students to see reading not as an unmanageable global entity but as one with component parts, some of which they already handle quite well. By the end of the program, students will be able to read long words by finding and reading the syllables within them. Students will read and use parts of words such as *cor, es,* and *cac* as building blocks for reading longer words such as *correspond, assess,* and *cactus.*

6. *Reading Multisyllabic Words*   This test reveals decoding ability by asking the student to read 40 multisyllabic words with short vowel sounds, such as *lamented* and *establishment.* The test has several purposes:

- To assess the students' decoding skills
- To show students that long words are built with one-syllable parts similar to those they were asked to read in the previous test, Reading One-Syllable Words and Word Parts
- To advise the students that decoding is the first area to be addressed in the hierarchy of reading skills
- To assure students that Starting Over was designed to give them the necessary skills to attack all 40 words, spell them, learn their meanings, write them in sentences, and comprehend them in paragraphs.

The Reading Subtest of the Wide Range Achievement Test   The WRAT reading subtest (Jastak & Jastak, 1978) reveals decoding ability by asking the student to read a list of 75 words that are arranged by school grade from 1 to 12 and are frequently misread by dyslexic students (e.g., *left* for *felt, preserve* for *persevere, who* for *how*). The WRAT reading subtest presents words of differing lengths that are both familiar and unfamiliar, are regular and irregular, and contain many different vowel and consonant combinations.

The Word Discrimination Test   The Word Discrimination Test (Huelsman, 1958) reveals ability to recognize the correct sequence of letters in a word by asking the student to read 96 items silently that each contain five groups of printed letters (e.g., *wouber wonder wouder wonber wondre*) and identify the real word in each group. This test reveals visual-perceptual skills with letter orientations and sequences that are frequently misread by individuals with dyslexia: m/n, u/n, and b/d.

TEACHING DURING PRETESTING

When testing is completed, the teacher shows the notated protocol to the student and points out possible evidence of dyslexia in incorrect responses. Then the teacher uses a Starting Over strategy to teach the student how to correct one error. For example, a student who identified the dictated short vowel sound /ĭ/ as long /ē/ during the test Recognizing Sounded Letters and who read the word part *wid* as "wide" during the test Reading One-Syllable Words and Word Parts would be shown the notated protocols and taught one Starting Over element, the short /ĭ/ sound. The teacher asks the student what a mosquito bite feels like. When the student responds, "Itchy," the teacher demonstrates how to tap the word with the thumb, index finger, and back to the thumb to represent the sounds: /ĭ//tchē//ĭ/. Going back to the thumb isolates the targeted vowel sound. (All Guide Words for the short vowel sounds contain the short vowel in the first syllable.) Next, the teacher demonstrates how to draw a picture that represents what it looks like to scratch an itchy bite (see Figure 16.1). Once the student has internalized the short /ĭ/, the word part *wid* will be shown again and the student will pronounce it in three steps: 1) with the consonants covered up and only the vowel articulated while drawing the first stroke of its picture (/ĭ/), 2) with the vowel and final consonant uncovered and spoken together (/ĭd/), and 3) with the initial consonant uncovered and the complete word part uttered together (/wĭd/).

Adults will finally understand the importance of phonological processing as they see how difficult it was for them to control and place letter sounds in various parts of words before they were taught how to learn and control sounds with an MSLE system. They are usually relieved to find out that they have dyslexia and that it is not a disease but a condition that they have just experienced as remediable. This is the initial undermining of their lifelong belief that they are "stupid" or "damaged."

Student Sensitivity to Test Taking

Many people approach tests with trepidation and anxiety. Those who have failed to learn to read are particularly vulnerable. Sensitivity in acknowledging their apprehension is especially necessary. By sharing the results and giving enlightening feedback, the teacher administering the tests can help students overcome their fears. Students learn that reading consists of component parts and gain the ability to recognize these parts. The more they learn about their own strengths and weaknesses, the more cooperative and ready they are to approach reading from new avenues. They should be told that these measures form a baseline of today's functioning. At the conclusion of the year, they will be tested again and be delighted with their progress.

CLASSROOM INSTRUCTION

Individuals who have demonstrated the characteristics of dyslexia are enrolled in class. On the first day of class several tests complete the baseline functioning. The

Review of Short-Vowel Sounds and Guide Words

Figure 16.1. Review of short vowel sounds and Guide Words. (From Knight, J.R. [1986]. *Starting Over: A literacy program* [p. 47]. Cambridge, MA: Educators Publishing Service; reprinted by permission.)

first are the standardized Tests of Adult Basic Education (TABE; McGraw-Hill, 1987), which consist of silent measures of vocabulary and comprehension. In addition, students are tested on alphabetizing, spelling, and oral reading comprehension, and they write a composition. Two tests, Reading One-Syllable Words and Word Parts (Knight, 1986; see Figure 16.2) and the TABE, also will serve as posttests at the end of the year.

Short Vowel Sounds

Diagnostic testing has revealed that the short vowel sounds, the sounds that are most frequently encountered in reading, are inordinately difficult for individuals with dyslexia to apprehend. The six other kinds of vowels—long vowels, vowel pairs, silent vowels, r-controlled vowels, irregular vowels, and the schwa— appear in fewer words on a page of print. Therefore, early acquisition of short vowel sounds is a vital tool in the student's mastery of decoding.

Every session in the unit on short vowel sounds begins with the same multisensory exercise that heightens awareness and embeds the sounds into long-term memory. Activities are provided to measure whether the students' recall of sounds has become automatic. Teachers never assume that a concept is learned simply because they introduced or taught it. The teacher does not model sounds but rather encourages and prompts the student with clues. The program seeks to make students independent—they have to search their memories for word-association clues and go through a series of steps before making any sounds. Independence is fostered and confidence is boosted as students rely more and more on themselves. Phonological awareness is heightened, patience and respect for each student's thinking process is developed, and a sense of protective community is nurtured.

The Alphabet

The next unit focuses on the alphabet. The unit enables students to memorize the alphabet's sequence; open the dictionary to the letter they want on the first attempt so that they do not have to turn one page at a time to find it; alphabetize words that have the same first, second, and third letters; and use the dictionary guide words at the top of each page to find the column in which the word is located. Once alphabet operations have been mastered, further practice is eliminated, but mastery is measured by occasional testing.

Consonants

The body of the program is organized around 21 consonant units; 1 or more of the 44 Guides to Spelling and Pronunciation are presented at the end of most units. The sequence of consonant presentation has been determined by the ease with which the consonant can be blended with the five short vowels. Blending is a skill that some students have great difficulty mastering. At the end of every other consonant unit, a test (Mastery Measure) is given. Most consonant units are made up of the following 10-part procedure.

1. *Phonological Awareness* Awareness of the physical aspects (e.g., phonetics) of the letter name and sound and the differences between them contributes to

Pretest 9   Reading One-Syllable Words—Individual

▶ *Teacher writes.*

Take the student's form and use it to write on. Say, "Look at your Pretest Form which you used earlier to read Pretests 4 and 5. Under Pretest 9, please read each word. If you cannot say the whole thing, say any part that you can. I'll write what you say and show it to you later." (Write exactly what the student says in the blanks below.)

Whole Words (1–20)		Word Parts (21–40)	
1. lax _lex_	11. wax ✓ _hard_	21. zam _zim_	31. lat _lots_
2. yen _yūn_	12. gel _gīl_	22. fes _fis_	32. bez _diss_
3. kin ✓ _King_	13. hip ✓	23. wid ✓	33. civ _cit_
4. got ✓	14. mob _mop_	24. hol _hōl_	34. tox _tix_
5. bum _boom_	15. dun _doon_	25. mul _mūl_	35. kum _Kūn_
6. jab _jub_	16. zag _zug_	26. rab _rob_	36. daz _duz_
7. rev _rēv_	17. vet _zēch_	27. pej _Kēf_	37. ques _quigs_
8. quiz _ques_	18. tic ✓	28. viv _vēn_	38. cig ✓
9. fop ✓	19. nod ✓	29. sof _soft_	39. jod ✓
10. sup _soop_	20. pus _pū_	30. yuc _yooch_	40. nug _noog nuj_

Evaluation: Evaluate the student's strengths and weaknesses below. Put the number correct to the left of the slash. The number to the right of the slash indicates the total number of items in each category.

Words		Consonants		Vowels
Whole Words (1–20)	6 /20	First Consonant	Last Consonant	Short Vowel
Word Parts (21–40)	3 /20			
Total Correct	9 /40	Total Correct 36 /40	Total Correct 25 /40	Total Correct 13 /40

Optional Letter Analysis: In the columns marked "Beginning of Word," "End of Word," and "Middle of Word," the numbers separated by commas indicate the words in which the letters are found in Pretest 9. If the letter has been read incorrectly, circle the appropriate number. Numbers below lines show the number of times the letter appears in the test. Put the number of correct pronunciations above the line. In the column marked "Substitution," write the letter that the student said instead of the printed one. Then fill in the "Reversals" section.

Figure 16.2. Pretest 9: Reading One-Syllable Words—Individual. (From Knight, J.R. [1986]. *Starting Over: A literacy program* [p. 29]. Cambridge, MA: Educators Publishing Service; reprinted by permission.)

phonological awareness. Before the exercise begins, most students are unaware that there are two sounds in the name of the letter *m* (the first consonant unit taught). A multisensory approach with emphasis on the tactile and kinesthetic channels elicits the sound from students, not through teacher imitation but by having students focus on how the placement of the tongue, teeth, and lips differs when saying the letter name and the letter sound. Students are instructed to press their lips together and hum. They alternate between the name and the sound, noticing when the lips are open and when they are closed. When students say the first sound in the letter name (*m*), they have apprehended the short vowel /ĕ/physically and realize that the lips are open. The short vowel sound, /ĕ/, is isolated, stretched, and connected to its Guide Word ending: *e . . . ddy*. With the index (pointer) fingertip, students trace the picture of an eddy on the palm of their hands (See Figure 16.1). They suddenly realize that the letter *m* has two sounds and that to extract only the sound /m/ from its letter name, they must remove the short vowel sound /ĕ/, which they are now able to hear and control.

2. *Handwriting*   The four forms of handwriting, upper- and lowercase print and cursive, are presented in one lesson to help students disentangle them for writing. Using a multisensory approach, students trace over the letter with their fingertip while describing the number, direction, and shape of strokes. Finally, they write the letter and short vowel word parts in their notebooks in print and script. To perfect the writing of the letter, the teacher points out the smallest details in the relationship of the letter strokes to their spatial environment.

3. *Blending Sounds to Build Word Parts*   The consonant is blended with each short vowel sound to form three different word parts:

a	e	i	o	u
am mam ma	em mem me	im mim mi	om mom mo	um mum mu

Although some individuals with dyslexia have difficulty with blending, they can largely overcome this problem by learning the vowel first. The vowel serves as an anchor both for the word and for students. It keeps the letters in order and eliminates out-of-sequence reading, which can be so bewildering for students. Once students have internalized the vowel (e.g., /ă/), it is repeated, stretched, and blended into the consonant sound to the right (e.g., /ăm/). When that word part is solid and spoken easily, the first consonant is connected, and the whole syllable is spoken at once as a single entity (e.g., /măm/). Blending from the vowel to the consonant on its right presents little difficulty, but blending from the first consonant to its neighboring vowel can be a problem for individuals with moderate to severe dyslexia. This difficulty is handled by having students blend no more than two entities at a time, such as a sound and a word part (e.g., /ă/ to /ăm/, /ăm/ to /lăm/, /lăm/ to /slăm/). This enables the student to focus on each sound in the final word and to realize that there are four sounds. When students listen to and say a word such as *slam* and are asked to count the number of sounds in it, few dyslexics say that there are four sounds. Most say that there are one (the whole word) or two (*sla* plus *m*). Few students can isolate the *s* and the *l*, because they hear only the initial sound clearly. Isolating individual sounds raises students' awareness of sounds and contributes to the skill of spelling.

4a. *Word Parts to Words*   A teacher clue elicits from students multisyllabic words that begin with each word part. For example, the clue for *am* is "an emergency vehicle that takes patients to the hospital." Starting with the thumb and using one finger per syllable, students tap the word on a hard surface to see and feel the number of syllables. Words that are not in the students' vocabularies, such as *mammal*, *ember*, or *nemesis*, are tapped into syllables and are sounded using the blending technique just described.

4b. *The Spelling Voice and the Schwa*   To teach students how to spell known and unknown words, the teacher pronounces the syllables with exaggerated long or short vowel sounds, and the students repeat and tap each syllable. Schwas are converted into long or short vowel sounds to make them identifiable. This technique of changing schwas is referred to as using the *spelling voice*. For example, the teacher uses the spelling voice for the *a* in the third syllable of ambulance and turns the schwa into a short vowel sound. Students isolate the vowel first and then add the surrounding consonants (*l*, *n*, *c*). Students then write the entire word. After it is written correctly, the word is adjusted back to the speaking voice and the students try to hear the schwa sound that, of course, speeds by almost unintelligibly in the unaccented syllable. This enables students to understand that if they do not learn how to use the spelling voice to remember a vowel that is pronounced with the schwa, then they will usually have to guess the spelling of the vowel.

The schwa was introduced to students briefly in an early lesson on vowel sounds. The teacher points out the sound frequently, and a formal lesson on it comes later in the program.

5. *Vocabulary*   To learn the meaning of a word, it is most important for one to be able to pronounce it. After decoding words, students are required to use their dictionaries to look up those that are unfamiliar or only vaguely known. Teachers translate the dictionary definitions into understandable language, lead a discussion of everything they know about the words, and help the class to compose short, simplified definitions that they write in their 4″ × 6″ spiral-bound vocabulary notebooks. Teacher-led discussions of a word such as *mammal* can bring the outside world of science, history, drama, and current events into the classroom by taking students from Darwin's theory of evolution, to the Scopes "Monkey Trial," to the continued hunting of whales for their ambergris in spite of a proposed voluntary moratorium. Because vocabulary is so difficult to acquire permanently, it is important to have oral discussion and visualization with each word. A 10-step vocabulary strategy for use when teaching unfamiliar words follows:

1. Help the students decode the word by having them use the guides they have learned thus far.
2. Talk about the word—make it come alive with background and stories.
3. Demonstrate how the word is used in a sentence.
4. Have the students find the word in their dictionaries, and read it aloud to them, if necessary.
5. Discuss multiple meanings.
6. Have students practice visualizing—to teach the word *avid*, have the students picture a person they know who is an avid reader, tennis player, or music lover engaged in the activity.
7. Have students draw the scene and write *avid* across the page.
8. With the students, compose a simplified, understandable definition, and write it on the board.
9. Have the students write the word in their 4″ × 6″ spiral-bound notebooks with the word on the left-hand page of the book and definition on the right-hand page.
10. Tell students that to memorize the words, they must study them three times within the next 24 hours and at least once a day for the next week.

6. *Writing Sentences*   Students weave at least two unrelated lesson words that contain the target consonant and vowel combinations into one sentence to get experience with syntactically difficult reading material. The following sentences were composed by a class, corrected by the teacher, and copied from the board into the students' large, 8½″ × 11″ spiral-bound notebooks (italics indicate the unrelated words): "Holding the *antler* above his head, *Andy* led *Nancy* and the *nanny* down the *narrow* path, where *Nancy* took a *nasty* fall," and "DDT was the *nemesis* of large *numbers* of birds because their eggshells became too *thin* to *withstand* the weight of the sitting birds' bodies."

Approximately two thirds into the first year, explicit instruction in narrative writing occurs. The words *topic* and *thesis* are defined, and students search for examples in well-written newspaper articles, essays, and works of literature. After thorough analysis, the students attempt to write their own opening paragraphs.

7. *Decoding Words and Reading Sentences*   As part of each consonant unit, all previously introduced consonants are brought back and recombined with the target consonant and short vowel sounds to produce more words and sentences, including sentences about world knowledge. For example, when the units on *m* and *n* have been completed, words such as *manner, mundane, nemesis,* and *namby-pamby* are decoded, defined, and read from the sentences in the textbook. As students advance, the single sentence that they have composed in the previous activity serves as an opening sentence for a paragraph they will write.

8a. *How to Read a Word: Finding the Syllables in 10 Steps*   A major aspect of decoding words correctly and independently is locating and reading the syllables within a word. Starting Over has reduced the number of syllable patterns taught to three, but even this small number is difficult for students to remember and use. Therefore, the program calls for decoding at least two words during each session using the 10-step procedure. After students have memorized the three regular syllable patterns, they learn a strategy for finding syllables in words with three, four, and five consecutive consonants (e.g., *erstwhile*).

The students are introduced to the abbreviations *V* for *vowel* and *C* for *consonant* and note that the three regular syllable patterns all begin and end with a vowel. The three patterns and 10 steps are shown in Figure 16.3; the target word, *sensitivity*, uses Patterns I and II.

Pattern III (two adjacent vowels) syllable division is taught later in the program because it requires knowledge of more than 20 vowel pairs. Pattern III has two possible syllable divisions. The first is V | V. This division means that the two adjacent vowels will produce two separate, distinct sounds and, therefore, will each belong to a different syllable. Examples are multisyllabic words that contain the letter *i* followed by a vowel: *radiate, carrier, skiing, patio,* and *medium,* as well as *miasma, biennial, biology,* and *triumphant.* These words require the teaching of two Guides (explained later in Step 9).

The second possibility for Pattern III is

$$\frac{\text{V}}{\cancel{\text{V V}}}$$

This means that the two adjacent vowels will produce one vowel sound and, therefore, will not be divided. Instead, the two *V*s will be struck through with one horizontal line, and one *V* will be written above the two *V*s to indicate that there

How to Read a Word

Syllable Finder Patterns

Pattern I   V C | C V
Pattern II   V | C V

                  V
Pattern III   V | V or V̶ V̶

Finding Syllables in 10 Steps

1. **Underline and count** the vowels.

     s e̲ n s i̲ t i̲ v i̲ t y̲

2. **Estimate** the number of syllables.
(Every syllable has one vowel sound.)

     5

3. **Label V to V** and **stop** to find the first syllable.
(Start with the first V, label each letter in turn, and stop at the next V.)

     V C C V
     s e̲ n s i̲ t i̲ v i̲ t y̲

4. **Decide** whether the pattern that has evolved is Pattern I, II, or III, **and divide** (draw the syllable division line).

     V C|C V
     s e̲ n|s i̲ t i̲ v i̲ t y̲

5. **Read the syllable.**

     V   (Read the vowel first.)

                 e̲

     VC   (Read the vowel and consonant together.)

                  e̲ n

     CVC   (Read as one.)

                  s e̲ n|

6. Cover the syllable and **find the next** syllable by repeating Steps 3–5.

     Label V to V.

                  V C|C V|C V

     Decide and divide.

                  s e̲ n|s i̲|t i̲ v i̲ t y̲

     Read the syllable.

                       i̲

                      s i̲

7. **Go back** and read syllables already decoded before going on to the next syllable.

     V C|C V
     s e̲ n|s i̲|

8. **Find the next** syllable and additional syllables by repeating.

     Label V to V.

                  V C|C V|C V|C V

     Decide and divide.

                  s e̲ n|s i̲|t i̲|v i̲ t y̲

     Read the syllable.

                      i̲

     Go back.

                  s e̲ n s i̲|t i̲|

(continued)

Figure 16.3. How to read a word.

Figure 16.3. *(continued)*

9. Say and tap each syllable evenly several times with spelling voice (exaggerate long or short vowel sounds) until you can **adjust** the word to your speaking voice (revert to schwa vowel sounds).		V C|C V|C V|C V|C V s e̱ n|s i̱ |t i̱ |v i̱ |t y i̱ |v i̱ s e̱ n|s i̱ |t i̱ |v i̱ |
10. **Write** the letters of each syllable with your **fingertip** on a hard surface, **and say** each syllable simultaneously (not the letter names); look away from the word, and say each syllable while writing with a pencil.		y |t y s e̱ n|s i̱ |t i̱ |v i̱ |t y s e̱ n|s i̱ |t i̱ |v i̱ |t y s e̱ n s i̱ t i̱ v i̱ t y

is one sound. When this occurs in a word, the pattern *V V*, disappears. The student must continue to label each letter until arriving at the next *V*, which will indicate the pattern that shows where to divide to find the syllable. An example follows:

$$\begin{array}{cc} V & V\ \ C\ V \\ \cancel{V}\ \cancel{V} & \cancel{V}\ \cancel{V} \\ a\ \underline{u}\ t\ \underline{o} & a\ \underline{u}\ t\ \underline{o} \end{array}$$

8b. How to Spell a Word: Sounding Syllables in 10 Steps To spell words correctly and independently, students are taught a procedure for tapping and sounding syllables, isolating vowels, and identifying consonants in words (see Figure 16.4). Spelling is more difficult to master than decoding because there are various ways to spell the same sound. Therefore, although students may be able to decode a written word that they have never seen before, it is often impossible for them to spell a word that they hear but have never seen. For example, a vowel plus the letter *l* at the end of a word can be spelled seven different ways that all sound alike: *mammal, level, middle, peril, missile, carol,* and *mogul.* In addition, vowels can lack clarity and are unrecognizable when they make the schwa sound, such as in the words *mammary, benefit, sudden, poison,* and *rumpus.* The spelling procedure parallels the 10-step decoding strategy described previously in that students again emphasize vowels and convert schwa sounds into short or long sounds.

9. Guides to Spelling and Pronunciation The English language has many silent letters and letters that produce unexpected sounds. For the most part, these letters are regular aspects of the language that appear the same way in countless words. To help students remember these language patterns, 44 Guides to Spelling and Pronunciation are taught throughout the program at the end of most consonant units. For example, the words *radiate, carrier, skiing, patio,* and *medium* are explained by the Guide: Inner *i*, "When Inner *i* is followed by a vowel near the end of a multisyllabic word, it usually sounds like long /ē/." The Guide: Alternate In-

How to Spell a Word

Sounding Syllables in 10 Steps

1.	**Say the word** in your regular *speaking voice:*	majesty	
2.	**Tap, count, and say syllables** using your thumb first and consecutive fingers for each subsequent syllable, replacing schwa sounds with short or long vowel sounds (*spelling voice*):	ma jes ty	
3.	**Draw the lines:**		

vowel lines   –   –   –

syllable lines   ___ ___ ___

4.	**Tap and say** first syllable:	ma
5.	**Isolate and write vowel:** connect vowel sound to its Guide Word ending, and write vowel on vowel and syllable lines:	<u>a</u> <u>a</u>
6.	**Fill in consonants:** repeat syllable, and fill in consonants before and after vowel.	<u>a</u> <u>ma</u>
7.	**Go back** to the beginning, tap, and say the syllables, stopping at the second tap and saying the short vowel sound instead of the schwa.	ma jes
8.	**Continue to the end** by repeating Steps 5–7 for each syllable.	<u>a</u> <u>e</u> <u>ma</u> <u>jes</u> <u>a</u> <u>e</u> y <u>ma</u> <u>jes</u> <u>ty</u> <u>ma</u> <u>jes</u> <u>ty</u>
9.	**Adjust;** say the word in your regular *speaking voice.*	ma jes ty
10.	**Write** the letters of each syllable with your **fingertip** on a hard surface, **and say** each syllable simultaneously (not the letter names). Do this three times: Look at the word, look away from the word, and look at the word again. Finally, look away from the word, and say each syllable while you write it with a pencil.	

Figure 16.4.   How to spell a word.

ner *i*, "When Inner *i* is followed by a vowel near the beginning of a multisyllabic word, it usually sounds like long /ī/," helps students remember how to pronounce words such as *miasma, biennial, biology,* and *triumphant.*

10. *Comprehension*   Teachers look for newspaper, textbook, and encyclopedia articles that contain words that students have previously decoded and spelled. Many are unfamiliar to students with limited reading experience. When

they see the words in print, their confidence in the program is heightened and they realize that they are learning vocabulary that is immediately useful and relevant to world events. The teacher provides background information orally and encourages discussion. Pairs of students read aloud to one another at the end of every lesson, even if only headings and captions are read. For example, articles containing the lesson word *amber* brought forth discussion of eras in the history of the earth. One class visited the Museum of Natural History's special exhibit on amber, saw the replica of the Russian amber room, learned about the Russian Revolution, and read the explanations in the glass cases.

Approximately two thirds of the way through the school year, explicit instruction in comprehension begins. Both dyslexic and nondyslexic individuals profit from instruction in how to find main ideas, predict outcomes, understand figurative language, and analyze characters and style. Extensive instruction in decoding and vocabulary development are prerequisites to instruction in understanding what is read. Although comprehension instruction is fairly useless if students cannot decode, one cannot wait for fluent and flawless decoding to begin to teach comprehension strategies. Regardless of the level of fluency, students read something from narrative passages every day, including that day's teacher's page in *Starting Over* (Knight, 1986). Students enjoy reading what they looked at and listened to earlier in the lesson when the teacher read the scripted teacher's page.

Daily Instruction

The following is a plan for a 3-hour session after approximately 6 months of instruction or two thirds through the school year. The strands of language skills are integrated into each 3-hour lesson. At this time explicit instruction in comprehension and expository writing begins.

9:00–9:10	Each day a different student writes on the board an abbreviated form of the short vowel chart and all of the guides to spelling and pronunciation learned thus far and leads classmates, who are writing in their notebooks and tracing on their palms.
9:10–9:25	Pairs of students read to each other from teacher-made practice sheets containing sounds, word parts, and words, such as *a, am, amber; mam, mammal; ma, majesty; ai, aim, maim;* and *ay, pay, payment.* A short spelling quiz on the studied words follows, and is collected, marked, and given back to the students.
9:25–9:35	A student at the board and the class at their desks decode two words using the Guide: How to Read a Word. Words are selected based on the guides, vowels, and consonants learned thus far. At the beginning of the year, *amnesty* and *nemesis* were decoded. At this point the words might be *jaundiced* and *intrinsic* because the students have covered vowel pairs, the three sounds of final *-ed,* and the two sounds of *c.*
9:35–9:45	A student at the board and the class at their desks spell two words dictated by the teacher, using the Guide: How to Spell a Word. At the beginning of the year, the words *sassafras* and *peristalsis* were selected. At this point the words might be *flaunted* and *illicit.*

9:45–10:15   The consonant unit on the letter *r* is begun; this unit includes a lesson on the physical aspects of the consonant and a lesson on the three *r*-controlled vowel sounds. The words *armor, ermine, irksome, sordid,* and *urban* are read and spelled using guides for reading and spelling. The students find the words in the dictionary, discussed them, write them in their small vocabulary notebooks, and use three or more of them in one written sentence. One group-composed sentence is put on the board and corrected for syntax, grammar, and usage. This type of lesson is the starting point for grammar lessons that the teacher will conduct at another time.

10:15–10:30   Students take a break.

10:30–11:15   Comprehension instruction begins. Reading material comes from various sources: newspaper articles on current or historical events in all fields of interest from science, to politics, to the arts; classic works of literature and poetry; and textbooks on specific subjects. The choice of reading material is governed by the administration's policies. Instruction begins with a specific strategy for finding the main ideas in sentences, paragraphs, and larger chunks of reading matter. Pairs of students read aloud to each other and work cooperatively on words that need to be decoded or defined. Lively discussions accompany their efforts to find those key words that reveal the meaning of each sentence. The teacher is free to work with pairs of students throughout the room. During the last 15 minutes of this part of the lesson, the teacher puts the students' comprehension outlines on the board and guides them into thinking logically about the decisions they have made regarding the meaning of the passage.

11:15–12:00   Writing instruction begins. Students are introduced to a standard format for expository writing: an introductory paragraph containing a topic and thesis, one paragraph containing opposing arguments, one or two supporting the thesis, and a final paragraph that draws conclusions and summarizes. The opening paragraph of a passage that was analyzed earlier for comprehension is now analyzed for writing structure. Students debate on a familiar issue about which they have an opinion. Students put unfamiliar words on the board and spell and define them using guides and strategies. The sentence writing that students have done during every session all year has prepared them to write an opening paragraph of their own.

Case Study of a Union Member

Simone was 45 years old when she joined the DC 37 program for dyslexic union members. At the time of her enrollment, she was an office aide who for 12 years had taken and failed tests that would have changed her employment status from provisional to permanent. She worried that something was wrong with her. Recognizing her symptoms in a union newspaper article announcing an upcoming information and testing session on dyslexia, she eagerly attended the meeting. Three years after starting class, she passed the test for permanent status as a secretary with a grade of 83. "I couldn't believe I got that high a mark. I screamed and hollered and cried for joy. I just couldn't stop crying." The test consisted of spelling, answering questions on silent reading passages and charts, and solving math problems. (See Table 16.1 for a summary of Simone's Starting Over test battery.)

Simone was born prematurely; at birth she weighed a little more than 2 pounds and had good sight in her right eye but only a trace of sight in her left eye. When in the second grade she had trouble learning to spell and read, the difficulty was attributed to her prematurity and visual impairment. When Simone entered the third grade, her mother found an outside tutor, but Simone's reading did not improve. Her three older siblings went through school successfully and all attended college. Simone's struggles resulted in her being held back in the sixth grade; later she attended a vocational high school, where she majored in nursing. She had enormous difficulty passing tests, but because she was a "good girl," she was promoted each year and graduated with her class. Over the years, she attempted to attend college but failed, so she took courses in office practices, computer literacy, and shorthand. At the city agency where she worked, she was considered a model employee, with few absences, an engaging personality, and a cooperative spirit. She explained, "If my supervisor told me or showed me how to do something, I grasped it immediately, but if I had to read about it, I was lost."

Simone said that when she cried with frustration and anger, "my mother would tell me that I was just as smart as my sisters and brother, that I had the gift of love, and one day I would rise above my learning problems. My mother was my inspiration. I admired her for her wisdom and knowledge. At age 65, a year before she died, she got her degree as a teacher. She was a fanatic for *The New York Times's* crossword puzzles. My father didn't have much education, and I think my dyslexia can be traced through him. He was a carpenter and welder, good with his hands, just as I found out I am."

Table 16.1.   Summary of tests taken by Simone

Test	Date of test 10/92	6/93	6/94	6/95
Knight Pretest #9, Reading One-Syllable Words and Word Parts (1986)	20	34	38	40
Wide Range Achievement Test (WRAT, Jastak & Jastak, 1978), Spelling I	5.0	5.6	6.3	7.9
WRAT, Reading I	7.0			9.1
Huelsman Word Discrimination (1958)[a]	7.8			
Tests of Adult Basic Education (TABE; McGraw-Hill, 1987), Level M (medium)	7.5	8.2	9.6	
Level D (difficult)				9.6

[a]Used only as a pretest for screening purposes

After embarking on her remedial instruction, Simone began to pursue a long-held desire to learn to paint. She had been watching instructional painting on television over the years, and one day she thought that if she could learn to read, then she might also be able to learn to paint. She began with watercolors and moved on to oils when her daughter presented her with an easel, tubes of paint, and a canvas. Later a colleague at work and a former junior high school teacher became her mentors. She recently had a show at the YMCA.

Simone said, "Now I always have a book in my hands, and I read like there's no tomorrow. I don't have to use the 10-steps in order to find the syllables any more. I look at a word, and somehow the syllables jump out. I just seem to see them without working at it. My dream is still to go to college, but I have not overcome my fear. A lot of people don't understand dyslexia, and they belittle us. All we need is just a little more time. I'm not going to give up my dream."

Case Study of a Young Man Recovering from Substance Abuse

Horace was the youngest of four children, all born and raised in the Bronx, New York. Horace attended a local public school, and he explained, "I knew from the second grade that I just couldn't seem to learn to read." He repeated the fourth grade which, he said, "did me no good at all and made it obvious to everybody that I was a real dummy. There was a lot of . . . abuse from my family, especially from my older brother, who tried to help for a while and finally gave up, calling me all kinds of insulting names." In the seventh grade, he began working in a local supermarket and increasingly took to cutting school. Instead of being scolded or helped by his teachers, he was ignored and promoted to the eighth grade and later to the ninth grade. High school became a drudgery. Horace said, "No matter how many classes I cut, I didn't fail. That's when I realized that it didn't matter whether I went to school or not, and I dropped out. From then on, my life went downhill. All I could do well in was hanging around. I soon got involved with alcohol and then drugs."

Two years later, he married a young woman who had never abused drugs. He attempted to clean up and remained drug free for 2 years. During that time, Horace and his wife had two children. Horace's search for permanent employment led only to temporary, menial jobs that didn't require a high school diploma or reading and writing skills. By age 20, he was back on drugs. Several years later, after he had dropped out of two residential therapeutic communities within 3 months of voluntary enrollment, he explained, "I lost my wife and my kids and ended up homeless, sleeping on the train, and eating out of garbage cans." By age 28, however, he was living in his third therapeutic community and had been sober for 3 months when he began Starting Over.

Horace was elated with the diagnosis of dyslexia. "It cleared up all the fears I had had about being too stupid to learn. I ran around the treatment center telling everyone over and over that I was dyslexic." Horace was present for almost the entire school year—he attended 155 out of 159 days from October to June. He remained in residential treatment after his Starting Over graduation. Later he celebrated a second graduation, this time from his treatment house, and a third on completion of a 9-month vocational training course in air conditioning and refrigeration repair. As of 1999, Horace was remarried and had been employed for the past 2 years by a major international airport. He said, "I have been drug free for 5 years. I am learning in a way I always wanted to but never imagined I actually would. My plan is still to go to college. I will do it." (See Table 16.2 for a summary of Horace's Starting Over test battery.)

LENGTH OF TIME FOR GAINS

Dyslexic Union Members

The DC 37 union members with dyslexia typically attended 3-hour Starting Over classes twice per week. After work they traveled to classes at union headquarters from locations throughout the city. Holding classes at union headquarters offered students several advantages: job safety in the confidentiality offered by the separation from workplace supervisors, a choice of other DC 37 Education Fund classes for lifelong learning if diagnosis ruled out dyslexia, a union-based college for those who graduated from the dyslexia program and wished to continue their education, and the camaraderie of other adults with dyslexia.

Classes met on two nonconsecutive weekdays. Such scheduling has the disadvantage of gaps between instructional days, but working adults can hardly handle more than 2 evenings per week. The greater the number of days with no instruction, the more material is forgotten, which necessitates a longer review period at the beginning of each session. To make up for these losses and because DC 37 realized that the maximum of 180 hours of instruction per year was inade-

Table 16.2.   Summary of tests taken by Horace

	Date of test	
Test	10/92	6/93
Knight Pretest #9, Reading One-Syllable Words and Word Parts (1986)	17	34
Wide Range Achievement Test (WRAT, Jastak & Jastak, 1978), Spelling I	4.6	6.2
WRAT, Reading I	6.7	8.5
Huelsman Word Discrimination (1958)[a]	4.2	
Test of Adult Basic Education (TABE; McGraw-Hill, 1987), Level M (medium)	7.9	
Level D (difficult)		9.0

[a]Used only as a pretest for screening purposes

quate for students with dyslexia, the classes were open ended. That is, if students did not attain their goals by the end of the year, then they were welcome to return after summer break and remain in class until they reached their personal objectives. They attended faithfully and seriously, leaving when life problems caused a break in attendance and returning when they could. It took most students 2–3 years to achieve their various goals, such as passing the high school equivalency examination, gaining admission to college, passing an exam to receive an upgrade in their job title or to move from provisional to permanent employment status, helping their children and grandchildren with homework, and reading for their own pleasure and continued learning.

Dyslexic Adults Recovering from Alcoholism and Substance Abuse

The students in the Starting Over program for dyslexic adults recovering from alcoholism and other substance abuse, all of whom were welfare recipients living in publicly supported residential therapeutic communities, attended 3-hour classes 5 days per week for 8½ months, for a total of 480 hours of instruction from October to June. No enrollments were accepted after the second week of classes because of the sequential nature of the program, which builds on a newly developing foundation, and because of the term of instruction had a fixed end date.

Absenteeism and attrition are major obstacles to success for adults in educational programs. Although most substance abuse programs report high rates of turnover for clients in residential treatment and in education classes held at the treatment facilities, more than 70% of the students enrolled in Starting Over completed the program while remaining in drug treatment. The consistency and intensity of 15 hours per week of daily instruction resembled a part-time work week and served to instill the employment values of reliability and dependability; the learning skills of memorizing, reading, writing, and questioning; and the social skills of trusting and bonding with peers and supervisors.

The project was funded by the New York State OASAS for 8 consecutive years (1987–1995). Knight and Randell (1995) reported on testing, conducted at the end of the first 5 years of the program, of 409 clients who were reading between grade levels 4.0 and 8.0. Of the 409 clients, 291, or 71%, were found to have dyslexia. Of the 291 clients with dyslexia, 133 enrolled in the Starting Over program and 96 graduated. Sixteen classes (two per year for 8 years) received almost 9 months of instruction, 480 hours from October to June. Posttests of decoding (Reading One-Syllable Words and Word Parts, Knight, 1986) and of vocabulary and comprehension (TABE, McGraw-Hill, 1987) revealed statistically significant improvement on all reading measures: decoding, vocabulary, and comprehension. Grade equivalents showed that on entry, the average reading level was grade 5.8; on completion it was grade 7.7.

The goals of OASAS—recovery and improved employment functioning—meant that students at reading levels below grade 4.0 could not be admitted. With only 8½ months of remedial instruction, there would be little chance that such students would reach grade level 8.0, the reading level at which most training programs with an employment ladder begin. Clients reading near an 8.0 grade level, however, might improve enough to pass the high school equivalency examination and have many more training and employment opportunities open to them. Even with 480 hours of instruction, the Starting Over staff were aware that graduation in June should not be the end of remedial instruction because the students were just entering a period in which they could finally "read to learn." For in-depth comprehension and writing skill development, they would have needed to attend 3-hour classes for 2 nights per week while also employed or attending vocational training.

SUPPORT STAFF

Adults in literacy programs cannot achieve grade-level gains with reading instruction alone. Many adults in ABE and literacy programs exhibit self-defeating behaviors in areas that are not academic yet have an impact on learning and independence. It is important to implement a holistic approach in helping these students achieve their potential. For instance, the Starting Over program attended by adults recovering from substance abuse had three staff members: an academic teacher who worked 5 days per week, a life skills/vocational teacher who spent 1 day per week with the whole class, and a licensed social worker who worked 1 day per week to help individual students understand their socioemotional stresses. All staff members received 60 hours of Starting Over training prior to the first day of class and follow-up training once per week during the year during a regularly scheduled meeting. At the weekly meeting, staff members discussed particular students from the perspective of their own disciplines. Thus, the whole person was better understood and served by the entire staff.

The DC 37 program also had a rich variety of services available to all union members as well as a counselor who provided information and support to the students. Several times a year, the counselor met with the Starting Over representative to prepare group sessions on topics of interest to union members, such as parenting issues, dealing with hostility on the job, the Americans with Disabilities Act of 1990 (ADA; PL 101-336), and the definition of *reasonable accommodation* (required in most workplaces by PL 101-336) as it relates to testing and work assignments. The counselor was also available for individual counseling.

SUMMARY

In the early 1960s, the government recognized the threat of illiteracy to economic well-being and national security (Knight, 1998b). Thirty years later, in the 1990s, ever-increasing numbers of adults showed poor reading ability (Kirsch, Jungblut, Kolstad, & Jenkins, 1993); functional illiteracy was continuing to grow. *Functional illiteracy* refers to people age 16 and older who have reading grade levels that do not exceed 4.0. Their reading material consists of short sentences with simple construction and vocabulary. Reading material for adults, however, expresses complex thoughts that require an understanding of complex sentence structure and advanced vocabulary (to eliminate verbosity). Although adults who read at a grade level of 4.0 are actually reading, they are functioning as though they were illiterate in terms of the reading needs of an adult.

With further investigation into the innate nature of adults with reading difficulties and with the development of a definition of dyslexia, it became apparent that persistent, immutable difficulties experienced by adults with functional illiteracy were not caused by poor motivation but by undiagnosed and untreated learning disabilities, including dyslexia, of which the primary characteristic is poor phonological processing ability.

Starting Over, an MSLE program, trained its teachers to diagnose and teach a group of union members and a group of adults who were unemployed and recovering from substance abuse. The training for the teachers and support staff was intensive and ongoing for the duration of both projects. The students examined sounds fully, slowly, sequentially, individually, and with deliberate repetition, then they immediately blended the sounds to form words, which they defined and used in written sentences. Comprehension instruction and writing were a part of every session. The teaching proceeded not simply on an upward path but on an upward, spiral path; previously introduced information came back in every lesson. Information from all subject areas was introduced in a way that enhanced learning by reasoning, thinking, creating, and verbalizing rather than by mere rote memorization.

Students learned to trust the teacher and each other. They worked in pairs on all skill areas and learned to function independently. Their self-esteem was greatly enhanced as they saw themselves as capable learners in every session.

To retain students over the long remediation period, every session had to demonstrate that they had mastered some small element in the reading, spelling, and writing process. Early in the year, multisensory learning was viewed as a new and unattractive experience. Initially students were reluctant to participate in a process that asked them to utter sounds aloud and within earshot of their classmates while they used their fingertip as a pencil and the palm of their hand as paper to trace what they needed to learn. One day during the first week of class, a student confessed her embarrassment at never having been able to memorize her sister's telephone number. They were very close and telephoned each other every day. The student always had to look up the number and have it in view while dialing. During a 20-minute lesson, she wrote the number on her palm and then on the tabletop with her fingertip, said it aloud, found the relationship of one digit to another, wrote it with a pencil, looked at and drew the pattern formed by the digits on the telephone's number pad, and finally called her sister on a public telephone without looking at the written page. Every day for a week, she called her sister while the class looked on. She truly had memorized the number. The other students found this experience to be so remarkable that they tried the exercise and found that it worked for them, too. They realized that multisensory learning not only motivated and taught them but also brought excitement and commitment to learning.

In 10 months of instruction, children may have 1 hour per day of communication arts instruction, or approximately 180 hours of language instruction per year. By the end of the school year, however, the adults who were recovering from substance abuse had received 480 hours of instruction, and the union members had received 180 hours of instruction. The latter group took two to three times as long as the substance abusers to achieve their goals.

Considering the length of time and intensity of instruction that adults with dyslexia need to overcome severe phonological difficulties, it is understandable that short-term programs that do not enhance weak phonological abilities fail to achieve results and why it has been so enormously difficult to teach ABE students throughout the years. This difficulty, however, exists not merely because students need considerable time to learn to decode, spell, write and comprehend. Teachers also need to learn about dyslexia, about the sounds and linguistic regularities of the language, and how to deliver these elements to students who may have quit school years earlier but still want to learn. Highly trained professional teachers who are committed to the long period of time needed for remediation and to the continual honing of their own skills, especially their expertise with MSLE techniques, are clearly what adults with dyslexia needed then and still need.

REFERENCES

Adams, M.J., Foorman, B.R., Lundberg, I., & Beeler, T. (1998). *Phonemic awareness in young children: A classroom curriculum.* Baltimore: Paul H. Brookes Publishing Co.

American Psychiatric Association. (1994). *Diagnostic and statistical manual of mental disorders* (4th ed.). Washington, DC: Author.

Americans with Disabilities Act (ADA) of 1990, PL 101-336, 42 U.S.C. §§ 12101 *et seq.*

Banks, S.R., Guyer, B.P., & Guyer, K.E. (1995). A study of medical students and physicians referred for learning disabilities. *Annals of Dyslexia, 45,* 233–245.

Bat-Hayim, M.L. (1996). Analyzing cohesion in language samples of college students: A diagnostic tool. *Annals of Dyslexia, 46,* 123–155.

Denckla, M.B. (1994). Measurement of executive function. In G.R. Lyon (Ed.), *Frames of reference for the assessment of learning disabilities: New views on measurement issues* (pp. 117–142). Baltimore: Paul H. Brookes Publishing Co.

Elbro, C., Nielsen, I., & Petersen, D.K. (1994). Dyslexia in adults: Evidence for deficits in non-word reading and in the phonological representation of lexical items. *Annals of Dyslexia, 44,* 205–226.

Ellis, W., & Cramer, S.C. (1996). Introduction. In S.C. Cramer & W. Ellis (Eds.), *Learning disabilities: Lifelong issues* (pp. xxvii–xxxi). Baltimore: Paul H. Brookes.

Galaburda, A.M., Sherman, G.F., Rosen, G.D., Aboitiz, F., & Geschwind, N. (1985). Developmental dyslexia: Four consecutive patients with cortical anomalies. *Annals of Neurology, 18,* 222–232.

Huelsman, C.B., Jr. (1958). *Word Discrimination Test.* Oxford, OH: Miami University Alumni Association.

Jastak, J.F., & Jastak, S. (1978). *Wide Range Achievement Test.* Wilmington, DE: Jastak Associates.

Kirsch, I.S., Jungblut, A., Jenkins, L., & Kolstad, A. (1993). *Adult literacy in America: National adult literacy survey.* Washington, DC: U.S. Department of Education.

Knight, J.R. (1986). *Starting Over: A combined teaching manual and student workbook for reading, writing, spelling, vocabulary, and handwriting.* Cambridge, MA: Educators Publishing Service.

Knight, J.R. (1997). *Adults with dyslexia: Aspiring and achieving.* Orton Emeritus Series Baltimore: International Dyslexia Association.

Knight, J.R. (1998a). Assessing learners' phonological awareness, spelling, and decoding skills. *Linkages, 5*(1), 11–14.

Knight, J.R. (1998b). The link between learning disability and instruction. *Literacy Harvest, 7*(1), 11–16.

Knight, J.R., & Randell, J. (1995). Efficacy of Starting Over for improving the reading of adult dyslexic substance abusers in residential treatment. In C.W. McIntyre & J.S. Pickering (Eds.), *Clinical studies of multisensory structured language education* (pp. 233–243). Dallas, TX: Shelton School, International Multisensory Structured Language Education Council.

Lyon, G.R. (1995). Toward a definition of dyslexia. *Annals of Dyslexia, 45,* 3–27.

Lyon, G.R. (1996). The state of research. In S.C. Cramer & W. Ellis (Eds.), *Learning disabilities: Lifelong issues* (pp. 3–61). Baltimore: Paul H. Brookes Publishing Co.

McGraw-Hill. (1987). *Tests of Adult Basic Education (TABE)*. Monterey, CA: CTB/McGraw-Hill.

Pennington, B.F. (1991). *Diagnosing learning disorders*. New York: The Guilford Press.

Pennington, B.F. (1995). Genetics of learning disabilities. *Journal of Child Neurology, 10*, 69–77.

Shaywitz, S.E., & Shaywitz, B.A. (1996). Unlocking learning disabilities: The neurological basis. In S.C. Cramer & W. Ellis (Eds.), *Learning disabilities: Lifelong issues* (pp. 255–260). Baltimore: Paul H. Brookes Publishing Co.

Shaywitz, S.E., Shaywitz, B.A., Pugh, K.R., Skudlarski, P., Fulbright, R.K., Constable, R.T., Bronen, R.A., Fletcher, J.M., Liberman, A.M., Shankweiler, D.P., Katz, L., Lacadie, C., Marchione, K.E., & Gore, J.C. (1996). The neurobiology of developmental dyslexia as viewed through the lens of functional magnetic resonance imaging technology. In G.R. Lyon & J.M. Rumsey (Eds.), *Neuroimaging: A window to the neurological foundations of learning and behavior in children* (pp. 79–94). Baltimore: Paul H. Brookes Publishing Co.

Stone, B., & Brady, S. (1995). Evidence for phonological processing deficits in less-skilled readers. *Annals of Dyslexia, 45*, 51–78.

Truch, S. (1994). Stimulating basic reading processes using auditory discrimination in depth. *Annals of Dyslexia, 44*, 60–80.

Voeller, K.K.S. (1994). Techniques for measuring social competence in children. In G.R. Lyon (Ed.), *Frames of reference for the assessment of learning disabilities: New views on measurement issues* (pp. 523–554). Baltimore: Paul H. Brookes Publishing Co.

Wise, B.W., & Olson, R.K. (1995). Computer-based phonological awareness and reading instruction. *Annals of Dyslexia, 45*, 99–122.

Yancey Padget, S., Knight, D.F., & Sawyer, D.J. (1996). Tennessee meets the challenge of dyslexia. *Annals of Dyslexia, 46*, 51–72.

17

Working with the High-Functioning Dyslexic

Susan H. Blumenthal

The population of high-functioning dyslexic adults is a specific but quite diverse group of individuals. They are studying and working in a variety of fields and include college students, graduate students, physicians, lawyers, and clergymen. Some adults, especially those in graduate school, are required to do tremendous amounts of reading each week. Other graduate students conduct experiments in science research, which may require less reading than is necessary in liberal arts programs. In science settings, however, graduate students need to perform sequential, multistep experiments with relative independence over a period of several days. Frequent shifting from abstract conceptualization to sequenced detail and back again requires a high degree of organization, which can be troublesome for some dyslexics.

Not all high-functioning dyslexics are in school. Some dyslexic adults have already completed school and are working in a business setting. Whether a person runs his own business or is in a corporate setting, he or she usually has to do background reading in trade or professional journals to keep abreast of developments in the field. In addition, individuals in professional positions often have to write memos and reports on a regular basis as part of their job.

Virtually all high-functioning dyslexic adults are ambitious and highly motivated, but they also suffer from chronic feelings of inadequacy, stress, and low self-esteem regarding their ability to learn. Almost all of them had a difficult beginning in the early grades of elementary school and continued to function quite unevenly during their school years.

EMOTIONAL REPERCUSSIONS

Despite being above average or quite superior in general ability, nearly all of the high-functioning dyslexic adults who seek help with reading and writing skills experience anxiety about some aspects of their work and learning. They often do not know why they have so much difficulty with written language. Through the years, they have tried both to compensate for and to hide the problem. They may have never read a book all of the way through but will rarely miss class so that they can pick up the necessary information from discussion. They may have to write multiple drafts of a term paper but often will ask and be allowed to give an oral presentation or work in tandem with another student. So many of these students have been told to "try harder" throughout their school careers. Nearly every dyslexic adult who goes for a psychoeducational consultation or evaluation thinks that he or she is "lazy," that everyone else is smarter, or that there is something wrong with his or her brain. It does not matter whether they graduated from a state school or an Ivy League school, nor does it matter whether they were inducted into Phi Beta Kappa. They almost always are plagued by varying degrees of self-doubt.

There are important differences between children and adults who have learning difficulties that can have an impact on intervention. First, their basic attitudes generally are different. When children are referred for language intervention, they often are resistant at first. They have been identified as not doing well in school, and both the children and the parents may be upset with their school performance and/or with the school staff. In contrast, adults usually are highly motivated to improve their language skills. Many are self-referred or are referred by other professionals, such as psychotherapists or college teachers. Consequently, adults with learning difficulties often have definite goals. In addition, they often are relieved when they realize that they can get help.

A second difference between children and adults with learning difficulties is awareness. Children's awareness of their learning needs and difficulties usually are unformulated. In some way, they sense that there is something wrong. They say, "Reading is not hard for me, I just don't like it." Adults are much more aware of how learning difficulties, especially reading difficulties, have affected their lives. They may feel self-conscious in a social group—not because they lack social skills but because they do not make the same kind of contributions as others. They may not make the same mental associations because they lack the underlying foundation of knowledge, which is often derived from reading. For example, a 35-year-old physician with a persistent reading problem came for help with this comment, "I feel I am shallow, compared to all my friends. They read all of the time."

Another difference between children and adults with learning disabilities is how they cope. Children are part of an established support system; they are evaluated, tested, promoted to or held back from the next grade, and are often the focus of parent–teacher conferences. The responsibility of learning or not learning is shared. Adults with learning disabilities invariably seem to have a secret lives. They do not have the same support system as children do. Adults have to work in an increasingly independent manner, and they worry about being "found out." Many adults with learning disabilities have learned to hide their problems and compensate as much as possible. Often, they focus on avoidance in order to escape potential humiliation.

Finally, the beginning of the referral process is also different for adults and children. Children are usually referred or evaluated because they are failing or not doing well in school. Adults are referred for a variety of reasons. Some adults experience a change in their work requirements or in their educational setting, and they find that they cannot meet the expected level of the new requirements. For example, a member of the Coast Guard with severe dyslexia was promoted to petty officer. Instead of working on machines, at which he was an expert, he now had to do considerable paperwork and report writing. His performance ratings, which were formerly consistently high, fell below average. In another instance, an ambitious 31-year-old account executive who had a history of dyslexia was quite successful on her job. She had excellent verbal skills and was effective at meetings. Her new boss, however, insisted that there be more memos and outlines of marketing goals and fewer face-to-face meetings. The account executive knew that if she wanted to be promoted, then she would have to get her ideas down in writing.

Some adults who return to school for a higher degree refer themselves for a psychoeducational evaluation. For example, a successful 47-year-old business-woman with a bachelor of arts degree decided to apply for a master of business administration program. She referred herself for evaluation because she suspected that she had a previously undiagnosed learning problem. When her son was diagnosed with dyslexia, she recognized similar patterns in her own academic life.

More adults are being referred by mental health workers, personnel in the workplace, and college and university faculty to explore whether there is an undetected learning problem. As awareness increases about the different forms that learning problems can take, psychotherapists, job supervisors, and professors have begun to notice areas of discrepancy in people who otherwise are functioning well. For example, an administrator at a university was referred for a psychoeducational evaluation after his boss wrote, "The communication area is of great concern and an obstacle to Mr. K's career development. He exceeds expectations in personal skills and in commitment to all aspects of his job. I recommend that he get help for problems in writing and other communications skills."

EVALUATION AND ASSESSMENT

The first component of a comprehensive assessment for an adult involves the gathering of information about the individual's early developmental history, educational and medical history, and, if appropriate, employment history. The individual's own perception of the problem is particularly helpful. The latter information can be obtained from a writing sample called Educational Memories (Blumenthal, 1981), which is described later in this section.

The purpose of the assessment is to try to understand and evaluate the client's presenting problems to develop a treatment plan. The assessor tries to determine why he or she is having difficulty functioning in an academic or a work setting and explore the client's capabilities and learning patterns to see what interferes with learning. Current information is as important as the individual's history. If the individual is in school, then it is important to read several recent term papers as well as look over class notes from lectures. Individuals with jobs can bring in reports, memos, or letters that are representative of work demands.

There is no specific test battery for diagnosing learning disabilities. Psychologists who specialize in working with people who have dyslexia or other types of learning disabilities use many of the same tests in their evaluation as are used in traditional psychological evaluations, but they view the results in a particular way (see Chapter 5 for more on types of assessment tests). That is, during assessment of learning disabilities, qualitative information is always an important supplement to the quantitative results. The evaluator wants to know exactly what the client said and how he or she responded to each task. A trained diagnostician always administers tests in a standardized manner according to the test manual but views each test as a vehicle for deriving other important, perhaps subtle currents of information. By listening carefully and recording precisely what the client says, an evaluator can pick up clues about receptive and expressive language problems, confusion in the use of prepositions, word substitutions, and so forth. Although this ancillary information may not directly affect the overall test results, it is important because it helps show vulnerabilities in the client's learning and performance and often illuminates why his or her performance in school or on the job has been uneven.

A typical test battery to identify learning disabilities in adults includes the Wechsler Adult Intelligence Scale–III (Wechsler, 1991); a silent reading test such as the Nelson-Denny Reading Test (Brown, Bennett, & Hanna, 1981) or the Gates-MacGinitie Reading Tests–3 (MacGinitie & MacGinitie, 1989); the Wide-Range Achievement Test–3 (Wilkinson, 1993), which has Word Recognition, Spelling, and Math Computation subtests; a test of oral reading such as the Gray Oral Reading Test (Wiederholt & Bryant, 1992) or the Diagnostic Assessments of Reading with Trial Teaching Strategies (DARTTS; Roswell & Chall, 1992); a design copying test such as the Bender Visual Motor Gestalt Test (Bender, 1938); and several writing samples (usually one written during the session and two written at home between testing sessions), including Educational Memories (Blumenthal, 1981). Depending on the client's presenting problems, other tests may be included, such as House-Tree-Person Drawing (Buck, 1970), selected cards form the Thematic Apperception Test (Muray & Bellak, 1973), and a sentence completion test such as the Rotter Incomplete Sentences Blank (The Psychological Corporation, 1992). Sometimes a client has had a prior psychological examination but has not undergone reading tests or a writing evaluation. Although it is not necessary to redo what has been done already, reading and writing assessment should be done before the specialist begins to work with the client.

After the testing is completed, the evaluator interprets the findings and explains them to the client. It is important for the evaluator as well as the remedial specialist (if the specialist is different from the evaluator) to present the results in as constructive a manner as possible. When the evaluator uses trial teaching techniques and judiciously chosen teaching materials, the client can begin to sense how he or she can make progress. After test findings were explained to one young physician and he had begun working on his problems, he wrote, *My diagnosis as dyslexic, i.e., reading more slowly in order to understand, was both difficult and refreshing. At first I had attached a stigma to it, yet it was also refreshing, since it validated my life experience. I now feel in control. Adequate time to read translates into adequate time to process and understand.*

Educational Memories

The Educational Memories writing sample measure provides information that cannot be obtained through typical diagnostic tests. Between the initial telephone call and the time of the first testing appointment, clients receive a writing assignment that focuses on their school memories. Clients are asked to relate their own version of their educational experience, including both positive and negative memories. They are to write a first draft only, by hand, on 8½" × 11" paper. They are to avoid talking to family members or using a dictionary or any other reference source. Educational Memories allows evaluators to get to know more about a client and at the same time obtain a writing sample for close examination. Most individuals write seven to nine handwritten pages.

Educational Memories serves as a valuable part of the diagnostic examination for a number of reasons. First, it is possible to find out what insights the client has about his or her own difficulties. Second, the writing sample reveals information about the individual's tendency to blame him- or herself or others for any difficulties faced. Third, the sample gives a sense of the emotional impact of years of struggling with school and/or work. Finally, the writing sample offers an initial view of the person's ability to organize information. This sample also allows an examination of handwriting, grammar, syntax, vocabulary, and spelling. The Educational Memories sample also is a useful part of the diagnostic process because it helps diagnosticians differentiate between people who have learning difficulties and people who do not. People with learning problems rarely report positive memories about school. Their negative memories always center around problems of mastery. In contrast, people with no learning difficulties have many more positive memories of school, and their negative memories relate not to mastery but instead to specific social problems (e.g., *I was never popular. I didn't get invited to the parties*) or to the harshness of particular teachers.

Following are excerpts from the Educational Memories samples of four individuals, which illustrate how painful the introduction to school can be, particularly in the beginning years when children are especially vulnerable.

Bobbie

Bobbie, a 45-year-old woman with learning and memory problems, admitted during her first session that she has never read a book all of the way through. She is now in a graduate program with approximately 1,000 pages per week of assigned reading, such as Freud, D.W. Winnicott, and Melanie Klein. Bobbie wrote, *I always have difficulty remembering what I read, and also I have trouble with facts and names. The memory of my education goes back to my very first day at school. I sat there and they debated whether or not I was retarded, because I did not know my name. I had been called Bobbie all my life, and had no idea my given name was Roberta.*

Lana

A 30-year-old woman studying for her bachelor of science degree in physical therapy, Lana, wrote, *From the time I was around 8 years old, I have had this underlying feeling of inadequacy and inferiority, which is very tied into my feelings about school. The two are almost synonymous. My driving force to get my B.S. is to rid myself of this burden.*

Derek

A 27-year-old law student recalled the following in his write-up: *I attended private school from nursery through third grade, and it was there where I encountered the most academic difficulty. The school told my parents that I was "unteachable." This attitude is reflected in a progress report from the third grade in which it was stated they no longer measured my advancement on a scale with other students: "His grades reflect individual progress rather than third-grade expectations." These are particularly painful years to remember as my self-esteem was significantly diminished.*

Mark

A 22-year-old dental student wrote the following: *My earliest academic memories are filled with anxiety—feeling the inability to master all of the spelling words for the Monday morning quiz. As I grew older, reading quickly and accurately became more important. I always had to work longer and concentrate more intently than my peers. Finally, my compensatory mechanisms of using extra time were inadequate, since I was confronted with timed exams, and no matter how much I prepared I was faced with my nemesis, only a limited amount of time to read. This forced me to skim over material rather than master it, and I therefore could not answer questions on topics I was familiar with.*

THE MOST COMMON NEEDS OF HIGH-FUNCTIONING DYSLEXICS

Individuals with learning difficulties or dyslexia usually need help in one or more of the following areas: silent reading comprehension skills, vocabulary development, expressive language (writing) skills, spelling, study skills, and managing or allocating time in a constructive manner. Each person may have a greater or lesser degree of difficulty with any one of these areas and may not have difficulty with all of them. It is particularly important to remember that each person presents a unique combination of strengths as well as weaknesses. The remediation plan has to be tailored to that person's specific needs. Often the client manifests competence in unexpected areas, as well as surprising gaps in background knowledge. Information gathered from the individual's history, diagnostic study, and examination of current work as well as trial teaching will help to pinpoint areas that need attention.

There are several important goals in treatment. The first goal is to change the individual's perception of him- or herself from someone who *cannot* learn to one who *can* learn. This is best accomplished by helping the person to become an active learner. Many dyslexic readers are too passive in relation to the material they read. As a result, their retention, understanding, and even appreciation is affected. Being an active learner means thinking about and evaluating the material being read. Active learning involves bringing prior information to the discussion of the subject at hand. The active reader tries to discern the author's point of view. Encouraging the transition from a passive to a more active approach to reading requires guidance from the remedial specialist. The remedial specialist needs to know when to pose evocative questions, how to elicit information, and when to prepare the client to develop insights about the material. For example, Evelyn, an ambitious college graduate, was running a successful business and wanted to go to graduate school for her master of business administration degree. The evaluation showed that she had a slow reading rate and had difficulty retaining what she read. Evelyn thought that she often missed main ideas, which undermined her confidence in general. An intelligent woman, she was quite interested in world affairs. To improve her reading comprehension and retention of information, she was encouraged to read the editorial columns in the daily newspaper. Instead of skimming articles and retaining a minimal amount, as she had done formerly, Evelyn was asked to approach the reading material differently, in a four-step approach.

1. First, she should read the headline and subhead and before reading further, ask herself, "What do I think this article is about?" By posing this question, she immediately became more active and focused on the article's topic.
2. Next, she should read the article and then ask herself, "What did the author say?"
3. Then she should ask, "What did I learn that was new?"
4. Finally, she should ask, "What is my opinion about this subject? Do I agree or disagree?"

After using this approach, Evelyn wrote a one-page essay about the newspaper column, which she brought to the next session. The entire assignment took her about 1 hour at home. This active approach stimulated her ability to concentrate and fostered her retention. It also improved her writing skills. After approximately 2 months of remediation, Evelyn commented, "At first it seemed like I was taking baby steps, but the way I read is really changing. When we went out to dinner with friends, it was amazing, I found I had facts and opinions and held my own in the discussion." Evelyn also worked with a variety of other standardized reading comprehension materials, such as *Six-Way Paragraphs (Advanced)* by Pauk (1983), and in doing so improved her concentration, reading comprehension, and writing skills. At the end of the year, she took the Graduate Management Admissions Test (GMAT) with extended time and was accepted into business school, where she did well.

When the therapeutic alliance is optimal and the demands of the remedial work are challenging but not overwhelming, progress can be made. The client often will report a sense of excitement about his or her own potential being realized. For example, one graduate student declared, "I looked at this assignment and said, 'I know you, you sucker! I can do it.'" Another client said, "I know that what is coming next will be hard, but now I think there is nothing I can't handle."

The second goal of remediation is to help the individual to develop an awareness of his or her own thinking process. As individuals become aware of their own thinking, positive changes occur, and thinking, reading, and writing become more efficient. It is possible to stimulate and activate cognitive processes such as reasoning, organizing, generalizing, and planning so that these cognitive processes are enhanced across a broad range of content areas. One way to encourage this kind of awareness of how one thinks is through the use of Process Notes (Blumenthal, 1981).

When the clients are disturbed about their reactions to their pattern of work habits or ability to sustain attention, they can be taught to be more aware of how they think of what interrupts their reasoning and what helps them to continue their work. When the client faces obstacles in doing his or her work, the remedial specialist can encourage the client to write Process Notes, that is, to evaluate in writing his or her own reactions to the assignment. This often helps the client to develop organizing principles, which facilitates his or her work.

For example, Process Notes were eventually used by Ted, a dyslexic doctoral student who referred himself for evaluation after he failed his written comprehensive exams. The members of the examining committee had harsh comments and remarked on how "poorly written" and how "disorganized" Ted's written effort was. They raised questions about Ted's suitability in a doctoral program, perhaps forgetting that he had completed all of the coursework up to that point with excellence. None of the committee members thought about the discrepancy between Ted's record and his performance on the comprehensives, yet *unevenness* in performance is the hallmark of almost all learning disabilities.

One of the first steps in helping Ted was for the remedial specialist to read Ted's comprehensive exam. Although the exam was more than 35 handwritten pages long, it was necessary to read it carefully to understand how Ted performed under pressure, to evaluate exactly where he needed help, and to develop a treatment plan. Although Ted experienced both anger and mild depression in reaction to his failure, his drive to improve his writing was prodigious. He responded well to the varied writing assignments that the remedial specialist gave him, most of which he completed in the library between sessions. During sessions, all completed work was read aloud, sentence by sentence, and discussed in relation to clarity, organization, and effectiveness. Although the remedial specialist made no marks on Ted's paper, every unclear sentence was discussed. In essence, the remedial specialist *modeled an active approach* for Ted by questioning unclear areas rather than by writing correct answers. After the 20th session, the specialist encouraged Ted to write Process Notes. Ted wrote the following passage after the 21st session of work:

> I began writing this time before I began typing—I began to frame this essay in my mind ahead of time. I asked a main question, and then made myself ask "What does another person reading this have to know in order to understand both the question and the answer?" I asked myself, "Does the piece follow a logical and easily understood order?" and "Does each paragraph contain a logical order too? Do all the paragraphs fit together?" Although there were a good many spelling lapses, the general ordering to the ideas seem OK to me—and this is encouraging to me. I would have to say a guarded yes to my questions.

The working relationship between the remedial specialist and the client is never a static one. It draws its strength from the balance between necessary support and the increasing autonomy of the student as he or she becomes more able to compensate for his or her difficulties. In this particular case, we see that Ted has developed an awareness of the specific elements of effective and communicative writing. The revelation that one's writing always needs to be understood by others continued to transform his efforts, and he eventually integrated this principle into most of his writing. By the end of the year, he retook the comprehensive exams and passed with high commendations.

Finally, the third goal of treatment is to reduce anxiety related to learning. A client can decrease anxiety while working on the area of his or her greatest vulnerability if a positive therapeutic alliance has been established, if materials appropriate to the client's intellectual level are used, and if each defined goal or task is broken down into manageable parts. Achievement of all three goals of treatment—helping the individual to change his or her self-perception, to develop an awareness of his or her thought processes, and to reduce anxiety—can help the individual to achieve a degree of mastery. The following two case reports illustrate these points.

Janet

The emotional repercussions of learning disabilities can interfere with a sense of positive self-worth and cause a person to feel intense shame. Janet, a friendly 30-year-old who works for a large corporation, graduated from a small liberal arts college with a degree in marketing.

Early History

Janet had difficulty learning to read in the early grades. During reading instruction, she was placed in a corrective reading group that met five times per week for 1 hour each day. Janet recalls that reading was always difficult for her. In high school, her parents helped her with assignments. They helped her review before tests and made editorial and spelling changes on her papers. She graduated from high school with a C average. Janet's anxiety heightened in college, and she often stayed up all night before an exam. She made it a point to find a study group. Her friends read her papers and made corrections before she handed them in. She did well enough so that no professor ever identified her as someone who needed to be referred for psychoeducational evaluation. After passing all of her courses, she graduated in 4 years.

Work History

After college, Janet worked in sales. Her organizational ability was praised, but she decided to change jobs because she wanted a position that included some travel. She took a job with the large corporation for whom she currently works. Her new job required interpersonal and organizational skills and also involved some travel. After 1 year, she had her first job review. She was rated outstanding in interpersonal skills and in working as a member of a team. In fact, she was rated well above average in every category except writing and communication skills. The job review noted, *Written work is dramatically inadequate for her level of responsibility*. She was told that the quality of her written work would keep her from being promoted. Janet's boss told her that she thought that Janet had some kind of learning disability and strongly urged her to get help if she wanted to advance on the job.

Testing and Remediation

Janet was extremely anxious when she first consulted the psychoeducational diagnostician and wept helplessly when she talked about her learning problems. Confronting her problems with learning was so traumatic that a month passed after the first interview before she called to begin work. Her parents were supportive both emotionally and financially. Janet asked her parents not to tell anyone else in her family that she was getting help for her learning problems. She told her boss but did not tell any of her close friends. She felt stigmatized and very ashamed.

An intelligence test showed that Janet had average ability, but the unevenness of her subtest scores showed that she had higher potential ability. For example, her general knowledge clearly had been inhibited by lack of background reading. She also experienced considerable anxiety when asked to answer questions and do specific tasks; this anxiety had a definite negative impact on the intelligence test results.

On the Word Recognition subtest of the WRAT–R, Janet scored at the sixth percentile, which is equivalent to approximately an eighth-grade skill level. Her oral and silent reading were approximately at the 10th-grade level. When answering questions about the silent reading passages, Janet read the passages and had to look back at them to find every answer.

She was asked to write several short summaries. Although it was evident that she could express herself verbally, she was very uncertain about how to put what she wanted to say in writing. Her fear about making spelling errors made her choose a simple vocabulary that made her writing seem less mature.

The evaluation was stressful. The findings were interpreted and explained to her in as positive a manner as possible, but Janet felt despair about making progress. It seemed likely that Janet had had severe reading problems when she was a youngster. There was no indication in her history or in the current evaluation, however, that suggested that she would be unable to make progress during remediation, and the evaluator conveyed this positive outlook to her.

The Work

The first goal of treatment was to change Janet's perception of herself from *someone who could not learn* to *someone who could learn* by having her work on appropriate materials within the context of a supportive relationship. It was also necessary to reduce Janet's anxiety and despair related to learning.

Because of Janet's intense anxiety in relation to reading, writing, and words in general, it was particularly important for the remedial specialist to be supportive and nonpressuring and at the same time choose materials that were mature in format and content and appropriate to Janet's reading level. Janet and the remedial specialist met once a week, before Janet was due at work. Remediation focused on oral reading; vocabulary development; silent reading comprehension; expressive language skills, including letter and memo writing; spelling; and word analysis. Janet reviewed expressive writing and vocabulary activities during the week at home.

Janet's first writing assignments were to write about members of her family. These assignments required no advance reading. Writing impressions about family and friends usually tends to be less stressful than a more formal assignment. The remedial specialist made no corrections on these first few writing assignments. After a few weeks the specialist asked Janet to summarize an article of her choice from a newspaper. Janet was able to find articles she could read in USA *Today*. Because she rarely had looked at a newspaper, she and the specialist looked at one together to see how to locate news articles, the weather section, and human interest stories. The specialist asked her to choose a newspaper article that appealed to her, read the article at home, and then summarize it in writing. Janet underlined any words in the article that she did not know or words that she thought she would have trouble defining. Each week at her remedial session, she read the summary aloud. Again, the specialist made no corrections at the time of the reading. Instead, the specialist chose one aspect of the writing—usually grammar, spelling, or general usage—for teaching during the next session. In this way, Janet felt less threatened because she was not corrected during her presentation and because skills were taught separately. She began incorporating the grammar and usage lessons into her writing. After approximately 8 months, Janet started reading *The New York Times* instead of USA *Today*. This change boosted her self-esteem, because her family and friends also read *The New York Times*. She generally found at least one article of interest to write about.

The newspaper reading was important to remediation because Janet avoided reading in general and never read the newspaper at all. After she had been attending remediation sessions for a while, Janet started to read the newspaper once per week and consequently had more to contribute when she socialized with her co-workers. Each week she added new words to her vocabulary by underlining new words at home. During remediation sessions, she and the specialist discussed and defined each word with the aid of a dictionary. By herself, Janet felt intimidated by the dictionary, but she did use it during sessions. She wrote each new word on a 3″ × 5″ index card with the definition on the reverse side. She also added a sentence using the word to help her to retain the word. The specialist also encouraged Janet to keep and bring to her sessions a list of any unknown words that she might hear at work. In this way all of the new words studied were ones that Janet herself had selected rather than words from a list in a vocabulary book.

During each session Janet read silently a short selection and answered accompanying comprehension questions. She and the remedial specialist discussed any incorrect responses. The questions that posed the most problems for Janet were questions that required inferential thinking, a skill that is essential for advanced reading comprehension. Inferential thinking involves making accurate judgments and drawing conclusions about what is read. It was necessary for Janet to approach the text in a more interactive manner than she was accustomed to. She also tended to make literal interpretations that limited her understanding of subtleties. The remedial specialist helped her to make more accurate inferences in the following way. Through guided discussion, Janet was encouraged to make relationships between events in a passage, as she and the specialist returned to the text for additional analysis of the content. The specialist helped Janet to recognize that she often could use some prior knowledge to figure out an answer. Increased self-monitoring of her own thought processes was also encouraged. In this way, Janet began to derive more meaning from what she read.

So that Janet could improve her spelling skills, misspelled words were identified both in her weekly writing assignments and in the memos or reports that she wrote for her job. When the words were common and likely to be used frequently, she copied them in a small, alphabetized notebook that she could carry in her pocketbook. The remedial specialist reviewed the words with Janet during the weekly sessions and added to the list each week so that Janet became familiar with the words. When she needed to use a word in her writing, she referred to her "personal dictionary." As time went on, she memorized many of the words, and they were dropped from the list. New words were added as Janet began to expand her vocabulary. In this way, her spelling skills improved steadily and so did her confidence in including a more varied vocabulary in her writing.

Although Janet was reading at the high school level, she was not confident about applying word analysis skills or syllabification skills to figure out new multisyllabic words. Because review of basic word analysis skills was a painful reminder of early school failures, word analysis was taught in conjunction with the words from newspaper articles that Janet mispronounced. For example, when she was not able to pronounce *mirth*, an opportunity arose for the remedial specialist to introduce the pronunciation of the special letter combinations *ir*, *ur*, and *er* and to select different words for teaching and practice at the following session. Teaching was thus tied to *use* and did not take on the qualities of *drills*. Eventually, all of the necessary word analysis skills were reviewed.

Although Janet was motivated and conscientiously completed her writing and vocabulary review at home, she continued to hide her efforts from her friends and close family members. After approximately 8 months of remediation, Janet received a promotion and a pay bonus. Her boss no longer criticized her writing and communication skills. Janet was more confident and handled pressure and stress on her job with greater equanimity. She still tended to procrastinate when she had to write memos and letters but brought them to the remedial sessions more readily to work on them with her remedial specialist. Janet still found reading to be a struggle, but she was more willing to try to get information from books and began to read some self-help books related to career advancement.

After 1½ years of remedial sessions, Janet had less anxiety and increased confidence about reading and writing. As a result, she was able to learn and retain more easily. At work she became more willing to write her memos and letters and did not automatically think that whatever she writes is of poor quality. Her vocabulary expanded, and she realized that she was aware of words in a way that she had not been before. She made an effort to retain what she knew by reviewing and by trying to use the words in conversation.

Roy

Many individuals with learning disabilities or symptoms of mild dyslexia who have struggled for years in school tend to become discouraged and take an increasingly passive approach to academic work. This was the case with Roy, an articulate 24-year-old college graduate who was distressed about his future. He wanted to decide on a career but did not think he could do anything well.

Early History

Roy's earliest memory of school was of feeling frightened. In the first and second grade, he did not make sufficient progress in reading and was assigned to remedial reading classes. In addition, he went to tutors periodically throughout elementary school. He never read for pleasure and read only what was assigned. Roy described elementary school as "frustrating." Roy chose to attend an alternative high school that offered smaller classes and more individual attention to each student. He became a student government leader but never excelled in his studies. In college, he graduated with a B-minus average and felt he had not learned as much as he would have liked. Roy stated that he never put his full effort into schoolwork. He told himself that if he did not do well, then he could also comfort himself with the fact that he had not tried very hard.

Testing and Remediation

After college, Roy was evaluated by a neuropsychologist who administered a comprehensive testing battery. Roy had done mediocre academic work throughout college, and the testing showed Roy to have uneven abilities. He had above-average ability in verbal and math areas but read very slowly and had a relatively limited vocabulary. He had extensive word retrieval problems. He also had difficulty interpreting visual or pictorial material. The neuropsychologist discouraged Roy from attempting graduate school. No silent reading test was administered at the evaluation. Instead of choosing a career, Roy, with the encouragement of his family, decided to seek remediation for his learning difficulties.

Roy was interested in learning more about his problem and wanted to improve his reading skills, but he was ambivalent about working on anything academic.[1] The remedial specialist needed a baseline measure because there was no current information about how well he could read textbook-like material. The Nelson-Denny Reading Test (Brown et al., 1981) was administered. The specialist made a mark on Roy's answer sheet when the standard time had passed but then allowed him to complete the test to find out his accuracy if he had sufficient time to finish the test. The results (relative to the results of typical college seniors) were as follows:

Area tested	Standard time percentile	Extended time percentile
Vocabulary	12	82
Reading comprehension	31	85

The results indicated that although Roy had a slow rate of reading, he definitely could understand difficult material when he had sufficient time. At this point, Roy was quite discouraged and did not see himself as capable of doing well in school because he had never done so.

Many students who read slowly and struggle constantly to keep up with their work also never learn how to study effectively or how to sustain effort in order to master material for a difficult course of study. Roy had shown very uneven ability on the intelligence test, but he had average ability, and the pat-

---

[1]Symptoms of mild dyslexia often have a major impact on motivation and performance. The ambivalence about doing sustained work often masks feelings of lowered self-confidence.

tern of scores suggested that he had higher potential ability. The silent reading test helped confirm his good basic ability. That Roy said he had never put in full effort was also taken into account by the remedial specialist when she was devising a plan of treatment for him. She interpreted and explained the results of the reading test to Roy in as positive a manner as possible; that is, she told him that the results showed that he had good basic ability and that although he had a slow rate of reading, he definitely could improve. She also told him that he expressed his ideas well in writing.

It is possible to help an individual change from being a passive reader to being an active one, if appropriate materials are chosen and if assignments are presented both supportively and incrementally. It was important that Roy not be overwhelmed. The plan was to help him gradually to perceive himself as a learner, as someone who could sustain effort even with difficult material. That Roy enjoyed expressing his ideas in writing was incorporated into the plan.

Roy came to weekly 1-hour remedial sessions and spent approximately 2 hours per week working at home. Each week he was assigned a short story by a writer such as Raymond Carver, Ernest Hemingway, George Orwell, Eudora Welty, or Italo Calvino. Roy was always able to complete each assignment because the stories were short. He felt positive about being able to do the assignments and, at the same time, learned about many new authors. After reading the week's story at home, he wrote a one- or two-page summary that included a discussion about the story's main theme. After a few weeks, he was also assigned to read an editorial essay in *The New York Times* by a regular editorial writer. Roy also read and summarized these point-of-view articles at home. He was encouraged to agree or disagree with the columnist at the end of his summary. Roy was slowly but systematically beginning to acquire information both from literature and from current events. Roy liked to write, and the act of writing required him to become more interactive with the text. He began to discuss the new information with his family and his friends and engage more actively in discussion about politics.

Each week, Roy brought in a list of new words from the reading selection. Roy had an excellent speaking vocabulary but had a much more limited reading vocabulary because of his limited reading experience. He therefore had many new words to discuss each week. He and the remedial specialist chose 10 words per week for inclusion on 3" × 5" cards and wrote the definitions on the reverse sides and sentences from the article or book that included the new words. Roy and the remedial specialist discussed the meanings in the sessions, and Roy reviewed the words at home. Roy's vocabulary gradually improved. Other topical articles were introduced, for example, essays by Elisabeth Kübler Ross and Betty Friedan, to broaden both his interests and his knowledge base. Finally, the remedial specialist asked Roy to get a book by a professional photographer. Every other week he wrote an essay about a photograph of his choice. He had to discern the story the photographer appeared to convey. The book contained no explanatory text, so Roy's entire essay had to be rooted in what he saw in the photograph. He got practice in interpreting visual and pictorial material, which had been identified as a problem area in his neuropsychological testing. His observations became more acute, and with practice he began producing integrated essays that incorporated most of the visual details as well as the underlying drama in the photographs.

Roy's anxiety about learning and reading gradually lessened. All of Roy's written assignments were read aloud and discussed at remedial sessions. He received general positive feedback as well as specific suggestions for improving his essays. At the end of 3 months, Roy began to think of himself as both well informed and well read. He saw that he had learned a great deal and had developed his own opinions about world events. He felt so energized by all of the information that he was absorbing and learning that he declared, "This has been the most exciting 3 months of my life!"

At this point, Roy began to have hope for his future. He decided that he might like to go to medical school. First, he had to prove to himself that he could put forth the effort in a sustained way. He and his remedial specialist found an undergraduate science course that he could take on a noncredit basis. He attended each week, did the reading and assignments, took the exams, and saw that he could master the material.

Next, as part of this new long-range plan, Roy had to apply for a program where he could take all of his pre-med requirements because he had not been a science major in college. He took these background science courses over a 2-year period so that he and his remedial specialist could concentrate on effective study skills. It was necessary for him not only to become an active learner but also to begin to work in an increasingly independent manner. The remedial specialist encouraged him to sit near the front of the lecture room, prepare for class *before* going to the lecture, take complete notes, and review the notes *after* the lecture, underlining important points in red pencil. He learned to apply these study skills as the first term progressed. Before the midterm exams, the specialist encouraged Roy to go to his professors during office hours to ask questions about anything that was not clear. He first wrote out a list of the questions and left space for the answers. Roy was surprised to find that he was the only student who visited during office hours, so each professor spent the entire hour with him. In addition, Roy and the remedial specialist looked over the questions together to see whether his questions were based on insufficient information, misreading the text, or topics that were not covered in lectures. He could then zero in on any vulnerable area when he studied.

During his first term, Roy definitely became a more active learner. He was introduced to the SQ3R method of study (Robinson, 1946), which helped him to be less overwhelmed by the science texts. These texts were difficult, but it was particularly helpful for him to find out that most of the information in each paragraph is represented in the first sentence of the paragraph and that the remaining sentences in the paragraph support the first sentence with details.

Roy remained motivated throughout the 2 years, even though the courses were difficult and demanding. At the end of the 2 years, he had earned seven As and one B. He took the Medical College Admissions Test (MCAT) with extended time because he had a diagnosis of dyslexia. His score on the MCAT was above average, and Roy was accepted to medical school. Although Roy's reading rate had improved, it still was slower than that of the average student. Consequently, he requested and was granted extended time on examinations in medical school. Roy continued to do well in medical school.

SUMMARY

Although the two individuals described in these case studies are quite different, they both made a lot of progress and developed a greater sense of self-confidence. Although learning differences in high-functioning dyslexics vary greatly, all individuals have the potential to make progress. It is important for each client to have a thorough and competent evaluation (which is interpreted to the client in the most positive manner possible), from which an effective treatment plan can be developed. When a treatment plan is successfully implemented, the clients take an active role in their own learning. Often when clients understand their strengths and weaknesses, they can advocate for the necessary accommodations in school or on the job. When these accommodations are made, clients can show the extent of their knowledge better. They perform better, receive recognition for their improved performance, can sustain hope about the future, and often achieve their goals.

REFERENCES

Bender, L. (1938). *Bender Visual Motor Gestalt Test.* San Antonio, TX: The Psychological Corporation.

Blumenthal, S. (1981). *Educational memories.* Unpublished manuscript.

Brown, J.I., Bennett, J.M., & Hanna, G.S. (1981). *The Nelson-Denny Reading Test.* Chicago: Riverside.

Buck, J.N. (1978). *The House-Tree-Person Technique* (Rev. manual). Los Angeles: Western Psychological Services.

MacGinitie, W.H., & MacGinitie, R.H. (1989). *Gates-MacGinitie Reading Tests—Third Edition.* Chicago: Riverside.

Murray, H.A., & Bellak, L. (1973). *Thematic Apperception Test (TAT).* San Antonio, TX: The Psychological Corporation.

Pauk, W. (1983). *Six-way paragraphs (Advanced).* Providence, RI: Jamestown Publishers.

Robinson, F.P. (1946). *Effective study.* New York: HarperCollins

Roswell, F.G., & Chall, J.S. (1992). *Diagnostic Assessments of Reading with Trial Teaching Strategies (DARTTS).* Chicago: Riverside.

The Psychological Corporation. (1992). *Rotter Incomplete Sentences Blank* (2nd ed.). San Antonio, TX: Author.

Wechsler, D. (1991). *Wechsler Adult Intelligence Scale–III.* San Antonio, TX: The Psychological Corporation.

Wiederholt, J.L., & Bryant, B.R. (1992). *Gray Oral Reading Test–Third Edition (GORT–3).* Austin, TX: PRO-ED.

Wilkinson, G.S. (1993). *Wide Range Achievement Test–Third Edition: Manual.* Wilmington, DE: Jastak Associates.

18

Parenting the Child with Dyslexia

Betty S. Levinson

It is important to help the dyslexic child and the family understand the nature and implications of dyslexia. Although advancements have been made in diagnostic and instructional procedures for dyslexia, there has been no parallel gain in counseling for families who have progressed beyond the diagnostic phase. This chapter deals with issues relating to parenting a dyslexic youngster including the similarities to and the differences from raising a nondyslexic child. Furthermore, this chapter stresses the desperate need that parents of dyslexics have for sound, realistic guidance and the possible resultant despair and loss of human potential when appropriate advice is absent.

This chapter also addresses the language problems that often accompany dyslexia. Parents typically seek help from well-trained, knowledgeable professionals after witnessing the negative impact that these problems have on the child both in school and at home. Finally, this chapter provides guidelines for assessing the training and qualifications of professionals who counsel parents of dyslexics. Intervention practices are compared with research findings and the clinical experience of professionals who have worked with dyslexics and their families over the years.

THE WAY THINGS ARE

When discussing child-rearing issues with the parents of dyslexic youngsters, it becomes apparent that these children are different from groups of young people with other disabilities. Children who have a physical disability or severe cognitive impairments are observably different to both laypeople and professionals.

In this chapter, the word *parents* denotes the child's primary caregivers.

The child with a specific language-based learning disability such as dyslexia, however, is said to have an "invisible condition," which often goes undetected. Dyslexia's early signs vary greatly and are frequently mistaken for a developmental lag (Bernstein & Tiegerman, 1997). Consequently, by the time parents and teachers become convinced the child needs help, the mystery surrounding the disability has deepened, and confusion has taken over.

Dyslexia is a language-based communication problem. Its remediation requires that several key concepts about communication be kept in mind. First, most communication problems are related to the language, *not* to the person. That is, the individual's thoughts are appropriate, but language is received and expressed differently. Second, language is anything that transmits a message and, depending on the situation, can include the following:

- Words and other vocal sounds
- Silence
- Pitch, tone, and rhythm of voice
- Gestures
- Facial expressions
- Postures
- Body language
- Signs
- Clothing worn or objects carried
- Distance from other people or objects

Dyslexia is a disorder that interferes with communication—the acquisition, processing, and transmission of language—and consists of the symptoms illustrated in Figure 18.1.

It is crucial to consider genetic factors when dealing with dyslexia. There is a high incidence of specific language disability among the parents of dyslexics. Their own language processing and general communication difficulties can complicate the assessment and intervention process. Unless this possibility is considered (and appropriate training is introduced), the ability of parents to assist their children will be reduced significantly. In other words, often the parents *along with* the child should receive help for specific language disability.

In four family studies that addressed rates of recurrence and possible mechanisms of transmission of dyslexia, Pennington, Gilger, Olson, & DeFries (1992) showed that there is a very high and consistent occurrence of dyslexia among siblings of dyslexics—ranging across studies from 38.5% to 43%. Dyslexia rates among parents of dyslexics are also high (ranging from 27% to 49%) and is consistent across studies. A dyslexic child is eight times as likely to have a parent with dyslexia as the general population (whose risk is only 5%)—a higher level than that found in many familial behavior disorders. These extensive longitudinal studies report strong evidence that dyslexia is both familial and heritable.

Arnold (1978) reminded professionals about the need to identify the parents' situation, to empathize with their feelings, and to enter into a cooperative alliance. A survey of parents of dyslexics would likely show that parents' experiences with professionals have been in direct contrast to Arnold's prescription. This discrepancy stems not from the helpers' unwillingness to assist but from a lack of knowledge about *how* to help.

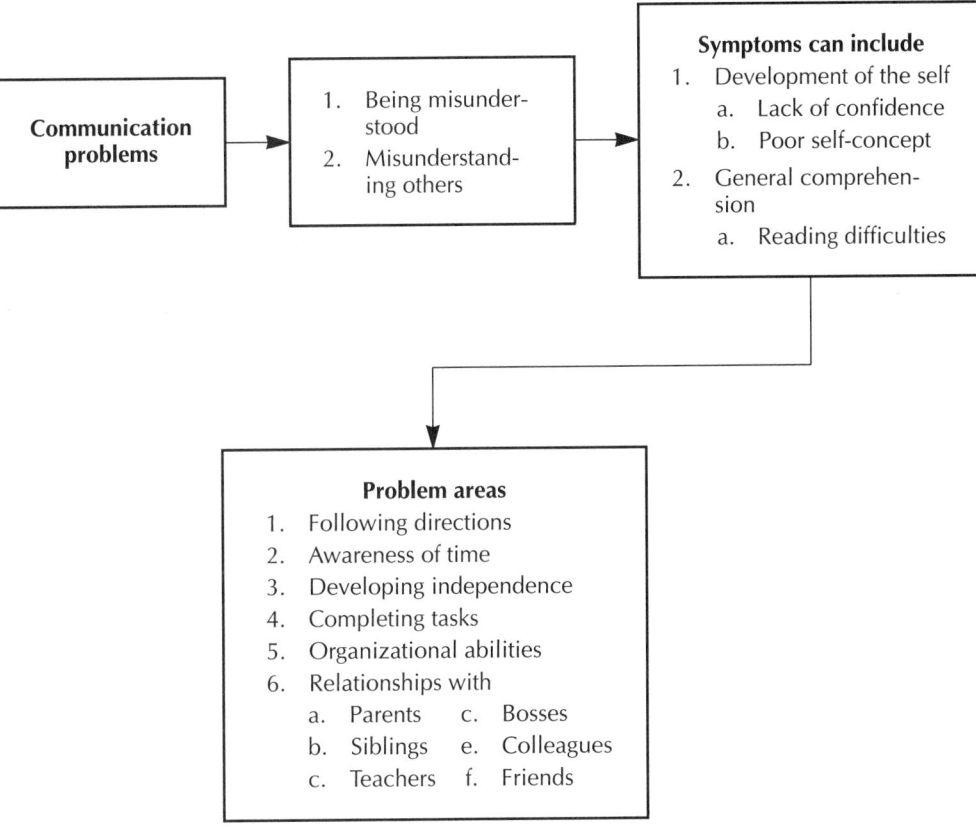

Communication problems →
1. Being misunder-stood
2. Misunderstanding others
→
Symptoms can include
1. Development of the self
   a. Lack of confidence
   b. Poor self-concept
2. General comprehension
   a. Reading difficulties

Problem areas
1. Following directions
2. Awareness of time
3. Developing independence
4. Completing tasks
5. Organizational abilities
6. Relationships with
   a. Parents   c. Bosses
   b. Siblings   e. Colleagues
   c. Teachers   f. Friends

Figure 18.1. Symptoms of and problems resulting from communication problems such as dyslexia.

Until the 1980s, many "how to" books written for parents and the general public about dyslexia failed to take into account both the probable genetic factors (within parents) and many teachers' lack of training concerning typical language development in children. Consequently, advice that intended to help missed the target. Parents who have dyslexia cannot implement suggestions that they are unable to assimilate, and most teachers cannot intervene in the manner prescribed by the "how to" books because they lack appropriate training and necessary background information.

For instance, a parent might complain that weekends are a disaster. With several children in the family, all of whom have activities, homework, and chores, the child with dyslexia seems to be the only one who cannot remember his or her responsibilities, cannot follow a task through to completion, and complains about everything. Often this occurs to the point that either the parent does things for him or her or asks another child to do it.

One can readily see what the result of this approach will be. The parent becomes angry, despairing, and overwhelmed with a feeling of inadequacy. The child enlisted to help feels angry and burdened. This child with dyslexia gets the message that people are angry with him or her, which is true; that the parent does not love him or her, which is not true; and that he or she does not have to do what he or she does not want to do, which is certainly not true.

Rather, the parents should have a session with the learning disabilities specialist during which they go over everyone's weekend expectations and then reconsider the findings in the dyslexic child's diagnostic reports. Symptoms therein, such as memory problems, organization, timing, retrieval, and insecurity difficulties, all would suggest why the child with dyslexia fails to carry out an oral list of instructions.

The learning disabilities specialist can then explain to the parents new ways to approach weekends and can try role-playing strategies to help the child succeed. It is suggested that the entire family be included in the weekend plans to avoid singling out the child with dyslexia. One option is for the family to get together on Friday evening to list all of the chores and activities that need to be accomplished that weekend. Each individual should have his or her own list containing specific times to start and (if possible to determine) to stop. The overall family schedule contains breaks, fun time, telephone time, and so forth. There is also a box to check off each task when it is finished.

This arrangement provides parents with a way to monitor their child with dyslexia from beginning to the end. Any interruption during the process can be handled so that the list of tasks is completed without conflict or repeated failures.

This scheduling method is a didactic approach. It involves heightening awareness, teaching, monitoring, and following up. The helping professional (HP) never presumes that parents readily understand or can implement the necessary changes without rehearsing the script. The HP accepts that parents may lack the necessary repertoire of constructive behaviors and require explicit instruction.

BACKGROUND KNOWLEDGE

Knowledge of typical language development must be a large part of professional training. One cannot recognize what is different unless he or she knows what is typical. Information from standard texts on child development cover the physical, emotional, psychological, and social arenas, which must be part of the knowledge base of individuals who work with the parents of dyslexics. Professionals also need a thorough understanding of dyslexia's neurobiological underpinnings, particularly the development of language and information processing. Understanding the neurobiological substrates that are involved in communication (e.g., see Chase, Rosen, & Sherman, 1996) increases the professional's comprehension of the causation of language difficulties and aids in conveying this information to parents.

Enhancing Communication with Parents

The professional who lacks adequate communication skills to translate complex information into understandable language leaves parents in the same state as when they initially arrive at the office—unable to understand the reasons behind their child's difficulties and lacking the knowledge about how to help their youngster. Unless parents understand this, the professional may be contributing unwittingly to an increase in parental depression, feelings of hopelessness, and anger. In addition, the child is not being helped.

To enhance communication with parents, the professional must be aware of the major difficulty that dyslexics often have with nonliteral language, such as id-

ioms, proverbs, metaphors, similes, and slang, and of their tendency often to become overloaded auditorially. Other symptoms such as problems with time management and the inability to organize a response rapidly can interfere with communication if a parent also has dyslexia. Consequently, HPs must be vigilant
about the language they use. It should be simple but not demeaning. To ensure
that parents have understood, it is imperative for the HP to ask for frequent feedback: "Just so that I can be sure that my explanation was clear, tell me in your
own words what we just talked about."

To address some of these communication difficulties, professionals and parents are advised to gain the listener's attention, speak concisely (using short sentences), eliminate figures of speech, and provide concrete examples from the family's daily experiences with the child. Doing so helps the parent make an
immediate connection and illustrates (for the parent) useful behaviors that, in
turn, bring more immediate positive changes.

Factors that Interfere with Communication

An example of the confusion that can happen (and what helps clear up the misunderstanding) when highly figurative language is used came up during a counseling session with a British-born mother married to an American. All three of her
children were born in America; two are dyslexic. Everyone in the family, parents
and children, were very intelligent. The mother continually reported, however,
that the only child in the family with whom she did not have communication
problems was her youngest boy, the one who was not dyslexic.

One day Mrs. C came to her counseling session quite distressed. She told the
following story. Her oldest child, a 14-year-old girl, came home, dropped her
books on the floor in the living room, threw her jacket on a chair, took a snack out
of the refrigerator (leaving the refrigerator door open), and left her dirty glass
and plate on the table. She then went into her parents' bedroom, sprawled herself
across the freshly made bed while she used her parents' telephone to call a friend,
and continued to munch on some crackers.

Mrs. C walked in the bedroom and screamed, *"I'm speechless! Can you throw
any light on this situation? Do you know how often you drive me around the bend? Do
you have bats in your belfry? Oh, God! I think I'm losing it!"*

At that point, the daughter (who was still on the telephone) turned to her
mother and said, "What did you lose?"

Obviously, the mother became more upset and thought that her daughter
was giving a smart-mouthed reply. It was even more obvious that the daughter
had misunderstood her mother's tirade and only grasped the fact that her mother
seemed upset. The girl later said that she was genuinely concerned about her
mother's loss, which was totally "lost" on the mother who stomped out—crying
in frustration—and called her HP for an extra session that week.

In part, the mother's session proceeded as follows:

Therapist: Try to tell me exactly what happened. I want to hear it all because I
know how frustrating this was for you. [This gave the mother a
chance to be heard in an environment in which she feels listened to
and understood.]

Mrs. C: I'm not sure I can remember much, except how inadequate these
            blowups make me feel, but I'll try. [She went on to relate the story in
            a disorganized way, interrupting herself many times. The therapist
            recorded the session with Mrs. C's permission while helping her to
            organize her thoughts and also wrote down all of Mrs. C's nonliteral
            language and behaviors that might have interfered with communica-
            tion.]

Therapist: Oh, my! I certainly can feel that you're upset, given how often you
            experience these situations that seem unforgivable, given that your
            daughter is so bright and already 14 years old. By now you had a
            right to expect more appropriate behavior. That is, if she were not
            dyslexic.

Mrs. C: Thank you for listening and understanding. But tell me what to do.
            It's upsetting the whole family.

Therapist: All right, I'll try. I know when we met to discuss the findings from
            the tests that I gave you a lot of information all at once. It was too
            much for any parent to remember to use in situations at home. So let
            me use your difficult time to go over some issues and to suggest
            ways to handle them in the future.

            First, as you entered the house and followed the trail your daugh-
            ter left, your agitation mounted as you climbed the steps that led to
            your bedroom. By the time you saw her, you were angry and cer-
            tainly could not be expected to reflect on the symptoms that often co-
            exist with dyslexia, such as difficulties with nonliteral language,
            problems when too many words are used, problems responding to
            questions, lack of ability to focus, and defensiveness (primarily be-
            cause these youngsters feel as though they are constantly displeasing
            someone). Instead of yelling at the child, it's necessary, initially, to
            gain the child's attention.

            I can go through your story and suggest a different approach to
            help you develop some effective ways to bring about change. Now,
            the next time you see the items your daughter leaves strewn about,
            you might begin an inner dialogue: *Yes, she has a problem. Which symp-
            tom does this resemble—lack of focus? disorganization?* Next, you need to
            take some deep breaths. Try to assess the situation quickly. Then in
            some way other than screaming, *"I'm speechless,"* get your daughter's
            attention, and make eye contact.

            Next, ask your daughter to please come to see you as soon as she is
            off the telephone. Or, hand her a note that says, *Please end your con-
            versation, now, and come see me in the kitchen.* Once your daughter gets
            to the kitchen, try to smile at her, as difficult as this may be for you.
            Ask how her day was. Keep looking at her. Then say what you want
            her to hear: "I came into the house and I saw your book bag on the
            floor, your jacket on the chair, your dirty dishes on the table, and
            then found you on my bed eating crackers and getting crumbs all
            over." You need to say this neutrally.

            At this point, become an actress. Begin to laugh, and say, "You
            were expecting me to yell and punish, right? Well to tell you the

truth, I felt like it. But that's what I've done many times. Obviously, it doesn't work. So let's try to work this out together. Here's my thought on the subject. Number one, I love you. Second, I don't think you do this kind of thing on purpose. Third, I think when you come home you do things without thinking too much about them. So let's you and I look at what happened today. Let's see if together we can plan some ways to prevent this kind of thing from happening."

Next, the therapist gave Mrs. C a list of suggestions and role-played with her to develop a plan for monitoring her daughter's progress. Mrs. C laughed as she and the therapist went over these things. She said that she saw the situation more clearly now. She went over her language and saw how it might seem incomprehensible to her daughter. She and the therapist both laughed.

Years later, Mrs. C reminded her therapist of this incident. She told her therapist how she brought it up with her daughter (now married, with three children of her own, all of whom have dyslexia). During their conversation, her daughter said, "I still don't have any idea what a belfry is. And Dad used to say, 'Hold your horses.' Pretty confusing, since I didn't have any. And you used to say, 'Don't count your chickens before they hatch.' I didn't have any of those either."

The daughter then listed a few other sayings her parents used, such as "Kill two birds with one stone," and "Don't cut off your nose to spite your face." The daughter said that her parents spoke like that so much that she often failed to understand. Yet they would invariably end up asking, "Do you understand?" She said it made her feel dumb and angry.

Unfortunately, her parents did not realize the impact of their daughter's language problems and how it led to her rebellious behavior. Because her language difficulties were discovered so late, they led to continual conflicts among family members.

Although the role playing and counseling were effective to some degree with Mrs. C, the truly beneficial outcome was that the daughter, now the mother of Mrs. C's three grandchildren, became more knowledgeable about dyslexia—its symptoms and what must be done. She identified it in her own children before their teachers recognized it. The daughter asked an advocate to help her at school meetings. Although the daughter had learned a great deal, she wanted an advocate to ensure that communication between her and school personnel would be effective for her children. In addition, this young mother is continuing to role-play with a therapist to acquire better communication skills.

Mrs. C stated that gaining a sense of humor is essential for parents. She learned to laugh at what used to make her cry. She said it also helped her when other parents of dyslexics shared their frustrating language experiences. Mrs. C remembered a friend who came to her and said, "You won't believe this. My son came to me yesterday and asked when his piano lesson was. I said, 'Tomorrow.' Then today he asked again when was his piano lesson going to be. I said, 'Today.' Then he said, 'But you told me tomorrow.'" In complete frustration, Mrs. C's friend had smacked her forehead, only to have her sweet little boy ask her whether she had a headache.

Mrs. C and her friend laughed, and one funny story after another followed. Mrs. C ended by telling her friend that when she was a little girl in England during World War II, she heard two adults speaking about two children who had been blown up. For days afterward she remembers looking up in the sky for the children. She was only 5 years old at the time, when such a concrete interpretation would have been considered normal and funny. For the dyslexics, this concreteness goes on long beyond the time when it is considered developmentally appropriate. Therefore, dyslexics must be taught the whole range of language skills, including use of nonliteral language; these skills are essential for their socialization. In addition, it is important for the HP to explain to parents the difficulties that dyslexics have with nonliteral and abstract language.

One more brief vignette, involving Mrs. C, her dyslexic daughter, and Mrs. C's dyslexic granddaughter, exemplifies dyslexia's genetic factor. One afternoon Mrs. C's daughter called to say, "I think dyslexia has struck again." When queried, her daughter reported that Mrs. C's granddaughter (age 9, IQ above 129), overheard that her mother's friend would not be going to the park with them because "he was all tied up." The granddaughter volunteered to help, saying, "Don't worry. I'll come right over and untie you, and then we can all go to the park."

For those who are not dyslexic, stories such as Mrs. C's bring laughter and amusement. For those who have difficulties with language, these stories may conjure up memories of embarrassment, withdrawal from social situations, and instances of limited comprehension in academic reading and conversation.

A Helpful Device

Ask the child's parents to keep a journal of how each day went (including tasks finished/unfinished) so that adjustments can be made when needed. Keeping a record that includes their successes is important. Parents, similar to their children, often remember their failures but not their successes. Keeping records or journals is one of the most difficult tasks for parents to accomplish. Therefore, the HP should assist parents in devising a simple record-keeping system. For instance, a checklist of chores could be set up as a seven-column chart (one column for each day of the week). Each chore (one row for each chore) that the child finishes would be checked off using the child's favorite color. No crosses or Xs should be used to indicate unfinished chores; empty boxes seem to bring about more positive results.

The chart in Figure 18.2 brought about positive changes for John, a 9-year-old whose mother kept insisting that he *never* does what is asked of him, although John maintained that he does his chores most of the time. The goal was to see whether the boy could have all of the boxes filled in for a day. At the end of each day, mother and son would count the checks for that day. They enjoyed the fact that the checks showed that he was really trying and that he had accomplished some of what was expected. The mother was to smile, give him a hug, and say, "Nice try! We'll see how tomorrow's chart looks. Before you go to bed, let's just see if you can say what happened that made you leave some of today's boxes empty. Maybe we can figure out something together so that all of the boxes will have checks soon."

Even when all of the boxes for the day are checked, no special award should be offered. This author has found over the years that most children find it a chal-

CHORE	M	T	W	T	F	S	S
1. Brush teeth	✓	✓		✓	✓	✓	✓
2. Feed dog	✓	✓	✓	✓	✓	✓	✓
3. Walk dog		✓	✓	✓	✓	✓	✓
4. Start homework w/o nagging			✓	✓	✓	✓	✓
5. Take bath w/o arguing	✓		✓	✓		✓	✓
6. Clear room floor before bed		✓			✓	✓	
7. Layout clothes for next AM		✓	✓		✓	✓	✓

Figure 18.2. Chore chart for John, a 9-year-old with dyslexia.

lenge to fill all of the boxes—first for a day, then for a week. After the 7-day check-list has been used for a while, the parent can explain to the child that when all (or almost all) of the boxes are filled for 4 weeks, perhaps the chart won't be needed anymore.

The next week, John and his parents decided to stop using the chart, there was a real setback. His mother reported that John had stopped doing some of his chores. The HP advised her to say to her son, who had a real interest in becoming a scientist, "You know, John, some scientists need a checklist most of the time to be sure they remember all of the necessary steps when they do an experiment. Maybe you will need to do this for a while longer. Let's try it for a few more weeks."

After another week, the mother and son had a session with the therapist about what happened and to discuss the empty boxes (see Figure 18.2).

Monday John said, "I forgot to walk the dog because I was late for school." His mother suggested that she could wake him a little earlier. John did not agree that his mother had to nag him to do his homework. His mother followed one of the therapist's prior suggestions (when you are not sure about how to handle a situation, give yourself time to think before you attempt to deal with it) and let John's statement stand. John said his mother didn't remind him to clear his bedroom floor and lay the next day's clothes out before going to bed; she said that she would remind him to look at the chart before he went to bed the next night.

Tuesday When asked about the empty box for #4, *Start homework w/o nagging,* John stated, "I hate homework." His mother said she understood but that maybe the next night he could just begin his homework by telling her how much he hates it and then ask for help. (This seemed to help; for the next 4 nights, John's mother did not have to nag him to start his homework.) When asked what happened on Sunday, John laughed and said that he didn't have any homework. Then they both laughed, and his mother said, "He should have given himself a check. Then he will reach his goal sooner."

Wednesday   When asked why he didn't put a check in the box for #6, *Clear room floor before bed*, John laughed again and said, "There was nothing to pick up."

Thursday   The same thing happened as on Wednesday, and John added, "I'm a little more careful now about leaving things on the floor, because I hate picking up."

Friday   John's excuse for arguing about taking a bath was "I guess I'm a regular boy."

Saturday   Mother and son celebrated because all of the day's boxes had checkmarks. Mom spontaneously offered him the opportunity to watch an especially long television show that would end past his bedtime.

Sunday   John laughed as he explained why he didn't clear his floor before going to bed; his dad had said that he would do it for him because John had been trying so hard all week. His mom was so pleased with his honesty that she said he deserved a check in that box anyway.

The following weeks had some ups and downs, but the one wonderful result was the lessening of conflict and the family's working together more positively. When John was asked how everything was going, he said, "You know, they smile at me now!" His mom cried when he said this and told me later that she never realized how angry and sullen she looked most of the time.

THE PARENTS' PLIGHT

When parents learn that their child is dyslexic, they frequently experience a mixed sense of relief (Houston, 1987). They are comforted to finally know what is causing their child's problems, and they feel apprehension that they, too, may have the same problem with language. Parents may feel this apprehension when the diagnosticians describe the child's difficulties and give details concerning its negative impact on functioning at home and in the classroom. Hearing this information often triggers memories about their own past (or present) functioning.

As intervention progresses, the parents' memories of their own childhood experiences at home and at school may enhance their understanding and increase their level of empathy. This increased understanding may provide an opportunity for the parents to receive help and make changes that they never thought possible. Although the parents' discovery of their own problems can be difficult, gradually the process results in positive attitudinal changes that lead to better relationships with their dyslexic child and with others.

If a parent discovers that he or she has dyslexia, then he or she may feel other emotions, such as denial, anger, fear, guilt, shame, loss, and panic. Some psychologists suggest that parents go through stages similar to those experienced when grieving after the loss of a loved one. The important point is that most parents, when given appropriate professional support and understanding, work through this spectrum of normal feelings. Through education and increased knowledge that the outlook for their youngster can be a positive one, parents can become strong advocates for their children. Many enter the field of language disorders or become advocates for other children.

Parents' initial negative feelings change as they observe progress such as obtaining an appropriate school placement, the implementation of the correct approach to teaching language skills. The child's improvement and successes change everyone's negative feelings. Given the right information and support, the parents feel more adequate and regain confidence in themselves. When taught properly, the child also gradually gains confidence in him- or herself as a learner, and this leads to greater self-esteem and a more typical childhood.

Helping Parents Help Children

Teaching children with dyslexia properly means addressing such stress areas for dyslexics as inability to follow directions, not having a sense of time, lack of organization, failure to complete assignments on time, leaving chores until the last minute, forgetting tasks such as homework, and being resistant when help is offered. Each of these requires a teaching approach that includes a multisensory plan—one that encompasses structure, organization, integration, and feedback.

Professionals need to become familiar with material that deals with organizational skills and time management. Then they can teach parents how this information can be applied to every facet of a child's functioning such as the child's morning routines, daytime activities, playtime, homework, and bedtime routines. The use of lists, calendars, and organizers of all types should be a focus in such learning (see Chapter 13).

Organization and time management must be a family affair. Every child and adult living under the same roof participates in and benefits from strategies that improve organization and time management. The advantage of such approaches is that they increase everyone's efficiency without placing a constant focus on one child and his or her problems. The plan, however, must be designed to fit the individual needs of the family. A plan that is effective for one family may not be suitable for another—only the general guidelines remain the same.

In addition, time, money, and progress all need to be discussed with the parents when intervention is being formulated. If the child attends a local inclusive school, then the more individual sessions with direct explicit instruction, the better. Ideally, 1 hour per day, five times per week, provides the level of intensity from which most children benefit. This frequency of sessions, however, is rarely affordable; therefore, it is recommended that the child have individual sessions with the HP no less than three times per week. Anything less than this ignores the dyslexic's difficulty with memory and the need for frequent and intensive reinforcement.

Less experienced or uncertified tutors may recommend one session per week. Such an approach is both unproductive and harmful. Under such a regimen the dyslexic child will not acquire the necessary skills, and both child and parent will become discouraged and believe that they are at fault rather than blame the once-a-week schedule. The child will feel an additional reason to believe that he or she is "dumb"—and may feel that even with help (which, of course, is not of an appropriate intensity), he or she cannot learn. Moreover, when more appropriate, more intense help is found, the child who has failed recently will be less likely to want to try again—he or she may reason, "Why risk another failure?"

Helping Parents Who Feel Overwhelmed

Sometimes when parents learn more about the recommended intervention plan, they feel overwhelmed. They lament about how much time it will take. This is when professional support is most necessary. It often helps to remind parents of the enormous amount of time they now expend in coaxing, nagging, arguing, and battling resistance—most of which ends in failure for both the child and the parents. The HP can make this amount of time concrete by examining a situation the parents have related to the HP.

Help for the parent can vary from several sessions per week with telephone feedback to one session per week with a therapist—until both parent and therapist agree that enough new parenting strategies have been learned. Parents should feel confident to move ahead on their own, with only an occasional session for monitoring.

Parents' resistance to change is no different from their child's opposition to change. In part such resistance stems from a neurological rigidity coupled with a fear of failure. Resistance may also result from past successes that could not be sustained. When the professional communicates his or her understanding of these fears to the parents, along with reassurances that the HP will be there to help, the parents' courage to try once again can be rebuilt. Much effort and many attempts are necessary before success is achieved, but it will happen.

Attention-Deficit/Hyperactivity Disorder

Language processing difficulties in a dyslexic child are frequently misidentified as attention-deficit/hyperactivity disorder (ADHD). This, in turn, often leads to the suggestion of a trial on medication. Regardless of whether the child is later determined to have ADHD, it is good for the HP to remember, as Healy (1990) stated, that teaching the parents of children with ADHD techniques to control behavior is at least as effective as, if not superior to, the use of Ritalin alone:

> Whether we want to admit it or not, the way the parents and/or caregivers interact with children is critically important to teaching them how to pay attention. These interactions also communicate subtle messages about what is appropriate to pay attention to, the thing most children diagnosed with these difficulties don't seem to understand.

The Competence of Professionals

In addition to dealing with their own difficulties with dyslexia, parents of children with learning disabilities must cope with questions concerning the competence of the professionals working with their child. Most often, more than one professional is involved in the intervention process. When team members disagree concerning a diagnosis or a course of action, the situation becomes highly problematic. Nothing is as destructive to a child and his or her family and can shake the confidence of parents more than observing conflicts among several professionals on whose knowledge they depend. The likelihood of such a traumatic situation is reduced when each person serving the family has been well-trained in parent–professional relationships and can work with the others as a team to help the child and the family.

When the parents first become involved with their child's intervention, their focus is usually on why their child cannot read or succeed in school. To them academic achievement is the issue. As they become more knowledgeable, parents gain a greater awareness of the wide, negative effects that untreated dyslexia can have on children—diminished self-esteem, restricted socialization, delayed emotional development, and lifelong effects from depression. More often than not, there is no overall structure to the oral and/or written suggestions or reports given to parents. At its crux, this material deals only with how to bring help to the child through others. The crucial contribution that parents can make to assist in their child's remediation process is often omitted. As a consequence, coexisting problems in social, emotional, and behavioral areas frequently remain unresolved, and family difficulties persist.

During the initial stage of seeking information, parents often feel overwhelmed. These feelings are often exacerbated by the difficulties the parents themselves may have with sorting out relevant information and understanding their role and by their perception that the professionals dealing with them (e.g., diagnosticians, physicians, teachers, special educators) do not agree on a definition of dyslexia (see Chapter 14), what constitutes a specific language-based learning disability, and what interventions have had demonstrated success.

Planning, timing, organization, and memory difficulties all affect the parents' ability to understand and follow through with suggestions made by professionals. These capabilities constitute an individual's executive functioning ability. They are often poorly developed in dyslexics, including parents who have dyslexia. It is not unusual to hear a psychologist, a psychotherapist, or a speech-language pathologist tell another professional (with great exasperation) how a client's parents failed to carry out a series of remedial suggestions. Such exclamations reflect the professional's inability to recognize in one or both parents symptoms that are similar to those in the child (client). Moreover, such professionals need to appreciate how their own lack of knowledge about effective interventions can produce such negative outcomes with parents. Mental health professionals who have obtained additional training in this area report increased successes in working effectively with the parents of dyslexic children.

If parents are to play their critical role in helping their dyslexic child, then the HP must develop and model a structured multisensory program for them. Parents of youngsters with learning disabilities continue to have more responsibility for their child over a significantly longer period of time than the parents of a nondyslexic (Fine, 1980). To help their child with organizing the basic routines of daily life, parents must become involved in showing their youngster how to do the following: ask the right questions; talk through problems; plan ahead; and, in general, insert language between impulse and behavior. Professionals often urge parents to talk with their children; certainly, this is a reasonable suggestion. This advice ignores the fact, however, that many of these parents do not know how to talk to children; they themselves need to be taught that skill.

An emphasis among the helping professions is teaching professionals-in-training to empower those whom they are assisting. When this principle is misunderstood, it can become not only less than helpful but also dangerous. Parents who feel inadequate, have little knowledge about learning problems, and few skills in this area initially cannot be empowered. To attempt to do so would be similar to telling a 6-year-old who has never been off a farm that he or she is empowered to cross a major street in a large metropolitan city. No one would do such a thing before instructing, practicing, and making certain that the child has the "tools" to cross the street without getting injured.

DIAGNOSIS AND BEYOND

It is difficult for parents to project themselves (and their child) into the future. Telling them about all of the past and present famous/successful dyslexics is hardly reassuring. Once they hear the word *dyslexia*, emotional and intellectual turmoil often sets in. Parents frequently pass through several stages: denial, anger, guilt, shame, blame, overprotection, and (finally) emotional adaptation (Fine, 1980). They certainly will have little idea about the competencies needed by the professionals who will work with their child and/or provide support. The HP needs to be prepared to deal directly with three questions the parents will bring up immediately:

1. *"Will he or she get better?"*   The HP must assure the parents that dyslexia is not new, that there are approaches for treating this condition that have proven successful, and that dyslexia is not a disease.
2. *"How long will it take?"*   The HP's experience will help parents understand that they cannot expect overnight "cures." Dyslexia's neurological factors preclude cures, but remediation can be attained with appropriate intervention. The process takes time, yet progress will be seen by the child, the parents, and the teachers.
3. *"How much will it cost?"*   Not only is the diagnostic and intervention process both bewildering and overwhelming to the client's parents, often it also is financially burdensome. Many parents will be unable to follow through with an elaborate evaluation or afford multiple sessions. Has help become unattainable? No!

The HP must indicate to the parents the difference between the ideal situation and reality. The emphasis should be on describing a step-by-step process. Explanation should focus on how much can be accomplished with *some* good information and on the need to begin intervention immediately. The HP should reassure parents that he or she will monitor the situation and seek further evaluations and/or intervention only when needed and in a way that will be affordable.

At this time, outreach is crucial; the list of community resources that the HP has built becomes essential. Knowing which professionals or agencies offer help and use sliding-scale fees is very helpful. It is necessary for parents to be aware that the public school system is bound by law to provide help (e.g., the Individuals with Disabilities Education Act [IDEA] Amendments of 1997, PL 105-17). The more the HP demonstrates an unwillingness to give up seeking affordable help from professionals and legally required supports from schools, the less likely the parents will be to give up. Parents model the HP's actions and gain confidence in doing so.

The parents' next set of questions may include "Why didn't the school pick this up sooner?" or "Why can't the teacher help?" The parents' anguish about every aspect of their child's life will most likely be directed at the teachers and at the person who has just delivered the diagnosis of dyslexia. This situation requires that the HP be able to display a high degree of empathy and patience and have the ability to cope with a great deal of anger without taking it personally or withdrawing from it.

Parents are often furious at the school system. They blame the school not only for failing to detect their child's condition earlier or even denying its existence but also for causing it. The HP must be careful not to appear to support this view by agreeing with the parents. Although the parents' frustration and anger with the school may be somewhat justified, seeing only the negatives will not help. Parents need to be guided in a more beneficial direction.

At this stage of the helping process, the HP's ability to accept the parents as they are and convey genuine respect for them and their situation is crucial. Establishing this type of atmosphere allows the parents to feel safe enough to hear what they must do. It enables them to become constructive members on the intervention team that will help their child.

INTERVENTION STRATEGIES

Houston (1992) asked the following: What good does it do to diagnose dyslexia, pinpoint the specific difficulties of the client, and then send the individual to someone for remediation if that person does not know what to do about alleviating the various problems? The way to avoid this dilemma lies in the HP's being well informed about research on effective intervention approaches, knowing how to gain access to appropriate community resources, and having a list of well-trained academic therapists to whom parents can be referred.

Most books on dyslexia for parents (or professional books written on this subject) indicate that dyslexia can affect every aspect of a child's life. They tend to reassure both parents and educators that all is "treatable": that with proper intervention at home and at school, the child will succeed or can fulfill his or her potential. As a result, false hopes of quick remediation may be raised.

Parents of dyslexics may have read books or taken their child to participate in study groups for typical children, only to find such experiences of little or no help with their child. A whole new body of knowledge needs to be integrated with what they already know.

When interventions are designed and implemented for the dyslexic child, consideration must be given to the parents' own difficulties—often caused by dyslexia—in following through on an intervention plan. Giving a list of suggestions to parents is often as ineffective as presenting the dyslexic child with a similar set of instructions. Typically, scheduled activities are forgotten, the list is lost, or the date and/or time of appointments is confused. Professionals who are attempting to help the child may become frustrated with the parents. Consequently, attention needs to be given both to the parents' training program and to the child's intervention plan.

Parent Intervention

Parents need help not only with their own emotions but also with the school system and its teachers as well as their friends, neighbors, and extended family. Grandparents can be a real source of help to both the parents and the dyslexic child. Or, they may be a great impediment by further undermining the confidence of the dyslexic child's parents at a time when they are feeling most inadequate and are questioning their ability to parent their child. It is often helpful to suggest that the grandparents visit the HP for their own session during which the diagnosis is interpreted and a plan is developed containing specific ways in which the grandparents can assist.

The dyslexic child's siblings are another group about which the parents will need guidance. Issues arise regarding the siblings of all children who are experiencing problems. If the parents do not bring up the subject, then the HP must not let it remain ignored. The well-trained HP will explain the issues directly to the brothers and sisters of the dyslexic child. When this is not possible, the information is conveyed by the parents. The HP, however, must assist the parents concerning how the message is to be delivered. The tone must be one that mutes difficulties and highlights strengths. The dyslexic child is not "a problem," rather he or she is someone who has some difficulties with language and some skills in other areas, just as the siblings may be good at some activities but not others. For example, some dyslexics are quite talented musically. One such youngster might be the one chosen to sing a solo in the school chorus. This child's sibling, who is doing well in school, might be extremely embarrassed if asked to sing alone before a group of peers. The sibling with a "musical disability" can hide this lack of skill better. He or she is never considered as a child with a disability but merely as one who cannot carry a tune. The HP should have a repertoire of stories similar to the above example. The intent of telling such stories is to make clear that the dyslexic child has a disability only in certain environments.

After hearing some of these examples, one 14-year-old boy said, "Oh, I get it. It was like me in Algebra. I just couldn't understand the teacher. A few other kids couldn't either, but my best friend could. That made me feel dumb. I was getting Ds and Es. After Christmas, when we got back to school, we had a new teacher. The other one went skiing and got badly hurt. With the new teacher I began to get Bs and even As, sometimes. My parents asked me if I was working harder. I said, 'No. In fact I had to work harder with the other teacher because I couldn't understand his accent.' My parents never thought of that as being my problem and neither did I, until I realized how clearly my new teacher spoke." Then he laughed and said, "Maybe I have an auditory processing problem like my brother. I sure hope he gets teachers who speak the way he understands."

Even when the parents have been fortunate enough to secure a thorough, competent evaluation, their initial understanding of its implications may be hazy. Consequently, assisting parents becomes a process of educating them over a period of time. In addition, the HP will need to provide support to the parents as they cope with the many emotional issues that continue to appear during the course of intervention. Consequently, the HP's assistance cannot be hurried, unsystematic, or brief. It must be thorough, comprehensible, and sufficiently flexible so that as changes occur over time, the type of support provided is appropriately modified.

Language learning disabilities change over time as the child develops and use of language becomes more complex. In a parallel fashion, the parents' problems also change as the dyslexic child develops. Although this also can be said about most children without dyslexia, the parents of a dyslexic youngster are confronted by a different timetable. In addition, they continually battle with the problem of how to help without adding to their child's negative self-esteem. For example, during adolescence, when most youngsters are beginning to individuate (start to separate from parents) and need less help from parents, the dyslexic child still needs assistance. The dyslexics' wish to be more like their peers leads them to deny their learning needs and causes conflicts at home when they refuse the help offered by their parents.

In this situation, the HP, parents, and the adolescent dyslexic need a session together. During their interaction, the following should be outlined: where the client was when he or she began the intervention, the progress that has been made, the areas of difficulty that remain, and new problems that may occur and that can result in a setback in school performance. The consequences of a child's refusal to participate in intervention and how this will limit his or her choices in the future must also be discussed.

At the end of the session, the HP must give a clearly written document (in bullet style) to the client. The HP should explain that the client can use this document to monitor his or her situation and to know when to ask for or to reinstate help.

Consequently, the document must include clear descriptions of early warning signs, such as slipping grades; increased time to complete homework; a number of assignment deadlines missed; increasingly frequent conflicts with teachers and parents; the dyslexic's own disappointment regarding progress; and the secretly felt anxiety, stress, and/or depression.

Both the joint session and the resulting document need to have a positive thrust. They should not be viewed as a warning or a prediction of doom and gloom. The session ends with positive statements by the HP that commend the client on the progress made and that indicate that the dyslexic may be making the right decision for the moment but also mention the hope that the client's good judgment will allow him or her to seek help when needed. The client should not be made to feel that this refusal of help is a step backward but rather an opportunity to grow and gain control over the situation.

The parents will need support at this time. They also will benefit from suggestions and guidelines as to what to say and do as time passes and the client makes no request for help. Parents need to know which clues signal that it is time to step in and when it is okay to allow the consequences of failure to provide the child with an impetus to seek help again.

The HP needs to make certain that the dyslexic child's parents understand how important it is that they encourage and support their youngster; unconditional love needs to be not just the order of the day but also the order of a lifetime. Parents need to hear that they—with guidance from the HP—must become their child's advocate. Primarily, it will be the parents who will have to deal with the school system and find ways to elicit cooperation and understanding from their child's teachers. Finally, the overarching directive for parents is patience, patience, patience.

Child Intervention

The professional helping the parents must be knowledgeable about the child's needs. The process of designing intervention for the dyslexic youngster begins with the development of an organizing structure. Both the parents and the HP must help the client become organized. For example, a written activity schedule needs to be generated—one that describes what is to happen and when it is to occur; a regular routine needs to be established and followed; an uncluttered, quiet workplace must be established for the child; and the parents should provide help with their youngster's school assignments. Getting organized is a monumental task, especially when the parents have their own problems in this area. Hence, the HP needs to teach such skills and help parents monitor the home front. (See

Chapter 15 for tips on arranging the home environment for better organization and study.)

Once an intervention strategy for a dyslexic child has been implemented, close monitoring becomes a high priority. This will allow modifications to be made promptly when progress is not occurring as anticipated.

Often, when intervention is implemented but the child's academic progress is not evident and coexisting emotional problems increase, the original learning disability diagnosis is questioned. Both parents and professionals may begin to believe that the child's emotional and psychological difficulties are the "real" cause. These issues, rather than the lack of a well-integrated intervention strategy, become the focus of attention. Rarely does the focus shift to more intensive help for the family. At this critical juncture, mental health services are often suggested. Such a recommendation fosters a greater loss of self-esteem and increased feelings of inadequacy in both the child and the parents.

Many professionals believe that prior to a shift away from school- and home-based intervention, the first attempts at adjusting a chosen intervention approach should include the following: effecting environmental changes at home and at school, securing an adequate academic program, offering more parental support, systematic monitoring, and making frequent reevaluations. A trial on medication should be the last resort.

MOTHERS, FATHERS, AND DYSLEXIC CHILDREN

The parenting roles of *both* the mother and the father have frequently been stressed as fathers have received more encouragement to participate actively in the home and in child rearing.[1] This reflects changes in society as well as an increase in knowledge of men's and women's emotions and ways of interacting. Although many professionals recognize that the heavier burden of parenting still rests with the mother (even when both parents hold jobs outside the home), there is a noticeable trend toward the father's greater involvement. To make generalizations in this area, however, would be a mistake, except that it is wise—although not always necessary—to encourage both parents to participate. Sometimes, in fact, this encouragement may have a negative effect.

The HP needs to assess the personalities—strengths and weaknesses—of the client's parents. If one parent is more articulate with adults, then he or she may need to take the lead in school conferences. The more nurturing parent—not always the mother—needs to be encouraged to interact more directly with the child. What comes naturally to each parent will allow each to help his or her child more authentically and successfully. In addition, this approach helps each individual to feel more adequate with regard to his or her parenting skills.

Thus, the HP plays a very positive role for the parents by aiding them in discovering how each can best help and by showing each how to help the child. This directs their attention to how their spouse's strengths are an asset, thereby reducing the adversarial, conflictual environment that often develops. Parents must be trained in how to establish a co-equal relationship to help their dyslexic child.

---

[1]Dr. Alan Wachtel and Dr. Betty Levinson each have created audiotapes on the role of fathers, which might be useful both for HPs and for parents. These audiotapes are available from the International Dyslexia Association, 8600 LaSalle Road, Chester Building, Suite 382, Baltimore, Maryland 21286.

In cases in which only one parent is the child's primary caregiver or only one parent is participating in intervention, a support network needs to be established. The HP should see to it that no single parent or guardian is left alone to deal with the complexities brought on by dyslexia.

THE TRAINING REGIMEN FOR THE HELPING PROFESSIONAL

As of 1999, there were no national standards for HPs who lead parent groups. If professionals are to be adequately trained to help parents assist their dyslexic child or to serve as direct agents of change, then minimum training requirements need to be put in place; these include the following:

- *Knowledge concerning typical child development*   HPs must understand the stages of development in order to help parents of a dyslexic child appreciate the complex nature of the physical, psychological, social, and language forces that influence children's behavior during each age period. Expectations for the dyslexic, who develops differently in certain areas, must be explained in terms of what constitutes normal development (Berk, 1996).
- *Knowledge about neurobiology*   HPs should have an understanding of neurobiology to answer parents' "why" questions about dyslexia, which is a neurobiologically based syndrome. HPs need to learn some basic neurology, neuroanatomy, and a working knowledge of neuropsychology. "Models [of human behavior] which leave out man's physical organism are bound to be inadequate for the task of making behavior intelligible" (Guthrie, 1950).
- *Knowledge about language development*   At a minimum, HPs should be familiar with the descriptive view of language development, which holds that a language disorder is "any disruption in the learning or use of the conventional system of arbitrary signals used by persons in the environment as a code for representing ideas about the world" (Bloom & Lahey, 1978).
- *Knowledge of assessment procedures*   HPs must understand assessment procedures; however, it must be stressed that the child is not a number, does not always fit into a discrepancy formula, and must never be dismissed as having "no problem" based on measurements alone. As Einstein stated, "Not everything that counts can be counted and not everything that can be counted, counts" (as cited in Wechsler, 1991)
- *Up-to-date information concerning direct intervention techniques*   HPs must stay current about direct intervention techniques in use, particularly in regard to the teaching of language (reading, writing, spelling). The research literature (e.g., Brady & Moats, n.d.) supports code-based techniques for such teaching and strategies that include a simultaneous, multisensory, language-based approach.
- *An awareness that dyslexia's symptoms change*   HPs must recognize that the symptoms of dyslexia change as the client's language becomes more complex and as the client moves from oral to reading/written expression.
- *An ability to deal with the complexities and controversies concerning ADHD*   HPs should have an understanding of issues pertaining to ADHD, which can co-occur with dyslexia.
- *Supervised experience and training in intervention techniques*   HPs should learn how to implement intervention procedures that are structured and organized.

Such intervention should include a monitored program for the dyslexic youngster's parents, which can be intertwined with the intervention provided for the child.

- *Role playing and practicum experiences* The student-professional learns by doing; supervision during training must be part of the curriculum.

The well-trained professional who is helping the parents of a dyslexic child needs to be knowledgeable about the use of multiple therapies—often including the use of medication. (The use of medication is a highly charged topic for parents, teachers, and professionals.) If interventions are to be beneficial, then parents must have confidence in the competence of the professional making the suggestions. This, in turn, requires that the HP be knowledgeable and experienced and, most important, have a track record of successful past work with dyslexic children. Professionals should take a stand on issues (e.g., the use of medication) by drawing support from a knowledge base that justifies the actions they take. Consequently, the student-professional needs to read widely—across disciplines—to serve both children and their parents effectively. It is most important that practitioners be knowledgeable about these two issues:

1. *Differing definitions of dyslexia, learning disabilities, and specific language disability—and the confusions that still persist in the field* For example, the Orton Dyslexia Society (ODS), now known as the International Dyslexia Association, has published two definitions of dyslexia (1984; 1994, as cited in Lyon, 1995),[2] neither of which deal with often-found coexisting conditions such as difficulties with organization, timing, memory, and integration. It is when conditions such as these are addressed that the parents usually need to become involved.

2. *The major controversies in regard to diagnosis and intervention* What constitutes a comprehensive evaluation for children suspected of having dyslexia is not agreed on. Recommendations often vary, depending on what is available and how costly it will be. There also is no general agreement as to what the intervention for dyslexia should be. Its complexity precludes a quick and simple prescription.

Similar to the Hula-Hoop and other fads, the quick, unsubstantiated cures for learning disabilities come and go—vision training, tinted lenses, certain drugs, megavitamins, special diets, and neurological training. Vulnerable parents—those with children whose problems are not being remedied rapidly—are often ready to accept well-publicized claims about "successful" new approaches. What complicates matters is that frequently there is a professional in the community who supports one of these therapies or a handful of parents who swear by

---

[2]"Dyslexia is a neurologically-based, often familial, disorder which interferes with the acquisition and processing of language. Varying in degrees of severity, it is manifested by difficulties in receptive and expressive language, including phonological processing, in reading, writing, spelling, handwriting, and sometimes in arithmetic. Dyslexia is not a result of lack of motivation, sensory impairment, inadequate instructional or environmental opportunities, or other limiting conditions, but may occur together with those conditions. Although dyslexia is life-long, individuals with dyslexia frequently respond successfully to timely and appropriate intervention." (ODS, 1984)

See Chapter 14 for the 1994 ODS definition of dyslexia.

such a therapy because of how their child has been helped. HPs must exercise extreme caution when they are working with parents who reveal they have already started using one of these controversial therapies with their youngster. Undermining or criticizing the parents' action can lead to the premature termination of the HP's own intervention process. The HP can say, "I do not wish to undermine your previous choice, but I wonder if you would read some material that I have that raises questions about the effectiveness of the approach you have tried." The HP should then present material from reputable sources.

Properly Trained Helping Professionals

Research stresses the need for properly trained professionals in the learning disabilities/dyslexia field. The need is becoming increasingly apparent and is being addressed by an ever greater emphasis on preservice and in-service training for HPs. No longer is it appropriate for physicians, psychologists, psychiatrists, social workers, educators, speech-language pathologists, audiologists, occupational therapists, and members of any other discipline involved in helping dyslexics and their families to be knowledgeable only in their own field of expertise. Dyslexia is a complex condition that requires a multidimensional intervention approach.

Along with understanding the child's condition, it is necessary for the HP to attend equally intensively to the parents' needs on a continuing basis. To help the parents help their child, the HP should give them information about child development. Parents of dyslexics should understand differences in the learning patterns of children. Professionals working with dyslexia must be knowledgeable and able to communicate accurate information on these topics. An HP can overcome a lack of training by working in a multidisciplinary setting.

Professionals who help dyslexics usually have not been exposed to a special curriculum to teach them how to support their client's parents. At best, training in how to assist these parents is generic. Most often it involves addressing only the anxieties, fears, denial, depression, and confusion that parents experience at the outset of an intervention with their dyslexic child. Professionals must also learn what information parents need and must know how to convey this material so that parents will not only understand what is to be done, but also will carry out the necessary actions.

To the student-professional, all of this may seem overwhelming and give rise to such questions as the following:

1. If my way of communicating is difficult for these parents to understand, then does that mean I cannot help them?
2. How do I assess this situation, and what can I do about it?

The answer to the first question is that the student-professional can help the parents provided that he or she becomes knowledgeable about dyslexia and the other areas listed previously. Then the student–professional follows specific guidelines for effective communication and consistent monitoring (outlined later in this chapter).

With regard to the second question, the key is for the student-professional to consult with an already trained HP who can assess both the student's knowledge about dyslexia and his or her style of communication. As stated previously, it is also necessary for the student to learn by doing, in a practicum situation that includes systematic supervision.

Professionals must be trained so that they can help parents understand and accept the following: 1) the most current, widely accepted definition of dyslexia; 2) the fact that a thorough multidisciplinary evaluation has shown that their child is dyslexic; and 3) that specific interventions, based on research findings, will benefit their child.

It is of utmost importance that professionals avoid defining dyslexic children only in terms of their problem. The dyslexic child is a child *with* a specific problem and he or she is not *the* problem. Similarly, a child with blond hair is still a child first and foremost and would not be referred to as only *a blond*, which would ignore all of his or her other attributes.

Often when others hear the term *dyslexia*, it elicits a stream of negative verbalizations. Rarely do people respond, "Oh, he must be very bright," or, "Oh, she must be very talented." It is disheartening for the HP to hear this negativity about dyslexia. Often when parents or teachers of dyslexics are asked to name one positive trait, they cannot. Consequently, from the very outset, professionals dealing with dyslexia must emphasize the client's strengths.

THE HELPING PROFESSIONAL'S LIBRARY

The well-trained HP needs to have a complete library of books, videotapes, and audiotapes that can be lent to and read by the parents of a dyslexic child. Providing books to the parents will be useful only when the HP offers additional, concrete help regarding how to use such information. No book should be given to the parents unless the HP has read it. This will ensure that the book is relevant to the client's situation. The HP could devote part of each session to planning with the parent how information in the book can be used with the child.

There are many well-written books on dyslexia for parents and teachers, such as the following:

- *What's Wrong with Me?: Learning Disabilities at Home and School* (Cicci, 1995)
- *Overcoming Dyslexia* (Hornsby, 1984)
- *Understanding Dyslexia* (Houston, 1992)
- *Understanding Learning Disabilities: A Parent Guide and Workbook* (National Center on Learning Disabilities/Learning Disabilities Council, 1991)
- *The Dyslexic Scholar* (Nosek, 1995)

In addition, excellent videotapes are available, such as *How Hard Can This Be?: F.A.T. City* (Eagle Hill School & Rosen, 1989), *Keeping Ahead in School* (Levine, 1990), and a series on learning disabilities—*LD/LA: Learning Disabilities/Learning Abilities* (Birsh, 1997)—that clarifies dyslexia as being distinct from other learning disabilities and explains that ADHD is different from a learning disability. Among some excellent reference books are *No Easy Answers: The Learning Disabled Child at Home and at School* (Smith, 1979), *Succeeding Against the Odds* (Smith, 1991), and *The Misunderstood Child* (Silver, 1988). Both Smith and Silver focused on learning disabilities; dyslexia as a *specific* learning disability is not always addressed in these texts as it is in books on dyslexia.

Much new material is being published (books, audiotapes, videotapes, CD-ROMs; see Appendix B); the best advice to parents may be to check with their local dyslexia organization and HP. Special-needs librarians in public libraries can also be quite helpful.

Reading may be a problem for the parents because they have no time or have reading difficulties of their own. In such situations the HP might suggest that the parents obtain an audiotape of the book so that they could play it in their car. Driving to appointments may give some parents their only opportunity to listen to the audiotapes.

It is important that the HP keep current with the resources available for parents and teachers. Many parents will hear something on the radio, see something on television, or read an article in the newspaper or on the Internet about dyslexia, learning disabilities, or ADHD. Frequently, this will precipitate a call or visit from the parents because they want to discuss what they have just learned. Parents want professionals to have opinions on such matters. Not only do they want to know what the HP thinks, but they also want those opinions to be supported by up-to-date research information.

HELPING PARENTS PRIORITIZE

Because many professionals are involved in treating dyslexics, the HP must help parents set priorities and should recognize the critical nature of timing. All forms of intervention need to be considered in light of what will keep the situation for both child and parents as normal as possible. Often, parents express a desire to deal with all of the issues simultaneously, assuming that such an approach will hasten success. Not only is this far from the truth, but attacking all of the issues at once also can have the opposite effect—that of leading the child to feel like a "basket case." For example, some evaluations end with a statement recommending speech and language help, academic therapy, occupational therapy, computer keyboard training, and psychotherapy (individual and family). Needless to say, no child or family could tolerate all of this help at once financially, emotionally, or practically—in terms of time. It is possible, however, to prioritize and address a few issues at a time.

Depending on the age of the child, usually it is most urgent to secure academic therapy and to counsel the parents briefly. Other interventions should be postponed, if at all possible. If it seems urgent to implement many therapies at first, then placement in a special school is warranted—one in which help is part of everyday school activity and in which the child will not be seen as being different from the other students.

Decisions about priorities should be made by a team consisting of all of the professionals that assessed the child. Each team member should be able to justify his or her list to the satisfaction of all team members. This should be done at a meeting designed specifically for that purpose.

THE HELPING PROFESSIONAL AS ADVOCATE

In addition to helping the child at home, the parents will have to communicate with the school. Therefore, the HP must ensure that the dyslexic child's parents are knowledgeable about due process requirements, PL 105-17, the Family Educational Rights and Privacy Act of 1974 (PL 93-380), and the difference between advocacy and direct intervention.

Although the dyslexic child's parents must play the major role in being advocates for their youngster, particularly with the school system, they will need the guidance of the HP. This, in turn, means that the HP must develop considerable expertise.

QUALITIES NECESSARY IN HELPING PROFESSIONALS

If HPs are to help the parents of dyslexics be advocates for their children, then HPs must know what constitutes a comprehensive evaluation, who are the well-trained people in the community, and how to build a link between evaluation and help from these individuals. Professionals in a helping role must have the following qualities:

1. HPs must have a high level of empathy and a great deal of patience.
2. HPs must have the ability to listen with a "third ear"—to really hear what is being said while remembering that the parents may also be struggling with language.
3. HPs must be able to deal with the frustration and anger of others without taking it personally.
4. HPs must be able to offer emotional support while also teaching parents in concrete ways; suggestions that are only given orally and are given without any follow-up often are useless.
5. HPs must be willing to secure additional knowledge (beyond coursework requirements) by reading, obtaining more academic training, and attending workshops and discussion groups in which experienced people in the field participate.
6. Early on, HPs must meet with other family members (even briefly) so that advice given later in the helping process will be more practical and relevant to the family.
7. HPs must be nonjudgmental and flexible when relating to others.
8. HPs must be able to empathize with the parents and communicate that empathy to the parents. This is crucial for building a trusting relationship in which the parents feel safe enough to try the HP's suggestions. For the parents, who already may feel inadequate, to risk trying is to risk failure. Unless they feel safe, they will often give up trying to help their child.
9. If the HP has children with dyslexia, then he or she must avoid frequent use of his or her children as an example. Not all children with learning disabilities present in the same way. Moreover, the client's parents may conclude that their youngster's situation is even more unfortunate because they lack the knowledge to help that the HP has. When such examples are used sparingly and appropriately, however, they can build the parents' confidence because they convey that you really do understand their situation.
10. The HP should recognize, as Carl Rogers once said, that being trustworthy does not mean being rigidly consistent but being dependably real. In other words, the HP should be consistent because the information is based on valid data and, therefore, is to be trusted.

Many other desirable qualities in HPs could be enumerated, but the list grows daunting. If a student-professional thinks that he or she does not have some of the listed qualities, then they can be developed. Many of these attributes can be acquired through experience and direct teaching. Openness and a willingness to learn, coupled with meaningful interactions with experienced professionals, will help the student-professional become an effective agent of change for the parents of dyslexic children. It will also mean that the HP will become a never-to-be-forgotten friend to both the child and the family.

The last but undoubtedly the most important quality the helping professional must have is a genuine sense of humor. It has been written that

> Joy and laughter are indispensable to emotional well being. To make others laugh is a talent but to be able to laugh at ourselves is as necessary to living as air is to breathing. Humor, when properly used, is a means of lessening personal hostility and dispelling self-hatred. Moreover, laughter is often effective in expressing the truth. We can often say in jest the things we would not dare to express directly. *In situations of emotional tension, humor frequently helps those involved to gain the perspective they need to look at the situation realistically.* ("Jewish Spirituality and Peace of Mind," n.d., p. 5)

Dyslexic children and their parents must see others smile at them. Expressions of tension, discouragement, and frustration will appear on the faces of the professionals involved in helping dyslexics. Unlike normal youngsters, who see lots of smiles, dyslexics are often robbed of this aspect of childhood. No child's world should be populated chiefly by serious faces.

The kind of humor that HPs should have is more than a knack for telling or laughing at jokes. It involves not taking oneself too seriously, appreciating the occasional absurdity of the human condition, and being able to smile and shake one's head at the kind of situations we all get ourselves into.

CONCLUSION

Those who diagnose and treat children with dyslexia need to be alert to the role that genetic factors play in this syndrome. Consequently, the well-trained HP will do more than merely recommend that parents of a dyslexic child complete a series of events. Knowledgeable HPs will monitor subsequent interventions and guide parents step by step through the process. Only in this way will the child with dyslexia be able to realize his or her true potential. Only in this way will everyone—child, parent, and society—benefit from the intellectual talent that lies within a child, for example, who says while riding in the car with his or her mother that she would see better if she turned on the "shinwield wiper."

REFERENCES

Arnold, E.L. (1978). *Helping parents help their children.* New York: Brunner/Mazel.

Berk, L.E. (1996). *Infants, children, and adolescents* (2nd ed.). Needham Heights, MA: Allyn & Bacon.

Bernstein, D.K., & Tiegerman, E. (1997). *Language and communication disorders in children* (4th ed.). Needham Heights, MA: Allyn & Bacon.

Birsh, J.R. (1997). *LD/LA: Learning disabilities/learning abilities* [Videotape series]. West Tisbury, MA: Vineyard Video Productions.

Bloom, L., & Lahey, M. (1978). *Language development and language disorders*. New York: John Wiley & Sons.

Brady, S., & Moats, L. (n.d.). *Informed instruction for reading success: Foundations for teacher preparation* [Position paper]. Baltimore: International Dyslexia Association.

Chase, C.H., Rosen, G.D., & Sherman, G.F. (Eds.). (1996). *Developmental dyslexia: Neural, cognitive, and genetic mechanisms*. Timonium, MD: York Press.

Cicci, R. (1995). *What's wrong with me?: Learning disabilities at home and school*. Timonium, MD: York Press.

Eagle Hill School & Rosen, P. (Producers). (1989). *How difficult can this be?: F.A.T. city* [Videotape]. Alexandria, VA: PBS Video.

Family Educational Rights and Privacy Act of 1974, PL 93-380, 20 U.S.C. §§ 1221 *et seq.*

Fine, M.J. (1980). *Handbook on parent education*. New York: Academic Press.

Guthrie, E.R. (1950). The status of systematic psychology. *The American Psychologist, 5*(4), 97–101.

Healy, J.M. (1990). *Endangered minds*. New York: Simon & Schuster.

Horsnsby, B. (1984). *Overcoming dyslexia*. London: Martin Dunitz Ltd.

Houston, A.M. (1987). *Common sense about dyslexia*. Lanham, MD: University Press of America.

Houston, A.M. (1992). *Understanding dyslexia*. Lanham, MD: University Press of America.

Individuals with Disabilities Education Act (IDEA) Amendments of 1997, PL 105-17, 20 U.S.C. §§ 1400 *et seq.*

Jewish spirituality and peace of mind: Daily meditations. (n.d.). Hoboken, MJ: Ktav Publishing.

Levine, M. (1990). *Keeping ahead in school* [Audiotapes and book]. Cambridge, MA: Educators Publishing Service.

Levinson, B. (1987). *Fathers: Critical determinants of a child's success*. Chevy Chase, MD: National Institute of Dyslexia.

Lyon, G.R. (1995). Toward a definition of dyslexia. *Annals of Dyslexia, 45*, 3–27.

Nosek, K. (1995). *The dyslexic scholar*. Dallas, TX: Taylor Publishing Co.

NCLD/Learning Disabilities. (1991). *Understanding learning disabilities: A parent guide and workbook*. Richmond, VA: Author.

Pennington, B.F., Gilger, J.W., Olson, R.K., & DeFries, J.C. (1992). The external validity of age versus IQ-discrepancy definitions of reading disability: Lessons from a twin study. *Journal of Learning Disabilities, 29*, 562–573.

Silver, L.B. (1988). *The misunderstood child*. New York: McGraw-Hill.

Smith, S.L. (1979). *No easy answers: The learning disabled child at home and at school*. New York: Bantam Doubleday Dell.

Smith, S.L. (1991). *Succeeding against the odds*. New York: Penguin Putnam.

The International Dyslexia Association. (1984). *The reprint series on dyslexia*. Baltimore: Author.

Wechsler, D. (1991). *Wechsler Intelligence Scale for Children–Third Edition*. San Antonio, TX: The Psychological Corporation.

Appendix A

Glossary

Anne M. Glass

Accent Stress or emphasis on one syllable in a word or on one or more words in a phrase or sentence. The accented part is spoken louder, longer, and/or in a higher tone. The speaker's mouth opens wider while saying an accented syllable.

Accommodations Modifications within the general classroom to enable students to keep up with the education program, such as intensive instruction; reduced assignments; adapted test procedures; and use of computers, calculators, and tape recorders.

Addend A number to be added to another. The numbers 1 and 2 are addends in $1 + 2 = 3$.

Affix A letter or a group of letters attached to the beginning or ending of a base word or word root that adds to or changes its meaning or grammatical form and creates a derivative. *See also* Prefix, Suffix.

Affricate A complex speech sound consisting of a stop consonant followed by a fricative (e.g., /ch/ in *chair*, /dz/ in *rods*).

Agraphia *See* Specific agraphia.

Air writing *See* Sky writing.

Allophones Slight variations in production of vowels and consonants that are predictable variants of a phoneme (e.g., /p/ in *pot* and *spot*, /a/ in *fast* and *tank*).

Alphabet A series of letters or signs arranged in a fixed sequence, each of which represents a spoken sound of that language. Knowledge of the 26 letters of the English alphabet is essential to the language skills—phonics, reading, writing, and spelling.

Alphabetic language A language in which letters are used systematically to represent speech sounds, or phonemes.

Alphabetic principle The relationship between letters ordered left to right in a written word and the phonemes ordered in a specific temporal sequence in the spoken word; knowledge of the alphabetical principle is essential to the ability to read an alphabetic language.

Amanuensis A person, such as a teacher, who writes while another person, such as a student, dictates words, sentences, or stories.

Analytic Pertaining to instruction or a process that separates the whole into its constituent parts to reveal the relationships of the parts. Analytic phonics separates the whole word into

---

Some definitions are adapted from Fromkin and Rodman (1988), Harris and Hodges (1981), Lerner (1997), Moats (1995), and *Stedman's Medical Dictionary* (1990).

its constituent parts so students can deduce the phonic relationships of the separate ortho-graphic patterns.

Anaphora Use of a pronoun or a definite article to refer to something already mentioned (e.g., The turtle moved slowly. *It* crept along the road).

Anglo-Saxon The language of the Germanic peoples (Angles, Saxons, and Jutes) who settled in Britain in the 5th and 6th centuries A.D. Anglo-Saxon was the dominant language in Britain until the Norman Conquest in 1066.

Antonyms Words of opposite meaning.

Appositive A noun that is placed after a noun to explain it more fully and usually has modi-fiers (e.g., Susan B. Anthony, *an influential suffragist,* appears on the silver dollar).

Arbitrary learning New learning that has no logical connection to already acquired knowl-edge or practical relationships (in contrast to learning through guided discovery).

Articulation The position of the mouth, tongue, lips, and teeth in the vocal production of speech.

Aspiration The push of air that accompanies the production of some consonants (e.g., /t/ in *top*).

Assessment Collection of information to make decisions about learning and instruction.

Attention-deficit/hyperactivity disorder (ADHD) Disorder characterized by difficulty with attending to and completing tasks, impulsivity, and/or hyperactivity that frequently co-occurs with but is not a learning disability. Also called *attention deficit disorder (ADD), at-tention disorder.*

Auditory discovery Listening and responding to guided questions to discover new informa-tion, such as when students echo words dictated by the teacher to discover a new common sound.

Automaticity Ability to respond or react without attention or conscious effort. Automaticity in word recognition permits full energy to be focused on comprehension.

Base word A word to which affixes are added (e.g., *whole* in *unwholesome*). A base word can stand alone.

Blend Two or more adjacent consonants (a *consonant blend*) or two or more adjacent vowels (a *vowel blend*) whose sounds flow smoothly together; to combine sounds of letters to produce a word or to sound out.

Blending Fusing individual sounds, syllables, or words into meaningful units (e.g., saying /m/ /ă/ /p/ as "map"; saying "tooth" and "brush" as "toothbrush").

Bottom-up process *See* Text-driven process.

Bound morpheme A morpheme that must be attached to other morphemes (e.g., *ed* in *spotted, s* in *boys, pre* in *preview*).

Breve The curved diacritical mark (˘) above a vowel in a sound picture that indicates a short sound in a closed syllable, in which at least one consonant comes after the vowel in the same syllable (e.g., ĭt, căt, blĕnd; exception: dĭvide).

Chameleon prefix A prefix whose final consonant changes based on the initial letter of the root (e.g., *in-* changes to *ir-* before *responsible*). *See also* Euphony.

Checkpoint *See* Marker.

Circumflex A diacritical mark (ˆ) placed over certain vowels when coding or when writing a sound picture to indicate an unexpected pronunciation. The circumflex is used in the Alpha-betic Phonics (Cox, 1992) code to indicate when a vowel-*r* combination is accented (e.g., âr, êr, îr, ôr, ûr). The circumflex is also used over the circled *a* to indicate the /aw/ pronunciation before /l/ in a monosyllabic word (e.g., b(ⓐ)ll).

Closed syllable A syllable ending with one or more consonants (e.g., *mat, hand*). The vowel usually is short. *See also* Open syllable.

Closure A statement summing up the focus of a lesson activity as a sign of completion; point at which a student is able to function comfortably at grade level in the general classroom (e.g., after remedial language therapy). The student may require temporary supports while mak-ing the transition to independence, such as tutoring in academic subjects, lessening of pres-sure, or tapering off of remediation.

Cloze technique Any of several ways of measuring a student's ability to restore omitted por-tions of an oral or written message from its remaining context. Also called *fill-in-the-blank technique.*

Clue *See* Context clue; *see also* Marker.

Coarticulation The phenomenon of word pronunciation in which adjacent sounds often are spoken in such a way that one phoneme overlaps, is changed by, and/or modifies another.

Code   A system of signs and signals used for communication. A system of words or other symbols arbitrarily used to represent longer words or ideas.

Cognates   *See* Voiced–voiceless cognates.

Cognitive strategies   Self-regulating mechanisms including planning, testing, checking, revising, and evaluating during an attempt to learn or problem-solve. Use of cognitive strategies is a higher order cognitive skill that influences and directs the use of lower-order skills.

Combination   A pattern of letters in a single syllable that occurs frequently together. The pronunciation of at least one of the component parts is unexpected, or the letters stand in an unexpected sequence (e.g., *ar, er, ir, or, qu, wh*).

Combining form   A root with which other roots and/or affixes may be combined to form compound words or derivatives (e.g., *auto, hemi, bio*). Combining forms are usually of Greek origin.

Compound word   A word composed of two or more smaller words (e.g., *doghouse*). A compound word may or may not be hyphenated depending on its part of speech.

Concept of a word   Understanding that sentences are made up of strings of words; the ability to count words in oral sentences and to match spoken words to printed words as demonstrated by pointing to the words of a text while reading. *See also* Finger-point reading.

Concept-driven process   Theoretical view of reading as a process that consists of using one's experiences and expectations to react to text (Harris & Hodges, 1981). Also called *top-down process*.

Conjunction   A part of speech that serves to connect words, phrases, clauses, or sentences (e.g., *and, but, as, because*). Also called *connectives*.

Consonant   One of a class of speech sounds in which sound moving through the vocal tract is constricted or obstructed by the lips, tongue, or teeth during articulation.

Consonant blend   *See* Blend.

Consonant digraph   *See* Digraph.

Consonant prefix   A prefix with a consonant as the final letter. The spelling of a consonant prefix may change for euphony (e.g., *ad-* becomes *at-* in *attraction*, *in-* becomes *ir-* in *irresponsible*).

Consonant suffix   A suffix beginning with a consonant (e.g., *-ful, -ness*).

Consonant-*le* syllable   A syllable in final position of a word that ends in a consonant, an *l*, and final silent *e* (e.g., *mid<u>dle</u>, ri<u>fle</u>.*) *See also* Final stable syllables.

Consonant-vowel-consonant (C-V-C)   A word or syllable composed of letters with a consonant-vowel-consonant pattern. These short words/syllables are a common starting point for reading phonetically regular words.

Context clue   Information from the immediate setting in which a word occurs, such as surrounding words, phrases, sentences, illustrations, syntax, or typography, that might be used to help determine the meaning and/or pronunciation of the word. Also called *contextual clue*.

Cooperative learning   Instructional approach in which students work together rather than compete to solve a problem or complete a task.

Cornering   Use of thumb, index finger, and middle finger to expose only the guide words in the corners of dictionary pages in rapid succession to find the page on which the entry word is defined.

Corrective feedback   Teacher responses during and following performance of a skill that is sensitive to the student's level and that guides him or her closer to mastery.

Criterion-referenced test   Test in which performance is assessed in terms of the kind of behavior expected of a person with a given score. A criterion-referenced test permits descriptions of a child's domain of knowledge represented in the test, allows an item-by-item description of knowledge attained and knowledge yet to be acquired, and may be standardized or informal.

Cross-modal integration   Combination of information received as visual, auditory, kinesthetic, and tactile input.

Curriculum-referenced test   Test in which items are taken from the curriculum used in the child's classroom so that he or she is not tested on material that has not been taught. A curriculum-referenced test provides a good match between assessment and instruction and may be standardized or informal.

Cursive handwriting   Joined, rounded handwriting; writing with the slanted strokes of successive characters joined and the angles rounded.

Decode   Word recognition in which the phonic code is broken; to determine the pronunciation of a word by noting the position of the vowels and consonants.

Deictic term   A word whose use/meaning changes based on context (e.g., *I, you, tomorrow, here, there*).

Derivation   The process of building a new word from another word by adding affixes. For example, *deconstructing* is a derivative of *deconstruct*, which in turn is derived from *struct*. *See* Etymology.

Derivational morpheme   Morpheme added to a base word that changes the part of speech of the base word (e.g., *-ness* changes adjective *careless* into noun *carelessness*).

Derivative   A word made from a base word by the addition of one or more affixes.

Detached syllable   *See* Nonsense word.

Diacritical marking   A distinguishing mark used in dictionaries and phonics programs to indicate the pronunciation of a letter or combination of letters.

Dictionary technique   A procedure for achieving rapid and efficient use of the dictionary.

Digraph   Two adjacent consonants or two adjacent vowels in the same syllable representing a single speech sound (e.g., *sh* in *wish*, *ee* in *feet*). *See also* Diphthong, Quadrigraph, Trigraph.

Diphthong   Two adjacent vowels in the same syllable whose sounds blend together with a slide or shift during the production of the syllable (e.g., *oy* in *toy*, *ow* in *cow*).

Directionality   The direction used in a language for reading and writing. English is governed by left-to-right directionality.

Discovery words   Group of related words used during guided discovery teaching to help students perceive a principle, pattern, or feature of the language.

Discrimination   The process of noting differences between stimuli. Auditory discrimination involves listening for the position of a particular sound in a word.

Dividend   In division, the total amount that is to be divided into a given number of parts (divisor) (e.g., 15 is the dividend in $15 \div 3 = 5$).

Division radical   Mathematical symbol ($\overline{)}$) used when writing long division facts.

Divisor   In division, the number that the total (dividend) is divided by (e.g., 3 is the divisor in $15 \div 3 = 5$).

Double deficit   Deficit in phonological awareness and rapid serial naming.

Dysarthria   Neurological oral-motor dysfunction including weaknesses of the musculature necessary for making the coordinated movements of speech production.

Dysgraphia   Extremely poor handwriting or the inability to perform the motor movements required for handwriting. The condition is associated with neurological dysfunction.

Dyslexia   "One of several distinct learning disabilities. It is a specific language-based disorder of constitutional origin characterized by difficulties in single word decoding, usually reflecting insufficient phonological processing. These difficulties in single word decoding are often unexpected in relation to age and other cognitive and academic abilities; they are not the result of generalized developmental disability or sensory impairment. Dyslexia is manifested by variable difficulty with different forms of language, often including, in addition to problems with reading, a conspicuous problem with acquiring proficiency in writing and spelling." (The Orton Dyslexia Society Research Committee, 1994, as cited in Lyon, 1995, p. 9)

Dyspraxia   Sensorimotor disruption in which the motor signals to the muscles, such as those necessary for speech production, are not consistently or efficiently received.

Ellipsis   Deletion of information from a portion of the discourse immediately preceding (e.g., "Do you like tortillas? *I do*").

Embedded clause   A clause enclosed within a sentence (e.g., The hummingbird, *whose wings beat very rapidly*, has brilliant plumage).

Embedded phonics   Phonological awareness and phonics taught implicitly through the reading of real words in text.

Emergent literacy   A level of cognitive maturation characterized by well-developed oral language ability, exposure to written language, and metalinguistic awareness.

Entry word   Word that is defined in a dictionary or glossary; may be divided into syllables.

Eponyms   Places, objects, or actions that are named after an individual (e.g., *sandwich, Fahrenheit, diesel*).

Etymology   The study of the origins and historical development of words.

Euphony   Beautiful or pleasing sound (from Greek). A desire for euphony may explain why, in the development of the English language, the last letters of certain prefixes have changed to match the first letter of the base words or stems. The result is easier to say and often results in a double consonant (e.g., *irregular*, not *inregular*). This knowledge is an aid to spelling.

Exaggerated pronunciation Overpronunciation of a word as an aid to spelling. Dyslexic students are encouraged to develop and to practice exaggerated pronunciation at first as needed to strengthen auditory memory. Thus, vowel sounds in unaccented syllables are not reduced to the indistinguishable schwa sound but are pronounced phonetically (e.g., the closed syllable in *vital* is exaggerated as /tăl/ to emphasize the *a*). Also called *spelling pronunciation* or *spelling voice*.

Expository writing Writing that explains or informs, including persuasive or descriptive writing and compare-and-contrast compositions.

Fernald method Technique for learning words that involves the visual, auditory, kinesthetic, and tactile (VAKT) modalities. The student looks at a word while saying and tracing it.

Figurative language *See* Nonliteral language.

Figure–ground perception The ability to attend to one aspect of a visual field while perceiving it in relation to the rest of the field; ability to identify and focus on salient information.

Final Pertaining to or occurring at the exact end; the very last letter or sound in a word or syllable. Z is the final letter of the alphabet.

Final stable syllables Syllables with nonphonetic spellings that occur frequently in final position in English base words (e.g., *tle, sion, cial*).

Fine motor skills The strategic control of small sets of voluntary muscles such as in writing, grasping small objects, controlling eye movements, or producing speech.

Finger agnosia A kinesthetic feedback disorder in which the fingers do not report their location to the brain.

Finger-point reading A form of pretend reading in which prereaders point their fingers at the words on a page as they recite the story from memory and synchronize spoken words with words in print. Finger-point reading is facilitated by the ability to segment phonemes and match them with written letters. *See also* Concept of word.

Flap The reduction of /t/ and /d/ in the American English pronunciation of *ladder* and *latter* formed by the tongue flapping on the alveolar ridge.

Fluency in reading Ability to translate print to speech with rapidity and automaticity that allows the reader to focus on meaning.

Formal tests *See* Standardized tests.

Formative data Information about a child's progress in acquiring particular skills or knowledge to be applied to short-term instructional goals; usually collected using criterion- and curriculum-referenced tests.

Fragment A phrase or subordinate clause that is used incorrectly as a sentence (e.g., *The girl who was standing.*).

Free morpheme A morpheme that can stand alone as a whole word (e.g., *box, plant, tame*). Also called *unbound morpheme*. *See also* Bound morpheme.

Frequency The number of times an event occurs in a given category (e.g., frequency in English of multiple spellings of the long /ū/ sound as in *cube, human*, and *statue*) that provides the order of introduction for reading and spelling.

Fricative A consonant produced by a partial obstruction of the airflow, which creates friction and slight hissing noise (e.g., /s/, /f/).

Functional neuroimaging Pictures of brain activity of awake subjects performing specific tasks that allow researchers to investigate which brain areas are used during certain tasks. *See also* Neuroimaging.

Gerund An English word ending in *-ing* when used as a noun (e.g., She loves *dancing* and *singing*).

Glide A vowel-like consonant (i.e., /w/ and /y/) produced with little or no obstruction of the air stream in the mouth; also called *semivowel*.

Grapheme A letter or letter cluster representing a single speech sound (e.g., *i, igh*).

Graphic organizers Visual displays of information to help a student compose written material or study for tests (e.g., outlines, semantic maps, story grammars/diagrams).

Graphomotor Pertaining to the skillful coordination of the muscle groups involved in handwriting.

Graphophonemic Pertaining to letter–sound patterns.

Guide letters The first few letters in a word that guide the reader in alphabetizing the word or finding it in the dictionary.

Guide words   The two words usually found in the upper corner of each dictionary page indicating the first and last words on the page.

Guided discovery teaching   Manner of presenting new material or concepts so that they can be deduced or discovered by the students. Only material that relates logically to their previous learning or that evolves through reason or sequence will lend itself to the students' discovery. Students will remember more readily that which they have been allowed to discover. Successful discovery teaching requires careful preparation.

Heterogeneous practice   A spelling or reading practice session with more than one focus used only after the student has mastered each of the concepts contained in the practice.

Homogeneous practice   A spelling or reading practice in which every word contains the same pattern or rule that is the single focus of the practice.

Homophones   Words that sound like another but have different spellings and meaning (e.g., *bare* and *bear; fourth* and *forth*).

Imagery training   Training in the use of language to create sensory impressions and in the formation of imaginative mental images while reading or listening.

Inclusion   The opportunity for all students with disabilities to have access to and participate in all activities of the neighborhood school environment. A placement where all students receive services, including specialized services, in the general education setting.

Independent level   That level of academic engagement in which an individual works independently without need for instructional support. Independent-level behaviors demonstrate a high degree of accuracy, speed, ease, fluency, and mastery.

Indo-European   A family of languages consisting of most of the languages of Europe, as well as those of Iran, the Indian subcontinent, and other parts of Asia.

Inflectional morpheme   A morpheme added to the end of a word that shows tense, number, or person of a verb; plural or possessive of a noun; or comparative form of adjectives (e.g., *-ed* in *floated, -s* in *tales, -er* in *thinner*).

Informal tests   Tests that are structured but not standardized; they typically follow the format of standardized tests, but presentation can be modified to probe the students' responses in ways that are not permissible with standardized tests.

Initial   The first or beginning sound or letter in a word or syllable. *A* is the initial letter of the alphabet.

Interdisciplinary studies   Learning through a series of experiences around a given theme connecting multiple subject areas (e.g., history, geography, art, music). Also called *thematic units, theme cycles, central subject curriculum, central study,* and *integrated curriculum.*

Invented spelling   Encouraged from preschool to first grade to help students develop phonemic awareness and apply their knowledge of sounds, symbols, and letter patterns to the task of spelling. The use of invented spelling is temporary until regular orthography is learned.

Irregular word   Word that has an unexpected spelling either because its orthographic representation does not match its pronunciation (e.g., *colonel*) or because it contains an infrequent orthographic representation of a sound (e.g., *soap*).

Juncture   The transition or mode of transition from one sound to another in speech; a pause that contributes to meaning of words (e.g., to make a *name* distinguishable from *an aim*) or rising juncture as in a question.

Key word   A word emphasizing a particular letter–sound association that serves as the key to unlock the student's memory for that association (e.g., *apple* for /ă/, *igloo* for /ĭ/).

Kinesthetic   Pertaining to the sensory experience stimulated by bodily movements and tensions; often pertaining to the student's feeling of letter shapes while moving parts of the body through space.

Kinesthetic memory   A voluntary motor sequence that is recalled by the student after repeated practice and training, such as daily writing of cursive letter shapes while associating them with the name and sounds represented by each.

Labiodental fricative   A sound in which the lower lip (*labio*) and the upper teeth (*dental*) touch and partially obstruct the air flow (e.g., /f/, /v/).

Laterality   The tendency to use either the left or the right side of the body; handedness.

Lax vowel   *See* Short vowel.

Learning disabilities   "A generic term that refers to a heterogeneous group of disorders manifested by significant difficulties in the acquisition and use of listening, speaking, reading, writing, reasoning, and mathematics abilities, or of social skills. These disorders are intrinsic to the individual and presumed to be due to central nervous system dysfunction. Even though a learning disability may occur with other handicapping conditions (e.g., sensory impairment, mental retardation, social and emotional disturbance), with socioenvironmental influences (e.g., cultural factors), and especially with attention deficit disorder, all of which may cause learning problems, a learning disability is not the direct result of those conditions or influences." (The Interagency Committee, 1985, as cited in Kavanagh & Truss, 1988, pp. 550–551)

Learning strategies model *See* Cognitive strategies.

Left angular gyrus Part of the left hemisphere of brain that is the primary location for translating visual-orthographic information into phonological representations (linking symbol to sound).

Letter cluster Group of two or more letters that regularly appear adjacent in a single syllable (e.g., *oo, ng, th, sh, oi, igh*). *See also* Combination, Digraph, Diphthong, Quadrigraph, Trigraph.

Letter–sound correspondences *See* Phonics.

Lexical Of or relating to words or the vocabulary of a language or the meaning of the base word in inflected and derived forms.

Lexical cohesion Planning and organizing of the content of a message before it is communicated.

Lexicon A body of word knowledge, either spoken or written.

Linguistic Denoting language processing and language structure.

Linguistics Study of the production, properties, structure, meaning, and/or use of language.

Linkages The associations developed in language training between students' visual, auditory, kinesthetic, and tactile perceptions by seeing the letter, naming it, saying its sound, and writing it in the air and on paper.

Liquid A class of consonants that contains /l/ and /r/ of American English.

Literacy socialization As a result of being read to, the development of the sense that marks on a page relate to the words being said, that there is a correct way to manipulate books, and that there is a positive connection between reading and nurturing experiences (Snow & Dickinson, 1991).

Long vowel A vowel sound that is produced by a slightly higher tongue position than the short vowels. The long sounds represented by the written vowels (i.e., *a, e, i, o,* and *u*) are usually the same as their names. When coding or when writing a sound picture, any long vowel is marked by a macron. Also called *tense vowel.*

Long-term memory Permanent storage of information by means of primarily semantic links, associations, and general organizational plans; includes experiential, semantic, procedural, and automatic habit memories.

Macron The flat diacritical mark (¯) above a vowel in a sound picture that indicates a long sound (e.g., /fāvor/).

Marker A distinguishing feature of a word that signals the need to apply a spelling rule or a coding for reading. The student may literally place a mark at each crucial point as a reminder. Also called *checkpoint, clue.*

Mastery Proficiency in specific subskills of a new task. Based on the "bottom-up" notion of gaining automatic recall of basic information or learning to automaticity; also called *overlearning.*

Meaning-based word As a result of compounding, a word whose meaning may not always be inferred from the meaning of its components (e.g., *greenhouse, flyleaf*).

Medial The letters or sounds that occur in the interior of a word or syllable. All of the letters in the sequential alphabet are medial except *A* and *Z. Medial* is not a synonym for *middle.*

Metacognition The deliberate rearrangement, regrouping, or modal transfer of information; the conscious choice of the strategies used to accomplish a task and processes to provide feedback on learning and performance.

Metalinguistics Awareness of language as an entity that can be contemplated; crucial to early reading ability, to understanding discourse patterns in the classroom, and to analyzing the language being used to teach the language that must be learned.

Metaphor A word or phrase that means one thing is used, through implication, to mean something else (e.g., "His remark created a blizzard of controversy"). *See also* Simile.

Middle Equidistant from two extremes. *Middle* and *medial* are not synonymous. The middle letters of the alphabet are *M* and *N*.

Miscue Used by reading specialists to refer to inaccurate reading responses to written text during oral reading.

Missing addend equation Addition equation in which only one addend and the sum are given (e.g., 5 + ____ = 10); the student must provide the missing addend.

Mnemonic strategies Any formal scheme designed to improve memory, including using keywords, chunking, rhyming, and visualizing. Arbitrary learning is more difficult for the dyslexic student than learning that is related and logical, so devices for grouping needed facts are essential.

Modality A specific sensory pathway. Multisensory instruction engages simultaneously the student's visual, auditory, and kinesthetic/tactile senses.

Model A standard or example provided by the teacher for imitation or comparison (e.g., a model of syllable division procedure before a reading practice); a structure or design to show how something is formed (e.g., teacher skywrites a cursive letter).

Monosyllable A word of one syllable containing one vowel sound.

Morpheme The smallest meaningful linguistic unit. A morpheme may be a whole word (e.g., *child*), a base word (e.g., *child* in *childhood*), a suffix (e.g., *-hood* in *childhood*), or a prefix (e.g., *un-* in *untie*). *See also* Derivational morpheme, Inflectional morpheme.

Morphological In linguistic terms, pertaining to the meaningful units of speech; a suffix, for example, is a morphological ending.

Morphology The internal structure of the meaningful units within words and the relationships among words in a language; also the study of word formation patterns.

Multiple meanings Different meanings for the same word; characteristic of English language. Students with learning disabilities often have difficulty with multiple meanings of words.

Multiple regression analysis A statistical method that relates a dependent (or criterion) variable (y) to a set of independent (or predictor) variables (x) by a linear equation for the purposes of prediction, controlling confounding variables, evaluating sets of variables, accounting for multivariate interrelationships, and analyzing variance and covariance on levels of independent variables (Fruchter, as cited in Corsini & Auerbach, 1996).

Multiple spellings The various ways in which a sound may be spelled (e.g., long /ā/ may be spelled *a, ay, ei, eigh, ey,* or *ai*).

Multiplicand The number in a multiplication equation that states the size or amount that is to be multiplied (e.g., 5 is the multiplicand in $3 \times 5 = 15$).

Multiplier The number in a multiplication equation that states how many times a certain size is to be produced (e.g., 3 is the multiplier in $3 \times 5 = 15$). Also called *operator*.

Multisensory Involving three or more senses, usually visual, auditory, kinesthetic, or tactile.

Multisensory structured language education (MSLE) Instructional approach that incorporates the simultaneous use of auditory, visual, kinesthetic, and tactile sensory modalities to link listening, speaking, reading, and writing together.

Multisyllabic Of or pertaining to a word of more than one syllable (e.g., *fantastic*). Also called *polysyllabic*.

Narrative Composition containing a sequence of events, usually in chronological order.

Nasals A sound produced in which air is blocked in the oral cavity but escapes through the nose. The first consonants in *mom* and *no* are nasal sounds.

Neuroimaging Diagnostic method of viewing brain structures and activity through the use of nuclear technology, such as magnetic resonance imaging, in which the patient's body is placed in a magnetic field and resulting images are processed by computer to produce an image of contrasting adjacent tissues. *See also* Functional neuroimaging.

Neuropsychology The study of areas of the brain and their connecting networks involved in learning and behavior.

Nonliteral language Language that avoids use of the exact meanings of words and uses exaggeration, metaphors, and embellishments. Also called *figurative language*.

Nonsense word A word having no meaning by itself, the spelling of which is usually phonetic. Reading and spelling nonsense words are phonic reinforcement for students who have already memorized a large number of words. Nonsense words provide the teacher with needed material for teaching older students to apply phonetic decoding. Also called *detached syllable, nonsense syllable, nonword, pseudo word*.

Norm-referenced test Assessment of performance in relation to that of the norm group (cohort) used in the standardization of the test. Norm-referenced tests produce scores that permit comparisons between a student and other children of the same age. All norm-referenced tests are standardized.

Oddity task   Task or question in which student is presented with several items and must select the one that does not fit with the rest (e.g., *"Ball, call, tall, hop.* Which of these words doesn't belong?"). Also called *odd-one-out task, odd-man-out task.*

Onset   The initial written or spoken single consonant or consonant cluster in a word (e.g., /s/ in *sit,* /s/ /t/ /r/ in *strip*).

Open syllable   A syllable ending with a vowel (e.g., the first syllables in *labor* and *freedom*). *See also* Closed syllable.

Operator   *See* Multiplier.

Orthography   The writing system of a language; correct or standardized spelling according to established usage.

Orthographic memory   Memory of letter patterns and word spellings.

Orton-Gillingham approach   Multisensory method of teaching language-related academic skills that focuses on the structure and use of sounds, syllables, words, sentences, and written discourse. Instruction is explicit, systematic, cumulative, direct, and sequential.

Otitis media   Inflammation of the middle ear that can lead to temporary conductive hearing loss or, sometimes, permanent hearing loss. A young child who experiences hearing loss from otitis media may have resulting speech or language difficulties.

Overlearning   *See* Mastery.

Paralinguistic aspect of phonology   *See* Suprasegmental.

Pause   A break, stop, or rest in spoken language; one of the suprasegmental aspects of language.

Phoneme   An individual sound unit in spoken words; the smallest unit of speech that makes one word distinguishable from another (e.g., /f/ makes "fat" distinguishable from "vat"; /j/ makes "jump" distinguishable from "chump").

Phoneme awareness   *See* Phonemic awareness.

Phoneme deletion   *See* Sound deletion.

Phonemic awareness   Awareness of the smallest units of sound in the speech stream and the ability to isolate or manipulate the individual sounds in words. Also called *phoneme awareness.*

Phonetic   Pertaining to speech sounds and their relation to graphic or written symbols.

Phonetically regular words   *See* Regular words.

Phonetics   The system of speech sounds in any specific language.

Phonics   Paired association between letters and letter sounds; an approach to teaching of reading and spelling that emphasizes sound–symbol relationships, especially in early instruction.

Phonological   Pertaining to a speaker's knowledge about sound patterns in a language.

Phonological awareness   Both the knowledge of and sensitivity to the phonological structure of words in a language. It involves the ability to notice, think about, or manipulate sound segments in words. Phonological awareness can progress from rhyming; to syllable counting; to detecting first, last, and middle sounds; to segmenting, adding, deleting, and substituting sounds in words.

Phonological loop   Part of short-term memory that can store small bits of speech information as they are being processed.

Phonological rules   Implicit rules governing speech sound production and the sequence in which sounds can be produced.

Phonology   The science of speech sounds, including the development of speech sounds in one language or comparison of speech sound development in different languages.

Place of articulation   The place in the oral cavity where the stream of air is obstructed or changed during the production of a sound.

Place value   The position of a digit in a numeral or series (e.g., the ones place, the tens place, the hundreds place).

Polyglot   Made up of several languages; English is a polyglot language.

Pragmatics   The set of rules that dictates behavior for communicative intentions in a particular context and the rules of conversation or discourse.

Précis   Condensation in the student's own words of the author's essential message, thesis, moral, or purpose.

Prediction chart   Chart on which students make initial predictions about a story and then modify as they read the story.

Prefix An affix attached to the beginning of a word that changes the meaning of that word (e.g., *tri-* in *tricycle*). *See also* Consonant prefix, Vowel prefix.

Prephonetic stage Stage in spelling development in which not all of the sounds of the word appear (e.g., *JS* for *dress*).

Print awareness Children's appreciation and understanding of the purposes and functions of written language.

Print handwriting Unconnected letters formed using arcs and straight lines. Also called *manuscript handwriting*.

Prosody *See* Suprasegmental.

Proprioception An individual's subconscious perception of movement and spatial orientation coming from stimuli within the body.

Pseudoword *See* Nonsense word.

Quadrigraph Four adjacent letters in a syllable that represent one speech sound (e.g., *eigh*).

Quotient In division, the number of shares contained in a total (dividend) (e.g., 5 is the quotient in $15 \div 3 = 5$).

R-controlled Pertaining to the phenomenon in English when an *r* colors the way the preceding vowel is pronounced. For example, the *a* in *bar* is influenced by the *r* and sounds different from the *a* in *bad*.

R-controlled syllable A syllable containing the combination of a vowel followed by *r*. The sound of the vowel often is not short but instead may represent an unexpected sound (e.g., *dollar, star, her*).

Rapid serial naming Task, most often administered to prereaders, in which individual is asked to name quickly a series of printed objects or blocks of color repeated over and over in random order.

Reading disability *See* Dyslexia.

Reading precursors Experience and skills that lead to learning how to read (e.g., listening to books read aloud, letter naming, phonological awareness, motivation).

Recognition The act of identifying a stimulus as the same as something previously experienced (e.g., auditory recognition is involved in listening for a particular sound).

Regrouping New mathematical term for *carrying* (in addition) and *borrowing* (in subtraction); necessary in our base-10 positional notation system.

Regular words Words that are spelled the way they sound. Also called *phonetically regular words*.

Relative clause A dependent clause introduced by a relative pronoun such as *who, that, which,* or *whom* (e.g., We bought ice cream from the man *who was standing on the corner*).

Review Look over again; bring back to awareness. Used twice in a multisensory lesson to increase automatic reaction to symbols for reading and spelling and to make a brief reference to the day's new material.

Rime The written or spoken vowel and the final consonant(s) in a syllable (e.g., *at* in *cat, itch* in *switch*).

Root word A content word (noun, verb, adjective, verb) to which affixes can be added (e.g., *hat, group, green, happily*). Some word roots, of Greek or Latin origin, to which affixes are attached are morphemes that generally cannot stand alone as a word in English (e.g., *cred, dict, struct, tele*).

Rule word A word that carries information indicating when a letter should be dropped, doubled, or changed (e.g., *shiny, rabbit, bountiful*).

Run-on sentence Two main clauses run together without any punctuation or conjunction separating them (e.g., *It began raining they parked the car*).

Schema Student's prior knowledge and experience relevant to the new topic insofar as it contributes to a frame of reference, factual or attitudinal, for the new information creating links or structures through which the new information can be assimilated. Also called *schemata.*

Schwa An unaccented vowel whose pronunciation approximates the short /ŭ/ sounds, such as in the first and last *a* in *America* or the second *a* in *sandal*.

Segmental Feature of a word that can be divided or organized into a class.

Segmentation Separating a word into units, such as syllables, onsets and rimes, or individual phonemes, for the purpose of reading or spelling. Also called *unblending*.

Selective attention The ability to attend to certain stimuli while ignoring other stimuli; in working memory, putting ideas "on hold" while working on other ideas.

Self-contained classroom A classroom in which students are taught all, or nearly all, subjects together by the same teacher; often used to refer to a classroom in which all of the students receive special education services.

Semantic Concerning the meaning of words and the relationships among words as they are used to represent knowledge of the world.

Sentence expansion Addition of who, what, where, when, and/or how to a sentence kernel (e.g., *Yesterday when I was at the store, I saw the woman with the brown dog* is an expansion of *I saw the woman*).

Short vowel A vowel that is pronounced with a short sound, an arbitrary sound that is unrelated to any aspect of the letter, such as the name of the letter. A short vowel usually occurs in a closed syllable and is marked with a breve. Also called *lax vowel*.

Short-term memory Memory that lasts only briefly, has rapid input and output, is limited in capacity, and depends directly on stimulation for its form. Short-term memory enables the reader to keep parts of the reading material in mind until enough material has been processed for it to make sense. Also called *working memory*. *See also* Phonological loop, Visuospatial loop.

Sibilant A speech sound that is uttered with or accompanied by a hissing sound (i.e., /s/, /ks/, /z/, /ch/, /sh/, /j/, and /zh/).

Sight word A word that is immediately recognized as a whole and does not require decoding to identify. A sight word may or may not be phonetically regular (e.g., *can, would, the*).

Simile An explicit comparison of two unlike things, usually with the word *like* or *as* (e.g., "Her tousled hair was like an explosion in a spaghetti factory"). *See also* Metaphor.

Simultaneous Oral Spelling (S.O.S.) A structured sequence of procedures to teach the student how to think about the process of spelling; student looks and listens to the word, unblends it, spells it aloud, writes it while naming each letter, codes it, and reads it aloud for proofreading (Cox, 1992).

Situation A feature in a word that provides clues about how to spell or read a word. The situation refers to the position of letters or sounds, placement of accent, and the influence of surrounding sounds or letters.

Sky writing Technique of "writing" a letter or word in the air using arm and hand of writing hand. Use of upper arm muscles during sky writing helps the student retain kinesthetic memory of the shape of letters. Also called *air writing*.

Sound deletion Early literacy task in which student is presented with a word and is asked to say all of the sounds in the word except one (e.g., "Say *bat* without the /b/"). Ability to delete sounds is an important component of phonemic awareness. Also called *phoneme deletion*.

Sound dictation Teacher pronounces individual phonemes, words, or sentences, and student responds with spellings of each; review with a sound or spelling deck to develop automaticity in translating sounds to spellings.

Sound picture Letter or word written with diacritical markings indicating pronunciation (e.g., kŭp for *cup*).

Sound–symbol correspondences *See* Phonics.

Specific agraphia Acquired disorder in which ability to form letter shapes, letter sequences, and motor patterns is impaired.

Spelling-based pronunciation, spelling voice *See* Exaggerated pronunciation.

SQ3R *See* Survey, Question, Read, Recite, Review.

Standardized tests Tests that are standardized using a carefully selected sample of people representative of the larger group of people for whom the test was created; must be administered and scored following procedures prescribed in the manual accompanying the test.

Stop A consonant that is produced with a complete obstruction of air (e.g., /p/, /t/, /k/).

Stress *See* Accent.

Subskill A skill that is part of a more complex skill or group of skills. Subskills of reading include phonological awareness and knowledge of letter–sound correspondences.

Suffix A morpheme attached to the end of a word that changes the form or use of that word in a sentence (e.g., *-s* in *cats*, *-ing* in *lettering*). Suffixes include inflected forms indicating tense, number, person, and comparatives. *See also* Consonant suffix, Vowel suffix.

Summative data Information about the accumulation and integration of knowledge to be applied to long-term comprehensive teaching goals; typically collected using norm-referenced measures but may be collected with curriculum- and criterion-referenced tests.

Suprasegmentals   The musical qualities of language, including intonation, expression, stress, pitch, juncture, and rhythm, which are significant in our ability to communicate and comprehend emotions and attitudes.

Survey, Question, Read, Recite, Review (SQ3R)   Study method in which student surveys the assignment, poses a question, reads to answer the question, recites the answer to the question, and reviews the material read (Robinson, 1946).

Syllable   A spoken or written unit that must have a vowel sound and that may include consonants that precede or follow that vowel. Syllables are units of sound made by one impulse of the voice.

Syllable division   The process of breaking down multisyllabic words into separate syllables for greater ease in pronunciation.

Syllable patterns   There are four major syllable division patterns in English: VCCV, VCV, VV, and VCCCV.

Syllable types   There are six syllable types in English: closed, open, vowel-consonant-*e*, *r*-controlled, vowel pair (vowel team), and consonant-*le*. *See also specific syllable types.*

Synonyms   Words of similar meaning.

Syntax   The system by which words may be ordered in phrases and sentences; sentence structure; grammar.

Synthetic   Pertaining to instruction or process that begins with the parts and builds to the whole. Synthetic phonics starts with individual letter sounds that are blended together to form a word. *See also* Analytic approach.

Tactile   Relating to the sense of touch.

Target word   A word that is being looked for in a dictionary or other reference source.

Tense vowel   *See* Long vowel.

Text-driven process   Theoretical view of reading as a process that consists of accurate sequential reading of every word. Comprehension is viewed as text driven rather than concept driven. Also called *bottom-up process.*

Top-down process   *See* Concept-driven process.

Tracking   The ability to fingerpoint while reading a text, demonstrating the concept of a word.

Transitional stage   Stage in spelling development in which a child's spelling is very similar to conventional spelling of a word (e.g., *DRES* for *dress*).

Trigraph   Three adjacent letters in a syllable that represent one speech sound (e.g., *tch, dge*). *See also* Digraph, Quadrigraph.

Umbrella theme   In interdisciplinary instruction, theme studied with respect to various school subjects and disciplines (e.g., the umbrella theme *water* can be studied as a vital part of life, as a cycle, and as a means of transportation).

Unblending   *See* Segmentation.

Unbound morpheme   *See* Free morpheme.

Unstable digraphs   Adjacent vowels that appear in distinct syllables and therefore have distinct sounds (e.g., *theatre, create, theory*).

Unvoiced consonant   *See* Voiceless consonant.

Verbal rehearsal   Strategy that can be used to help hold information in short-term memory.

Verbalization   After the discovery of a rule for reading, spelling, or strokes of a letter shape, students verbalize the pattern or rule .

Visual, auditory, kinesthetic, tactile (VAKT)   *See* Fernald method.

Visual discovery   Information gained by sight; guided discovery of a reading or spelling rule through looking at written language.

Visual hints   *See* Context clues.

Visuospatial loop   Part of short-term memory that can store print or graphic information.

Voiced consonant   A consonant articulated with vocal vibration (e.g., /z/).

Voiced–voiceless cognates   Phonemes produced in the same place of the mouth, in the same manner, but that vary in the voicing characteristic (e.g., /k/ and /g/).

Voiceless consonant   A consonant articulated with no vocal vibration (e.g., /s/). Also called *unvoiced consonant.*

Vowel   A class of open speech sounds produced by the easy passage of air through a relatively open vocal tract. English vowels include *a, e, i, o, u,* and sometimes *y*.

Vowel blend   *See* Blend.

Vowel digraph   *See* Digraph.

Vowel pair (vowel team) syllable A syllable containing two adjacent vowels that have a long, short, or diphthong sound (e.g., *meet, head, loud*).

Vowel prefix A prefix with a vowel as the final letter.

Vowel suffix A suffix beginning with a vowel, such as *-ing* and *-ed*.

Vowel-consonant-*e* syllable A one-syllable word or a final syllable of a longer word in which a final silent *e* signals that the vowel before the consonant is long (e.g., *cake, rope, cube, five, athlete*).

Watch Our Writing (W.O.W.) A checklist designed to help students write accurately, comfortably, and legibly: Place feet flat on the floor, sit up straight, slant the paper at a 45° angle, rest arms on the desk, and hold the pencil lightly while pointing its upper end toward the shoulder of writing arm.

Whole-language approach A perspective on teaching literacy based on beliefs about teaching and learning that include the following: Reading can be learned as naturally as speaking; reading is focused on constructing meaning from text using children's books rather than basal or controlled readers; reading is best learned in the context of the group; phonics is taught indirectly during integration of reading, writing, listening, and speaking; teaching is child centered and emphasizes motivation and interest; instruction is offered on the basis of need.

Word blindness Term used in the late 19th and early 20th centuries for *dyslexia*. *Word blindness* now refers to *alexia*, the loss of ability to read because of brain injury.

Working memory *See* Short-term memory.

REFERENCES

Corsini, R.J., & Auerbach, A.J. (Eds.). (1996). *Concise encyclopedia of psychology* (2nd ed.). New York: John Wiley & Sons.

Cox, A.R. (1992). *Foundations for literacy: Structures and techniques for multisensory teaching of basic written English language skills*. Cambridge, MA: Educators Publishing Service.

Fromkin, V., & Rodman, R. (1988). *An introduction to language* (4th ed.). Austin, TX: Holt, Rinehart & Winston.

Harris, T.L., & Hodges, R.E. (1981). *A dictionary of reading and related terms*. Newark, DE: International Reading Association.

Kavanagh, J.F., & Truss, T.J. (Eds.). (1988). *Learning disabilities: Proceedings of the national conference*. Timonium, MD: York Press.

Lerner, J.W. (1997). *Learning disabilities: Theories, diagnosis, and teaching strategies* (7th ed.). Boston: Houghton Mifflin.

Lyons, G.R. (1995). Toward a definition of dyslexia. *Annals of Dyslexia, 45*, 3–27.

Moats, L.C. (1995). *Spelling: Development, disabilities, and instruction*. Timonium: York Press.

Robinson, F.P. (1946). *Effective study*. New York: HarperCollins.

Snow, C., & Dickinson, D. (1991). Skills that aren't basic in a new conception of literacy. In A. Purves & E. Jennings (Eds.), *Literate systems and individual lives: Perspectives on literacy and schooling*. Albany, New York: SUNY Press.

Stedman's medical dictionary (25th ed.). (1990). Baltimore: Lippincott Williams & Wilkins.

Appendix B

Materials and Sources

Holly Baker Hill

GENERAL RESOURCES

**Institutions and Organizations Offering
Training in Multisensory Structured Language Education**

Arizona Multisensory Training Institute
1300 North 77th Street
Scottsdale, AZ 85257
602-425-9221

*Brighton Academy/Dyslexia Association
of Greater Baton Rouge, Inc.*
9150 Bereford Drive
Baton Rouge, LA 70809
225-923-2068; 225-923-2071
sgibson@brightonacademy.com

DuBard School for Language Disorders
The University of Southern
Mississippi
Box 10035
Hattiesburg, MS 39406
601-266-5223

Dyslexia Specialist Certificate Program
Learning Disabilities Program
Sammartino School of Education
Fairleigh Dickinson University
302 Bancroft Hall
1000 River Road
Teaneck, NJ 07666
201-692-2089

EDMAR Educational Associates
Post Office Box 2
Forney, TX 75126
972-564-5005
mtaysmith@aol.com

Garside Institute for Teacher Training
The Carroll School
Baker Bridge Road
Lincoln, MA 01773
781-259-8340

*Hardman & Associates, Inc./Dyslexia
    Research Institute*
4745 Centerville Road
Tallahassee, FL 32308
850-893-2216

Herman Method Institute
4700 Tyrone Avenue
Sherman Oaks, CA 91423
818-784-9566

*Language! National Institute for
    Continuing Education*
Post Office Box 865
Gulf Breeze, FL 32562
805-934-0554
read@nice-usa.com
www.nice-usa.com

Lindamood-Bell Learning Processes
416 Higuera Street
San Luis Obispo, CA 93401
800-233-1819; 805-541-3836
www.lblp.com

*Literacy Education and Academic
    Development, Inc. (LEAD)*
Post Office Box 262
Argyle, TX 76226
940-464-3752
lead1234@gte.net

*Massachusetts General Hospital Reading
    Disabilities Unit*
Language Disorders Unit
A.C.C. Room 737
Massachusetts General Hospital
Boston, MA 02114
617-724-2764

*Multisensory Language Therapy Training
    of New Mexico*
6344 Buenos Aires, NW
Albuquerque, NM 87120
505-898-7500

*Multisensory Teaching of Basic Language
    Skills*
Department of Curriculum and
    Teaching
Teachers College, Columbia
    University
Box 31
New York, NY 10027
212-678-3080

Neuhaus Education Center
4433 Bissonnet Street
Bellaire, TX 77401
713-664-7676

Payne Education Center of Ardmore
Post Office Box 1807
Ardmore, OK 73401
405-226-2341

*Payne Education Center of Oklahoma
    City*
3240 West Britton Road, #103
Oklahoma City, OK 73120
405-755-4205
payneedu@accessacg.net

Project Read
Language Circle Enterprise
Post Office Box 20631
Bloomington, MN 55420
800-450-0343; 612-884-4880

Reading Reform Foundation of New York
333 West 57th Street, Suite 1L
New York, NY 10019
212-307-7320

*Scottish Rite Learning Center of West
    Texas*
602 Avenue Q
Post Office Box 10135
Lubbock, TX 79408
806-765-9150

*Southern Methodist University Learning
    Therapy Program*
Post Office Box 750384
Dallas, TX 75275
214-768-7323

Southwest Multisensory Training Center
9550 Forest Lane, Suite 600
Dallas, TX 75243
214-349-7272

Spalding Education Foundation
2814 West Bell Road, Suite 1405
Phoenix, AZ 85023
602-866-7801
spalding@neta.com

Starting Over
c/o Joan Knight
317 West 89th Street, #9E
New York, NY 10024
212-769-2760

Stern Center for Language and Learning
135 Allen Brook Lane
Williston, VT 05495
800-544-4863
www.sterncenter.org

Stratford Friends School
5 Llandillo Road
Havertown, PA 19083
610-446-6381

Texas Scottish Rite Hospital for Children
2222 Welborn Street, Room 425
Dallas, TX 75219
214-559-7800

The Centers for Youth and Families
6601 West 12th Street
Post Office Box 251970
Little Rock, AR 72225
501-666-8686

The Greenwood Institute
Rural Route Box 270
Putney, VT 05346
802-387-4545
grnwood@sover.net

The June Shelton School
15720 Hillcrest Road
Dallas, TX 75248
972-774-1772

The Slingerland Institute
Security Pacific Plaza
411 108th Avenue, NE
Bellevue, WA 98004
206-453-1190

James P. Williams Memorial Foundation
2117-B Knickerbocker Road
San Angelo, TX 76904
915-655-2231

Wilson Language Training
175 West Main Street
Millbury, MA 01527
800-899-8454; 508-865-5699
www.WilsonLanguage.com

Accrediting Organizations

*Academic Language Therapy Association
  (ALTA)*
4020 McEwen, Suite 105
Dallas, TX 75244
972-907-3924

*Academy of Orton-Gillingham
  Practitioners and Educators*
East Main Street
Post Office Box 234
Amenia, NY 12501
914-373-8919

*International Multisensory Structured
  Language Education Council (IMSLEC)*
c/o The June Shelton School
15720 Hillcrest Road
Dallas, TX 75248
972-774-1772

Organizations

Alliance for Technology Access
2175 East Francisco Boulevard, Suite L
San Rafael, CA 94901
415-455-4575

Center for Accessible Technology
2547 Eighth Street 12A
Berkeley, CA 94710
510-841-3224
www.el.net/CAT/

*Center of Minority Researchers in Special
    Education (COMRISE)*
Curry School of Education
University of Virginia
405 Emmet Street
Charlottesville, VA 22903
804-924-1022

*Children with Attention Deficit Disorders
    (CHADD)*
499 Northwest 70th Avenue, Suite 308
Plantation, FL 33317
305-587-3700
www.chadd.org

Division for Learning Disabilities (DLD)
The Council for Exceptional Children
    (CEC)
1920 Association Drive
Reston, VA 22091
703-620-3660
cec@cec.sped.org
www.cec.sped.org

*ERIC Clearinghouse on Disabilities and
    Gifted Education*
1920 Association Drive
Reston, VA 22091
800-328-0272
ericec@cec.sped.org
www.cec.sped.org/ericec.htm

*Federal Resource Center for Special
    Education*
1875 Connecticut Avenue, NW, Suite
    900
Washington, DC 20009
202-884-8215
frc@aed.org
www.dssc.org/frc

HEATH Resource Center
American Council on Education
1 Dupont Circle, NW, Suite 800
Washington, DC 20036
800-544-3284

*Learning Disabilities Association of
    America (LDA)*
4156 Library Road
Pittsburgh, PA 15234
412-341-1515
www.ldanatl.org

*National Attention Deficit Disorder
    Association (ADDA)*
Post Office Box 1303
Northbrook, IL 60065
DearADDA@aol.com
www.add.org

*National Center for Learning Disabilities
    (NCLD)*
381 Park Avenue South, Suite 1401
New York, NY 10016
888-575-7373; 212-545-7510
www.ncld.org

*National Clearinghouse for Professions
    in Special Education (NCPSE)*
The Council for Exceptional Children
    (CEC)
1920 Association Drive
Reston, VA 20191
800-641-7824

*National Information Center for Children
    and Youth with Disabilities (NICHCY)*
Post Office Box 1492
Washington, DC 20013
800-695-0285
nichcy@aed.org
www.nichcy.org

The International Dyslexia Association
Chester Building, Suite 382
8600 LaSalle Road
Baltimore, MD 21286-2044
800-222-3123; 410-296-0232
info@interdys.org
www.interdys.org

Trace Research and Development Center
University of Wisconsin–Madison
S-151 Waisman Center
1500 Highland Avenue
Madison, WI 53705
608-263-5776; 608-263-5910
trace.wisc.edu

Publishing Companies and Distributors

Academic Communication Associates
Publication Center, Department 698
4149 Avenida de la Plata
Post Office Box 586249
Oceanside, CA 92058
760-758-9593
acom@acadcom.com

Academic Therapy Publications
20 Commercial Boulevard
Novato, CA 94949
800-422-7249

Paul H. Brookes Publishing Co.
Post Office Box 10624
Baltimore, MD 21285
800-638-3775
www.brookespublishing.com

Brookline Books
Post Office Box 1047
Cambridge, MA 02238
800-666-BOOK; 617-868-0360

C TECH
Post Office Box 30
2 North William Street
Pearl River, NY 10965
800-228-7798

CEC Publications
The Council for Exceptional Children
1920 Association Drive, Department
   K7082
Reston, VA 20191
888-CEC-SPED

Center for Applied Research in Education
Book Distribution Center
Route 59 at Brook Hill Drive
West Nyack, NY 10995

Communication Skill Builders
555 Academic Court
San Antonio, TX 78204
800-221-8378
www.hbtpc.com

Continental Press
520 East Bainbridge Street
Elizabethtown, PA 17022
800-233-0759

Corwin Press, Inc.
2455 Teller Road
Thousand Oaks, CA 91320
805-499-9774

Educators Publishing Service, Inc.
31 Smith Place
Cambridge, MA 02138
800-225-5750
www.epsbooks.com

Franklin Electronic Publishers, Inc.
1 Franklin Plaza
Burlington, NJ 08016
800-266-5626; 609-234-4333
www.franklin.com

Flyleaf Publishing Company
Post Office Box 185
Lyme, NH 03768
603-795-2875

Gander Publishing
416 Higuera Street
San Luis Obispo, CA 93401
800-541-3836

High Noon Books
20 Commercial Boulevard
Novato, CA 94949
800-422-7249

Jamestown Publishers
NTC Contemporary Publishing
  Group
4255 West Touhy Avenue
Lincolnwood, IL 60646
800-323-4900
www.jamestownpublishers.com

Kurzweil Educational Systems, Inc.
411 Waverley Oaks Road
Waltham, MA 02154
800-894-5374

Lawrence Erlbaum Associates, Inc.
10 Industrial Avenue
Mahwah, NJ 07430
800-926-6579

Lindamood-Bell Learning Processes
416 Higuera Street
San Luis Obispo, CA 93401
800-233-1819; 805-541-3836
www.lblp.com

LinguiSystems, Inc.
3100 4th Avenue
East Moline, IL 61244-9700
800-776-4332
linguisys@aol.com

Modern Learning Press, Inc.
Post Office Box 167, Department 390
Rosemont, NJ 08556
800-627-5867

MTS Publications
Post Office Box 2
Forney, TX 75126
972-564-5005

PRO-ED
8700 Shoal Creek Boulevard
Austin, TX 78757
800-897-3202
www.proedinc.com

Recorded Books, Inc.
270 Skipjack Road
Prince Frederick, MD 20678
800-638-1304

Recordings for the Blind and Dyslexic
20 Roszel Road
Princeton, NJ 08540
800-803-7201; 609-452-0606
www.rfbd.org

*Region XIII TAAS/Education Service
  Center*
5701 Springdale Road
Austin, TX 78723
512-926-5593

Riverside Publishing Company
8420 Bryn Mawr Avenue
Chicago, IL 60631
800-767-8378
www.riverpub.com

Saxon Publishers, Inc.
1320 West Lindsey Street
Norman, OK 73069
800-284-7019

Singular Publishing Group, Inc.
401 West "A" Street, Suite 325
San Diego, CA 92101
800-774-8398

Slosson Educational Publications, Inc.
Post Office Box 280
East Aurora, NY 14052
888-756-7766

Smart Stuff & Good Ideas
56 Ludlow Street
New York, NY 10002
800-20-SMART

*Social Work, Psychology, and
  Disabilities Video Collection*
Fanlight Productions
47 Halifax Street
Boston, MA 02130
800-937-4113

Sopris West
Post Office Box 1809
Longmont, CO 80502
800-547-6747

Teachers College Press
1234 Amsterdam Avenue
New York, NY 10027
800-575-6566

Vineyard Video Productions
Post Office Box 370
West Tisbury, MA 02575
800-664-6119
VVP@capecod.net

Walker & Company
435 Hudson Street
New York, NY 10014
800-AT-WALKER; 212-727-8300

Windsor Corporation
1620 Seventh Street West
Saint Paul, MN 55102
800-321-7585

York Press
Post Office Box 504
Timonium, MD 21094
800-962-2763

Zaner-Bloser
2200 West Fifth Avenue
Post Office Box 16764
Columbus, OH 43216
800-421-3018

Teacher References

Adams, M.J. (1990). *Beginning to read: Thinking and learning about print.* Cambridge: The MIT Press.

Blachman, B.A. (Ed.). (1997). *Foundations of reading acquisition and dyslexia: Implications for early intervention.* Mahwah, NJ: Lawrence Erlbaum Associates.

Bowler, R. (Ed.). (1987). *Intimacy with language: A forgotten basic in teacher education.* Baltimore: The International Dyslexia Association.

Brady, S., & Moats, L.C. (1997). *Informed instruction for reading success: Foundations for teacher preparation.* Baltimore: The International Dyslexia Association.

Chall, J.S. (1983). *Stages of reading development.* New York: McGraw-Hill.

Chall, J.S. (1996). *Learning to read: The great debate* (3rd ed.). Orlando, FL: Harcourt Brace & Co.

Chase, C.H., Rosen, G.D., & Sherman, G.F. (Eds.). (1996). *Developmental dyslexia: Neural, cognitive, and genetic mechanisms.* Timonium, MD: York Press.

Clark, D.B., & Uhry, J.K. (1995). *Dyslexia: Theory and practice of remedial instruction* (2nd ed.). Timonium, MD: York Press.

Cox, A.R. (1983). Programming for teachers of dyslexics. *Annals of Dyslexia, 33,* 221–233.

Cox, A.R. (1992). *Foundations for literacy: Structures and techniques for multisensory teaching of basic written English language skills.* Cambridge, MA: Educators Publishing Service.

Ehri, L.C., & Williams, J.P. (1995). Learning to read and learning to teach reading are both developmental processes. In F.B. Murray (Ed.), *A knowledge base for teacher educators.* San Francisco: Jossey-Bass.

Ellis, W. (Ed.). (1991). *All language and the creation of literacy.* Baltimore: The International Dyslexia Association.

Hulme, C., & Joshi, R.M. (1998). *Reading and spelling: Development and disorders.* Mahwah, NJ: Lawrence Erlbaum Associates.

Hulme, C., & Snowling, M. (Eds.). (1997). *Dyslexia: Biology, cognition and intervention.* London: Whurr Publishers Ltd.

Learning disabilities: Preservice preparation of general and special education teachers. (1998, January–February). *LDA Newsbriefs,* 3–7.

Lehr, F., & Osborn, J. (Eds.). (1994). *Literacy for all: Issues in teaching and learning.* New York: The Guilford Press.

Lyon, G.R. (Ed.). (1994). *Frames of reference for the assessment of learning disabilities: New views on measurement issues.* Baltimore: Paul H. Brookes Publishing Co.

Lyon, G.R. (1995). Toward a definition of dyslexia. *Annals of Dyslexia, 45,* 3–27.

McIntyre, C., & Pickering, J.S. (1995). *Clinical studies of multisensory structured language education for students with dyslexia and related disorders.* Salem, OR: International Multisensory Structured Language Education Council.

Moats, L.C. (1994). The missing foundation in teacher education: Knowledge of the structure of spoken and written language. *Annals of Dyslexia, 44,* 81–102.

Orton, J.L. (1966). The Orton-Gillingham approach. In J. Money (Ed.), *The disabled reader: Education of the dyslexic child* (pp. 119–145). Baltimore: The John Hopkins University Press.

Pressley, M. (1998). *Reading instruction that works.* New York: The Guilford Press.

Shapiro, B.K., Accardo, P.J., & Capute, A.J. (Eds.). (1998). *Specific reading disability: A view of the spectrum.* Timonium, MD: York Press.

Snow, C.E., Burns, M.S., & Griffin, P. (1998). *Preventing reading difficulties in young children.* Washington, DC: National Academy Press.

Vail, P.L. (1991). *Common ground: Whole language and phonics working together.* Rosemont, NJ: Modern Learning Press.

World Wide Web Sites

Disabilities, Opportunities, Internetworking, and Technology (DO-IT)
weber.u.washington.edu/~doit
Promotes use of technology among academics and professionals with disabilities; offers on-line library access

Disability Resources, Inc.
www.geocities.com/~drm
Guide to other World Wide Web resources

Equal Access to Software and Information (EASI)
www.isc.rit.edu/~easi
Resources on access to technology

Federal Resources for Excellence in Education (FREE)
U.S. Department of Education
www.ed.gov/free
Resources for teaching and learning

LD Online
www.ldonline.org
Clearinghouse for learning disabilities

LD Resources
www.ldresources.com
Software for people with learning disabilities

One A.D.D. Place
www.oneaddplace.com
Checklists and other resources

Videotapes

Birsh, J.R. (Consulting Ed.), Potts, M., & Potts, R. (Producers). (1997a). *LD/LA: Learning disabilities/learning abilities: Videotape I. Introduction: Understanding learning disabilities through demonstration and description.* West Tisbury, MA: Vineyard Video Productions. (Available from Paul H. Brookes Publishing Co., Post Office Box 10624, Baltimore, MD 21285; 800-638-3775)

Birsh, J.R. (Consulting Ed.), Potts, M., & Potts, R. (Producers). (1997b). *LD/LA: Learning disabilities/learning abilities: Videotape II. The teaching: What students need.* West Tisbury, MA: Vineyard Video Productions. (Available from Paul H. Brookes Publishing Co., Post Office Box 10624, Baltimore, MD 21285; 800-638-3775)

Birsh, J.R. (Consulting Ed.), Potts, M., & Potts, R. (Producers). (1991). *Teaching the learning disabled: Study skills and learning strategies.* West Tisbury, MA: Vineyard Video Productions.

Dyslexia: A different kind of mind. (1997). Princeton, NJ: Films for the Humanities and Sciences. (Available from the publisher, Post Office Box 2053, Princeton, NJ 08543; 800-257-5126)

Dyslexia: Finding the answers. (1999). Baltimore: The International Dyslexia Association.

CHAPTER 1—MULTISENSORY INSTRUCTION

Professional Journals

American Educator
Annals of Dyslexia
Annals of Neurology
Brain and Language
Child Development
Cognition and Instruction
College English
Developmental Psychology
Dyslexia: An International Journal of Research and Practice
Educational Psychologist
Exceptional Children
JAMA: The Journal of the American Medical Association
Journal of Child Neurology
Journal of Child Psychology and Psychiatry and Allied Disciplines
Journal of Consulting and Clinical Psychology
Journal of Educational Psychology
Journal of Experimental Child Psychology
Journal of Experimental Psychology: Learning, Memory, and Cognition
Journal of General Psychology
Journal of Learning Disabilities
Journal of Psycholinguistic Research
Journal of Psychology
Journal of Special Education
Journal of Speech and Hearing Disorders
Learning Disabilities Quarterly
Learning Disabilities: A Multidisciplinary Journal
Learning Disabilities: Research and Practice
Nature

Neurology
New England Journal of Medicine
Perspectives
Reading and Writing: An Interdisciplinary Journal
Reading Research Quarterly
Remedial and Special Education
Science
Scientific Studies of Reading
TEACHING Exceptional Children
The Journal of Educational Research
The Reading Teacher
Topics in Language Disorders
Trends in Neurosciences

CHAPTER 2—DEVELOPMENT OF ORAL LANGUAGE AND ITS RELATIONSHIP TO LITERACY

Teacher References

Baron, N. (1992). *Growing up with language.* Reading, MA: Addison Wesley Longman.
Catts, H.W., & Kamhi, A.G. (1999). *Language and reading disabilities.* Needham Heights, MA: Allyn & Bacon.
Hulit, L., & Howard, M. (1993). *Born to talk: An introduction to speech and language development.* New York: Macmillan.
Owens, R. (1996). *Language development: An introduction* (3rd ed.). Columbus, OH: Charles E. Merrill.

Instructional Materials

Dandy Lion Publications
3563 Sueldo Street, Suite L
San Luis Obispo, CA 93401
800-776-8032
dandy@dandylionbooks.com
www.dandylionbooks.com

Janelle Publications
Post Office Box 811
DeKalb, IL 60115
800-888-8834
info@janellepublications.com
www.jannellepublications.com

The Speech Bin
1965 25th Avenue
Vero Beach, FL 32960
800-4-SPEECH

Thinking Publications
424 Galloway
Eau Claire, WI 54703
800-225-4769
www.ThinkingPublications.com

Professional Journals

Journal of Speech and Hearing Disorders
Language, Speech, and Hearing Services in the Schools
Topics in Language Disorders

CHAPTER 3—PHONOLOGICAL AWARENESS AND READING: RESEARCH, ACTIVITIES, AND INSTRUCTIONAL MATERIALS

Teacher References

Blachman, B.A., Ball, E.W., Black, R., & Tangel, D.M. (1994). Kindergarten teachers develop phoneme awareness in low income inner-city classrooms: Does it make a difference? *Reading and Writing: An Interdisciplinary Journal, 6,* 1–18.

Clark, D.B., & Uhry, J.K. (1995). *Dyslexia: Theory and practice of remedial instruction* (2nd ed.). Timonium, MD: York Press.

Cunningham, A.E. (1990). Explicit instruction in phonemic awareness. *Journal of Experimental Child Psychology, 50,* 429–444.

Griffith, P.L., & Olson, M.W. (1992). Phonemic awareness helps beginning readers break the code. *The Reading Teacher, 45,* 516–523.

Stanovich, K.E., Cunningham, A.E., & Cramer, B. (1984). Assessing phonological awareness in kindergarten children: Issues of task comparability. *Journal of Experimental Child Psychology, 38,* 175-190.

Torgesen, J.K. (1995). Phonological awareness: A critical factor in dyslexia. *Orton Emeritus Series.* Baltimore: The International Dyslexia Association.

Uhry, J.K. (1993). Predicting reading from phonological awareness and classroom print: An early reading screening. *Educational Assessment, 1,* 349–368.

Yopp, H.K. (1995). A test for assessing phonemic awareness in young children. *The Reading Teacher, 49,* 20–29.

Curricula, Guides, and Activities

Bear, D.R., Invernizzi, M., Templeton, S., & Johnston, F. (1996). *Words their way: Word study for phonics, vocabulary, and spelling instruction.* Upper Saddle River, NJ: Prentice-Hall.

Blachman, B.A., Ball, E.W., Black, R., & Tangel, D.M. (2000). *Road to the code: A phonological awareness program for young children.* Baltimore: Paul H. Brookes Publishing Co.

Gentry, J.R. (1982). An analysis of developmental spelling in GYNS AT WRK. *The Reading Teacher, 36,* 192–200.

Goldsworthy, C.L. (1998). *Sourcebook of phonological awareness activities: Children's classic literature.* San Diego: Singular Publishing Group.

Griffith, P.L., & Olson, M.W. (1992). Phonemic awareness helps beginning readers break the code. *The Reading Teacher, 45,* 516–523.

Opitz, M.F. (1998). Children's books to develop phonemic awareness—for you and parents too! *The Reading Teacher, 51,* 526–528.

Yopp, H.K. (1992). Developing phonological awareness in young children. *The Reading Teacher, 45,* 696–703.

Yopp, H.K. (1995). Read-aloud books for developing phonemic awareness: An annotated bibliography. *The Reading Teacher, 48,* 538–542.

Instructional Materials

Adams, M.J., Bereiter, C., Hirshberg, J., Anderson, V., & Case, R. (1995). *Framework for effective teaching: Sounds and letters* (Teacher's guide). New York: McGraw-Hill.

Adams, M.J., Foorman, B.R., Lundberg, I., & Beeler, T. (1998). *Phonemic awareness in young children: A classroom curriculum.* Baltimore: Paul H. Brookes Publishing Co.

Byrne, B., & Fielding-Barnsley, R. (1991). *Sound foundations.* Artamon, New South Wales, Australia: Leyden Educational Publishers. (Available from the publisher, 36 Whiting Street, Artamon, New South Wales 2064, AUSTRALIA)

Carreker, S. (1992). *Reading readiness.* Bellaire, TX: Neuhaus Education Center.

Catts, H.W., & Vartiainen, T. (1993). *Sounds abound: Listening, rhyming, and reading.* East Moline, IL: LinguiSystems.

Conocimiento fonémico [Trans. and adapted by Sánchez Hart Consultants from *Phoneme awareness* by M.T. Smith, 1997]. Forney, TX: MTS Publications.

Lindamood auditory conceptualization complete kit. (1971). Austin, TX: PRO-ED.

Lindamood, P., & Lindamood, P. (1998). *Lindamood phoneme sequencing program for reading, spelling, and speech: Teacher's manual for the classroom and clinic* (LiPS). Austin, TX: PRO-ED.

Smith, M.T. (1999). *Phoneme awareness: Assessment, instruction, practice.* Forney, TX: MTS Publications.

Torgesen, J.K., & Bryant, B. (1993). *Phonological awareness training for reading* [Kit]. Austin, TX: PRO-ED.

Torgesen, J.K., & Bryant, B. (1994). *Test of Phonological Awareness* (TOPA) [Complete kit]. Austin, TX: PRO-ED.

Assessment Tools

Denckla, M.B., & Rudel, R.G. (1976). *Rapid Automatized Naming Test.* Baltimore: Kennedy Krieger Institute.

Lindamood, C.H., & Lindamood, P.C. (1971). *The LAC Test: Lindamood Auditory Conceptualization Test.* Austin, TX: PRO-ED.

Robertson, C., & Salter, W. (1997). *The Phonological Awareness Test.* East Moline, IL: LinguiSystems.

Sawyer, D.J. (1987). *Test of Awareness of Language Segments.* Austin, TX: PRO-ED.

Smith, M.T. (1999). Phoneme awareness: Assessment, instruction, practice. Forney, TX: MTS Publications.

Stanovich, K.E., Cunningham, A.E., & Cramer, B. (1984). Assessing phonological awareness in kindergarten children: Issues of task comparability. *Journal of Experimental Child Psychology, 38,* 175–190.

Torgesen, J.K., & Bryant, B.R. (1994). *Test of Phonological Awareness* (TOPA). Austin, TX: PRO-ED.

Wagner, R., Torgesen, J.K., & Rashotte, C. (1999). *Comprehensive Test of Phonological Processing.* Austin, TX: PRO-ED.

Yopp, H.K. (1995). A test for assessing phonemic awareness in young children. *The Reading Teacher, 49,* 20–29.

Videotapes

Birsh, J.R. (Consulting Ed.), Potts, M., & Potts, R. (Producers). (1997). *LD/LA: Learning disabilities/learning abilities* (Videotapes I–IV). West Tisbury, MA: Vineyard Video Productions. (Available from Paul H. Brookes Publishing Co., Post Office Box 10624, Baltimore, MD 21285; 800-638-3775)

Software

Erickson, G.C., Foster, K.C., Forster, D.F., Torgesen, J.K., & Packer, S. (1992). *Daisyquest.* Scotts Valley, CA: Great Wave Software.

Erickson, G.C., Foster, K.C., Forster, D.F., Torgesen, J.K., & Packer, S. (1993). *Daisy's castle*. Scotts Valley, CA: Great Wave Software.

Resources for Parents[1]

Adams, M.J., Foorman, B.R., Lundberg, I., & Beeler, T. (1997a). Appendix F: Annotated bibliography of rhyming stories. In *Phonemic awareness in young children: A classroom curriculum* (pp. 159–169). Baltimore: Paul H. Brookes Publishing Co.

Adams, M.J., Foorman, B.R., Lundberg, I., & Beeler, T. (1997b). Appendix G: Poems, fingerplays, jingles, and chants. In *Phonemic awareness in young children: A classroom curriculum* (pp. 171–175). Baltimore: Paul H. Brookes Publishing Co.

Brown, M.W. (1983). *Four fur feet*. New York: Bantam Doubleday Dell.

Buller, J., & Schade, S. (1989). *I love you, good night*. New York: Simon & Schuster.

Carter, D. (1990). *More bugs in boxes*. New York: Simon & Schuster.

de Regniers, B., Moore, E., White, M., & Carr, J. (1988). *Sing a song of popcorn*. New York: Scholastic.

Deming, A.G. (1994). *Who is tapping at my window?* New York: Penguin USA.

Ehlert, L. (1989). *Eating the alphabet: Fruits and vegetables from A to Z*. Orlando, FL: Harcourt Brace & Co.

Emberley, B. (1992). *One wide river to cross*. Boston: Little, Brown.

Geraghty, P. (1992). *Stop that noise!* New York: Crown.

Gordon, J. (1991). *Six sleepy sheep*. New York: Puffin Books.

Hague, K. (1984). *Alphabears*. New York: Henry Holt.

Krauss, R. (1985). *I can fly*. New York: Young Scott Books.

Kuskin, K. (1990). *Roar and more*. New York: HarperCollins.

Lewison, W. (1992). *Buzz said the bee*. New York: Scholastic.

Martin, B. (1989). *Chicka chicka boom boom*. New York: Simon & Schuster.

Marzollo, J. (1989). *The teddy bear book*. New York: Dial.

Obligado, L. (1983). *Faint frogs feeling feverish and other terrifically tantalizing tongue twisters*. New York: Viking.

Ochs, C.P. (1991). *Moose on the loose*. Minneapolis, MN: Carolrhoda Books.

Otto, C. (1991). *Dinosaur chase*. New York: HarperCollins.

Parry, C. (1991). *Zoomerang-a-boomerang: Poems to make your belly laugh*. New York: Puffin Books.

Patz, N. (1983). *Moses supposes his toeses are roses*. Orlando, FL: Harcourt Brace & Co.

Pomerantz, C. (1993). *If I had a paka*. New York: Mulberry.

Prelutsky, J. (1982). *The baby Uggs are hatching*. New York: Mulberry.

Prelutsky, J. (1989). *Poems of A. Nonny Mouse*. New York: Alfred A. Knopf.

Raffi, D. (1989). *Down by the bay: Raffi songs to read*. New York: Crown.

Sendak, M. (1990). *Alligators all around: An alphabet*. New York: HarperCollins.

Seuss, Dr. (1963). *Dr. Seuss's ABC*. New York: Random House.

Seuss, Dr. (1965). *Fox in socks*. New York: Random House.

Seuss, Dr. (1974). *There's a wocket in my pocket*. New York: Random House.

Shaw, N. (1989). *Sheep on a ship*. Boston: Houghton Mifflin.

---

[1]With the exception of Adams, Foorman, Lundberg, and Beeler (1997), these parent resources are adapted from Yopp, H.K. (1995). Read-aloud books for developing phonemic awareness: An annotated bibliography. *The Reading Teacher, 48*(6), 538–542. Copyright © International Reading Association; adapted by permission.

Showers, P. (1991). *The listening walk*. New York: HarperCollins.

Silverstein, S. (1964). *A giraffe and a half*. New York: HarperCollins.

Staines, B. (1989). *All God's critters got a place in the choir*. New York: Penguin.

Van Allsburg, C. (1987). *The alphabet theatre proudly presents the Z was zapped: A play in twenty-six acts*. Boston: Houghton Mifflin.

Winthrop, E. (1986). *Shoes*. New York: HarperCollins.

CHAPTER 4—ALPHABET KNOWLEDGE: LETTER RECOGNITION, NAMING, AND SEQUENCING

Teacher References

Balmuth, M. (1982). *The roots of phonics*. New York: Teachers College Press.

Dowdell, D. (1965). *Secrets of the ABC's*. Fayetteville, GA: Oddo Publishing.

Fisher, L.E. (1978). *Alphabet art: Thirteen ABC's from around the world*. New York: Macmillan.

Logan, R.K. (1986). *The alphabetic effect*. New York: William Morrow and Company, Inc.

Museum of the Alphabet. (1990). *The alphabet makers*. Huntington Beach, CA: Summer Institute of Linguistics.

Ogg, O. (1971). *The 26 letters*. New York: Thomas Y. Crowell. (Out of print but still available in libraries).

Patton, S.J. (1989). *Alphabetic: A history of our alphabet*. Tucson, AZ: Zephyr Press.

Curricula, Guides, and Activities

Cox, A.R. (1992). *Foundations for literacy: Structures and techniques for multisensory teaching of basic written English language skills*. Cambridge, MA: Educators Publishing Service.

Gillingham, A., & Stillman, B.W. (1997). The *Gillingham manual: Remedial training for children with specific disability in reading, spelling, and penmanship* (8th ed.). Cambridge, MA: Educators Publishing Service.

Hogan, E.A., & Smith, M.T. (1987). *Alphabet and dictionary skills guide*. Cambridge, MA: Educators Publishing Service.

Instructional Materials

Alphabet Strips and Three-Dimensional Alphabet Letters
Abecedarian, 9311 Claridge Drive, Houston, TX 77031
Set of 26 plastic uppercase block letters (1¼", nonmagnetic, blue)
Set of 26 plastic lowercase letters (1¼", nonmagnetic, red)
Set of 33 plastic lowercase letters for Spanish (1¼", nonmagnetic, green)
Plastic classroom-size uppercase alphabet strip (3" × 48")
Plastic individual uppercase alphabet strip (2" × 17½")

Dominie Press, Inc., 1949 Kellogg Avenue, Carlsbad, CA 92008; 800-232-4570; FAX: 619-431-8777
Set of 36 plastic uppercase block letters (1¼", magnetic)
Set of 36 plastic lowercase block letters (1¼", magnetic)

Spanish edition of uppercase letters
Spanish edition of lowercase letters

Educators Publishing Service, Inc., 31 Smith Place, Cambridge, MA 02138;
  800-225-5750
Set of plastic uppercase block letters (magnetic)
Laminated individual alphabet strip (2½" × 22½")

MTS Publications, Post Office Box 2, Forney, TX 75126; 972-564-5005
Plastic alphabet strips with uppercase block letters on the top of the strip and
  lowercase block letters on the bottom (2½" × 16")
Plastic alphabet mat with uppercase block letters in an arc (11" × 17")

Other materials available from Educators Publishing Service, Inc.
Advanced Reading Deck (grapheme[s] on cards)
Dictionary Technique (Skeleton Dictionary, four envelopes of words to be
  alphabetized, and a teacher's key)
Initial Reading Deck (picture[s] and grapheme[s] on cards)
Missing Letter Deck (uppercase block letters on cards)
Phonics Drill Cards (available with or without pictures)
Skeleton Dictionary (guide-word practice dictionary)
Teacher's Hand Pack for Classroom Use (letters of the alphabet, phonograms,
  digraphs, and letter combinations)

CHAPTER 5—A SHORT HISTORY OF THE ENGLISH LANGUAGE

Teacher References

Adams, M.J. (1990). *Beginning to read: Thinking and learning about print.* Cambridge:
  The MIT Press.
Balmuth, M. (1992). *The roots of phonics.* Timonium, MD: York Press.
Bryson, B. (1990). *The mother tongue: English and how it got that way.* New York: William
  Morrow.
Chall, J.S. (1996). *Learning to read: The great debate* (3rd ed.). Orlando, FL: Harcourt
  Brace & Co.
Chall, J.S., & Popp, H.M. (1996). *Teaching and assessing phonics.* Cambridge, MA:
  Educators Publishing Service.
Claiborne, R. (1983). *Our marvelous native tongue.* New York: Times Books.
Jesperson, O. (1982). *Growth and structure of the English language* (10th ed.).
  Chicago: University of Chicago Press.
Male, M. (1996). *Technology for inclusion: Meeting the special needs of all students.*
  (3rd ed.). Needham Heights, MA: Allyn & Bacon.
Martin, H.-J. (1994). *The history and power of writing.* Chicago: University of Chicago Press.
McCrum, R., Cran, W., & MacNeil, R. (1986). *The story of English.* New York: Viking.
Pinker, S. (1994). *The language instinct: How the mind creates language.* New York:
  William Morrow.

Curricula, Guides, and Instructional Materials

Adams, M.J., Foorman, B.R., Lundberg, I., & Beeler, T. (1998). *Phonemic awareness in
  young children: A classroom curriculum.* Baltimore: Paul H. Brookes Publishing Co.

Bear, D.R., Invernizzi, M., Templeton, S., & Johnston, F. (1996). *Words their way: Word study for phonics, vocabulary, and spelling instruction.* Upper Saddle River, NJ: Prentice-Hall.

Ehrlich, I. (1972). *Instant vocabulary.* New York: Pocket Books.

Fifer, N., & Flowers, N. (1989). *Vocabulary from classical roots.* Cambridge, MA: Educators Publishing Service.

Fry, E.B., Polk, J.K., & Fountoukidis, D.L. (1996). *The reading teacher's new book of lists.* (3rd ed.). Upper Saddle River, NJ: Prentice-Hall.

Gillingham, A., & Stillman, B.W. (1997). *The Gillingham manual: Remedial training for children with specific disability in reading, spelling and penmanship* (8th ed.). Cambridge, MA: Educators Publishing Service.

Henry, M.K. (1990). *WORDS: Integrated decoding and spelling instruction based on word origin and structure.* Austin, TX: PRO-ED.

Henry, M.K., & Redding, N.C. (1996). *Patterns for success in reading and spelling: A multisensory approach to teaching phonics and word analysis.* Austin, TX: PRO-ED.

Kleiber, M.H. (1993). *Specific language training: A systematic study of Latin and Greek roots. An Orton-Gillingham curriculum for adolescents.* New York: Decatur Enterprises.

Marcellaro, E.G., & Ostrovsky, G.R. (1998). *Verbal vibes with Latin.* Sacramento: Lumen Publications.

Moore, B., & Moore, M. (1997). *NTC's dictionary of Latin and Greek origins.* Chicago: NTC Publishing Group.

Robinson, S.R. (1989). *Origins: Vol. 1. Bringing words to life.* New York: Teachers and Writers Collaborative.

Robinson, S.R., & McAuliffe, L. (1989). *Origins: Vol. 2. The word families.* New York: Teachers and Writers Collaborative.

Steere, A., Peck, C.Z., & Kahn, L. (1971). *Solving language difficulties.* Cambridge, MA: Educators Publishing Service.

Software

Sound American: Pronunciation guide for American English with directions in numerous languages [CD-ROM]. San Luis Obispo, CA: Gander Publishing.

Resources for Parents

Beal, G. (1992). *Book of words: A–Z guide to quotations, proverbs, origins, usage, and idioms.* New York: Kingfisher Books.

Brook, D. (1998). *The journey of English.* New York: Clarion Books.

CHAPTER 6—TEACHING READING: ACCURATE DECODING AND FLUENCY

Teacher References

Adams, M.J. (1990). *Beginning to read: Thinking and learning about print.* Cambridge: The MIT Press.

Adams, M.J. (1994). Phonics and beginning reading instruction. In F. Lehr & S. Osborn (Eds.), *Reading, language, and literacy* (pp. 3–23). Mahwah, NJ: Lawrence Erlbaum Associates.

Adams, M.J. (1995, Summer). Resolving the "great debate." *American Educator, 7–20.*

Bear, D.R., Invernizzi, M., Templeton, S., & Johnston, F. (1996). *Words their way: Word study for phonics, vocabulary, and spelling instruction.* Upper Saddle River, NJ: Prentice-Hall.

Beck, I.L., & Juel, C. (1995, Summer). The role of decoding in learning to read. *American Educator, 8–42.*

Blachman, B.A. (1991). Getting ready to read: Learning how to print maps to speech. In J.F. Kavanagh (Ed.), *The language continuum: From infancy to literacy* (pp. 41–62). Timonium, MD: York Press.

Chall, J.S. (1983). *Stages of reading development.* New York: McGraw-Hill.

Chall, J.S. (1992). The new reading debates: Evidence from science, art, and ideology. *Teachers College Record, 94,* 315–328.

Chall, J.S., & Popp, H.M. (1996). *Teaching and assessing phonics.* Cambridge, MA: Educators Publishing Service.

Cox, A.R. (1992). *Foundations for literacy: Structures and techniques for multisensory teaching of basic written English language skills.* Cambridge, MA: Educators Publishing Service.

Fry, E.B., Polk, J.K., & Fountoukidis, D.L. (1996). *The reading teacher's new book of lists* (3rd ed.). Upper Saddle River, NJ: Prentice-Hall.

Honig, B. (1996). *Teaching our children to read: The role of skills in a comprehensive reading program.* Thousand Oaks, CA: Corwin Press.

Honig, B., Diamond, L., & Nathan, R. (1998a). *Reading research anthology.* Novato, CA: Academic Therapy Publications.

Honig, B., Diamond, L., & Nathan, R. (1998b). *Teaching reading sourcebook.* Novato, CA: Academic Therapy Publications.

Liberman, I.Y., & Liberman, A.M. (1990). Whole language vs. code emphasis: Underlying assumptions and their implications for reading instruction. *Annals of Dyslexia, 40,* 51–89.

Liberman, I.Y., Rubin, H., Duques, S.L., & Carlisle, J. (1985). Linguistic skills and spelling proficiency in kindergartners and adult poor spellers. In D.B. Gray & J. Kavanagh (Eds.), *Biobehavioral measures of dyslexia* (pp. 163–176). Timonium, MD: York Press.

Mather, N. (1992). Whole language reading instruction for students with learning disabilities: Caught in the crossfire. *Learning Disabilities Research and Practice, 7,* 87–95.

Richardson, S. (1991). The alphabetic principle: Roots of literacy. In W. Ellis (Ed.), *All language and the creation of literacy* (pp. 57–62). Baltimore: The International Dyslexia Association.

Snow, C.E., Burns, M.S., & Griffin, P. (Eds.). (1998). *Preventing reading difficulties in young children.* Washington, DC: National Academy Press.

Vail, P.L. (1991). *Common ground: Whole language and phonics working together.* Rosemont, NJ: Modern Learning Press.

Williams, J. (1991). The meaning of a phonics base for reading instruction. In W. Ellis (Ed.), *All language and the creation of literacy* (pp. 9–19). Baltimore: The International Dyslexia Association.

Multisensory Structured Curricula

Bertin, P., & Perlman, E. (1980). *Preventing academic failure.* Cambridge, MA: Educators Publishing Service.

Carreker, S. (1999). *Corrective reading.* Blacklick, OH: SRA/McGraw-Hill.

Cox, A.R. (1992). *Foundations for literacy: Structures and techniques for multisensory teaching of basic written English language skills.* Cambridge, MA: Educators Publishing Service.

Dillon, S. (1987). *Sounds in syllables.* Albuquerque, NM: S.I.S. Publishing Co.

duBard, N.E., & Martin, M.K. (1994). *Teaching language deficient children: Theory and application of the Association Method for multisensory teaching* (Rev. ed.). Cambridge, MA: Educators Publishing Service.

Enfield, M.L., & Greene, V. *Project read.* Bloomington, MN: Language Circle Enterprise.

Gillingham, A., & Stillman, B.W. (1997). *The Gillingham manual: Remedial training for students with specific disability in reading, spelling, and penmanship* (8th ed.). Cambridge, MA: Educators Publishing Service.

Greene, J.F. (1995). *Language! A reading, writing, and spelling curriculum for at-risk and ESL students* (grades 4–12). Longmont, CO: Sopris West.

Henry, M.K., & Redding, N.C. (1996). *Patterns for success in reading and spelling: A multisensory approach to teaching phonics and word analysis.* Austin, TX: PRO-ED.

Herman, R.D. (1993). *The Herman Method for reversing reading failure.* Sherman Oaks, CA: The Herman Method Institute.

Jolly phonics. Chigwell, Essex, United Kingdom: Jolly Learning. (Available from the publisher, Tailours House, High Road, Chigwell, Essex IG7 6DL, UNITED KINGDOM; info@jollylearning.co.uk)

Knight, J.R. (1986). *Starting over: A combined teaching manual and student textbook for reading, writing, spelling, vocabulary, and handwriting.* Cambridge, MA: Educators Publishing Service.

LEAD Educational Resources. *LEAD program: Logical encoding and decoding.* Bridgewater, CT: Author. (Available from the author, 144 Main Street North, Bridgewater, CT 06752; 860-355-1516)

Lindamood, P., & Lindamood, P. (1998). *Lindamood phoneme sequencing program for reading, spelling, and speech: Teacher's manual for the classroom and clinic* (LiPS; 3rd ed.). Austin: TX: PRO-ED.

Pickering, J.S. *Sequential English education* (SEE). Dallas, TX: The June Shelton School.

Reading mastery. Blacklick, OH: SRA/McGraw-Hill.

Simmons, L. (1997). *Saxon phonics.* Norman, OK: Saxon Publishers.

Slingerland, B.H., & Aho, M. (1994–1996). *A multi-sensory approach to language arts for specific language disability children* (Rev. ed., Vols. 1–3). Cambridge, MA: Educators Publishing Service.

Smith, M.T. (1996). *MTA reading and spelling program* (Kits 1–7). Cambridge, MA: Educators Publishing Service.

Smith, M.T. (1996). *Multisensory teaching system for reading* (MTS). Forney, TX: MTS Publications.

Sonday, A. (1997). *The Sonday system: Learning to read* [Learning plan and word books]. Cambridge, MA: Educators Publishing Service.

Spalding, R.B., with Spalding, W.T. (1990). *The writing road to reading: The Spalding Method of phonics for teaching speech, writing, and reading* (4th rev. ed.). New York: Quill.

Texas Scottish Rite Hospital for Children. *Dyslexia training program: Teacher's guides and student's books.* Cambridge, MA: Educators Publishing Service.

Texas Scottish Rite Hospital for Children. *Texas Scottish Rite Hospital literacy program: Program guides and student books* (Vols. 1–4) Cambridge, MA: Educators Publishing Service.

The Calfee Project: Project READ. *Project READ.* Stanford, CA: Stanford University.

Traub, N., with Bloom, F. *Recipe for reading: A structured approach to linguistics.* Cambridge, MA: Educators Publishing Service.

Wickerham, C.W., & Allen, K.A. (1993). *Multisensory reading and spelling* (Books 1–4). The Woodlands, TX: Apple Core Press. (Available from the publisher, 11 Rosethorn Place, The Woodlands, TX 77381; 713-367-3715)

Wilson, B.A. (1988). *Wilson reading system: Teacher's guide and student material.* Millbury, MA: Wilson Language Training. (Available from the publisher, www.WilsonLanguage.com)

Instructional Materials

Biddle, M.L., & Raines, B.J. (1980). *Situation learning: Teacher guides and student workbooks* (Vols. 1–3). Cambridge, MA: Educators Publishing Service.

Erwin, P. (1992). *Winston grammar cards.* San Diego: Farnsworth Books.

Gillingham, A., & Stillman, B.W. (1959). *Phonetic word cards: Remedial training for children with specific disability in reading, spelling, and penmanship.* Cambridge, MA: Educators Publishing Service.

Greene, J.F., & Woods, J.F. (1992). *J & J language readers for reading/language delayed and ESL/EFL students* (Levels I–III). Longmont, CO: Sopris West.

Hall, N., & Price, R. (1993). *Explode the code.* Cambridge, MA: Educators Publishing Service.

Henry, M.K. (1990). *WORDS: Integrated decoding and spelling instruction based on word origin and structure.* Austin, TX: PRO-ED.

Henry, M.K., & Redding, N.C. (1996). *Patterns for success in reading and spelling: A multisensory approach to teaching phonics and word analysis.* Austin, TX: PRO-ED.

McCracken pocket charts. Seattle, WA: School Art Materials. (Available from the publisher, Post Office Box 94082, Seattle, WA 98124; 800-752-4359)

Montgomery, D.B. (1975). *Angling for words: The teacher's line.* Novato, CA: Academic Therapy Publications.

Neuhaus Education Center. *Procedure charts: LLP, WOW, SOS, Dict, Demo, Copy.* Bellaire, TX: Author.

Region XIII TAAS/Education Service Center. (1998). *Reading activities supporting the Texas reading initiative* [Instant word recognition, six types of syllables, two-syllable word puzzles, and multisyllabic word puzzles]. Austin, TX: Author.

Sands, E.M. *SANDS reading cards* [Picture sound cards, letter sound cards, audiocassette]. New York: Davick House. (Available from the publisher, Post Office Box 150136, Kew Gardens, NY 11415)

Smith, M.T. *MTA reading and spelling program* (Kits 1–7). Cambridge, MA: Educators Publishing Service.

Smith, M.T. (1987–1993). *MTA reader series.* Cambridge, MA: Educators Publishing Service:
Brubaker, S., & Jackson, N. (1988a). *Tracks.*
Brubaker, S., & Jackson, N. (1988b). *Wishes.*
Brubaker, S., Crouch, J., & Jackson, N. (1989). *Hurdles.*
Jackson, N. (1987). *Pals.*
Sokoloski, B. (1993). *Kids and critters.*

Smith, M.T. (1996). *Multisensory teaching system for reading.* Forney, TX: MTS Publications.

Texas Scottish Rite Hospital for Children. *Dyslexia training program: Teacher's guides and student's books* (Vols. 1–4). Cambridge, MA: Educators Publishing Service.

Texas Scottish Rite Hospital for Children. *Texas Scottish Rite Hospital literacy program: Program guides and student books* (Vols. 1–4) Cambridge, MA: Educators Publishing Service.

Wilson, R.Q., & Rudolf, M.K. (1986). *Merrill linguistic reading program* (4th ed.). New York: Merrill.

Videotapes

Beckham, P.B., & Biddle, M.L. (1988). *Dyslexia training program videotapes.* Dallas: Texas Scottish Rite Hospital, Child Development Division.

Birsh, J.R. (Consulting Ed.), Potts, M., & Potts, R. (Producers). (1997a). *LD/LA: Learning disabilities/learning abilities: Videotape II. The teaching: What students need.* West Tisbury, MA: Vineyard Video Productions.

Birsh, J.R. (Consulting Ed.), Potts, M., & Potts, R. (Producers). (1997b). *LD/LA: Learning disabilities/learning abilities: Videotape III. Reading is not a natural skill: Teaching children the code to unlock language.* West Tisbury, MA: Vineyard Video Productions. (Available from Paul H. Brookes Publishing Co., Post Office Box 10624, Baltimore, MD 21285; 800-638-3775)

Keagy, J., & Sanders, A. (1991). *Literacy program videotapes.* Dallas: Texas Scottish Rite Hospital, Child Development Division.

Software

Cambridge Development Laboratory, Inc., 86 West Street, Waltham, MA 024551; 800-637-0047.

Dyslexia training program supplement. Richardson, TX: SofDesign International.

Kurzweil 3000 [Provides visual and auditory feedback with printed material]. Waltham, MA: Kurzweil Educational Systems. (Available from Kurzweil Educational Systems, 411 Waverley Oaks Road, Waltham, MA 02452; 800-894-5374; www.lhsl.com/education)

Lorien textHelp! [Vocabulary support package]. Antrim, Northern Ireland: Lorien Systems. (Available from the Lorien Systems, Enkalon Business Centre, 25 Randalstown Road, Antrim BT41 4LJ, NORTHERN IRELAND; 01849 428105; justine@loriens.com; www.texthelp.com)

ULTimate reader [Speaks back electronic printed matter]. Wauconda, IL: Don Johnston, Inc. (Available from Don Johnston, Inc., Post Office Box 639, Wauconda, IL 60084; 800-999-4660; info@donjohnston.com; www.donjohnston.com)

World Wide Web Sites

Center for the Improvement of Early Reading Achievement
www.ciera.org
Practical applications of research cited

Junior Great Books
www.greatbooks.org
Reference for parents, professionals, and children

Resources and Organizations for Parents

Hall, S.L., & Moats, L.C. (1999). *Straight talk about reading: How parents can make a difference during the early years.* Chicago: Contemporary Books.

International Reading Association (IRA)
Public Information Office
800 Barksdale Road
Post Office Box 8139
Newark, DE 19714
302-731-1600
www.reading.org

The International Dyslexia Association (IDA)
8600 LaSalle Road
Chester Building, Suite 382
Baltimore, MD 21286
800-ABC-D123
info@interdys.org
www.interdys.org

CHAPTER 7—TEACHING COMPREHENSION FROM A MULTISENSORY PERSPECTIVE

Teacher References

Bell, N. (1986). *Visualizing and verbalizing for language comprehension and thinking.* Paso Robles, CA: Academy of Reading Publications.

Carreker, S. (1993). *Multisensory grammar and written composition.* Houston, TX: S.S. Systems. (Available from the publisher, 5434 Darnell Street, Houston, TX 77096)

Cox, A.R. (1992). *Foundations for literacy: Structures and techniques for multisensory teaching of basic written English language skills.* Cambridge, MA: Educators Publishing Service.

Greene, V.E., & Enfield, M.L. (1989). *Framing your thoughts: The basic structure of written expression.* Bloomington, MN: Language Circle Enterprise.

Hagood, B.F. (1997, March–April). Reading and writing with help from story grammar. *Teaching Exceptional Children,* 8–14.

Smith, M.T. (1997). *Phoneme awareness.* Forney, TX: MTS Publications.

Smith, M.T., & Hogan, E.A. (1991). *MTA: Teaching a process for comprehension and composition.* Forney, TX: MTS Publications.

Curricula, Guides, and Activities

Carreker, S. (1992). *Language enrichment.* Bellaire, TX: Neuhaus Education Center.

Greene, J.F. (1995). *Language! A reading, writing, and spelling curriculum for at-risk and ESL students* (Grades 4–12). Longmont, CO: Sopris West.

Smith, M.T. (1987a). *MTA for reading and spelling* (Kits 1–7). Cambridge, MA: Educators Publishing Service.

Smith, M.T. (1987b). *MTA: Teaching a process for comprehension and composition.* Forney, TX: MTS Publications.

Instructional Materials

Bell, N., & Lindamood, P. (1993). *READ ALOUD books: The adventures of Gunny and Ivan* (Level I). San Luis Obispo, CA: Gander Publishing.

Bell, N., & Lindamood, P. (1997). *READ ALOUD books: The adventures of Gunny and Ivan* (Level II). San Luis Obispo, CA: Gander Publishing.

Bell, N., & Lindamood, P. (1993). *Vanilla vocabulary: A visualized/verbalized vocabulary program* (Level I). San Luis Obispo, CA: Gander Publishing.

Bell, N., & Lindamood, P. (1997). *Vanilla vocabulary: A visualized/verbalized vocabulary program* (Level II). San Luis Obispo, CA: Gander Publishing.

Bush, C.S. (1989). *Language remediation and expansion: 150 skill-building reference lists.* Austin, TX: Communication Skill Builders.

Carlisle, J. (1982–1983). *Reasoning and reading* (Levels 1 & 2). Cambridge, MA: Educators Publishing Service.

Carlisle, J. (1987). *Beginning paragraph meaning: Beginning reasoning and reading.* Cambridge, MA: Educators Publishing Service.

Ervin, J. (1993). *Early reading comprehension in varied subject area and reading comprehension in varied subject matter* (Books A & B). Cambridge, MA: Educators Publishing Service.

Erwin, P. (1992). *Winston grammar cards.* San Diego: Farnsworth Books.

Erwin, P. (1992). *The Winston grammar program.* Cambridge, MA: Educators Publishing Service.

Evans, A.J. (1979). *Reading and thinking: Exercises for developing reading comprehension and critical thinking skills* (Books I & II). New York: Teachers College Press.

Fadiman, C. (1985). *The world of treasury of children's literature* (Vols. 1–3). Boston: Little, Brown.

Fifer, N., & Flowers, N. (1990). *Vocabulary from classical roots* (Books A–C). Cambridge, MA: Educators Publishing Service.

Fry, E.B., Polk, J.K, & Fountoukidis, D.L. (1996). *The reading teacher's new book of lists* (3rd ed.). Upper Saddle River, NJ: Prentice-Hall.

Greene, V.E., & Enfield, M.L. (1987a). *Report form comprehension guide.* Bloomington, MN: Language Circle Enterprise.

Greene, V.E., & Enfield, M.L. (1987b). *Story form comprehension guide.* Bloomington, MN: Language Circle Enterprise.

Gwynne, F. (1970). *The king who rained.* Upper Saddle River, NJ: Prentice-Hall.

Gwynne, F. (1976) *A chocolate moose for dinner.* Upper Saddle River, NJ: Prentice-Hall.

Gwynne, F. (1980). *The sixteen hand horse.* Upper Saddle River, NJ: Prentice-Hall.

Hall, K.L. (1996). *Reading stories for comprehension success: 45 high-interest lessons that make kids think* (Grades 1–3 & Grades 4–6). West Nyack, NY: Center for Applied Research in Education.

Johnson, K., & Bayrd, P. (1983–1988). *Megawords: Multisyllabic words for reading, spelling and vocabulary* (Books 1–8). Cambridge, MA: Educators Publishing Service.

McCall, W.A., & Crabbs-Schroeder, L. (1979). *Standard test lessons in reading* (Books A–F). New York: Teachers College Press.

Panman, S., & Panman, R. (1986). *Writing guides: Step-by-step individualized instruction.* New Paltz, NY: Active Learning Corporation.

Reading activities supporting the Texas reading initiative [Foam squares for use with Multisensory grammar and written composition by S. Carreker, 1993]. Austin, TX: Region XIII TAAS/Education Service Center.

Reading for comprehension (Levels AAA–I). Elizabethtown, PA: Continental Press.

Smith, M.T., & Hogan, E.A. (1991). MTA: *Teaching a process for comprehension and composition.* Forney, TX: EDMAR Educational Associates.

Verbal expression (Vols. I & II). (1991). Bellaire, TX: Neuhaus Education Center.

CHAPTER 8—TEACHING SPELLING

Teacher References

Cox, A.R. (1992). *Foundations for literacy: Structures and techniques for multisensory teaching of basic written English language skills.* Cambridge, MA: Educators Publishing Service.

Moats, L.C. (1995). *Spelling: Development, disability, and instruction.* Timonium, MD: York Press.

Curricula, Guides, and Activities

Carreker, S. (1992). *Scientific spelling* (Grades 1–8). Bellaire, TX: Neuhaus Education Center.

Carreker, S. (1999). *Basic language skills.* Bellaire, TX: Neuhaus Education Center.

Cox, A.R. (1992). *Alphabetic phonics.* Cambridge, MA: Educators Publishing Service.

Enfield, M.L., & Greene, V. *Project Read.* Bloomington, MN: Language Circle Enterprise.

Gillingham, A., & Stillman, B.W. (1997). *The Gillingham manual: Remedial training for children with specific disability in reading, spelling, and penmanship* (8th ed.). Cambridge, MA: Educators Publishing Service.

Hall, N.M. *Spellwell.* Cambridge, MA: Educators Publishing Service.

Henry, M.K. (1990). *WORDS: Integrated decoding and spelling instruction based on word origin and structure.* Austin, TX: PRO-ED.

Rak, E.T. *The spell of the word* (Grades 7–Adult). Cambridge, MA: Educators Publishing Service.

Rome, P.D., & Osman, J.S. *The language tool kit.* Cambridge, MA: Educators Publishing Service.

Rudginsky, L.T., & Haskell, E.C. (1985). *How to spell* (Grades 1–12). Cambridge, MA: Educators Publishing Service.

Simmons, L. (1997). *Saxon phonics.* Norman, OK: Saxon Publishers.

Slingerland, B.H., & Aho, M. (1994–1996). *A multi-sensory approach to language arts for specific language disability children* (Rev. ed., Vols. 1–3). Cambridge, MA: Educators Publishing Service.

Smith, M.T. *MTA reading and spelling program* (Kits 1–7). Cambridge, MA: Educators Publishing Service.

Texas Scottish Rite Hospital for Children. *Dyslexia training program: Teacher's guides and student's books* (Vols. 1–4). Cambridge, MA: Educators Publishing Service.

Wickerham, C.W., & Allen, K.A. (1993). *Multisensory reading and spelling* (Books 1–4). The Woodlands, TX: Apple Core Press. (Available from the publisher, 11 Rosethorn Place, The Woodlands, TX 77381; 713-367-3715)

Wilson, B.A. (1988). *Wilson reading system: Teacher's guide and student material.* Millbury, MA: Wilson Language Training. (Available from the publisher, www.Wilson Language.com)

Instructional Materials

Bear, D.R., Invernizzi, M., Templeton, S., & Francine, J. (1996). *Words their way: Word study for phonics, vocabulary, and spelling instruction.* Upper Saddle River, NJ: Prentice-Hall.

Bell, N. (1997). *Seeing stars: Symbol imagery for phonemic awareness, sight words, and spelling.* San Luis Obispo, CA: Gander Publishing.

Electronic spellers. Burlington, NJ: Franklin Electronic Publishers, Inc.

Manupulative four-leaf clover [For teaching the Doubling Rule]. Austin, TX: Region XIII Education Service Center. (Available from Region XIII Education Service Center, 5701 Springdale Road, Austin, TX 78723; 512-926-5593)

McCracken pocket charts. Seattle, WA: School Art Materials. (Available from the publisher, Post Office Box 94082, Seattle, WA 98124; 800-752-4359)

Videotapes

Birsh, J.R. (Consulting Ed.), Potts, M., & Potts, R. (Producers). (1997a). *LD/LA: Learning disabilities/learning abilities: Videotape II. The teaching: What students need.* West Tisbury, MA: Vineyard Video Productions. (Available from Paul H. Brookes Publishing Co., Post Office Box 10624, Baltimore, MD 21285; 800-638-3775)

Birsh, J.R. (Consulting Ed.), Potts, M., & Potts, R. (Producers). (1997b). *LD/LA: Learning disabilities/learning abilities: Videotape III. Reading is not a natural skill: Teaching children the code to unlock language.* West Tisbury, MA: Vineyard Video Productions. (Available from Paul H. Brookes Publishing Co., Post Office Box 10624, Baltimore, MD 21285; 800-638-3775)

CHAPTER 9—TEACHING HANDWRITING

Teacher References

Cox, A.R. (1992). *Foundations for literacy: Structures and techniques for multisensory teaching of basic written English language skills.* Cambridge, MA: Educators Publishing Service.

Gillingham, A., & Stillman, B.W. (1997). *The Gillingham manual: Remedial training for children with specific disability in reading, spelling and penmanship* (8th ed.). Cambridge, MA: Educators Publishing Service.

Curricula, Guides, and Activities

Bertin, P., & Perlman, E. (1980). *Preventing academic failure.* Cambridge, MA: Educators Publishing Service.

duBard, N.E., & Martin, M.K. (1994). *Teaching language-deficient children: Theory and application of the Association Method for multisensory teaching* (Rev. ed.). Cambridge, MA: Educators Publishing Service.

Enfield, M.L., & Greene, V. *Project read.* Bloomington, MN: Language Circle Enterprise.

Herman, R.D. (1993). *The Herman Method for reversing reading failure: Teacher's guide, set A.* Sherman Oaks, CA: The Herman Method Institute.

Knight, J.R. (1986). *Starting over: A combined teaching manual and student textbook for reading, writing, spelling, vocabulary, and handwriting.* Cambridge, MA: Educators Publishing Service.

Slingerland, B.H., & Aho, M. (1994–1996). *A multi-sensory approach to language arts for specific language disability children* (Rev. ed., Vols. 1–3). Cambridge, MA: Educators Publishing Service.

Smith, M.T. *MTA reading and spelling program* (Kits 1–7). Cambridge, MA: Educators Publishing Service.

Smith, M.T. *MTS handwriting program.* Forney, TX: MTS Publications.

Sonday, A.W. (1992). *Fundamentals of reading success: An introduction to the Orton-Gillingham approach to teaching reading and spelling.* Cambridge, MA: Educators Publishing Service.

Spalding, R.B., with Spalding, W.T. (1990). *The writing road to reading: The Spalding Method of phonics for teaching speech, writing, and reading* (4th rev. ed.). New York: Quill.

Texas Scottish Rite Hospital for Children. *Dyslexia training program: Teacher's guides and student's books* (Vols. 1–4). Cambridge, MA: Educators Publishing Service.

Wilson, B.A. (1988). *Wilson reading system.* Millbury, MA: Wilson Language Training.

Handwriting and Keyboarding Curricula

Bertin, P., & Perlman, E. (1980). *Preventing academic failure handwriting program.* Cambridge, MA: Educators Publishing Service.

Cavey, D.W. (1993). *Dysgraphia: Why Johnny can't write. A guide for teachers and parents* (2nd ed.). Austin, TX: PRO-ED.

Duffy, J. (1974). *Type it.* Cambridge, MA: Educators Publishing Service.

Johnson, W.T., & Johnson, M.R. (1977). *Beginning connected, cursive handwriting.* Cambridge, MA: Educators Publishing Service.

Johnson, W.T., & Johnson, M.R. (1975). *Let's write and spell.* Cambridge, MA: Educators Publishing Service.

King, D.H. (1986). *Keyboarding skills.* Cambridge, MA: Educators Publishing Service.

King, D.H. (1987). *Cursive writing skills.* Cambridge, MA: Educators Publishing Service.

Phelps, J., & Stempel, L. (1985). *CHES's Handwriting improvement program* (CHIP). Dallas: CHES. (Available from the publisher, Post Office Box 25254, Dallas, TX 75225)

Slingerland, B.H., & Aho, M.S. (1971a). *Manual for learning to use cursive handwriting.* Cambridge, MA: Educators Publishing Service.

Slingerland, B.H., & Aho, M.S. (1971b). *Manual for learning to use manuscript handwriting.* Cambridge, MA: Educators Publishing Service.

Smith, M.T. *Handwriting masters guide.* Cambridge, MA: Educators Publishing Service.

Smith, M.T. *Handwriting practice guide.* Cambridge, MA: Educators Publishing Service.

Smith, M.T. *MTS handwriting program.* Forney, TX: MTS Publications.

Instructional Materials

All the write news [Fits over pencil to assist grip]. Los Angeles: Thē Pencil Grip. (Available from the publisher, Post Office Box 67096, Los Angeles, CA 90062; 888-PEN-GRIP; 310-788-9485)

Pencil grips. Dallas, TX: CHES. (Available from the publisher, Post Office Box 25254, Dallas, TX 75225)

Writing frame (#C1590011) [Metal frame to help writer's grip and shaping of letters]. Columbus, OH: Zaner-Bloser.

Videotapes

Allen, K. (Director). *Help your child with handwriting.* Bellaire, TX: Neuhaus Education Center.

Multisensory typing program. Dallas: Texas Scottish Rite Hospital for Children, Child Development Division.

Software

Mavis Beacon teaches typing for kids. Novato, CA: Mindscape, Inc. (Available from the publisher, 88 Rowland Way, Novato, CA 94945; 415-897-9900)

Texas Scottish Rite Hospital for Children. *Keyboarding for written expression.* Dallas, TX: Author.

CHAPTER 10—COMPOSITION: EXPRESSIVE LANGUAGE AND WRITING

Teacher References

Vail, P.L. (1981). *Clear and lively writing: Language games and activities for everyone.* Rosemont, NJ: Modern Learning Press.

Curricula, Guides, and Activities

Carlisle, J.F. (1998). *Models for writing.* Novato, CA: Academic Therapy Publications.

Cheney, T.A.R. (1983). *Getting the words right: How to rewrite, edit, and revise.* Cincinnati, OH: Writer's Digest Books.

Clark, D.B., & Uhry, J.K. (1995). *Dyslexia: Theory and practice of remedial instruction.* (2nd ed.). Timonium, MD: York Press.

Collins, K.M., & Collins, J.L. (1996, October). Strategic instruction for struggling writers. *English Journal, 5*(6), 54–61.

Deshler, D.D., Ellis, E., & Lenz, B.K. (1996). *Teaching adolescents with learning disabilities: Strategies and methods* (2nd ed.). Denver, CO: Love Publishing.

Gunning, T.G. (1996). *Creating reading instruction for all children* (2nd ed.). Needham Heights, MA: Allyn & Bacon.

Johnson, D.J., & Grant, J.O. (1989). Written narratives of normal and learning disabled children. *Annals of Dyslexia, 39,* 140–158.

Kamhi, A.G., & Catts, H.W. (1989). *Reading disabilities: A developmental language perspective.* Boston: Little, Brown.

King, D.H. (1989). *Writing skills levels 1 and 2* (Grades 4–6 & 7–9). Cambridge, MA: Educators Publishing Service.

Levy, N.R. (1996, November). Teaching analytical writing: Help for general education middle school teachers. *Intervention, 32*(2), 95–96.

Maria, K. (1990). *Reading comprehension: Instruction, issues, and strategies.* Timonium, MD: York Press.

State University of New York & New York State Education Department. (1987). *The arts and learning: The write way on.* Albany: Authors.

State University of New York & New York State Education Department. (1988a). *English language arts syllabus K–12* (1988). Albany: Authors.

State University of New York & New York State Education Department. (1988b). *Helping student writers.* Albany: Authors.

Instructional Materials

Biddle, M.L. (1998). *Written basic English for dyslexic students.* Cambridge, MA: Educators Publishing Service.

Composition in the English language arts curriculum K–12. (1986). Boston: McDougal, Littell.

Region XIII TAAS/Education Service Center. *Reading activities supporting the Texas reading initiative* [Manipulative paragraph writing outlines]. Austin, TX: Author.

CHAPTER 11—MULTISENSORY MATHEMATICS INSTRUCTION

Teacher References

Burns, M. (1987). *50 problem solving lessons.* White Plains, NY: Cuisinaire Dale Seymour Publications. (Available from the publisher, Post Office Box 502, White Plains, NY 10602)

Burns, M. (1992). *About teaching mathematics: A K–8 resource.* Sausalito, CA: Math Solutions Publications.

Fennema, E., Carpenter, T.P., & Lamon, S. (Eds.). (1991). *Integrating research and teaching and learning mathematics.* Albany: SUNY Press.

Gardener, H. (1991). *The unschooled mind: How children think and how schools should teach.* New York: Basic Books.

Grouws, D.A. (1992). *Handbook of research on mathematics teaching and learning.* New York: Macmillan.

Jordon, N.C., & Montani, T.O. (1996). Mathematics difficulties in young children: Cognitive and developmental perspectives. *Advances in Learning and Behavioral Disabilities, 10A,* 101–134.

Kamii, C. (1985). *Young children reinvent arithmetic: Implications of Piaget's theory.* New York: Teachers College Press.

MacNeal, E. (1994). *Mathematics: Making numbers talk sense.* New York: Viking Penguin.

Montessori, M. (1964). *The Montessori method.* Cambridge, MA: Robert Bentley.

National Council of Teachers of Mathematics. (1991). *Professional standards for teaching mathematics.* Reston, VA: Author.

Pimm, D. (1990). *Speaking mathematically: Communication in mathematics classrooms.* New York: Routledge.

Sawyer, W.W. (1964). *Introducing mathematics: Vision in elementary mathematics.* London: Penguin Books, Ltd.

Steen, L.A. (1997). *Why numbers count: Quantitative literacy for tomorrow's America.* Reston, VA: National Council of Teachers of Mathematics.

Stern, M., & Gould, T. (1988–1992). *Structural arithmetic workbooks and teacher's guides 1–3.* Cambridge, MA: Educators Publishing Service.

Thiessen, D., Matthias, M., & Smith, J. (1998). *The wonderful world of mathematics: A critically annotated list of children's books in mathematics.* Reston, VA: National Council of Teachers of Mathematics.

Trafton, P.R. (Ed.). (1989). *New directions for elementary school mathematics.* Reston, VA: National Council of Teachers of Mathematics.

Tuley, K., & Bell, N. (1998). *On cloud nine: Visualizing and verbalizing for math* [Includes kit and graded workbooks]. San Luis Obispo, CA: Gander Publishing.

Instructional Materials/Manipulatives

Base ten blocks [Plastic blocks with units marked, used to demonstrate place value: tens, hundreds, and thousands]. White Plains, NY: Cuisinaire Dale Seymour Publications.

Cuisinaire rods [Colored plastic rods with sizes in centimeters, units not marked]. White Plains, NY: Cuisinaire Dale Seymour Publications.

Structural arithmetic materials [Includes wooden number blocks 1–10 with units marked, numerals, and devices into which the blocks fit; counting board; pattern boards; number track; and dual board for place value]. Cambridge, MA: Educators Publishing Service.

Unifix cubes [Set of colored interlocking plastic cubes and devices into which they fit]. White Plains, NY: Cuisinaire Dale Seymour Publications.

Assessment Tools

Ginsburg, H. (1987). *Assessing the arithmetic abilities and instructional needs of students.* Austin, TX: PRO-ED.

National Council of Teachers of Mathematics. (1995). *Assessment standards for school mathematics.* Reston, VA: Author.

Videotapes

Birsh, J.R. (Consulting Ed.), Potts, M., & Potts, R. (Producers). (1997). *LD/LA: Learning disabilities/learning abilities: Videotape VI. Teaching math: A systematic approach for children with learning disabilities.* West Tisbury, MA: Vineyard Video Productions. (Available from Paul H. Brookes Publishing Co., Post Office Box 10624, Baltimore, MD 21285; 800-638-3775)

Birsh, J.R. (Consulting Ed.), Potts, M., & Potts, R. (Producers). (1991). *Teaching the learning disabled: Study skills and learning strategies.* West Tisbury, MA: Vineyard Video Productions.

World Wide Web Sites

Centre for Innovation in Mathematics Teaching, University of Exeter, United Kingdom
www.ex.ac.uk/cimt/
Research and curriculum development in mathematics teaching

Math Parent Handbook: A Guide to Helping Your Child Understand Mathematics
www.eduplace.com/math/res/parentbk/
Houghton Mifflin Mathematics Center discussion forums and materials

Mathematics Learning Forum, Bank Street College
www.bnkst.edu/mlf/
On-line seminars for elementary and middle school teachers for refining teaching practices

Sunburst Communications Inc.
www.sunburst.com
Software and other electronic resources

Organizations

National Council of Teachers of Mathematics
1906 Association Drive
Reston, VA 20191
800-235-7566
www.nctm.org

CHAPTER 12—APPLYING MULTISENSORY TECHNIQUES TO INTERDISCIPLINARY STUDIES

Teacher References

Baskwill, J. (1988). Themestorming. *Teaching K–8, 19*, 80–82.

Briggs, J.E. (1996). The Friends' central fall project: Teacher conversation and collaboration in the construction of thematic curriculum. *Dissertation Abstracts International, 57*(04), 1464A. (University Mircofilms No. AAG96-27891)

Del Soldo, L. (1989, Spring/Summer). Sports and games: A lower school thematic project. *Friends' Central Forum, 4–9.* (Available from Stratford Friends School, 5 Llandillo Road, Havertown, PA 19083)

Eisner, E.W. (1990). The role of art and play in children's cognitive development. In E. Klugman & S. Smilansky (Eds.), *Children's play and learning: Perspectives and policy implications.* New York: Teachers College Press.

Five, C.L., & Dionisio, M. (1996). *Bridging the gap: Integrating curriculum in upper elementary and middle schools.* Portsmouth, NH: Heinemann.

Gallas, K. (1992). Arts as epistemology: Enabling children to know what they know. In M.R. Goldberg & A. Phillips (Eds.), *Arts as education* (pp. 19–32). Cambridge, MA: Harvard Educational Review.

Gardner, H. (1985). *Frames of mind: The theory of multiple intelligences.* New York: Basic Books.

Gardner, H. (1991). *The unschooled mind: How children think and how schools should teach.* New York: Basic Books.

Griss, S. (1989). *Minds in motion: A kinesthetic approach to teaching elementary curriculum.* Portsmouth, NH: Heinemann.

Harris, N. (1980). *Thematic teaching—1980: A manual of the thematic process for teachers.* Dover: Independent School Association of Massachusetts.

Healy, J. (1990). *Endangered minds: Why children don't think and what we can do about it.* New York: Simon & Schuster.

Jacobs, H.H., Hannah, J., Manfredonia, W., Percivalle, J., & Gilbert, J. (1989). Descriptions of two existing interdisciplinary programs. In H.H. Jacobs (Ed.), *Interdisciplinary curriculum: Design and implementation* (pp. 39–52). Alexandria, VA: Association for Supervision and Curriculum Development.

Katz, L.G., & Chard, S.C. (1989). *Engaging children's minds: The project approach.* Greenwich, CT: Ablex Publishing Corp.

Leland, C.H., & Harste, J.C. (1994). Multiple ways of knowing: Curriculum in a new key. *Language Arts, 71*(5), 337–345.

Lewis, M.E.B. (1993). *Thematic methods and strategies in learning disabilities: A textbook for practitioners.* San Diego: Singular Publishing Group.

Manning, M., Manning, G., & Long, R. (1994). *Theme immersion: Inquiry-based curriculum in elementary and middle schools.* Portsmouth, NH: Heinemann.

McMillan, E. (1994–1995, Fall–Winter). A bridge grows in 1A. *Friends' Central Forum,* 24–27. (Available from Stratford Friends School, 5 Llandillo Road, Havertown, PA 19083)

Reed, E.W. (1997–1998, Winter). Projects and activities: A means, not an end. *American Educator.*

Rogovin, P. (1998). *Classroom interviews: A world of learning.* Portsmouth, NH: Heinemann.

Short, K., Schroeder, J., Laird, J., Kauffman, G., Ferguson, M., & Crawford, K. (1996). *Learning together through inquiry.* Monroeville, PA: Stenhouse Publishers.

Walmsley, S.A. (1994). *Children exploring their world: Theme teaching in elementary schools.* Portsmouth, NH: Heinemann.

Instructional Materials

Cobblestone Publishing
7 School Street
Peterborough, NH 03458
Historical materials for middle-level learners and teachers, including theme packs, books, primary source material, and magazines for thematic curricula

Documentary Photo Aids
Post Office Box 956
Mt. Dora, FL 32757
Science and social studies visual aids

Heinemann
361 Hanover Street
Portsmouth, NH 03801
info@heinemann.com
www.heinemann.com
Books, videotapes, and professional development resources for K–8 teachers

Primary Source
Post Office Box 381711
Cambridge, MA 02238
Professional development and curriculum resources in social studies

Stenhouse Publishers
Post Office Box 360
York, ME 03909
800-988-9812
info@stenhouse.com
www.stenhouse.com
Professional books on expanding classroom curriculum

Zephyr Press
Post Office Box 66006
Tucson, AZ 85728
neways2learn@zephyrpress.com
www.zephyrpress.com
Learning packets on a number of science and social studies themes as well as workbooks and activities to accompany Howard Gardner's (1985) *Multiple Intelligences*

Videotapes

Birsh, J.R. (Consulting Ed.), Potts, M., & Potts, R. (Producers). (1991). *Teaching the learning disabled: Study skills and learning strategies.* West Tisbury, MA: Vineyard Video Productions.

PBS Video
1320 Braddock Place
Alexandria, VA 22314
703-739-5000
Videotapes and supplemental teacher materials

Software

Tom Snyder Productions
80 Coolidge Hill Road
Watertown, MA 02172
Software for science and social studies

Organizations

National Council for Teachers of English
1111 West Kenyon Road
Urbana, IL 61801

National Council for the Social Studies
3501 Newark Street, NW
Washington, DC 20016

CHAPTER 13—ORGANIZATION AND STUDY SKILLS

Teacher References

Aaron, P.G., & Baker, C. (1991). *Reading disabilities in college and high school: Diagnosis and management.* Timonium, MD: York Press.

Calfee, R.E. (1983). The mind of the dyslexic. *Annals of Dyslexia, 33,* 28.

Cristensen, C.R., Garvin, D.A., & Sweet, A. (1991). *Education for judgment: The artistry of discussion leadership.* Boston: Harvard Business School Press.

Gaddes, W.H., & Edgell, D. (1994). *Learning disabilities and brain function: A neuropsychological approach.* (3rd ed.). New York: Springer-Verlag.

Galaburda, A. (Ed.). (1993). *Dyslexia and development: Neurobiological aspects of extraordinary brains.* Cambridge, MA: Harvard University Press.

Kamhi, A.G., & Catts, H.W. (1989). *Reading disabilities: A developmental perspective.* Boston: Little, Brown.

Levine, M. (1987). *Developmental variation and learning disorders* (2nd ed.). Cambridge, MA: Educators Publishing Service.

Shaywitz, S.E. (1998). *Current concepts in dyslexia.* New England Journal of Medicine, 338, 307–312.

Steeves, K.J. (1983). Memory as a factor in the computational efficiency of dyslexic children with high abstract reasoning ability. *Annals of Dyslexia, 33,* 141–152.

Tuley, A.C. (1998). *Never too late to read: Language skills for the adolescent dyslexic (based on the work of Alice Ansara).* Timonium, MD: York Press.

Wiig, E.H., & Semel, E. (1990). *Language assessment and intervention for the learning disabled.* Columbus, OH: Charles E. Merrill.

Curricula, Guides, and Activities

Abbamont, G.W., & Brescher, A. (1997). *Test smart: Ready-to-use test-taking strategies and activities for grades 5–12*. West Nyack, NY: Center for Applied Research in Education.

Askov, E.N., & Kamm, K. (1982). *Study skills in the content areas*. Needham Heights, MA: Allyn & Bacon.

Bragstad, B.J., & Stumpf, S.M. (1987). *Study skills and motivation: A guidebook for teaching*. Needham Heights, MA: Allyn & Bacon.

D'Angelo Bromley, K. (1996). *Webbing with literature: Creating story maps with children's books*. Needham Heights, MA: Allyn & Bacon.

Deshler, D.D., Ellis, E., & Lenz, B.K. (1996). *Teaching adolescents with learning disabilities: Strategies and methods* (2nd ed.). Denver, CO: Love Publishing.

Devine, T.G. (1987). *Teaching study skills: A guide for teachers* (2nd ed.). Needham Heights, MA: Allyn & Bacon.

Ellis, E.S. (1984). An instructional model for integrating content-area instruction with cognitive strategy instruction. *Reading and Writing Quarterly, 1*, 63–90.

Foss, J. (1986). The tutor–student instructional interaction. *Annals of Dyslexia, 36*, 15–27.

Langan, J. (1979). *Sentence skills: A workbook for writers*. New York: McGraw-Hill.

McNeil, J.D. (1992). *Reading comprehension: New directions for classroom practice*. New York: HarperCollins.

Roman, N.V. *Get set for reading test preparation for reading assessment*. Elizabethtown, PA: Continental Press.

Strichart, S.S., & Mangrum, C.T., II. (1993). *Teaching study strategies to students with learning disabilities*. Needham Heights, MA: Allyn & Bacon.

Tonjes, M.J., & Zintz, M.V. (1992). *Teaching reading, thinking, study skills in content classrooms* (3rd ed.). Dubuque, IA: William C. Brown.

Vurnakes, C. (1995). *The organized student: Teaching time management*. Torrance, CA: Frank Schaffer Publications, Inc.

Instructional Materials

Ayto, J. (1990). *Dictionary of word origins*. New York: Arcade.

Benne, B. (1988). *WASPLEG and other mnemonics: Easy ways to remember hard things*. Dallas, TX: Taylor Publishing Co.

Budworth, J. (1991). *Instant recall: Tapping your hidden memory power*. Holbrook, MA: Bob Adams, Inc.

Buzan, T. (1991). *Use both sides of your brain* (3rd ed.). New York: E.P. Dutton. [Note-taking system is not recommended; for mind-map design and enhancement only.]

Bywaters, D. (1998). *Affix and root cards*. Cambridge, MA: Educators Publishing Service.

Cherry, R.L. (1989). *Words under construction*. Tucson: University of Arizona Press.

Danner, H.G., & Noël, R. (1996). *Discover it!: A better vocabulary the better way*. Occocquan, VA: Imprimus Books.

Gilbert, S. (1990). *Go for it: Get organized. The perfect time-management system for busy teens*. New York: Morrow Junior Books.

Kesselman-Turkel, J., & Peterson, F. (1982). *Note-taking made easy*. Chicago: Contemporary Books.

Lakoff, G., & Johnson, M. (1983). *Metaphors we live by*. Chicago: University of Chicago Press.

Makkai, A., Boatner, M.T., & Gates, J.E. (1995). *A dictionary of American idioms.* Hauppage, NY: Barron's Educational Series, Inc.

Merriam Webster's collegiate dictionary (10th ed.). (1993). Springfield, MA: Merriam-Webster.

Moore, B., & Moore, M. (1997). *NTC's dictionary of Latin and Greek origins.* Lincolnwood, IL: NTC Publishing Group.

Morwood, J., & Warman, M. (1990). *Our Greek and Latin roots.* London: Cambridge University Press.

Murray, C., & Munro, J. (1989). *30 roots to grow on.* Cambridge, MA: Educators Publishing Service.

Partridge, E. (1966). *Origins: A short etymological dictionary of modern English.* New York: Greenwich House.

Roget's thesaurus (5th ed.). (1992). New York: HarperCollins. [Note: Only this version is recommended.]

The Oxford dictionary and thesaurus (American ed.). (1996). New York: Oxford University Press.

Trudeau, K. (1995). *Megamemory.* New York: William Morrow & Co.

Wycoff, J. (1991). *Mindmapping: Your personal guide to exploring creativity and problem-solving.* New York: Berkley Books.

Videotapes

Birsh, J.R. (Consulting Ed.), Potts, M., & Potts, R. (Producers). (1991). *Teaching the learning disabled: Study skills and learning strategies: Videotape III. Organizing time, materials, and information.* West Tisbury, MA: Vineyard Video Productions.

Software

Anderson, L. *Inspiration* [Outlining and graphic organizer software]. Portland: University of Oregon.

CHAPTER 14—ASSESSMENT OF PROGRESS

Teacher References: General Assessment

Cohen, L., & Spenciner, L. (1998). *Assessment of children and youth.* Reading, MA: Addison Wesley Longman.

Choate, J.S., Enright, B.E., Miller, L.J., Poteet, J.A., & Rakes, T.A. (1995). *Curriculum-based assessment and programming.* Needham Heights, MA: Allyn & Bacon.

Darling-Hammond, L., Ancess, J., & Falk, B. (1995). *Authentic assessment in action.* New York: Teachers College Press.

Idol, L.A., Nevin, A., & Paolucci-Whitcomb, P. (1996). *Models of curriculum-based assessment.* Austin, TX: PRO-ED.

Kubiszyn, T., & Borich, G. (1993). *Educational testing and measurement: Classroom application and practice* (5th ed.). Boston: Houghton Mifflin.

Nitkop, A.J. (1996). *Educational assessment of students.* Upper Saddle River, NJ: Prentice-Hall.

Salvia, J., & Ysseldyke, J.E. (1998). *Assessment* (7th ed.). Boston: Houghton Mifflin.

Wiggins, G. (1993). *Assessing student performance: Exploring the purpose and limits of testing.* San Francisco: Jossey-Bass.

Teacher References: Reading and Writing Assessment

Anthony, R., Johnson, T., Midelson, N., & Preece, A. (1991). *Evaluating literacy: A perspective for change.* Portsmouth, NH: Heinemann.

Barr, R., Blachowicz, C.L.Z., & Wogman-Sadow, M. (1995). *Reading diagnosis for teachers: An instructional approach* (3rd ed.). Reading, MA: Addison Wesley Longman.

Clay, M.M. (1995). *An observation of early literacy attainment.* Portsmouth, NH: Heinemann.

Glazer, S.M., & Brown, C.S. (1993). *Portfolios and beyond: Collaborative assessment in reading and writing.* Norwood, MA: Christopher Gordon.

Hewett, G. (1995). *A portfolio primer: Teaching, collecting, and assessing student writing.* Portsmouth, NH: Heinemann.

Kibby, M.W. (1995). *Practical steps for informing literacy instruction: A diagnostic decision-making model.* Newark, DE: International Reading Association.

Miller, W.H. (1995). *Alternative assessment techniques for reading and writing.* West Nyack, NY: Center for Applied Research in Education.

Rhodes, L.K., & Shanklin, N.L. (1993). *Windows into literacy.* Portsmouth, NH: Heinemann.

Roskos, K., & Walter, B.J. (1994). *Interactive handbook for understanding reading diagnosis.* Upper Saddle River, NJ: Prentice-Hall.

Rumsey, M.B. (1992). *Dyslexia training program: Schedules I–III progress measurements teacher's guide and student's book.* Cambridge, MA: Educators Publishing Service.

Valencia, S.W., Hiebert, E.H., & Afflerback, P.P. (Eds.). (1994). *Authentic reading assessment: Practice and possibilities.* Newark, DE: International Reading Association.

Walker, B.J. (1996). *Diagnostic teaching of reading: Techniques for instruction and assessment* (3rd ed.). Upper Saddle River, NJ: Prentice-Hall.

Videotapes

Birsh, J.R. (Consulting Ed.), Potts, M., & Potts, R. (Producers). (1997a). *LD/LA: Learning disabilities/learning abilities: Videotape I. Introduction: Understanding learning disabilities through demonstration and description.* West Tisbury, MA: Vineyard Video Productions. (Available from Paul H. Brookes Publishing Co., Post Office Box 10624, Baltimore, MD 21285; 800-638-3775)

Birsh, J.R. (Consulting Ed.), Potts, M., & Potts, R. (Producers). (1997b). *LD/LA: Learning disabilities/learning abilities: Videotape IV. Children & parents & schools & strengths.* West Tisbury, MA: Vineyard Video Productions. (Available from Paul H. Brookes Publishing Co., Post Office Box 10624, Baltimore, MD 21285; 800-638-3775)

Resources for Parents

Greene, J.F., & Moats, L.C. Testing: *Critical components in the clinical identification of dyslexia.* Baltimore: The Orton Dyslexia Society.

Hurford, D.M. (1998). *To read or not to read: Answers to all your questions about dyslexia.* New York: Scribner.

Smith, C., & Strick, L. (1997). *Learning disabilities: A to Z.* New York: The Free Press.

CHAPTER 15—TRANSITION TO THE GENERAL CLASSROOM AND CONTENT AREAS

Teacher References

Barkley, R.A. (1995). *Taking charge of ADHD: The complete, authoritative guide for parents.* New York: The Guilford Press.

Boggeman, S., Hoerr, T., & Wallach, C. (1996). *Succeeding with multiple intelligences: Teaching through the personal intelligences.* St. Louis: The New City School.

DuPaul, G.J., & Stone, S.L. (1994). *ADHD in the schools: Assessment and intervention strategies.* New York: The Guilford Press.

Goldstein, S., & Goldstein, M. (1990). *Managing attention disorders in children: A guide for practitioners.* New York: John Wiley & Sons.

Goldstein, S., & Goldstein, M. (1995). *Intervention: Attention-deficit/hyperactivity disorder* (2nd ed.). Salt Lake City, UT: Neurology, Learning, and Behavior Center.

Learning disabilities: Preservice preparation of general and special education teachers. (1998, January–February). *LDA Newsbriefs,* 3–7.

Quinn, P.O., & Stern, J.M. (1991). *Putting on the brakes: Young people's guide to understanding attention deficit hyperactivity disorder* (ADHD). New York: Magination Press.

Scruggs, T.E. (1992). *Teaching test-taking skills: Helping students show what they know.* Cambridge, MA: Brookline Books.

Stainback, S., & Stainback, W. (Eds.). (1992). *Curriculum considerations in inclusive classrooms: Facilitating learning for all students.* Baltimore: Paul H. Brookes Publishing Co.

Stainback, S., & Stainback, W. (Eds.). (1996). *Inclusion: A guide for educators.* Baltimore: Paul H. Brookes Publishing Co.

Wood, J.W. (1992). *Adapting instruction for mainstreamed and at-risk students* (2nd ed.). Upper Saddle River, NJ: Prentice-Hall.

Wood, J.W. (1993). *Mainstreaming: A practical approach for teachers* (2nd ed.). New York: Macmillan.

Instructional Materials

Abbamont, G.W., & Brescher, A. (1997). *Test smart: Ready-to-use test-taking strategies and activities for grades 5–12.* West Nyack, NY: Center for Applied Research in Education.

Adams, M.J., Foorman, B.R., Lundberg, I., & Beeler, T. (1998). *Phonemic awareness in young children: A classroom curriculum.* Baltimore: Paul H. Brookes Publishing Co.

Fry, E.B., Polk, J.K., & Fountoukidis, D.L. (1996). *The reading teacher's new book of lists.* (3rd ed.). Upper Saddle River, NJ: Prentice-Hall.

Hall, N., & Price, R. (1993). *Explode the code.* Cambridge, MA: Educators Publishing
    Service.
Parker, H.C. (1994). *The ADD hyperactivity workbook for parents, teachers and kids.*
    Plantation, FL: Specialty Press, Inc.
Smith, M.T. *Phoneme awareness, assessment, instruction, practice.* Forney, TX: MTS
    Publications.
Smith, M.T. *MTS reading program.* Forney, TX: MTS Publications.

Organizations

> *National Transition Alliance for Youths with Disabilities (National Transition
>   Network, Academy for Educational Development, and Transition Research Institute)*
> Transition Research Institute at Illinois
> University of Illinois
> 113 Children's Research Center
> 51 Gerty Drive
> Champaign, IL 61820
> 217-333-2325

> *National Transition Network (NTN)*
> Institute on Community Integration
> University of Minnesota
> 430 Wulling Hall
> 86 Pleasant Street, SE
> Minneapolis, MN 55455
> 612-626-8200

CHAPTER 16—READING AND WRITING INSTRUCTION IN ADULT BASIC EDUCATION

Teacher References

Adams, M.J. (1990). *Beginning to read: Thinking and learning about print.* Cambridge:
    The MIT Press.
Chall, J.S. (1996). *Learning to read: The great debate* (3rd ed.). Orlando, FL: Harcourt
    Brace & Co.
Clark, D.B., & Uhry, J.K. (1988). *Dyslexia: Theory and practice of remedial instruction*
    (2nd ed.). Timonium, MD: York Press.
Cramer, S.C., & Ellis, W. (Eds.). (1996). *Learning disabilities: Lifelong issues.* Baltimore:
    Paul H. Brookes Publishing Co.
Gardner, H. (1985). *Frames of mind: The theory of multiple intelligences.* New York:
    Basic Books.
Gottesman, R.L., Bennett, R.E., Nathan, R.G., & Kelly, M.S. (1996). Inner-city adults with
    severe reading difficulties: A closer look. *Journal of Learning Disabilities, 29*(6), 589–597.
Gould, S.J. (1981). *The mismeasure of man.* New York: W.W. Norton.
Harrison, E. (1994). Starting Over at John F. Kennedy High School. In National Center
    for Learning Disabilities (Ed.), *Their world* (pp. 60–61). New York: National Center
    for Learning Disabilities.
Hirsch, E.D. (1987). *Cultural literacy: What every American needs to know.* Boston:
    Houghton Mifflin.

Kirsch, I.S., Jungblut, A., Jenkins, L., & Kolstad, A. (1993). *Adult literacy in America: National adult literacy survey.* Washington, DC: U.S. Department of Education.

Knight, J.R. (1998). The link between learning disability and instruction. *Literacy Harvest, 7*(1), 11–16.

Knight, J.R., & Randell, J. (1994). Substance abuse rehabilitation and learning to read. In National Center for Learning Disabilities (Ed.), *Their world* (pp. 56–59). New York: National Center for Learning Disabilities.

Lyon, G.R. (Ed.). (1994). *Frames of reference for the assessment of learning disabilities: New views on measurement issues.* Baltimore: Paul H. Brookes Publishing Co.

Lyon, G.R. (1995). Toward a definition of dyslexia. *Annals of Dyslexia, 45,* 3–27.

Pennington, B.F. (1991). *Diagnosing learning disabilities.* New York: The Guilford Press.

Shaywitz, S.E. (1996). *Dyslexia.* Scientific American, 98–104.

Tuley, A.C. (1998). *Never too late to read: Language skills for the adolescent with dyslexia (based on the work of Alice Ansara).* Timonium, MD: York Press.

Curricula, Guides, and Activities

Knight, J. (1986). *Starting over: A combined teaching manual and student textbook for reading, writing, spelling, vocabulary, and handwriting.* Cambridge, MA: Educators Publishing Service.

Multisensory reading and spelling (Student, teacher, and masters books 1–4). Bellaire, TX: Neuhaus Education Center.

Wilson, B.A. (1988). *Wilson reading system.* Millbury, MA: Wilson Language Training.

Instructional Materials

Local newspapers
The New York Times

Videotapes

Texas Scottish Rite Hospital for Children. *Literacy program videotapes.* Dallas: Author.

Professional Journals

LINKAGES: Linking Literacy and Learning Disabilities
National Adult Literacy and Learning Disabilities Center
1875 Connecticut Avenue, NW, Ninth Floor
Washington, DC 20009
800-953-2553; 202-884-8185
info@nalldc.aed.org
www.LD-READ.org

Literacy Harvest
Literacy Assistance Center
84 Williams Street, 14th Floor
New York, NY 10038
www.lac.nyc.org

Organizations

Literacy Assistance Center
84 Williams Street, 14th Floor
New York, NY 10038
www.lacnyc.org

New York City Learning Disability Network
VESID
116 West 32nd Street, Seventh Floor
New York, NY 10011
212-630-2384

National Adult Literacy and Learning Disabilities Center
1875 Connecticut Avenue, NW, Ninth Floor
Washington, DC 20009
800-953-2553; 202-884-8185
info@nalldc.aed.org
www.ld-read.org

The International Dyslexia Association (IDA)
8600 LaSalle Road
Chester Building, Suite 382
Baltimore, MD 21286
800-ABC-D123; 410-296-0232
info@interdys.org
www.interdys.org

CHAPTER 17—WORKING WITH THE HIGH-FUNCTIONING DYSLEXIC

Teacher References

Blumenthal, S.H. (1981a) *Educational memories as a diagnostic measure.* Unpublished manuscript. (Available from the author, SHB280@aol.com)

Blumenthal, S.H. (1981b). *Process notes as a cognitive mediator.* Unpublished manuscript. (Available from the author, SHB280@aol.com)

Gerber, P.J., Ginsberg, R., & Reiff, H.B. (1992). Identifying alterable patterns in employment success for highly successful adults with learning disabilities. *Journal of Learning Disabilities, 25*(8), 475–487.

Gerber, P.J., Ginsberg, R., & Reiff, H.B. (1996). Reframing the learning disabilities experience. *Journal of Learning Disabilities, 29*(1), 98–101.

Reiff, H.B., Gerber, P.J., & Ginsberg, R. (1994). Instructional strategies for long term success. *Annals of Dyslexia, 44,* 270–288.

Reiff, H.B., Gerber, P.J., & Ginsberg, R. (1997). *Exceeding expectations: Successful adults with learning disabilities.* Austin, TX: PRO-ED.

Roswell, F., & Chall, J. (1994). *Creating successful readers.* Chicago: Riverside.

Instructional Materials

Cooley, T. (1993). *The Norton sampler: Short essays for composition* (4th ed). New York: W.W. Norton.

Milan, D. (1991). *Developing reading skills* (3rd ed.). New York: McGraw-Hill.

Milan, D. (1992). *Improving reading skills* (2nd ed.). New York: McGraw-Hill.

Pauk, W. (1983a). *Six-way paragraphs: Advanced level* (Rev. ed.). Providence, RI: Jamestown Publishing.

Pauk, W. (1983b). *Six-way paragraphs: Middle level* (Rev. ed.). Providence, RI: Jamestown Publishing.

Books by Adults with Learning Difficulties

Hampshire, S. (1982). *Susan's story.* New York: St. Martin's Press.

Simpson, E.M. (1998). *Reversals: A personal account of victory over dyslexia* (Reissue ed.). New York: Noonday Press.

West, T.G. (1991). *In the mind's eye.* Buffalo: Prometheus Books.

World Wide Web Sites

National Adult Literacy and Learning Disabilities Center
www.novel.nifl.gov/nalldtop.htm
Information on learning disabilities and adult literacy

Rebus Institute
www.cenatica.com/rebus
By and for adults with learning disabilities and attention-deficit/hyperactivity disorder (ADHD)

Organizations

Learning Disabilities Association of America (LDA)
4156 Library Road
Pittsburgh, PA 15234
412-341-1515
www.ldanatl.org

National Center for Learning Disabilities (NCLD)
381 Park Avenue South, Suite 1401
New York, NY 10016
888-575-7373; 212-545-7510
www.ncld.org

The International Dyslexia Association (IDA)
8600 LaSalle Road
Chester Building, Suite 382
Baltimore, MD 21286-2044
800-ABC-D123; 410-296-0232
info@interdys.org
www.interdys.org

CHAPTER 18—PARENTING THE CHILD WITH DYSLEXIA

Teacher and Parent References

Barkley, R.A. (1995). *Taking charge of ADHD: The complete, authoritative guide for parents.* New York: The Guilford Press.

Betancourt, J. (1993). *My name is ~~Brain~~ Brian.* New York: Scholastic.

Cicci, R. (1995). *What's wrong with me?: Learning disabilities at home and in school.* Timonium, MD: York Press.

Clark, D.B., & Uhry, J.K. (1995). *Dyslexia: Theory and practice of remedial instruction* (2nd ed.). Timonium, MD: York Press.

Corcoran, J. (1994). *The teacher who couldn't read.* Colorado Springs: Focus on the Family Publishing.

Cordoni, B. (1987). *Living with a learning disability.* Carbondale: Southern Illinois University Press.

Dwyer, K. (1991). *What do you mean I have a learning disability?* New York: Walker & Co.

Gehret, J. (1990). *Learning disabilities and the don't give-up kid.* Fairport, NY: Verbal Image Press.

Griffith, J. (1998). *How dyslexic Benny became a star.* Dallas, TX: Yorktown Press.

Hall, S.L., & Moats, L.C. (1999). *Straight talk about reading.* Chicago: Contemporary Books.

Hallowell, D.M., & Ratey, J.J. (1994a). *Answers to distraction.* New York: Bantam Doubleday Dell.

Hallowell, D.M., & Ratey, J.J. (1994b). *Driven to distraction.* New York: Pantheon Books.

Hampshire, S. (1982). *Susan's story.* New York: St. Martin's Press.

Honig, B. (1996). *Teaching our children to read.* Thousand Oaks, CA: Corwin Press.

Hurford, D.M. (1998). *To read or not to read.* New York: Scribner.

Huston, A.M. (1992). *Understanding dyslexia: A practical approach for parents and teachers.* Lanham, MD: Madison Books.

Janover, C. (1988). *Josh: A boy with dyslexia.* Burlington, VT: Waterfront Books.

Landau, E. (1991). *Dyslexia.* New York: Franklin Watts.

Lauren, J. (1997). *Succeeding with LD: 20 true stories about real people with LD.* Minneapolis, MN: Free Spirit.

Levine, M. (1990). *Keeping ahead in school* [Audiotapes and book]. Cambridge, MA: Educators Publishing Service.

Levine, M. (1993). *All kinds of minds.* Cambridge, MA: Educators Publishing Service.

Marek, M. (1985). *Different, not dumb.* New York: Franklin Watts.

National Center for Learning Disabilities. (1997–1998). *Their world.* New York: Author.

National Council on Learning Disabilities. (1991). *Understanding learning disabilities: A parent guide and workbook.* New York: Author.

Osman, B.B. (1995). *No one to play with: Social problems of LD and ADD children.* Novato, CA: Academic Therapy Publications.

Osman, B.B. (1998). *LD and ADHD: A family guide.* New York: John Wiley & Sons.

Parents Educational Resource Center. (1995). *Bridges to reading.* San Mateo, CA: Author.

Parker, H.C. (1994). *The ADD hyperactivity workbook for parents, teachers and kids.* Plantation, FL: Specialty Press, Inc.

Quinn, P.O., & Stern, J.M. (1991). *Putting on the brakes: Young people's guide to understanding attention deficit hyperactivity disorder* (ADHD). New York: Magination Press.

Rawson, M.B. (1988). The many faces of dyslexia. *Monographs of the Orton Dyslexia Society, 5.*

Sedita, J. (1993). *Landmark study skills guide.* Prides Crossing, MA: Landmark Outreach Program. (Available from the publisher, Box 79, Prides Crossing, MA 01965)

Silver, L.B. (1992). *Attention-deficit hyperactivity disorder: A clinical guide and treatment.* Washington, DC: American Psychiatric Press, Inc.

Silver, L.B. (1998). *The misunderstood child: A guide for parents of learning disabled children* (3rd ed.). New York: Random House.

Silver, L.B. (1999). *Dr. Larry Silver's advice to parents on ADHD* (2nd ed.). New York: Times Books.

Simpson, E.M. (1998). *Reversals: A personal account of victory over dyslexia* (Reissue ed.). New York: Noonday Press.

Smith, S.L. (1987). *No easy answers: The learning disabled child at home and at school.* New York: Bantam Doubleday Dell.

Vail, P.L. (1987). *Smart kids with school problems: Things to know and ways to help.* New York: E.P. Dutton.

Vail, P.L. (1991). *About dyslexia: Unraveling the myth.* Rosemont, NJ: Modern Learning Press.

Vail, P.L. (1994). *Emotion: The on-off switch for learning.* Rosemont, NJ: Modern Learning Press.

West, T.G. (1943). *In the mind's eye.* Buffalo, NY: Prometheus Books.

Instructional Materials

Schmidt, J.J. (1997). *Making and keeping friends: Ready-to-use lessons, stories, activities for building relationships* (Grades 4–8). West Nyack, NY: Center for Applied Research in Education.

Videotapes

Birsh, J.R. (Consulting Ed.), Potts, M., & Potts, R. (Producers). (1991). *Teaching the learning disabled: Study skills and learning strategies.* West Tisbury, MA: Vineyard Video Productions. (Available from Paul H. Brookes Publishing Co., Post Office Box 10624, Baltimore, MD 21285; 800-638-3775)

Birsh, J.R. (Consulting Ed.), Potts, M., & Potts, R. (Producers). (1997a). *LD/LA: Learning disabilities/learning abilities: Videotape IV. Children & parents & schools & strengths.* West Tisbury, MA: Vineyard Video Productions. (Available from Paul H. Brookes Publishing Co., Post Office Box 10624, Baltimore, MD 21285; 800-638-3775)

Birsh, J.R. (Consulting Ed.), Potts, M., & Potts, R. (Producers). (1997b). *LD/LA: Learning disabilities/learning abilities: Videotape V. ADD/ADHD/LD: Understanding the connection.* West Tisbury, MA: Vineyard Video Productions. (Available from Paul H. Brookes Publishing Co., Post Office Box 10624, Baltimore, MD 21285; 800-638-3775)

Eagle Hill School & Rosen, P. (Producers). (1989). *How difficult can this be? F.A.T. city.* Alexandria, VA: PBS Video. (Available from the publisher, 1320 Braddock Place, Alexandria, VA 22314; 703-739-5000)

Guilford Publications (Producer) & Barkley, R.A. (Director). (1992a). *ADHD in the classroom: Strategies for teachers.* New York: Guilford Publications.

Guilford Publications (Producer) & Barkley, R.A. (Director). (1992b). *ADHD—What do we know?* New York: Guilford Publications.

WETA-TV (Producer) & Lavoie, R. (Director). (1994). *Learning disabilities and social skills with Richard Lavoie: Last one picked…first one picked on.* Alexandria, VA: PBS Video. (Available from the publisher, 1320 Braddock Place, Alexandria, VA 22314; 703-739-5000)

World Wide Web Sites

LD Online
www.ldonline.org
Find help and exchange ideas

Matrix Parent Network
marin.org/edu/matrix/index.html
Support for parents

Parents Helping Parents
www.php.com/
Resources and links to other World Wide Web sites

Professional Journals

Parent Journal: A Quarterly Publication for Parents of Children with Learning Differences
Parents Educational Resource Center
1650 South Amphlett Boulevard, Suite 300
San Mateo, CA 94402
650-655-2410

Organizations

Children with Attention Deficit Disorders (CHADD)
499 Northwest 70th Avenue, Suite 308
Plantation, FL 33317
305-587-3700

Division for Learning Disabilities (DLD)
The Council for Exceptional Children
1920 Association Drive
Reston, VA 22091
703-620-3660

ERIC Clearinghouse on Disabilities and Gifted Education
The Council for Exceptional Children
1920 Association Drive
Reston, VA 22091
800-328-0272; 703-264-9474
www.cec.sped.org/ericec.htm

Independent Educational Consultants Association
4085 Chain Bridge Road, Suite 401
Fairfax, VA 22030
703-591-4850
iecaassoc@aol.com
www.educationalconsulting.org.

Learning Disabilities Association of America (LDA)
4156 Library Road
Pittsburgh, PA 15234
412-341-1515
www.ldanatl.org

National Center for Learning Disabilities (NCLD)
381 Park Avenue South, Suite 1401
New York, NY 10016
888-575-7373; 212-545-7510

*National Information Center for Children
   and Youth with Disabilities (NICHCY)*
Post Office Box 1492
Washington, DC 20013
800-695-0285

*National Library Service for the Blind and
   the Physically Handicapped (Talking
   Books)*
The Library of Congress
1291 Taylor Street, NW
Washington, DC 20542
800-424-8567

*Parents Educational Resource Center
   (PERC)*
Charles and Helen Schwab Foundation
1650 South Amphlett Boulevard, Suite
   300
San Mateo, CA 94402
800-230-0988
infodesk@schwablearning.org
www.perc-scwhabfdn.org

Recordings for the Blind and Dyslexic
20 Roszel Road
Princeton, NJ 08540
800-803-7201; 609-452-0606
www.rfbd.org

*Technical Assistance for Parent Programs
   (TAPP)*
Federation for Children with Special
   Needs
95 Berkeley Street, Suite 104
Boston, MA 02116

*The International Dyslexia Association
   (IDA)*
8600 LaSalle Road
Chester Building, Suite 382
Baltimore, MD 21286-2044
800-ABC-D123; 410-296-0232
info@interdys.org
www.interdys.org

Index

Page numbers followed by *f* indicate figures; those followed by *t* indicate tables.

DATE DUE

JUN 29 2000		
APR 1 6 2008		